Preaching in the
Last Days

Preaching in the
Last Days

THE THEME OF 'TWO WITNESSES'
IN THE SIXTEENTH
AND SEVENTEENTH CENTURIES

Rodney L. Petersen

New York   Oxford
OXFORD UNIVERSITY PRESS
1993

Oxford University Press

Oxford   New York   Toronto
Delhi   Bombay   Calcutta   Madras   Karachi
Kuala Lumpur   Singapore   Hong Kong   Tokyo
Nairobi   Dar es Salaam   Cape Town
Melbourne   Auckland   Madrid

and associated companies in
Berlin   Ibadan

Copyright © 1993 by Rodney L. Petersen

Published by Oxford University Press, Inc.
200 Madison Avenue, New York, New York 10016

Oxford is a registered trademark of Oxford University Press, Inc.

Library of Congress Cataloging-in-Publication Data
Petersen, Rodney Lawrence.
Preaching in the last days : the theme of 'two witnesses' in the
sixteenth and seventeenth centuries / Rodney L. Petersen.
p. cm.   Includes bibliographical references and index.
ISBN 0-19-507374-6
1. Bible. N.T. Revelation XI, 3-13—Criticism, interpretation,
etc.—History. I. Title.
BS2825.P384   1993   228'.06—dc20   92-27964

246897531

Printed in the United States of Americaon
acid-free paper

To George H. Williams
for a vision of faith in time

to Karlfried Froehlich
for the technique of history

to my parents
for introductions and sustaining love

and to my son, Eliot,
may he walk in the way of hope

As depicted by Lucas Cranach in the Luther Bible, 1522, December edition, as found in Philipp Schmidt. *Die Illustration der Lutherbibel, 1522–1700. Ein Stück abendländischen Kulter- und Kirchengeschichte mit Verzeichnissen der Bibeln, Bilder und Künstler.* Basel: F. Reinhardt, 1962.

The Two Witnesses

(3) "And I will grant my two witnesses authority to prophesy for one thousand two hundred and sixty days, wearing sackcloth."

(4) These are the two olive trees and the two lampstands that stand before the Lord of the earth. (5) And if anyone wants to harm them, fire pours from their mouth and consumes their foes; anyone who wants to harm them must be killed in this manner. (6) They have authority to shut the sky, so that no rain may fall during the days of their prophesying, and they have authority over the waters to turn them into blood, and to strike the earth with every kind of plague, as often as they desire.

(7) When they have finished their testimony, the beast that comes up from the bottomless pit will make war upon them and conquer them and kill them, (8) and their dead bodies will lie in the street of the great city that is prophetically called Sodom and Egypt, where also their Lord was crucified. (9) For three and a half days members of the peoples and tribes and languages and nations will gaze at their dead bodies and refuse to let them be placed in a tomb; (10) and the inhabitants of the earth will gloat over them and celebrate and exchange presents, because these two prophets had been a torment to the inhabitants of the earth.

(11) But after the three and a half days, the breath of life from God entered them, and they stood on their feet, and those who saw them were terrified. (12) Then they heard a loud voice from heaven saying to them, "Come up here!" And they went up to heaven in a cloud while their enemies watched them. (13) At that moment there was a great earthquake, and a tenth of the city fell; seven thousand people were killed in the earthquake, and the rest were terrified and gave glory to the God of heaven. Revelation 11:3-13 (NRSV).

Preface

Christian eschatology and apocalyptic speculation have been the subjects of a spate of books in recent years, but detailed studies of particular themes are needed. This book is an effort in that direction. The study of specific texts can reveal the changes in detail that become new trends and outlooks. Apocalyptic symbols have been read in different ways in the history of biblical exegesis. Without going extensively into the effects of different schemes of history, one may say that the images in the book of Revelation (the Apocalypse) have been understood in a literal or prima facie way, in a spiritual or allegorical manner, or further, in such a way as to introduce a third, temporal factor that affected the symbol's literal value. This last, more typological method of understanding was quite popular among reformers in the sixteenth century.

Various studies have been done on the figure of Antichrist, the epitome of evil associated with specific visions in the Apocalypse. Here we will study that human agency which is the positive counterpart to Antichrist, the two witnesses (Rev. 11:3-13). They appear in the dark days of the Church to preach or prophesy with the powers attributed to the prophets of Israel. It appears as if they warn of the deceptions of Antichrist. Having completed their testimony, they are slain by the beast from the bottomless pit, only to be resurrected and vindicated in their ascent to heaven. The sounding of the seventh trumpet (Rev. 11:15) now rings the apparent end of history. The text is suggestive yet openended. Many have speculated on the identity of these prophetically mantled witnesses, or martyrs, and have associated theological themes with them: (1) a time of culminating evil, (2) the final proclamation of hope through prophetic word, and (3) the consequent end of history associated with divine judgment and government. The lines of speculation about the identity and time of these witnesses, established early in the history of the Church, find expression in medieval literature, art, and drama and take on increased social implications in reformist exegesis. This interest is visible in the proliferation of commentaries on the Apocalypse in the sixteenth and seventeenth centuries, and in popular literature as well. The effect of the narrative outlined by our text continued to draw attention after the Reformation, developing an even clearer visibility in subsequent Protestant polemics. In fact, we may say that the two witnesses become an image for self-interpretation, part of the message-oriented reform movement called Protestantism.

Finally, although this study is especially concerned with the exegetical history of a particular passage of Scripture, it is hoped that by investigating the different ways in which interpretation has been done, we might better understand the resulting behavior of those who have attempted to live in faithfulness to the *sacra pagina*.

Newton, Mass.   R. L. P.
July 1992

Contents

List of Illustrations

Preaching in the
Last Days

1

Adventual Prophets

Introduction to an Idea

Narratives play an important role in our lives. The stories that we tell ourselves or those to which we listen shape our self-understanding and, hence, the ways in which we interact in our world. Stories and images that have become a part of sacred traditions play an even greater role in this regard. Biblical narratives, as "mysterious and 'fraught with background'" as they may be,[1] call forth an interpretation from those of us who read them. And, particularly in the case of sacred texts like the Bible, such interpretation makes claims upon us that call us from the world of definition into that of ethics and political action.[2]

The theme of this study, the history of the interpretation of the "two witnesses" in the book of Revelation, and then the subsequent significance of that image for Protestantism, is the story of the ways in which such a narrative developed. The following pages will take us through the development of a matrix for reading our text, steps of self-understanding as related to that text, and an account of the wider social perception of its meaning and implications for the arena of ecclesial and political action. For, in addition to its earlier medieval function and influence, the text of "two witnesses" played a role in helping to establish a sense of Protestant identity during the period of religious reform and confessional realignment in the sixteenth and seventeenth centuries.

The passage where our two witnesses are found, Revelation 11:3–13, and the other biblical stories or allusions suggested to the mind of the reader in the account of the two witnesses, had a certain reactive effect. It provided an opportunity, a locus in the Christian Scriptures, for further defining the movement that, since the German Imperial Diet of Speyer (1529), became known as Protestantism. Following Western society's religious rupture, our passage of the two witnesses became increasingly important among Protestants who sought a larger narrative so as to understand their own break from the Western Catholic and Roman Church. Through the use of this biblical text a certain representation of reality was permitted that provided fertile ground for speculation about one's place in history, task in the world, and position vis-à-vis other Christian communities, which would extend well into the nineteenth century.

Some turned to this passage to find a model for prophetic warning. Others found a measure of self-identification as they pushed for a radical revision of Christendom. In doing either, such reading of our text raises the question of the way in which the symbolism of suggestive texts calls forth, for legitimation or censure, specific models for ethical emulation. Such symbolic modeling is central to Christian theology. Indeed, humankind, the first Adam, is said to have been made male and female in the image, or model, of God (Gen. 1:26–27), shattered yet deepened in likeness through a primordial disobedience (Gen. 2:17; 3:22). The second Adam, Jesus Christ, is referred to as the only perfect image of God, elliptically by the disciple John (John 1:1–18) and directly in Pauline theology (1 Cor. 11:7; Col. 1:15). And we are instructed to be "renewed in knowledge in the image of [the] Creator" through Christ (Col. 3:1–11). Yet, as the Church turned its attention beyond Christ for additional models who were to be emulated in different circumstances, their paucity in the sacred writings and the Church's outright embarrassment over some would contribute to the development of ways of reading and interpreting texts that would mark the development of hermeneutics in the churches.[3]

The text of Revelation 11:3–13 provides no direct reference to any particular model for behavior, but is suggestive in its symbolism of a plethora of models found in the "background" of Scripture. Such imagery is set forth in the context of thematic ideas found elsewhere in the book of Revelation, or Apocalypse, but is dramatically encapsulated in our text on what appears to be the plane of history. For example, there is the theme of Judgment. Purity of doctrine and practice must be maintained, or reestablished, in the face of defection. Our narrative catches up both a prophetic challenge and an apocalyptic preoccupation with synchronism and chronology.[4] Significantly, in the face of a possible predetermined historical periodization, an opening is offered by our theme for human effort and autonomy through an identification with our two witnesses. In prophesying like an Enoch or an Elijah, in constructing the New Jerusalem along lines laid down by a Joshua or Zerubbabel, various people who read our text acknowledged that there is room here for human agency.[5]

Finally, different visions for the future have been found in the passage of the two witnesses: further revelation, a new era in history, and a final call to salvation as human history moves toward a divine closure.[6] But for most commentators it was not ultimately important who the witnesses themselves were in the text. As a part of penultimate history preceding the Last Judgment, the witnesses became, for some, a symbolic vignette in the continuing struggle of truth with falsehood. Such would hold for those primarily convinced that the binding of Satan (Matt. 12:29; 16:19) occurred in the days of Christ's ministry and death and that the Christian millennial (one thousand years) age of bliss (Rev. 20:4–5) fell together with the life and expansion of the Church according to Augustine's teaching (amillennialism). For others, the two witnesses were those reconstructing Jerusalem, the new society of progress and immediate spiritual perceptivity as all the promises of God would be realized on earth prior to the Last Judgment (Dan. 7:27; Isa. 54) in what would be called postmillennialism, the belief that the return of Christ to judgment will not occur until the kingdom of God has been established on earth (Lactantius). Finally, for others our witnesses were resurrected preachers from the past called forth to herald hope in the darkest days of a mounting crescendo of evil either at the end of Augustine's "amillennial" age of history or for "premillennialists," prior to a disjunctive and divinely instituted millennium (Tertullian). The tradition of interpretation behind our passage draws upon and deepens such themes through 1500 years of interpretation prior to sixteenth-century religious upheaval.

Before turning to the Protestant use of our text, its history in preaching and biblical interpretation through early Christian and medieval tradition will be sketched.[7] This is done to lay out the major themes that develop in association with the two witnesses. Doing this will help us to understand the significance of the text. Following this, our attention will run from the apocalyptic ferment coincident with Martin Luther's vision of spiritual and consequent social reform to the work of Anglo-American commentators on the Apocalypse in the seventeenth century. In terms of formal commentary on the text, this period is roughly bounded by the appearance of the first Protestant commentary on the book of Revelation, written by Francis Lambert (1528), to the work of the English apocalypticist Thomas Goodwin (1600–1680). Except for greater specificity in interpretation, this period sets the major lines for later and contemporary interpretations of Revelation.

Exegesis of the Text

Exegesis is the explanation and critical interpretation of a text.[8] Narratives, such as that of the two witnesses, come to us through texts. Literary texts are composed of symbols that yield multiple meanings evident in the history of ways in which a text has been read; because reflection is language and language lacks a single voice, our study reveals something of the way in which there is a textuality to our text.[9] Each reading carries with it aspects of legitimacy, although in its reflections on the texts of Scripture, churches, as communities of Christian faith, have been generally guided in their assessment of a text's meaning by its "critical," "canonical," and "contextual" relationships.[10] Any particular reading may or may not be the best reading of a text. However, every way in which a text is read tells us about its significance, if not its proper meaning.

Our study will reflect something of the scope of perspectives that have been brought to and have arisen from Revelation 11:3–13. For if our study is to be anything other than an intramural theological exercise, the investigation of our text's meaning must be more than a cataloging of the history of interpretation as it relates to this aspect of the Apocalypse. Rather, it will reflect something about the way in which symbols open a path to reflection, and reflection to meaning. Through the study of the history of how a text has been understood, we gain both an awareness of the plurality of meanings elicited, and also learn something of its trajectory of meaning through time. This trajectory may not satisfy us with the exact meaning of our text, but it does map out a certain legitimate field of interpretation.[11]

The study of the reactive effect of a text such as ours, as long as the study avoids an "inner emigration" or commitment to a "sectarian stance," can help to provide a "dialogic" path between our text's meaning in the history of the Church with other theological disciplines and with a general hermeneutical quest for the understanding of texts.[12] It moves on to understand the text as shaping and being reflectively shaped by tradition and communal piety (i.e., the sense of our text in calling forth faith in a design though dimly perceived). A spiritual, or charismatic, reading of our text in addition to a focus upon its ethical significance may provide further ways of understanding but must stand together with a widened view of critical reflection.[13]

Our exegesis begins with understanding our text's context. This will help to make sense of the different ways in which it has been used. Our two witnesses appear in an interlude in the Apocalypse, somewhat independent of the surrounding visionary material, or, perhaps, as part of an increasing intensity marked by divine judgments organized around three sets of seven symbols: the opening of a seven-sealed book (Rev. 6:1–8:1), the blowing of seven angelic trumpets (8:2–11:19), and the pouring forth of seven bowls of divine wrath (16:1–21). The two witnesses appear between the sounding of the sixth and seventh apocalyptic trumpets (9:13–11:14 and 11:15ff).[14] Many, having read this material, find this interval to be parallel to that between the sixth and seventh seals (6:12–7:17 and 8:1ff.) elsewhere in Revelation.[15]

Chapters 10 and 11 in the Apocalypse are often seen to be bound together under the sounding of the sixth trumpet, perhaps determinative of an historical era opened up by the seventh apocalyptic seal (8:2). As chapter 10 begins we are met with the description of a mighty angel who hands the seer a scroll (10:1–2). This scroll, called a small book (*biblaridion*) as opposed to the book (*biblion*) mentioned in Revelation 5:1, is to be devoured (10:8–10). Our seer is then instructed to prophesy again before all the world (10:11). This is followed by the measuring of the temple (11:1–2)[16] and the appearance of the adventual witnesses (11:3–13).

The appearance of these witnesses, or prophets, their task, and the powers given them are described briefly (11:3–6). They prophesy for 1260 days (11:3).[17] When they finish their work, the beast from the pit[18] slays them, leaving their bodies exposed in a great city for three and a half days (11:7–10). After this they return to life and ascend to heaven amid the terror of all who had rejoiced in their death (11:11–13). Then the seventh trumpet sounds a final period of tribulation (11:14) prior to the establishment of the kingdom of the Lord (11:15).[19] Rich in symbolism, intriguing in specificity, chapter 11 has been seen by many commentators to provide a summary for the entire Apocalypse. Who are these prophets who have the power to destroy their enemies with fire from their mouths, to call out famine and plagues upon the earth? From where do they come? Why do they appear? What of the beast that arises to slay them? What does one make of their later resurrection?

In wrestling with the context of our text, some have held that the vision is rooted in the Hebrew Scriptures, or Old Testament. Revelation 11:14 seems derived from a vision in the book of Zechariah (4:3, 11, 14). The power of the witnesses (11:4–6), the fire that proceeds from their mouths, reminds one of Elijah's encounter with the prophets of Baal (2 Kings 1:10, 12; cf. Jer. 5:14)[20]; their power to cause a great drought of Elijah's encounter with Ahab (1 Kings 17:1); and their ability to turn water into blood or strike the earth with plagues with the mighty deeds of Moses (Exod. 7:14–18ff.; 8:12). Throughout Revelation 11:3–13, allusions can be found to the books of Ezekiel, Daniel, and Zechariah. Visions such as these gain added significance within the structural whole of the Apocalypse. They have led some commentators to suggest that our passage developed out of a refashioned Jewish source, used now to predict the repentance of the Jews and their turn to Jesus as the Messiah in the last days.[21] Others have argued that our passage and its symbolism reflect fragments of Jewish Zealot literature.[22]

While important parallels may be found in Jewish literature, the appearance of two witnesses prior to the Last Judgment seems unique. It underscores the Christian nature of this vision, whatever its earlier source in literature or prophetic inspiration. Some have argued that pre-Christian authors knew of forerunners to the last days but not of two definite prophets coming together in time, purpose, and martyrdom.[23] Echoes of the expectation of returning prophets with adventual significance are contained in the Gospels (e.g., Mark 6:14–16; 8:27–30; 9:11–13). In some of Israel's earliest records can be found the hope for a future prophet of the stature of Moses (Deut. 18:15). Later, Isaiah (40:3) speaks of a voice crying in the wilderness and Malachi (3:1) of one who will prepare the way for the Messiah. In Malachi 4:4–5 we find an allusion to two individuals, Moses and Elijah, but only Elijah is spoken of as returning before the day of the Lord (Judgment). His is the name that will be most frequently associated with the two witnesses. The idea of such forerunners, heralds of a king, is an expectation that may grow out of an Oriental background as some have argued. Still, the duality of our martyred witnesses appears to have refashioned an earlier expectation.[24]

The purpose of the appearance of the two witnesses is to prophesy—but whether this is a call to repentance or includes the foretelling of future events is left unanswered. Called by God (Rev. 11:3), identified with respect to God (11:4), and only then with regard to their task, our prophets are "the two olive trees and the two lampstands that stand before the Lord of the earth" (11:4),[25] apparently channels of God's grace or power, his light or direction. They appear to have the powers and miraculous gifts attributed to prophets from the past. Dressed in sackcloth like Elijah, like other prophets of the Old Testament, or like John the Baptist, their appearance calls forth humility and penitence (cf. Isa. 22:12; Jer. 4:8). However esoteric their prophecy, repentance in word and deed seems implied. They preach for a period of 1260 days (11:3), perhaps prophetic years, prior to completing their testimony (11:7). The question of the individuality or symbolic nature of our two witnesses is tried to an understanding of the time lying before us, be it years or days.[26]

The witnesses appear to begin their testimony before the revelation of the apocalyptic beast, living indefinitely into the period of its manifestation. However, the language of the text implies designation rather than time (11:7).[27] Much depends upon the associations one draws here: How are these events related to the wider set of visions under the sixth trumpet (9:13–11:14)? What bearing does other bestial symbolism (13:1–18; 17:8) or the prophecy of the "lawless one" (2 Thess. 1:8) have upon our text? Questions such as these open up the wider issues of the relationship between Revelation 11:3–13 and apocalyptic material elsewhere.

The adventual prophets appear to bridge history and eschatology. Finishing their testimony, they face martyrdom,[28] slain by the beast (11:7). Their bodies are left exposed in a "great city" (11:8), which may be Jerusalem, Rome, or simply the world.[29] But after three and a half days (11:9, 11) the witnesses appear vindicated by their resurrection and by their ascent to the heavens (11:11–12). Furthermore, their message seems confirmed by a great earthquake, ending our scenario with the destruction of a tenth of the city, the death of 7000 people, and the submission of the remnant of God (11:13).

From what little has been said about the context of our text, it can be seen that the imagery of this passage is related not only to Christian eschatological and apocalyptic speculation, but also to the rich history of Jewish prophecy and apocalypse. Even restricting ourselves to the canonical New Testament, we find many parallel themes (cf. Mark 13:5–37; Matt. 24:4–36; Luke 21:8–36); however, this is not the place for a full discussion of such literature.[30] Still, we may note that Paul presents a series of events prior to the "day of Christ."[31] He writes of growing defection from the gospel, of the appearance of the man of sin (2 Thess. 2:3; 4:8), who has often been connected with the beast of Revelation 11:7 and 13:1–11.[32] In both books the wicked one comes shortly before the end to Jerusalem, Rome, or the remnant of the Roman Empire.

Paul's description of these events is briefer than that found in the Apocalypse, and neither he nor the synoptic apocalypses describe the appearance of adventual witnesses. Accordingly, such prophets are not always a part of events listed for the apocalyptic scenario, prior to the Last Judgment, in the history of exegesis.[33] Indeed, such treatment in Scripture indicates that an extended discussion of their appearance is often an indication of a heightened preoccupation with apocalyptic identity and time-consciousness.[34]

The work of these prophets, apparently directed to those who have already been acquainted with the word of God, visualizes ideas found elsewhere in that word, that the Judgment of the Lord begins within the house of God (1 Peter 4:17). For many who would be called Protestants, this was the reality they felt they experienced as they looked to a Church that they believed had lost both its doctrinal accuracy and moral purity. Revelation 11:3–13 (together with 11:1–2) is a visual elaboration of the call for measured purity either along traditionally prophetic or radically apocalyptic lines. It found its place in renewal and reformist movements from the later Middle Ages through the development of Protestantism.

Revivified Prophets

The earliest tradition of the Church held that the two witnesses were to be two prophets out of Israel's past brought back for a final mission on earth.[35] Elijah's name has long been connected with Revelation 11. The grounds for this reside in possibly Jewish and certainly Christian apocalyptic speculation and upon suggestive remarks in the synoptic Gospels,[36] particularly the association of John the Baptist with the memory of Elijah (Luke 1:17; Matt. 11:14).[37] Jesus was believed

by some to be the final Elijah (e.g., Mark 6:15; 8:28). Disclaiming such association, he identified the Baptist as having performed Elijah's work in the account
of the Transfiguration (Mark 9:11–13). But for many John only partially performed
those tasks assigned to Elijah (Mark 9:12; Mal. 3:1–3; 4:5–6). According to
the Gospel of John, the Baptist denied the association (John 1:21, 25).[38] From the
Transfiguration and the double prophecy of Christ in the Old Testament, Justin
Martyr (c. 100–165) inferred a coming of Elijah prior to each Advent, but there
is no reference to our text.[39] While he discusses our witnesses elsewhere, Tertullian
(c. 160–225) knows of a single return of Elijah in the same body in which he
left this world.[40] Lactantius (c. 240–320) clearly connects Elijah's name with Revelation 11:3–13,[41] thereby illustrating how the tradition of Elijah's return, a theme
distinct from that of this study, is often woven into the interpretation of our
text.

Whereas the tradition of Elijah's return has been clear, the identity of a second prophet has varied.[42] Moses is often referred to as Elijah's colleague, following the account of Jesus' Transfiguration. The expectation of a leader like Moses
(Deut. 18:15), and the mysterious nature of his death (Deut. 34:6),[43] make the idea
plausible. Similar arguments can be found for other contenders. Jeremiah, called
a prophet to the nations (Jer. 1:5), is seen by some not to have fulfilled his mission in his day, and therefore is pictured here. The Evangelist John, thought not
to have experienced death (John 21:22–23), is given a renewed opportunity to
preach the gospel. Others described Elijah's colleagues simply as the apocalyptic
"prophets."[44]

Nevertheless, Enoch has usually been associated with Elijah in this projected
hope for returning prophets prior to the end of history. According to tradition,
Enoch was "translated," or caught up deathless from the earth to a heavenly realm
(Gen. 5:22–24; Eccles. 44:16; Heb. 11:5)[45] for the sake of his sanctity in the age
before the Mosaic law. The Gospel of Nicodemus offers a paradisal vision of the
exalted state of Enoch and Elijah, who await the coming of Antichrist. At this
time they will reappear on earth together with other adventual signs and wonders
of God.[46] They, perhaps with the addition of Adam, Moses, Jeremiah, Mary the
Mother of our Lord, and John the beloved disciple, all inhabit a kind of terrestrial
paradise, the conditions of which will one day be those of the entire world when
the kingdom of God is established.[47]

As Enoch was translated, so Elijah arose to heaven in a fiery chariot, and while
the present location of these prophets was a subject of speculation, many exegetes
were led to opine that the prophets would have to be recalled in order to die.
Their righteousness, together with a kind of sanguineous suffering for the truth,
formed a mysterious bond between human effort and the purposes of God.[48] Like
Elijah, Enoch's momentous return was tied to interests of prophecy and judgment.[49]
Thus, it became quite plausible in the work of early commentators on our text for
Enoch and Elijah to be the two who would appear prior to the end of history.
Their last call to repentance and prophetic challenge of the beast, or Antichrist,
would call forth not only their own martyrdom—and the death they had once
eluded, yet (as human) had to face—but also the final blast of the angelic seventh
trumpet (11:15) announcing the eternal establishment of Christ's kingdom.

If one considers the texts of Mark 9:12–13 and Revelation 11:3–13 together, the prominence of Elijah and Enoch is striking. Their reappearance, rather than that of Moses and Elijah, which might seem more obvious simply on the basis of our text alone, attests to the strength, according to some commentators, of the Enoch tradition in pre-Christian and early Christian understanding.[50] Having carefully studied apocalyptic literature in the common era in an effort to define the tradition that generated accounts of heroes arising to check an embodiment of evil, later defined as Antichrist, Bousset summarized the differences that he found. His conclusions, which can be summarized in the following five points, are: (1) The Johannine seer probably assumed Moses and Elijah to be the two witnesses whereas the tradition promoted Enoch and Elijah; (2) in the Johannine vision the beast appears from the pit after the witnesses have completed their testimony; in the tradition the order is reversed; (3) whereas the witnesses in the book of Revelation are capable of causing great plagues, in the tradition these plagues are brought on by God; (4) while in the Johannine vision the witnesses do not develop any particular posture toward the beast, in the tradition they instruct the faithful and actively oppose the beast, fomenting rebellion against him; (5) the Johannine witnesses are resurrected and ascend to heaven. Their ressurection, Bousset concluded, constituted a unique contribution of the author of the Apocalypse upon tradition.[51]

Other early texts like the Ethiopic Apocalypse of Peter and the Coptic Apocalypse of Elijah further define the witnesses' identity and tasks. In the former, the martyrdoms of Enoch and Elijah are not specifically mentioned, but they are said to come at the end of the age to instruct against the deception of false Christs.[52] In the latter they encounter the "son of Lawlessness" and are slain by him (35:1–14). They return with the Lord at Judgment and slay Antichrist (42:1–17).[53] In light of this material, Jeremias[54] and Jean Marc Rosentiehl[55] argue differently from Bousset; they find a Jewish origin of our text related to and extended into Revelation 11. However, Bauckham adds a word of caution to such argumentation. He carefully works his way through Bousset's sources, concluding that the unique contribution of Revelation 11 to the tradition of returning prophets was not their resurrection but their martyrdom. Faced with the difficulty of precisely describing the provenance of our text, he attempts a classification of the witnesses' tasks, thereby delineating pre-Christian and Christian contributions to their work and identity.[56]

Tertullian and Hippolytus (c. 170–236) present us with the clearest datable references to our two witnesses.[57] Both follow a literal pattern of exegesis and indicate that these two prophets are actual persons.[58] They are Enoch and Elijah, the two prophets who did not experience death.

Tertullian argues that the two have been preserved until the last days in order to expose and fight Antichrist. Accordingly, they will appear with Antichrist at the end of history, extinguishing him with the blood of their martyrdom.[59] The theme of martyrdom is one often associated with the work of God's witnesses in the history of the exegesis of Revelation 11. Protestant commentators will be quick to draw it out. Not only do the two witnesses return for this task because of their righteousness but, as Tertullian argues against Epicurus and Menander (who claimed deathlessness for their followers), they too must yet experience death like all others.[60]

Hippolytus, using Daniel's seventy prophetic weeks as a guide to divide the last days, places the appearance of Enoch and Elijah in the first half of the end time.[61] They mark the impending Judgment by preaching penance. Such "prophesying" is an important theme for later reformist groups. The witnesses are precursors of the Second Advent as John the Baptist preceded the first. They preach the imminent return of Christ, performing signs and wonders as they call for repentance. They are slain because they will not honor Antichrist, whose rule occurs in the last half of Daniel's prophetic week, a period of three and a half years (cf. Rev. 11:7–10). Hippolytus cites Malachi 4:5–6 in support of his contention that one of the witnesses is Elijah but merely asserts that the second will be Enoch.[62] He does not mention their resurrection.

Both Tertullian and Hippolytus refer unhesitatingly to the witnesses as Enoch and Elijah, but the ambiguity respecting their number, identity, and tasks has fostered continued speculation about the threads of tradition behind the text. What is clear and central to the point of this chapter of Revelation is that in the earliest history of the Church our text was associated with specific figures, their penitential attitude, proclamation, and final martyrdom set in the context of an apocalyptic horizon.

The thrust of this early and literal exegetical tradition was enhanced by the work of such later commentators as Victorinus of Pettau (d.c. 304), for whom the identity of the witnesses is correlated with several references in the Apocalypse.[63] These prophets now become pictured under a wider canopy of visionary images. Victorinus, referred to as the first exegete of the Western Church, is cited by later critics both for his comprehensiveness and his contribution to a theory of recapitulation in his interpretation of the Apocalypse.[64] Victorinus found similar spiritual truths embedded in different but logically parallel symbols. His commentary, the earliest example of a continuous systematic analysis of Revelation, displays such methodology in his interpretation of our theme.

The vision of the angel with the seal of the living God (Rev. 7:2) is understood to be Elijah. Victorinus gives him a threefold task: (1) to anticipate the time of Antichrist; (2) to preach penance, turning the hearts of fathers to their children and children to their fathers (Mal. 4:5–6); and (3) to convert to faith many from Israel as well as from the Gentile nations.[65] This image comes together with the warning cry of the eagle who flies across the heavens (Rev. 8:13), that is, the Holy Spirit speaking, as it were, through the mouths of the prophets (11:3).[66] These are the ones whose time and identity are discussed in Revelation 11:2ff. One is said to be Elijah, Victorinus writes; the name of the second is not clear. Many have suggested Elisha, Moses, or others, Victorinus states. He notes, however, that he is of the opinion that the second witness is Jeremiah, the prophet to the nations (Jer. 1:5), who must yet complete his prophetic mission.[67]

These prophets appear for three and a half years (11:3). The woman (i.e., the Church), driven to the wilderness for 1260 days, is nourished by their word (12:6–14).[68] They perform their work, then are slain by the beast (11:7) in Jerusalem. Antichrist now reigns, tormenting the earth for a second period of three and a half years. At the end of this time the witnesses are resurrected.[69] Further illustrations are given as Victorinus continues to draw our attention to the work of these adventual witnesses, but in particular to the return of Elijah.[70] Other symbols are explained through the same method of recapitulation. Angelic trumpets (8:2–11:19) and bowls of divine wrath (16:1–21) mark the pattern of an imminent future portending God's reign, which will follow the destruction of Babylon, or Rome.[71] The narrative of Revelation 11 is seen to come together with the current period of persecution that lay before the churches under Diocletian's reign. For Victorinus, these were the days of the sixth seal (8:2). The witnesses might now appear to perform their task.[72]

The work of Victorinus summarizes for us important perspectives on the literal and specific identity of the two witnesses through a method of recapitulative exegesis. By working as he did, Victorinus added life and visionary breadth to what otherwise might have been the witnesses' slight appearance in the Apocalypse. This added significance to what was believed to be the pattern of events involved in their imminent return to history and their role in portending imminent Judgment. The witnesses were to be two in number. They were prophets, probably reappearing from the past. These prophets would be recognized by characteristics recalling earlier prophetic activity, and by signs of penitence as they prophesied in the last days. Slain by Antichrist, they would then be resurrected prior to or as a part of the general resurrection to Judgment, depending upon whether a particular exegete found a grounding in the text for a space of time between their history and that of the Last Judgment.

Victorinus's way of reading our text was handed down to the medieval Church under the authoritative name of Jerome (c. 342–420), who, however, was uncomfortable with Victorinus's millenarian viewpoint and, therefore, editorally revised Victorinus's commentary on the Apocalypse. Jerome's edition gave an abiding, if marginal, stamp of orthodoxy in the Western Church to the understanding of the witnesses and to the method of exegesis developed by Victorinus, including traces of its implicit chiliasm (belief in a millennium). However, Jerome's own work would move questions concerning the witnesses' identity and tasks in a highly symbolic direction. Such would add to their significance by deepening the kind of figural, or symbolic, scriptural associations correlated with them, even as it would move speculation upon their immediate, and literal, return ever further to the margins of orthodoxy.

Symbolic Representation

Jerome helped lead the way toward a more symbolic reading of our text.[73] The earlier literal personification was eclipsed by a growing spiritual or allegorical understanding. Such tendencies were systematically elaborated by the exegete Tyconius (d.c. 400) under whose influence Jerome fell.[74] The years surrounding the first century A.D. were marked by major shifts in Christian thinking related to the Church's new orientation toward the larger culture. Such shifts can be seen in fresh interpretations of the book of Revelation.[75]

A refashioned "representative" understanding of the witnesses may be found in Jerome's work, later cited authoritatively. Jerome reflects on the interpretation of the Apocalypse in his commentary on Isaiah. Reading the book of Revelation in a literal fashion, he fears, will cast one together with the Judaizers who failed to see the first Advent of the Messiah, and carnally look for Christ's kingdom. However, to interpret the Apocalypse spiritually would be to understand it differently from such authorities as Irenaeus, Tertullian, Victorinus, and Lactantius.[76]

This dilemma is reflected in the pattern of Jerome's own exegesis. First, he argues, Enoch and Elijah continue to exist. They were bodily caught up, raptured to a paradisal state without experiencing death, having led lives that were pleasing to God.[77] Then, commenting upon Malachi 4:5-6 (the prophecy of Elijah's return before the Day of the Lord), Jerome argues symbolically that insofar as Elijah did return, he came in the person of John the Baptist. The passage in Malachi is to be spiritually understood, indicating the continual preaching of the spiritual message of the law and the prophets.[78]

In a letter to his devotee, Marcella (386), Jerome emphasizes (in the names of Paula and Eustochium, his female companions in Palestine) that a spiritual or figurative interpretation is to be given to the return of Enoch and Elijah despite the expectation that their return was required for their prophesied conflict with Antichrist and their experience of death.[79] Marcella seems unwilling to come to Jerusalem, fearing, perhaps, that it is the city in which the witnesses are to be slain (11:8). In some of his earliest commentaries, Jerome had argued that Jerusalem was as Sodom and Egypt (*In Zeph.* 2:9). When Christ was rejected by the Jews, Jerusalem lost her holy status (*In Matt.* 27:51-53). Now, Jerome urges Marcella to leave Rome, referred to as Babylon (soon to be sacked by Alaric and the Vandals!) and join the three of them in retreat at Jerusalem and Bethlehem. They seem to anticipate Marcella's argument by contending that Revelation 11 can mean something other than the literal Jerusalem. In fact, the city described here, Jerome argues, represents the entire world.

The case is still not entirely clear. Jerome writes again, answering five questions on such topics as the identity of spiritual things, the quality of Christ's person following his Resurrection and the status of those who remain alive at the second Advent.[80] In his answer, Jerome outlines an anthropology that will be of continuing importance in the Church affecting our conception of the witnesses: Adam's sin brought death. As heirs of Adam we sin and die. However, Enoch and Elijah were so free from sin that they were translated without having experienced death. Leaving the world in their bodies, they remain in them, but, as such, are not in the same heavenly realm as other deceased saints. They will return to our realm to engage in battle with Antichrist. Reflecting the ambiguity of the tradition, Jerome adds that whether they will die at this time is difficult to know. Affirming the importance of a spiritual interpretation of the text, Jerome goes no further, fearing acquiescence to Jewish fables.[81]

Jerome's thinking, even in its uncertainty, is part of a general move from a prevailing realistic literal hermeneutic to one that is more allegorical and representative.[82] The attempt to find the spiritual significance of the text had been largely defined by the exegetical concerns of Tyconius,[83] who had argued that the book of Revelation was not an historical outline of present and imminent history. Rather, it is a picture of prophetic tension in the days defined by the Messiah's first Advent. Tyconius, important in his own right, is worth noting at this point not only because of his influence on Jerome, but also because of his influence upon Augustine, who largely adopts, and then bears to the medieval period, Tyconius's method of reading Scripture.[84]

Tyconius's work represented in its contours contemporary religious conflict in North Africa between Catholic and Donatist religious communities, and it stands in contrast to it.[85] Persecution from Catholic and Roman Imperial interests, as experienced by Tyconius's Donatist associates, could be viewed as part of a perennial moral conflict described in Revelation. Therefore, the text was of use to his radical colleagues; for Tyconius this did not necessarily imply an imminent end to history, though such has often been affirmed by later interpreters.[86] Tyconius's own sense of the end was probably more muted.[87] This appears to be borne out not only in the way in which he was used by immediate successors but also in the prevailing spirit behind medieval apocalyptic iconography.[88]

According to Tyconius, the witnesses are not two personalities. Rather, they represent the pure Church, the Lord's body in the world, prophesying and preaching through the two testaments.[89] Later medieval commentators would further this perspective. However, it is the message-oriented reform movement, Protestantism in the years of its formation, that will be most marked by this conception of our text. The work of the prophets is carried out in the entire age of the Church. For Tyconius, this period can be interpreted as 350 years, calculated from the "1260 days" of their prophetic activity.[90] The beast who rises to slay the witnesses, leaving them to lie in the great city (11:7–10), is symbolic of worldly power.[91] The true Church exists in a persecuted and martyred condition in the midst of the world.[92] Under the impact of Tyconius's fifth exegetical rule, the meaning of this period is not so straightforward. Different temporal indicators may reveal the same spiritual relationships.[93] Therefore, the work of the witnesses also falls under the millennial age of the Church. This is adumbrated by the 1260 days of protection and nourishment given the woman (12:6) who flees before the wrath of the seven-headed, ten-horned dragon (Satan).[94]

What of our adventual witnesses? It would appear that Tyconius, differing from his Donatist associates, felt that it was impossible to divide the current Church into communities of true and faithless Christians. They were pictured together as one in the sun-draped woman of the Apocalypse (12:1).[95] Yet, within this image were two bodies of believers.[96] One group is symbolized by the solar apparel of the woman, the Church purified and baptized into Christ.[97] The other is adumbrated under the moon upon which the woman is standing.[98] The dragon shown to attack the woman (12:3)[99] is said, in its seven heads, to represent all of the kings of the world. Its ten horns symbolize all kingdoms. Is this the time for the revelation of the pure? For some of Tyconius's colleagues, current persecution represented a final growth of evil.[100] In this context a separation would occur in the Church. This would be followed by the resurrection of the witnesses, Christ's true disciples, and the Second Advent (Coming) of Christ.[101] Is this the end? Viewed from the perspective of Tyconius's exegetical rules, the vision is complex. It appears to describe the perennial struggle of the Church. The Church's qualities of perfection are "eschatologized," reserved for God's end.[102]

Tyconius's view of the Apocalypse marked a fresh point of departure for conceiving of the time and identity of the witnesses. His significance appears in his influence upon Augustine (354–430), who found Tyconius's exegetical methodology and conception of the Church useful.[103] Tyconius's idea of two bodies in the world, one of Christ and the other of the Devil, was now re-conceived by Augustine as two cities.[104] Augustine conveyed the implied temporal dualism to the medieval period, but gave no pointed consideration to our two prophets. However, Augustine does have an impact upon later reflection concerning the witnesses. Not only does this come through the moral dualism he finds in history, but also in three further respects: First, he notes the appearance of Elijah prior to the Day of Judgment based upon Malachi 4:4–6.[105] His reference to the work of this one prophet will lend legitimacy to speculation on the adventual witnesses for some later commentators. In fact, Augustine is cited (mistakenly) for his spiritual interpretation of our text, illustrating the intertwining of the Elijah tradition.[106] Elijah is to return to become the agent of the Jews' conversion to the Messianic character of Jesus.[107] Second, Augustine's seriated understanding of time will contribute to the nature of later speculation[108]; the two witnesses, or their corporate representation, will replace the return of Elijah within the framework of a definite chronology. Finally, Augustine's influence will affect speculation on the growth of evil, even the manifestation of Antichrist at the end of the age, but he concludes that the only certainty is that such a time of evil will come.[109] He does not, however, explicitly connect Elijah's return with this intensification of evil (as others will do), although both events precede a Second Advent of the Messiah.[110] Still, in the four areas touched upon above—moral dualism, Elijah's return, seriated time, and a final intensification of evil—we see themes that bear directly upon our text.

Augustine's student and bishop of Carthage, Quodvultdeus (d.c. 453), forced to flee the city at the invasion of the Vandals, lived with a keen sense of end-time events, including an interest in our two witnesses.[111] Quodvultdeus's view illustrates the way in which the witnesses continued to be seen by some as returning revivified prophets despite the growth of symbolic representation in their understanding. He expected a final mission of righteousness by both Enoch and Elijah. As God sent Moses and Aaron against Pharaoh and his magicians, Peter and Paul against Nero and his accomplice (by tradition) Simon Magus, so Enoch and Elijah will be sent against Antichrist and his false prophets in the closing days of history.[112] Our witnesses appear in the first half of a final historical period divided into the "Half-time with the Signs of Antichrist" and the "Glory and Kingdom of the Saints," a division based upon a conflation of prophetic texts (Dan. 7:25; 12:7; cf. 9:24–27; and Rev. 12:14; cf. 11:2–3, 11). Quodvultdeus cites Tyconius for exegetical support.[113]

Before moving further into the Western and medieval tradition of apocalyptic speculation, several things need to be said about how our text was read in the Eastern churches. First, it should be noted, the book of Revelation was generally excluded from liturgical use in the churches of the East.[114] The book had been assessed critically by Eusebius of Caesarea and others charged with the promotion of a canon of Scripture in the East. Insofar as apocalyptic themes were developed, they were not as directly dependent upon the book of Revelation as in the West.[115] Interestingly, the Antichrist legend, cited earlier in connection with Bousset, plays a more central role in many of the Greek or Byzantine apocalypses than does the book of Revelation,[116] envisaging conflict between Antichrist and a Last Roman/Byzantine emperor, even a call for participation in a holy war. However, in the commentaries of Oecumenius, Andreas of Caesarea, and Arethas of Caesarea (following Andreas closely), a strong spiritual accent dominates the interpretation of the text.[117] This spiritual emphasis, added to Tyconius's stress on the corporate personality of the witnesses, will be attractive to later Protestant exegetes who will find in the works of Andreas and Arethas perceived patristic testimony to the book of Revelation, lending legitimacy to our text.[118]

The oldest Greek commentary appears to be that by Oecumenius (early sixth century), probably a contemporary and supporter of the Monophysite Patriarch of Antioch, Severus (c. 465–538).[119] This alignment is indicative of a profound mystical interpretation. Oecumenius establishes a common catena—the adventual witnesses are Enoch and Elijah; they appear before the second Advent to fight Antichrist (a more combative posture than given them in the Apocalypse); they will be slain by his cunning following their testimony; their martyrdom is a sign for those who are laden with guilt. However, Oecumenius draws out the layered symbolism of the text by turning to "the ineffable prophet," Zechariah (Zech. 4:11–14). There the symbolism of the olive trees and lampstand (picked up in Rev. 11:4) is said to refer to two who offer special service to the Lord of the earth. The spiritual and perceptual implications of this allusion, not to mention the strength of the reference to Zerubbabel and Joshua in Israel's history, draw out the spiritual and mystical significance of our text in Oecumenius's day.[120]

This spiritual lesson of the text is highlighted in the works of Andreas, archbishop of Caesarea (Cappadocia).[121] While Andreas makes no reference to other formal expositions on the book of Revelation prior to the one in his preface,[122] he does point to work on apocalyptic themes by Gregory of Nazianzus, Cyril of Alexandria, Papias, Irenaeus, Methodius, and Hippolytus.[123] Having done this, three levels of meaning are given to our text: (1) a literal or outward identification, (2) a tropological or moral import, and (3) a mystical or speculative significance. Such levels of interpretation will meld together with similar emphases in exegesis to provide models for legitimate reading of texts. For Andreas, both the time and the conflict of the Church on earth, revealed mystically in the Apocalypse, are part of a temporal procession returning from division to unity in God. The first six seals binding the apocalyptic scroll are connected with this sequence.[124] The seven trumpets and vials herald the judgments and plagues of the last days. The two adventual witnesses (11:3), Enoch and Elijah, appear at the end of the age, the time pictured under the sixth seal, for three and one-half years (figured on the basis of a year of 360 days).[125] Dressed in sackcloth, they preach against apostasy and the deceptiveness of Antichrist, a Jewish ruler from the tribe of Dan who deceives his people, establishes a throne in Jerusalem, and imitates David.[126] They are a final antidote to his poison. The miraculous strength in their work counters his machinations. Although slain by Antichrist, who now rules in a period of infidelity, the witnesses' subsequent resurrection together with a glorification of Christian martyrs concludes with the sounding of the seventh trumpet (11:11, 15) and the end of the age.[127]

In conclusion, we return to the West by turning to Primasius of Hadrumetum, a Latin contemporary of Oecumenius. Primasius wrote in the tradition of Tyconius.[128] The witnesses retain their corporate identity and symbolize "the church preaching and prophesying through the two testaments of scripture."[129] His discussion reflects Tyconius's fourth exegetical rule: While many may be included within his model (e.g., the two sons of Zebedee in the early Church) God alone knows what they are like and how they will appear.[130] Primasius offers an extended discussion of the qualities of the witnesses based upon the imagery of the text (11:4–6). When he comes to their slaying by Antichrist (who has grown up in the tribe of Dan), Primasius becomes more specific about their identity, namely that although Elijah's return was associated with John the Baptist, this does not preclude his return prior to the second Advent to fulfill completely the prophecy of restitution given by Malachi.[131] The validity of a literal interpretation of the text, perhaps illustrative of a domesticated apocalypticism, was now permitted by the Latin Church as long as it did not upset its prevailing theology. Indeed, Primasius's allegorical commentary can be seen to represent general apocalyptic tendencies through the tenth century.[132]

Notes

1. See Erich Auerbach, *Mimesis: The Representation of Reality in Western Literature*, trans. by Willard R. Trask (Princeton: Princeton University Press, 1953), introductory pages and p. 12. The significance of latent meaning in the Bible is heightened to the breaking point for many today in light of its simultaneous claim to truth. The function of narrative and its recovery is pioneered by Hans W. Frei, *The Eclipse of Biblical Narrative: A Study in Eighteenth and Nineteenth Century Hermeneutics* (New Haven: Yale University Press, 1974); cf. Lawrence Stone, who writes about the significance of the return to narrative in historical writing in "The Revival of Narrative: Reflection on a New Old History," *Past and Present*, 85 (1979):3–24.

2. Robert Bellah notes the role of the Bible in "communal re-creation." He continues, citing a respondent, "'The texts don't create our world. But Christians in every age use it, together with the rest of their culture, to create images and discourses to know the world and act in it.'" See Robert Bellah et al., *The Good Society* (New York: Knopf, 1991), pp. 206–11. Language, as a medium of power by all groups, is forcefully argued in terms of representation in the social world by Pierre Bourdieu in "Social Space and the Genesis of 'Classes,'" *Language and Symbolic Power* (Cambridge: Harvard University Press, 1991):229–51. The relationship between the hermeneutical decisions involved in language and the interpretation of texts as applied to the shaping of communities, preeminently the Church, is discussed by Stanley Hauerwas in *A Community of Character. Toward a Constructive Christian Social Ethic* (Notre Dame, Ind.: University of Notre Dame Press, 1981).

3. See Augustine, *De doctrina christiana*, III, xii–20, in *St. Augustine on Christian Doctrine*, trans. by D. W. Robertson (Indianapolis: Bobbs-Merrill, 1958–83), p. 91. Roland

Bainton traces the importance of such symbolic models and the theological ingenuity which they inspired since Origen in "The Immoralities of the Patriarchs According to the Exegesis of the Late Middle Ages and of the Reformation," in HTR, 22 (1920):39–49. Issues of culture, special revelation, natural law, and argument by definition were used to explain such behavior as the incest of Lot, and the polygamy of Abraham and Jacob. The necessity of models as exemplars of the biblical narrative is illustrated early in the Church in such works as Jerome's *De viris illustribus* (c. 392/3), the significance of such highlighted by Peter Brown in *The Cult of the Saints* (Chicago: University of Chicago Press, 1981).

4. A clear definition of the terms "eschatological" and "apocalyptic" is found in Bernard McGinn, *Visions of the End: Apocalyptic Traditions in the Middle Ages* (New York: Columbia University Press, 1979), pp. 28–32. The former refers to the Greek word *eschatos*, or last things; the latter to attitudes and ideas sparked by apocalypses, a literary genre, offering visions of end-time events. The preeminent example of this in the Christian world is the Apocalypse of John, or the book of Revelation. (The former term, a latinism, more characteristic of Roman Catholicism, than the latter, popular since the sixteenth century in the West.) By way of distinction, "prophecy," spiritually inspired preaching, may be fore-telling or forth-telling. I add a further term in this study, "adventual," as suggested by George H. Williams, to denote those persons or events that appear on the plane of history prior to the end. See Hillel Schwartz, "The End of the Beginning: Millenarian Studies, 1965–1975," *Religious Studies Review*, 2 (1976):1–15; for a focus on medieval Christendom, see Bernard McGinn, "Awaiting an End: Research in Medieval Apocalypticism, 1974–1981," MH, n.s. 11 (Totowa, N.J.: Rowman and Littlefield, 1982), pp. 263–89; and Ann Williams, ed., *Prophecy and Millenarianism: Essays in Honor of Marjorie Reeves* (Essex: Longman, 1980). Particular studies of apocalyptic literature include Paul Hanson, ed., who grounds such in Jewish prophecy, *Visionaries and Their Apocalypses* (Philadelphia: Fortress Press, 1983). See also the systematic analysis of John Collins as well as Walter Schmithals's explanation of the inner spirit of apocalyptic thinking. The essays and accompanying bibliography of commentaries and ancillary readings on prophecy and the Book of Revelation in the book edited by C. A. Patrides and Joseph Wittreich form a convenient place to begin a study of the effect of the Apocalypse upon the Anglo-American world: *The Apocalypse in English Renaissance Thought and Literature* (Ithaca, N.Y.: Cornell University Press, 1984).

5. The use of biblical models to effect moral reform in society is as old as biblical literature is sacred. For examples, see John Bossy, "Holiness and Society," *Past and Present*, 75 (1977):119–37; and Robin Horton, "A Definition of Religion and Its Uses," *Journal of the Royal Anthropological Institute*, 90 (1966):211. Recent scholars who have worked in this area include Mary Douglas, Janet Nelson, and W. H. C. Frend.

6. Frank Kermode discusses the ways in which conceptions of finality shape narrative in *The Sense of Ending: Studies in the Theory of Fiction* (London: Oxford University Press, 1967).

7. Use of our text in preaching may illustrate relative degrees of dissatisfaction with the state of Christendom. On such potential "decay" see Erich Seeberg, *Gottfried Arnold: Die Wissenschaft und die Mystik* (Darmstadt: Wissenschaftliche Buchgesellschaft, 1964), pp. 257–80); viz. Heinrich Bornkamm's caution of Seeberg's typology in John Headly, *Luther's View of Church History* (New Haven: Yale University Press, 1963), pp. 156–57.

8. While appreciating deconstructive insight into texts (*pace* Kermode or, with differences, Derrida), Ronald F. Thiemann urges an alternative to the polarities of epistemological foundationalism and literary/cultural relativism through the invitation to faith offered by persuasive texts. See "Radiance and Obscurity in Biblical Narratives," in

Constructing a Public Theology: The Church in a Pluralistic Culture (Louisville, Ky.: Westminster/John Knox Press, 1991), pp. 45–62. Thiemann's reasoning follows a path opened by Hans Frei and Robert Alter.

9. The function of symbols as avenues to reflection is explored against the background of current hermeneutical theory (*pace* Hans Georg Gadamer with further nuances from Jürgen Habermas) by Paul Ricoeur, *Hermeneutics and the Human Sciences: Essays in Language, Action, and Interpretation*, John B. Thompson, ed. (Cambridge: Cambridge University Press, and Paris: Editions de la Maison des Sciences de l'Homme, 1981).

10. Ever since the time of the theologian Origen (d.c.254) a fourfold pattern of exegesis —finding in the text literal, allegorical (or typological), tropological, and anagogical levels of meaning—has held sway. Although, for Protestants in particular, a literal sense of the text has been underscored, other senses of the text are often operative in the life of the churches. See Gabriel Fackre, *The Christian Story* (Grand Rapids, Mich.: Eerdmans, 1987), pp. 158–60. Classic studies on the ways in which the Bible has been read include Ernst von Dobschütz, "Vom vierfachen Schriftsinn," in *Harnack-Ehrung* (Leipzig: J. C. Hinrichs, 1921), pp. 1–13; Beryl Smalley, *The Study of the Bible in the Middle Ages* (Oxford: Clarendon Press, 1941); Henri de Lubac, *Exégèse médiévale: Les quatres sens de l'Ecriture*, 2 vols. (Paris: Aubier, 1959–1964); and Gerhard Ebeling, "Hermeneutik," RGG, 3 (1959): 244–62. Commentaries used throughout this study include R. H. Charles, *A Critical and Exegetical Commentary on the Revelation of John*, 2 vols. (Edinburgh: T. & T. Clark, 1920); P. E.-B. Allo, *L'Apocalypse* (Paris: Librairie Victor Lecoffe, 1921); Charles Brütsch, *Die Offenbarung Jesu Christi* (Zürich: Zwingli Verlag, 1970); J. Massyngberde Ford, *Revelation* (New York: Doubleday, 1975); John M. Court, *Myth and History in the Book of Revelation* (Atlanta: John Knox Press, 1979); and Robert Mounce, *The Book of Revelation* (Grand Rapids, Mich.: Eerdmans, 1977).

11. Note Augustine's argument in the opening pages of *De doctrina christiana*, that the Spirit speaks through all to teach each one humility in order that we might listen to one another, in *On Christian Doctrine*, p. 6.

12. The terms are Karlfried Froehlich's in "Church History and the Bible," as he sketches the contributions of the discipline of Church history, in *Biblical Hermeneutics in Historical Perspective*, Mark S. Burrows and Paul Rorem, eds. (Grand Rapids, Mich.: Eerdmans, 1991), p. 15.

13. Apart from the horizon of historical, and thereby communal, reflection, Frank Kermode's charge that "inside" and "spiritual" (as opposed to "outside" and "carnal") interpretations of a text are finally illusory, is cogent. See *The Genesis of Secrecy: On the Interpretation of Narrative* (Cambridge: Harvard University Press, 1979). Communal reflection has followed four different paths in seeking to understand the symbolism of the Apocalypse: (1) preterist (the text was written for and is best understood in terms of events in the days of its author); (2) historicist (the text forecasts human history between the two Advents of Christ); (3) futurist (except for the first three chapters, the text is exclusively concerned with events at the end of history); (4) idealist (the text is primarily concerned with ideas and principles that may occur in any age).

14. Three exegetical studies on Rev. 11 have been of help throughout this work: Donatus Haugg, *Die Zwei Zeugen: Eine exegetische Studie über Apok, 11:1–13* (Münster: Aschendorffschen Verlagsbuchhandlung, 1936); Johannes Munck, *Petrus und Paulus in der Offenbarung Johannis* (Copenhagen: Rosenkilde og Bagger, 1950); and André Feuillet, "Interpretation of Chapter 11 of the Apocalypse," in *Johannine Studies*, trans. by T. E. Crane (Staten Island, N.Y.: Alba House, 1964).

15. See the method of recapitulation further in this study as developed by Victorinus of Pettau (d.c. 304) and more systematically by Joachim of Fiore (c. 1132–1202).

16. The measuring and desolation of the temple (11:1–2), prophesying days of the witnesses (11:3), and their death and resurrection (11:8–10) are related by many exegetes to the mystery of the Church perhaps delineated in chapters 12 and 20 of Revelation. See Pierre Prigent, *Apocalypse 12, Histoire de L'exégèse* (Tübingen: J. C. B. Mohr, Paul Siebeck, 1959). More recently, and with contemporary political implications, see Craig A. Blaising and Darrell L. Bock, eds., *Dispensationalism, Israel and the Church. The Search for Definition* (Grand Rapids, Mich.: Zondervan, 1992).

17. Much is made by different interpreters of the parallel between this period of time and previously mentioned periods of 42 months (Rev. 11:2). If we assume Rev. 11:2–3 to be concurrent, this taken together with the time cited in Rev. 11:9, 11 can be equalled with the mystic number seven. Here a further comparison is made by some with Dan. 9:24–27.

18. The figure of Antichrist, believed by many to be described in chapters 13 and 17, is often identified as the beast from the pit (Rev. 11:7). The term "Antichrist" as such is not used in the book of Revelation (cf. 1 John 2:18, 22; 4:3; 2 John 7). See Richard Emmerson, *Antichrist in the Middle Ages* (Seattle: University of Washington Press, 1981), pp. 34–73, who presents a consideration of the medieval exegetical tradition; cf. Wilhelm Bousset's earlier study, *The Antichrist Legend*, trans. by A. H. Keane (London: Hutchinson, 1896).

19. God's intervention in the destruction of Babylon (chapters 19–22) is often associated with Rev. 11:11–13; the establishment of God's kingdom (chapter 20) with Rev. 11:15.

20. The conflict between Elijah and Baal worship is drawn out by Leah Bonner, *The Stories of Elijah and Elisha as Polemics against Baal Worship* (Leiden: E. J. Brill, 1968). A parallel moral conflict is seen to exist by prominent Protestant exegetes in the sixteenth century, often against an apocalyptic horizon.

21. I. T. Beckwith, *The Apocalypse of John* (New York: Macmillan, 1919), pp. 586–90; cf. George E. Ladd, *A Commentary on the Revelation* (Grand Rapids, Mich.: Eerdmans, 1972), pp. 149–51.

22. Charles, *Revelation of John*, Vol. 1, p. 270; cf. G. Bornkamm, "Die Komposition der apokalyptischen Visionen in der Offerbarung Johannis," ZNW, 36 (1937):137–49.

23. Richard Bauckham, "The Martyrdom of Enoch and Elijah: Jewish or Christian?" JBL, 95 (1976):447–58; cf. Oscar Cullmann, *The Christology of the New Testament* (rev. ed.) (Philadelphia: Westminster Press, 1959), pp. 16ff.; and Barnabas Lindars, "Enoch and Christology," *Expository Times,* 92 (1981):295–99.

24. Based upon Wilhelm Bousset and the argument that the Apocalypse of Elijah lies behind our text, Jeremias argues that the witnesses are Moses and Elijah, a tradition lost in later Judaism but preserved by early Christianity. Johannes Munck argues the reverse, that the book of Revelation is the source for a later confused rendering of the account in the Coptic *Apocalypse of Elijah: Die Religion des Judentums im späthellenistischen Zeitalter. Handbuch zum NT,* Hans Lietzmann, ed. (Tübingen, 1926), p. 261. See Court, *Myth and History,* pp. 90–99.

25. Cf. Zech. 4:2–14.

26. Compare this period with other times of prophetic calamity, e.g., 1 Kings 18:1–46 (Luke 4:25), Dan. 7:25; 12:7; and Rev. 11:2.

27. I am following Henry Alford, who calls attention to the present participle "*anabainon,*" in *The Greek New Testament*, Vol. 4, p. 660.

28. Ideas connected with the term "witness" are developed by A. A. Trites, *The New Testament Concept of Witness*, SNTS monograph 31 (Cambridge: Cambridge University Press, 1977). The term "martus" occurs in the Apocalypse five times: Rev. 1:5; 3:14; 2:13; 17:6; 13:15.

29. Beckwith, *Apocalypse of John*, p. 591; Alford, *The Greek New Testament*, Vol. 4,

p. 661. Beckwith argues for Jerusalem, connecting Rev. 11:8 with 11:1–3; through a closer textual study Alford points to "the great city" depicted in succeeding visions. The effect is not slight both in its bearing upon literal or symbolic exegesis, but also upon Jewish-Christian relations.

30. Arguing that Christianity began as an apocalyptic sect within Judaism, Norman Perrin presents a brief but helpful thematic overview of apocalyptic literature in early Christianity, "Apocalyptic Christianity, The Synoptic Source 'Q,' The Apocalypse Discourses, The Book of Revelation," in Hanson, ed., *Visionaries*, pp. 121–45.

31. For example, 1 Cor. 15; 1 Thess. 4:13–18; 5:1–11. Earlier H. A. A. Kennedy argued for verbal coincidences between synoptical and Pauline eschatology and a unity of underlying ideas. See *St. Paul's Conceptions of the Last Things* (London, Hodder & Stoughton, 1904). Cf. Leonard Goppelt who stresses the role of typology in apocalyptic reality forged by God's work in Jesus for Paul, in *Typos: The Typological Interpretation of the Old Testament in the New* (Grand Rapids, Mich.: Eerdmans, 1982), pp. 233–37; and J. Christiaan Beker, *Paul the Apostle* (Philadelphia: Fortress Press, 1980).

32. Beda Rigaux, *Saint Paul, Les Épitres aux Thessaloniciens* (Gembloux: J. Duculot, 1956), pp. 259–80.

33. For example, on their absence see William Heist, *The Fifteen Signs Before Doomsday* (East Lansing: Michigan State College Press, 1952); on their inclusion, cf. Ernst Wadstein, *Die eschatologische Ideengruppe: Antichrist-Weltsabbat-Weltende und Weltgericht* (Leipzig: O. R. Reisland, 1896), p. 31; H. T. Musper, *Der Antichrist und die fünfzehn Zeichen: Faksimile-Ausgabe des einzigen erhaltenen chiroxylographischen Blockbuchs* (Munich: Prestel Verlag, 1970), pp. bl. 4r-v, 12rb-vb.

34. Diachronic thinking, characteristic of the West, is seen today as reflecting relative or actual moral declension from Christian ideals. See Gerhart Ladner, "Medieval and Modern Understanding of Symbolism: A Comparison," *Speculum*, 54 (1979):230–31.

35. Leonhard Atzberger gives an introduction to early Christian apocalyptic in *Geschichte der christlichen Eschatologie innerhalb der vornicänischen Zeit* (Freiburg im Breisgau: Herdeer'sche Verlagshandlung, 1896); more recently, see Brian E. Daley, *The Hope of the Early Church* (Cambridge: Cambridge University Press, 1991).

36. Jeremias, TDNT, 2 (1964):928–34. Elijah's prominence derives from his defense of Israel's religion against the cult of Baal (1 Kings 17:1–2 Kings 2:12). This is heightened in tradition through his rapture (2 Kings 2:11) and the prophecy of his return (Mal. 4:5). The traditional tasks associated with his return are to purify the priesthood, restore Israel, and prepare for or establish universal restitution. These are tasks that will be central to later Protestant efforts. Morris M. Faierstein argues that there is a lack of evidence for the idea of the return of Elijah as the forerunner of the Messiah in the first century. If such is a "*novum*" in the NT (p. 86), the apocalyptic significance is heightened. See "Why do the Scribes say that Elijah must come first?" JBL, 100.1 (1981):75–86; cf. Mal. 3:1; 4:4–5, and the Jewish interests illustrated by L. Ginzberg, *An Unknown Jewish Sect* (New York: Jewish Theological Seminary, 1976), p. 212.

37. Jeremias, ibid., pp. 936–38. The spirit and power of Elijah were passed to Elisha (2 Kings 2:9–15), similarly, perhaps, to John the Baptist. As Elijah preached against the idolatry of Ahab and Jezebel, so the Baptist preached against the sins of Herod and Herodias.

38. See J. L. Martyn, "We Have Found Elijah," in *Jews, Greeks and Christians*, R. Hammerston-Kelly and R. Scroggs, eds. (Leiden: E. J. Brill, 1976), pp. 181–219.

39. *Dialogue with Trypho, 49*. In *Saint Justin Maryr*, Thomas B. Falls, ed. *The Fathers of the Church*, Vol. 6 (Washington, D.C.: Catholic University of America, 1948, repr. 1965), pp. 221–23. Cf. Atzberger, *Geschichte*, pp. 147–48.

40. *De anima*, 50, 35. Tertullian *Opera*, II, CSEL 2, pp. 818–21; cf. *De resurrectione*, 22. Note allusion to Mal. 4: 5 and possible Rev. 12:6 (cf. 1 Kings 17:2–6), p. 949.52.

41. *Divinarum Institutionum Liber* 7.17; *Opera Omnia*, Samuel Brandt, ed. CSEL, Vol. 19.1, pp. 638–40.

42. Haugg, *Zwei Zeugen*, pp. 79–114.

43. In later rabbinic tradition the soul of Moses is said to be preserved under God's altar, HDB, 3, p. 450.

44. *Carmen de duobus populis*, CCL, 128, pp. 103–5. On the "*prophetae*," pp. 104–5, vv. 856–64; on Elijah, pp. 103–4, vv. 833, 839, 850; cf. *Instructiones* ("De Antechristi Tempore"), ibid., pp. 33–34.

45. On the state of the righteous after death in early Christian thought, see Atzberger, *Geschichte*, pp. 79–92.

46. H. C. Kim, *The Gospel of Nicodemus* (Toronto: Pontifical Institute of Medieval Studies, 1973), chapters 25, 26; pp. 46–47; cf. IV Ezra 1:39; Irenaeus, *Adversus Haereses* 5.5.1; and *Apocalypse of Paul* 20, NTA, 2, pp. 772, 755–98.

47. The stories that develop around such figures illustrate the idealism of the age in which they were written or became popular. See NTA, 2, pp. 174–78.

48. Lindars argues that 1 Peter demonstrates how Christian theology absorbed this understanding; see "Enoch and Christology," pp. 295–99.

49. The Similitudes of Enoch (1 Enoch 37–71) proclaim the establishment of God's kingdom by his anointed one, a figure of supernatural stature. His return together with that of others (Moses, Baruch, Ezra) seems attested to in IV Ezra 6:26 (cf. 7:28; 13:52). A prophetic and judgmental task was reserved for Enoch (1 Enoch 1:9; Jude 14). The esteem in which Enoch was held and the expectation of his return led R. H. Charles to write that Enoch's influence upon the NT writers was "greater than that of all the other apocryphal and pseudepigraphical books taken together" (R. H. Charles, ed., *The Book of Enoch* [Oxford: Oxford University Press, 1893], p. 41; cf. Stone, "Enoch and Apocalyptic Origins," in Hanson, ed., *Visionaries*, pp. 92–100).

50. Bousset argues such as part of his effort to find the root of what he identified as the "antichrist legend," *Antichrist Legend*, pp. 19, 208. Bousset holds back on giving the origin of the idea of two witnesses, arguing only that it cannot have been Jewish as only Elijah's return was expected. He suggests a wider Near Eastern or Sibylline origin (p. 211).

51. Ibid., pp. 203–11.

52. Apocalypse of Peter, Ch. Maurer, ed., NTA, 2, pp. 663–83; chapters 1 and 2, pp. 668–69. In the same volume are references to Enoch and Elijah in the Apocalypse of Paul, chapters 20, 51; pp. 772, 755–98.

53. *Die Apokalypse des Elias*, in *Texte und Untersuchungen*, Georg Steindorff, ed. 17, 3a (Leipzig: J. C. Hinrichs'sche Buchhandlung, 1899), pp. 93–95, 103–5. Dated as late as the fourth century by some (Weinel), many place it considerably earlier.

54. TDNT, 2 (1964):339–40.

55. *L'Apocalypse d'Elie* (Paris: Geuthner, 1972), p. 70.

56. Bauckham's outline is based upon: (1) the conception of their identity; (2) how they destroy Antichrist; and (3) how they expose Antichrist. Bauckham finds the idea of martyrdom introduced into the further, probably Christian, development ("Martyrdom," pp. 457–58).

57. On matters of dating, see August Strobel, *Untersuchungen zum eschatologischen Verzögerungsproblem auf Grund der spätjüdisch-urchristlichen Geschichte von Habakuk 2, 2ff.* (Leiden: E. J. Brill, 1961), pp. 137–47.

58. R. H. Charles finds traces of a contemporary-historical method of exegesis here. See *Studies in the Apocalypse* (Edinburgh: T. & T. Clark, 1913), pp. 7–11.

59. *De anima* 50, CSEL (Reifferscheid and Wissowa, eds.), 20 (Vienna: Hoelder, Pichler, Tempsky, 1890), pp. 380–82.

60. Tertullian argues elsewhere that Enoch and Elijah have been translated and are now learning what it means for the flesh to be exempt from humiliation, teaching us that the Lord is more powerful than natural laws (*De carnis resurrectione* 58, CSEL, 47, p. 119). But the consummation of Christian hope is not yet (*De car. res.* 22, p. 56). Nor was Elijah reproduced in John the Baptist, who came in the spirit and power of Elijah. Elijah must come again but not after his death; rather, after his translation (*De anima* 35, pp. 361–62; cf. on Enoch, *Adversus Iudaeos* 2, CSEL, 70, p. 258).

61. *Demonstratio de Christo et Antichristo* 43, 46–47, in Migne, *Patrologia Graeca*, Vol. 10 (Paris, 1865), cols. 761A–88, esp. 761/2A, 765/6AB, and 781/2AB; cf. *In Danielem* 50 *et passim*, in M. Lefevre, ed., *Sources Chrétiennes*, Vol. 14 (Paris: Editions du Cerf, 1947), pp. 366–69. Hippolytus argues that Christ was born in the middle of the sixth millennium, leaving 470 years yet to elapse from the death of Christ to the end of the world (*In Dan.* 4:23–24).

62. Johannes Munck argues that Hippolytus (and Ps.-Hippolytus) originates the line of mistaken exegesis yielding Enoch and Elijah as our witnesses, in *Petrus und Paulus in der Offenbarung Johannis* (Copenhagen: Rosenkilde og Bagger, 1950), pp. 81–120.

63. *Commentarius in Apocalypsin*, Johannes Hausleiter, ed., CSEL, 49 (Vienna: Hoelder, Pichler, Tempsky, 1916). A newly discovered text (*Editio Victorini*) is juxtaposed here to Jerome's revision.

64. Wilhelm Bousset, *Die Offenbarung Johannis* (Gottingen: Vandenhoeck und Ruprecht, 1906), p. 54; cf. Charles, *Studies in the Apocalypse*, pp. 10–11.

65. *Editio Victorini*, pp. 80–82.

66. Ibid., p. 86.

67. Ibid., p. 98.

68. Ibid., pp. 110–114.

69. Ibid., pp. 98–104.

70. Ibid., p. 130 (Rev. 14:8).

71. Ibid., pp. 84–86. The trumpets and bowls of wrath are correlated as follows: (1) Rev. 8:7 and 16:2; (2) Rev. 8:8–9 and 16:3; (3) Rev. 8:10–11 and 16:4–7; (4) Rev. 8:12 and 16:8–9; (5) Rev. 9:1ff. and 16:10–11; (6) Rev. 9:13ff. and 16:12–16; and (7) Rev. 11:15–16 and 16:17–21.

72. Ibid., p. 82.

73. We will follow the commentary tradition on Rev. 11. I have been guided by Bousset, *Offenbarung*, pp. 49–108 and by Charles, *Studies in the Apocalypse*, pp. 1–102.

74. Charles, *Studies in the Apocalypse*, pp. 11–15.

75. Yves Christe argues that iconographic apocalyptic expression after the fourth century reflects more the immanence of Christ at his first Advent rather than the imminence of a future parousia. See "Traditions littéraires et iconographiques dans l'interpretation des images apocalyptiques," in *L'Apocalypse de Jean . . . Actes du colloque de la Fondation Hardt* (Genève: Librairie Droz, 1979), pp. 110–111.

76. *In Isaiam Lib, XVIII*, cited in Bousset, *Offenbarung*, p. 62.

77. *In Amos* 9:2, CCL 76.1, p. 337.79–85; *In Zachariam* 4:11,14, CCL 76.1, p. 785. 284–6.

78. *In Malachiam* 4:5–6, CL 76.1, pp. 941–942.83–115. Jerome connects the prophecy of Malachi with the Transfiguration as well as with the person of John the Baptist.

79. *Epistula* XLVI.6, CSEL, 54, pp. 333–36.

80. *Epistula* LIX.3, CSEL, 54, pp. 543–44.

81. Ibid., p. 544.6–14.

82. Bousset, *Offenbarung*, p. 62.

83. Tyconius's commentary is available only in fragments preserved in revisions and in the quotations of later authors. Two important critical texts are available: (1) a reconstruction from the commentary on the Apocalypse by Beatus of Liebana, in *Beati in Apocalypsin libri XII*, Henry A. Sanders, ed. (American Academy in Rome, 1930); (2) a critical edition of *The Turin Fragments of Tyconius' Commentary on Revelation*, Francesco LoBue, ed. (Cambridge: Cambridge University Press, 1963). The LoBue text, *Tyconii Afri in Apocalypsin*, will be used. When a variant is quoted, the name of the commentator will be given. Wilhelm Kamlah argues that Tyconius's hermeneutic dominates apocalyptic and, thereby, historical understanding from the fourth century through the twelfth when, with Joachim of Fiore (c. 1135–1202), a new pattern of understanding Scripture emerges. See Kamlah, *Apokalypse und Geschichtstheologie: Die mittelalterliche Auslegung der Apokalypse vor Joachim von Fiore* (Berlin: Emil Ebering, 1935), pp. 9–10.

84. See Augustine, *De doctrina christiana*, III.xxx, 42-xxxvi, 56, CCL 32, pp. 102–16. Tyconius's seven rules for interpretation are literary analogies to (1) the Lord and his body, (2) the twofold division to the body of the Lord, (3) the promise and the law, (4) species and genus, (5) of times, (6) recapitulation, (7) the devil and his body. This is not the place to expand on the meaning of these rules. The critical edition of Tyconius's hermeneutical treatise is "The Book of Rules of Tyconius," ed. F. C. Burkitt, in *Texts and Studies*, Vol. 3 (Cambridge: Cambridge University Press, 1894); cf. Karlfried Froehlich, *Biblical Interpretation in the Early Church* (Philadelphia: Fortress Press, 1984), pp. 104–32.

85. On the apocalyptic dimensions, see R. A. Markus, *Saeculum: History and Society in the Theology of St. Augustine of Hippo* (Cambridge: Cambridge University Press, 1970), p. 55; cf. W. H. C. Frend, *The Donatist Church: A Movement of Protest in Roman North Africa* (Oxford: Clarendon Press, 1952); and T. W. MacKay, "Early Christian Exegesis of the Apocalypse," *Studia Biblica*, 3 (1978):257–63.

86. Kamlah, *Apokalypse*, pp. 10–11; cf. Traugott Hahn, *Tyconius-Studien* (Leipzig: Scientia Verlag, 1900), pp. 5–6,87.

87. Frederiksen (Landes) reads Tyconius's Apocalypse in the context of his Rules. See Landes, "Tyconius and the End of the World," *Revue des études augustiennes*, 28 (1982):59–75. She writes that Tyconius's moral-typological emphasis enables him to use the Apocalypse for three purposes: (1) to illustrate the unity of the OT and NT; (2) to resolve contradictions in scriptural interpretation; and (3) to guide the reader through prophecy (p. 73).

88. For example, Primasius, Bede, Caesarius of Arles, Apringius, and Beatus; on the methodological difficulty with the iconographic evidence, see Christe, "Traditions littéraires et iconographiques," p. 125.

89. In LoBue ed., *Apocalypsin*, p. 143, par. 334.

90. Ibid., p. 143, par. 336; cf. p. 157, par. 379.

91. Ibid., p. 153, par. 368.

92. Ibid., pp. 154–62, pars. 370–94.

93. The fifth exegetical rule: "De temporibus," in Burkitt, ed., *Book of Rules*, pp. 55–56. This appears to provide for a complete recapitulation of apocalyptic symbolism. Landes uses rules 3 ("De promissis et lege") and 6 ("De recapitulatione") to establish her argument for concurrent symbolism. See Landes, "Tyconius," pp. 63–66.

94. In LoBue, ed., *Apocalypsin*, pp. 190–92, pars. 484–89; cf. Burkitt, ed., *Book of Rules*, pp. 60–61.

95. Ibid., p. 178, par. 441.

96. Ibid., p. 178, par. 443. Note the nature of this division in the Church out of the second exegetical rule, "De Domini corpore bipertito." Burkitt, ed., *Book of Rules*, pp. 8–11.

97. Ibid., p. 178, par. 444; note the Pauline argument connected with this Church, "baptized into Christ," having "put on Christ" (Gal. 3:27). Here is an illustration of the third exegetical rule of Tyconius, "De promissis et lege." Burkitt, ed., *Book of Rules*, pp. 12–31.

98. Ibid., p. 181, par. 453.

99. Ibid., p. 182, pars. 456–57. The dragon: "Id est diabolus." Here and in the symbolism of the dragon's array is illustrated Tyconius's seventh exegetical rule, "De diabolo et corpore eius." See Burkitt, ed., *Book of Rules*, pp. 70–85. H. Rauh, *Das Bild des Antichrist im Mittelalter: Von Tyconius zum deutschen Symbolismus*. Vol. 9: *Beiträge zur Geschichte der Philosophie und theologie des Mittelalters*, n.s. (Münster: Aschendorf, 1973), pp. 98–121.

100. Ibid., pp. 186–87, par. 468–74. The growth of evil is traced in a series of ten steps from the beginning of new spiritual perception to the open reign of evil. This may be related to Tyconius's sixth exegetical rule, "De recapitulatione," in Burkitt, ed., *Book of Rules*, pp. 66–70.

101. Ibid., p. 164, pars. 398–99.

102. I am following Landes. She writes: "His exegetical rules are *mystical*, his Apocalypse commentary thoroughly allegorical. His genius, in fact, lay in reversing the values of the old categories which had for so long served millenarian speculation, anti-Roman sentiment, and perfectionist ecclesiologies" ("Tyconius," p. 72).

103. Julien Ries summarizes Tyconius's importance for Augustine's hermeneutics in his anti-Manichaean period, in "La bible chez s. Augustin et chez les manichéens," *Revue des études augustiniennes*, 10 (1964):309–29, esp. pp. 309–10.

104. *De civitate dei*, xx.7.33–43, CCL 48, p. 709. Note chaps. 7–17. Peter Brown discusses further influences in *Augustine of Hippo, a Biography* (Berkeley: University of California Press, 1969), p. 314.

105. Ibid., xx.29–30, pp. 752–58.

106. Cf. Peter John Olivi (below). Bousset writes that Augustine's allegorization is checked by his interest in God's actual participation in history which is seen, for him, in the return of Elijah (Mal. 4:5–6), the four secular world kingdoms (Dan. 7), a final rebellion of lawlessness (2 Thess. 2), in addition to Creation and Incarnation. In *De civitate dei*: On Elijah, xx.29–30; the four kingdoms, xx.23; the rebellion, xx.29; as cited in Bousset, *Offenbarung*, p. 61.

107. *De civitate dei*, xx.29.7–11, p. 752; cf. *Apocalypse of Peter* (NTA, 2, p. 669): the two witnesses, Elijah and Enoch, instruct the House of Israel; and Jerome, *In Esaiam* 5.23.18, CCL, 73, p. 222.

108. Earlier, Augustine drew upon psychological-developmental terminology to understand time, then, more normatively, turned to the Jewish model of Creation; see R. A. Markus, *Saeculum*, pp. 32, 70; cf. Ernst Lewalter, "Eschatologie und Weltgeschichte in der Gedankenwelt Augustins," ZKG, 53 (1934):1–51; Roderich Schmidt, "Aetates mundi. Die Weltalter als Gliederungsprinzip der Geschichte," ZKG, 67 (1955):288–317; and G. Folliet, "La typologie du sabbat chez St. Augustine," *Revue des études augustiniennes*, 2 (1956):371–91.

109. *De civitate dei*, xx.19; in reference to 2 Thess. 2:1–11; cf. Luneau, *L'Histoire du salut chez les Pères de l'église*, pp. 314–21. His emphasis is not so much on the intensification of evil as on perennial conflict (ibid., xviii, 52–53); cf. Herbert A. Deane, *The*

Political and Social Ideas of St. Augustine ["New York: Columbia University Press, 1963], pp. 72–76).

110. Ibid., xx,29–30.

111. The effect of Hippolytus's apocalyptic dating, compounded by the then-current social crisis in the collapse of Rome, is summarized by McGinn, *Visions of the End*, pp. 51, 62.

112. *Livre des promesses et des predictions de Dieu*, in R. Braun, ed., *Sources chrétiennes*, Vol. 102 (Paris: Cerf, 1964), pp. 623–34. An English translation of this portion may be found in McGinn by which I am guided; *Visions of the End*, pp. 53–54.

113. Landes, "Tyconius," p. 67. She cites Burkitt's contention that the earliest reference to Tyconius's *Rules* after Augustine is in *Liber de promissionibus*. McGinn adds that this "typological method of exegesis . . . foreshadows" that of the later, more systematic work of Joachim of Fiore (*Visions of the End*, p. 298, n. 14; cf. pp. 54, 298 n. 16).

114. Josef Schmid, ed., *Studien zur Geschichte des griechischen Apokalypse-Texts, Der Apokalypse-Kommentar des Andreas von Kaisareia*, 3 books in 2 vols. (Munich: Karl Zink Verlag, 1955). According to tradition, Hippolytus wrote a commentary on the book of Revelation, but no Greek author who knows Hippolytus's other works mentions it (Vol. I.1, pp. 157ff.), an absence reflected in Byzantine iconography generally until the late fifteenth century when such imagery becomes prominent in, e.g., the fortress churches of Bucovinia (Romania). See N. Thierry, "L'Apocalypse de Jean et l'iconographie byzantine," *L'Apocalypse*, ed. Yves Christe, pp. 319–39. On Byzantine apocalypticism generally, see Paul J. Alexander, *The Byzantine Apocalyptic Tradition* (Berkeley: University of California Press, 1985).

115. Paul J. Alexander, "The Diffusion of Byzantine Apocalypses in the Medieval West and the Beginnings of Joachimism," in Ann Williams, ed., *Prophecy and Millenarianism*, pp. 53–106. Note Alexander's discussion of the Tiburtine Sibyl (cf. McGinn, *Visions of the End*, pp. 45–50, 294–95) and the somewhat more prominent role given to the witnesses in Pseudo-Ephraem, pp. 61–62. For the Tiburtine Sibyl, see Ernst Sackur, ed., *Sibyllinische Texte und Forschungen, Pseudomethodius, Adso und die Tiburtinische Sibylle* (Halle: Niemeyer, 1898; repr., Turin, 1963), p. 186. For Pseudo-Ephraem, see C. P. Caspari, *Briefe, Abhandlungen, und Predigten aus den zwei letzten Jahrhunderten des kirchlichen Alterthums und dem Anfang des Mittelalters* (1890; repr., Brussels: Culture et Civilisation, 1964), pp. 108–220. In both of these apocalypses the Antichrist appears before the two witnesses. See Bousset, *Antichrist Legend*, p. 208.

116. Bousset cites early fears of heretical associations with the Apocalypse, *Offenbarung*, pp. 26–30. The later social-political context will encourage the use of apocalyptic themes; cf. McGinn, *Visions of the End*, p. 66.

117. On Oecumenius and Andreas, see below; Arethas wrote c. 900. See J. Schmid, *Studien, Vol. I: 1 Einleitung*, pp. 96–97.

118. For example, Heinrich Bullinger will often refer to Arethas whose commentary was first issued as a supplement to the Catena of Oecumenius at Verona (1532); Latin translation by Hentenius at Paris (1547). Andreas's commentary was first printed, albeit in an inaccurate Latin form, by Peltanus (1574).

119. The text was rediscovered by Franz Diekamp and published by H. C. Hoskier, ed., *The Complete Commentary of Oecumenius on the Apocalypse* (Ann Arbor: University of Michigan Press, 1928), pp. 1–25.

120. Ibid., p. 128.21–21. References from the OT and NT are drawn in as well (Mal. 4:4–5; Gen. 5:22; Matt. 11:14; Heb. 11:5); cf. p. 129.4–21.

121. Schmid, *Studien, Vol. I:1, Introduction and Text*. The commentary probably dates from the late sixth or early seventh century A.D.

122. There was an apocalypse attributed to Methodius of Patara, which is not considered here as there is no direct reflection of the canonical book of Revelation. See Sackur, ed., *Sibyllinische Texte*, pp. 59–96.

123. Schmid, *Studien, Vol. I.1: Text*, p. 10. Note his divisions of the text: 24 logoi, corresponding to the 24 elders of the Apocalypse, and 72 kephalaia, related to the threefold distinction of body, soul, and spirit (3×24 = 72).

124. Ibid., pp. 59–73. Six "times" are mentioned: (1) the era of the Apostles and conversion of the Gentiles, (2) an era of martyrdom, (3) a time of apostasy, (4) a period of famine and pestilence like that under Maximin, (5) the cry of the martyrs for vengeance, and (6) a transition time to the days of Antichrist. The adventual witnesses appear in the final period.

125. Ibid., p. 113.1–8.

126. Ibid., pp. 114–15; 79.3.3. For this Jewish haggadic interpretation, see Bousset, *Antichrist Legend*, pp. 171–74; cf. Emmerson, *Antichrist in the Middle Ages*, pp. 34–73.

127. Ibid., pp. 117–18. Arethas of Caesarea (In *Apocalypsin*, PG, 106, cols. 487ff.) retains Andreas's role for the witnesses: Enoch and Elijah preaching against apostasy for three and a half years (PG, 106, col. 649).

128. *Commentariorius super Apocalypsim*, PL, 68.793–936. Others who follow Tyconius are summarized by Bousset, *Offenbarung*, pp. 65–72.

129. Ibid., col. 866.39–41. "Ecclesia duobus Testamentis praedicans et prophetans."

130. Ibid., cols. 866–867 (Matt. 26:37).

131. Ibid., cols. 869–870.

132. Bousset finds Primasius's adoption of Tyconius's exegetical method of recapitulation important for later exegetes who will follow Primasius; *Offenbarung*, p. 66.

2

Witnesses Through History

Doorkeepers to the Future

An awakened interest in the Apocalypse can be discerned in the Carolingian Age with Bede "the Venerable" (c. 673–735), whose commentary on the book of Revelation evinces historical movement under apocalyptic symbolism. Together with Ambrosius Autpertus (d. 778 or 781), Bede carries us forward to the sharpened historical and polemical exegesis associated with apocalyptic thought in the twelfth and thirteenth centuries.[1] The question of the identity of our two witnesses placed within a firm temporal framework will take on a new liveliness in the period ahead.[2]

Bede acknowledges dependence upon Tyconius, in the introduction to Bede's own commentary, listing the seven exegetical rules.[3] The thrust of his work emphasizes a typological rather than allegorical conception of our witnesses (i.e., it is more atuned to historical models, in a fixed biblical pattern, rather than to symbolic truth).[4] Bede shows a greater interest in history than either Tyconius or Primasius. The world, he argues, entered its sixth and last age.[5] Into this thinking, drawn from Augustine,[6] Bede found an integral sense of development, a process similar to that which he observed within each day of Creation: initial creative activity, development, and decline.[7]

Bede used the seals of the Apocalypse to picture a similar division in the sixth age, as in every other, in distinction from Augustine, who had left the last period undifferentiated.[8] The opening of the first seal was symbolic of the primitive Church's triumph. The next three reveal forms of warfare against the Church: the attack of tyrants, consequent martyrdom, false brethren and heretics. The fifth seal, not a part of the historical sequence, reveals the glory of deceased martyrs. The sixth seal represents the time of Antichrist's persecution. The seventh seal marks the beginning of eternal rest.[9]

The witnesses retain the corporate identity given them by Tyconius and Primasius. They are the Church formed from two peoples, Jews and Gentiles, with Christ as its head. Their work is carried on throughout history, perceived under all seven seals, as unbelievers tread down the Church of Christ.[10] At the same time Bede recognizes a more particular interpretation of the two witnesses. They may also be Enoch and Elijah, who will appear in their particularity under the sixth seal, at the time of Antichrist's persecution, to perform their ministry of confirming hearts prior to their death.[11] Bede's debt to Augustine, Tyconius, and

Primasius is evident. The witnesses retain a corporate identity but now in an innovative way that begs for further identification in the "evening" of the sixth age prior to the opening of the seventh seal.[12]

A strong moral thrust is added to the temporal tendencies that we find in Bede's work by that of the commentary on the Apocalypse by Ambrosius Autpertus.[13] Intent on discovering the mystical or spiritual sense of the text, he not only follows Bede but also draws on the allegorical and recapitulative exegesis of Tyconius and Primasius.[14] Autpertus's moral interests are developed in relation to Jerome, and Gregory the Great. Israel's prophets are held up as examples for moral modeling in relation to our text.[15] He follows the Victorinus/Jerome text in his discussion of the Church, but he differs on particular issues.[16] For example, the two witnesses are not Elijah and Jeremiah (Victorinus), but the prophetic Church strengthened by the two testaments, gathered out of two peoples, Jews and Gentiles, quickened by the two commandments of love.[17] For both Bede and Autpertus, the witnesses are models of proclamation and spirituality in the period of time opened up by Christ's first Advent, but are such without the exclusion of a more particular personification in history's closing days.[18] This double conception of their identity and work will be further developed, albeit stressed differently in various commentators, in the years stretching from the Carolingian Renaissance to the ecclesiastical and imperial disputes of the twelfth century.

For example, in such commentaries as that by the Spanish presbyter and Benedictine monk Beatus of Liebana (d. 798),[19] who wrote with a keen sense of the end, yet in dependence particularly on Tyconius,[20] our witnesses, Elijah and a second unnamed prophet, are expected to appear together before the end.[21] The importance of Beatus is his usefulness for reconstructing the Tyconian text and in his influence upon apocalyptic iconography.

In the commentary attributed to Alcuin (c. 735–804),[22] the Carolingian schoolmaster, a work that evinces the influence of Bede and Autpertus,[23] Bede's division of history and Tyconius's exegetical rules are first cited as guiding principles.[24] Alcuin notes the work of Victorinus and Tyconius, and then discusses the spiritual value to be gained by studying the Apocalypse.[25] When Alcuin addresses the question of the witnesses' identity, he notes the interpretation of Victorinus but believes it is better to understand them literally as the revivified Enoch and Elijah. Yet, following Tyconius's fourth exegetical rule, he concludes that one may find in their persons a figurative description of the Church. Again, this Church is based upon two testaments, two peoples (Jew and Gentile), and two love commandments. However, Alcuin adds another part—and two kinds of martyrdom (physical and monasticism)—and concludes that the time of their ministry is the whole age of the Church.[26]

The witnesses and their foe, Antichrist, are perceived symbolically in Haimo of Halberstadt.[27] Our prophets preach repentance, and work in their humility for restitution. The whole Church is understood in their persons and preaching,[28] both now as well as at the end of history. He adds, pointedly, that at the time of their appearance prior to the reign of Antichrist, there will be a spirit of deception, persecution, and Jewish perfidy that will not destroy the work of the Church.[29]

This recapitulative, allegorical, or at times typological, interpretation contin-ues in Walafrid Strabo (c. 808–849),[30] Berengaudus (ninth century),[31] Anselm of Laon (d. 1117),[32] and Bruno of Segni (d. 1123).[33] Both Strabo and Berengaudus add historical concerns in their understanding of apocalyptic symbolism. Strabo carefully correlates periods of history since the inception of the Church with the seven seals.[34] Berenguadus connects a long systematic outline of history with the seals and their apocalyptic symbolism.[35] God's saints, our witnesses, are tested in seven days of world history as was the faith of Israel in its seven-day journey around Jericho.[36] The angel of Revelation 10 is the Christ at his Incarnation. The book given to John (Rev. 10:9) is the Scriptures, to be preached by John, by all apostles, and by Christian teachers.[37] This history continues in chapter 11, which pictures the Church from the expulsion of the Jews (Rev. 11:1–2) to their return. They will be called back to true worship by Enoch and Elijah, the two who will fulfill the prophecy in a specific way and fight Antichrist. They will precede the Second Coming of the Lord as John the Baptist preceded the first.[38]

Disclosing Deception

The intriguing question of the identities of the two witnesses is also found out-side of the commentary tradition. The play *Antichrist* (c. 1160),[39] dependent upon the work of Adso Dervensis (d. 992),[40] presents one of the more complete apoca-lyptic plots found in medieval literature. It introduces us to the growing use of apocalyptic themes, particularly their politicization in the papal-imperial conflicts that characterize the period ahead. With the Carolingian Renaissance well behind us, *Antichrist* leads us into a period in which our two witnesses will be drawn upon as symbolic representations of virtue among competing claims to social legitimacy.

The play offers an implicit criticism of the medieval Church, which, under Pope Gregory VII, had sought to reorganize itself independent of the political intent of society. Antichrist is at first defeated by the Germanic King, then converts the King by his miracles. Next, Synagoga and the Jews are converted by Antichrist, but Enoch and Elijah draw them to Christ.[41] They preach for three and a half years, "unmask" Antichrist,[42] but are finally killed by him. He, in turn, is destroyed by Christ. The appearances and works of the witnesses help to mark the last stage of history as time hastens to final Judgment.

Whether in drama or in commentary, our witnesses now become useful sym-bols for reformist purposes in an envisioned development of history.[43] By the elev-enth century, new questions were being raised about the Church's place in society. These pertained not only to issues of political order, such as how Church and civil ideals were to relate, whether canon law was definitive in civil court, and who was to govern the Church. Such questions inevitably opened up the debate about the nature of history and of historical periodization, which had been worked out by authorities like Augustine or Bede.[44] In different ways commentators, and other social theorists of the day, sought a deepened understanding of patterns of political and religious legitimacy through society's heritage of biblical narrative. Augustine's sixth age, contemporary history for medieval Europe, had been defined through recourse to such narratives and in particular to apocalyptic symbolism.[45] Against such a backdrop, political and religious debates naturally draw forth a more focused use of the symbol of returning prophets, associated with our text, even as the symbol offered fruther development to the theme of Antichrist.

Such a symbolic understanding of history was developed by Rupert of Deutz (1070–1129/1135?) in support of monastic reform with its attendant social implications.[46] History, viewed as the unfolding or historical working out of the trinitarian godhead (Father, Son, and Holy Spirit), was divided into periods reflective of the personalities and work of each of the members of the Trinity: an historical age before the law (i.e., before God had begun to reveal his nature [*ante legum*]), an age characterized by the revelation of his law for humankind (*sub lege*), an age revealing his graciousness (*sub gratia*), and eventuating in an age of the Spirit. Each age was further divided into periods characterized by particular virtues that were, at the time, proper for the whole Church through all of history.[47] These virtues marked a growth in grace through history and provided a set of spiritual symbols and examples available for polemical purpose.[48] Rupert's eschatological mysticism is reflected in his treatment of Antichrist, the beast of the Apocalypse, and the two witnesses. In Rupert's elaborate historical scheme Antichrist is not denied a final appearance, but may be seen spiritually as internal decay and hypocrisy.[49] Our prophets, in association with models drawn from all of Scripture, define through their preaching and gifts the spirituality of the Church.[50] As Rupert writes:

> Accordingly, by these two [Enoch and Elijah], the witnesses of Christ are distinguished both today and to the end of the age; some are witnesses who live faithfully in the peace of holy church; they have given and will not cease giving their witness to the truth by speaking and writing; some are witnesses who have shed or will shed their blood in persecution, fighting for the integrity of the faith.[51]

Honorius of Autun (early twelfth century)[52] continued the interest in historical periodization that we noted with Rupert of Deutz. Honorius marked history by a continuous line of ten "ordines" or "states" of the Church (five before and five after Christ), each indicating specific conflict between God and Satan. The witnesses appear at the end of time but are not given sustained attention.[53] Their traditional tasks, the conversion of the Jews and heathen, are seen to occur fully only after the defeat of Antichrist in a lengthened time between this apocalyptic conflict and the Last Judgment.[54] Otto of Freising (c. 1110–1158) finds Enoch and Elijah to be examples of rightousness in their day who will attempt to lead the world to the truth in the end times. They fail and are slain, but appear by their actions to hasten the return of the Lord.[55] Otto's contemporary, Hildegard of Bingen (1098–1179), has the two witnesses appear primarily to console the faithful during Antichrist's reign.[56]

In the more optimistic historical understanding of Anselm of Havelberg (1100–1158), the new orders in the Church are given deepened spiritual significance. Anselm's use of apocalyptic symbolism to understand reform[57] adds significance to the adventual witnesses for later authors.[58] Successive states of the Church, natural change or *mutatio*, are foreshadowed in the seven apocalyptic seals. The present Church is located under the fourth of seven periods,[59] a time of conflict between false and true disciples. The end is still distant.[60]

More immediate conflict characterizes the work of Gerhoh of Reichersberg (1093–1169), as he put the periodization of Church history at the service of reform[61] and provided, thereby, a role for the two witnesses. Despite Gerhoh's commitment to holiness and social purity, a certain ambiguity in his work exists as he at first wrote in defense of the papacy (viewing emperor Henry IV as Antichrist).[62] Following Jerome's reflection on our two witnesses, Gerhoh found in these symbols a spiritual work of the law and the prophets in the Church,[63] without denying a possible literal interpretation, arguing that before the end new spiritual men living in a state of apostolic purity would reform the Church.[64] Later, Gerhoh grew disillusioned with the Church's leadership, and he charted a less obvious path of reform: The black night of history is periodically broken by the night "watches" of those who name evil and deception for what they are. These latter hold the truth of Christ aloft like a light. They are, in order of historical appearance, the apostles, martyrs, doctors, and in Gerhoh's own day, the "poor in spirit" (*beati pauperes spiritu*). The might of Antichrist's last storm is breaking out, but the Church will only be finally cleansed following the Second Advent.[65] Both the witnesses and Antichrist are part of the continuum of history yet point to spiritual realities beyond it.

Orders for Church Renewal

This optimistic historical perspective came as the result of the exegetical work of Joachim of Fiore (c. 1132–1202),[66] whose work ensures the greater visibility of our theme and establishes an apocalyptic tradition from which Protestants and others will draw in the years ahead.[67] The identity of the two witnesses is further defined in line with Tyconius's corporate emphasis by the thirteenth century so as to symbolize, primarily, two new religious orders that would reform the Church and characterize it in an age of the Spirit. Two questions were dominant for Joachim and have remained so for Joachite studies: (1) the nature of the Trinity, and (2) the historical implications of the Trinity with reference to apocalyptic figural imagery.[68] By tying the resolution of history to an internal development modeled on the procession of the Spirit from the Father and Son, Joachim gave immediacy and significance to the time, work, and identity of the two witnesses. Their appearance, and the nature of their work, drew one to the tension in Christian history between a mounting crescendo of evil or the onset of a Millennial age. In doing this, Joachim appears to have built upon an exegetical foundation found in the trinitarian reflection of Rupert of Deutz, the optimism about new orders in Anselm of Havelberg, and the expectation of new spiritual men in Gerhoh of Reichersberg.[69]

From the time Joachim received papal permission to give himself fully to his scriptural research (Pope Lucius III, 1182), he developed the reputation of a prophet, while claiming himself the more modest gift for exegesis.[70] Central to Joachim's understanding was that as inner relations of the Trinity worked themselves out toward history's consummation, all of the biblical figural patterns and spiritual graces had to be brought to completion.[71] The two witnesses were part of the rich prophetic fabric delineated by Joachim, especially in his work on the agreement of the Old and New Testaments[72] and in his commentary on the Apocalypse.[73]

Joachim sketched two eras of history, in the *Liber concordiae*, growing out of the two testaments of Scripture, each finding its resolution in the First or Second Advent of Christ.[74] This conception is overlaid by a trinitarian perspective, delineating three states of history: the first, from Adam to Christ; the second, from Ozias (Uzziah) to Joachim's day; the third, reflecting the double procession of the Spirit from the Father and Son, from Elisha and again with Benedict of Nursia to the consummation of history.[75] Joachim's commentary on the Apocalypse focuses on the history of the Church, although the seven-sealed book (Rev. 5:1) adumbrates the history of both testaments. It opens with a series of tables, diagrams, and a summary of his intent. One of the first illustrations represents Joachim's three overlapping eras: the time between the present and the consummation is characterized by the two witnesses or witnessing orders of Revelation 11.[76] Then, Joachim repeats in summary form the historical vision elaborated in *Liber concordiae*.[77] History may be seen as three spiritual states, or as two ages running from Jacob to Christ, then from Christ to the consummation.[78] As the seven-sealed book is opened, seven parallel eras of history are revealed.[79] The opening of the seventh seal, revealing sabbath rest and Last Judgment, is preceded by a coming of Elijah, as the First Advent was preceded by John the Baptist. In this way Elijah expresses the identity of the two witnesses yet is seen to return singly prior to the end (Rev. 11:3–13; 19:17–18).[80] As the end of Book II of *Liber concordiae* makes clear (4–8:1), the opening of the last seal (8:1) reveals more than simply the immediate end. In the age of the Church, depicted in detail under the vision of seven trumpets in Book III (Rev. 8:2–11:18), Joachim identifies the trumpet-bearing angels as preachers similar to the priests who circled Jericho. What the latter did in a week is analogous to what preachers do in the sixth age after which the world will fall.[81]

In the midst of the conflict revealed by the sixth trumpet, a mighty angel (Rev. 10), a preacher in the spirit and power of Enoch, if not Enoch himself, descends from heaven to earth (i.e., from the contemplative to the active life). Through his preaching, respite is given amid tribulation. He will announce the coming Judgment,[82] and orders John (representative of the monastic life) to take and eat the book (10:8–10).[83] This carries us to a vision of the temple and the holy city, church, and empire. The Greek church, not under the papacy, is the temple's outer court (11:1), cast out, given to the Saracens.[84] When he comes to the witnesses, Joachim raises two questions: (1) Who are they? and (2) Are they to be understood figuratively? His answer: They are Enoch and Elijah; but, personally, he adds, he believes they are Moses and Elijah—the two appearing at Christ's Transfiguration. Joachim then cites Jerome's opinion that the book of Revelation is best understood spiritually.[85]

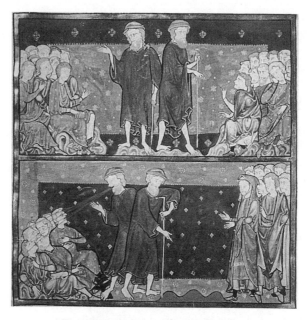

The Preaching of the Two Witnesses

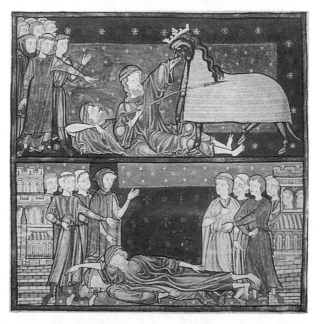

The Slaying of the Two Witnesses

As depicted in illuminations in an Apocalypse, probably made for Queen Eleanor, ca. 1242–50, Trinity College, Cambridge, England. Discussion in Frederick van der Meer. *Apocalypse, Visions from the Book of Revelation in Western Art*. London: Thames and Hudson, 1978.

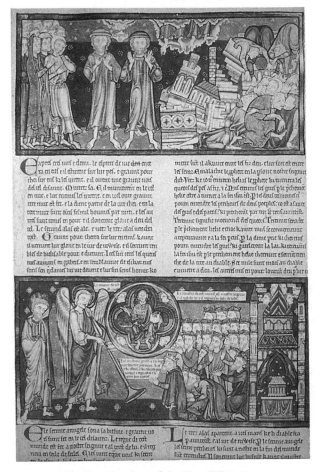

The Resurrection of the Two Witnesses

The witnesses are to be two individuals or two spiritual orders coming in the spirit and power of Enoch and Elijah to preach and fight against Antichrist.[86] Two orders of clerics and monks, modeled on Moses and Elijah, point toward and anticipate the third spiritual state.[87] As pictured in Revelation 14:14–15, one order, that of Moses, appears upon a cloud like the Son of Man. It imitates the life of Christ and the apostles. Its members preach and teach the gospel as part of a final proclamation. The second appears like a man leaving the heavenly temple, crying out for the destruction of the ungodly. This order, characterized by Elijah, imitates the life of the angels.[88] In Joachim's *Liber concordiae*, our two witnesses, together with other paired images, describe the nature of these orders. They are similar to the two olive trees or lampstand of the prophet Zechariah, the raven and dove sent out from Noah's ark after the Flood, and the two women who followed Christ, Mary and Martha. Other examples of paired heralds foreshadowing a new spiritual age are given.[89]

The time of their preaching and penitential activity can be interpreted in both a general and a specific sense. It is found in the forty-two generations of clerical and monastic witnessing orders, the second state, and in that period which grows into the third state of history as Antichrist treads down the holy city.[90] The slaughter of the two witnesses reveals the fate of all preachers of truth. It is best understood spiritually, following Jerome; but Joachim leaves room for a literal fulfillment, at least in the person of Elijah, prior to the war of Antichrist against the elect.[91] Following the reign of Antichrist (only forty-two months for the sake of the elect), there will come a period on earth when all of the promises pertaining to the kingdom of God will be fulfilled.[92] This is the time of the imprisonment of the beast (Rev. 20:2–3). After this, Satan will be released in the form of a second Antichrist only to be finally defeated.[93]

These final events are further nuanced in an oration attributed to Joachim.[94] This text adds additional reflection on Revelation 11 and 19, drawing on the example of three periods of Jewish war and peace.[95] Joachim postulates a parallel situation for the Church between the Incarnation and the Second Advent: (1) persecution ending in the peace of Constantine; (2) an imminent attack upon the people of God by beast and dragon followed by the rule of the people of God (the consummation of Joachim's sixth era); and (3) the unloosing of Satan who, together with Gog and Magog, wages war upon the saints. Prior to the outbreak of this final war, Elijah, not two witnesses, will appear to preach and convert the Jews.[96]

That Joachim was influential, even within his own generation, is without debate.[97] Who his heirs were is a moot point—whether the free-thinking sects of the later Middle Ages or the Franciscans and others within the Church.[98] When the orders of Dominic and Francis appeared in the thirteenth century, they seemed to express concretely the aspirations embodied in Joachim's prophecies.[99] Within the Franciscan Order itself there developed a strong attachment to the Joachite prophecies, particularly among the Spirituals with their strict adherence to a literal interpretation of Francis's Rule.[100] Having caught the imagination of his age, Francis embodied for many the dramatic sense of history defined by Joachim's figural imagery.[101]

Pseudo-Joachite works, which begin to appear by the middle of the thirteenth century in the context of heightened Spiritualist and papal-imperial tension, fed off an impending sense of the consummation of history sparked by such symbolic associations. The pseudo-Joachite *Commentary on Jeremiah*,[102] pointedly forecasted A.D. 1260 as the end of the forty-two months of affliction experienced by the Church.[103] The complexity of Joachim's end-time vision devolved into two orders, symbolized in our witnesses.[104] These symbolic witnesses took on political significance and were charged to perform a salvific role while Antichrist, or his instrument (Frederick II), chastened a fallen Church.[105]

Joachite ideas as they touch on our text are found in early Franciscan consciousness.[106] Salimbene of Parma emphasized the role of the adventual witnesses in conflict with a spiritual Antichrist in the Church.[107] Gerard of Borgo San Donnino's *Introduction to the Eternal Gospel* found Joachim to be the prophet of the new truth of the Spirit in an age foreshadowed by new spiritual disciples.[108] The

Apostolic Brethren, Flagellants, and other late-thirteenth-century movements appeared to some to embody this expectation.[109] It was Bonaventure's more moderate work that prevailed at least within the Church.

Francis was more than merely another saint for Bonaventure.[110] Although he suffered the wrath of the Spirituals,[111] many have argued for an abiding Joachite influence upon Francis. Without entering into that debate,[112] we may note that in Bonaventure's official biography of Francis, the *Legenda Maior* (1263), Francis is declared to have come in the spirit and power of Elijah. He is the second angel of the Apocalypse, "ascending from the sun and having the sign of the living God" (Rev. 7:2),[113] a vision frequently set parallel to our text. The apocalyptic significance is highlighted by Francis's reference to himself as the "herald of a great king":[114] as "*praeco Dei*," a resurrected John the Baptist and second Elijah. In Francis, Elijah has appeared as a singular image conflated with Revelation 11.[115]

This view of Francis makes sense within Bonaventure's vision of history, developed, to be sure, in relation to Augustine, but also shaped by Joachim.[116] Christ's First Advent divided two separate but parallel periods of time figurally depicted by the testaments. Each era was further divided into seven parallel periods adumbrated by the Creation days. Bonaventure viewed his own day and the proximate future under the signs of the church at Philadelphia (Rev. 3:7–13), the sixth seal (Rev. 6:12–17), and the sixth trumpet (Rev. 9:13–11:15), including thereby the time of our witnesses, implying thereby the imminent second Advent.[117] Nevertheless, the full extent to which Francis was identified with apocalyptic imagery in Franciscan mysticism is difficult to assess. For Bonaventure and others the symbolism of the text was important, but it was valued precisely because of the way in which Francis caught the imagination of his generation with his protest against growing wealth and commercialization. He desired to live out the gospel literally, to image the Evangel without encumbrance. His life, the life sought by the Franciscan Spirituals, pictures the appearance and tasks of the two "sack-clothed" witnesses.

There is no ambiguity about the symbolic value of our witnesses in the works of Peter John Olivi (c. 1248–1298) and Ubertino da Casale (c. 1259–1330). Olivi,[118] a Franciscan Spiritual, defended the strict observance of Francis's Rule. Censured for heresy (1283), later cleared (1287), he was venerated by many after his death. Olivi's *Postilla super Apocalypsim* (c. 1297) was popular and reflected the continuing apocalyptic tension of the period.[119] It is sometimes suggested that by 1297 Olivi believed that the expected apocalyptic pseudo-pope had arrived in the person of Boniface VIII (1294–1303).[120] His spiritual opposite, Olivi believed, was Francis. Like the angel with the face like the sun (Rev. 10:1), like Enoch and Elijah, he is the Elijah of the sixth age ready to wage war on Antichrist.[121] While applying the imagery of our text to Francis, Olivi also uses it to discuss two orders given the task of converting the world. He writes:

> According to Augustine, Gregory, and Richard, these two witnesses are literally Elijah and Enoch, and this is generally held. However, by them are also designated two orders of preachers, one of which will be more dedicated to exterior rule and suffering whence it is designated in John 21 by Peter to whom Christ said: feed my sheep, etc., and when you are old you will stretch out

your hands, i.e., on a cross, and follow me, i.e., to the cross. Indeed, the other is given more to contemplation and peace whence it is designated by John of whom Christ said: I will that he remains this way till I come.[122]

Olivi's commentary on the Apocalypse attracted wide attention. It became an "underground" canon of apocalyptic literature that persisted into the sixteenth century. Its visionary challenge was heightened by the martyrdom of four Spirituals in Marseilles (May 7, 1318).[123] Here were "witnesses" slain for the truth by Antichrist, becoming thereby the embodiment of the symbolism of our text and who represented the spiritual thrust of our text.

Olivi's fellow instructor at Florence, Ubertino da Casale, was also explicit in pointing to our text to draw out the apocalyptic sense of the times. Having attacked the Church for is carnality, he was suspended from the Franciscan Order and retired to Mt. Alverna where Francis had received the stigmata. Here (1305) Ubertino wrote *The Tree of the Crucified Life of Jesus*,[124] drawing relationships between his Order and the ministry of Jesus and commenting on the Apocalypse. In this classic expression of apocalyptic mysticism,[125] the two beasts (Rev. 13:1,11) have arisen, Boniface VIII and Benedict XI,[126] but are countered by the renovation of the evangelical life in Francis, the second (spiritual) of three comings of Christ.[127] The two witnesses, Enoch and Elijah, are mysteriously understood as the Franciscan and Dominican Orders. Enoch and Elijah themselves will come literally to herald Christ's third coming at Judgment.[128] Through voluntary poverty, in the present sixth age of the Church, the witnesses battle the mystical Antichrist.[129]

Spiritual apocalyptic speculation continued in such figures as Jacopone da Todi (c. 1230–1306) and Angelo of Clareno (c. 1255–1337).[130] Contrariwise, Thomas Aquinas (c. 1225–1274) emerged as the chief critic of their theology of history,[131] giving scant attention to our witnesses in contrast with the Spirituals. Aquinas's treatment of our theme (and of Antichrist) is *ad hoc* or simply illustrative. He writes that during the time when Antichrist rules, it is believed that God will call the witnesses, Enoch and Elijah, from the terrestrial paradise.[132] When Antichrist comes it will be with "all power and signs and lying wonders and with all wicked deception."[133] This mystery of evil is at work now in a collective sense,[134] but there is no parallel argument for the two witnesses.[135]

The Joachite view of history tended to find more of a role for outstanding prophets in the tradition of our witnesses. Francis was a new man, in Spiritualist exegesis, effecting a new covenant with a Spirit-filled band of prophets.[136] Aquinas's theology of history ran differently. His two eras of old and new law (OT, NT) appear to leave little room for fresh prophetic insight, and even provide a braking force for religious enthusiasm. The state of the new law (gospel) is imperfect, but no state of present life can be better than that embodied in and brought by Christ. Two points stand out: First, nothing can be nearer to the final goal than that which immediately drives us to that goal. This is the gospel, and Aquinas cites Hebrews 10:19: "We enter the sanctuary by the blood of Jesus." Second, the state and condition of humanity may change; the nature of the new law may be experienced in different ways depending upon persons, places, and times. The grace of the Holy Spirit may indwell perfectly or imperfectly.

In other words, there are degrees of reception of the Spirit as Thomas points out in a gloss on Romans 8.[137]

Thomas argues more pointedly: (1) Perfection can only be achieved in heaven, not in some further age on earth. (2) The Church's theology of the Spirit has always emphasized the fact that the Spirit was given when Christ was glorified—not separately or at a different time, as taught by Montanus and Priscilla. We have already been told all that we need to know about the future. (3) Thomas emphasized immanence over economy with respect to the Trinity and history. (4) Finally, the gospel of Christ is the only gospel of the kingdom. This is to be publicly proclaimed throughout the world. When the Church has been established among all peoples, then the end will come.[138]

If we contrast for a moment the theology of Aquinas against the Joachite visions of history that have developed we can note that piety is often symmetrically related to eschatology. Or, to put it differently, along with a new understanding of the movement of history comes a new piety or idea about individual morality, ethic for nature of the Church and community, and consequent politics.[139] This is strikingly borne out as one analyzes the development of various sects in the thirteenth and fourteenth centuries. While there are many factors at work in religious dissension,[140] an investigation into such groups for their understanding of history and appropriate behavior, then also for their recourse to symbolism and whether that might include our text, could be fruitful and illustrative of the intertwining of biblical interpretation with historical reflection. What was the meaning of our text for such groups as the Beguins, the Apostolic Brethren, the Fraticelli, and other Church reform- or renewal-minded groups who appear to take up the tasks of the adventual witnesses? Examples do exist like that of Prous Boneta (d. 1325), who was executed as a heretic after confesing that Olivi surpassed Francis in importance; that Francis was a latter-day Elijah and Olivi a latter-day Enoch.[141] She was not alone.[142]

In the *Inquisitor's Manual*, designed by the Dominican Bernard Gui (1261–1331), the characteristics attributed to suspect groups or individuals reveal traits that we have seen in the exegesis of Revelation 11.[143] Suspects were to be asked whether they were followers of Olivi and whether Francis was the renovator of the Church in the sixth age.[144] Questions like these, together with the coarse garb, penitential appearance, and apostolic-evangelical intent of suspected persons, picture literally the interpretation of our text. The adventual witnesses were available models within as well as outside of accepted piety.[145] They provided a symbolic avenue for redemptive prophetic activity or, coupled with historical periodization, an apocalyptic path toward social perfectionism. The potential of this symbol for social exploitation is evident.[146]

Aquinas's criticism of Joachite history was pointedly refuted by Arnold of Villanova (c. 1240–1312)[147] for whom Thomas was prefigured in the star which fell from heaven (Rev. 9:1).[148] Disappointed with the papacy of Boniface VIII and Clement V, Arnold promoted an apocalyptic piety of great lay appeal with hopes focused upon Frederick II, Aragonese king of Sicily (1296–1337).[149] But, it is another Franciscan, Peter Aureoli, who carries us forward to new emphases in the exegesis of our witnesses. For Aureoli and his fellow Franciscan, Nicholas of Lyra, the book of Revelation became a "prophetic compendium" of Church history between the two Advents.[150] Although an opponent of the Spirituals and of a third historical age, Aureoli drew upon the work of Joachim and Olivi. He marked out seven epochs in Church history, the seventh falling after Judgment.[151] Many of the favorite Spiritualist images are turned to the support of the Church. For example, Gregory VII, not Francis, is the sixth trumpeting angel. Still, appearing in the sixth epoch are the two witnesses, the Franciscan and Dominican Orders. The first resurrection (Rev. 20:5) is the renewal of piety through their efforts.[152]

The identity of the witnesses changes dramatically in the work of Nicholas of Lyra (1270–1340), regent master at Paris, one of the best-equipped scholars in his day. Lyra drew widely upon the work of Jewish writers, particularly the commentator Rashi (1040–1105), in his effort to combat allegory in favor of a more literal sense of the text.[153] His commentary on both the Old and New Testaments, earning him the title "Postillator," was widely used. In his discussion of the Apocalypse (1329), he identified the two witnesses as Pope Silverius (c. 536) and Patriarch Mennas of Constantinople (522).[154] The significance of this identification lies not so much in these individuals as in the precedent that is set for a specific identification of the prophetic vision with historical events.[155] Such focus upon particular individuals or events will be of determinative influence through the balance of the later Middle Ages and into the sixteenth century.

Members of Christ's Body

Our path to the sixteenth century must go by way of the late medieval Hussite revolt in central Europe. Several of its Czech reformers speculate on the identity and role of our witnesses, symbolic of Christ's true Church and mystical body (Eph. 5:23–27) at work in Church renewal and social reform. A spiritual and corporate sense of the text is underscored in Matthew of Janov (c. 1355–1394); however, as reform trailed off into radical Hussitism, the polemical periodization of history becomes more evident, calling forth the search for individual personalities to fill out the identities of the two witnesses.

The reform had its origin in the desires of the king, Emperor Charles IV (1347–1378), and in a succession of preachers, beginning with Conrad of Waldhausen, called by the king to preach in Prague. Critical of privileged wealth and clerical or monastic simony, Conrad anticipated many of the religious themes that interest us—particularly the visible purity of the Church, Christ's body. This theme runs throughout the movement from Milíc of Kromeríz (or Kremser) (d. 1374), often referred to as the father of Bohemian reform, into the split between Utraquists and Taborites[156] to the later Bohemian Brethren. In his brief work, *Libellus de Antichristo*, Milíc reminds his readers of the close connection among the proclamation of the gospel, the coming of Antichrist, and the Lord's return to rule. On the basis of detailed calculations he was convinced that Antichrist was already at large.[157] At first, believing Antichrist to be an individual, Milíc later developed a general and representative conception that became normative for Czech reform.[158] Placing his confidence in the promise of a New Jerusalem, he attempted to establish a foretaste of this hope by founding a school for preachers and a house for repentant prostitutes in Prague. Frequent reception of the Eucharist in bread and wine, became the eschatological symbol of one's new status in Christ.

Specific references to our theme appear in the work of Milíc's disciple, Matthew of Janov, the chief biblical theorist for the Czech reform. His primary work, *Regulae veteris et novi testimenti* (begun in 1388),[159] had as its aim the recovery of the apostolic life. Critical of papal or curial institutionalism and moral hypocrisy, it distinguished true from false Christians against an eschatological horizon. Reform was to be carried out by a holy people within the existing Church. Preaching, a key to Janov's program, was oriented to an immanent (Matt. 13:41) as well as imminent (Rom. 9:28) understanding of eschatology. With the triumph of ecclesial hypocrisy (c. 1200), Antichrist had been slowly growing in power. Rather than being some figure reserved for the future (Jew, pagan, or Saracen), Antichrist was best understood as a hypocritical Christian, conceived corporately and spiritually, both singly as well as a body with many members.[160]

At the height of Antichrist's power, inspired prophets, preaching with the zeal, innocence, and humility of Enoch and Elijah, will begin to slay Antichrist.[161] This is the work of the preachers and teachers in the Bohemian reform,[162] specifically that of Conrad of Waldhausen and Milíc.[163] Their program is outlined in the following way: (1) The true Church is distinct from the current political-ecclesiastical alliances with Rome, Avignon, and Greek Orthodoxy. (2) Spiritual and sacramental communion are not separate. (3) Those who are worthy of communion repent, although sinlessness is impossible. (4) The benefits of frequent communion are enumerated. (5) The authority of individual conscience is underscored. (6) The objection by priests to full and frequent communion lies in fear and pride. (7) Sacramental, not merely spiritual, communion is advocated. (8) Frequent communion is a panacea for the moral and spiritual ills of the Church, a weapon for slaying the "*mysticus Antichristus.*"[164] This is the work of the Church, a picture of the renovation promised as part of Elijah's return before the end of the age.

Bohemian students were increasingly attracted to Oxford rather than to Paris for study as the Great Schism (1378–1417) in the Latin Church continued. This had the effect of adding the influence of John Wyclif to the Bohemian reform. John Hus (1369–1415) employed much of Wyclif's theology, particularly the idea of the indestructibility and purity of Christ's Church, his mystical body, and pure bride (Eph. 5:23–27).[165] This church was grounded in the grace of predestination, not in the habitual grace of the visible church. Furthermore, adhering to the wrong visible church could mean complicity with an anti-church, even Antichrist, an issue already implied by Janov.[166] Schism could only come to the body of Antichrist, not Christ's true body. The current ecclesial turmoil raised the historical question of when Antichrist had entered the institutional Church. Wyclif argued that after the Church's first 1000 years Satan had been loosed in the world.[167] The visible church declined markedly from that date despite the efforts of Francis and Dominic. Their followers furthered the decay, becoming avenues for Antichrist.[168] Perhaps Wyclif's own poor preachers were part of an effort at restoring what had been lost.[169] According to his tract, *Of Good Prechyng Prestis*, preachers are to apply God's law, expose Antichrist, and promote love.[170] Such tasks form the body of work given our witnesses. In the Lollard commentary on Revelation, written by a student of Wyclif,[171] the two witnesses are identified with true doctrine and emerge triumphant over Antichrist, the papacy, and its adherents.[172] Hus's own eschatology was sharpened in its historical dimensions when he came under attack by the papacy.[173] Called before the Council of Constance (1414), Hus was martyred on July 6, 1415. The precise reasons for this are not our concern. However, his death was significant for the theme of two adventual witnesses. From 1415 on, Hus's martydom along with that of his fellow preacher, Jerome of Prague (c. 1370–1416), became both image and fulfillment in the minds of many of the death of the adventual witnesses (Rev. 11:7–10).

More immediately, Hus's death revealed the divided character of the national movement, perpetrated in the later Hussite wars.[174] The Hussite party soon split into two major factions, moderates around Jakob von Mies (Jakubek, d. 1429) and separatists who evinced an acute apocalyptic adventism exemplified in preachers like John Zizka and Nicholas of Dresden.[175] Prior to Hus's death, the more moderate Jakubek had held an academic debate at the university (1412), arguing that preachers in the spirit of Elijah were already in the world prior to the return of the Lord.[176] One of Jakubek's Bethlehem sermons argued that Hus was one who had come as a second Elijah to fight anti-Christian viciousness and clerical simony.[177] Hus's preaching was a sign of the approaching end. However, Jakubek's way of reading Scripture was more symbolic than that of his more extreme Hussite compatriots. The restoration of holy communion under the forms of both bread and wine (*sub utraque specie* = Utraquists) was itself sufficiently symbolic of one's new life in Christ.

The more radical and separatist Hussites took the name "Taborites" from their fortified stronghold south of Prague, a name resonant with the story of the "eschatological" transfiguration of Jesus, reportedly on Mt. Tabor in Galilee (Matt. 17:1–13). Many of the disaffected Taborites saw themselves witnessing the drama of the destruction of the world, which must come following the revelation of Antichrist. They grew in strength after the death of King Wenceslaus (1419), as their leader Zizka spread the "Kingdom of God" by force. For some this event was to occur in 1420.[178] Christ would come disguised as a robber in a period marked by retribution, fire, and the sword for his enemies. Following the cataclysm a state of innocence would be established, to which the elect, like Enoch and Elijah, would be called.[179]

Taborite hope intensified from 1421 to 1436. Its apocalyptic dimensions were stressed by leaders like the exiled English Wycliffite, Peter Payne. Guided by the Four Prague Articles, the Taborites defended themselves and sent out missionaries with the Word.[180] While general scriptural injunctions, prophetic immediacy, penitential asceticism, and evangelistic intent are the controlling motifs, it is difficult not to see some connection with our two witnesses. Janov had used the two witnesses as a way of talking about Christ's body in conflict with that of Antichrist.[181] Christ's final witnesses personify the spiritual qualities associated with Enoch and Elijah; these qualities were evident for many in Conrad and Milíc as well as in Hus and Jerome. We have an example of this attitude in the Taborite work *De Anatomia Antichristi*,[182] where the witnesses of truth continue their fight with the beast without weariness, perhaps a word to those whose zeal was flagging at this point.[183]

Our interest in the Hussite-Taborite movement must end here. Specific use of our text has not always been clear, with the important exception of Matthew of Janov. An apocalypticism that expected the appearance of Enoch and Elijah did attract, however, other contemporary reformers. It is visible among at least one group of Waldensians.[184] Such a group in the vacinity of Augsburg believed that "they would remain until the future judgment, but secretly until the advent of Elijah and Enoch, then openly; . . ."[185] Furthermore, a group of flagellants in the area of Thuringia believed their leader, Konrad Schmid, to be the Enoch of our adventual pair. When he was slain (1414), his followers expected him to return as a last emperor or even as the Son of man.[186]

Fringe groups such as these and the general appeal of our text seem to have been sufficiently important so as to lift up our text in two academic disputations at the University of Erfurt, Luther's later home. The first was held in 1466 against the heresy of the Wirsberger brothers, who in some sense saw themselves as the two witnesses of the book of Revelation.[187] The second, in 1486, was focused against continuing apocalyptic unrest represented by two elements: one group which identified with the views of Giovanni Nanni (1452–1502), denying any further personal appearances of the two witnesses and Antichrist, and declaring Muhammad to have been the true personal Antichrist; and another group of people who calculated when the Last Day might be.[188] In both disputations, arguments were presented that, among other things, looked for the personal return of Enoch and Elijah as the two witnesses of the Apocalypse, prior to the Day of Judgment.

Heralds of the Second Advent

The theme of the two witnesses did not only appear in direct biblical exposition but also found its way into artistic expression. While there is scant use of the Apocalypse in the Church's liturgy and only one occurrence of our text in the early liturgies of the Church,[189] the book was regularly read in monastic communities.[190] By the later medieval period our theme became more prominent in drama and visual representation, in addition to the exegetical literature already noted.[191] The Antichrist plays of the fourteenth and fifteenth centuries draw upon our text[192]; as the Gospels acknowledged a prophetic tradition pointing to the First Advent, so in contemporary drama an oral tradition was utilized that included signs of Doomsday[193] pointing to Christ's Second Advent. In the Chester *Prophets of Antichrist* play (c. 1328), the witnesses identify the machinations of Antichrist and warn of impending doom.[194] This gave special prominence to the witnesses' conflict, which for many would be acted out on the stage of history.

In painting and illumination, our theme begins to appear clearly in the Carolingian Apocalypse cycles[195] together with other illustrations of the text. By the fourteenth and fifteenth centuries pictures of the two witnesses are not difficult to find.[196] A Dutch block-book attributed to Laurens Janszoon Coster (b. 1405) illustrates the activities of our witnesses.[197] The two prophets prophesy before what

The Two Witnesses and Late Medieval Dissent

From a Dutch block-book (c.1420), probably the work of John or Lawrence Coster at Haarlem. As found in Heinrich T. Musper, *Die Urausgaben der holländischen Apokalypse und Biblia pauperum*, 3 volumes. München: Prestel Verlag, 1961. Atlas I, p. 17.

appear to be the soldiers of Antichrist. In a second scene they are beheaded. Then follows a picture of the seduction of Antichrist, followed by another illustrating his destruction. This last scene is viewed by the witnesses through a door as though they are looking in on the "inner" story of history. In another block-book of the same period such images are repeated.[198]

Echoes of prophetic utterances with an acute apocalyptic horizon can be found in many places in the later Middle Ages.[199] This wider field of prophetic and

apocalyptic vision from St. Bridget of Sweden (1303–1373) to continuing interest in Joachite speculation evident in Venetian circles, and elsewhere on the eve
of the Reformation, provides the context for reading our text.[200] For example, the
work of Savonarola (1452–1498) was identified by some as that of a final Elijah,[201]
an idea picked up by a later Reformed chiliast, Jacob Brocardo.[202] The optimistic
restitution heralded by Guillaume Postel (1510–1581)[203] or Michael Servetus
(1511–1553)[204] drew upon the theme of adventural witnesses, as both writers
developed strains of Renaissance mysticism, mediation, and prophecy in looking
forward to a new world order.[205] If late medieval learning was one path to
reform,[206] another came through the mystical, even apocalyptic, piety that included
our theme of adventural witnesses. Many people believed they were living in the
last days, which, on the basis of Daniel's envisioned empires or apocalyptic prognostication, implied an imminent Advent however precisely interpreted.[207] If the
history of New Israel ran parallel to that of Old Israel, then the turning point in
time might be at hand. As the old era ended with Malachi's prophecy of Elijah's
return, so the new era could be seen to end with adventural witnesses or at least a
final Elijah heralding the coming Advent.

Through the centuries, the wider story of historical self-understanding affected
the precise interpretation of our theme. The breadth of permissible meanings was
broadly defined in the exegesis of the early Church. Varying conceptions of the
witnesses' time, identity, and tasks were laid out. The possibility of a literal identification with one or two prophets was not lost, but a symbolic representation
was added by Tyconius and similarly inclined exegetes. Tyconius's exegetical rules
gave strength to the recapitulative methodology pioneered by Victorinus. A range
of images was now conflated with our prophets, illustrating the tasks of Christ's
body, his Church, in the era of the Church marked by the First Advent.

The temporal, or apocalyptic, horizon was not completely lost but it was muted.
Drawn into the reformist impetus following the Hildebrandine (Pope Gregory VII,
1073–1085) reforms, the apocalyptic systematization of Joachim of Fiore and his
successors gave renewed attention to our prophets. The two witnesses were no
longer seen as representatives of the entire Church, but rather as two preachers or
reforming orders within the Church. This understanding was placed within a framework of temporal periodization related to the septenary imagery of the Apocalypse, which gave our prophets a leading role in demarcating the end of the era
or in characterizing the new. Nicholas of Lyra set the entire drama into a firm
historical mold, specifically matching vision with event. Finally, in the Hussite-
Taborite movement, especially in Matthew of Janov, our two witnesses became
those preachers and teachers calling for reform in terms of the word. Tied neither
to emperor nor to pope or Church, their thrust was doctrinal and moral. Their
vision of reform included a call for social change in terms of apostolic
purity. They were to slay Antichrist through their preaching and teaching. John
Hus's death galvanized this message, offering a model of intractability and of
final obedience to God.

There is no uniform way in which Protestants will appropriate this tradition.
Some will reject it outright, others will follow it only at points and then cautiously.
Some, more inclined toward Joachite interests, will adopt it wholly. Our text will

play a role in Protestant-Roman Catholic polemics.[208] Generally, however, Protestant exegetes will adopt a Tyconian reading together with varying degrees of historical periodization, influenced only in part by Joachite prophecies. This is not to say that Catholic commentators in the sixteenth and seventeenth centuries did not use our text[209]; indeed, Protestant historicist appropriation helped to stimulate Jesuit preterist and futurist explanations of the Apocalyptic drama with their appropriate modification to the interpretation of Revelation 11. Our study will illustrate how the theme of two adventual witnesses helped to form Protestant self-understanding. This will now be demonstrated by focusing attention on the major lines of Protestant development.

Notes

1. *Explanatio Apocalypsis*, PL, 93, cols. 129–206. Wilhelm Kamlah maintains that the "door" from the Patristic to the Medieval Age is through Bede and Ambrosius Autpertus. See *Apokalypse und Geschichtstheologie* (Berlin: Emil Ebering, 1935), pp. 12–13. The awakened interest in apocalyptic speculation in the Carolingian Age is illustrated by C. Heitz as part of his general thesis, followed here, that "chaque profond changement de société a été précédé par une vogue notable de la pensée apocalyptique," in "Rententissement de l'Apocalypse dans l'art de l'époque carolingienne," *L'Apocalypse* (Genève: Droz, 1979), ed. Christe, p. 217. See also Richard K. Emmerson and Bernard McGinn, eds. *The Apocalypse in the Middle Ages.* (Ithaca, N.Y.: Cornell University Press, 1992).

2. Both later Carolingian and eventually Protestant commentators on the Apocalypse will cite Bede along with the earlier tradition out of which his work grows. R. H. Charles, *Studies in the Apocalypse* (Edinburgh: T. & T. Clark, 1913), pp. 13–15; cf. Wilhelm Bousset, *Die Offenbarung Johannis* (Gottingen: Vandenhoeck und Ruprecht, 1906), p. 67.

3. Bede, *Apocalypsis*, PL, 93, cols. 131–33.

4. Gerald Bonner argues for the dominance of typological thinking in Bede's works in *Saint Bede in the Tradition of Western Apocalyptic Commentary* (Jarrow Lecture, 1966), pp. 5, 31–29. This, contrary to R. W. Southern, who argues that Bede's chronological interests continued to remain subsidiary to the symbolic value of the text (Southern, "Aspects of the European Tradition of Historical Writing. Vol. 3: History as Prophecy," *Transactions of the Royal Historical Society*, 22 [1972]:164–65).

5. Richard Emmerson gives a tabular presentation of these ages in *Antichrist in the Middle Ages* (Seattle: University of Washington Press, 1981), p. 18.

6. See in Augustine, *De civitate dei*, XXII, 30 (CCL, 48.865–6); cf. XX.7, as transmitted to Bede's generation in the chronology of Isidore of Seville's "Etymologiae" ("De discretione temporum"), 5, 39 [PL, 82, cols. 334–28]).

7. R. W. Southern writes, "Each age acquired a distinct momentum . . . an act of restoration, succeeded by a period of divergent development, leading to a general disaster which set the scene for the new act of restoration." See "Aspects of the European Tradition of Historical Writing. Vol. 2: Hugh of St. Victor and the Idea of Historical Development," *Transactions of the Royal Historical Society*, 21 (1971):162.

8. Bede divides his commentary into three books (I:1–8,1; II:8,2–14,20; III:15–22,21), which conflate apocalyptic imagery in the manner prescribed by Tyconius's sixth rule ("De recapitulatione"). The chronological interest is characteristic.

9. Bede, PL, 93, cols. 146–54; on *Antichrist*, col. 148C.

10. Ibid., col. 162C.

11. Ibid., col. 164C.

12. Ibid., col. 154C. The significance of this seal is discussed by Wilhelm Bousset, *The Antichrist Legend* (London: Hutchinson, 1986), p. 149. Robert E. Lerner shows that the period marked by the opening of the seventh seal was, for Bede, typologically similar to Christ's life between his Crucifixion and Resurrection. It was a testing prior to the heavenly reward. Jerome developed this idea from Dan. 12 and an apparent surplus of 45 days between the end of Antichrist's reign and the Last Judgment. Jerome's surplus would, in succeeding centuries, provide a point of departure for Christian chiliasm (Robert E. Lerner, "Refreshment of the Saints: The Time After Antichrist as a Station for Earthly Progress in Medieval Thought," *Traditio*, 32 [1976]:97–144). Lerner's argument is part of his larger point that chiliasm, the expectation of a disjunctive and beneficient earthly millennial age prior to the Last Judgment, was not merely a *factum* of religious fanaticism or social unrest, but derivative of the biblical exegetical tradition. See his *Powers of Prophecy: The Cedar of Lebanon Vision from the Mongol Onslaught to the Dawn of the Enlightenment* (Berkeley: University of California Press, 1983); and cf. Norman Cohn's *The Pursuit of the Millennium: Revolutionary Millenarians and Mystical Anarchists of the Middle Ages* (New York: Oxford University Press, 1970) who drew a closer relationship among chiliasm, social unrest, and religious fanaticism and whose work inspired sociological explanation for later millenarian studies.

13. *Expositio in Apocalypsim*, CCL, Continuatio Mediaevalis 27, 27A, 27B; ed. Robert Weber (Turnhout: Brepols, 1975–79).

14. Bousset, *Offenbarung*, p. 68.

15. *Expositio in Apocalypsim*, p. 365.

16. Ibid., p. 228 (Rev. 6:12).

17. Ibid., p. 414.41–46 (Matt. 22:37–40).

18. See in Yves Christe for iconographic depiction, "Traditions littéraires et iconographiques . . . des images apocalyptiques," *L'Apocalypse de Jean* (Geneva: Librairie Droz, 1979), pp. 111–13.

19. *Beati in Apocalypsin libri XII*, ed. Henry A. Sanders (American Academy in Rome, 1930); the work was prior to that by Autpertus.

20. Bousset, *Offenbarung*, pp. 68–69; cf. Bernard McGinn, *Visions of the End* (New York: Columbia University Press, 1979), p. 77.

21. *In Apocalypsin*, p. 448. The importance of Beatus is his usefulness for reconstructing the Tyconian text and in his influence upon apocalyptic iconography. One illustrated Beatus Apocalypse identifies the witnesses as: "duo testes elias et jheremias" (fol. 104r). See Peter Klein, *Der altere Beatus-Kodex Vitr. 14-1 der Biblioteca Nacional zu Madrid: Studien zur Beatus-Illustration und der spanischen Buchmalerei des 10, Jahrhunderts* (Hildesheim: George Olms Verlag, 1976), Vol. 2, illus. 49; on the role of the Beatus codices, cf. Wilhelm Neuss, *Die Apokalypse des hl. Johannes in den altspanischen und altchristlichen Bibel-Illustrationen*, 2 vols. (Münster: Aschendorff, 1931).

22. *Commentariorum in Apocalypsin libri quinque*, PL, 100, cols. 1085–1156. For attribution, see "Alcuin," DTC, 1, pp. 687–94.

23. Bousset, *Offenbarung*, p. 69.

24. Alcuin, *Apocalypsis*, PL, 100, col. 1087.

25. Ibid., cols. 1088–89.

26. Ibid., col. 1147C.

27. *Expositio in Apocalypsin*, PL, 117, cols. 937–1220; cf. Bousset, *Offenbarung*, p. 69.

28. Ibid., col. 1070BC.

29. Ibid., cols. 1072D–73C.

30. *In Apocalypsin*, PL, 114, col. 730D.

31. Berengaudus (Pseudo-Ambrose), *In Expositionem Apocalypsis Admonitio*, PL, 17, cols. 868B–71D.

32. *Enarrationes in Apocalypsin*, PL, 162, cols. 1540B–41D. A present and future role is held for Antichrist and the witnesses. The latter are given a moral and penitential role.

33. *Expositio in Apocalypsin*, PL, 165, col. 662B. The witnesses are not the whole Church but its teachers, or doctors.

34. *In Apocalypsin*, PL, 114, col. 7212C.

35. *Apocalypsis*, PL, 17, cols. 812–42.

36. Ibid., cols. 773C–74D.

37. Ibid., cols. 863D–67A.

38. Ibid., col. 868B. "Testes duos Dominus Eliam et Enoch vocat, qui adventum eius secundum praecurrent, sicut Joannes praecurrit primum."

39. *The Play of Antichrist*, trans. with introduction by John Wright (Toronto: The Pontifical Institute of Medieval Studies, 1967); cf. McGinn, *Visions of the End*, pp. 117–21. On early medieval conceptions of Antichrist, see D. Verhelst, "La préhistoire des conceptions d'Adson concernant l'Antichrist," RTAM, 40 (1973):52–103. Verhelst argues that Adso's conception of Antichrist was influenced by Bede's work.

40. *Adso Dervensis, De ortu et tempore Antichristi*, ed. D. Verhelst, CCL, Continuatio Mediaevalis, 45 (Turnholt: Brepols, 1976), pp. 28.153–60. The two witnesses are said to prepare the elect for war and convert the Jews. In his essay on Antichrist (*Libellus de Antichristo*, PL, 101) Adso follows Augustine on the conversion of the Jews prior to Antichrist's reign. Only Elijah performed this task in Augustine (cf. Mal. 4:5–6). For Adso, it is the task of the witnesses. Further influences on Adso's work, including the debated relation to Pseudo-Methodius, are discussed in McGinn, *Visions of the End*, pp. 73, 82–84; cf. Donatus Haugg, *Die Zwei Zeugen*, (Münster: Aschendorfschen Verlagsbuchhandlung, 1936), p. 108.

41. Wright, *Play of Antichrist*, pp. 93–94.

42. Ibid., p. 95.360–65.

43. Barbara Nolan, *The Gothic Visionary Perspective* (Princeton: Princeton University Press, 1977), pp. 5–29.

44. Kamlah, *Apokalypse*, p. 105. McGinn finds in the emergence of the high medieval papacy a third turning point following (1) the conversion of the Roman Empire and (2) the rise of Islam as inspiring of new apocalyptic creativity in medieval history; see McGinn, *Visions of the End*, p. 33.

45. Marjorie Reeves presents various images used in defining a deepened understanding of history: the pilgrimage, the genealogy of Christ (Jesse Tree), days of Creation ("History and Prophecy in Medieval Thought," MH, n.s. 5 [1974]:51–75); cf. Southern, "Idea of Historical Development," p. 163.

46. John H. van Engen, *Rupert of Deutz* (Berkeley: University of California Press, 1983), pp. 262–74; cf. Wolfgang Beinert, *Die Kirche—Gottes Heil in der Welt* (Münster: Verlag Aschendorff, 1973), pp. 12–37, 229–68. On Rupert's influence into the sixteenth century, see Johannes Beumer, "Rupert von Deutz und sein Einfluss auf die Kontroverstheologie der Reformationszeit," in *Catholica*, 22 (1968):207–16.

47. *De Trinitate*, "Prologus," PL, 167, cols. 197–200. An English translation is in McGinn, *Visions of the End*, p. 110. The relation of this scheme to an identical one in Rupert's commentary on the Apocalypse is shown by van Engen, *Rupert of Deutz*, pp. 227–81. Van Engen draws out the importance of Rupert for new historical and typological concerns, breaking with Tyconian allegory; ibid., pp. 279–80.

48. Beinert, *Die Kirche*, p. 325; cf. Rupert on the letters to the seven churches (Book II).

49. *In Apocalypsim*, PL, 169, col. 1029D; cf. Beinert, *Die Kirche*, pp. 345–46.

50. *In Apocalypsim*, PL, 169, cols. 1021–34. Note the abundant use of OT imagery used to fill out the witnesses' identity. Van Engen draws out the importance of preaching for Rupert in this connection. See *Rupert of Deutz*, pp. 271–72.

51. *In Apocalypsim*, PL, 169, col. 1022D.

52. Beinert, *Die Kirche*, pp. 38–50.

53. I am following Beinert, ibid., p. 344.

54. *Expositio in Cantica Canticorum*, PL, 172, cols. 471–72; cited in Lerner, "Refreshment of the Saints," pp. 111–12. Lerner shows Honorius to be the first to contradict the idea (established by Jerome, Bede, and Haimo) that the time on earth between the end of Antichrist and the Last Judgment is brief. The task assigned to Enoch and Elijah is placed in this lengthened period. The implications of this for later Protestant millenarianism are replete. Cf. Marie Thérèse d'Alverny, "Le Cosmos symbolique du XIIe siècle," in *Archives d'Histoire doctrinale et litteraire du Moyen-Age*, 28 (1953–54):31–81.

55. *The Two Cities, A Chronicle of Universal History of the Year 1146 A.D.*, trans. by C. C. Mierow (New York: Columbia University Press, 1928), p. 461 (Book viii.5). Note the entrance of Enoch into Otto's neo-Augustinian history.

56. *Scivias sive Visionum ac Revelationum* ("Visio Undeccima"), PL, 197, cols. 712, 720.

57. See L. F. Barmann, "Reform Ideology in the Dialogi of Anselm of Havelberg," CH, 30 (1961):379–95; but without specific treatment of our theme.

58. On Premonstratensian eschatology, see Guntram Bischoff, "Early Premonstratensian Eschatology: The Apocalyptic Myth," in *The Spirituality of Western Christendom*, E. R. Elder, ed. (Kalamazoo, Mich.: Cistercian Publications, 1976), pp. 41–71. The author contends that a more optimistic, even chiliastic, vision of history was developed prior to Joachim of Fiore by Premonstratenians like Eberwin of Steinfeld.

59. *Dialogi* I.5, PL, 188, cols. 1159–60.

60. I am following Kamlah, *Apokalypse*, pp. 66–70; cf. Reeves, "History and Prophecy," pp. 55–56.

61. See Peter Classen, *Gerhoch von Reichersberg: Eine Biographie mit einem Anhang uber die Quellen, ihre handschriftliche überlieferung und ihre Chronologie* (Wiesbaden: 1960), esp. pp. 89–90; cf. Beinert, *Die Kirche*, pp. 50–68, n. p. 59; on Gerhoh's theology, see Erich Meuthen, *Kirche und Heilsgeschichte bei Gerhoh von Reichersberg* (Leiden: E. J. Brill, 1959), pp. 94–110.

62. Beinert shows both clerical and humanist parties appealing to Gerhoh in the sixteenth century (*Die Kirche*, pp. 66–67).

63. *Gerhohi . . . Opera Inedita*, ed. by O. Van Den Eynde I. Tractatus et libelli . . . (Rome: Spicilegium Pontificii Athenaei Atoniani 8, 1955), pp. 159–60; 162.4–5; cited in Meuthen, *Kirche*, pp. 140–41. See *Libri III de Investigatione Antichristi* (c. 1160).

64. *Epistolae*, PL, 193, cols. 489–618, esp. 564–70; cf. Meuthen, *Kirche*, pp. 140–42.

65. *De Quarta Vigilia Noctis* (1165). I am guided by Beinert, *Die Kirche*, pp. 339–47; note the chart on p. 347; cf. McGinn, *Visions of the End*, pp. 104–7.

66. For a summary of Joachite studies, see Morton W. Bloomfield, "Recent Scholarship on Joachim of Fiore and his Influence," in Ann Williams, ed., *Prophecy and Millenarianism* (Essex: Longman, 1980), pp. 21–52; cf. Bernard McGinn, "Awaiting an End," MH, n.s. 11 (Totowa, N.J.: Rowman and Littlefield, 1982), for further research. Especially important are the studies by Marjorie Reeves, *The Influence of Prophecy in the Later Middle Ages: A Study of Joachimism* (Oxford: Clarendon Press, 1969), and *Joachim of Fiore and the Prophetic Future* (London, 1976; New York: Harper and Row, 1977); cf. review by David Flood, "A Study in Joachimism," in CF, 41 (1971):131–40; and Bernard McGinn, "Apocalypticism in the Middle Ages: An Historiographical Sketch," *Medieval Studies*, 37 (1975):

252–86, esp. pp. 276–83; cf. the earlier scholarship of Herbert Grundmann, *Studien über Joachim of Floris* (Leipzig, 1927; repr., 1966). The impact of Joachite thought is treated by Delno West, *Joachim of Fiore in Christian Thought: Essays on the Influence of the Calabrian Prophet*, 2 vols. (New York: Burt Franklin, 1975).

67. Bousset, *Offenbarung*, pp. 73–75; cf. Charles, *Studies in the Apocalypse*, pp. 15–27.

68. Reeves analyzes Joachim's *figurae* in "The Abbot Joachim's Sense of History," in *1274-Année Charnière-Mutations et Continuités* (Paris, Centre National de la Recherche Scientifique, 1977):782–95; cf. Bernard McGinn, "Symbols in the Thought of Joachim of Fiore," in Williams, ed., *Prophecy and Millenarianism*, pp. 143–64.

69. Reeves argues that in Joachim's emphasis upon a future manifestation of the Spirit's fullness in the course of historical development, a new feature is added to the history of Christian thought. See "The Originality and Influence of Joachim of Fiore," *Traditio*, 36 (1980):169–316.

70. Reeves, *Influence of Prophecy*, pp. 3–15. In the Augustinian tradition, prophetic inspiration, grounded in a recognized authority, was valid, whereas human speculation was not. Echoes of this argument can be seen in both Joachim and his later disputant, Thomas Aquinas (cf. Augustine, *De civitatis dei*, XVIII.52).

71. Joachim's emphasis is upon a sixth followed by a seventh, or sabbatical, age within history rather than upon concurrently running sixth and seventh ages (as had been argued by Augustine, cf. chapter 1). Reeves writes, "The acid test for distinguishing a Joachimist form an anti-Joachimist viewpoint lies in the interpretation of the seventh age" (with B. Hirsch-Reich, *The Figurae of Joachim of Fiore* [Oxford: Clarendon Press, 1972], p. 301; cf. p. 12). Reeves and Hirsch-Reich indicate that the "kaleidoscopic quality" of these patterns make Joachim subject to various interpretations (p. 260).

72. *Liber concordiae novi ac veteris testamenti* (Venice, 1519; repr. Frankfurt: Minerva, 1964). A section of Book II is translated in Bernard McGinn, *Apocalyptic Spirituality* (New York: Paulist Press), pp. 120–34. E. Randolph Daniel views the *Liber concordiae* as the exegetical introduction to Joachim's major works. The spiritual significance of agreement between the Old and New Testaments is also presented in Joachim's *Psalterium decem cordarum* . . . (repr. Frankfurt: Minerva, 1965); cf. Reeves on editions, *Influence of Prophecy*, pp. 512, 514.

73. *Expositio magni prophete Abbatis Joachim in Apocalypsim* (Venice, 1527).

74. *Liber concordiae*, fol. 19r.

75. Ibid., fol. 10r.

76. *Expositio*, fol. A3r. Note other paired spiritual heroes and the parallels drawn with Israel's entrance into the promised land (Josh. 4); cf. Reeves and Hirsch-Reich, *The Figurae*, p. 260.

77. *Expositio*, fols. 1v–26v; cf. Reeves and Hirsch-Reich, *The Figurae*, p. 265, n. 24.

78. Ibid., fol. 5r; cf. 37v.

79. These eras are: (1) Jacob to Moses and Joshua, a parallel to the period running from Christ's Resurrection until the death of John the Evangelist; (2) Joshua to Samuel and David, a parallel to the time from John the Evangelist to Constantine; (3) David to Elijah and Elisha, paralleling Constantine to Justinian; (4) Elisha to Isaiah and Hezekiah, paralleling Justinian to Charlemagne; (5) Isaiah to the Babylonian captivity, paralleling Charlemagne to the present; (6) the Jews' return from the captivity to Malachi's death, paralleling the present and revelation of new Babylon until the time when Babylon will be destroyed; and (7) the time from Malachi's death to John the Baptist or Christ and the end of the first "status," paralleling the destruction of the second "status," opening of Sabbath rest and Last Judgment. *Expositio* (intro.), fols. 6v–13r; cf. (Book II) fols. 113v–123r.

80. Ibid., fol. 6v; cf. fols. 145v–149v, fol. 109v; cf. on the return of Elijah, Reeves and Hirsch-Reich, *The Figurae*, pp. 134–45, 138–40.

81. The seven trumpets signify: (1) the apostles, (2) martyrs of the Church, (3) teachers who opposed Arianism; (4) monks and virgins overrun by the Saracens, (5) the conflict between children of the spirit and those of the flesh (Manichees, Waldensians, Cathari); (6) Christian preachers who loose the evil angels; (7) the full revelation of OT mysteries. *Expositio*, fols. 123r–153r.

82. Ibid., fols. 137r–140v. Joachim writes that this preacher could be Elijah or Enoch, but he prefers Enoch because Elijah is one of the two adventual witnesses.

83. Ibid., fols. 141v–142v.

84. Ibid., fols. 143v–145v.

85. Ibid., fols. 146r–v, 148r–v.

86. Specific application of Joachim's figural formulae is complex, and a full analysis is beyond this effort. A focused treatment of the corporate identity of the witnesses is found in *Expositio*, fols. 148v–150v; cf. fols. 175r–176r; cf. Reeves, *Influence of Prophecy*, pp. 133–292.

87. McGinn indicates that they prefigure, but are not to be identified with, the *ordo monachorum* of the third state; *Visions of the End*, pp. 316–17, n. 52.

88. *Expositio*, fols. 175v–176r. Portions are translated in McGinn, *Visions of the End* pp. 136–37.

89. Reeves cites *Liber concordiae*, fols. 68r, 76v, *et passim*, in *Influence of Prophecy*, pp. 142–43.

90. As symbolized in Isaiah (*ordo clericorum*) and then in Elisha and Benedict of Nursia (*ordo monarchorum*) in its double foundation. See *Expositio*, fol. 146v; cf. fols. 5r–v; cf. Alfred-Felix Vaucher, "Les 1260 jours prophetiques dans les cercles joachites," *Andrews University Seminary Studies*, 3 (1965):42–48.

91. Ibid., fols. 176r, 207v–209r.

92. During the general tribulation occurring in the 42nd generation, a new leader or pontiff in the Church will arise, the "angel ascending from the rising of the sun" (Rev. 7:2). This is the time of the reign of the Lord of Hosts. Bernard McGinn finds Joachim as the first to see in this angelic figure a leader of the last days (*Visions of the End*, p. 316, n. 45). It should be noted that Victorinus had already identified this angel with Elijah who comes before Antichrist to restore the Church through penitence, offer comfort in time of persecution, and convert many Jews and Gentiles (*Commentarii in Apocalypsin*, p. 80).

93. I am following McGinn's translation of *Libro delle Figure* in *Visions of the End*, pp. 137–38; the end of the world is interpreted as the world's last hour (1 John 2:18), leaving room for a fuller development of apocalyptic history.

94. E. R. Daniel, "Abbot Joachim of Fiore: The *De Ultimis Tribulationibus*," in *Prophecy and Millenarianism*, Ann Williams, ed., pp. 165–89; cf. 167–71 for authenticity.

95. The three periods are: (1) Moses to David, followed by the peace of Solomon; (2) the Babylonian exile of Israel, followed by her restoration; (3) the conquest of Alexander and the Seleucid kings, followed by the coming of John the Baptist in the spirit of Elijah (ibid., p. 176).

96. Ibid., p. 178.

97. Morton Bloomfield and Marjorie Reeves, "The Penetration of Joachimism into Northern Europe," *Speculum*, 29 (1954):772–93; cf. Reeves, *Influence of Prophecy*, pp. 37–44.

98. Herbert Grundmann contends that Joachim's proper heirs were the free-thinking sects attempting to break with religious authoritarianism. Later, following the work of Tondelli, Grundmann modified this view, offering them a measure of orthodoxy (*Studien*

über Joachim, pp. 182ff.). Ernst Benz held that the Spiritual Franciscans were the heirs of Joachim, but their "reformation" was rejected by ecclesial authority (*Ecclesia Spiritualis* [Stuttgart: W. Kollhammer, 1934]).

99. Reeves cites the joint encyclical issued in 1255 by the generals of the two orders, Humbert de Romanis and John of Parma, describing the orders in Joachim's parallel twos (*Influence of Prophecy*, pp. 146–47).

100. Ibid., pp. 45–58; cf. Ruth Kestenberg-Gladstein, "The Third Reich: A Fifteenth-Century Polemic against Joachimism, and Its Background," *Journal of the Warburg and Courtald Institute*, 18 (1955):245–95. She holds that Joachim's followers generally held three points: (1) an imminent future will soon overtake an imperfect present; (2) the present is evolving into that future perfected state; (3) a heightened sense of anticipation is present among the believers.

101. Reeves writes about the Franciscans: "Thus they transformed Joachim's system into a drama shaped by the clues he had given and leading towards a final act which would embody his expectation. . . . For those who were too impatient to wait for divine intervention to reshape the authority of the Church the revolutionary implications of Joachimism offered an opportunity to cast themselves in the key roles in the final age." In "History and Prophecy," pp. 62–63, 67.

102. The text is only available in several sixteenth-century editions. Reeves argues for Cistercian rather than Franciscan origin; *Influence of Prophecy*, pp. 156–58, n. 1; cf. pp. 56, 397–98; and Benz, *Ecclesia Spiritualis*, pp. 182–91.

103. Leroy Froom, *The Prophetic Faith of Our Fathers* (Washington, D.C.: Review and Herald, 1948), vol. 1, p. 727.

104. Benz, *Ecclesia Spiritualis*, pp. 182–83.

105. McGinn, "Angel Pope and Papal Antichrist," CH, 47 (1978):155–73; and Brian Tierney, *Origins of Papal Infallibility: Sovereignty and Tradition in the Middle Ages* (Leiden: E. J. Brill, 1972), pp. 58–82.

106. Reeves, *Influence of Prophecy*, pp. 37, 52, 173–250.

107. Benz, *Ecclesia Spiritualis*, pp. 191–93; cf. Delno West, "Between Flesh and Spirit: Joachite Pattern and Meaning in the *Chronica* of Fra Salimbene," JMH, 3 (1977):339–52; cf. Jacques Paul, "Le Joachimism et les Joachimites au milieu du XIIIe siècle d'après le témoignage de Fra Salimbene," in *1274 Année Charnière*, pp. 797–813.

108. Reeves, *Influence of Prophecy*, pp. 59–70.

109. Ibid., pp. 52–55; 242–50.

110. See Joseph Ratzinger, *The Theology of History in St. Bonaventure*, trans. by Zachary Hayes (Gr. 1959; Chicago: Franciscan Herald Press, 1971), pp. 31–55.

111. Angelo Clareno's *Historia septem tribulationum*, ed. F. Ehrle, ALK, 2 (1866): 271ff. connects him with the fourth and fifth persecutions. Ernst Benz supplies examples of our adventual witnesses in sectarian polemics in *Ecclesia Spiritualis*, pp. 335, 350, 374, 390; on Francis as Elijah, see pp. 70, 92–93, 121, 167, 332.

112. See McGinn, "The Significance of Bonaventure's Theology of History," in *Celebrating the Medieval Heritage: A Colloquy on the Thought of Aquinas and Bonaventure. The Journal of Religion*, 58 (1978, suppl.):565–81.

113. *Legenda Maior S. Francisci*, Praef. 2; 13.10; Marion A. Habig, ed., *St. Francis of Assisi. Writings and Early Biographies. English Omnibus of the Sources for the Life of St. Francis* (Chicago: Franciscan Herald Press, 1973), p. 632, 736.

114. *Legenda Maior* 2.5; Habig, *Writings*, p. 643; n. pp. 631–32.

115. Ratzinger cites Bonaventure, *Hexaemeron*, XV, 28, in *St. Bonaventure*, p. 33; cf. William Bouwsma, *Concordia Mundi: The Career and Thought of Guillaume Postel, 1510–1581* (Cambridge: Harvard University Press, 1957), p. 76.

116. Ibid., pp. 1–55. Bonaventure, following Joachim, understood history as arising from the concord of the OT and NT. Other contemporary ways of understanding history were: (1) seven ages from Adam through Christ and the Church (Augustine); (2) five ages based upon the parable of the workers in the vineyard, Matt. 20:1–16 (Gregory the Great and Honorius of Autun); and (3) the three ages of nature, law and gospel, or grace (Paul).

117. The full spiritual conditions of Augustine's seventh age are yet to come, though they are already found in those who enter the spiritual state in this age. This is the basis for hope in world transformation. See Ratzinger's diagram, *St. Bonaventure*, p. 21.

118. Franz Ehrle, "Petrus Johannes Olivi, sein Leben und seine Schriften," ALK, 3, (1887):409–552; cf. Raoul Manselli, "Une grande figure Serignanaise: Pierre Jean Olivi," *Etudes Franciscaines*, 12 (1972):69–83; and David Burr, "The Persecution of Peter Olivi," *Transactions of the American Philosophical Society*, 66 (1976):44–66.

119. Bousset, *Offenbarung*, pp. 78–79. E. R. Daniel contends that it was Olivi, not Bonaventure, that brought together the Franciscan eschatology with Joachim's theology of history. See E. R. Daniel, *The Franciscan Concept of Mission in the High Middle Ages* (Lexington: University of Kentucky Press, 1975), p. 27; cf. McGinn, "Awaiting an End," p. 275.

120. The significance of this possibility is highlighted in Olivi's understanding of history: Seven ages in the OT correspond to the first five eras of the world week (seven larger eras), forming the age of God the Father. The seven ages of the Church fall in the sixth world week, lasting from Incarnation to Judgment. The first ages of the Church correspond to the time of God the Son, the latter two to the time of God the Spirit, opening into the seventh world week, a time of immense spiritual significance. Olivi believes that he stands at the end of the fifth and beginning of the sixth age of the Church, a time of a new spiritual illumination. See Burr, "Persecution," pp. 17–24, 72–73.

121. As Christ introduced the sixth age of history, so Francis came in parallel fashion. See Burr, ibid., pp. 19–20.

122. Olivi continues by noting that these two represent a common evangelical spirituality, which will characterize a final age as Enoch and Elijah did earlier periods. See Olivi, *Postilla*, as found in J. J. I. von Döllinger, ed., *Beiträge zur Sektengeschichte des Mittelalters, Vol. II: Dokumente vornehmlich zur Geschichte der Valdesier und Katharer* (Munich: C. H. Beck'sche Verlagsbuchhandlung, 1890), p. 564.

123. Malcolm Lambert, "The Franciscan Crisis under John XXII," FS, n.s. 32 (1972): 123–43; and Kestenberg-Gladstein, "Third Reich," pp. 248–66.

124. *Arbor vite crucifixae Jesu* (Venice, 1488 repr. ed. Torino, 1961). Some pertinent texts are translated in McGinn, *Visions of the End*, pp. 212–15. Augustine, Jerome, Richard of St. Victor, and esp. Joachim are cited as authorities.

125. Gordon Leff, *Heresy in the Later Middle Ages: The Relation of Heterodoxy to Dissent c. 1250–c. 1450* (New York: Barnes & Noble, 1967), Vol. 1, p. 152–53.

126. *Arbor vite*, sig. Fiiiv–Fvr.

127. Ibid., sig. Cr, Ciiir.

128. Ibid., sig. Fiiir.

129. Ibid., sig. Cr.

130. McGinn, *Visions of the End*, pp. 205–7.

131. Bernard McGinn, "The Abbot and the Doctors: Scholastic Reactions to the Radical Eschatology of Joachim of Fiore," CH, 40 (1971):30–47; cf. Y.-D. Gelinas, "La critique de Thomas d'Aquin sur l'exégèse de Joachim de Flore," in *Tommaso d'Aquino nel suo settino centenaria* (Rome, 1974), I, pp. 368–75; and cf. Peter Meinhold, "Thomas von Aquin und Joachim von Fiore und ihre Deutung der Geschichte," *Saeculum*, 27 (1976): 66–76.

132. *Summa theologiae*, 3a, 49, 5, 2 (abbr. used: part, question, article, reply).

133. Ibid., 3a, 49, 2, 3.

134. This parallels Tyconius's seventh rule ("De diabolo et corpus eius"); cf. *Summa theologiae* 3a, 8, 8.

135. *Summa theologiae*, 3a, 8, 8 ad 1, 3. One day Antichrist will be embodied in the "man of sin" and will "sit in the temple of God . . . as if he were God" (2 Thess. 2:3–10).

136. Olivi's sermon on Francis as filled with the Spirit so as to become another man follows 1 Sam. 10:6, which talks of being so filled with the Spirit that one is turned into another person. See Ernst Benz, "Die Kategorien des eschatologischen Zeitbewusstseins," *Deutsche Vierteljahresschrift für Literaturwissenschaft und Geistesgeschichte*, 11 (1933): 203–5, 215.

137. Benz, "Aquinas," p. 82.

138. *Summa theologiae*, 1a2ae, 106, 4.

139. This point was raised by Ernst Benz in relation to medieval eschatological and apocalyptic ideas among sectarian Christian groups. See Benz, "Die Kategorien des eschatologischen Zeitbewusstseins.

140. Earlier reform in the Church had led to the development of new religious orders now forced out of the Church. Leff classifies such groups: (1) radical Franciscans including the Beguins and Joachites, (2) Eckhartian Mystics and Free Spirits, and (3) Cathars, Waldensians, Lollards, and Hussites seeking to restore the true church, in *Heresy*, Vol. 1, p. 15. Cf. Ernst Warner, "Popular Ideologies in late Medieval Europe: Taborite Chiliasm and Its Antecedents," *Comparative Studies in Society and History*, 3 (1960):344–63; Marjorie Reeves, "Some Popular Prophecies from the Fourteenth to the Seventeenth Centuries," in *Popular Belief and Practice*, G. J. Cuming and D. Baker, eds. (Cambridge: Cambridge University Press, 1972):107–34.

141. William May, "The Confession of Prous Boneta, Heretic and Heresiarch," in *Essays in Medieval Life and Thought* (New York: Columbia University Press, 1955), pp. 3–30, esp. pp. 18–19.

142. Leff, *Heresy*, Vol. 1, pp. 212–30.

143. Bernard Gui, *Manuel de l'Inquisition*, ed. and trans. by G. Mollat (Paris: Société d'édition "les Belles lettres," 1964), Vol. 1, 84–94, 108–38, 138–66. Cf. W. L. Wakefield and A. P. Evans, *Heresies of the High Middle Ages* (New York: Columbia University Press, 1969), p. 425.

144. Ibid., Vol. 1, pp. 108–10, 144–52.

145. See Anthony of Florence, *Summa Theologica*, 4 vols. (Verona: Ex typ., 1740; repr. 1959), IV, cols. 722–28. Emmerson cites examples in the theological compendia of the thirteenth and fourteenth centuries, in *Antichrist in the Middle Ages*, pp. 77, 95–101.

146. Cola di Rienzo (c. 1314–1354), e.g., used the prophecy of the two adventual witnesses by writing (letter 49) that God "had intended to punish the people and the Church and wound them terribly with these scourges before the coming of St. Francis, but at the insistency of Dominic and Francis, who he claimed had held up the then collapsing Church of God by preaching in the spirit of Enoch and Elijah, the Judgment of God was put off until the present time. . . ." Cited in McGinn, *Visions of the End*, p. 242. See Duncan Nimmo, "Poverty and Politics: The Motivation of Fourteenth Century Franciscan Reform in Italy," in *Religious Motivation: Biographical and Sociological Problems for the Church Historian* D. Baker, ed. (Oxford: Clarendon Press, 1978): pp. 161–78.

147. Arnold can be seen as the second of three types of Franciscans: radical followers of Olivi, exponents of a Spiritual lay movement, and (with Peter Aureoli) those faithful to the Church. See Ernst Benz, "Die Geschichtstheologie der Franziskaner-spiritualen des 13, und 14. Jahrhunderts nach neuen Quellen." *Zeitschrift für Kirchengeschichte*, 52 (1933), p. 92.

148. Cited by McGinn, *Visions of the End*, p. 225.

149. Benz, "Geschichtstheologie," pp. 99–111.

150. The term is Charles's from *Studies in the Apocalypse*, pp. 27–30.

151. His ages are: (1) the time of the apostles, (2) persecution under the Caesars, (3) the Church's prosperity under Constantine, (4) division and dissension brought by heretics and schismatics, (5) the peace of the Church under Charlemagne and Christian emperors, (6) persecution by Antichrist, (7) the messianic kingdom following the Last Judgment.

152. Benz, "Geschichtstheologie," pp. 113–19.

153. See Herman Hailperin, *Rashi and the Christian Scholars* (Pittsburgh: University of Pittsburgh Press, 1963), pp. 137–246. Lyra's concern with the literal meaning was not new, and he never rejected an allegorical sense *per se*, but emphasized a double literal understanding of the text. See Heiko Oberman, *Forerunners of the Reformation* (Philadelphia: Fortress Press, 1966/81), p. 286; and Henri de Lubac, *Exégèse médiévale: Les quatres sens de l'Ecriture*, Vol. 2 (Paris: Aubier, 1959–1964), pp. 344–67.

154. *Postilla super Apostolorum, Epistolas canonicales, et Apocalypsim* (Mantua: Paulus de Butzbach, 1480) *ad loc*. Obtained by courtesy of the University of Illinois. The pages are unnumbered, but the text remains divided into chapter headings.

155. The seals describe the events in history through Domitian; the seven trumpets, history from Arius through Patriarch Anthemus; chapter 12 of Revelation pictures the conflict between Chosroes of Persia and the Byzantine general and emperor Heraclius. The first beast is the son of Chosroes, the second is Muhammad. Rev. 14 tells of Charlemagne, the seven vials represent the history of the Crusades, and Rev. 20 the conflict between Pope Calixtus and Henry V.

156. I am guided by Howard Kaminsky, who gives ample attention to the development of Taborite chiliasm, in *A History of the Hussite Revolution* (Berkeley: University of California Press, 1967). Kaminsky offers an overview of sources, pp. 344–45 (n. 88), and prints a number of them in appendix III (pp. 517–50).

157. Milíc of Kromeríz, *Libellus de Antichristo*, in Janov's *Regulae veteris et novi testamenti* (Vol. 3), Vlastimil Kybal, ed. (Oeniponte: Libraria Universitatis Wagnerana, 1911), pp. 368–81; cf. Matthew of Janov's "Narratio de Milicio," pp. 333–57. Milíc derived the idea that Antichrist would appear in 1365 on the basis of the following: 1260 day-years as derived from Dan. 12:11 added to the 33 day-years of Jesus' earthly life and the 42 years from Jesus' Crucifixion to the destruction of Jerusalem. Added together, this yields 1365 (Vol. 3, 372–73). Amadeo Molnár writes that whereas Cola looked for renewal through the emperor, Milíc had not yet lost hope in the pope although he placed his confidence in the proclamation of the Word. See "Die eschatologische Hoffnung als Grundlage der Böhmischen Reformation," in *Von der Reformation zum Morgan*, Josef L. Hromadka, ed. (Leipzig: Koehler und Amelang, 1959), pp. 59–187, esp. pp. 63–66.

158. Paul DeVooght, *L'Hérésie de Jean Huss*, Bibliothèque de la Revue d'histoire ecclésiastique. Fasc. 34 (Louvain, 1960):7–21.

159. R. R. Betts, "The Regulae Veteris et Novi Testamenti of Matej z Janova," *The Journal of Theological Studies*, 32 (1931):344–51. On the edition by V. Kybal, see above. Kestenberg-Gladstein, "Third Reich," p. 288, n. 112, sees stronger resemblances to Olivi than Joachim; Leff finds Janov's ideas distinctly individual and dissimilar from either, in Leff, *Heresy*, p. 615.

160. Ibid.

161. Note the connection between the slaying of Antichrist with "the spirit of christ's mouth" (2 Thess. 2:8) and Janov's preachers. Earlier commentators connect the slaying of Antichrist with Christ or a divine agent. Janov, *Regulae*, Vol. 3, p. 20.

162. Ibid., Vol. 3, pp. 351–52; cf. Vol. 2, pp. 40–41.

163. Amadeo Molnár, "Le mouvement préhussite et la fin des temps," in *Communio Viatorum*, 1 (1958):30.

164. The articles are summarized from Betts, "Regulae," pp. 348–51.

165. The standard work on Wyclif remains H. B. Workman, *John Wyclif: A Study of the English Medieval Church*, 2 vols. (Oxford: Oxford University Press, 1926); Oberman presents an English translation of portions of Hus's *De ecclesia* (1413) in *Forerunners*, pp. 218–37; Hus on the purity of the Church (p. 218); his definition of the Church and refutation of Tyconius (p. 231).

166. Janov, *Regulae*, Vol. 2, pp. 157–58.

167. Bousset, *Offenbarung*, p. 81; and Michael Hurley, "'Scriptura sola' Wyclif and his critics," *Traditio*, 16 (1960):301.

168. Workman discusses the prevalence of Joachite ideas at Oxford and Wyclif's early attraction to the Franciscan Spirituals, whom he later rejected; see *John Wyclif*, vol. 2, pp. 97–108; Emmerson notes that 20 percent of Wyclif's sermons cite the work of Antichrist, in *Antichrist in the Middle Ages*, p. 71.

169. Workman, *John Wyclif*, Vol. 2, pp. 201–20; Emmerson writes that Wyclif may have seen "himself as filling the role of Elias, although he makes no claim to be a prophet," in *Antichrist in the Middle Ages*, p. 71.

170. Cited by Gotthard Victor Lechler, *John Wycliffe and His English Precursors*, trans. by Lorimer, rev. by S. G. Green (London: Religious Tract Society, 1904), pp. 208–21.

171. Bousset, *Offenbarung*, pp. 81–82. The work, *Commentarius in Apocalypsin* (c. 1390), is attributed to John Purvey and was of use to Luther (ed. by him, 1528) through its identification of the papacy with Antichrist. See Anne Hudson, "Contributions to a Bibliography of Wyclifite Writings," *Notes and Queries*, n.s. 20 (1973):443–53.

172. Ibid., p. 82, n. 2.

173. The theme of Antichrist is central to Hus's work, *De ecclesia*. Similarities and differences with Wyclif on this topic are raised by Johann Loserth in *Wiclif and Hus*, trans. by M. J. Evans (London: Hodder and Stoughton, 1884; 1st ed., Prague and Leipzig, 1884), pp. 181–291; cf. Matthew Spinka, "Was Hus an Independent Thinker?" in *John Hus and the Czech Reform* (Hamden, Conn.: Archon Books, 1966), pp. 3–11. Molnár, "Hoffnung," p. 72.

174. Kaminsky, *Hussite Revolution*, pp. 97–140.

175. Ibid., pp. 310–60.

176. Leff, *Heresy*, p. 685.

177. Reference to the witnesses is found in the Taborite work *De Anatomia Antichristi* (c. 1421). Janov is frequently cited and the suggestion is made that the warfare between Jerusalem and Babylon continues through all history. The two witnesses are interpreted (with Janov) as faithful preachers.

178. Leff, *Heresy*, p. 691; cf. Kaminsky on stages of chiliastic development and secession, in *Hussite Revolution*, pp. 336–52.

179. Lawrence of Brezova's treatise on Tabor reads: "The elect . . . will be brought back to the state of innocence of Adam in Paradise, like Enoch and Elijah, and they will be without any hunger or thirst, or any other spiritual or physical pain."

180. Molnár, "L'évolution de la théologie hussite," pp. 150–52; cf. Kaminsky's lists of chiliast literature, *Hussite Revolution*, pp. 344–60.

181. Janov, *Regulae*, Vol. 3, pp. 13–15, 40–41, 351, 356. Molnár cautions that Janov's emphasis is more upon Antichrist than upon the two witnesses, in *A Challenge to Constantinianism, The Waldensian Theology in the Middle Ages* (Geneva: WSCF, 1976), p. 58.

182. (Pseudo) Ioannes Huss, *De Anatomia Antichristi* (1525). Printed in 1525, and

attributed to Hus, it originated in Taborite circles in 1421; cf. Kestenberg-Gladstein, "Third Reich," p. 289, n. 114.

183. Ibid., p. 73b.

184. Molnár writes that apocalyptic thought was generally muted among the Waldensians. See *Die Waldensergeschichte und europäisches Ausmass einer Ketzerbewegung* (Gottingen: Vandenhoeck und Ruprecht, 1980), p. 234. However, Moneta notes that Peter Waldo was viewed by his followers as a returning Elijah.

185. J. J. I. Döllinger, *Beiträge zur Sektergeschichte des Mittelalters*. Vol. 2. (Munich: C. H. Beckische Verlagsburchhandlung, 1890), p. 364.

186. Ernst Wadstein, *Die eschatologische Ideengruppe* (Leipzig: O. R. Reisland, 1896), pp. 31–32. This group was one used by Norman Cohn to illustrate aberrant forms of Christian spirituality which he believed contributed to National Socialism in Germany. See his *Millenarians and Mystical Anarchists of the Middle Ages* (rev. ed.) (New York: Oxford University Press, 1970), pp. 145–46.

187. In the 1450s and 1460s two brothers, Janko and Livin of Wirsberg, claimed to be precursors of a coming saviour who would inaugurate a last historical age. See Wadstein, *Die eschatologicshe Ideengruppe*, pp. 122–23, 183; cf. Kestenberg-Gladstein, "Third Reich," pp. 256–57 and 257–66, where the author of the disputed question, Johannes Dorsten, is discussed. Kestenberg-Gladstein prints the Latin text on pp. 266–82; see esp. p. 278 for the two witnesses. Issues of the nature of mortality and immortality would be dealt with at the Fifth Lateran Council (1512–1517).

188. Ludger Meier O. F. M., "Die Rolle der Theologie im Erfurter Quodlibet," RTAM, 17 (1950):298. The book of the Italian Dominican Giovanni Nanni (1452–1502) is entitled *De futuris Christianorum triumphis in Saracenos* (1st ed., 1480). He viewed Muhammad as the literal Antichrist, but taught against a literal return of Enoch and Elijah.

189. The Mozarabic liturgy offers the most readings from the Apocalypse among the ancient rites. The one exception is found here with the reading of Rev. 10:8–10 and 11:1,3,4,15 on the festival of Saints Peter and Paul in the *Liber comicus* (Spain, c. 656–67). F. van der Meer, *Maiestas Domini. Théophanies de l'Apocalypse dans l'art chrétien* (Roma/Paris: Société d'edition les "Belles Lettres," 1938), p. 469.

190. Van Engen, *Rupert of Deutz*, p. 275.

191. Although we have primarily followed the commentary tradition, Emmerson presents helpful examples from medieval preaching and other literature. He draws attention to preaching guides such as the *Compendium theologicae veritatis* (c. 1265) of Hugh Ripelin of Strassburg, the *Tractatus de victoria Christi contra Antichristum* (1319) of Hugh of Newcastle; and the *Postilla* of Nicholas of Lyra; in *Antichrist in the Middle Ages*, pp. 77, 106.

192. See the Italian Doomsday play from Perugia (c. 1320–1340), e.g., the German Corpus Christi cycle from Künzelsau (c. 1479), *Ludus de Antichristo* (12th century), *Jour de Jugement* (c. 1330), and the Chester Corpus Christi cycle (c. 1328); ibid., pp. 164–65, 180–87.

193. William Heist, *The Fifteen Signs Before Doomsday* (East Lansing: Michigan State College Press, 1952), pp. 94–95, 108–25.

194. Linus Urban Lucken, *Antichrist and the Prophets of Antichrist in the Chester Cycle* (Washington, D.C.: Catholic University of America Press, 1940), pp. 102–3, 181 212 (Rev. 11:3–12).

195. Peter K. Klein, "Les cycles de l'Apocalypse du haut Moyen Age (ix–xiie s.)," in *L'Apocalypse*, pp. 135–86, esp. pp. 140–41; van der Meer, *Maiestas Domini*, p. 298; and idem, *Apocalypse. Visions from the Book of Revelation in Western Art* (London: Thames and Hudson, 1978), pp. 29, 194; pl. 148; cf. Wilhelm Neuss, *Die Apokalypse*, pp. 143–55.

196. See an illustration of true preaching in, e.g., Schedel's *Liber Chronicarum* (Augsburg, 1497), reproduced in Steven Ozment, *The Age of Reform, 1250–1550: An Intellectual and Religious History of Late Medieval and Reformation Europe* (New Haven: Yale University Press, 1980), p. 111.

197. H. Th. Musper, *Die Urausgaben der holländischen Apokalypse und Biblia pauperum* (Munich: Prestel Verlag, 1961), pp. 25, 35–36; Tafelband I, Apokalypse, plates 17–19.

198. H. Th. Musper, *Der Antichrist und die Fünfzehn Zeichen. Faksimile—Ausgabe des einzigen erhaltenen chrioxylographischen Blocksbuchs* (Munich: Prestel Verlag, 1970). Note 1.4r–v, Bl.12rb, and Bl.12vb, all of which deal with the two adventual witnesses. Cf. Hans Preuss, *Die Vorstellungen vom Antichrist in späteren Mittelalter bei Luther und in der Konfessionellen Polemik* (Leipzig: J. C. Hinrichs, 1906), p. 273.

199. Many of these prophecies have been collected by Hans Preuss, *Martin Luther. Der Prophet* (Gütersloh: C. Bertelsmann, 1933), esp. pp. 4–23; cf. J. Rohr, "Die Prophetie im letzten Jahrhundert vor der Reformation als Geschichtsquelle und Geschichtsfaktor," *Historisches Jahrbuch*, 19 (1898):29–56, 547–66; esp. p. 38; and Will-Erich Peuckert, *Die Grosse Wende, Das apokalyptische Saeculum und Luther* (Hamburg: Claassen und Goverts, 1948).

200. Bernard McGinn, "Venetian Joachite Circles: c. 1450–1525," typescript, 1982 (pp. 1–27), by courtesy of the author.

201. Donald Weinstein, *Savonarola and Florence. Prophecy and Patriotism in the Renaissance* (Princeton: Princeton University Press, 1970), p. 159; cf. H. Heermann, *Savonarola. Der Ketzer von San Marco* (Munich: C. Bertelsmann Verlag, 1977), pp. 148–66, 204–8.

202. Jürgen Moltmann, "Jacob Brocard als Vorläufer der Reigh-Gottes-Theologie und der symbolisch-prophetischen Schriftauslegung des Johann Coccejus," ZKG, 71 (1960):115.

203. Bouwsma, *Concordia Mundi*, pp. 157–62. Bouwsma cites Postel, *Candelabri interpretatio . . .* (1548) and *Restitutio rerum omnium . . .* (1522), p. 301.

204. *Christianismi Restitutio* (Vienne, 1553; repr., 1966), p. 447.

205. Reeves, *Joachim of Fiore*, pp. 83–115.

206. Heiko Oberman, *The Harvest of Medieval Theology. Gabriel Biel and Late Medieval Nominalism* (Grand Rapids, Mich.: Eerdmans, 1967), pp. 5–7.

207. This sense of impending doom was not unreasonable: Saracen destruction of the Byzantine Empire seemed to portend the end as that event was understood through the lens of texts from Daniel, 1 Thessalonians, and the Apocalypse. In Russia, the fall of Contantinople (1453) was viewed as divine judgment upon the Patriarch for concessions made to Rome at the Council of Florence (1439).

208. Bousset, *Offenbarung*, pp. 84–91; Reeves, *Joachim of Fiore*, pp. 136–65.

209. Some Franciscans and Jesuits will do so confidently; cf. Bousset, *Offenbarung*, pp. 91–95; of Reeves, *Joachim of Fiore*, pp. 116–35. She details the ways in which Catholic thinking develops ideas of a *renovatio mundi* out of late medieval lines of thought. With application to the New World, see John Leddy Phelan, *The Millennial Kingdom of the Franciscans in the New World: A Study of Writings of Geronime de Mendieta (1525–1604)* (Berkeley: University of California Press, 1970) and, as applicable to Columbus, see John V. Fleming, "Christopher Columbus as a Scriptural Exegete," in Mark Burrows and Paul Rorem, eds. *Biblical Hermeneutics in Historical Perspective* (Grand Rapids, Mich.: Eerdmans, 1991), pp. 173–86.

3

The Dawn of Reformation Preaching

Power to Prophesy

Reformation preaching, concerned with particular religious abuses, was shaped by prophetic anticipation.[1] Whether in Italy, among apocalyptic Spiritualists who drew inspiration immediately from Savonarola and more distantly from Joachite spirituality, or in Spain among mystically oriented Alumbrados in search of a "third church," or in the heartland of the empire, in central Europe, among such peasant movements as associated with the visionary Johann Eberlin of Günzberg, one can discern such expectation. Deepened biblical study, whether Humanist or mystical in intent,[2] the search for a universal science,[3] astrology,[4] and divination[5] were all used to strengthen the prophetic vision despite caution and censure from the Fifth Lateran Council (1512–1517).

Much of this prophecy was linked to particular events at the close of the fifteenth and early sixteenth centuries. New economic conditions in central Europe were leading to an upheaval in social relations.[6] The fall of the Byzantine Empire and the arrival of Turkish armies from the east into European precincts offered a sense of the impending Judgment of God upon the last of the kingdoms envisioned by the biblical prophet Daniel. Finally, continued anxiety over religious and institutional failure in the Church contributed to the popularity of apocalyptic prophecy, fear of false prophets, and search for true ones.[7] Competing theories about who such prophets were grew through the sixteenth century, sometimes including one who would appear like an earlier paragon of virtue, perhaps a restored Enoch or Elijah.

Luther and many of his reform-minded contemporaries were affected by this wide expectation, though not uniformly. To the extent that literate Christians followed an understanding of history generated by the biblical text, it was possible to believe that social turmoil was indicative of that larger turmoil in the moral order that tended toward the final calamitous days preceding Judgment or millennial bliss.[8] In fact, what is noteworthy about the period is not how people's lives were affected by social and economic realities, but how they may have shaped their lives differently by idealistic conceptions drawn from the biblical text. To the extent that the Bible was read, the book of Daniel (7:1–28) was frequently understood to present a vision of empires or kingdoms through the course of history that ended with Rome, the Holy Roman Empire of the sixteenth century being understood as

59

the final shadow of that larger political reality. Accordingly, as the papacy became identified with Antichrist, which itself had been equated with the "little horn" (Dan. 7:8) arising on the head of the final beast, so the age could be perceived as falling in a penultimate way to portentous divine events. Variants of this perspective were held by both those counted as working for reform together with the prevailing social order ("magisterial" reformers) as well as those apart from that order ("radicals"). Views ranged from an "historicist" and "futurist" identification of contemporary or soon-to-be events to the distrust of contemporary interpretations characterized by Calvin's belief that all of the events in Daniel's prophecy were fulfilled by the time of Christ or shortly thereafter.[9]

Attempts are made in theology to distinguish between a prophetic and apocalyptic appropriation of Christian hope or eschatology, the former emphasizing present moral principles, the latter focusing more upon a clear development of the historical process.[10] Our focus upon the time, identity, and work of the two adventual witnesses draws out this distinction. The tradition of the final appearance of Enoch and Elijah was familiar in the sixteenth century.[11] Luther knew of it,[12] was associated with it, and rejected the literal application to himself,[13] but this association surfaces again in later polemical Lutheranism.[14] While not all religious radicals shared a sharply defined apocalyptic expectation, such is increasingly evident through the career of Thomas Müntzer. In his appropriation of Elijah's mantle, Müntzer found his identity in an image promising historical deliverance through the purification of society. That image took on greater chiliastic proportions as he found his work increasingly frustrated when local princes failed to heed his call. In appropriating this image he helped to stamp a line of spiritual consciousness that can be traced from him through Hans Hut, the Strassburg prophets, and Melchior Hoffman, each of whom conditioned early phases of radical reform in the sixteenth century.[15]

The Spirit of Elijah

When Thomas Müntzer (c.1490-1525)[16] wrote to Nikolaus Hausmann in the summer of 1521, clarifying what it meant for him to come in the spirit of Elijah, he was describing the nature of his reforming vision by drawing upon a fiery tradition of prophetic invective.

> Beloved, the justice of God's mandates in which I have earnestly directed my steps, according to his declaration, has instructed me that it teaches the modesty of the spirit, not of the flesh; this should be clear to all the elect people of God in the candlestick of truth; this is also not opposed to that most modest servant, the prophet Elijah when he slew one thousand prophets of Baal (except 150 priests). For he was most modest precisely at the time when to carnal people he appeared to be in raging fury.[17]

Müntzer saw himself coming in the spirit of Elijah, not in a general sense, but increasingly with the consciousness of being placed in a unique situation in order to fulfill a prophetic role.[18] That mission was the cleansing of Christendom of false belief and easy Christianity in a historical period marked by impending cataclysmic events. As was said of Elijah of old, "you troubler of Israel" (1 Kings 18:17), so it was said of Müntzer. The question that lies before us is to what extent Müntzer's identification with Elijah moves toward our theme of two adventual witnesses. To answer this question several of his letters and theological treatises will be studied. While his direct citation of the Apocalypse is surprisingly infrequent,[19] the structural development of his ideas and the frequent citation of prophetic and apocalyptic material from the Old Testament, which seems parallel to our interests, lends support to the idea that Müntzer's thought moves toward an appropriation of our theme.

The person of Elijah was not the only prophetic model appealed to by Müntzer. Rather, following an initial period at Zwickau as an erstwhile ally of Martin Luther, Müntzer used a variety of prophetic models to define his ministry. These are, for example, the new Jeremiah in the "Prague Manifesto" inveighing against false religion,[20] the new Daniel in his "Sermon Before the Princes" offering spiritual direction to the princes of Saxony,[21] the new Baptist of the "Special Exposé" working in the spirit of Elijah,[22] and finally as Elijah in his "Defense,"[23] opening the way to a new apostolic chiliastic church.[24]

Müntzer was at first caught up in the reforming momentum centered around Luther.[25] During this initial phase of Müntzer's career he gives evidence of interest not only in the Church's liturgical practices but also of a spiritual desire for religious authenticity.[26] This latter mystical concern continues throughout his life, deepens his sense of alienation from the Lutheran establishment, and heightens his interest in apocalyptic prophecy.

Müntzer was forced to leave Zwickau in mid-April 1521, following increasing controversy, and civic and anticlerical unrest.[27] In the early summer of that year he wrote his letter of self-defense to Nikolaus Hausmann. It is here that the Elijah connection begins to emerge. Müntzer wrote that he felt called to Bohemia for the sake of the Cross. He defended himself as an Elijah, exposing the false faith and carnality of the modern prophets of Baal. That Müntzer may be thinking of more than simply the Old Testament model of Elijah is indicated by the apocalyptic horizon evident in the letter:

> Now is the time of Antichrist, as Matthew 24 most clearly manifests. When the Lord says that the gospel must be proclaimed in the whole world, then the abomination of desolation will be seen. But the reprobate are not going to believe just as they clung to a straw in the days of Noah. All those who say that the pope is the superior Antichrist err. Indeed he is his true herald. But the fourth beast will rule the whole world and its reign will be greater than all.[28]

Curiously, the same day on which the letter to Hausmann was dated, Müntzer wrote to Marcus Thomae (Stübner), hinting at some urgent cause in danger of being thwarted by Satan.[29] By September, Müntzer was in Prague, a city experiencing neo-Utraquist strength.[30] He was probably welcomed in Bohemia because he was perceived as a follower of Martin Luther.[31] The religious turmoil may have been attractive to Müntzer because of its roots in radical Hussite-Taborite thinking. Three of the leaders appear to be self-styled prophets. At least one, Matej

Poustevnik (Matthew the Hermit), from western Bohemia, seems to have followed an apocalyptic pattern of thought.[32]

In November 1521 Müntzer issued his "Prague Manifesto."[33] At least three factors here may establish a growing connection between Müntzer and our theme. First, Müntzer opens the treatise by eulogizing the memory of John Hus. He will sound the trumpet of that "holy warrior."[34] Müntzer is beginning in a way that would appeal to his audience. Of course, Hus's place in Taborite thinking was not simply that of a national hero. Janov's theology of witnesses, as developed in earlier Hussite-Taborite thinking, continued in effect in the early sixteenth century, holding open a special place for Hus.[35] This should alert us to possible implications for our theme. The structure of the manifesto appears to reflect an elaboration of Müntzer's earlier letter to Hausmann. There we caught a reference to the work of Elijah against an apocalyptic horizon. Both ideas are strengthened here. Following an invective against priestly hypocrisy and false faith,[36] Müntzer proposes: "I will bring destruction to the enemies of faith before your eyes in the spirit of Elijah."[37] As in ancient Israel, so also in Christendom, the faith had been seriously compromised.[38] Having exposed such false faith, Müntzer promises to help build the new apostolic church in Bohemia.[39] The apocalyptic horizon is developed more fully, perhaps with a greater sense of immediacy as Sultan Suleiman II had recently demanded tribute of Hungary.[40] Müntzer warns of the coming separation of the wheat from the tares,[41] of judgment brought by God through the Turk,[42] even of the coming of the "personal Antichrist" to rule, whose short reign will be followed by that of the elect.[43] Such a warning was defined in medieval exegeses as the work of a final Elijah, often conflated with the tasks of our two witnesses. An additional factor is introduced, not clearly evident in Müntzer's letter to Hausmann, the announcement of a new apostolic church.[44] Its significance will be developed in relation to our theme after we note Joachite and other apocalyptic intimations in Müntzer's later works.

The prophetic and apocalyptic interests in Müntzer's "Prague Manifesto" surface several months later during a period of apparent wandering and instability for Müntzer. Shortly after Luther's return from the Wartburg to slow or block the revolutionary, even apocalyptic, program of Andreas Karlstadt and Gabriel Zwilling,[45] Müntzer wrote to the learned colleague of Luther, Philipp Melanchthon (1497–1560), whose own work was later to give rational and systematic form to Lutheranism. Müntzer complained to an apparently receptive Melanchthon:[46] "Our dearest Martin acts ignorantly." He refuses "to offend the little ones who as little ones are accursed like children a hundred years old in wickedness."[47] Müntzer lashes out at Luther's apparent timidity in failing to perceive the nature of the times:

> Indeed, the persecution of Christians is already in the public places, and I don't know why you think it is something still to be expected. Dear brother, stop waiting; the hour has come! Do not hesitate for summer is at the door. Do not seek the favor of your princes, for if you do you will behold your own destruction.[48]

Given the work of Melanchthon together with Karlstadt and Zwilling, Müntzer might have expected some support, but received none.[49] The interesting thing about this statement is what it implies with respect to the time of the two witnesses. If

Müntzer saw himself related in some way to our theme, perhaps his reference here is to their slaying. This letter and the "Prague Manifesto" alone outline the complete scenario; judgment and tribulation, persecution and the reign of Antichrist followed by that of the elect and the new apostolic church. The vision of Isaiah 65:17–25, forecasting the new heavens and a new earth after current persecution, was the one that Müntzer was seriously trying to convey to Melanchthon. Yet it was precisely at this time that Luther at first hesitatingly, then more openly, backed away from a literal, even an individual, understanding of the witnesses, stressing only their representational proclamation of the Word.[50] Furthermore, in 1522 Luther will publish his New Testament containing a negative appraisal of the book of Revelation.[51] At this point, Luther and Müntzer are moving in opposite directions in terms of apocalyptic paradigms.

This division is also evident in matters of spiritual authority. It becomes evident in a letter Müntzer wrote to Luther shortly after becoming the preacher at St. John's Church in Allstedt. Now he makes his break from Luther, establishing what Carl Hinrichs has referred to as a "counter-Wittenberg."[52] Müntzer writes Luther, politely acknowledges his effort at reform, and then proceeds to differ radically in his view of faith. What is characteristic of the text of Revelation 11:3, and clearly of Müntzer, is the immediacy of prophetic revelation, the fact that Müntzer views himself as God's witness.[53]

Earlier Luther had urged Melanchthon to find out whether those who were calling themselves "prophets" could prove their calling.[54] Now in the months after Luther's debates with the "Zwickau Prophets" (e.g., Michael Cellarius and Gerhard Westerburg), Müntzer's own program was threatened. In September the local lord, Count Ernst of Mansfeld, forbade attendance at Müntzer's services. In return, Müntzer leveled an apocalyptic warning at the count, closing his letter as Elijah might have done with Ahab, "Thomas Müntzer a destroyer of the ungodly."[55] The Elector, Frederick the Wise, having caught wind of the disturbance, wrote to his city warden, Hans Zeiss, requesting information. Müntzer, probably tipped off by Zeiss, wrote to Frederick and asserted his divine call to the prophetic task in Allstedt,[56] appealing to the Imperial Mandate, which allowed the proclamation of the gospel. Müntzer defended his efforts with a further apocalyptic thrust, interpreting the danger for the ruler who fails to carry out the mandate of Romans 13 in light of Revelation 6.[57]

Throughout the fall of 1523 an increasing cleavage grew within the reforming movement, in Wittenberg and elsewhere.[58] Stressing the Christian's life of trial, Müntzer published two theological treatises summarizing the false faith of Christendom and the hypocrisy of her religious leaders. While the "Imaginary Faith" (*Von dem getichten glauben*) focuses upon an externalized faith symbolized in infant baptism, it is in the "Protestation or Demonstration" (*Protestation odder Empietung*) that we receive a further intimation of possible connections with our theme.[59] The clearest hint is a marginal reference to Malachi 3, the promise that before the Day of Judgment a messenger will be sent to herald the coming Advent.[60]

In the context of Müntzer's desire for a cleansing of Christendom, the reference is at least indicative of his own prophetic consciousness. I would argue further in light of what we have seen in Müntzer's letter to Hausmann, a possible

hint on the same day to Stübner, the structure of the "Prague Manifesto" and remarks dropped along the way to Melanchthon, Luther and even Frederick the Wise,
that this intimation suggests once more an apocalyptic paradigm which may be
defined by Revelation 11. That we are not pressing the evidence too hard is indicated in a somewhat defensive letter written to Zeiss in December.[61] Müntzer must
have been accused of a latent or growing Joachimism in the previous months. He
defends his teaching against those who mock it as similar to the Joachite "eternal
gospel." After repeating themes raised in his treatise "Imaginary Faith," Müntzer
writes that he respects Abbot Joachim. However, he argues that his own teachings are from a higher source and that he has only read the (ps.-Joachite) commentary on Jeremiah.[62]

It is of interest that there is no criticism of Joachim here. Furthermore, Müntzer
appears to claim similar ideas but derived from Scripture.[63] The door to a distinct
Joachite influence is not shut. Rather, he widens it. In *On Jeremiah,* at least three
things stand out: a coming time of suffering; a pressing apocalyptic horizon that
offers a new order of existence following that suffering; and a special place for
new spiritual prophets.[64] All of these items appear in some form in this letter. The
time of suffering is now.[65] The apocalyptic horizon is evident in the marginal
references at the end of the first paragraph (Isa. 54 and Jer. 31).[66] A definite seven-
year deadline appears to have been preached in Wittenberg in 1521–1522 by the
"Zwickau Prophets."[67] Even the emphasis upon new spiritual prophets is here,
though not specifically, perhaps for reasons of humility or even self-preservation.
Müntzer does imply his genuine faith as opposed to the false faith of others, his
having been tested while others are untested and, by implication, unfit for ministry. He has been taught by God while the teaching of others is suspect.[68]

To this point, specific evidence connecting Müntzer with our passage is lacking, although parallels are evident.[69] A Joachite connection would make more lively
Müntzer's allusion to doing the work of Elijah in his earlier letter to Hausmann,[70]
or to his work as an agent of the new apostolic church in the "Prague Manifesto."[71]
Such a connection with Joachim would also draw in Revelation 11 and Müntzer's
conception of his own prophetic role on the threshold of a new age. From such a
perspective his covenanted following, or *Bund*, with all of its spiritual and redefined baptistic understanding, can be seen to stand next to the corporate enter-
prise of earlier Cistercians, Spiritual Franciscans, and Taborites—all of whom had
tried to usher in the kingdom of God but failed.[72]

In the spring of 1524, events moved along precipitously for Müntzer. When
the chapel of Mallerbach, belonging to the Cistercian nunnery at Naundorf, was
destroyed by Müntzer's *Bund*, events hastened toward Müntzer's final break with
established authority. The nuns appealed to the Elector for redress. Although a
directive was issued to apprehend the guilty, the city council of Allstedt defended
the violence, placing blame upon civil toleration of idolatry.[73] The letter was probably drafted by Müntzer. It reflects themes of Christian political legitimacy to be
developed in his "Sermon Before the Princes."[74]

Following further violence, Müntzer was granted his hearing. The princes, not
uniformly opposed to Müntzer,[75] came to Allstedt to hear him preach. On July
13, 1524, Müntzer delivered the "Sermon Before the Princes" (*Fürstenpredig*),[76]

"the high-water mark of torrential Revolutionary Spiritualist counterreformation directed against Luther."[77] Müntzer's defense of himself, an exposition of Daniel 2, stresses the importance of conformity to Christ's suffering and the nature of political legitimacy as mediated through elaborate figural imagery. We need not give a summary of this work as it is thoroughly analyzed by Hinrichs.[78] However, several points concerning prophecy and history do need to be raised as they touch upon our purpose.

First, Müntzer identifies himself as a new Daniel, prepared to offer prophetic guidance to the princes as the prophet Daniel had once been asked to do for Nebuchadnezzar. But this model is best viewed in the context of Müntzer's conception of a final historical mission modeled on the work of Elijah, the nature of which has already been pointed out.[79] Its widest implications are best understood under the figural imagery of our text as will be more clearly evident in Müntzer's final treatises. Whether as Daniel of old, or as a prophetic Daniel standing within a final Elijah mission, Müntzer's pattern of thought seems to carry affinity with themes traditionally associated with our two witnesses.

The historical perspective in this sermon draws out the connection. Müntzer presented his credentials to the princes as a new Daniel.[80] Such a prophet was needed in the present perilous days of the Church. Revelation did not conclude with the end of the apostolic age, but it was neglected though apostasy, rejected by godless men and idolatrous priests.[81] This religious declension has a history. It was pointed out as early as Hegesippus in Eusebius, signifying an early fall of the Church.[82] This fall finds itself within the wider historical context in which Müntzer understands his message to come. Appealing to one of the standard models for historical interpretation, the variegated image envisioned by Nebuchadnezzar (Dan. 2),[83] Müntzer argues that decisive Reformation is imminent. The fifth monarchy, the Holy Roman Empire, symbolized in the feet of mixed clay and iron of the bodily image, is rapidly coming to an end.[84] The stone made without hands will crush this final kingdom (Dan. 2:34).[85] This destruction is the prelude to the establishment of God's kingdom (Dan. 2:44, cf. 7:27). It stands parallel in spiritualist exegesis to the new dominion under Christ and the kingdom of the saints as in Revelation 11:15 following the end of the second prophesied woe and the work of God's last prophets. Such a connection is not unwarranted. Immediately after asking the princes to play the role of the godly Jehu (2 Kings 9–10) Müntzer connects the nature of the present to the apocalyptic picture sketched out in the book of Revelation.[86] Any possible Joachite influence upon Müntzer would now imply life at the juncture of the sixth and seventh ages, the time of our two witnesses.

If a new Elijah mission is called for and envisioned prophetically as the agency to carry society into the new age, then Müntzer's call for a new Daniel to arise and lead the army of God finds its best historical perspective.

> Therefore a new Daniel must arise and interpret for you your vision, and this [prophet], as Moses teaches (Deut. 20:2), must go in front of the army. He must reconcile the anger of the princes and the enraged people.[87]

Immediately prior to this Müntzer lifted up the role of John the Baptist, one who provided such leadership and chastening in the days of the fourth kingdom, the Roman Empire, and First Advent of Christ.[88] John the Baptist was seen in his day as performing the work of Elijah. Müntzer's focus upon Daniel in filling out the lineaments of this idea is appropriate in terms of his audience and the political dimensions of the task. Here, the Marxist interpretation of Müntzer finds, in my opinion, its greatest justification. Müntzer argues that the nature of the time is recognized best by the poor and the peasants when compared to the nobility.[89] A new democracy of the spirit is heralded, which draws upon Joel's prophecy (Vulgate, 2:27–32) that God's spirit will be poured out upon all flesh in the last days.[90] Yet this could as easily be a Franciscan argument, giving further support to the claim of Joachite influence.[91]

Müntzer proceeds to draw out the political implications of this mission. Those who claim that the duty of princes is only to maintain civil unity have made fools of the people.[92] The decisive conflict stands before society, "the process of ending the fifth monarchy of the world is in full swing."[93] Christ came not with peace but with a sword (Matt. 10:34), Müntzer claims.[94] These are not days of peace but of conflict. The wicked who hinder the gospel are to be eliminated, for they destroy the dominion of Christ. Good government begins with their eradication. If the princes do not lead the people, then the people will rise up under prophetic leadership to execute righteous judgment.[95] It is the work of Elijah, which both draws the Church "back again to its origin" and leads forward "in the time of harvest."[96] Demonstrating his rhetorical skills as a righteous latter-day Elijah, Müntzer prophesies:

> The weeds must be plucked out of the vineyard of God in the time of harvest. Then the beautiful red wheat will acquire substantial rootage and come up properly (Matt. 13:24–30). The angels [v. 39], however, who sharpen their sickles for this purpose are the serious servants of God who execute the wrath of divine wisdom (Mal. 3:1–6).[97]

The Sword of Gideon

Spiritual prophets faced tasks other than preaching repentance and true faith. More was called for in Elijah's encounter with the priests of Baal (1 Kings 18). Israel did not conquer the land by the sword but rather through the power of God. The sword, Müntzer argues, was their means, even as eating and drinking is a means for living. So today the sword is necessary but one conquers through the power of God.[98] Soon he will conclude a letter, citing Revelation 11, "Thomas Müntzer with the sword of Gideon."[99]

Müntzer seems to have felt that the princes never caught the drift of his message; at least it was not received as he had hoped. Well they might not have.[100] One who was not present but appears to have caught the drift was Duke George of Saxony. Müntzer's disciples in Sangerhausen were quickly tossed into prison.[101] Two days after delivering his sermon Müntzer dashed off a letter to his followers encouraging them to stand firm.[102] God would not forget them but would turn their sorrow to joy.[103] Having written the authorities,[104] Müntzer wrote again to his imprisoned disciples. Like the apostle Paul he brings them "grace and peace."[105]

Two references are of interest: citing John 16:1, Müntzer writes that those who fear God should expect persecution; citing 2 Timothy 3:1, he argues that such persecution should be expected in the perilous times of the last days.[106] This theme of the persecution or even martyrdom of the saints should not surprise us if these are the days of Antichrist and concomitantly the time of adventual witnesses.[107]

Toward the end of July 1524 a series of letters to city warden Hans Zeiss were drafted that continue this apocalyptic rhetoric and draw us even more pointedly to Revelation 11. After warning Zeiss in his first letter not to turn believers over to the godless,[108] Müntzer emphasizes his two characteristic themes: the value of suffering and the current apocalyptic horizon. What is of particular interest is Müntzer's response to one of four unknown questions that comes toward the end of this letter. After noting that there is no Christian renewal without suffering,[109] Müntzer adds that the true Christian who is detached from this world can look forward to "good days," clearly prefigured by the Evangelist John, and by Enoch and Elijah. The exegesis behind his reference to Enoch and Elijah is clear.[110] The inclusion of the Evangelist John was established in late medieval piety by virtue of his apparent purity, possible warrant in John 21:22–23, and the promise that John, the seer of the Apocalypse (usually identified with the Evangelist), was promised a further chance to proclaim the gospel (Rev. 10:11).[111]

If the form of the future is clarified by these figures, the time of their appearance is either here or near. This need not be a literal return of those prophets of old. However, their work, or a prophetic witness modeled upon their activity, is expected. This implies the kind of persecution and martyrdom envisioned in the text. The apocalyptic time clock is ticking.

Müntzer's letter is quickly followed by two more to Hans Zeiss. In his next letter Müntzer again underscores the imminence of the apocalyptic events: "the renewal of the world is at the door."[112] Then in a letter written on July 25, 1524, Müntzer hints at the nature of the new order, reporting on a sermon he gave on 2 Kings 22-23.[113] Interviewed by the authorities in Weimar on the first of August,[114] Müntzer appears to have then been abandoned by key supporters in Allstedt.[115] On the seventh or eighth of August 1524, he fled the city and headed to nearby Mühlhausen, which was also in social and religious turmoil. Here the fiery reformer Heinrich Pfeiffer had been calling for a larger representation of the citizenry on the town council. Müntzer joined the conflict and through his rhetoric became one of the leaders of the movement.[116]

Müntzer and Pfeiffer were eventually expelled from Mühlhausen. However, sometime in the late summer Müntzer drafted his inflammatory "Manifest Exposé" (*Ausgedrückte Entblössung*),[117] and appears to have had it printed by the book publisher and distributor Hans Hut of Bibra.[118] Steven Ozment's analysis of this work, a "masterpiece of dissent," is helpful.[119] Müntzer draws the connection between his interior or mystical basis of authority and his growing dissent from both the religious[120] and now civil authorities.[121] The themes are similar to the ones already noted: "No fear, no grace,"[122] and God can do the impossible.[123] True authority is found in spiritual immediacy.[124] What is of particular note for our purposes is the way in which Müntzer argues for a new spiritual leader, a "new John."[125] Having known suffering and the "trial of unbelief," this prophet would be able to expose the godless by raising up God's truth. Drawing upon Luke 1:15–17, Müntzer writes:

> John is a very different kind of preacher, a witnessing angel of Christ, displayed in every true preacher. Everyone should have this praise, like John, not through the merits of works but on account of his earnestness born of valiant sobriety, an earnestness which suppresses lust and strips the powers of the soul so that the depths of the spirit could be seen in them. For it is there [in the depths of the spirit] that the Holy Spirit must speak, Psalm 84 [85:8ff.].[126]

Müntzer had already found a measure of self-identity in earlier prophetic models, but what is of particular interest in this model is the way in which the idea of a "new John" can be seen as part of Müntzer's larger vision of a final "Elijah-mission" in the closing days of history.[127] Particular warrant for this may be found in the "Expose" through Müntzer's following remark:

> If the holy church is to be renewed through the bitter truth, a grace-filled servant of God must step forth in the spirit of Elijah (Matt. 17:3; 1 Kings 18:1; Rev. 11:3) and he must bring all things into a right direction.[128]

As John the Baptist bore the mantle of Elijah in his day, introducing the revelation of the First Advent (John 1:29, 36), so Müntzer and all true preachers of the gospel stand in a new, decisive Elijah-configuration in the early years of the sixteenth century. The Elijah of the Old Testament defines the model; the current apocalyptic crisis determines the context now even as in the days of the first Advent.

Following closely upon the completion of his "Manifest Exposé," Müntzer wrote his "Defense" (*Hochverursachte Schutzrede*),[129] a bitter invective against Luther: "O doctor lügner [liar], you wily fox."[130] Begun in late summer or early fall, the pamphlet, addressed to Jesus Christ, was printed at Nürmberg in December 1524:[131]

> Highly motivated defense and answer against the spiritless, soft-living piece of flesh at Wittenberg who has sullied pitiable Christendom through the theft of holy Scripture.
>
> Thomas Müntzer of Alstedt
From the cave of Elijah whose seriousness spares no one.[132]

This title is fascinating. The continued polemic against Luther's misuse of Scripture and compromise is evident. As the Scriptures were used by the early Pharisees to crucify Christ, so, Müntzer argues, is he now being persecuted by present pharisees.[133] Again, Müntzer writes as one doing the work of Elijah, a theme that has been continuously present at least since the letter to Hausmann,[134] recently expressed in the "Exposé."[135] However, we now note a difference. In previous references our attention has been drawn to the story of the victorious Elijah, the one who encounters the prophets of Baal and defeats them (1 Kings 18). Now the reference is to Elijah in self-imposed exile. Perhaps as Ahab had related to Jezebel the story of Elijah's victory, Müntzer now felt that Luther was complaining to the princes in his "Brief." So Müntzer runs, as Elijah ran, deserted by his followers in Allstedt.[136] He finds his cave as did Elijah.[137] But Müntzer knows that the story of Elijah does not end here. It was at the cave that Elijah was restored, that his vision was renewed. It was here that the inner voice of God was heard (1 Kings 19:12). As Elijah emerged from the cave to anoint new followers and discover 7000 supporters, so will Müntzer emerge by the spring of 1525.

Again, more is implied by Müntzer's reference than the recalling of that earlier prophetic figure. In the same line we are finally confronted by the cryptic reference to Revelation 11.[138] Here both the reforming and the apocalyptic Elijah are implied. As was evident in the "Exposé," this role could be filled, and was, by John the Baptist, but now a "new John" is required, in the apocalyptic framework of the last days sketched out in Revelation 11. Several features in the "Defense," touch upon our theme.

First, the nature of spiritual authenticity is placed in an apocalyptic framework. After criticizing vehemently that "scribe" and "liar" Luther,[139] Müntzer cites the prophetic warning of Micah 3 where false prophets are said to preach for monetary gain.[140] The end of chapter 3 of Micah foresees the plundering of Zion, which was something, we may plausibly argue, Müntzer foresaw for Europe, with the Turks pressing at the borders. Micah 4:1 then opens with a prophecy that following such destruction the Lord's kingdom will be established. Spiritual knowledge will be immediate, his reign will be over all. These are themes that should all be familiar to us now: moral denunciation, prophesied destruction, and an imminent new age with a "new apostolic church."[141] Is it too much to see in Müntzer a prophet of doom and of the new era, one who knows he is filling out the lineaments of Revelation 11:3?

Second, Müntzer's idea of the rule of the elect, developed out of an apocalyptic framework, is quite visible in this treatise. He writes, referring to his "Sermon to the Princes," that the elect possess "the sword and the key of loosing." While this could merely be a reference to present political legitimacy, I suspect more is involved. Müntzer bases his argument upon apocalyptic texts (e.g., Dan. 7:27; Rev. 6:15).[142] Furthermore, toward the end of the treatise we encounter the imminence of Judgment. It will come upon that "rabid fox," Luther, "who barks hoarsely before dawn."[143] Citing a German proverb, Müntzer writes that such Judgment will come upon all who jump "into the well" after Luther.[144] That this is more than simply Judgment in the present order seems evident from Müntzer's next statement: "Ezekiel 13 and Micah 3 give you the answer."[145] Ezekiel 13 certainly emphasizes the swiftness of Judgment. It is an open criticism of prophets who cry "peace" for Jerusalem when "there is no peace" (Ezek. 13:16). Micah 3 draws us back to the idea raised earlier in the treatise: the destruction of Zion to be followed by God's kingdom. Is Müntzer thinking of a coming Armageddon?[146] It would appear so. Certainly none of these ideas are new.[147] They were evident in the "Prague Manifesto." The question is a real one. However, from what we have seen, it would appear that there is an apocalyptic structure to Müntzer's thinking from a time well before his "Sermon Before the Princes" and clearly prior to the "Defense."

Finally, we come to one of the more intriguing allusions in this document. Müntzer closes by indicating that he will play the David to Luther's Saul: "David will teach them. Saul also began well, but David after a long delay had to carry it out."[148] David sallied forth with new vigor from the cave Adullam (1 Sam. 22:1–2) to defeat Saul. Elijah heard the inner voice of God and left his cave to anoint Elisha and discover 7000 cohorts. So also would Müntzer now leave his self-imposed exile. He points this out as one filling the large role of Elijah, a prophet of Judgment and final witness at the edge of history.

Four months later, on the eve of the Peasants' War, Müntzer repeats several of the points made in the "Defense" in a letter to his followers at Eisenach.[149] Counseling the fear of God, he writes that "now the whole world starts understanding God's truth, and the zeal against tyranny is the proof." Citing Daniel 7, Müntzer argues that power will pass to the common people. Citing Revelation 11 he argues that the kingdom of this world will become Christ's.[150] It appears from this that Müntzer has a keen sense of the material manifestation of God's kingdom. Now in the end of times God is calling forth a new spirit of prophecy. Müntzer seems to identify with the work of Jeremiah, Daniel, John, Gideon, but especially Elijah—and not merely Elijah of old, but now the apocalyptic Elijah at the end of the age. He points the way: Choose for or against the coming kingdom of God.

As is evident from the pamphlet literature between the years 1518–1524,[151] there were many calls for reform during this period in central Europe. Reform in society was sought by jurists and humanists like Ulrich von Hutten as well as by theologians like Martin Luther. What was marginal in one reformer's cries was often central for another. The precise nature of Müntzer's vision of reform is beyond the focus of our analysis. He seems to have envisioned some kind of utopian-communistic order. Perhaps his vision incorporated something of the radical Taborite idea of an in-breaking, other-worldly society.[152] It may also have received certain lineaments from the concept of an ideal monastery. In any case, it seems strongly egalitarian, involving his *Bund*, a community of the covenanting elect radically divided from the rest of society.[153] This new order would be inaugurated by God when the time was ripe. Schwarz writes that Müntzer's vision may be that of the medieval *status innocentiae*, the present condition experienced by Enoch, Elijah, and the Evangelist John in medieval speculative theology.[154] The spiritual condition implied in their persons is to be the norm for all Christians even in an earthly kingdom of God.

Having gone to seek support for the reform of Church and society in the south German countryside and cities,[155] Müntzer was again in Mühlhausen by early 1525. Together with others he succeeded in replacing the town council with his "eternal council" representing the interests of those seeking a more radical direction for the Reformation.[156] In April 1525, Müntzer issued his revolutionary "Call to the Allsteters" (*Anruf an die Allstedter*).[157] Again calling his brothers to live in the fear of God, he brings home the social dimension of his interior mystical call:

> I tell you again, if you won't suffer for God, then you will be Devil's martyrs. . . .
> Get going, and fight the battle of the Lord! It is high time, keep the brethren together so that they do not mock the divine witness, or they will all be destroyed.[158]

One hears the call for martyrdom—either for or against the Lord. The mention of the "divine witness" is intriguing. Whether Müntzer is thinking of the general prophetic thrust of his message or of a final divine witness at the end of history is difficult to tell. From what we have noted earlier, I would suggest both and argue that he continues to be fascinated by a kind of final "Elijah-mission" in history. All of Europe, he cries, is awake to what is going on: "The master wants to start the game; the scoundrels must be routed."[159]

Armed with banners upon which were symbols of the new covenant, sword and rainbow, Müntzer, his comrade Heinrich Pfeiffer, and others took up the sword.[160] However, in taking the sword, this "warrior-priest" and his followers hastened instead the wrath of Landgrave Philip of Hesse who now, with his army, defeated the peasants in a battle at Frankenhausen, May 14, 1525. Whether Müntzer's forces had hoped to institute God's kingdom, perhaps forcing God's hand, or were simply, like other peasant groups, attempting to redress ancient grievances is something we will never fully know. Captured, Müntzer recanted and was beheaded along with others.[161] It is said that he smiled at the very end.[162] Was this the sarcastic smile of one who has bettered his foes in matters of principle? Or was it the smile of a martyr, another Hus?[163] We are left to speculate how and if this final picture relates to the martyr's mantle, which falls upon the two witnesses in Revelation 11:7. However it is finally determined, Müntzer's memory lived on, even as that of an adventual Elijah.[164]

Prophets of a Last Chance

Whether or not Müntzer's prophetic mantle fell upon Hans Hut[165] has been central to Hut studies. Hut (c. 1490–1527), a bookbinder and salesman at Bibra in the neighborhood of Meiningen, helped to spread the new evangelical faith through the sales and distribution of Reformation tracts. He was present at Frankenhausen, knew Müntzer, and was later re-baptized by Hans Denck (May 26, 1526).[166] More than this, Hut was to become an Anabaptist preacher of such notable success, particularly in Franconia. He is recognized as having brought more people to Anabaptism in his brief ministry of one year and a quarter than any other Anabaptist leader.[167] His disciple, Ambrose Spitelmeier, called Hut "a servant of God and an apostle sent by God to this last and most dangerous time."[168]

There is evidence that Hut found more significance in Müntzer than merely that of the one who bore the mantle of a prophet. It appears that he regarded Thomas Müntzer and Heinrich Pfeiffer as prophets conforming in some way to the vision of our text. Whether an identification was made and to what extent is difficult to ascertain fully. In any event, we have here echoes of the kind of earlier apocalyptic thinking associated with Spiritual Franciscanism and other Joachite-inspired movements. There is plausibility to the association; related visions of history appear to have been preached by those around Müntzer and with whom Hut may have come into contact.[169] Hut suggests the identity of the two witnesses when, following the Peasants' War, he started to date the approaching cataclysm in terms of the deaths of Müntzer and Pfeiffer.[170] The question of whether Hut connected the interpretation of Revelation 11 with Müntzer and Pfeiffer is important not only for what it may say about Hut and Hut's relationship to Müntzer, but also for how Müntzer and Pfeiffer may have been perceived in the popular imagination.[171]

How are we to evaluate this possibility? The contacts, brief as they apparently were between Hut and Müntzer, have been clearly set forth in the literature: two brief encounters, and then the continuing debate.[172] Hut apparently carried with him on his missionary journeys a small book entitled "Of the Mystery of Baptism." Was this his? Did it ultimately derive from Müntzer?[173] Following the debacle of the Peasants' War, Hut preached a sermon at Bibra (May 31, 1525) that paralleled Müntzer's rhetoric.[174] Soon thereafter he was forced to leave the city, reappearing a year later in Augsburg where he requested re-baptism at the hands of the pacific Denck. Is this a new Hut?[175]

There is something to the idea of a change in Hut. However, such a change would appear to have less to do with the spiritualization of an apocalyptic vision and more with Hut's reworking of the apocalyptic timetable in light of a new understanding of the Peasants' War and of Müntzer. When Hut later retracted the content of the message preached at Bibra, saying his mind had changed on the matter of civil violence, his remarks had nothing to do with the question of how acute his apocalyptic understanding of the present may have been. What one may note is a shift from the primacy of Judgment to that of proclamation in a period of last days filled with prophetic significance. If this is the nature of the change on Hut's part, he may have conceived of Müntzer and Pfeiffer in some way as our two witnesses. This appears plausible from what little evidence remains: the Nikolsburg disputation, the "Martyrs' Synod," the trial reports from the Augsburg interrogations, and finally some later recollections by former disciples.

Hut's frenetic missionary activity took him throughout Franconia, Moravia, and Austria. In the Nikolsburg debates, which took place in the spring of 1527, the nature of his apocalypticism became a point of dispute with Balthasar Hubmaier.[176] Although we shall probably never know the full scope of the discussions,[177] they appear to be shaped by two primary issues: the question of support by arms and taxes for the civil government under the imminence of the Turkish threat, and the nature of Christian eschatology. The latter issue reaches into Hut's understanding of baptism. Eschatological concerns constitute the largest number of items mentioned in the confession of Hans Nadler of Erlangen in February 1529: (1) baptism, (2) the Lord's Supper, (3) Gods justice, (4) Gods judgment, (5) the end of the world, (6) the coming kingdom, and (7) the return of Christ.[178]

Both issues, the question of whether to help defend the prevailing order, and the understanding of last things, were related ethically and prophetically, insofar as prophecy touches upon political events. From this perspective two things are striking about the Nikolsburg discussions. First, one must question Hut's motivation for pacifism.[179] If we assume that Hut continued to follow Müntzer's teachings in some respect, then we must ask whether his "pacifism" followed from Christian conviction about war itself or from his belief that the Turk might carry out the cleansing act of God in society. We have little direct evidence, but the latter conclusion seems warranted in light of later memories of Hut's teachings.[180] Furthermore, it appears that Hut believed that when the proper time arrived God would give the sword to the righteous to participate in the cleansing of society.[181] It would appear that Hut's "pacifism" only served to allow the Turk to perform his God-ordained act of purification. In other words, Turkish havoc was merely the prophesied period of biblical tribulation before the Parousia, or Second Coming.[182]

This apocalyptic horizon lends plausibility to Hut's use of our text. The same is true of his conception of baptism.[183] There is not a great deal of direct evidence, but from the treatise "Of the Mystery of Baptism," as well as other memories of Hut, a case can be made for the significance of our text in Hut's baptismal thinking. The treatise begins by counseling the "pure fear of God" in this "last and most dangerous age" of history. Those with proper spiritual discernment are able to observe:

> How all those things which from the beginning have been foretold and preached by the prophets, patriarchs, and apostles as to happen, are now at work afresh and will be restored, as Peter prophesied to us beforehand in the Acts of the Apostles, . . .[184]

Hut follows this remark with language reminiscent of Müntzer as he criticizes carnal and "scribal" approaches to Scripture, which Müntzer associated with the teachers in Wittenberg.[185] Having developed his understanding of baptism in terms of the missionary command and call to suffering, Hut emphasizes a baptism of tribulation: "So this water of all tribulation is the real essence and power of Baptism, in which a man is submerged into the death of Christ."[186]

Baptism connotes disjunction and separation through suffering, crucifixion, and tribulation. It is for those who smell the smoke of the end of the age.[187] Gottfried Seebass uses the textual associations found in Hut's biblical concordance[188] to draw out the full apocalyptic significance of baptism; its characteristic features appear in Hut's association of baptism (article 81) with apocalyptic sealing (Rev. 7:3) and the command given to the prophet Ezekiel (Ezek. 9:4) to mark those to be saved from the imminent destruction (cf. Ezek. 14).[189]

To this understanding of baptism must be added the nature of Hut's preaching. Hut was perceived as teaching that the cessation of the sacrifice and the abomination of Daniel 9:27 were in process of fulfillment.[190] In his concordance Hut associates Gabriel's revelation of the seventy weeks (Dan. 9) with Daniel's vision of the last days (Dan. 12) and with the conflict of the woman and dragon (Rev. 12).[191] The implications for Hut's understanding of baptism are intriguing. In light of the apocalyptic sealing adumbrated by Revelation 7:1-4 one is drawn to the conclusion that Hut's frenzied ministry of one year and a quarter represented an attempt to call out from society the 144,000 who would be saved (Rev. 7:4).[192]

Escaping from Nikolsburg, Hut continued the work of a prophet of penance throughout the following months of his freedom. Like Müntzer, he followed his sense of divine commission with a belief in visions.[193] Like an Amos, called of God, he warned of God's visitation in the midst of the sins of the new Israel. As it was in the days of Noah and Lot so God's Judgment would come in these times. Seebass sketches ways in which Hut carried out the work of a new Moses, Elijah, or John the Baptist, a final prophet of repentance and Judgment.[194] The picture is given added plausibility by similar activities of Hut's chief disciples, Ambrose Spitelmeier, Leonard Schiemer, and John Schlaffer.[195] All of these features, the apocalyptic significance attributed to the Turk, Hut's conception of apocalyptic baptism, and his prophetic work in the closing days of history, point to the importance of Revelation 11 for Hut's thinking.

The next significant appearance of Hut is at the so-called Martyrs' Synod in August 1527.[196] Here again it seems that Hut invested particular apocalyptic significance in the persons of Müntzer and Pfeiffer. The central issue discussed at this assembly of Anabaptist leaders related to the coming of the kingdom, missionary efforts, and the further organization of the movement.[197] As is clear from many later texts, Hut was believed to have taught that Judgment and radical social change would occur in three and a half years.[198] Certainly the idea of living within the last three and one-half years of history would bear upon the questions of missionary effort and ecclesial organization.

Under interrogation in October of the same year Hut was to deny that he had fixed a date for the culmination of history. Later evidence shows that it is difficult to take his denial at face value.[199] Klassen argues that Hut often cited Matthew 24 where Christ refers to the idea that no one can know the day and the hour when the Lord will come.[200] Still, one is faced with the problem of what such a statement says. It does not rule out an attempt to plot the year of the Advent, an activity associated with Hut. Significantly, Matthew 25:13 is not found in his concordance where he associates passages of Scripture that appear to refer to the end.[201]

The scope of Hut's apocalyptic teachings, whatever they may have been at this point, appear reflected in a letter probably written by Hut to his followers.[202] He tells them not to be offended if they do not yet understand the apocalyptic mysteries.[203] There appear to be further allusions to themes that we encountered in Müntzer, including a stress upon the fear of God, the present period constituting dangerous last times, and the reconstruction of a Church that has been wasted and broken down. As with Münster, the present state of Christendom appears to be a disaster. Rather than calling for the apocalyptic war for the construction of God's new society, Hut seems to say that the Church is to be rebuilt through the creation of conventicles of believers awaiting the imminent end of all things and God's power as it will be given for the final cleansing of society. Hut apparently signed the letter as Müntzer is remembered to have signed his, "from the cave of Elijah."[204]

Following the "Martyrs' Synod" Hut and a number of his colleagues were seized by the authorities of Augsburg. Hut was placed on trial for heresy September 16, 1527.[205] Subsequent hearings were held until his death by suffocation in his call from a fire of uncertain origin.[206] The apocalyptic re-baptizer was now twice burned, as his charred body was put to the stake the following day, December 7, 1527.

Both by virtue of Hut's own trial reports as well as those of his followers, a picture of Hut's eschatology emerges: a final period of three and one-half years of history for penance and proclamation, a cleansing war led by the Turk with the elect of God joining in at God's command, and a prophesied Parousia at Pentecost 1528.[207] All of this was to occur in the period of three and one-half years following the Peasants' War with the death of our witnesses. With regard to his own role, Hut appears as a final prophet sealing those who are willing to undergo tribulation in the present to be spared that which is to come.[208] Did Hut find in Müntzer and Pfeiffer the two adventual witnesses? It is difficult to answer "no" to that question if one considers the way in which Revelation 11, together with the texts that traditionally are quoted alongside of it, help to chart the way from the present to the predicted end on Pentecost 1528.

Because of his untimely death, Hut did not witness the denouement of the apocalyptic scenario, the conclusion to the final period of history set in motion by the death of the witnesses, Müntzer and Pfeiffer. With growing persecution in Augsburg many of Hut's disciples sought asylum in Strassburg.[209] They came awaiting a sign from God before drawing their sword in the end-time conflict. Although Hut was not to see the outcome of his vision, others were to see such a conclusion, especially as similar speculation centered around the person and teachings of Melchior Hoffman.

Notes

1. Such expectations are organized by Hans Preuss around hopes for a messianic king, an angelic pope, and a new prophet or prophets of God in *Martin Luther, Der Prophet* (Gütersloh: C. Bertelsmann, 1933), pp. 4–23. Paul Russell illustrates the importance of prophecy as social dissent on the eve of the Reformation in "'Your Sons and Daughters Shall Prophesy . . .' (Joel 2:28): Common People and the Future of the Reformation in the Pamphlet Literature of Southwestern Germany to 1525," AHR, 74 (1983):122–39; cf. Gerald Strauss, *Manifestations of Discontent in Germany on the Eve of the Reformation* (Bloomington: University of Indiana Press, 1971). See also Walter Klaassen's *Living at the End of Ages. Apocalyptic Expectation in the Radical Reformation* (Lanham, Maryland: University Press of America, 1992).

2. On the former, Paul Oskar Kristeller, *Renaissance Thought: The Classic, Scholastic, and Humanist Strains* (New York: Harper and Row, 1961); on the latter, see below.

3. Stewart C. Easton, *Roger Bacon and His Search for a Universal Science* (New York: Columbia University Press, 1952).

4. Dietrich Kurze, *Johannes Lichtenberger: Eine Studie zur Geschichte der Prophetie und Astrologie* (Lübeck: Matthiesen, 1960).

5. Aby Warburg, *Ausgewalte Schriften und Wurdigungen* (Baden-Baden: Saecula Spiritula, 1979).

6. Bernd Moeller, *Reichsstadt und Reformation* (Gütersloh: Gerd Mohn, 1962), pp. 54ff; and Peter Blickle, *The Revolution of 1525: The German Peasants' War from a New Perspective*, trans. by Thomas A. Brady, Jr., and H. C. Erik Middelfort (Baltimore: The Johns Hopkins University Press, 1981; orig. German ed., 1977), pp. 3–13. Such economic dislocation has been used by Marxist historians to explain the rise of chiliasm in the sixteenth century. See Georg Lukacs, *Geschichte und Klassenbewusstsein: Geschichte der bürgerlichen Gesellschaft* (4th ed.) (Neuwied and Berlin, 1971). Ernst Warner argues that as Müntzer became an "ideologist of poverty," he "dropped his career of a prophet . . . and founded a political party, or Bund" ("Popular Ideologies in Late Medieval Europe: Taborite Chiliasm and its Antecedents," in *Comparative Studies and History*, 3 [1960]:363).

This does not do justice to Müntzer's final speech before the battle of Frankenhausen, as recognized by Warner, nor does it take into account Müntzer's deepening alienation from the religious establishment, yet appropriation of the prophetic model of a final Elijah. As the Elijah of old cleansed society of the worship of Baal, so a final Elijah (Rev. 11:3–13) might cleanse society in preparation for the kingdom of Christ.

7. Johann Friedrich, *Astrologie und Reformation* (Munich: Universitäts-Buchhandlung, 1864), pp. 46–50; cf. Preuss, *Martin Luther, Der Prophet*, pp. 11–33.

8. H. C. Erik Midelfort, "Social History and Biblical Exegesis: Community, Family, and Witchcraft in Sixteenth-Century Germany," in David C. Steinmetz, ed., *The Bible in the Sixteenth Century* (Durham, N.C.: Duke University Press, 1990), pp. 7–20.

9. Richard Muller, "The Hermeneutics of Promise and Fulfillment in Calvin's Exegesis of the Old Testament Prophecies of the Kingdom," in Steinmetz, ed., *The Bible in the Sixteenth Century*, p. 71. A useful summary of eschatological and apocalyptic thinking in the period is found in George H. Williams, *The Radical Reformation* (Kirksville, Mo.: Sixteenth Century Journal Publishers, 1992), sec. 11.4. In our study Williams's first edition (1962) will be referred to except as otherwise noted.

10. Hans Preuss, "Apokalyptische und prophetische Frömmigkeit seit Ausgang des Mittelalters," *Zeitschrift für den evangelischen Religionsunterricht*, 14 (1907):117–18; cf. Wilhelm Gussmann, "D. Johann Ecks Vierhundertvier Artikel zum Reichstag von Augsburg 1530," in *Quellen und Forschungen zur Geschichte des Augsburgischen Glaubensbekenntaisses*, Vol. 2 (Kassel: Edmund Pillardy, 1930), pp. 267–68.

11. Gottfried Seebass, "Apokalyptik/Apokalypsen VII. Reformation und Neuzeit," in *Theologische Realenzyklopädie*, Vol. 3 (Berlin and New York: Walter de Gruyter, 1978), pp. 280–81.

12. WA, 10.I.1, pp. 147.14–18. Our discussion will be presented later in this chapter.

13. WA, 10.I.2, pp. 191.31-5.

14. Gussmann, "D. Johann Ecks Vierhundertvier Artikel," pp. 251–61. The focus is usually upon Luther as Elijah, but our theme and its citation are evident. This connection will be discussed later in this chapter.

15. The transition to pacifism and a transposition of apocalyptic fervor to a missionary or quietistic conventicular movement is seen in the *Geschichtsbuch* (*Chronicle*). See in Williams, *Radical Reformation*, pp. 151–52.

16. The pioneer studies on Thomas Müntzer in this century were done by Heinrich Böhmer, Karl Holl, and Annemarie Lohmann: Böhmer, *Studien zu Thomas Müntzer* (Leipzig, 1922); Holl, "Luther und die Schwärmer," chapter 7 of *Gesammelte Aufsätze zur Kirchengeschichte*, Vol. 1 (Tübingen: J. C. B. Mohr-Paul Siebeck, 1923), pp. 420–67; Lohmann, *Zur geistigen Entwicklung Thomas Müntzers* (Leipzig: Teubner, 1931). For work through 1976, see Hans J. Hillerbrand, *Thomas Müntzer: A Bibliography* (Sixteenth Century Bibliography, Vol. 4; St. Louis, Mo.: Center for Reformation Research, 1976). Eric W. Gritsch summarizes a history of scholarship of the Müntzer-Luther relationship, "Thomas Müntzer and Luther: A Tragedy of Errors," in Hans J. Hillerbrand, ed., *Radical Tendencies in the Reformation: Divergent Prospectives*, Vol. 9. *Sixteenth Century Essays and Studies* (Kirksville, Mo.: Sixteenth Century Journal Publishers, 1988), pp. 54–83. Abraham Friesen's biography sketches Müntzer's identity in terms of the intellectual and social factors that shaped him. See *Thomas Müntzer: A Destroyer of the Godless* (Berkeley: University of California Press, 1990); cf. Williams, *Radical Reformation*, chapters 3, 4, 9, 11.

17. *Thomas Müntzer, Schriften und Briefe, Kritische Gesamtausgabe*, Günter Franz, ed. (Gütersloh: Mohn, 1968), p. 372.3-9; cf. pp. 504.27-31; 494.18-23. Hausmann was a follower of Luther and pastor in Zwickau. Müntzer appears fearful that his efforts will be thwarted. See also Otto Clemen, "Sechs Briefe aus der Reformationszeit," ZKG, 23 (1902):434.

18. Reinhard Schwarz highlights the development of Müntzer's understanding of the cleansing of society along lines suggested by the prophet Elijah, now set within an acute apocalyptic framework. Schwarz offers precision to our understanding of Müntzer's eschatology by drawing out its affinities with a Taborite apocalyptic-chiliastic tradition, setting it in contrast to Luther, in *Die apokalyptische Theologie Thomas Müntzers und der Taboriten* (Tübingen: Mohr, 1977), pp. 8, 62–64. Gordon Rupp finds Müntzer's apocalyptic consciousness to be more similar to that of Luther than Bockelson's or even Hoffman's, in *Patterns of Reformation* (Philadelphia: Fortress Press, 1969), pp. 302–3; cf. "Thomas Müntzer: Prophet of Radical Christianity," JBL, 48 (1965/66):466–68; and "Word and Spirit in the First Years of the Reformation," ARG, 49 (1958):13–26.

19. Schwarz cites this as a characteristic of Taborite apocalyptic thinking (*Die apokalyptische Theologie Thomas Müntzers*, p. 49).

20. Franz, *Schriften*, p. 506.6-11.

21. Ibid., p. 257.19-22.

22. Ibid., p. 300.14-31. Steven Ozment finds Müntzer following the two prophetic models of Daniel and John the Baptist. See *Mysticism and Dissent, Religious Ideology and Social Protest in the Sixteenth Century* (New Haven: Yale University Press, 1973), pp. 79, 93–97.

23. Franz, *Schriften*, p. 322.1-7.

24. The dimensions of this new Church are sketched out, e.g., in the "Prague Manifesto" (Franz, *Schriften*, p. 504.30) and the "Defense" (pp. 328.27–329.4).

25. The earliest indication that Müntzer had joined in the reforming efforts of Luther may be seen in a letter from Christian Döring to Müntzer, January 11, 1519. See in Franz, *Schriften*, p. 351.

26. Lohmann argues that two of Müntzer's early letters reveal a desire for spiritual immediacy rather than deep skepticism as contended by Heinrich Böhmer, *Studien zu Thomas Müntzer*; Lohmann, *Zur geistigen Entwicklung*, p. 10; cf. Franz, *Schriften*, pp. 352-54.

27. John S. Oyer, *Lutheran Reformers against Anabaptists* (The Hague: Martinus Nijhoff, 1964), p. 16; cf. J. K. Seidemann, *Thomas Müntzer: Eine Biographie* (Leipzig, 1842), pp. 107–8.

28. Franz, *Schriften*, p. 373.4-10.

29. Ibid., p. 370.6-10.

30. Jarold Knox Zeman, *The Anabaptist and the Czech Brethren in Moravia, 1526–1678: A Study of Origins and Contacts* (The Hague: Mouton, 1969), p. 62.

31. Lohmann, *Zur geistigen Entwicklung*, p. 18; cf. Rupp, who suggests a parallel with Luther before the Diet of Worms (*Patterns of Reformation*, p. 303).

32. The names of the other two prophets: Jan Kalenec of Prague and Vaclav of Lilec, Utraquist priest and rector of a Hussite monastery. (See Zeman, *The Anabaptists and Czech Brethren*, p. 65.)

33. For earlier critical discussion, see O. Clemen, "Das Prager Manifest Thomas Müntzers," ARG, 54 (1933):75–81; and Lohmann, *Zur geistigen Entwicklung*, pp. 18–30. Eric W. Gritsch sees in this work "more a radicalized Lutheran theology than a restatement of Taborite ideology," *Reformer without a Church: The Life and Thought of Thomas Muentzer 1488[?]–1525* (Philadelphia: Fortress Press, 1967), p. 60. Thomas Nipperdey develops the socio-theological implications of Müntzer's move away from Luther at this point [*Refor-mation Revolution, Utopie* (Gottingen: Vandenhoeck und Rupprecht, 1975), pp. 38–76]. Goertz claims that Müntzer never was a Lutheran but both men had shared a general spiritual affinity. See Gottfried Marow, "Thomas Müntzer als Theologe des Gerichts. Das 'Urteil'—ein Schlüsselbegriff seines Denkens," ZKG, 83 (1972):195–225; and Hans-Jürgen Goertz, "'Lebendiges Wort' und 'totes Ding.' Zum Schriftverständnis

Thomas Müntzers im Prager Manifest," ARG, 67 (1976):153–78; also Goertz, "The Mystic with the Hammer: Thomas Müntzer's Theological Basis for Revolution," MQR, 50 (1976):90–91.

34. Franz, *Schriften*, p. 495.2: "des heiligen kempers."

35. Ruth Kestenberg-Gladstein, "The Third Reich: A Fifteenth-Century Polemic Against Joachim and Its Background," *Journal of the Warburg and Courtald Institute*, 18 (1955), p. 289, n. 114. Note Hus's reputed authorship of an *Anatomia Antichristi*, published in 1525.

36. Franz, *Schriften*, e.g., p. 502.6-24.

37. Ibid., p. 504.19-31.

38. Note the historical dimensions of this spiritual declension, ibid., p. 504.2–4. On the theme of the "fall of the Church" among sixteenth-century radicals, see Franklin H. Littell, *The Origins of Sectarian Protestantism: A Study of Anabaptist Views of the Church* (3d ed.) (New York: Macmillan, 1964), pp. 46–78; cf. for Müntzer, Wolfgang Ullmann, "Das Geschichtsverständnis Thomas Müntzers," in *Thomas Müntzer, Anfragen an Theologie und Kirche*, Christoph Demke, ed. (Berlin: Evangelische Verlagsanstalt, 1977), pp. 46–56.

39. Franz, *Schriften*, p. 504.30-31.

40. See Franz's n. 138 to p. 502.24.

41. Ibid., p. 504.14-15.

42. Ibid., pp. 504.34–505.1.

43. Ibid., p. 505.1-4.

44. Franz, *Schriften*, p. 504.30-31.

45. The apocalyptic ideas attributed to the Zwickau prophets and the effect of their preaching in Wittenberg are discussed by Paul Wappler, drawing upon Karl Müller (*Wittenberger Bewegung* [Leipzig: Heinsius, 1911], pp. 159–60). Wappler cites the expectation of the transformation of the world in five to seven years in the apparent preaching of Stübner and the others [*Thomas Müntzer in Zwickau und die "Zwickauer Propheten"* (Zwickau: R. Zückler, 1908, pp. 45, 56, 65].

46. Wappler cites Melanchthon's evident apocalyptic consciousness in his letter to Spalatin, Dec. 27, 1521 (CR, 1, p. 515), shortly before Müntzer writes to Melanchthon (ibid., p. 59). As is evident from Luther's reply to Melanchthon (whose initial letter is lost) it is apparent that Melanchthon was impressed by the Zwickau prophets. From the previously cited letter we may assume this attraction included their apocalyptic ideas (LW, 48, p. 365).

47. Franz, *Schriften*, p. 381.20–21.

48. Ibid., p. 381.22–24 (guided by Ozment, *Mysticism and Dissent*, p. 71).

49. Karlstadt opposed Müntzer's program of violent revolution but did write a friendly, though critical, letter to Müntzer in December 1522. See Franz, *Schriften*, pp. 386–87; according to Lohmann, a possible allusion to Müntzer's use of the ps.-Joachite Jeremiah commentary might be found on p. 386.16-21 (*Zur geistigen Entwicklung*, pp. 35–36). See Ronald J. Sider, ed., *Karlstadt's Battle with Luther. Documents in a Liberal-Radical Debate* (Philadelphia: Fortress Press, 1978), pp. 36–48.

50. Compare WA, 10.I.1, pp. 147.14–148.18.

51. WA, DB, 7, p. 404.

52. Carl Hinrichs, *Luther und Müntzer* (Berlin: Walter de Gruyter, 1952), p. 1.

53. Franz, *Schriften*, p. 390.26-27; p. 391.23-29 (guided by Rupp, *Patterns of Reformation*, pp. 186–87).

54. LW, 48, pp. 364–67. Letter from Luther to Melanchthon, January 13, 1522. "I definitely do not want the 'prophets' to be accepted if they state that they were called by mere revelation, since God did not even wish to speak to Samuel except through the authority and knowledge of Eli [1 Samuel 3:4ff.]" (p. 366). That Luther is familiar with

and uses the language of German mysticism is indicated in the following portion of the letter.

55. Franz, *Schriften*, p. 394.36.

56. Ibid., pp. 395-97. Note the frequent citation of Scripture and the more moderate way in which the letter closes, "a servant of God" (p. 397.19), in comparison with that to Ernst of Mansfeld (p. 394.36).

57. Ibid., pp. 396.27–397.3.

58. The Saxon court stopped at Allstedt in November on its way to the Diet in Nuremberg. Müntzer was interviewed by Spalatin but unfortunately there is no record of the interrogation. See Irmgard Hoss, *Georg Spalatin, 1484–1545: Ein Leben in der Zeit des Humanismus und der Reformation* (Weimar: H. Böhlaus Nachfolger, 1956), p. 265.

59. James M. Stayer edited and translated these into English, "Thomas Müntzer's Protestation and Imaginary Faith," MQR, 57 (1983):99–130; cf. Franz, *Schriften*, pp. 217–40; and Siegfried Bräuer and Wolfgang Ullmann, *Theologisch Schriften aus dem Jahr 1523* (Berlin: Evangelische Verlagsanstalt, 1982), pp. 18–51. On problems of dating, see Stayer, p. 102, n. 12.

60. Stayer (p. 101, n. 11). See the opening of the document: Franz, *Schriften*, p. 225 bottom.

61. It is dated 2 December 1523, in Franz, *Schriften*, pp. 397–98. An English translation is available in Stayer, "Thomas Müntzer's Protestation and Imaginary Faith," pp. 129–30.

62. Franz, *Schriften*, p. 398.13-18.

63. Joachim would have argued similarly. In fact, his typology draws upon all of Scripture, demonstrated in *Concordia novi et veteris testamenti, Expositio* and in ps.-Joachite sources (see Marjorie Reeves, *The Influence of Prophecy in the Later Middle Ages* (Oxford: Clarendon Press, 1969), pp. 145–60). Mosei Smirin argues that Müntzer also knew the *Concordia novi et veteris testamenti*, "Thomas Müntzer und die Lehre des Joachim von Fiore," *Sinn und Form*, 4 (1952):69–143.

64. Written by a group of Joachim's disciples to explain the delay of the second Advent, *figurae* from Scripture were used to outline a revised apocalyptic timetable to understand the significance of current events. Israel and Judah represented the Greek and Roman churches, both opposing the advent of a new spiritual age. As Egypt and Chaldea once made Israel and Judah suffer for their sins, so also would the new age be preceded by a time of suffering [cf. Herbert Grundmann, *Studien über Joachim von Floris* (Leipzig, 1927), pp. 192ff.]. In this time prophets would appear. Our text and others are used to describe them (Reeves, *Influence of Prophecy*, pp. 140–44, 147–48; p. 148, n. 13, offers specific references). The commentary was printed three times in the sixteenth century: 1516, 1525 (both Venice), and 1577 (Cologne). See Morton Bloomfield, "Joachim of Flora," *Traditio* 13 (1957):251.

65. Franz, *Schriften*, pp. 397.29–298.1.

66. Ibid., p. 398.6-7. It is of interest that Müntzer writes that he has to cloak the full implication of his teaching by simply citing Scripture chapters (p. 398.8-11). Schwarz presents a precedent for such apocalyptic citation and expectation in Taborite chiliasm, *Die apokalyptische Theologie Thomas Müntzers*, p. 18.

67. Wappler, *Thomas Müntzer in Zwickau*, p. 65. Bailey concurs and presents a picture of Müntzer working speculatively with various dates to plot the cataclysm. His work is intriguing. While the evidence does not clearly lead to such dating, his speculation is within the bounds of possibility ("Müntzer and the Apocalyptic," p. 35).

68. Franz, *Schriften*, p. 398.3-7.

69. Abraham Friesen argues that there is no irrefutable evidence of a Müntzer-Joachim relationship, but there is much to be said for the connection based upon circumstantial

evidence, current ideas in Erfurt (and Wittenberg), as well as structural similarities found in Müntzer's thought, in "Thomas Müntzer and the Old Testament," MQR, 47 (1973), p. 13. Siegfried Bräuer and Wolfgang Ullmann argue that there is insufficient evidence for the Joachite connection [*Theologische Schriften aus dem Jahr 1523* (Berlin: Evangelische Verlagsanstalt, 1982), p. 21].

70. Franz, *Schriften*, p. 372.3-9.

71. Ibid., p. 504.30-1.

72. According to Hinrichs, the origin of Müntzer's "Bund der Auserwählten" is suggested by the eschatological rule of the elect as prophesied in Dan. 7:27 (*Luther und Müntzer*, p. 41).

73. Details are given in Hinrichs, *Luther and Müntzer*, pp. 11–14; cf. Ozment, *Mysticism and Dissent*, p. 75.

74. Franz, *Schriften*, p. 405.25-36.

75. Rupp presents the varying attitudes, *Patterns of Reformation*, p. 200; cf. George Williams and Angel Mergal, *Spiritual and Anabaptist Writers* (Philadelphia: Westminster Press, 1958), pp. 47–48.

76. The German text is in Franz, *Schriften*, pp. 241–63, an English translation by Williams is available in *Spiritual and Anabaptist Writers*, pp. 49–70.

77. Williams and Mergal, *Spiritual and Anabaptist Writers*, p. 47.

78. Hinrichs, *Luther und Müntzer*, pp. 5–76. Note esp. the analysis of Dan. 2, pp. 41–44.

79. In the documents already cited from Franz, *Schriften*, these include the prophet as Elijah confronting the prophets of Baal (372.3-9); as Jeremiah against false religion (506.6-11); as a pathfinder to the new Church (504.29), even with sickle if necessary (504.19-22, 262.2-4); as offering apocalyptic or prophetic judgment (394.36), and with potential Joachite affinities (398.3-7).

80. Ibid., p. 257.19-22.

81. Ibid., pp. 248.29–249.7.

82. Franz, *Schriften*, p. 243.22-23; cf. in the "Prague Manifesto," p. 504.2-4. Wolfgang Ullmann notes the similarity of this kind of historical thinking with that of Tertullian and Montanist speculation ("Geschichtsverständnis Thomas Müntzers," p. 50). The relationship to Tertullian's apocalyptic speculation has already been cited and helps to mark a different, more immediate apocalyptic program from that of Luther. See Schwartz, *Die apokalyptische Theologie Thomas Müntzers*, p. 2, n.s. 4,5.

83. Franz, *Schriften*, pp. 255.23–256.9. The image was used by such sixteenth-century annalists and historians as Johannes Sleidanus (1506–1556); cf. Erich Seeberg, *Gottfried Arnold* (Darmstadt: Wissenschaftliche Buchgesellt Schaft, 1964), pp. 257–58. Both Ullmann ("Geschichtsverständnis Thomas Müntzers," pp. 51–56) and Hinrichs, *Luther und Müntzer*, pp. 46–48, 54–57) draw out the significance of this image and its interpretation for Müntzer.

84. Franz, *Schriften*, p. 256.5-19.

85. Ibid., p. 256.20-21: "Dann der stein, an hende [cf. Dan. 2:34] vom berge gerissen, ist gross worden. Die armen leien und bawrn sehn yn viel scherffer an dann yr [die Fürsten]."

86. Ibid., p. 257.12-15; cf. Hinrichs, *Luther und Müntzer*, p. 59.

87. Ibid., p. 257.19-22.

88. Ibid., p. 256.11-14.

89. Ibid., p. 256.20-21. The social horizon was one of widespread peasant unrest. See Williams, *Radical Reformation*, chapter 4.

90. Ibid., p. 255.15-22; cf. Hinrichs, *Luther und Müntzer*, pp. 43–44, 55–59.

91. The implication, of course, is that the poor may more easily discern the nature of the kingdom as they are unencumbered by the things of this world (Matt. 19:24).

92. Müntzer is probably thinking of the intent and effect of Luther's eight "Invocavit" sermons (WA, 10.III). Here and elsewhere Luther advocated freedom for preaching the gospel but not for social disruption. Cf. Hinrichs, *Luther und Müntzer*, p. 63.

93. Franz, *Schriften*, p. 255.28-30 (Williams's translation, p. 63).

94. Ibid., p. 258.1-3.

95. Ibid., pp. 261.12–262.4. Note the conflation of Dan. 7:27 with Rom. 13:3-4; cf. Hinrichs, *Luther und Müntzer*, p. 64.

96. Ibid., cf. p. 261.27-8, p. 262.1-2.

97. Ibid., pp. 261.28–262.4 (guided by Williams, p. 69).

98. Franz, *Schriften*, p. 261.12-16.

99. Ibid., p. 464.7.

100. Müntzer was not the only one of this period to establish political legitimacy for the elect based upon Dan. 2:34,42 and 7:27. Giovanni Nanni defended the temporal power of the papacy on a similar basis in *De futuris Christianorum triumphis in Saracenos* (cf. Luther's Preface in WA, 50, pp. 96–105).

101. Hinrichs, *Luther und Müntzer*, p. 65.

102. Franz, *Schriften*, pp. 408–9. Ozment summarizes Luther's lack of patience with Müntzer by this point (*Mysticism and Dissent*, pp. 76–77).

103. Ibid., p. 409.14-18. Note further apocalyptic themes: the destruction of tyrants (p. 109.2-3) and the need for "bold preachers" (p. 409.11).

104. Ibid., pp. 409–10.

105. Ibid., pp. 411–15; cf. Hinrichs, *Luther und Müntzer*, pp. 66–68.

106. Ibid., p. 411.9-14.

107. This was the point made earlier to Hausmann (ibid., p. 373.4-6); and raised with Melanchthon (ibid., p. 381.20-3).

108. Ibid., pp. 416–19.

109. Ibid., p. 419.9-12.

110. Ibid., p. 419.12-15: "Wer dozu kommen ist, der mag myt sicherm gewyssen vil fuglicher gute tage dan bose erwelen, welchs in Johanne dem evangelisten und in Helia [und] in Enoch clerlich angezeygt ist." I am following Schwarz (*Die apokalyptische Theologie Thomas Müntzers*, pp. 46–48). On the nature of that time, see chapter 2; cf. Robert E. Lerner, "Refreshment of the Saints," *Traditio*, 32 (1976), pp. 113–16.

111. Schwarz, *Die apokalyptische Theologie Thomas Müntzers*, pp. 47–53.

112. Franz, *Schriften*, p. 420.25-7.

113. Ibid., p. 421.3-10.

114. Hinrichs, *Luther und Müntzer*, pp. 75–78.

115. Hinrichs, *Luther und Müntzer*, pp. 75–78; ibid., pp. 91–92, 126–30.

116. Hinrichs, *Luther und Müntzer*, pp. 136–42; cf. Rupp, *Patterns of Reformation*, pp. 221–27.

117. Franz, *Schriften*, pp. 265–319. See pp. 265–66 for discussion of the editions. They are analyzed by Hinrichs, *Luther und Müntzer*, pp. 77–142. Franz prints two versions of this work. Version "A" is longer and carries a greater sense of apocalyptic urgency. Version "B" is a revised version which was given to the censor. Version "A" will be cited here.

118. Hinrichs, *Luther und Müntzer*, p. 135.

119. Ozment, *Mysticism and Dissent*, pp. 79–97. The term is Ozment's.

120. Franz, *Schriften*, p. 315.15-24.

121. Ibid., pp. 284.11–285.3.

122. Ozment, *Mysticism and Dissent*, pp. 79–97. The term is Ozment's.

123. Franz, *Schriften*, pp. 281.12–282.21.

124. Ibid., pp. 292.33–293.8.

125. Ibid., pp. 296.31–297.3.

126. Ibid., pp. 306.28–307.3: "Johannes [Luke 1:15–17] ist aber vil ein ander prediger, ein bezeügender engel Christi, in eynem yeden rechten prediger angezeygt. Das lob müss ein yeder haben, wie Johannes, nicht von der werck ver dienst, sonder von des ernstes wegen, den die tapffer nüchterheyt gepyret, der sich zur entfrembdung der lüst erstreckt, da die krefft der selen emplösset werden, auff das der abgrund des geystes erscheyne durch alle krefft, da der heylig geist sein einrreden thün müss, psal. 84 [Ps. 85:9ff.]" (cf. Ozment's translation, p. 94).

127. I am guided by Schwarz, *Die apokalyptische Theologie Thomas Müntzers*, pp. 48–53.

128. Franz, *Schriften*, p. 300.14-31: "So die heylig kirch sol durch die bitter warheit vernewt werden, so müss ein gnadenreycher knecht Gottes herfür treten im geyst Helie, Math. am 17., 3. regum 18, apoca. 11 [Matt. 17:3, 1 Kings 18:1, Rev. 11:3], und müss alle ding in den rechten schwanck bringen." Müntzer continues, "Warlich, ir wirt vil müssen erweckt werden, auff das sie mit dem allerhöchsten eyfer durch brünstigen ernst die Christenheyt fegen von den gotlosen regenten": "In fact, many will have to be raised up. . . ."

129. Franz, *Schriften*, pp. 321–43; for editions and introduction, pp. 321–22. An English translation, less the expanded title, may be found in Reinhard P. Becker, ed., *German Humanism and Reformation* (New York: Continuum Press, 1983), pp. 274–90; cf. Hans J. Hillerbrand, "Thomas Muentzer's Last Tract Against Martin Luther: A Translation and Commentary," MQR, 38 (1964):20–36.

130. Franz, *Schriften*, p. 343.9; cf. pp. 323.5 and 339.28–340.15!

131. The treatise is a conscious "reply" to Luther's open criticism of radicalism and implicitly of Müntzer in "Ein Brief an die Fürsten von Sachsen von dem aufrührischen Geist" (publ. August 1524), WA, 15, pp. 210–21. Hillerbrand notes the frequent references in Müntzer's treatise to the "Brief" and the fact that Müntzer's opening paragraph is specifically patterned on Luther's work ("Thomas Müntzer's Last Tract," p. 22).

132. Ibid., p. 322.1-7: "Hochverursachte schutzrede und antwort wider das geistlosse, sannftlebende fleysch zu Wittenberg, welches mit verkärter weysse durch den diepstal der heiligen schrift die erbermdliche Christenheit also gantz jämerlichen besudelt hat. "Thomas Müntzer. Alstedter. Auss der Hölen Helie I K 19:9ff.; Mt. 17:1ff.; Lk. 1:11, 2:36f.; Offb. 11:3, welches ernst niemant verschonet, 3. Regum 18, Matthei 17, Luce 1; Apocali. undecimo. Anno MCXXIII."

133. Ibid., p. 324.3-11.

134. Ibid., p. 372.3-7.

135. Ibid., p. 300.14-31.

136. Franz, *Schriften*, pp. 342.17–343.3.

137. The Scriptural allusions do not end here. Müntzer tells us at the end of this treatise (ibid., pp. 342.17–343.3) that a new David is called for to replace the compromises of Saul. It was precisely in the cave Adullam (1 Sam. 22:1), to which a fearful David had fled, that David gathers his forces for eventual victory over Saul. See below.

138. Ibid., p. 322.7.

139. Ibid., p. 323.4-5.

140. Ibid., p. 325.11-15. The Marxist interpretation of Müntzer by M. M. Smirin may be developed plausibly here as it is the false princes and priests (Luther's Party) who rob the people (People's Party, or Reformation) for unlawful gain, though such fails to deal fully not only with Müntzer's mysticism, but especially his Joachimite-Taborite eschatology. Smirin, *Die Volksreformation des Thomas Müntzers und die grosse deutsche Bauernkrieg*, 2nd ed. (Berlin, 1965), esp. pp. 88–89, chapters 2–4.

141. Ibid., p. 504.30-1.

142. Ibid., pp. 328.26–329.4: "Eines saget er, und das allerbeschaydenste verschweyget er, wie ich klärlich vor den fürsten ausspraytete, dass ein gantze gemayn gewalt des schwertz hab wie auch den schlüssel der auflösung, und sagte vom text danielis 7; Apocalip. 6 und Romano 13; I. Regum 8. dass die fürsten keine herren, sonder diener des schwerts sein, sye sollens nicht machen, wie es yenen wol gefellet, Deutro 17. sye sollen recht thun." Later Rev. 11:15 will be added to this defense (p. 463.11-13).

143. Ibid., p. 339.30-1.

144. Ibid., pp. 339.31–340.15.

145. Ibid., p. 340.16: "Ezechiel saget dirs am 13. und Micheas am 3."

146. Bailey argues for such ("Müntzer and the Apocalyptic," p. 36).

147. Rupp raises the question whether Müntzer's thought became more radical or whether his failure to win the princes to his cause in July caused him to become "more explicit." In *Patterns of Reformation*, p. 228.

148. Ibid., pp. 342.27–343.1.

149. Ibid., pp. 463-4 (May 9, 1525).

150. Franz, *Schriften*, p. 463.8-19: "Die reyne rechtschaffene forcht Gottes zuvorn, lieben brueder. Nachdem Gott ytzt dye ganze welt sonderlich fast bewegt zu erkentnus gottlicher warheit und dieselbige sich beweyset mit dem aller ernsten eifer uber dye tyrannen, wie das clerlich Daniel am vii. underschied sagt, das die gewalt soll gegeben werden dem gemeinen volk, auch ists angezaygt Apoca. am XI. ca., das das reych dieser welt soll Christo zustendigk sein." Note the way he signs the letter, "Thomas Müntzer with the sword of Gideon," p. 464.7.

151. Analyzed by Hillerbrand, "Peasants War," in Lawrence Buck and Jonathan Zophy, *The Social History of the Reformation* (Columbus: Ohio State University Press, 1972), pp. 117ff; see also the collection of articles in *Bauernkriegs-Studien*, Bernd Moeller, ed., (*Verein für Reformationsgeschichte*, 189; Gütersloh: Gerd Mohn, 1975); and Blickle, *Revolution of 1525*, in particular the chapter on "The Twelve Articles," pp. 25–57.

152. Schwarz illustrates the relationship between Müntzer's chiliastic idea of the Kingdom and that evident in Taborite speculation (*Die apokalyptische Theologie Thomas Müntzers*, pp. 2–4, 56–59, *et passim*); cf. Gerhard Zschäbitz, *Zur mitteldeutschen Wieder-täuferbewegung nach dem Grossen Bauernkrieg* (Berlin: Rutter und Loenig, 1957–58), p. 38.

153. Hinrichs, *Luther und Müntzer*, pp. 44–46.

154. Schwarz, *Die apokalyptische Theologie Thomas Müntzers*, p. 55. Much of the speculation for this idea was systematized by Bonaventure in whose thought paradise, the present place of the witnesses, is located somewhere between earthly, therefore finite, considerations and a pure vision of God. In general, this idea is part of the broad Augustinian tradition inherited by the Middle Ages, which provided a definition for paradise: *ubi feliciter vivitur*. For some, the nature of this space and the quality of the lives of those living there would become the content of the hope for the nature of the kingdom of God on earth, prior to the Last Judgment and final placement in heaven or hell. See Schwarz, *Die apokalyptische Theologie Thomas Müntzers*, pp. 54–56.

155. Rupp summarizes some of the literature on the spreading peasant insurrections throughout central Europe in the mid-70s (*Patterns of Reformation*, pp. 231–34).

156. Williams, *Radical Reformation*, pp. 75–78.

157. Note its source in Luther's "Eine schreckliche Geschichte und ein Gericht Gottes über Thomas Müntzer" (WA, 18, p. 367). Franz, *Schriften*, pp. 454–56.

158. Ibid., pp. 454.6–454.12 (guided by Rupp, pp. 239–40).

159. Ibid., p. 454.13-14: "der meyster will spiel machen, die bösswichter mussen dran."

160. Ibid., p. 469.11-470.
161. Ibid., p. 550.
162. Rupp, *Patterns of Reformation*, p. 247.
163. Franz, *Schriften*, p. 495.1-5. That Müntzer saw his death in a religious framework seems indicated in a last letter to his disciples (ibid., p. 473.7-13).
164. Zschäbitz, *Wiedertäuferbewegung*, pp. 23–27; Paul Wappler, *Die Täuferbewegung in Thüringen von 1526–1584* (Jena: Verlag von Gustav Fischer, 1913), nr. 54b, p. 429; cf. Nipperdey, *Reformation, Revolution, Utopie*, p. 38.
165. Gottfried Seebass's *Habilitationsschrift* is the most extensive work on Hut and supersedes earlier studies ("Müntzers Erbe. Werk, Leben und Theologie des Hans Hut" [ms. Erlangen, 1972]). The appendices are a valuable source for documents by or about Hut drawn from a wide variety of archives (pt. 2, pp. 1–75). Seebass presents a helpful bibliographic survey in the opening pages and elsewhere, stressing the difficulties of working with all kinds of documents either authored by or derivative of Hut directly or through his disciples (pp. 1–7; cf. pp. 336–41). On the larger context in which Hut can be placed, see Williams, *Radical Reformation*, chapter 7.
166. Most of what we know about Hut is gained from admissions, often under torture, following his arrest in Augsburg, September 15, 1527. The court records were assembled, not always fully, by Christian Meyer, "Zur Geschichte der Wiedertäufer in Oberschwaben. I: Die Anfänge des Wiedertäuferthums in Augsburg" *Zeitschrift des Historischen Vereins für Schwaben und Neuburg 1* (1874):207–53. Seebass includes additional materials in the appendix to "Hans Hut."
167. R. F. Loserth, art. "Hans Hut," *Mennonite Encyclopedia*, Vol. 2, p. 849.
168. The statement was in answer to a question about the identity of his baptizer, Hut, "ein diner gottes und ein gesandter apostel von got zu diser letzter und aller geverlichsten zeit." In Karl Schornbaum, ed., *Quellen zur Geschichte der Wiedertäufer. Vol. 2: Markgraftum Brandenburg, Bayern, I. Abteilung Quellen und Forschungen zur Reformationgeschichte 16* (Leipzig, 1934), p. 26.18-20.
169. Wappler writes of the preaching of the Zwickau Prophets: "So werde der Tzürke (der damals unter Suleiman II. schon Ungarn bedrohte) Deutschland einnehman und in kurzem, in etwa 5-7 Jahren sich eine solche Veränderung in der Welt vollziehen, dass kein Unfrommer oder böser Sünder mehr solle lebendig bleiben."
170. Seebass argues that Hut at first followed Müntzer and saw the Peasants' War as the final cleansing conflict before the establishment of God's new order (cf. Meyer, "Anfänge," p. 241). However, in the period between that war and his baptism by Denck, Hut began to plot the end from the events of that war.
171. Loserth writes that "Hut's preaching on the return of Christ was entirely based on the Bible and was purely religious. He kept himself aloof from any political or revolutionary tendencies" (ME, 2, p. 847). This interpretation is followed by Robert Friedmann ("Thomas Müntzer's Relation to Anabaptism," MQR, 31 [1957]: 75–87) and Herbert Klassen ("The Life and Teachings of Hans Hut," [in 2 parts] MQR, 33 [1959]:171–205, 267–304). Klassen points to the growing influence of ideas characteristic of Denck following Hut's re-baptism (ibid., p. 280). On the other hand, several historians have argued for the influence of Müntzer upon South German Anabaptism through the teaching of Hut. Following Wappler, Holl, Böhmer and Müller, they include Zschäbitz (*Wiedertäuferbewegung*, pp. 26–31), Grete Mecenseffy ("Die Herkunft des oberösterreichischen Täufertums," ARG, 47-2 [1956]: 252–59), and Rupp (*Patterns of Reformation*, pp. 331–32). Seebass argues that Hut's views are derived from the same late medieval mystical and apocalyptic ideas which influenced Müntzer, ("Hans Hut," pp. 341–44).
172. Seebass, "Hans Hut," pp. 166–84; cf. Klassen, "Life and Teachings of Hans Hut,"

pp. 267–70; the first encounter came when Müntzer stayed with Hut for a night and a day in the summer of 1524, leaving an exposition on the first chapter of Luke, "Die Entblössung," for publication by him (Meyer, "Anfänge," p. 243 [no. XII]).

173. Lydia Müller published the text from a Budapest manuscript: Von dem geheimnus der tauf, baide des zaichens und des wesens, ein anfang eines rechten warhaftigen Christlichen lebens; Joan: 5, in *Glaubenszeugnisse oberdeutscher Taufgesinnter*, I (*Quellen und Forschungen zur Reformationgeschichte*, Vol. 20 (Leipzigg: M. Heinsius Nachfolger, 1938), pp. 12–28. A translation, "Of the Mystery of Baptism," appears in Rupp, *Patterns of Reformation*, pp. 379–99. Seebass writes that the question of the treatise's original authorship remains unanswered ("Hans Hut," p. 63).

174. Hut's message is reflected in the Augsburg interrogations, where he admitted to have said that the time had now come for the peasants to seize power: "sy die underthanen solten alle oberkait zu tod schlagen, dann es were die recht zeit jetzo hie, und sy hetten den gewalt in der handt, wie er dann sollichs hievor anzaigt hette" (Meyer, "Anfange," p. 241).

175. Klassen divides Hut's activities into two periods on either side of his re-baptism. The first runs from the collapse of the Peasants' War to the baptism (May 26, 1526), the second from that baptism to his death (December 6, 1527); Klassen, "Life and Teachings of Hans Hut," MQR (July 1959):177–79, 180–85. On debate over Denck's role in the baptism of Hut, see Williams, *Radical Reformation*, p. 234; cf. Werner Packull, "Gottfried Sebass on Hans Hut: A Discussion," MQR, 49 (1975):57–67.

176. Seebass, "Hans Hut," pp. 252–79; cf. Torsten Bergsten, *Balthasar Hubmaier, Anabaptist Theologian and Martyr*, trans. by I. J. Barnes and W. R. Estep; ed. by W. R. Estep (Valley Forge, Pa.: Judson Press, 1978), pp. 316–77.

177. The issues which were discussed have been confused with the points contained in an apparent forgery called the "Nikolsburg Articles," perhaps the work of Urbanus Rhegius. The relationship is discussed by Wilhelm Wiswedel, art. "Nikolsburg, Articles of," ME, 3, pp. 886–88; Bergsten holds that Hubmaier composed the Articles (*Hubmaier*, pp. 365–70) but variants existed earlier (Williams, *Radical Reformation*, chapter 7).

178. Schornbaum, *Bayern* I, p. 153.22-29.

179. Stayer writes that the real point of debate was Hut's chiliasm, that Hut never claimed to teach nonresistance ("Hans Hut's Doctrine of the Sword," MQR, 39 [1965]:181–91; esp. pp. 188–91).

180. The interrogations of some of Hut's disciples in later years reveal this conviction about the Turk: "So er kame, welche dan den willen des himlischen vaters theten, würden bleiben, und die fursten und die hern und alle, die den willen des himlischen vaters nit theten, zu tod schlahen" (Wappler, *Täuferbewegung*, p. 242; cf. pp. 231, 235, 240, 244, 280–82). See Clarence Bauman, *Gewaltlosigkeit im Täufertum. Eine Unter-suchung zur theologischen Ethik des oberdeutschen Täufertums der Reformationszeit* (Leiden: E. J. Brill, 1968), p. 59. Compare Müntzer in Franz, *Schriften*, pp. 504.34–505.1; p. 255.23-28.

181. Meyer, "Anfänge," p. 241 [nr. XI]. Under thorough questioning Hut admitted to have preached: "welcher zwien rockh hab, der soll ainen hingeben und ain schwertt darumb kauffen; . . alls Peterus dem Malchus das or abgehawen, derauff Christus gesagt, das er sein schwert einstecken, dann welcher mit dem schwert fecht, darumb gestraft werden solt; . . als Christus anzaigt, er sey nit komen, frid zu senden, sonder das schwert; . . am letzsten psalm: die heyligen werden frölich sein und zwayschneidende schwert in iren handen haben, auf das sy rach thun in den lendern under den völckern, zu pinden die konig mit ketten und die edeln mit eysenfässern, auf das sy an inen verbringen das gericht, davon geschriben ist." A similar statement in connection with a final three and a half years is found in Schornbaum, *Bayern* I, p. 188.20-31.

182. Each of the following agrees: Seebass, "Hans Hut," pt. 1, p. 391; Wappler, *Taüferbewegung*, p. 30; Stayer, "Hans Hut's Doctrine of the Sword," pp. 188–91; Zeman, *The Anabaptists and Czech Brethren*, pp. 185–86, 193–96.

183. Hut's conception of baptism will not be fully discussed here except to call attention to its apocalyptic association. See Williams, *Radical Reformation*, pp. 164, 172–73; Seebass, "Hans Hut," pt. 1, pp. 471–75.

184. Hut, "Of the Mystery of Baptism" (guided by Rupp, *Patterns of Reformation*, p. 379).

185. Ibid., pp. 380–82.

186. Hut, "Of the Mystery of Baptism" (Rupp, *Patterns of Reformation*, p. 390).

187. Ibid., p. 391–99. On a "baptism of fire" (associated with Hut) and the different theologies of baptism in the sixteenth century, see Williams, *Radical Reformation*, chapter 11.

188. Hut's concordance may be found in Seebass, "Hans Hut," pt. 2, pp. 3–9. Seebass lists 81 articles of association; cf. pt. 1, pp. 40–42; pp. 400, 471–75.

189. Ibid., pt. 2, p. 9. Hut baptized his followers with the "sign of Tau," a symbol he associated with that sign in Ezekiel and the Apocalypse. See Werner O. Packull, "The Sign of Thau: The Changing Conception of the Seal of God's Elect in Early Anabaptist Thought," MQR, 61 (1987):363–67.

190. Ibid., pt. 1, pp. 255–56.

191. Ibid., pt. 2, p. 9.

192. Ibid., pt. 1, p. 400.

193. Hut reveals in at least one place in the court trials that he believed God had through an angel called and empowered him to build up the Church: "er hab aus im selbs kain bruederschaft auffgericht, sonnder solichs aus dem bevelhe gots thun, der hat in gesandt und ime solhs durch ainen engel den got zu im geschickt, auszurichten und zu leren bevolhen" (Meyer, "Anfänge," p. 225 [nr. III]; cf. p. 240 [nr. XI] and its denial, p. 237 [VIII], p. 232 (nr. V).

194. Seebass, "Hans Hut," pt. 1, pp. 397–99.

195. Williams, *Radical Reformation*, pp. 167–76.

196. Hut referred to this "synod" as a "concilium" (Meyer, "Anfänge," p. 242 [nr. XI]). Williams finds eschatological overtones in this designation (*Radical Reformation*, pp. 261–76). Klassen writes that "the central theological problem discussed was probably Hut's eschatology" ("Life and Teaching of Hans Hut," p. 184).

197. Williams, *Radical Reformation*, p. 176–80; Seebass, "Hans Hut," pt. 1, pp. 307–20.

198. See the texts in Schornbaum, *Bayern I*, e.g., p. 112.9-14; p. 188.20-31; p. 198.32-35, and p. 199.17-26; Wappler, *Täuferbewegung*, pp. 244, 323. The forged Nikolsburg Articles purport to represent the opinions of Hut. It is of interest that each of three versions found in Strassburg specifically speak of the parousia as occurring within two years: Krebs-Rott, *Elsass* I, pp. 138–40 [nr. 116]. Citing version "A" (articles of the new sects or rabble-preachers): "Innerhalb zwey iaren wirt der Herr von himel komen vnd mit den weltlichen fürsten handlen vnd kriegen, vnd die Gottlosen werden vertilcket, aber die gottseligen vnd vsserwelten werden mit dem Herren herschen vff erden" (p. 139, nr. 5). The period of time mentioned is less than three and one-half years since the apocalyptic time-clock has already begun the countdown.

199. According to the September protocol Hut maintained: "das Christus in kurz zu richten komen werde, ... Aber auf was zeit und zu welher stund, das sei menigelich verporgen. Wiss solhs niemand, dann allein got" (Schornbaum, *Bayern* I, p. 44.15-16). Two months later Hut admitted: "Sein maynung sei gewesen, das got der her hab geben

zur buss vierthalbjar, wie in Apokalipsis am 13 [:5]. anzaigt werde: wer sich zur buss bekere, der werde verfolgt werden und müsse leiden, wie [II] Thimoth7 am 3. stände: wer gotseligklich leben werde, der muss verfolgnus leiden und Daniels am 12:7: sy werden all zerstret werden, da melde er auch vierthalb jar und zaige an darvon von theurung, pestilentz und krig und darnach werde der herr erst die seinen versammeln in allen landen und im einem jegklichen lande werden dieselben die oberkaiten und alle sünder strafen" (Meyer, "Anfänge," p. 239 [nr. X]).

200. Klassen, "The Life and Teachings of Hans Hut," p. 198.

201. Seebass, "Hans Hut," pt. 2, p. 9; cf. Seebass's comments, pt. 1, p. 387.

202. "Sendschreiben Hans Hut," in C. A. Cornelius, ed., *Geschichte des Münsterischen Aufruhrs*, 3 vols. (Leipzig: Weigel, 1860), I. pp. 251–52; also in L. Müller, *Glaubenszeugnisse oberdeutscher Taufgesinnter* (Leipzig: M. Heinsius, Nachfolger, 1938), pp. 11–12, note 4. First published by Urbanus Rhegius under the date of 1528, it lacks the names of addressor and addressee. Seebass concludes it is probably from Hut ("Hans Hut," pt. 1, pp. 20–21).

203. Idem., "Sendschreiben," p. 252.

204. "Hans Hut," aus der hölen Helie" (Meyer, "Anfänge," p. 240 [X]); cf. Seebass's version, "Hans Hut," pt. 2, p. 73, nr. 21.

205. "Hans Hut," pp. 113–149.

206. Meyer, "Anfänge," pp. 252–53 [XXI]; and Loserth, "Hans Hut," ME, 2, pp. 848–49; Williams, *Radical Reformation*, pp. 178–79.

207. Seebass summarizes Hut's reckoning: "Er erfuhr, wenn er nicht sogar Augenzeuge wurde, dass man die Köper Thomas Müntzers und Heinrich Pfeiffers nach ihrer Hinrichtung am 27. Mai 1525 nicht begraben, sondern auf Pfähle gesteckt hatte. Was lag also für ihn, der in beiden seine Lehrer verehrte, näher, als sie mit den beiden Propheten zu identifizieren, deren Leiber nach Apk. 11, 9 dreieinhalb Jahre unbegraben liegen sollten. Beide Propheten aber hatten nach Apk. 11, 3 zwölfhundertsechzig Tage, also wieder dreieinhalb Jahre, gepredigt. Rechnete man sie vom Mai 1525 zurück, so kam man in die Zeit des Auftretens der "Zwickauer Propheten" die ihrerseits eine grosse Veränderung nach sieben Jahren prophezeit hatten. Zu diesen sieben Jahren und den Ereignissen in ihrer Mitte passte dann auch Dan. 9, 27 dass nämlich der Bund eine Woche lang gestärkt werde, dass aber mitten in der Woche das Opfer aufhören werde. Hätte man nun vom Tod Müntzers korrekt die dreieinhalb Jahre, die als letzte Fluch- und Notzeit in der Schrift ofter gennant werden, gerechnet, so wäre man in den Ausgang des Jahres 1528 gekommen. Da aber die Notzeit nach Mt. 24, 22 verkürzt werden muss te, konnte man aufgrund des Gleichnisses vom Feigenbaum bereits um die Baumblüte, Pfingsten 1528, mit dem Ende rechnen" ("Bauerntum und Täufertum in Franken," pp. 147–48); see also "Hans Hut," p. 1, pp. 387–89.

208. Ibid., p. 149; cf. idem, "Hans Hut," pt. 1, pp. 394–99. Seebass raises the question of whether or not Hut may have seen himself as the gathering angel of Matt. 24:31 in a last period of time given for repentance ("Hans Hut," pt. 1, p. 394).

209. Klaus Deppermann, *Melchior Hoffman: Soziale Unruhen und apokalyplische Visionen im Zeitalter der Reformation* (Gottingen: Vandenhoeck und Ruprecht, 1979), pp. 174–86; cf. Zschäbitz, *Wiedertäuferbewegung*, pp. 49–64.

4

Identification or Representation

Messianic Troubles

Like Hans Hut, Melchior Hoffman (c. 1495-1543/4) was another highly successful lay preacher of Reformation times.[1] As Hut had been successful in carrying
the Anabaptist message to south and central Germany, so Hoffman was largely
responsible for helping to transmit the Anabaptist movement from southwest
Germany into and throughout northwestern Europe. Together with Müntzer and
Hut he exerted a wide influence among Anabaptists in central Europe and seems
to have made more of the prophecy of the adventual witnesses than perhaps even
Hut or Müntzer.[2] Furrier by trade but called by the Spirit to be a prophet, Hoffman
was won to the Lutheran cause by 1522. He became an itinerant evangelist and
was supported at various times by the guilds in Dorpat, merchants of Scandinavia,
the East Frisian chancellor Ulrich von Dornum, and even by Frederick I, king of
Denmark.

Hoffman's Reformation work can be divided into three fairly distinct phases.
First, we shall consider his work as a preacher in the Baltic states. Hoffman's
commentary on Daniel at this time reveals the initial shaping of his apocalyptic
self-consciousness. Second, while working as a Lutheran preacher in Schleswig-
Holstein, Hoffman engaged in a controversy with Nikolaus Amsdorf over apocalyptic themes including his interest in adventual witnesses. Finally, during his work
in and from Strassburg we find a clear development of the theme of the two end-
time prophets of our text.

Hoffman begins as a Lutheran. We first hear of him in 1523 as a preacher of
Luther's doctrine of justification by faith in the city of Wolmar, in Livonia. He
united this characteristically Lutheran doctrine with a lively sense of the impending Judgment of God.[3] This teaching soon brought him at odds with the traditional spiritual leaders in the Baltic area. Replaced by the reformer of Riga,
Sylvester Tegetmeyer, and forced to leave Wolmar, Hoffman was in Dorpat by
the fall of 1524.[4] Here he preached against images and auricular confession and
emphasized Lutheran doctrine with heavy apocalyptic overtones. Seeing him as a
cause of turmoil in the city,[5] the city council in the spring of 1525 summoned
him to bring forth a witness to the authenticity of his teachings from Luther if he
desired to continue to preach in the city. Hoffman sought to do this and immediately headed for Wittenberg. He was able to inspire sufficient trust there so that

when Luther and Johannes Bugenhagen decided to send letters to the Livonians, Hoffman was allowed to append a message of his own.[6] Hoffman appears a convinced Lutheran at this point, although with a heavy apocalyptic accent.[7] Returning to Dorpat, Hoffman alienated many by his preaching.[8] He was asked to leave the city and was in Stockholm by way of Reval in early 1526. During this first Baltic phase, his teachings seem to have departed increasingly from those of Luther in the interpretation of the apocalyptic prophecies. This can be seen in a work that Hoffman apparently published while at Stockholm, but especially in his treatise on the twelfth chapter of Daniel.[9] In his "Short Exhortation" Hoffman made use of apocalyptic language against Tegetmeyer.[10] But the commentary on Daniel 12 is more important for our purposes as it represents his first systematic treatment of apocalyptic imagery.

Whereas Luther reckoned generally that the Parousia of Christ would occur soon after the identification of the pope as Antichrist, Hoffman preached more precisely that the end time had already begun and would soon reach its climax. On the basis of his allegorical exegesis of Daniel 12, he argued that the last days were at hand.[11] The time of the sixth trumpet (Rev. 9:13-11:14) had arrived, the time of the unmasking of falsehood. Hoffman seems to imply that only seven years remain until the return of Christ.[12]

For Hoffman, the political and religious turmoil besetting Europe was an expression of God's anger as well as God's grace. He envisioned a last time of renewal as prophets and apostolic messengers would spread the word of God with preaching, not the sword.[13] This is the first phase of the messianic troubles; the godless will feel the condemnation and punishment of God's laws and the pope is recognized as blasphemer and Antichrist. At the climax, the two witnesses appear as Elijah and Enoch, removing the pope from God's sanctuary. They execute God's fury upon the godless for 1260 days (Rev. 11:3) or 1290 days (Dan. 12:11). In fact, Hoffman tells us, the two witnesses are currently alive although they are not yet known. The pope and the godless try to defend themselves against the godly persecution by calling upon Emperor Charles V, identified by Hoffman as the red dragon (Rev. 12:3). The dragon will persecute God's holy ones and slay the two witnesses. This ends the first period (three and one-half years) of the end time.[14]

After the slaying of the witnesses, a time of trouble follows for the godly in a parallel period of three and a half years, perhaps even 1335 days (Rev. 11:11; 12:14; Dan. 12:7; 12:12), like the days seen by Lot and Noah. Now the word of God is no longer preached openly, and Christians must flee to the wilderness for safety. In the world, "the sun of belief" goes down while the "moon of belief" arises in the hearts of believers; the latter will be a special spiritual knowledge unique to the last days. Powerful errors will issue forth in those days as one-third of all teachers teach error. Spiritual confusion will abound until the heathen nations of Gog and Magog fall upon both the godless and the spiritually renewed. The elect must now take up their cross but, in the midst of the world's night, Christ will appear to save the elect, judging all by the rule: "What you have done for the least of my brethren, you have done to me."[15]

Hoffman developed this scenario at a time of increasing apocalyptic fervor.

In fact, Deppermann argues that the literary pattern for Hoffman's treatise on Daniel 12 was Luther's interpretation of the gospel for the second Sunday of Advent (Luke 21:15–36), published in his "Kirchenpostille" (1522).[16] Further, in introducing two periods, each three and one-half years long and separated by the death of the two witnesses, Hoffman seems to have been influenced by the same interpretative tendencies that influenced Hans Hut, if not by Hut himself or his disciples. For Hoffman, the function of the witnesses is to proclaim the gospel, not to take up the sword. Hoffman combined the prophecies of Daniel and the Apocalypse in a realistic historical fashion. Spiritual men would be given the insight to discern these matters, rather than those whom the universities were turning out, preachers who lacked godly teaching and only built up what Hoffman identified as the hellish trinity of pope, emperor, and false teachers.[17] Throughout this early period strong lines of mystical apocalypticism are combined with a continued emphasis upon traditional Lutheran themes. Hoffman's preaching could produce not only great despair but also enthusiasm for what lay at time's doorstep.[18] This sense of living on the edge of history was so powerful for Hoffman that he would eventually be led to identify consciously with the role of Elijah *redivivus*.[19]

Driven out of Stockholm and then Lübeck, Hoffman moved on to Schleswig-Holstein where he continued his activity as a lay preacher.[20] Early in 1527 he worked with Marquard Schuldorp in the Nikolaikirche in Kiel, but the relationship was not smooth with either Schuldorp or the city council. Hoffman found himself faced with charges of radical apocalyptic and spiritualist teachings and association with Müntzer.[21] In the face of civic unrest and, to better his sullied credentials, Hoffman set out in the spring of 1527 to see Luther once again. On his way to Wittenberg, Hoffman stopped at Magdeburg to visit Luther's associate Nikolaus Amsdorf. Amsdorf had been outspoken in his criticism of Hoffman's exposition of Daniel 12. He seems to have been fearful of any repeat of the unrest associated with the Peasants' War. In an open letter to his Magdeburg congregation, Amsdorf ridiculed Hoffman's prediction of two adventual prophets who would prophesy for three and a half years followed by a period of persecution of equal length prior to Judgment. Hoffman was a self-styled prophet, without a proper calling. He and his false teaching were to be avoided.[22] Perhaps Hoffman sought to find reconciliation with Amsdorf at this time. He was, however, rebuffed by Amsdorf, who had little patience with him.[23]

Hoffman's trip to Wittenberg proved to be a disaster. Apparently neither Luther nor Johannes Bugenhagen approved of Hoffman's allegorical interpretation of Scripture. Later Luther was to write to Wilhelm Pravest in Kiel that Hoffman left in a huff. He was not fit for teaching nor was he called.[24] Still, the breach in relations did not prevent Hoffman from later sending to Luther his defense against what he believed to be Amsdorf's unwarranted criticism.[25] By the summer of 1527 Hoffman was back in Kiel and was perceived positively enough to continue in his work. In light of the controversy created by Hoffman's supervisor, Wilhelm Pravest, who at first culled Luther's favor and then turned on him, even Hoffman appeared not without redeeming qualities despite his radical preaching.[26]

From Kiel, Hoffman answered Amsdorf in a treatise defending his prophetic preaching, his status as a lay preacher, and his method of interpreting Scripture.[27]

He invited Amsdorf to substantiate his criticism through his own interpretation of the central apocalyptic texts of the Bible (Dan. 12; Joel 3; Matt. 24; Luke 21; 2 Thess. 2; Rev. 11 and 12). While no one knows the day or hour of Christ's return, still Paul summons us to watch for the clear sign of Christ's coming, namely the revelation of Antichrist, which is in process now. Hoffman continues by formulating his own teachings on the identity of the two witnesses and the time of the apocalyptic troubles more carefully than he had done in the treatise on Daniel 12: If he had maintained that the two witnesses already lived, he did not mean that they were now preaching.[28]

In a new reply Amsdorf repeated his earlier criticism: Hoffman's eschatological teaching was vain and useless. He neither disclosed who the witnesses were nor when the apocalyptic seven-year scenario was to begin. Christ and his apostles left the final date unspecified. In place of the simple and sincere teaching of Christ, Hoffman's trumpeted deep understanding of apocalyptic mysteries was only satanically inspired crafty wisdom. His teaching was superfluous and his preaching without a proper call.[29] The pamphlet was distributed by Marquard Schuldorp throughout Holstein.

Hoffman answered these charges in another pamphlet,[30] charging Amsdorf with a lying spirit and emphasizing the promise of Christ that all believers in God were called to be kings and priests (Rev. 1:6). With respect to Amsdorf's charge that Hoffman was a preacher without a proper call, Hoffman argued that he had been called by Frederick I, king of Denmark, to his work at Kiel. It was not he, Hoffman, who was the enthusiast and rebel; rather, it was Amsdorf. With respect to his prophecies concerning the adventual witnesses, Hoffman argued that under the criteria set forth by Amsdorf all Old Testament prophecies would then also be senseless for none announces the exact date of its future fulfillment.

By the summer of 1528, following further attacks by Amsdorf over Hoffman's calling and by Schuldorp over his spiritualist sacramental tendencies and moral indiscretion, Hoffman's authority was again questioned by Luther and Melanchthon. Writing to Crown Prince Christian of Denmark, Luther warned of Hoffman's damaging fantasies and slight emphasis upon the important elements of Christian doctrine—belief in Christ and love of one's neighbor.[31] Melanchthon wrote to King Frederick's advisor in Copenhagen, Peter Suave, on the same day, concerned that the king might be unaware of Hoffman's fanatical tendencies.[32]

A disputation was at last called by Frederick I to Flensburg, April 9, 1529.[33] Judged heterodox by the Lutheran establishment, Hoffman was banished. From this point he became more openly sacramentarian in his theology. For him this was a further indication that under the mask of the Reformation a new papacy was hiding.[34]

Hoffman now traveled to East Frisia where he met another disaffected reformer and acquaintance of Hut, Andreas Bodenstein von Karlstadt (c. 1480-1541).[35] From there he headed for Strassburg, the Alsatian city that had become a haven for many religious nonconformists.[36] Hoffman was able to establish an acquaintance with Martin Bucer, former Dominican, preacher of Lutheranism in the Alsace after 1523, and eventual leader of the Reformed Churches in Switzerland and S. Germany. However, the relationship did not last long.[37] Hoffman became increasingly associated with the strong currents of apocalyptic mysticism and Anabaptism in Strassburg, currents capable of stimulating powerful movements of religious and social ferment.[38]

Elijah and the Apostolic Messengers

Melchior Hoffman's theology was challenged and enriched by the contacts he made in Strassburg with two Anabaptist missionary groups: those gathering around William Reublin, Michael Sattler, and Pilgram Marpeck,[39] and those around Hans Denck and Jacob Kautz.[40] Most important, however, was the influence of a third group, the Strassburg prophets.[41] At its center were Lienhard and Ursula Jost and their visions, experienced around the time of the Peasants' War (1525) and in the years 1528-1529. Hoffman's closest followers, those who would make most concrete his prophetic interpretation of Revelation 11 and other apocalyptic texts, were to come from this group.[42]

Ursula Jost's visions dealt with imminent world destruction and renewal. Her prophesying, together with that of her husband and others, contributed to Hoffman's belief that the end times had actually begun. Many of her prophecies were collected by Hoffman in 1530 and published under the title, *Prophetische gesicht und Offenbarung der göttlichen würkung zu diser letsten zeit . . . (Prophetic Visions and Revelations of Godly Activity at This Last Time . . .).*[43] The title page to this work features an engraving showing the two adventual witnesses, Elijah and Enoch, mediating the divine revelation of the end time.[44] According to the introduction as well as in further visions, Ursula Jost was told by God to reveal the future.[45] According to her husband, who interpreted more concretely his wife's visions, Strassburg was to be the spiritual Jerusalem. Out of the city would proceed 144,000 apostolic messengers (Hut's converts?) as envisioned in Revelation 14:1. These would preach the true knowledge of Christ in the world and establish a unity between God and humanity based upon the covenant of belief.[46] Some of these prophecies reveal bitter disappointment with existing society and a latent readiness for revolutionary action under the leadership of a charismatic figure.

Many of these visions resembled the preaching of Hans Hut, whose ideas may have been mediated through Barbara Rebstock[47] and other Anabaptist refugees from Augsburg who continued to read current events into an apocalyptic scenario.[48] Such visions included the hope that after a time of imminent trouble, when the pious would find refuge in a free imperial city, saints would take dominion on earth. The Strassburg prophets did not summon believers to procure weapons. Hoffman forbade his apostolic messengers the use of the sword.[49]

A definitive break between Hoffman and the magisterial reformers came in April 1530 when he, together with others, requested a separate church for the Anabaptist community in Strassburg.[50] Hoffman fled Strassburg for Emden in East Frisia. Here he finally joined cause with the Anabaptists, preaching and administering adult baptism to hundreds of people.[51] In the same year he wrote about baptism in *The Ordinance of God*, which had strong eschatological overtones.[52]

By late 1530 Hoffman was back in Strassburg. His prophetic writings now were numerous. In addition to the publication of the visions of Ursula and Lienhard

The Two Witnesses and Spiritual Immedicay—The Dawn of Reformation Preaching

Title page from Melchior Hoffman's book on revelations, *Prophetische Gesicht und Offenbarung* (1530), as found in Peter Kawerau, *Melchior Hoffman als religiöser Denker*. Haarlem: De Erven F. Bohn, 1954.

Jost,[53] Hoffman had written *Prophecy from Holy Divine Scripture: Concerning the Distresses of This Last Time . . .*[54]; *Prophecy or Prediction from Holy Divine Scripture: Concerning all the Wonders and Signs . . .*[55]; and *An Exposition of the Secret Revelation of John . . . .*[56] These works, together with Hoffman's later commentary on Romans (1533),[57] provide the main source for Hoffman's later understanding of the place of the adventual witnesses. Together they betray a fascinating concern with a spiritualizing process in history that remains within a broadly conceived Augustinian vision of God's work in time.[58] But whereas Augustine had concentrated on the moral conflict inherent to every age, Hoffman's concern was with a heightened perception of God's developing plan of salvation, a plan marked by different covenant closures.[59]

Hoffman believed that this plan of salvation in history could be discerned in the book of Revelation.[60] Leaving aside his conception of spiritual development ever since the Fall of Mankind, Hoffman believed that God was now fully revealing his will through spiritual prophets who discerned his will in the Apocalypse.[61] The Revelation of John revealed three periods of renewal or awakening since the Resurrection of Jesus: in the Jewish and Gentile missions during the days of the apostles, in the Hussite movement, and in the Reformation of his own day—although Luther and the establishment that had formed around him held to an outmoded form of righteousness and so failed to carry through a complete reform.[62]

Within the time period since Christ, Hoffman elaborated a further distinction. He thought of the millennial kingdom of Christ as occurring in the first thousand years of the Church's history; later he placed more emphasis on a "fall" of the Church much earlier.[63] Deppermann summarizes Hoffman's understanding of this fall in the following way: (1) The Roman bishop appropriated the teaching authority over the entire Church, destroying the role of the laity and thus the original order of the early Church. (2) By his alliance with Constantine, the pope became a temporal prince making possible greater religious coercion and persecution. (3) The Mass replaced the true sacrifice of Christ. (4) The introduction of infant baptism under Innocent I (402–417) and Martin I (649–655) undermined the voluntary nature of the Church. (5) Finally, so-called saints, or new mediators, were introduced between God and man in violation of the explicit command against idolatry (Exodus 20:23).[64]

The beast of Rome was first wounded seriously by the preaching of Hus. The slaying of Hus in 1415 revealed the extent of the unholy alliance of emperor and pope in the attempt at undermining the gospel.[65] The Bohemian Brethren continued the work begun by Hus without, however, realizing the depth of satanic activity. Luther took up the process of reform again but, as Stayer quotes Hoffman, "for his own honor and gain has delivered Christ to crucifixion."[66] Now, as the imperial dragon and papal Antichrist are united on the devil's side, they are opposed by the "Spiritual Elijah" on God's side. The work of Elijah, Hoffman writes, was "to restore everything to its right order, so as to prepare the new heaven and new earth upon which justice will rule and dwell."[67]

In ways similar to Müntzer, Hoffman argued for the necessity of a final Elijah mission, drawing both upon the example of the prophet Elijah and the vision of our two witnesses. As Elijah preached repentance, so too would this latter-day prophet. Summarizing Hoffman, Stayer writes that "Elijah and Enoch, the other witness, were destined to the same fate as Jan Hus—the papal Antichrist would call a council and have them slain at it: 'How this death will occur will be shown in due time.'"[68]

Comparing Hoffman's earlier commentary on Daniel 12 (1526) with the apocalyptic works of 1529–1530, Deppermann argues that Hoffman retained essentially the same sense of the course of the last days.[69] For three and one-half years the gospel would be truly proclaimed with great success even among the Jews (Romans 11:25–32) by apostolic messengers.[70] Following the slaying of the witnesses (Enoch and Elijah), decreed by a general council in the middle of the seven last years of history, three and one-half years of persecution would ensue. During this time the powers of darkness—pope, emperor, and monks—would lead an attack upon the newly established "Spiritual Jerusalem" of God, seeking to destroy it.[71]

As this occurs the Turks, Gog, and Magog (Rev. 20:8), appear. They destroy those in league with anti-Christian forces. As chaos reaches a climax, Judgment breaks in, the kingdom of Christ begins.[72] Throughout this period of apocalyptic fury the true Church will be defended by two pious kings, one of whom Hoffman suggests would be the king of Denmark, Frederick I.

> For it says in Scripture that God alloted and reckoned two wings, two mountains, two horns, and that is two kings, with which he will keep and protect his beloved city and elect people, the New Jerusalem and Bride of the Lord Jesus Christ, four and a half times after the demise of the witnesses as it is described in chapter 12 of this book.[73]

Whether this marks the end of the world or a world revolution is a matter of debate.[74] What is of note is the way in which the account of adventual witnesses is appropriated and lends structure to history. Their preaching provides the model for the work of the 144,000 apostolic messengers whom God would awaken to carry out a final proclamation of the gospel. The fire that proceeds from their mouths (Rev. 11:5) is the fire of the spirit slaying the devil. The shutting of heaven (Rev. 11:6) is the suspension of the preaching of the gospel.[75] The death of the witnesses (Rev. 11:7) marks a change in the Church's condition in history's final countdown.

By 1531 Hoffman was again active in the Netherlands. His principal convert at Emden was John Volkerts (Trijpmaker), "the new Enoch." While in Amsterdam Trijpmaker was arrested and, together with nine other Anabaptists, beheaded on December 5, 1531.[76] In the face of this apparent setback Hoffman counseled a suspension of baptism and a revision of the eschatological timetable.[77] By December 1531, Hoffman was briefly back in Strassburg where his arrest was ordered and certain of his works proscribed.[78] However, in 1532 he was still publishing apocalyptic tracts.[79] His writing must have been popular as he issued a second edition of the prophetic visions of Lienhard Jost.[80] During this period of itinerant evangelical preaching Hoffman's ideas continued to develop more pointed apocalyptic overtones, evident in his commentary on Romans and other treatises based upon Pauline texts.[81] While Hoffman was in Frisia an old man prophesied that Hoffman would be imprisoned for a half year in Strassburg then freed to continue to spread the evangelical truth with the assistance of his supporters throughout the world.[82]

We learn from the later confession of Obbe Philips, a disenchanted Melchiorite, that meditation on this prophecy encouraged Hoffman to return to Strassburg in March 1533. He lived with his disciples in the city, continuing to preach on apocalyptic themes.[83] Hoffman sent a letter to the Strassburg city council in May together with his tract on the use of the sword, describing the strategic role to be played by Strassburg in the impending apocalyptic events.[84] Despite his continued deference to authority he was denounced by a former companion, Claus Frey, and charged with sedition.[85] Hoffman was arrested on May 20, 1533, and placed in prison.[86]

According to Obbe Philips this imprisonment seemed to fulfill in Hoffman's mind the prophecy of the Frieslander, confirming his sense of the impending final years of history.[87] He rejected Claus Frey's accusations[88] but was called back before the city council in June.[89] Judged heterodox in his Spiritualist view of the nature of Christ, his view of the Atonement, hermeneutics, understanding of baptism and forgiveness,[90] Hoffman was imprisoned and placed under custody but given several opportunities to recant.[91]

In Martin Bucer's treatise against Hoffman, written in the summer following Hoffman's imprisonment, Bucer systematically criticized Hoffman's Spiritualist-Anabaptist theology. He rejected Hoffman's idea of Rome as the spiritual Babylon, Strassburg as the spiritual Jerusalem, and the prophets of Strassburg as the 144,000 apostolic messengers, preaching the gospel in the last days.[92] Bucer begins the treatise by referring to Hoffman's supposed apocalyptic role:

> This Melchior Hoffman is seen by his disciples as a great prophet and apostle who was to be raised up in the Netherlands before the great day of the Lord and first bring the real Gospel to all the world.[93]

Throughout the following months the popularity of Hoffman in Strassburg and the Rhine valley is evident through references made to him.[94] Letters between the major reforming figures in the area discuss his person, ideas, and followers.[95] In the "revelations" of the Josts, special prophets in their own right, Hoffman was identified as the adventual Elijah.[96] For many, it seems, Hoffman was this witness, a part of the final apocalyptic scenario pictured in Revelation 11. In September 1534 Hoffman himself acknowledged to his jailor that he was the adventual Elijah foreseen in the Apocalypse.

> Melchior Hoffman said himself, among other things: that he was in the hands of my lords (the council) but that he advised them against doing violence to his innocent blood. One should know that one had in him the legitimate Elijah who should come before the judgment day of Christ. God had sent him to us and we did not want to know him. He would be the last; God would send us no one else, etc.[97]

Even as Hoffman held open this adventual role for himself, others were becoming identified, or were identifying themselves, as the second of the two adventual witnesses.[98] In his confession, Obbe Philips recalled that, with Hoffman and others of his followers in prison or killed, many others arose with further visions. So it was prophesied that either Cornelius Poldermann or Kasper Schwenckfeld was Enoch, and that the 144,000 apostolic messengers would leave Strassburg to preach throughout the earth when Hoffman was released from prison.[99] Philips related:

> Thereafter Elijah and Enoch would stand upon the earth as two torches and olive trees. No one might harm or hinder them; and they should be dressed in sacks; and, if anyone should hinder them, fire would go from their mouths and devour their enemies.[100]

As Philips continues, another prophet, Jan Matthijs, claiming to be Enoch and heir to Trijpmaker, appeared among the Anabaptist groups in the Netherlands in 1534.[101] Hoffman's ideas, always susceptible to misinterpretation, were concretized and perhaps distorted by this prophet (baptized by Hoffman), and by others who claimed to be followers of Hoffman's vision.[102] In terms of the political developments in the Rhineland, Hoffman's support of this disciple was one of his greatest mistakes. The Melchiorites, now dividing into peaceful and bellicose factions, were led on the militant side by Matthijs.[103] Throughout 1533 the city of Münster became dominated by "Anabaptists" (i.e., Melchiorites and followers of others like Bernhard Rothmann). With the reintroduction of baptism by Matthijs, an event only to be resumed in a future New Jerusalem, many began to see Münster rather than Strassburg as that Jerusalem.[104] With Melchiorites swarming in, the city was eventually taken over only to become a byword for the eccentricities of its ill-fated prophets.[105]

Philips tells us that while these events were taking place "Melchior was forgotten with his prophets and prophetesses, with his apostleship of 144,000 true apostles of Christ out of Strassburg, with his Elijah role, and all his boasting."[106] Hoffman languished in prison until his death in 1543 or 1544.[107] So also, Philips continues, Matthijs, our adventual Enoch, met his end in this world. Prior to the downfall of Münster (June 1535) to combined Catholic and Lutheran troops, Matthijs was beaten to death in a skirmish before the gates of the city in April 1534, despite prophecies of his resurrection.[108] Obbe Philips concludes:

> See, dear friends, how we have here the beginning and end of both Elijah and Enoch with their commissions, visions, prophecies, dreams, and revelations. What spirit compelled this performance, office, and commission, I will let each judge for himself.[109]

Luther the Prophet

A measure of late medieval prophetic and apocalyptic speculation coalesced around the name and efforts of Martin Luther (1483–1546). Müntzer, Hut, Hoffman, and even others like Zwingli and similarly inclined reformers, were caught up in the excitement. This sixteenth-century apocalyptic interest in Luther has long been recognized.[110] Our only effort is to see to what extent the theme of the adventual witnesses was a factor in this phenomenon and how it may have been used in the early development of Lutheranism.[111]

Luther himself was interested in prophetic and apocalyptic speculation. His understanding of his recovery of the gospel was set in this context.[112] He has even been characterized as more of a prophet of the last days than a reformer.[113] Luther was at first influenced by some of the same mystical and apocalyptic writings that had been important in the development of Müntzer, Hut, Hoffman, and others.[114] Both the radicals and Luther shared an interest in the steps to salvation outlined in this tradition. Part of the picture of salvation in medieval piety was shaped by the models of spirituality seen in Enoch, Elijah, and the Evangelist John. Speculation on their present existence could fire the imagination.[115] Apoca-

lyptic concerns even seem not to have divided Luther from Hoffman to the same
extent as they divided Amsdorf from Hoffman.[116] While such concerns are not
absent in Luther, they receive a qualitatively different emphasis, and they remain
more general and less focused.[117] Interestingly, while Luther disassociates himself from the idea of latter-day prophets, other elements in Lutheranism do
reflect upon his role as a prophet, even as one of the witnesses.[118] This identity
figured in popular imagination and is noted in the following acrostic:

> *Lautere Evangelisch leer*
> *Uberflüssige gnad des heyligen geists*
> *Trewlicher diener Christi*
> *H bedeut Heliam welche den Endchrist verraten*
> *E bedeut Enoch*
> *Rabi das er ist meister worden aller schriftschender.*[119]

If Luther can be considered as a prophet, his interest in Revelation 11 and
associated themes must be explored.

Following his denial at Leipzig (1519) of the primacy of the pope and the
infallibility of general councils, Luther's interest in apocalyptic material received
a new focus.[120] He increasingly identified with the reformer Hus, seeing in Hus's
work a restoration of evangelical light.[121] The Evangel had been raised up by Hus
and Jerome of Prague to challenge the papacy.[122] For Luther, Hus had correctly
distinguished between the organized church and Augustine's church of the elect.
The papacy was to be scored for its failure to perform its proper pastoral role in
society. By 1520, Luther drew a trajectory of true doctrine in the areas of salvation by grace and ecclesiology from Paul through Augustine and Hus to his own
reforming effort.[123] Later he would write critically of a misplaced emphasis upon
the visible papal church as the kingdom of God in the work of Giovanni Nanni.[124]
The papacy was Antichrist,[125] and Luther was called a Hussite![126] By 1521, a
reform movement centered around his person was well under way.

However, despite an apparent congruence of prophetic and doctrinal arguments,
Luther remained more uneasy with the book of Revelation than with other apocalyptic or prophetic texts of the Bible. The prophecies of Daniel came with that
seer's own inspired interpretation of them.[127] The description of Antichrist in
2 Thessalonians 2:3–4 was Pauline, and it interpreted for Luther developments in
the medieval Church. However, when Luther encountered the writings of others
on the Apocalypse,[128] and certain other works equally critical of the papacy,[129] he
grew more confident in his use of the text. Its message, together with the growth
of the Turkish threat, heresies, sects, and unbelief, signaled the end of the age.

As the question of Antichrist's identity was raised, it was natural to raise also
the question of whom the two witnesses might be.[130] One who asked it was the
Bohemian humanist Ulrichus Velenus in December 1520.[131] Velenus argues that
as Antichrist has been long in the world, so also have been his opponents, the two
witnesses.[132] Both bear moral-representational features. The argument reminds us
of the one advanced by Velenus's compatriot, Matthew of Janov. If the witnesses
were to be specific persons then, Velenus argues (following Jerome), one would

need a physical temple as well. However, all who preach and exhort against Antichrist may be seen as such witnesses. Among them one can point to several outstanding examples, especially Luther and Ulrich von Hutten.[133]

Luther was aware of this use of our text, even of the designation placed upon him as an Elijah.[134] However, while he may have at first entertained the thought of some usefulness of the title, he rapidly moved away from any appropriation of it; the name of Elijah stood for the Elijah spirit, the preaching of the gospel.[135] A revival of gospel hope set within the context of an apocalyptic framework guided Luther's eschatology. Although he believed his evangelical breakthrough might be fit into a temporal scheme of development, this was muted by his belief that the world's last hour began with Christ's first Advent.[136]

Luther has left a trail that allows us to follow the development of this perspective in those crucial early years. His thinking about the name of Elijah begins at least with the completion of his treatise to the German nobility.[137] A similar reference is found in a letter from the Wartburg, dated May 26, 1521, in which Luther wrote that he was only an "Elijah" in comparison with Melanchthon, his "Elisha."[138] In September, he writes somewhat remorsefully that he had failed to play the role of Elijah at the Diet of Worms.[139] More pointedly, in his sermon for Christmas Day, which he was preparing at this time, Luther dealt with the implied question of Hebrews 1:2, namely, Who should preach in "these last days." His answer is, Christ through the gospel. He is willing to entertain the idea of a returning Elijah, particularly in a representative sense, but does not extend such speculation to Enoch or the Evangelist John.

> What does one say then of Elijah and Enoch that they shall come against Antichrist? I answer: About the coming of Elijah I am caught between heaven and earth and waver much harder toward the idea that he will not come bodily, but I do not fight hard against it. I leave it to be believed or not, do what one will. I know well that St. Augustine says at one place [De civ. dei, xx, 29] . . . that the return of Elijah . . . is firmly in the mind of Christians. But I know well that no Scripture bears witness to it.[140]

Any scriptural expectation of a return of Elijah is fulfilled in John the Baptist as Christ himself says clearly in Matthew 11:14. Luther continues:

> Thus, I know nothing of a further return of Elijah. Except that his spirit, that is God's word, will be brought back again as is now going on. It is no longer of any doubt to me that the Pope, together with the Turk, is the Antichrist. Believe what you will.[141]

In a sermon listed for the day of John the Baptist, June 24, 1522, Luther asks the question of what it means to come in the spirit of Elijah. His answer includes the warning of coming wrath and the counsel of faith.[142] During Advent of 1522, Luther went further and clearly argued that there will be no other Elijah than John the Baptist. All the Laws and the prophets predict John. This is the way in which Malachi's prophecy must be understood.[143] The last preaching before the Day of Judgment is the preaching of the Evangel through which Christ comes to the whole world. It is for this that John came:

Therefore we hold to this, that the last preaching before Judgment Day is the Gospel through which Christ is come to all the world, and before this preaching and coming John came, and prepared the way.[144]

On the basis of the prophecy in Malachi, the Jews still look for a bodily Elijah before Judgment. Some Christians say that Elijah should return, others that Enoch should come as well, still others that John should return. But there is no scriptural warrant to expect an Enoch or John the Evangelist or any other personage.

If he (Malachi) speaks of the last day, the expectation of Elijah is certain, for God will not lie. But that Enoch or John should also come is not grounded in Scripture. Therefore it is to be held as a fable and a tale. But if he speaks of the future of Christ in flesh and word, it is certain that we have to await no further Elijah, but John is the same Elijah about whom Malachi preached.[145]

The question of adventual prophets continued to persist, but Luther's answer remained the same.[146] Later in his life, two years after the debacle at Münster, it is discussed in the annotations on the book of Matthew (1538) in relation to the Transfiguration of Jesus (Matt. 17:1–13).

An old opinion of the return of Elijah and Enoch after Antichrist is developed out of this place (where Christ says: Elijah will come and restore all things, etc.). It fills all the books and wanders about the whole church. For this reason this question would have to be treated here if we were able to state something beyond the authority of the ancients.[147]

Once again, Luther applies the prophecy of Elijah's return to John the Baptist. As the angel Gabriel in Luke 1:17 refers the prophecy of Malachi to John, so the words of Isaiah 7:14 apply to the child born of Mary. Just as another child is not expected of her, so there is no other Elijah than the one brought forth by Zacharias and Elizabeth. The angel offers the interpretation, and Christ clarifies it in Matthew 17:12 and 11:14 with the statement that Elijah has come in the person of John the Baptist.[148]

The apocalyptic significance of the times, however, continued to bear down upon Luther's interpretation; he believed he was living at the end of the time of witness. For Luther, three periods of history correspond to three witness-missions: Enoch is the witness of hope for those who lead lives of righteousness during the first period of history. Elijah is the witness to the rewards available for those who keep the Law at the time of the second world, the period of Mosaic law. Current history participates in the third and final world with Christ as its witness, the Evangel being his last word and his promise that the life which was lost in paradise will be restored.[149] Enoch and Elijah were witnesses to their respective ages and were translated to give hope to their time, not to be brought back at the end of history. Reflecting on his own role and that of his followers, Luther wrote at the end of his life:

I believe that we are the last trumpet which prepares for and precedes the advent of Christ. Therefore, although indeed we are infirm and scarcely do we sound in the presence of the world, yet we sound greatly in the assembly of the heavenly angels who will follow us and our horn and thus make the end.[150]

Luther had a strong sense of standing at the end of history, that perhaps his preaching was part of a final proclamation of the gospel before Judgment. However, he never conceived of himself in a unique way as one of the two adventual witnesses pictured in our text. This is different from what we have noted in Müntzer, Hut, and Hoffman. For both Müntzer and Hut a radical disjunction separates this age from the ideal order of God's kingdom. Adventual prophets serve as agents for bringing about a new congruity between future reality and present existence. Luther differs from Hoffman not only over the question of the appearance of adventual prophets, but also over their significance in the sequence of spiritual history. While Luther recognized the prophecy, knew of its association with Antichrist, he rejected any literal use of it. If prophets appeared in society they would be prophets primarily for their moral and spiritual qualities rather than because of the time of their appearance. Luther read the book of Revelation in the light of the moral conflict that it portrayed in what he perceived as the closing days of history. He never used the Apocalypse itself as the basis for special wisdom about the last days.[151] Just the opposite; when he did come to appropriate the book more fully it was to find in it a confirmation of God's graciousness through time.[152]

While Hoffman remained with Luther within a general Augustinian framework, never developing a future millennial age in a new historical era, still he found the future outlined and a deeper spiritual discernment called for in the text. As messianic troubles increase, God reveals deeper spiritual knowledge to his prophets and prophetesses. For Hoffman and kindred spirits this knowledge includes insight into God's plans for history and the necessary behavior appropriate for different historical periods (e.g., when to suffer the slanders of the ungodly, when to exercise righteous vengeance, what can be expected in the work of mission).[153] Hoffman's figural understanding of Scripture provided the rationale for reading into the apocalyptic scenario of Revelation 11 not only the means for marking out a final seven-year period of history, divided by the deaths of the two witnesses, but also a pattern for understanding the entirety of history.

Luther had much of the same sense of expectancy.[154] He perceived his own day as standing on the threshold of the return of the Lord.[155] However, proximity to the end did not mean new spiritual insight. Rather, it called for a greater degree of attention to the moral and doctrinal purity of the Church. Even as the Church, the body of Christ, will exist to the end of the world, so also will evil be manifest in a concrete form. This evil, even Antichrist, will find its way into the innermost courts of true religion symbolized in the temple of the Apocalypse (Rev. 11:1–2).[156] Luther believed that the last period of history belonged to this anti-Christian embodiment of evil. That period began in the seventh century with the agreement between the Emperor Phocas and Pope Boniface III recognizing the universal primacy of the Roman church.[157] It would last until the return of Christ, intensifying in the end with the exposure of evil.[158]

Having early in his work adopted the prevailing interpretation of the prophet Daniel's envisioned four world kingdoms, the last being that of Rome whose fall would coincide with the end of the world,[159] the book of Revelation came to more or less prefigure the chief eras of Church history in Luther's mind.[160] He drew the conclusion that the seals adumbrated physical or political evils; the trumpets represented the spiritual evils by which the Church suffers from the beginning of the Christian era to the present. The first four trumpeting angels represented works-righteousness (Tatian), enthusiasm (Marcion), philosophy (Origen), and the quest for unwarranted purity (Novatian).[161] The three woes that beset the Church (Rev. 9:1–12; 9:13–11:14; 11:15–19) are Arius, the Turks, and the papacy, particularly as the latter increased in dominion.[162] This pattern of declension in the era of Christ's first Advent paralleled that of previous historical eras which had ended with the Flood and the Advent of Christ. History ended with acts of God's Judgment, which was merciful even in its severity.[163]

Deeply impressed with papal hypocrisy, Luther interpreted the vision of the mighty angel who gives the sweet-bitter book to the seer (Rev. 10:8–10) of the papacy.[164] In chapter 11 of Revelation the popes are seen to measure the temple (Rev. 11:1–2) with their laws and regulations, establishing a mere formal church with an outward show of holiness. Then, for Luther, two comforting visions (*Trostbilder*) are given between this view of the papacy (ending at Rev. 11:2) and a further discussion of the two beasts (Rev. 13:1–18). These are the two witness-preachers (Rev. 11:3–13) and the woman who, together with her child, the true Church, is protected in the wilderness during the time of the beast's reign (Rev. 12:1–17).[165] Through the pressure of contemporary events Luther became more certain that God continually sends his Elijahs to work toward the restoration of his Church.[166] Luther's reading of the Apocalypse together with the book of Daniel encouraged him to think that a final flowering of the Church might now be occurring.[167]

Many people, however, were convinced that some of the general prophecies concerning the end were coming to a head in Luther. For some this was merely a recognition that Luther was a religious genius. Parallels were drawn between Luther and his enemies, and Christ or Paul, Peter, and Elijah and their enemies. For some Luther was more than this, perhaps the angelic preacher of Revelation 14:6 or even one of our adventual witnesses. As we have noted throughout, the roots for this identification reach back into biblical and legendary material developed throughout the medieval period. At any rate, the idea that Luther was either an Elijah of the last days, or one of the adventual witnesses of the Apocalypse, or at least a model prophet, is well attested.[168]

The Eternal Gospel

Whatever Luther's own reservations may have been, the pressure of the polemical situation pushed the designation forward. This was particularly true if the pope was conceived to be truly the Antichrist, standing parallel to the devil. Luther could then be seen as a human parallel to Christ, the counterpart to the evil that is becoming fully manifest in the last days.[169] In a popular work of the period, Michael Stifel, an Augustinian and disciple of Luther, identified Luther with the angel of Revelation 14:6, who proclaims the eternal gospel to all the inhabitants of the earth, warning of God's imminent Judgment.[170]

In tracing the origins of such honorific references to Luther, Gussman points out that the oldest mention takes us back to Huldrych Zwingli.[171] In a report to his friend and fellow reformer, Oswald Myconius of Luzern, dated January 4, 1520, Zwingli tells of his exchange of thoughts with Ulrich Zasius.[172] Zasius had praised Luther and Andreas Karlstadt, glorifying Luther as "theologorum Phoenix." Apparently, this gave Zwingli the courage to call Luther "Elijah," a title that Zasius in turn was not quite prepared to accept.[173]

Melanchthon did as much as any in stimulating this apocalyptic vision of Luther. Times had reached such a crisis point that extreme care and attention needed to be given to a proper understanding of the Bible. Biblical exegesis, the prophecy of Elijah, the precarious state of Christendom, and the Turkish menace—these and other signs all pointed to the fact that these times were indeed the last days.[174] In a letter written by Melanchthon to Georg Spalatin on February 3, 1521, Luther is referred to as "Hercules noster."[175] Again, Luther was one upon whom the spirit of Elijah had descended in his conflict with the prophets of the new Baal, the priests of the papacy, and Antichrist.[176] In writing to Spalatin a further time Melanchthon makes reference to the Apocalypse commentary by Joachim of Fiore in which the abbot illustrated how the papacy of the future would take on the characteristics of Antichrist. In this context, he refers to Luther as "the Elijah" in these latter times.[177]

This view of Luther began to catch on in the early 1520s. In a pamphlet that appeared in 1521 the writer rejoiced that God had sent Elijah out of paradise. Luther has come from God to reveal the secret and subtle conduct of Antichrist and his messengers. He is filled with the fervency of spirit characteristic of Elijah.[178] The phrases of the time that refer to Luther see him as the "Elijah of this most ruinous and last age," "Martin—in the spirit of Elijah," "God has awakened for us such an Elijah," "Elijah of the last times, who restores all things," and "Luther = Moses, John, Elijah and Enoch in one person." Others saw in Luther and Melanchthon the spirit of Elijah and Enoch and date letters from this "Elijah's" appearance.[179]

The social effect of such conceptions of Luther, in part engendered by him and in part by the hopes of those around him, gave shape to the movement he helped to spawn.[180] A new vision of history, a redefinition of Christian categories in line with that historical understanding, gave shape to a new understanding of the Church, a pattern that we have seen at work since the High Middle Ages.[181] The influence of this historical vision and its institutional embodiment was sufficiently persuasive to propel the Reformation in its Lutheran phase, as would also be the case for the Reformed, to its religious and political success. As would be the case for all later such corporate successes, the movement became "branded" and artistically depicted in the mind of the sixteenth century. The woodcuts produced by Lucas Cranach illustrated the new eschatological understanding as would scores of similar drawings through the next hundred years.[182] In a woodcut at the time of his death Luther is presented on a par with Moses who led the people out of Egypt, with Elijah who will restore all things, and with the prophet John Hus.[183]

Following Luther's death (1546) the idea of Luther as a God-ordained prophet, even a third Elijah, was further etched into people's minds by the polemical situation into which Lutheranism was now drawn. That situation could be defined as Lutheranism against competing confessional positions (Roman Catholicism, the Reformed, and perceived radicals in either confession and/or practice) as well as factional disputes within Lutheranism itself. Both sets of conflicts had their effect upon the way in which our text was read giving designation to Luther as the end-time prophet.[184]

Within Lutheranism this apocalyptic or acute prophetic consciousness grew through the sixteenth century. After open conflict developed between Melanchthon together with his colleagues (Philippists) and Nikolaus von Amsdorf and his colleagues (Gnesio-Lutherans) over theological compromise associated with the so-called Interims of 1548 (Augsburg and Leipzig), such sensibility was heightened in that line of Lutheran thought charted by Amsdorf and then Matthias Flacius Illyricus and the Magdeburg ministers.[185] Ritschl argues that the Gnesio-Lutherans, in their fear of Philippist synergism, furthered the idea that Luther had come as the third Elijah through whom God reestablished the true religion in the last times.[186]

Flacius's renowned effort to discover and lay out the history of that true religion, discerned wherever he discovered Luther's doctrine of the justification of faith by grace alone, is seen in its proper apocalyptic dress when we place his efforts in the context of a structure of history envisioned through our text. In the *Catalogus Testium Veritatis* (1556), Flacius notes those who were the true prophets of God while the Church came progressively under the influence of the "Papal Antichrist" until it was liberated by Martin Luther.[187] Here Flacius writes that God sends his Elijahs perpetually in order to console the Church. Quoting from Revelation 11, he notes that in the last time preachers will come like Enoch and Elijah to unveil the papal Antichrist.[188] Then, in his *Glossa Compendiaria*, Flacius speaks of our witnesses as prophets who testify to the truth and oppose error. They are not a literal Enoch and Elijah, an idea refuted by Christ and Jerome (in his letter to Marcella). Although it is difficult, he admits, to say much about when they will appear, the fact that the two witnesses are prophets, preachers, or pious doctors during the time of the greatest infamy of Antichrist is beyond doubt. Their death and resurrection illustrate the way in which parents are revivified in their children, or teachers in their disciples—as Elijah was in John the Baptist or Luther.[189] Earlier, in his inaugural address at the University of Jena (1557), Flacius made this more specific by pointing to Luther as the third Elijah who was sent by God before the Day of Judgment.[190]

Flacius's intent appears to have been to illustrate the point that truth is never fully defeated but has its witnesses in all periods of history. Still, Luther and the Reformation are cast into a light that makes the times not only one with that of earlier witnesses of the truth, but something distinctly more.[191] Flacius writes of Luther in terms of the expected twofold coming of Elijah, first in John the Baptist prior to the first Advent of Christ, and again in Luther before the second Advent. In both (this) "Elijah" is viewed as a precursor of the Advent of Christ.[192]

Similar apocalyptic reflection may be found among the Lutheran grouping centered around Andreas Osiander,[193] who feared that the Augsburg Interim represented the three and one-half years of final temptation of the elect prior to the emptying of God's vials of wrath envisioned in Revelation 11:11—implying in its way the identity of our witnesses. Other Lutherans like Andreas Musculus and Jacob Andreae shared this assessment. Nevertheless, Barnes argues, having culled a rich store of material, "Gnesio-Lutherans, Philippists and other factions did not differ in their central eschatological teachings."[194]

Following Osiander's death (1552), Johann Funck continued Osiander's theological efforts. Funck's commentary on Revelation understood the angel with the eternal gospel and the two adventual witnesses as referring to Luther.[195] The 1260 days of witness-preaching (Rev. 11:3) were viewed as 1260 years running from either A.D. 257 or 261 to A.D. 1517 or 1521. They corresponded to a period of religious declension in the Church beginning with the appearance of Paul of Samosata, the first significant heretic in the history of the Church in Funck's opinion. The power of the spirit of Antichrist was now broken with the evangelical preaching of Luther.[196]

The success of this view of Luther was grounded in the reformer's own self-consciousness. Luther believed his work had delivered a severe blow to the papacy.[197] God had brought about the Reformation because of the failure of pope and council to reform the Church. Therefore, in Luther's understanding, there remained nothing further than for Christ himself to reform the Church through the gospel.[198] For many of his followers this meant: Luther is the bearer of that gospel in the days of its final proclamation. He is the preaching angel with the "eternal gospel." He is a final witness as he preaches penance, encourages belief, the true worship of God, and warns of the approaching Judgment. He is God's man, the third Elijah who reveals the work of Antichrist before the arrival of Christ himself, an assessment shared by a wide body of Lutheran luminaries.[199]

As the sixteenth century moved on toward its own closure and the social apocalypse offered up in the Thirty Years War (1618–1648), this desire to make Luther and his prophetic standing absolute continued unabated in its search for confirming evidence in the wider realm of prophecies, signs, and wonders. Despite Luther's earlier caution, he had set a pattern for such apocalyptic corroboration, as prophecy and understanding sought to confirm each other. Reflection about the time and identity of our witnesses and the events of which they were purported to be a part continued to grow, fueled by factional debate and the polemics of the Reformation.

Earlier scholarship, such as that by Will-Erich Peuckert, has traced much of this apocalyptic interest in its highly speculative, astrological, and mystical dimensions, a kind of early modern "New Age" spirituality that the Lutheran establishment increasingly rejected by the early seventeenth century.[200] As Barnes demonstrates, this rejection of the validity granted apocalyptic speculation sundered a relationship between biblical prophecy and general knowledge that had a deep resonance upon the development of knowledge and understanding, releasing the quest for knowledge to follow a path of "rationalistic individualism" while believers backed away from the collective significance of apocalyptic hope to a quietistic devotion, which served to nurture a coming age of Pietism.[201] The identity of the adventual witnesses continued as a theme in the history of that Pietism,[202] but was muted in its apocalyptic and collective hope, the nature of which became more representative of Reformed meliorism, or theories of progress.

Such muted hopefulness was evident not only in Lutheran Orthodoxy; but even among the Melchiorites, now Mennonites, the two witnesses appear to have been redefined as "Christ Jesus, His Word and Spirit." Speaking pointedly of the tradition of Elijah's return, Menno Simons concludes:

> Therefore, one of two things must follow: either we are not going to have any Elijah any more, since John was the Elijah who was to come; or if an Elijah should still come, he must propose and teach us nothing but the foundation and Word of Christ according to the Scriptures. For Christ is the man who sits upon David's throne and shall reign forever in the kingdom, house, and congregation of Jacob.[203]

The prophets, our two witnesses, who had at first been so vivid in the minds of many at the onset of Luther's reform, were now largely symbolic of the consolation offered believers. The apocalyptic structure in which Luther's reform had been cast receded before new directions in society and a theology driven by a formal grace and forensic justification. It was now left to the Reformed to nuance the apocalyptic framework differently so as to provide, by way of a different historical paradigm, a way for our witnesses to become symbols of the reconstruction of Christendom, God's New Jerusalem.

Notes

1. Wolfgang Schäufele, *Das missionarische Bewusstsein und Wirken der Taufer* (Neukirchen: Neukirchen Verlag, 1966), p. 86; cf. Geroge Williams on the radical missionary impulse and early typologies for conceiving such, in *The Radical Reformation* (Philadelphia: Westminster Press, 1962), pp. 832–45.

2. Modern critical scholarship on Melchior Hoffman [variant spelling, Hofmann] begins with two studies in the nineteenth century: W. I. Leendertz, *Melchior Hofmann* (Haarlem: De Erven F. Bohn, 1883); and Friedrich Otto zur Linden, *Melchior Hofmann, ein Prophet der Wiedertäufer* (Haarlem: De Erven F. Bohn, 1885). Two recent studies deserve special mention: Peter Kawerau, *Melchior Hoffman als religiöser Denker* (Haarlem: De Erven F. Bohn, 1954); and Klaus Deppermann, *Melchior Hoffman: Soziale Unruhen und apokalyptische Visionen im Zeitalter der Reformation* (Göttingen: Vandenhoeck und Ruprecht, 1979). Deppermann traces the career of Hoffman, analyzes groups of his followers and relates his religious activity to its social context. Of special interest for this study is the extent to which Hoffman uses a theology of apocalyptic prophets. Deppermann's argument concentrates on an attempt to understand the development and change of Hoffman's ideas over time. In this he makes a significant advance over Kawerau's earlier topical approach to Hoffman. Further, Deppermann is interested as an historian in the social context for both Hoffman's ideas and the nature of his appeal as well as political opposition. Deppermann's study is now standard for all research on Hoffman and offers a helpful listing of Hoffman's works (pp. 345–49). See pp. 26–35 of Deppermann for historiographical summary.

3. Deppermann cites three possible influences upon Hoffman's eschatology in Livonia: (1) The apocalyptic ideas of the commentary on Revelation by John Purvey, student of Wyclif, published on Luther together with an introduction (1528). Purvey equated the papacy and Antichrist, arguing that the power of the word of Christ and the sword of the

emperor would destroy papal power. (2) The anti-papal apocalyptic propaganda of Johannes Hilten (late fifteenth century) who in his works on Daniel and Revelation prophesied that the papacy and monasticism would be destroyed around 1516 by an "irresistible monk." (3) Radical Hussite ideas which were current in the area. Hoffman will celebrate Hussitism as marking a third entrance of the Holy Spirit into the world, after the Jewish and Gentile missions of the early Church (Deppermann, *Hoffman*, pp. 70–71). Compare the older study by Leonid Arbusow, *Die Einführung der Reformation in Liv-Est- und Kurland* (Leipzig: M. Heinsius Nachfolger, 1921), pp. 154ff.; and Mark A. Noll, "Melchior Hofmann and the Lutherans: 1525–1529" (M.A. thesis, Trinity Evangelical Divinity School, Deerfield, Ill., 1972).

4. Deppermann, *Hoffman*, p. 49. Cf. Noll, "Hofmann," pp. 9ff; esp. Werner O. Packull who takes note of the social and psychological factors pushing Hoffman to the fringes in his "Melchior Hoffman's Experience in the Livonian Reformation: The Dynamics of Sect Formation," MQR, 59 (1985):130–46.

5. Deppermann, *Hoffman*, p. 50. Linden suggests that the Dorpat council was disturbed by Hoffman's allegorical and spiritualist emphasis as well as his chiliasm and possible associations with Müntzer (*Melchior Hofmann*, p. 58). Noll argues that there is little foundation for these claims at this period ("Hofmann," p. 23).

6. Luther, WA, 18, pp. 417–30. Hoffman's document "Jesus der christlichen gemeyn . . ." is found on pp. 426–30. Cf. Linden, *Melchior Hofmann*, p. 61; for an English translation, cf. Noll, "Hofmann," pp. 34–73.

7. Linden, *Melchior Hofmann*, p. 63; cf. Noll, "Hofmann," pp. 60–73. Hoffman appears to have satisfied the Wittenberg theologians on three important points: (1) righteousness through faith alone, (2) predestination, (3) renunciation of politically seditious ideas.

8. See the letter to Luther from the Livonians, WABr, 4, p. 202; cf. Noll, "Hofmann," p. 76.

9. Deppermann lists the two as nos. 2 and 3 on pp. 345–46. The titles are: "An de gelöfighen vorsambling inn Liflandt ein korte formaninghe . . . ," and "Das XII Capitel des propheten Danielis aussgelegt . . . ," 1526. I will rely upon Deppermann for my references to the Daniel commentary as its accessibility is limited.

10. Linden, *Melchior Hofmann*, p. 82.

11. Deppermann, *Hoffman*, pp. 65–68.

12. Ibid., p. 67. *Hoffman*, "Daniel," g1b–g2a, g4a as cited in Deppermann: "Und ist ytzt (1526) der schall der sechsten busaun/und ist eyn gut geschrey/von Christus und dem wort gottes über den falschen hirdten und endechrist und über seinem Anhangk. . . . Sobald die sybend busaun gehn wird und die sechst aus ist/sollen in der sybenden busaun alle ding erfüllet werden . . . die busaun soll clingen/oder der endechrist soll so lange regieren nemlich . . . fierd halb jar. . . . Auch sprechen etliche/so man den leuten wirt sagen/dass nicht mer auff erden zeit ist/biss zum Jüngsten Tag/dann syben jar . . . so werden die leute nicht arbeiten."

13. Ibid., p. 65.

14. Ibid., p. 66.

15. Ibid.

16. Deppermann, *Hoffman*, p. 67; cf. Luther, WA, 10.1.2, pp. 93–120.

17. Ibid., p. 69.

18. Ibid., pp. 71–72.

19. See above, p. 195.

20. Deppermann, *Hoffman*, pp. 84–85.

21. Ibid., pp. 89–96. On his work in Kiel, see Richard G. Bailey, "Melchior Hoffman: Proto-Anabaptist and [first] Printed in Kiel, 1527–1529," CH, 59 n. 2 (1990):175–90.

22. Nikolaus Amsdorf, "Ein vormanung an die von Magdeburg das si sich für falschen Propheten zu hüten wissen," (1527) in Leendertz, *Hofmann*, pp. 364–67; cf. Deppermann, *Hoffman*, pp. 97–98.

23. Luther, in a warning letter, had told Amsdorf not to receive Hoffman with kindness; Hoffman should return to his vocation and cease prophesying until properly heard and judged: "Melchiorem illum prophetam Livoniensem si venerit, ne suscipias amice, neque familiariter. . . . Si venerit, iube eum suae vocationi h.e. pellificio intendere et a prophetando vacare cessareque, donec in ecclesiam admissus fuerit, auditus et iudicatus." Luther to Amsdorf, May 17, 1527, in WABr, 4, p. 202.

24. Deppermann, *Hoffman*, pp. 98–99; cf. Luther's letter to Wilhelm Pravest, March 14, 1528, WABr, 4, p. 412.

25. See Luther's letter to Amsdorf, December 30, 1527, WABr, 4, p. 311.

26. Mark Noll, "Luther Defends Melchior Hofmann," SCJ, 4 (1973):47–60.

27. Deppermann, *Hoffman*, pp. 99–100; cf. no. 4, p. 346: "Dat Nikolaus Amsdorff der Meydeborger Pastor/nicht weth/wat he setten/schriuen edder swetzen schal/darmede he syne 17 gen bestedigen m7ge/und synen gruweliken anlop" (1528).

28. Ibid., p. 100.

29. Ibid., pp. 100–101.

30. Deppermann, *Hoffman*, pp. 101–2; cf. no. 5, p. 346: "Das Niclas Amsdorff der Magdeburger Pastor ein lugenhafftiger falscher nasen geist sey. . . ."

31. Luther to Prince Christian, July 7, 1528, WABr, 4, pp. 503–5.

32. Melanchthon to Peter Suave, July 7, 1528: CR, 1, p. 993.

33. Deppermann, *Hoffman* pp. 109–19.

34. Kawerau, *Hoffman religiöser Denker*, p. 94.

35. Deppermann, *Hoffman*, pp. 133–38.

36. Ibid., p. 149. Prior to Hoffman's arrival, Wolfgang Capito, together with Matthew and Catherine Zell, was largely responsible for Strassburg's relatively tolerant policy toward religious separatists. See James M. Kittelson, *Wolfgang Capito, From Humanist to Reformer* (Leiden: E. J. Brill, 1975), pp. 171–206.

37. Manfred Krebs and Hans Georg Rott, eds. *Quellen zur Geschichte der Täufer, Elsass I und II* (Gütertsloh: Gerd Mohn, 1959, 1960), p. 240.

38. Their popularity can be seen in the development of lay piety in Strassburg, e.g., in the preaching of Clement Ziegler, and in the appeal of special prophets, e.g., the visions of Venturinus (Krebs and Rott, *Elsass* I, pp. 253–56; WABr, 5, p. 425). On the social ramifications of religious nonconformity, see Claus-Peter Clasen, *Anabaptism. A Social History, 1525–1618* (Ithaca: University of Cornell Press, 1972), pp. 324ff; cf. Deppermann, *Hoffman*, pp. 140–44, who discusses such social factors contributing to apocalyptic speculation.

39. Deppermann, *Hoffman*, pp. 158–59, 231–35.

40. Ibid., pp. 163–69.

41. Ibid., pp. 178–86. Cf. Timotheus Wilhelm Rörich, "Zur Geschichte der Strassburgischen Wiedertäufer in den Jahren 1527 bis 1543," ZHT, 30 (1860):3–121.

42. Ursula Jost reports the date 1524 for the first visions and 1530 for the last. See Heinhold Fast, ed., *Der linke Flügel der Reformation* (Bremen: Schunemann Verlag, 1962), pp. 300–1, 304–5. Cf. Krebs and Rott, *Elsass* II, nr. 444, p. 184; of Williams's *Radical Reformation*, pp. 370–73, 388–90, 405–10.

43. The title is *Prophetische gesicht und Offenbarung/der götlichen würckung zu diser letsten zeit/die vom XXIIIj. jahr biss in dz XXX. einer gottes liebhaberin durch den heiligen geist geoffenbart seindl . . .* ; Deppermann, *Hoffman*, nr. 12, p. 347; for extracts, see Fast, ed., *Der linke Flügel*, pp. 298–308.

44. A reproduction is in Kawerau, *Hoffman religiöser Denker*, p. 100.

45. Fast, *Der linke Flügel*, pp. 300ff. See the introduction and vision 4. Fast includes the following visions among his extracts: introduction, 1, 2, 3, 4, 16, 32, 34, 41, 74, 75, 76, 77. Note the vision of a tree with many leaves out of the base of which came a brook. Two men appear who turn the course of the brook up the tree to feed the many leaves of the tree as well as to provide drink for a multitude drawn to it (p. 303, no. 34).

46. Krebs and Rott, *Elsass* II, no. 444, pp. 184–85. See also Williams, *Radical Reformation*, pp. 262–63; and Deppermann, *Hoffman*, pp. 181–85.

47. Krebs and Rott, *Elsass* II, no. 362, p. 13; nr. 540, p. 304.

48. Krebs and Rott, *Elsass*, I, no. 116, pp. 138–44.

49. James M. Stayer, *Anabaptists and the Sword* (Lawrence: Coronado Press, 1972), pp. 213–26, esp. p. 223.

50. Krebs and Rott, *Elsass* I, nr. 211, pp. 261–62. Note apocalyptic rationale based on Rev. 12.

51. See the evidence for this in Linden, *Melchior Hofmann*, pp. 225–38; cf. Stayer, *Anabaptists*, p. 211, for Hoffman's relations with other Anabaptist groups.

52. Deppermann, *Hoffman*, no. 14, p. 347: *Die Ordonnantie Godts/De welcke hy/door zijnen Soone Christum Jesum/inghestelt ende bevesticht heeft/op die waerachtighe Discipulen des eeuwigen woort Godts.* An English translation may be found in Williams and Mergal, *Spiritual and Anabaptist Writers* (Philadelphia: Westminster Press, 1958), pp. 182–203. Cf. Stayer, *Anabaptists*, pp. 212ff.

53. The collection of Lienhard's visions is apparently lost. See Krebs and Rott, *Elsass* I, no. 210, p. 259. For an indication of the contents and way in which Lienhard Jost made more concrete his wife's prophecies, see Krebs and Rott, *Elsass* II, no. 444, pp. 184–85.

54. Deppermann, *Hoffman*, no. 9, pp. 346–47 (1529): *Weissagung usz heiliger götlicher geschrifft. Von den trübsalen diser letsten zeit. . . .*

55. Ibid., nr. 10, p. 347 (1530): *Prophezey oder weissagung uss warer heiliger götlicher schrift. Von allen wundern und zeichen/biss zu der zükünfft Christi Jesu vnnsers heyllands. . . .*

56. Ibid., no. 11, p. 347 (1530): *Ausslegung der heimlichen Offenbarung Joannis. . . .* The dedicatory address to this work appears in Fast, ed., *Der linke Flügel*, pp. 308–18.

57. Ibid., no. 21, p. 348: *Die eedele hoghe ende troostlike sendebreif/den die heylige Apostel Paulus to den Romeren gescreeuen heeft. . . .*

58. Stayer, *Anabaptists*, p. 217.

59. Hoffman delineates his idea of covenant closures in *Das ware trostliche und freudenreiche Evangelion* (1531), no. 16, p. 348. See Deppermann, *Hoffman*, pp. 217–26. The idea that God has different ethical injunctions for different periods of history was developed by Bernhard Rothmann, who was commissioned during the period of the Anabaptist kingdom in Münster to explain the way of God to his elect. Unlike Hoffman, Rothmann believed that the age of the gospel, with its emphasis upon patience and suffering, had now been superseded by a third age, which held apostolic aggression to be both valid and virtuous. See Bernhard Rothmann, *Die Schriften Bernhard Rothmanns: Die Schriften der Münsterischen Täufer und ihrer Gegner*, Vol. 1. R. Stupperich, ed. (Münster, 1970), pp. 281, 323–33, 346.

60. My reading of Hoffman's *Offenbarung* is dependent upon selections found in Deppermann, Fast, and Stayer; here, see Fast, *Der linke Flügel*, p. 313.

61. Ibid., pp. 309–10.

62. Deppermann, *Hoffman*, p. 219; cf. Stayer, *Anabaptists*, pp. 217–18. On the possible connection between Hoffman's tripartite scheme of history and that of Peter John Olivi, see Werner O. Packull, "A Reinterpretation of Melchior Hoffman's Exposition against

the Background of Spiritualist Franciscan Eschatology with Special Reference to Peter John Olivi," in Irvin Horst, ed., *The Dutch Dissenters* (Leiden: Brill, 1986), pp. 32–65. Hoffman, like Olivi, kept all of Christian history under Christ and, therefore, can be seen as "Augustinian."

63. In his commentary on the Apocalypse Hoffman sketched his initial understanding of the millennium. In his exegesis of Romans, written three years later, he offered a more pessimistic outlook. See Stayer, *Anabaptists*, p. 217; Hoffman, *Offenbarung*, sig. X4vo, X5ro and *Römerbrief*, sig. O8vo.

64. Deppermann, *Hoffman*, pp. 219–20.

65. Deppermann quotes Hofmann: "Ich meyn zu Costentz hatt der grundt sich wol erzeiget/da das Evangelion verdampt ward/der zeug Gottes verbrant/und der Trach Sigismundus dem Bapst die füss küsset." Ibid., p. 220; Hoffman, *Offenbarung*, sig. K4b, P76–P8a.

66. Stayer, *Anabaptists*, p. 218.

67. Ibid., p. 219.

68. Ibid.

69. Deppermann, *Hoffman*, p. 224.

70. Ibid., pp. 223–24; quoting Hoffman, *Römerbrief*, sig. R8b–S1b.

71. Deppermann, *Hoffman*, p. 224.

72. Ibid., p. 225.

73. Our portion of the prologue reads: "Denn es steht in der Schrift, dass Gott zue dieser Zeit seiner geliebten Stadt und seinem auserwählten Volk, dem Neuen Jerusalem und der Braut des Herrn Jesu Christi zwei Flügel, zwei Berge, zwei Hörner, und das heisst: zwei Könige zugeteilt und zugerechnet hat, damit sie erhalten und beschützt wird, viereinhalb Zeit nach der Niederlage der Zeugen, wie es in diesem Buch zum 12. Kapitel dargestellt ist" (in Fast, *Der linke Flügel*, p. 311; the entire prologue, pp. 308–18). Hoffman's commentary on the Apocalypse was dedicated to Frederick I.

74. Stayer, *Anabaptists*, pp. 217–18. Stayer (n. 25) cites Linden, *Melchior Hofmann*, p. 201: "Denn Schauplatz dieses neuen Himmels denkt er sich wahrscheinlich auf der Erde; . . . wenn er die Entwicklung der Welt in einen geistig-leiblichen Zustand der höchsten Glückseligkeit auf der Erde ausmünden lässt. . . ."; Kawerau, *Hoffman religiöser Denker*, p. 76: "Der Jüngste Tag bringt nicht das Weltende, sondern die Weltrevolution und den Neuen Menschen."

75. Deppermann, *Hoffman*, p. 225.

76. See the report of Obbe Philips, in Williams and Mergal, *Spiritual and Anabaptist Writers*, p. 210.

77. Ibid., p. 211; cf. Williams, *Radical Reformation*, pp. 355–57; Deppermann, *Hoffman*, pp. 253–54.

78. Krebs and Rott, *Elsass* I, no. 280, p. 355. Deppermann refers to the period 1530–1533 as one of increasing social turmoil in Strassburg with growing apocalyptic concerns; see Deppermann, *Hoffman*, pp. 236–44.

79. Ibid., no. 298, pp. 411–12.

80. Ibid., no. 336, p. 553.

81. See in Deppermann's listing of Hoffmann's works, nos. 16–21, p. 348.

82. Obbe Philips in Williams and Mergal, *Spiritual and Anabaptist Writers*, p. 209.

83. This was now Hoffman's third definite stay in Strassburg, continuing from March 1533 until the end of his life in 1543: Krebs and Rott, *Elsass* II, nos. 362, 364, pp. 13–15; cf. Deppermann, *Hoffmann*, p. 253, n. 88.

84. Krebs and Rott, *Elsass* II, nos. 363–64, pp. 14–15.

85. Ibid., no. 362, p. 13; no. 370, p. 23; on the nature of the suspicions that Hoffman generated, see Stayer, *Anabaptists*, pp. 220–23.

86. Ibid., no. 420, p. 130.18-24. A description of Hoffman's imprisonment may be found in Obbe Philips' confession: Williams and Mergal, *Spiritual and Anabaptist Writers*, pp. 209–10.

87. Williams and Mergal, p. 210; cf. Deppermann, *Hoffman*, p. 253.

88. Krebs and Rott, *Elsass* II, no. 364, pp. 14–15.

89. Ibid., no. 380, pp. 70ff.

90. Ibid., and no. 387, pp. 91–92. On Hoffman's defense of himself, see nos. 398–99, pp. 100–10.

91. Ibid., no. 390, pp. 93–94; no. 395, p. 98; no. 400, pp. 110–11; cf. no. 397, pp. 99–100.

92. Ibid., no. 402, p. 113.33ff., pp. 114.1ff.

93. Ibid., no. 402, p. 122.205.

94. Obbe Philips writes that many preachers in Emden sought to imitate Hoffman: Williams and Mergal, *Spiritual and Anabaptist Writers*, p. 210.

95. For example, Krebs and Rott, *Elsass* II, nos. 471, 481, 484, 594, 677.

96. Fast, *Der linke Flügel*, p. 297. Obbe Philips writes that one of the prophetesses believed "Melchior was Elijah. She saw a white swan swimming in a beautiful river or watercourse, which swan had sung beautifully and wonderfully. And that, she interpreted to apply to Melchior as the true Elijah." In Williams and Mergal, *Spiritual and Anabaptist Writers*, p. 212.

97. Krebs and Rott, *Elsass* II, no. 607, p. 386.21-26: "Melchior Hoffmann selbsten etc. inter alia gesagt: er lig da in meiner herren gewalt; doch raht er jnen nit, dass sie sich an seinem unschuldigen blut vergreiffen. Man soll wissen, dass man den rechten Heliam, der vor dem jüngsten tag Christi kommen soll, an jm hab. Gott hab vns jn geschicht, und wir wollen jn nit kennen. Er sey der letst; gott werd vns kein mehr schicken, etc."

98. Krebs and Rott, *Elsass* II, no. 610, p. 388.30f. See here for added charges by the Strassburg council against Hoffman.

99. Williams and Mergal, *Spiritual and Anabaptist Writers*, pp. 211–12.

100. Ibid., p. 213.

101. Ibid., p. 214. Walter Klaassen sketches the parameter of prophetic themes in this region in "Eschatological Themes in early Dutch Anabaptism," in Horst, ed., *The Dutch Dissenters*.

102. Krebs and Rott, *Elsass* II, no. 617, p. 395, n. 9. Stayer lays out some of the ambiguity in Hoffman's teachings and ways in which it was possibly distorted by some Melchiorites (*Anabaptists*, pp. 211–26).

103. Obbe Philips, in Williams and Mergal, *Spiritual and Anabaptist Writers*, pp. 214–16. Jan of Leyden reports that Matthijs was the one to introduce "the use of the sword and violence against the government" into Melchioritism." Cf. Stayer, *Anabaptists*, p. 228.

104. Stayer, *Anabaptists*, pp. 227–80. On developments in Münster see the documents collected in *Das Taüferreich zu Münster 1534–1535. Berichte und Dokumente*, Richard van Dülmen, ed. (Munich: Deutscher Taschenbuch Verlag, 1974).

105. See Philips's confession in Williams and Mergal, *Spiritual and Anabaptist Writers*, pp. 220–23; cf. Stayer, *Anabaptists*, pp. 227–52; and Deppermann, *Hoffman*, pp. 288–93.

106. Williams and Mergal, *Spiritual and Anabaptist Writers*, p. 221. Werner Packull offers the hypothesis that a popular Hutterite commentary on the book of Revelation, previously thought to be an adaptation of Peter John Olivi's *Lectura super Apocalypsim*, represents an exegetical evolution from Hoffman's *Auslegung der heimlichen Offenbarung Joannis des hyeligen Apostels und Evangelisten* (1530). If correct, Packull writes, it is of note that Hoffman's authorship was so quickly lost to view. Packull surmises that this may have been due to the disfavor into which Hoffman's name fell in the 1530s ("A Hutterite Book of Medieval Origin 'Revisited. An Examination of the Hutterite Com-

mentaries on the Book of Revelation and Their Anabaptist Origin'," MQR, 56 [1982]:147–68, esp. pp. 153–55). The book in question exists in four codices. The one I examined (Codex G) probably represents "the harvest of the founding phase . . . of the early Anabaptist and Hutterite tradition" (ibid., p. 152). It is listed in Robert Friedmann, *Die Schriften der Huterischen Täufergemeinschaften* (Wich: Hermann Böhlaus Nachfolger, 1965), p. 57, vol. 10. The work argues that the witnesses are all true preachers and servants of the Word, not the bodily reappearing of Enoch and Elijah. This latter idea is criticized as a Jewish fable (fol. 286r-v). More work needs to be done with this text.

107. Deppermann, *Hoffman*, pp. 334–35. Based upon the appearance of a recanted Anabaptist Schwäbisch Hall and upon the fact that the last evidence of Hoffman only shows him near death, Werner Packull raises the question of whether this Hoffman is the same as our Melchior. It is possible, Packull concludes, but one cannot press the evidence, "Melchior Hoffman—A Recanted Anabaptist in Schwäbisch Hall?" MQR, 57 (1983):83–111, esp. p. 106.

108. Williams and Mergal, *Spiritual and Anabaptist Writers*, p. 221.

109. Ibid., p. 222. On the Melchiorite legacy as borne by Peter Tasch and George Schnabel in central Germany after 1535, see Williams's *Radical Reformation*, sec. 17.2, 3rd ed.; Tasch, acknowledging miscalculations on the identity of the witnesses foretold in Rev. 11:3, serves as a mediating figure from Melchioritism to the Reformed movement; see Werner O. Packull, "Peter Tasch: From Melchiorite to Bankrupt Wine Merchant," MQR, 62 (1988):276–95.

110. In 1930, Wilhelm Gussmann documented various titles bestowed on Luther in the sixteenth century in his study of Reformation catchwords: Exkurs I. "Elias, Daniel, Gottesmann," *Quellen und Forschungen zur Geschichte des Augsburgischen Glaubensbekenntnisses, II. D. Johann Ecks Vierhundertundvier Artikel zum Reichstag von Augsburg 1530* (Kassel: Edmund Pillardy, 1930), pp. 231–20. I have been guided by several studies including Hofmann, Gussmann, and Hans Preuss: *Die Vorstellungen vom Antichrist im späteren Mittelalter, bei Luther und in der konfessionellen Polemik* (Leipzig. J. C. Hinrichs, 1906), esp. pp. 208–9; and *Martin Luther. Der Prophet* (Gütersloh: C. Bertelsmann, 1933), pp. 36–72. The popularity of our theme is lifted up in the journal *History Today* (Vol. 33 [Nov., 1983]) in honor of the 500th anniversary of Luther's birth. See Bob Scribner, "The Reformer as Prophet and Saint. 16th-Century Images of Luther," pp. 17–21, esp. p. 20; and Ruth Kastner, "The Reformer and Reformation Anniversaries," pp. 22–26, esp. pp. 23–24.

111. Hans-Ulrich Hofmann, *Luther und die Johannes-Apokalypse: dargestellt im Rahmen des Auslegungsgeschichte des letzten Buches der Bibel und im Zusamemhang des theologicischen Enturicklung des Reformators.* Beiträge zur Geschichte der biblischen Exegese 24 (Tübingen: J. C. B. Mohr/Paul Siebeck, 1982): Exkurs I. "Luther und die Henoch-Elia-Tradition," pp. 656–61.

112. Preuss sees Luther's theology as more "prophetic" than "apocalyptic," but it is evident that as we see in relation to our text it is difficult to understand fully Luther's position apart from the apocalyptic construct within which he operated, albeit innovatively. See Preuss, *Martin Luther, Der Prophet*, pp. 210–15; cf. Ulrich Asendorf, *Eschatologie bei Luther* (Göttinger: Vandenhoeck und Ruprecht, 1967), pp. 228–32, *passim*, and Karl Holl, "Martin Luther on Luther," trans. by H. C. Erick Midelfort in Jaroslav Pelikan, ed., *Interpreters of Luther: Essays in Honor of Wilhelm Paruck* (Philadelphia: Fortress Press, 1968). Jaroslav Pelikan points beyond a polemical use of the Apocalypse to its paraenetic role in shaping Luther's thought about purgatory and works righteousness (viz. Rev. 14:13) in, "Some Uses of Apocalypse in the Magesterial Reformers," C. A. Patrides and Joseph Wittreich, eds., *The Apocalypse in English Renaissance Thought and Literature* (Ithaca, N.Y.: Cornell University Press, 1984), pp. 74–92.

113. Heiko A. Oberman in *Luther, Mensch zwischen Gott und Teufel* (Berlin: Severin und Siedler, 1982) shows the degree to which Luther saw himself in the shadow of the last days (p. 21) with its conflict between God and Satan, while avoiding religious dualism (pp. 79, 109). Luther's counsel of faith to avoid despair is reflected upon with implications for ethics by George W. Forell, *Faith Active in Love: An Investigation of the Principles Underlying Luther's Social Ethics* (New York: The American Press, 1954), p. 15.

114. Steven Ozment summarizes the importance of a book like the *Theologia Deutsch* for "radical reform movements" (*Mysticism and Dissent* [New Haven: Yale University Press, 1973], p. 14). Luther was the work's premier editor in the early sixteenth century (ibid., pp. 18–28; cf. WA, 1, pp. 378–79).

115. Reinhard Schwartz, *Die apocalyptische Theologie Thomas Müntzers und der Taboriten* (Tubingen: J. C. B. Mohr, 1977), pp. 50–55.

116. Deppermann, *Hoffman*, pp. 84–109.

117. Preuss distinguishes between the present orientation of the prophet and future orientation of the apocalypticist. The prophet's statements about the future arise out of general religious principles. Those made by the apocalypticist are more mechanistic and grow out of the hidden meaning of numbers and signs. Following these categories one could label Luther a prophet and Hoffman an apocalypticist (*Martin Luther. Der Prophet*, pp. 210–11). Cf. Gussmann, "Elias, Daniel, Gottesmann," pp. 268–69.

118. Gussmann cites examples, "Elias, Daniel, Gottesmann," pp. 244–67. Several of these will be considered later in this section; cf. also Albrecht Ritschl, "Die Entstehung der lutherischen Kirche," ZKG, 1 (1876):101–3.

119. The English translation is:
[L=] Pure evangelical teaching
[U=] Over flowing grace of the Holy Spirit
[T=] True servant of Christ
"H" stands for Elijah who discloses the Antichrist prior to the End
"E" stands for Enoch
[R=] He is the master of all messengers.
The acrostic was written by Haug Marschalck, "Von dem weit erschollenen Namen Luther, was er bedeut und wie er wirt missbraucht" (Strassburg, 1523); cited by Preuss, *Martin Luther. Der Prophet*, p. 34.

120. In 1521 Luther doubted that the Apocalypse was a genuinely apostolic book. Yet he wrote his "De Antichristo" (April 1521) using it and appealed to it in opposition to the Papal Bull issued against him (December 1520). The preface to the book of Revelation in the Luther Bible of 1530 was considerably more positive with regard to the Apocalypse, probably enhanced, in his view, by the siege of Vienna (1529) and impending Turkish onslaught. The 1534 preface was even more positive, provided one read the book of Revelation correctly. On this evolution in Luther see Hans-Ulrich Hofmann, *Luther und die Johannes-Apokalpyse*, p. 395.

121. Jaroslav Pelikan, "Luther's Attitude toward John Hus," *Concordia Theological Monthly*, 19 (1948):747–63. On Hus's prophecy that in 100 years his work would be taken up successfully and Luther's identification with that prophecy, cf. John Headley, *Luther's View of Church History* (New Haven: Yale University Press, 1963), pp. 225–28; WA, 30.3, p. 387.6-10, 18-22.

122. WA, 7, pp. 135–36; 431.20-36; 439.20-36; 439.24-34; WA, 44, p. 774.19-34.

123. WABr 2, p. 42.22-29.

124. WA, 50, pp. 98–105. Luther reacted to "Ioannis Nannis de monarchia papae disputatio" by editing this work with ironic glosses and a polemical postscript (1537).

125. Early in his career Luther occasionally referred to the Turk as Antichrist, a term he later reserved exclusively for the papacy for its alleged subversion of Christian truth.

See Scott Hendrix, *Luther and the Papacy* (Philadelphia: Fortress Press, 1981), pp. 21, 75–76; cf. Hans J. Hillerbrand, "The Antichrist in the Early German Reformation: Reflections on Theology and Propaganda," in *Germania Illustrata*, by Andrew C. Fix and Susan C. Karant-Nunn, eds. (Kirksville, Mo.: Sixteenth Century Journal Publishers, 1992), pp. 3–17.

126. WA, 50, p. 98.

127. Luther was easily drawn to the book of Daniel in the development of his historical perspective. "Vorrede vber den Propheten Daniel," WA D B 11, II, 13.

128. In particular, the commentary by John Purvey (c. 1390), published under the title *Commentarius in Apocalypsin ante centum annos editus 1528* (cf. WA, 26, p. 123).

129. See, e.g., a document describing the vision of Nicolaus von der Fluhe, and a collection of prophecies by the astrologer Johann Lichtenberger Hall, in "Luther's Eschatology," (*Augustana Quarterly*, 25, 1944) p. 17; cf. Dietrich Kurze, *Johannes Lichtenberger* (Lubeck: Matthiesen, 1960).

130. Preuss, *Antichrist*, pp. 49–50.

131. A. J. Lamping, *Ulrichus Velenus and His Treatise Against the Papacy* (Leiden: E. J. Brill, 1976). Lamping summarizes Velenus's argument: Papal claims have now been proven false. His fellow humanist Lorenzo Valla destroyed the myth of an historical basis for temporal power. Luther disproved the doctrinal basis for papal authority. Now the author sets out to disprove Peter's connection with Rome (p. 2).

132. Ibid., p. 220 (sig. Aiir): "Que quidem si carnaliter, atque in cortice futura credimus, Iudaicis fabulis, ut doctisimus Ieronimus ad Marcellam scribit, acquiescere necessum est, ut uidelicet rursus edificetur Ierusalem, & hostie offerantur in templo, & spiritali cultu imminuto, corporales reuiuiscant cerimonie: Sed quia totus ille liber Apocalypseos Ioannis, unde hec de Antichristo, Helia & Enoch opinio, spiritualiter intelligendus est, quum quot uerba tot mysteria habeat, Heliam Enoch & Antichristum iamdiu venisse, & tot annis tyrannidem suam in Ecclesia exercuisse, & etiam nunc exercere certum est."

133. Ibid., pp. 221–2 (sig. Aiiv–Aiiir). Velenus lists also Savonarola, Wyclif, Hus, Jerome of Prague, Reuchlin, and Pico della Mirandola.

134. Hans-Ulrich Hofmann, *Luther und die Johannes-Apokalypse*, p. 658; Gussmann, "Elias, Daniel, Gottesmann," pp. 241–44.

135. Headley, *Luther's View of Church History*, pp. 230–36; see pp. 215–16. See also WABr, 2, 167:7f.

136. Ulrich Asendorf, *Escahatologie bei Luther* (Gottingen: Vandenhoeck und Ruprecht, 1967), pp. 228–32. The nature of the apocalyptic dimension in Luther's thought can be tracked by his attitude toward the conversion of the Jews to Christianity, in medieval thought one of the functions of our witnesses. See Kurt Meier, "Zur Interpretation von Luthers Judenschriften," in J. Arkinson et al., *Vierhundertfunfzig Jahre lutherische Reformation, 1517–1967: Festschrift für Franz Lau* (Göttingen, Vanderhoeck u. Ruprecht, 1967).

137. See WABr, 2, 167:7f.

138. Ibid., p. 348.49-50.

139. Ibid., p. 388.23-25.

140. WA, 10.1.1, pp. 147.14–148.1.

141. Ibid., pp. 148.14-18.

142. WA, 10.3, p. 207.13-25.

143. WA, 10.1.2, pp. 191.31–195.4.

144. Ibid., p. 194.28-31.

145. WA, 10.2.3, p. 192.6-11.

146. Note the anti-enthusiast interpretation given our theme in Roth's Winterpostille (1528), WA, 21, pp. 38.37ff., 40.31ff.; I am in debt to Hans-Ulrich Hofmann for this reference (*Luther und die Johannes-Apokalypse*, pp. 660–61).

147. WA, 38, p. 661.22-26: "Vetus opinio de venturo Elia et Henoch post Antichristum ex hoc loco sympta (ubi Christi ait: Elias quidem venturus est, et restituet omnia, etc.) omnes libros implevit, et per totam Ecclesiam vagata est. Ideo hoc loco tranctanda esset ea quaestio, si idonei essemus ultra autoritatem veterum aliquid statuere."

148. Ibid., pp. 662.7–663.6; cf. WA, 13, In Mal., pp. 702.19–703.4.

149. WA, 42, pp. 252–57 (1535 *Genesis Commentary*), esp. p. 257.34-42. Luther writes: "We in the New Testament are in the third world, as it were, and we have a more out-standing example—Christ himself, our Deliverer, ascending to heaven with many of the saints. In every age God wanted to have at hand proofs of the resurrection of the dead in order to draw our hearts away from this detestable and troubled life, in which, as long as it seems good to God, we nevertheless serve him by performing our governmental and civic duties and also, above all else, by leading others to godliness and the knowledge of God" (I am citing from LW, pp. 350–51). Peter Meinhold has suggested that Luther was partly in debt to Carion and Melanchthon for his sense of this tripartite periodization and was influenced by the prophecy of Elias appearing in the Babylonian Talmud. Peter Meinhold, *Die Genesisvorlesung Luthers und ihre Herausgeber* (Stuttgart: W. Kohlhammer, 1936), p. 307.

150. WABr, 11, p. 59.5-9 (March 1545); in Headley, *Luther's View of Church History*, p. 256.

151. Luther does enter into a kind of prophetic numerology in his *Supputatio annorum mundi* (WA, 53, pp. 1–182), but never so far as to suggest a specific time for the second Advent or to offer secret spiritual counsel. He writes that this work was for his own use and is seen best as merely a further indication of the reality of, not his preoccupation with, apocalyptic aspects of eschatology.

152. Preuss contends that in Luther one finds a turn away from medieval "apocalyptic predictions" toward "prophetic-reformatory prophecy." He writes: "Es tritt bei ihm die grosse Wende von der apokalyptischen Wahrsagung des Mittelalters zu der prophetisch-reformatorischen Weissagung ein" (*Martin Luther, Der Prophet*, p. 84). See George Wolfgang Forell, "Justification and Eschatology in Luther's Thought," CH, 38 (1969):164–74. After drawing a close connection between justification by faith and eschatology, Forell writes, "Luther's understanding of justification by faith is developed against the background of what we would call realized eschatology" (p. 168); cf. Will-Erich Peuckert, who on this point overstates Luther's dependence upon a medieval eschatological framework: *Die Grosse Wende: Das apokalyptische Saeculum und Luther, Geistesgeschichte und Volskunde* (Hamburg: Classen & Geverts, 1948), vol. 2, p. 546.

153. Schäufele, *Missionarisches Bewusstsein*, p. 79; cf. Fritz Heyer, *Der Kirchenbegriff der Schwärmer, Schriften des Vereins für Reformationsgeschichte*, Vol. 56 (Leipzig: Heinsius Nachfolger, 1939), p. 41.

154. Headley draws together a variety of factors in late 1529 and 1530 that led Luther to perceive the imminence of the end: the prophesied geographical spread of the gospel having reached its (believed) spatial limits; the translation of the Bible into all languages; the pressing threat of the Turks and availability of certain prophecies like that of John Hilten (Headley, *Luther's View of Church History*, pp. 240–57). Headley cites various texts to substantiate his argument. Luther had only recently given a positive evaluation to the Apocalypse (WA DB, 7, pp. 406-8). Note in particular the letter to Nicholas Hausmann (WABr, 5, p. 176; cf. p. 28); cited by Headley (p. 245).

155. Luther prefaces his comments upon Dan. 12:11–12 with temporal speculation on Daniel's prophetic numbers 1290 and 1335. The "first time" stretches from John the Baptist to the days of Lewis of Bavaria, the second to near the time of the Great Schism and the Council of Constance. This dating in addition to the great prevalence of Epicureanism in society appears to make the end seem imminent (O. Albrecht, ed., "Luthers Arbeiten an

der Ueberstezung und Auslegung des Propheten Daniel in den Jahren 1530 und 1541," ARG, 23 [1926]:47).

156. WA DB, 7, p. 413.23-24.

157. Headley, *Luther's View of Church History*, pp. 106–61. In Dan. 11, Luther found a clear description of the papacy.

158. Ibid., pp. 252–57. Note the significance of "Epicureanism" in the last period of time since the revelation of Antichrist. Ever since Jerome, the period after the revelation of Antichrist prior to the second Advent was often viewed as a period for penance and preparation. See Robert E. Lerner, "Refreshment of the Saints," *Traditio*, 32 (1976): 101–5.

159. The "little horn" arising on the head of the fourth beast was usually identified by Luther with the Turk, God's scourge on Christendom for its sin, which would in its own time be judged and fall (Ezek. 39). See Headley, *Luther's View of Church History*, p. 228.

160. There is a somewhat fuller sense of identification between prophecy and event in the later preface of 1546 compared with the earlier one of 1530 (WA DB, 7, pp. 407, 409, 411, 413, 415, 417, 419, 421; (even-numbered pages refer to the earlier ed.); cf. Headley, *Luther's View of Church History*, pp. 106–56.

161. WA DB, 7, pp. 410.18–412.2; 411.26–413.2.

162. WA DB, 7, pp. 412.10-35, 413.10–415.2. Cf. the letter of Friedrich Myconius to Luther (December 2, 1529), WABr, 5 (no. 1501), p. 191.29-37.

163. Werner Elert, *The Structure of Lutheranism*, trans. by Walter A. Hanson (Saint Louis: Concordia Press, 1962).

164. This certainly illustrates the failure of the papacy for Luther. See Hendrix, *Luther and the Papacy*, p. 21; cf. Headley, *Luther's View of Church History*, p. 154. Luther gives to the "Fall" theory of the Church a different sense by virtue of his conception of papal moral failure (ibid., pp. 156–61, and p. 156, n. 36). Following this understanding, Antichrist is less a specific individual than a description of moral or doctrinal failure (e.g., the trumpets as well as the beasts).

165. WA DB, 7, pp. 412.25-29, 413.25-29.

166. WA, 26, p. 123.16-23. Warren Quanbeck traces the way in which Luther grew increasingly confident in his use of the Apocalypse. See "Luther and Apocalyptic," in *Luther und Melanchthon*, Vilmos Vajta ed., (Göttingen: Vandenhoeck und Ruprecht, 1961), pp. 119–28, esp. pp. 126–27.

167. Luther discerned his own time in chapter 12, chapter 11 being descriptive of the papal Antichrist. See W. A. Deutsche Bibel 11, II, 125, on Daniel's "weeks of years" (70 weeks of chapter 9) running from the assumed 490 years of the revelation to 7 years after Christ's Resurrection when the apostles turned from preaching to the Jews to the Gentiles. Luther's use of this apocalyptic history is noted by Richard Bauckham as an instance of the "continuity between prophecy and apocalyptic" where "the apocalyptists assumed the role of interpreters of prophecy" ("The Rise of Apocalyptic," *Themelios*, 3.2 [1978]:17). We have here an idea of reform, which can be said to rest, with some modification, upon an eschatology in the line of Tyconius.

168. See Preuss and Gussmann as cited above.

169. Preuss, *Antichrist*, pp. 208–9; cf. Robert Scribner, *For the Sake of Simple Folk: Popular Propaganda for the German Reformation* (Cambridge: Cambridge University Press, 1981), pp. 148–63.

170. *Bruder Michael Styfel Augustiner Von Esslingen, . . .* (Augsburg 1922).

171. Gussmann, "Elias, Daniel, Gottesmann," pp. 241–42.

172. CR, 94 (ZW, 7), no. 113, pp. 250–52. Note p. 250.11-15. On this letter see Gerhard

Ebeling, *Luther: An Introduction to His Thought*, trans. by R. A. Wilson (Philadelphia: Fortress Press, 1970), p. 21.

173. CR, 94 (ZW, 7), no. 100, pp. 218–22. "Utinam sit probus quispiam, qui Luterum commoveat, ne ita excurrat, sed modestiam, quam ubique tantisper laudat, teneat, aruo suo scroriam non miscreat! Tunc eum Heliam, et si quid amplius sit, nominabimus" (p. 222).

174. Peter Frankel, *Testimonia Patrum. The Function of the Patristic Argument in the Theology of Philip Melanchthon* (Geneva: Librarie E. Droz, 1961), pp. 329–30.

175. CR, 1 (*Melanchthonis Opera* 1), no. 100, p. 282.

176. CR, 1, no. 103, pp. 287–88: "Nam cum Lutherum tuemur, sincerae Theologiae et Christianae doctrinae caussam agimus, quam ille hactenus plane Heliae spiritu adserit."

177. CR, 1, no. 204, p. 565. Note also Melanchthon's letter to Michael Hummelberg, CR, 1, no. 205, pp. 565–66. Further references are cited by Gussmann, "Elias, Daniel, Göttesmann," p. 300, n. 39.

178. Hans Volz, *Die Lutherpredigten des Johannes Mathesius. Kritische Untersuchungen zur Geschichtsschreibung im Zeitalter der Reformation* (Leipzig: M. Heinsius Nachfolger Eger & Sievers, 1930), pp. 63–68; see note p. 65.

179. Preuss argues that Luther knew himself as having unique prophetic significance; in *Martin Luther. Der Prophet*, pp. 51–52, with references from Spalitian, Kettenbach, Rhegius, Brumfels, and others. This view is rejected by Headley who, together with Karl Holl, believes that the work of the gospel was preeminent in Luther's mind. The picture appears ambiguous with Luther and his fellow reformers finding identity between their work and that of OT prophets, as Mark Edwards demonstrates in *Luther's Last Battles: Politics and Polemics, 1531–46* (Ithaca: Cornell University Press, 1983), p. 103. Note in particular the letter from Wolfgang Richard to Luther (1523) in the collection of Luther's letters edited by Ernst Ludwig Enders, WABr, Vol. 4, p. 88.

180. In his study of Lutheranism in light of Apocalyptic and gnostic traditions, Robert Barnes argues that Luther's Reformation reinforced and enduringly perpetrated that tradition of expectancy more comprehensively in Lutheranism than in other contemporary movements of reform. See *Prophecy and Gnosis, Apocalypticism in the Wake of the Lutheran Reformation* (Stanford: Stanford University Press, 1988), pp. 2–3.

181. See chapter 2 of this text, and note Ernst Benz, "Kategorien des eschatologischen Zeitbewusstseins," *Deutsche Vierteljahresschrift für Literatur wissenchaft und Geistesgeschichte*, 11 (1933):200–99.

182. Peter Martin notes many of these in *Martin Luther und die Bilder zur Apokalypse* (Hamburg: F. Wittig, 1983). Placing such woodcuts and drawings next to the words of the text had the effect of lending such drawings added authority and, contrariwise, of giving interpretive shape to the text. See Barnes, *Prophecy and Gnosis*, pp. 55–59, who adds further illustrations of ways in which the veracity of Lutheranism was corroborated in the minds of the times. See John Bossy, *Christianity in the West, 1400–1700* (New York: Oxford University Press, 1985).

183. Georg Hirth, *Bilder aus der Lutherzeit: eine Sammlung von Porträts aus der Zeit der Reformation in getreuen Facsimile-Nachbildungen* (Munich: G. Hort, 1883), p. 35.

184. Ritschl, "Entstehung," pp. 102–3; cf. Ebeling, *Introduction*, p. 21. Barnes traces the broad lines of these conflicts with attention to detail from 1546–1630s, in *Prophecy and Gnosis* The flowering of apocalyptic *Flugschriften* cited by Barnes is reminiscent of similar Joachite pamphlets in the generation after Joachim's death.

185. Ritschl points by way of example to one Anton Otto zu Nordhausen, who affirmed in a letter to Justus Jonas (1555) that the sentences of Luther all descended from Christ. See Ritschl, "Entstehung," p. 102. On the controversy, see Robert Kolb, *Nikolaus von*

Amsdorf (1483–1565): Popular Polemics in the Preservation of Luther's Legacy (Nieuwkoop: De Graaf, 1978).

186. Ibid., pp. 102–3. There is a certain irony here considering Amsdorf's earlier hostility to Melchior Hoffman.

187. Flacius Illyricus, *Catalogus testium veritatis, qui ante nostram aetatem reclamarunt papae.* . . . (Basel, 1556; Ger. ed. Frankfurt, 1573). This is also the central theme running through Flacius's *Historia Ecclesiae Christi* (1559–1574). See Günther Moldaenke, *Schriftverständnis und Schriftdeutung im Zeitalter der Reformation, I. Matthias Flacius Illyricus* (Stuttgart: W. Kohlhammer, 1936), p. 320. Flacius's interest is in the legitimization of Luther's teachings, not apocalyptic speculation per se.

188. Flacius Illyricus, *Catalogus*, p. 5.

189. Matthias Flacius Illyricus, *Novum Testamentum . . . Glossa Compendiaria* (Basel, 1570), pp. 1352–53. this was implied in Hus's prophecy of the success of his teachings 100 years after his death. The influence of Tyconius is evident, but the work also cites Joachim's anti-papal prophecies but not any pertaining to a new earthly age.

190. S. L. Verheus, *Zeugnis und Gericht* (Nieuwkoop: B. DeGraaf, 1971), p. 49. We have noted that, whereas the return of Elijah in his singularity is not the same as the tradition of expectation derived from our text, ever since Augustine the two traditions have been frequently conflated.

191. Meinhold, *Geschichte*, p. 268; Herman Dietzfelbinger, "Vortrag des Landesbischofs der Evangelisch-Lutherischen Kirche in Bayern. Matthias Flacius . . . ," in Johannes Viebig, ed., *Matthias Flacius Illyricus, 1575–1975* (Regensburg: Lassleben, 1975), p. 15.

192. Moldaenke, *Schriftverständnis*, pp. 316–35.

193. Osiander's apocalyptic thought and biblical chronology, influential in Germany and upon English apocalypticism, is an illustration of the way in which such Lutheran speculation would find a wider audience over the next century. Cf. his *Conjecturae de ultimis temporibus, ac de fine mundi, ex sacris literis . . .* (Nuremberg, 1544). See Martin Stupperich, "Das Augsburger Interim als apokalyptisches Geschehnis nach den königsberger Schriften Andreas Osianders," ARG, 64 (1973):225–45.

194. Barnes, *Prophecy and Gnosis*, p. 65. In addition to his rich primary sources, Barnes notes the value of J. J. von Döllinger's study on the mind of the period, *Die Reformation, ihre innere Entwicklung und ihre Wirkungen im Umfänge Lutherischen Bekenntnisses* (Regensburg, 1846, 1848; repr., Frankfurt, 1962). As a corrective to Döllinger's pessimistic perspective on Lutheran social disintegration, Barnes cites the hope held by many in an imminent Kingdom of God (p. 282, n. 17) in Gerald Strauss, "The Mental World of a Saxon Preacher," in Peter Newman Brooks, ed., *Reformation Principle and Practice: Essays in Honor of Arthur Goeffrey Dickens* (London: Scolar Press, 1980).

195. *Apocalypsis. Der offenbarung Künfftiger Gesicht Johannis. . . . bis der Welt ende, Auslegung . . . Mit einer Vorrede Philip. Melanchth* (n.p., 1559); cf. Bousset, *Offenbarung*, p. 84.

196. Johannes Funck's chronological reflections may be found in his work, *Chronologia, hoc est. Omnivm temporvm et annorvm ab initio mvndi vsque ad resvrrectionem Domini Nostri Iesv Christi, computatio . . .* (Nuremberg, 1545).

197. WA, 10.2, p. 12.17-24; cf. Pelikan, "Luther's Attitude," pp. 747ff.

198. Asendorf, *Eschatologie*, pp. 214–17.

199. See Philipp Nicolai, Johann Gerhard, and Johann Valentin Andreae; e.g., David Chytraeus, *Explicatio Apocalypsis Johannis apostoli* (Wittenberg: J. Crato, 1564). Here the witnesses are seen as all true preachers during Antichrist's reign (calculated either from Alaric's sack of Rome in A.D. 412, or from Phocas's decree of Roman primacy in

606 until the end of the days of the Gentiles in 1672 or 1866). These witnesses, Chytraeus writes, have been recently detailed in the *Catalogues testium* of Flacius Illyricus. Bousset lists examples in *Offenbarung*, pp. 85–86; cf. R. H. Charles, *Studies in the Apocalypse* (Edinburgh: T. & T. Clark, 1913), pp. 27–28.

200. Will-Erich Peuckert, *Die Rosenkreutzer. Zur Geschichte einer Reformation* (Jena: Eugen Diederichs, 1928), pp. 8–10, 45–51, 78–80, 153–55; Roland Haase, *Das Problem des Chiliasmus uud der dreissigjährige Krieg* (Leipzig, 1933), pp. 90-91: and cf. Barnes, *Prophecy and Gnosis*, pp. 60–99, 228–66.

201. Barnes, *Prophecy and Gnosis*, p. 257. On the political dimensions of this turn from apocalyptic hope with possible implications for the reification of the state, see Koppel S. Pinson, *Pietism as a Factor in the Rise of German Nationalism* (New York: Columbia University Press, 1934), pp. 58–59, 78, 180–206.

202. Cf. Bousset, *Offenbarung*, pp. 99–101.

203. Menno Simons, *Fundamentum. Ein Fundament und klare Answeisung von der Seligmachenden Lehre unsers Herren Jesu Christi* . . . (1575 [Basel: Horst, 1740]), pp. 209–10, 381. The English text is from *The Complete Writings of Menno Simons*, ed. by J. C. Wenger, trans. by L. Verduin (Scottdale, Pa.: Herald Press, 1956), p. 220.

5

Bullinger and the Testimony
of the Church

Bullinger's Preachers

To the anxieties of the sixteenth century, whether political fears of internal social disintegration, Turkish advance into Europe, natural catastrophe, or even that of a fraudulent clergy,[1] Luther's answer was to preach the effective graciousness of God. Our two witnesses were actual or symbolic representatives of God's last call to humanity to accept that grace prior to Judgment. Heinrich Bullinger, and many of the reformers who would take the name "Reformed" as opposed to "Lutheran,"[2] nuanced this answer differently. Without denying the proffered grace of God, their preaching focused more upon God's promise given throughout the history of his people. Our witnesses became symbols of that promise.

Heinrich Bullinger (1504–1575), reformer of Zürich in Switzerland and successor to Huldrych Zwingli, writes about prophets as they herald God's promise.[3] The existence of the Christian ministry is a sign of God's care for humanity.[4] The work of that ministry, of prophets and preaching or prophesying, is to call people to live in terms of this covenant. Prophets are a part of Bullinger's concern for the restoration of the precepts of the covenant in the sixteenth century.[5] They call God's people to return to the theological simplicity and spiritual immediacy connoted for him by the covenant.[6] The way in which Bullinger's ideas of prophets, prophecy, and, indeed, the covenant are handled in his set of sermons on the Apocalypse, a book which he argues is a summary of biblical revelation, offers (1) an affective argument to his conception of the place of the covenant in shaping history, (2) a polemical yet effective vision of the Reformed pastor, and (3) lays an important part of the foundation for the later speculative development of the Apocalypse among Reformed churches and with implications for Protestant historiography.[7]

The vignette offered by Bullinger into the wide domain of prophets, prophecy, and historical understanding through the lens of the Apocalypse is appropriate in itself, but additionally from the perspective of social history.[8] Ideas of the Reformed ministry, developed in the light of Old Testament prophetic models in the context of a renewed sense of civic consciousness, are given polemical significance as understood through the Apocalypse, an important dimension of expanding Protestantism and Protestant conceptions of legitimate prophecy. Such views as used by reformers aligned with the office of the magistrate will in the evolution of social history become models for later religiously disaffected and socially marginalized groups seeking further reform.[9] The study of texts, then, and of their use continues to be of central historical importance. When we turn to Bullinger, we turn to one whose advice was sought and writings read through the bulk of the sixteenth century from the Kingdom of England to the Commonwealth of Poland-Lithuania.

The theme of two adventual witnesses provided a model for prophetic activity. It also helped to image the reconstruction of Christendom, drawing upon the examples of Joshua and Zerubbabel from the Old Testament. Our text was not the first to be used in this way,[10] nor was it initially of primary importance. It does not enter into Reformed consciousness in a significant way until after the shift to a more confident evaluation of the book of Revelation later in the sixteenth century, and the completion of Bullinger's series of sermons on the Apocalypse. Then it looms larger, in part from Bullinger's example. For this reason, we will begin with Bullinger, his understanding of the covenant, that covenant through the lens of the Apocalypse and, finally, the relation of such thinking upon his conception of history.

The Prophet and the Promise

In reaction to crisis and growing evil in the world, Bullinger referred to his predecessor, Huldrych Zwingli, as one who had performed the work of a prophet.[11] Whatever was said of the prophets of old can be said of Zwingli, Bullinger argued in a commemorative oration.[12] Rising in rhetorical flourish, Bullinger credits Zwingli with having shaken the reign of Antichrist, overthrown error and superstition: "For it was this one who restored the principle of the Testament and the eternal covenant and renewed what was worn out."[13] Zwingli was a prophet. Johannes Oecolampadius was another, as was Luther whose work *The Babylonian Captivity of the Church* was of major influence on Bullinger and his generation. Were there more? Our text will help to answer this question in Bullinger's later reflections. However, to place Bullinger's remarks in their proper context, his general conception of prophetic activity will have to be sketched briefly.

Bullinger begins his oration by providing a brief introduction to the office and function of a prophet. Tracing its existence among Greeks, Romans, Jews, and early Christians, he finds the office most clearly defined among the Hebrews.[14] Its function is divided between the interpretation of Scripture[15] and that of prophetic warfare against error and vice.[16] Taking his cue from Jeremiah and Paul, Bullinger writes that the activities which characterize the prophetic office are the explanation of the sacred Scriptures and their application.[17]

It is in the Scriptures, in the patriarchs, and Church fathers that one finds models for reform. Reform is needed when the visible marks of the Church become obscured as in the days of Elijah. This does not imply the destruction of the Church, which is always known by God. It is a call to renewed prophetic activity, the sincere preaching of God's Word and adherence to models of piety provided by the patriarchs.[18] The nature of this reform lies in an apprehension of God's covenant, his *testamentum.*

For Testament, which also is the title for all of Scripture, surely stands for the content of all of Scripture. Neither is this to be wondered at as something recent and devoid of meaning. For by the word *Testament* we understand the covenant and the agreement by which God agreed with the entire human race, to be himself our God, our sufficiency, source of good and horn of plenty. And this he would abundantly prove by the gift of the fertile earth and the Incarnation of his son. Man, however, ought to pursue integrity, that he may stand before God with a perfect and upright mind, that he may walk in his ways and commit himself totally to him, as to the highest God and most loving Father.[19]

The covenant served as the means by which Bullinger understood man's relationship to God. It was the center of his theological life and work.[20] God and his promises form the divine pole of what is essentially a bilateral pact.[21] Adherence or departure from the terms of the covenant gave an inner structure and meaning to history. The work of the prophet, whether in the days of Elijah, Jeremiah, and Isaiah or under the terms of the new dispensation, was the same: to call an erring people back to a salvific relation with God (i.e., to the terms of the covenant).[22] This was done by the Hebrew prophets before Christ, by Paul and by Church fathers like Athanasius.[23] It was to be done by prophets and pastors in Bullinger's own day.[24] A truly godly, covenanted people would establish a truly Christian commonwealth.[25] The prophet warns those who scorn God, Christ, and the Church. He admonishes people not to leave the living God but to live in faith and purity, finding consolation in God alone.[26]

This oration was not Bullinger's first attempt to define the work of a prophet. While teaching at Kappel he wrote *De propheta libri duo* (1525), stressing the work of the prophet as interpreter of Scripture and preacher of the Word, based upon Bullinger's early exegetical and homiletical training.[27] In 1528 Bullinger himself assumed the role of a prophet, calling for the repentance of the Swiss Confederacy.[28] When he took over the pulpit in Zürich as Zwingli's successor (December 13, 1531), he insisted upon the freedom of proclamation.[29] By 1532, having become the Antistes of the Zürich church, Bullinger's description of the work of a prophet included the exposition of Scripture and social or moral criticism of Church and society.

For Bullinger, Zwingli was not the only prophet in these days of crisis. He was part of a new outburst of prophetic zeal that stood in continuity with Moses, Isaiah, Paul, and Athanasius.[30] Bullinger referred to Zwingli as Zürich's local example of one filling the office of prophecy, but a singular and final expression of all the qualities that one would seek in the true prophet of God.[31] Much later, in 1557, Bullinger would write more generally that Christ always sends forth faithful preachers modeled on those prophets Enoch and Elijah, to oppose the abominations of Antichrist: "For since all times bring forth the faithful heralds of Christ, the Enochs and Elijahs, who oppose such abominations, Daniel is right in saying: 'and he waged war with the saints and prevailed against them.'"[32]

The idea of a prophet lay at the heart of the Zürich Prophezei, the beginning of the theological college in Zürich.[33] It was from this "bulwark of biblicism," as Büsser calls it, that preachers, teachers, and missionaries saturated in the Bible were sent out across Europe. If the government overlooked evil, it was the duty of the prophet to point it out. The office of the prophet involved exegesis and homiletics as well as social application or politics.[34] The times were evil. Signs of social disruption seemed to be increasing, but the existence of prophets was a sign of divine grace. God had not left his Church without consolation.[35] Describing such consolation will be central to the way in which Bullinger uses our text.

Bullinger explained current doctrinal and moral decadence similarly in several of his works. We can see in his analysis of the covenant how he sought to uncover the historical origin of institutions and doctrines and the departures from it.[36] The covenant originated in the agreement that God struck with Abraham: "That God has formed a pact with us . . . as is the custom among humans, is testified in the following words of Moses which we read in Genesis 17 after this sentence: when Abraham had begun to be ninety-nine years old, the Lord appeared to him and said to him: 'I am God almighty and all-sufficient. Walk before me and be whole.'"[37]

Here is "the source of our religion and first chapter of it."[38] Bullinger's interest in historical origins and their analogies in human experience comes out even more clearly in relation to departures from the covenant. He applied the same methodology to the Roman cult of images and the sacrifice of the Mass in two works written in 1528 and 1529, later printed together as *De origine erroris* (1539).[39] Here he pointed to parallels between the idolatry and errors of earlier ages and those that arose in Europe since the early Middle Ages. The real danger to the welfare of the Christian Church and the Christian republic lay not in the ravages of the Turks but in the hypocrisy and superstition of the "protectors" of the Church.[40]

Bullinger writes that after a period of initial monotheism, when God became known by many names reflecting his attributes,[41] impious men laid the foundation for idolatry by exploiting the names of God along with those of their ancient heroes.[42] A similar degeneration occurred among the Jews. They were led into the temptation of idolatry while sojourning in Egypt. Following their exodus, idolatry grew rapidly until it became manifest in the Baal worship of the time of Ahab.[43] Similarly, Roman saints were originally great martyrs or founders of particular orders. Venerated in commemoration, their images were soon worshipped and adored. Thus, abuses slowly crept into the Church; these were fully evident by the eleventh century.[44] The growth of such idolatry was furthered by barbarian invasions throughout the early Middle Ages, which affected both Church and society. The destruction of knowledge and education contributed to an illiterate and superstitious religion that, in turn, led to the adoration of saints.[45]

As Elijah called upon Israel to leave its Baals and "Jezebelism," so contemporary prophets and preachers were continuously calling upon Christendom to leave idolatry and superstition.[46] Jacob was blessed by God when he gave up the alien gods of Syria, burying them under the oak of Moreh in Schechem.[47] However, Israel did not forsake the gods of Egypt after her exodus. The people carried on their idolatry, polluted their pure religion, and fell away from the terms of the covenant.[48] By the time of Ahab and Jezebel, idolatry and superstition reached an insidious level.[49] Then Elijah appeared. He called the people to a clear decision between God and idolatry.[50] During the time of Bullinger, Christian society stood in a similar situation. Bullinger demonstrates this assertion by tracing the development of error in the medieval Church[51] and setting next to this history his treatise on the current errors and idolatry of the papal Church.[52] As the Jews had turned to the gods of Egypt and Canaan, so the papists had returned to the gods of the old Roman religion.[53] They changed only their names. Elijah had destroyed the prophets of Baal in his day, now Zwingli was called by his adversaries an "idol-smasher and impious iconoclast."[54] The work of the prophet in upholding the covenant will receive sustained treatment in Bullinger's sermons on the Apocalypse.

A Veiled History

The conflict between idolatry and the true God is expressed most clearly in the series of sermons Bullinger preached on the book of Revelation between 1555 and 1556. It is here within the Reformed tradition that the foundation is laid for a more focused attention upon the adventual witnesses. Bullinger's interest in the Apocalypse began early.[55] From the start of his ministry in Zürich he used its themes to promote religious reforms and to encourage his contemporaries to leave the scholastic teaching concerning the Lord's Supper, turning the threat (Rev. 14:9ff) that anyone who worships the beast will receive its mark and God's wrath against the medieval Roman Church. Well before Luther's positive reevaluation of the book of Revelation, Bullinger was attracted to the text, viewing the Apocalypse as the work of the Apostle John. While others such as Erasmus, Luther, Zwingli, and Oecolampadius read it with hesitation, Bullinger cited the text authoritatively and accorded it its recognized place in the Western canon.

Bullinger did not limit his interest in apocalyptic themes to the book of Revelation, but published in 1536 a commentary on 2 Thessalonians where he concentrated on the nature of Antichrist, correlating Paul's understanding of this epitome of evil with that presented in the book of Daniel.[56] Following Jerome, Bullinger connects the Roman Empire with the last empire spoken of in Daniel's vision (Dan. 7:1–28). After Constantine the process of the division of the Roman Empire begins until it is broken down into the various European nations, the ten divisions of Daniel's final empire prior to the revelation of Antichrist. This Antichrist is not one person but a name given to power set against God.[57] Three years later, Bullinger defended the apostolicity and canonicity of the book of Revelation in a statement attached to the Zürich Latin Bible (1539). He endorsed the principle of historicist exegesis, finding in the Apocalypse a forecast of Church history.[58] Then, in 1542, he dealt extensively with Matthew's apocalypse (chapter 24).[59]

Bullinger's interest in apocalyptic literature is evident, but having completed his series of New Testament commentaries in 1546, he appeared to have refrained from producing one on the Apocalypse. Instead, from 1555 through December 1556, he preached a series of sermons on the book of Revelation. The introduction of this series coincided with a sermon on the Last Judgment, dealing largely with Matthew 24.[60] The series was followed by two sermons comprising the work *On the End of the Age*.[61] By 1565 Bullinger completed two additional sermon series, one on the book of Jeremiah,[62] the other on Daniel.[63] In each of these Bullinger applied the significance of the prophetic message and the models found therein to the then current religious and social crises. Finally, in his *Epitome of Time*, appended to the commentary on Daniel, Bullinger sought to understand the historical development of evil and error up to the present.[64]

Bullinger's interest in prophetism, with an apocalyptic edge, is evident. It was stimulated by a variety of factors, especially his search for the cause of religious declension in history. By tracing the origin of error and setting it within the perspective of the covenant one could find an explanation for the current state of Christendom. Apocalyptic symbols were useful both because of the apparent temporal conflict with idolatry evident in the visions of the text and because their language draws so heavily upon allusions to the prophetic literature of the Old Testament. For someone writing within the historicist perspective of Nicholas of Lyra, such symbolism offered deepened prophetic insight into world history. The history of Israel was a figure for that of the new dispensation. There was, as it were, an invisible history behind the visible history of the world with its religious institutions. Such thinking can make lively use of our theme.

Bullinger's historical interest developed in tandem with that of his contemporaries. Several are cited in the preface to the series, particularly Theodor Bibliander, Martin Luther, Francis Lambert, and Sebastian Meyer.[65] Bullinger's allusions to the influence of the annotations of Erasmus of Rotterdam and Lorenzo Valla underscore the humanist influence which this series of sermons bears in its philological concerns and historical presentation of the growth of error, despite early humanist mistrust of the book.[66] Of medieval commentaries, Bullinger cites as of general influence on him the gloss of Walafrid Strabo, and, for his forecasting a sorry state for the Christian Church, Joachim of Fiore.[67] Bullinger's work gave evidence of a spiritual or allegorical emphasis characteristic of Tyconius, together with an affirmation of an end to history. Bullinger's use of patristic commentaries helped to quell any lingering Erasmian doubts of the legitimacy of the Apocalypse. Bullinger singles out works by Aretas, his predecessor Andreas, and Primasius as of help.[68] Each of these advocated strong spiritual interpretations of the imagery of the text, Primasius again drawing us back to the influence of Tyconius.[69]

In Bullinger's citation of the sources he used for his commentary, of note is the long list of commentators including Irenaeus, Joachim of Fiore, John of Salisbury, Savonarola, and Pico della Mirandola, who are drawn upon to attest to the growth of error in history as such error became embodied as Antichrist.[70] In light of these exegetical antecedents, it is clear that we can expect an important melding of the Tyconian and Joachite traditions in Bullinger's commentary.

This interweaving of representative interpreting of our text together with a specificity given to the development of evil and error in society will bear in a special way upon the interpretation of our text. A coherent explanation for the twin threat of Turkish armies and religious declension could be found in the narrative of the text together with the implication that God's true witnesses were those standing in opposition. Of course, many questions were left unanswered. Did Christendom face a war to be fought on secular grounds, hence by the Emperor Charles V? Was war against the Turk a Christian duty, a papal or holy war? Or, were the Pope and Turk both servants of the Antichrist, both to be resisted by every loyal citizen?[71]

Nevertheless, error there was and Bullinger argued that tyranny and lawlessness were increasingly evident in the papacy. This was the kingdom of Antichrist, growing daily, so "that the first beast might be worshipped, that is, that it might be given power once again, and the old idolatrous and superstitious cult renewed."[72] In the papacy, he argued, one finds the same cult, religion, and superstition as had existed in old Rome. Calling the reader's attention to his earlier work, *On the Origin of Error*, Bullinger adds: "But in the popish kingdom today, the actors only being changed, who can deny that the same cult, the same religion, even superstition is being renewed? I have treated these things at large in my book *De origine erroris*."[73]

The book of Revelation was of interest to Bullinger not only because it helped to explain the social reality in the sixteenth century, but because the doctrine found there was the same as that taught elsewhere in Scripture: It was a revelation of Jesus Christ.[74] Christ stands with the altar before the throne of God, which signifies his priestly role. He is always in the sight of the Father (Rom. 8; Heb. 9), continually interceding for us. Christ brings our prayers, those of the saints, before God. Saints are those who dwell on earth and are sanctified by the spirit of God, the blood of Christ, baptism, faith, and the Word.[75] The Apocalypse, a "paraphrase" of the prophets, directs us to Christ and his work at every juncture.[76]

> And I doubt, whether there exists in the canonical books after the prophecy of Isaiah, after the story of the Gospel, but especially after the Gospel of blessed John any other book which has more and more elegant descriptions of Christ, than this book. They are deceived and err completely, who are of the opinion that in this book the Gospel is rarely preached. But we should see descriptions of Christ throughout its parts.[77]

John is said to borrow illustrations from the rest of Scripture to explain the priesthood and kingdom of Christ. Bullinger writes approvingly of Oecolampadius's remark that in the book of Revelation the Evangelist John can be seen as the expositor of the prophets.[78] There is nothing said here that is contrary to the evangel. In the Gospels we read of coming persecution. In the Epistles we find that in the last times Antichrist will come even as many antichrists have already begun their work. The Apocalypse is merely "more painted, variable and polished. . . ."[79] Its doctrine is the same. Moreover, the Apocalypse tells the real story of the Church by summarizing the intent of the prophets for the new dispensation.

The style of the Apocalypse, however, is different from the rest of Scripture, although analogies exist. In the opening pages of the series Bullinger explains that style in his discussion of visions.[80] Three kinds of "prophesying" are distinguished, based on Moses' prophetic vindication before the murmuring of Miriam and Aaron.[81] First, there are visions. Many are found in Daniel. We read of one given to Peter, of another to Paul (Acts 16). The book of Revelation itself is cast in this form. Second, there are dreams like those sent to Pharaoh or Nebuchadnezzar and interpreted by Joseph and Daniel. The prophet Joel, in the second chapter of his book, spoke by visions and dreams. Finally, Moses included a skillful exposition of Scripture as a third form of prophecy. Many such prophecies were uttered by Moses and the Apostles. The Apocalypse is similar to this third type, a "skillful" or "eloquent exposition" of Scripture.[82] This concept of prophetic vision inevitably drives the expositor back to the rest of Scripture:

> For this book on account of the predictions of things to come is a prophecy of the New Testament. Moreover, a prophecy, that is, an exposition which opens up and illustrates the old prophets. . . . They therefore that shall frame their life after this book are blessed. For they flee the seduction of Antichrist, abide in the faith of Christ and live forevermore, etc.[83]

Bullinger cast his series of sermons into a structure that reflected his high Christology and emphasized the continual consolation of Christ and spiritual function of the ministry in every age, particularly the last and most severe.[84] Each sermon plays upon this theme. The first four, on the title and prologue of the Apocalypse, serve as an introduction and foundation for the rest of the series and outline Christ's qualities: the Lord, the faithful witness, first born of the dead, ruler over kings, and one who loves us incomparably.[85] The second section, sermons 5 through 22, develop Bullinger's central conception of Christ ruling his Church (Rev. 1:12–3:22). The letters to the seven churches provide a theological checklist for what Christ desires of his Church.[86] The third section, sermons 23 through 50 (Rev. 4–11), illustrates how God governs the world through Christ. Here the destiny of the Church is presented; persecution and martyrdom are its lot as the faithful do battle with Antichrist. This conflict, however, is not without its consolations; Bullinger sees them chiefly in chapters 10 and 11.[87] Here the regnant Christ is shown to stand with faithful preachers. The conflict between them and Antichrist is described in greater detail in the fourth division, sermons 51 through 65 (Rev. 12–14). While this section is not without its own consolation (chapter 14),[88] the emphasis is upon the nature of the beast and the parallel between old Rome and new Rome: the old political power with its manifest idolatry and the new shadow state with its idolatry centered in the papacy. In the fifth division, sermons 66 through 95 (Rev. 15–22), Bullinger delineates the torments of the ungodly and the rewards of the righteous. Finally, the last several sermons (Rev. 22:6–21) commend the book to its readers. A prophetic, or "insider's," look into history is given to Christ's Church, governed by his Spirit and Word through an ecclesiastical ministry.

Prophetic vision is appropriate to times of crisis. For a community faced with the loss of coherence and identity, apocalyptic literature can offer a balance and continuity with the past.[89] In days threatened by imminent disaster, as Israel in the time of Moses or Elijah, God makes his presence known to his Church. Bullinger provides insight into the way in which God does this in his comments on our text; he sends his prophets:

> Moreover, [God] openly affirms that he will send into the world teachers of the truth and of certain salvation who will sharply rebuke the wickedness and wicked men of the most corrupt last age. They shall preach Christ sincerely and accuse Antichrist most severely. These he shadows by the figure of the two excellent doctors who, he says, because of their liberty of preaching and constancy of faith, must be most cruelly slain by Antichrist.[90]

When these preachers are slain, God provides others.[91] The point here is that their fate directs our attention back to the Old Testament and its demonstration of the character of God's work with Israel. The style of the Apocalypse is related to its purpose: not the presentation of new knowledge but a rephrasing of what has been known since the covenant was first laid down. Bullinger notes: "The sum and end of this scripture is this, that Jesus Christ our Lord will never fail his church on earth but will govern it with his spirit and word through the ecclesiastical ministry. But that the church itself, while it remains in the world, shall suffer many things for the confession of Christ and the truth of his gospel."[92]

God's care for his crisis-worn Church comes through the ministry. This theme, present throughout the series, finds its most extensive treatment in the sermons on our text.[93] The qualities of Christ's ambassadors, his prophets, and preachers are stressed. They are an expression of God's mercy for a Church that knows tribulation. Tribulation, understood through the filter of the Apocalypse, helped to define where Christ's Church and its witnesses might be found.[94] Such tribulation was a sign of God's activity and cleansing, finding scriptural warrant in the Acts of the Apostles, in lists of upright martyrs (Heb. 11), and elsewhere.[95] Bullinger appears to identify the true Church with the persecuted and martyred Church.[96] The tendency to make this identification will grow with a new literalism in Protestant polemics after Bullinger and will be related to Revelation 11:3–13.

That others agreed with Bullinger's theology and ecclesial identification is seen in the ready translation of this series of sermons into languages from English to Polish within the century. Of particular interest is John Foxe's request of Bullinger for information on martyrs in the history of the Church.[97] It is Foxe, citing Bullinger in his own commentary on the Apocalypse, who will help to further this process of literalization, at least for the Anglo-American world.[98] The early Church had been persecuted by pagan Rome, the first beast of the Apocalypse. Now new Rome, the image of the beast, was persecuting those who stood for the ancient faith.[99]

The series found a ready audience, one that sought the consolation of Christ through the "prophetic" use of apocalyptic texts in the context of persecution. Its audience, a Church that conceived of itself as the true Israel to whom God was again sending his prophets, included the Marian exiles from Britain. Thomas Lever, speaking for this community, wrote to Bullinger:

> While others are wont to dedicate their writings to princes . . . you alone . . . have made choice of us poor exiles to whom to address your midnight studies and lucubrations. . . . But herein appears your zeal for the Lord's household

. . . in which we are deserted by our friends, laughed to scorn by many, spurned by others, assailed by reproaches and revilings by most, you alleviate by your learned discourses, that we may not sink under the pressure of these evils; and, like a good shepherd, you tend, strengthen, and cheer us all in our dispersion.[100]

Adventual Witnesses and the Growth of Evil

As we turn to Christ we see more clearly the mysteries of the kingdom of God. We come to understand the nature of the Church, her ministry, and how faithful pastors are to work "repairing and preserving" it.[101] Bullinger lays out his reasoning using the vision of seven churches.[102] Turning to Christ we learn of the destiny of his Church in the midst of adversity, and of the way in which God governs history.[103] The temple vision (Rev. 4:1–5:14) prepares us further as we learn of the government and order of the Lamb.[104] The nature of his rule is filled out in the visions of seals and trumpets. The seals represent a general prognostication of the nature of God's rule for all times and ages. They are followed by more specific visions following the opening of the seventh seal (Rev. 8:1).[105]

Drawing our attention to the seven trumpets (Rev. 8–11), symbolic of corrupt doctrine, heresy, and sects from John's day until the Last Judgment,[106] Bullinger illustrates the course of the Church as it progressed through the dangers of legalism,[107] sectarianism,[108] the pollution of pure doctrine (with the fall of a great prophet or preacher),[109] and Pelagianism.[110] These four trumpet disasters are followed by three "woes" introduced by the last three trumpets (Rev. 9:1). These signify the greatest dangers facing the Church since John's day: the Papacy,[111] Muhammadanism,[112] and the Last Judgment.

In contrast to the three woes, Bullinger finds three comforts in chapter 10 of Revelation: (1) the person and work of Christ, (2) the comfort of Scripture and preaching, and (3) the promise of restoration before the end. This restoration is said to be adumbrated under the person of the Evangel John: For under the person of John it is shown here that the evangelical and apostolic doctrine must be restored against Antichrist and Muhammad in the last times before Judgment.[113]

John is told to preach again (Rev. 10:11), a promise that he would yet preach after his exile. This is also a promise that before the Last Judgment preachers will preach before Antichrist with the spirit and doctrine of John. Drawing attention to Revelation 11, Bullinger cites Aretas, approving of his emphasis on the appearance of preachers in the spirit of Enoch and Elijah, not of their actual persons returning bodily to earth as is alleged by many common people.

> Aretas, bishop of Caesarea, an interpreter of this book, notes that from this text in John's book arose the opinion of the common people that John together with Enoch and Elijah would come again into the world before the judgment, i.e., corporally, and would preach earnestly and constantly against Antichrist. Aretas repeats this more fully in his exposition of chapter 11 when he comes to the words of John concerning the two witnesses, etc.[114]

Bullinger writes that he drew insight into the identity of our witnesses from Theodor Bibliander, Martin Luther, Francis Lambert, and Sebastian Meyer. Bibliander combined both the historical perspective of Nicholas of Lyra with the older exegetical interest in recapitulation.[115] For him, the trumpet visions carry us to our text, a description, in part, of the Council of Constance. Bibliander writes:

> The eleventh chapter, moreover, describes the battle of the Antichrist against two witnesses of Jesus, not simply against Elijah and Enoch, as Augustine reminds us, but also against the divine scripture of both testaments. At that time he commands the temple, that is, the priesthood, to be measured by the standard of the divine word, and since it in no way squares with this, to be rejected by the catholic and apostolic Church. That this was done at the Council of Constance, everyone can see who compares history diligently with this prophecy.[116]

The meaning of the passage agrees with a particular event in history. More than this, the spiritual qualities of our two witnesses are emphasized. They are not simply Enoch and Elijah but the Scriptures and the promise of God. Bibliander adds, "For if anyone desires to harm the two witnesses of Jesus, the old and the new testaments, in which is contained the testimony of the entire catholic church, fire will come out of their mouths and destroy their enemies."[117]

The history of the Church from Christ to consummation is illustrated, Bibliander contends, in the balance of the Apocalypse. Bullinger did not follow Bibliander precisely. For one thing, he finds our text illustrative of the spiritual ministry of the Church, not only the Scriptures. However, this is a ministry that grows out of the Scriptures.[118]

Bullinger mentions his debt to Luther both in the preface to this work and elsewhere[119] as having helped to define the nature of that conflict for him. Since we have already commented on Luther's use of our text, two extensive commentaries by former Franciscans should be mentioned. These works, by Francis Lambert (1528)[120] and Sebastian Meyer (1539),[121] were the first Protestant commentaries on the Apocalypse. Both will be discussed more fully in the next chapter. Bullinger builds on this to write that the spiritual qualities of Enoch and Elijah indicate the nature of the expected renewal. The example of Enoch, described in Genesis (given added significance in Sirach 44), is cited in his sermon on Revelation 10:8–11. Enoch was translated to heaven in order that through him the heathen might learn of another life for the servants of God. This was a polemic against the Epicureans, who believed there was no life other than this. However, while many argue that Enoch is preserved in heaven in order to return corporally in the last days, Bullinger contends:

> Here Enoch is seen to come spiritually to that last age which the Lord himself predicted would be similar to the one which preceded the Flood. For just as then most people despised the divine judgments thinking themselves to be safe, and neither feared any peril, or hoped for any better life: even so it is in the last age, in which Enoch constantly preaches in the person of those who build up and defend eternal life and the resurrection of the body against the Epicureans.[122]

If Enoch symbolized a warning and witness against a life lived without hope (Epicureanism), Elijah became a model for the work of the prophet against idolatry.[123] Bullinger's conception of the latter-day Elijah follows Aretas, thus buttressing his position with what he believes to be patristic precedent.[124] As in the case of Enoch, there is not to be a return of Elijah the Tishbite prior to the end of the age. The historical Elijah is not "thrust out of the heavenly palace, and again subject to corruption, and given to the cruel hands of antichristians who might tear him to pieces."[125] Rather, as Elijah appeared in strength and power in John the Baptist, the forerunner of Christ's first Advent, so Elijah's preaching will be heard again before the Last Judgment. Latter-day preachers will be filled with the spirit and power of Elijah. They will call people away from idolatry in a way similar to that of Elijah the Tishbite in the days of Ahab and Jezebel.

> Elijah cried out, How long do you limp on both sides: if the Lord is God, fol-
> low him: if Baal is God, follow him. Now the Elijahs will cry: if Christ is the
> perfection of the faithful, what need is there for man's inventions and consti-
> tutions in order to work perfection? If Christ is our justification, satisfaction,
> purification, our only intercessor and redeemer, why are these things attributed
> to human merit?[126]

Similarly, John the Evangelist will not return bodily to earth, but preachers filled with John's doctrine will preach the truth out of John's Gospel, Epistles, and Apocalypse.[127] These preachers or prophets of the last days will offer the con-solation of Enoch, the judgment of Elijah, and be filled with the doctrine of John the Evangelist.

John's call to preach against Antichrist's wickedness epitomizes the commis-sion given to others to preach against wickedness and idolatry in their times. First, his call is from God; John was told to go and preach. In a similar way Moses was called, and so are all prophets and apostles. To the one who is called, a com-mandment is given to take the book (Rev. 10:8). This is not merely any book but the one lying in Christ's (the mighty angel's) hand—that is, the Holy Scriptures, the sum of faith and doctrine.[128] Ministers must obey the commandment of God to take the book and seek to understand the Scriptures. Earlier Bullinger explained that Christ stands before us with his book open although Antichrist desires to see it shut. However, Antichrist cannot shut this gospel book, which lies open through preaching and printing.[129] The effect of the ministry of the witnesses and the preached Word will be sweet to the mouth yet bitter to the flesh.

With the vision come the gifts. Our adventual witnesses are equipped with God's Word. If the "champions of Antichrist" assail these prophets, then out of the Scriptures they will speak the Word of God, destroying their enemies "with the fire that goes out of their mouth."[130] Like Elijah they have the power to shut up the heavens, withholding the rain of God's grace: Where preachers are not heard, God's grace is not received.[131] Like Moses they have the power to turn water into blood (i.e., godly wisdom, grace, and relief into offense and punish-ment). The text implies that those who do not turn to Christ at the preaching of the prophets bring down damnation upon themselves.[132] In striking the earth with plagues, the witnesses, like Moses, demonstrate that God will punish sins with plagues. Finally, like Jeremiah, the witnesses are known for the strength of their preaching.[133] In ministers in whom these marks are seen one may find lawful proph-ets of God. In his sermon on Revelation 2:1–3, Bullinger reminds us that Christ, not the pope, carries the keys to heaven and hell. And Christ has delegated this power to his preachers.[134]

These gifts symbolize Protestant spirituality in the period lying before us: power through the Word, grace through preaching, damnation through rejection, and plagues for impenitence. It is with these weapons that the new temple is to be constructed. Christ vows that in the latter days his Church will be rebuilt through his ministers, though their number be small.[135] He promises as many as are needed. Their work is that of Enoch and Elijah, Joshua and Zerubbabel, Moses and Jeremiah. In fulfilling their task, "they imagine nothing out of their own minds, neither add to nor take away anything from God's word, but simply declare to the church of God the things they have seen in the story of the gospels and heard from prophets and apostles."[136] Bullinger continues:

> Thus much has he spoken concerning the preachers of the Gospel, who shall fight against Antichrist in that last age before the judgment, and shall build up the church and assure the believers. You yourself shall observe in what preachers you shall perceive these marks, and these shall you acknowledge as the lawful prophets of God. At the same time, you shall acknowledge how great a benefit of God it is to have true and faithful preachers of God's word. May the Lord our God confirm all ministers of his word in setting forth his truth to the world's end.[137]

Preaching, or "prophesying," follows the lines Bullinger laid down in *De prophetae officio*. Prophets teach, admonish, and console as did the Evangelist John, Elijah, and Enoch.[138] They are provided by God in order to rebuild his Church. This message of consolation is carried over into chapter 11 with the vision of the measurement of the temple (Rev. 11:1–2).[139] As Israel's temple had been devastated by the Chaldeans, both Church and Christendom of the time lay wasted by papists and Turks.[140] The pope and his priests are like the heathen. Rather than explain, they impugn the Scriptures.[141] They are permitted by God to trample over the holy city (i.e., persecute the Church, but only for a limited time).[142]

This period is spoken of as lasting forty-two months. However, Bullinger writes, the number is only to indicate that the time of tribulation has a definite duration, which is known to God.[143] It can be reckoned as running from the year A.D. 666, a number of mysterious significance mentioned in Revelation 13:18.[144] In the sermon on Revelation 11:3–6, Bullinger writes that during this time the Lord will send prophets—preachers who will maintain and defend the truth of the gospel, glorifying Christ. They will attack Antichrist,[145] destroying his kingdom. Again, a figurative period of time is given, 1260 days, a period similar to the mysterious times of trial in Revelation 12 and Daniel 7 and 12.[146] Bullinger argues against any specific three-and-one-half-year period as too brief for such momentous events:

> But who shall believe that within three and a half years all those things should be accomplished which he declared in the whole work? Why do they restrict the time of Antichrist to three and a half years, especially his persecution? Why don't they see the destruction of Antichrist, the peace of his saints and day of judgment to be the same day? . . . It is known to the Father alone. Therefore let them stop fighting the Gospel with their speculations.[147]

Hope is offered throughout the time of Antichrist's persecution, however long that time might be. This is clearly a task for later commentators to debate, particularly in light of the measured restoration Bullinger envisages for the Church even in days of a last conflict with Antichrist. Preachers throughout this period are spoken of as "two." This implies "not . . . only two," but "that the power of Christ in the world is small in the eyes of the worldly."[148] The appearance of the prophets in sackcloth underscores their diminutive status before the world. They are dressed as penitents for mourning. Faithful ministers and pastors who resist Antichrist at all times will appear this way. We are reminded by such dress of the prophets of old, particularly Enoch or Elijah, but we are not to look for their bodily return. Rather, as Jerome counselled Marcella, we should look for the spiritual interpretation of the text and not follow Jewish fables.[149]

If this restoration appears strange it is because of a general unfamiliarity with the book of Revelation in recent years. It was even condemned, Bullinger writes, by good and learned men who taught the same doctrine as that contained in the Apocalypse:[150] how Antichrist is to be refuted and slain.[151] This is done not in a corporeal but in a spiritual way, by preaching the doctrine found in the examples of Enoch, Elijah, and John.[152] The further imagery of the text reminds one of the renewal experienced by Israel following her return from the Babylonian captivity (Zech 2:1–5; 4:3–14). As God remembered Israel in the closing days of the old dispensation, so he is remembering the new Israel in the sixteenth century. The images of two olive trees and candlesticks standing before God (Rev. 11:4) reflect Zechariah (4:3–14) and his intent to describe the anointed ones (Zech. 4:14) to whom is given the task of national reconstruction.[153] Through God's Spirit, Zerubbabel is to complete the restoration of the temple. The vision of Joshua and Zerubbabel (godly prophet and prince) in the restored Jewish community, the golden lampstand and the two olive trees, carries with it connotations of national righteousness and renewal that reach back to Israel's earliest days (cf. Exod. 25:31–40) and carry us through the old dispensation into the new. Prophetic types point the way toward reform, the renewal of the Church, and reconstruction of Christendom.[154] Such thinking draws us back to the initial covenant between God and man. Adherence or departure from it tells the inner story of history.

Bullinger's commentary on our text has shown us something about the identity, spiritual qualities, and time of prophesying of our two witnesses. It has also shown us something of the goal of their preaching. Our text also opens up to a wider vision of organizing history. The resurrection of the witnesses (Rev. 11:11) illustrates God's promise of new prophets and our future resurrection.[155] Recently it was visible in John Hus, Jerome of Prague, Lorenzo Valla, and Savonarola, and now the kingdom of Antichrist is under full attack.[156] The sack of Rome (1527) appears to answer to the earthquake and destruction of the tenth of the city spoken of in our text (Rev. 11:13).[157] Bullinger's witnesses, the faithful preachers of all ages, are also more particularly depicted as time progresses toward a final conflict. That conflict is more fully pictured in sermons 51–65 (Rev. 12–14), where we find a fuller description of the conflict between the witnesses and the beast.[158] That beast, the spirit of Antichrist, is the general contamination of Christian doctrine pictured under the first four trumpets. It takes on greater specificity as the

Day of Judgment approaches,[159] following historical progression marked by the chief instruments of Satan against the Church: the old and new Roman empires.[160]

Believing the present to approximate history's last conflict brings out the tension inherent in the Tyconian tradition between the perennial spiritual truth of the Apocalypse and its specific applicability for the last days. Bullinger appears to argue that his is the time above all others for the adventual witnesses.[161] They stand at the threshold of a measure of restitution, at least the renewal of evangelical preaching prior to the Last Judgment as error and wickedness intensify.[162]

In his sermons on Revelation 13:1–11, Bullinger deals with what he refers to as the chief instruments of Satan, when they developed, and how they are determined.[163] His discussion is correlated with the visions of Daniel where he follows Jerome in interpreting as the Antichrist the little horn that arises among the ten horns of Daniel's final beast (Dan. 7:8).[164] He writes that old Rome fell around A.D. 480 when Odoacer invaded the city. Antichrist, or new Rome, originated with the claims to ecclesiastical dominion by Boniface III (607), who feared that such primacy might be given to Constantinople.[165] The actual "fall" of the Church is identified with the number "666" (Rev. 13:18), which implies a specific period from the date of John's vision (A.D. 97 for Bullinger) to the manifestation of open error in the Church. Adding 666 to 97 yields the year A.D. 763, the time of the reign of Pepin the Short. Pepin gave the former exarchate of Ravenna, claimed by Byzantium, to Rome, creating the papal state by this "donation."[166] Thus, Bullinger's conception of papal declension is tied to spiritual and temporal dominion: first property, then idolatry.[167]

A further "fall" came with Boniface VIII. In his Jubilee Year (A.D.1300) he arrogated to himself power that was not his. In causing all to worship him, he established an idolatry parallel to that of the days of Ahab and Jezebel and old Rome.[168] The story of the Middle Ages was one of the progressive subversion of the norms from the covenant. New Rome, the image of the beast, started to mock the things of Christ. As Christ produced miracles at Cana of Galilee, the papacy, following the example of Simon Magus, showed forth false miracles. As Elijah called down fire from heaven, the papacy issued excommunications. As the fire of the Holy Spirit descended upon the early disciples, so the papacy claimed that it could offer the grace of the Spirit.[169] Moreover, papal power is illusory power. In sermon 59, Bullinger calls papal Rome an empire that wishes to be seen in continuity with old Rome yet presents only a "show" of power.[170] It has no real authority, no actual legitimacy. Old Rome had a Senate, new Rome an imaginary Senate. Old Rome had its laws, new Rome its decretals, which, in the end, give all power to a pope who places himself above all laws. The beast, the false prophet, puts life into this image.[171]

As the Church was persecuted under old Rome, so it is also under new Rome. As the early Church faced ten persecutions yet was not defeated, such was also the experience of the Church through history. Bullinger writes that the Lord prophesied this future to his Church, reminding it of the consolation it would find along with the trials it would face.[172] Through persecution for the past 500 years the present Church has been linked to the early Church.[173] Even during Bullinger's time, he notes that "the ground is wet with the blood of martyrs."[174] To both churches the promise is given that the witnesses of Christ, his prophets and preachers, would complete their prophesying.[175]

Prophecies about witnesses and beasts, of their time, appearance, and number, should not lead to anxious speculation, Bullinger writes. The visions of consolation are meant to console us with the knowledge that God is omniscient, that all things are in his control.[176] The vision of the dragon and beasts, of their conflict with the woman and child, is contrasted by the vision of the Lamb on Mt. Zion accompanied by 144,000 persons marked with the name of the Father (Rev. 14:1).[177] This is the consolation: Christ stands with his Church throughout history. He knows its conflict. His gospel is continually sent forth, signified by the angel flying through the middle of the sky (Rev. 14:6). There will be no "peaceful kingdom" on earth before Judgment other than the Church.[178] He sends prophets and preachers to guide the way even in the most disastrous of times. They point to Christ, the one who together with the Father controls the destiny of Church and world. His person and his work are the guarantee and the illustration of God's covenantal goodness.[179] Bullinger notes, "By this enigmatic kind of speech the Lord has not defined a specific time or date; rather, he called the faithful to long-suffering, patience and constancy and commanded that we should not all too curiously search the instant of this time but leave it to Christ . . . ."[180]

In his criticism of Müntzer,[181] Hut[182] and the communalism, revolutionary spirit, and special revelations associated with their names, Bullinger helped to set the tone for the negative way in which Anabaptism would be perceived by many Protestants. They seemed to press for revelation beyond the stipulations of the covenant. But, while Bullinger eschews new religious revelation,[183] there appears a tension in his thought: If there is a final conflict, might such lead to a greater depth of spiritual perception as that conflict approaches? While Bullinger searches for historical reasons for the problems faced by the Church, nevertheless he tries to fit these into a pattern of the "fall" of the Church of varying significance.[184] His own narrative for the history of the Church, which has developed out of Bullinger's spiritual perception, comes into tension with a developing humanist interest in historical causation.[185] Bullinger's conception of the growth of error, personified in Antichrist, deepens (with ecclesial significance) the tension between history and theology.

Another strain in Bullinger's conception of history comes with declension from the covenant. The increase in such declivity appears to give an independent reality to wickedness, raising difficulties for understanding historical causation.[186] Moral failure affects history, and that history is conditioned by a growing spiritual power that may or may not take on a "borrowed" reality, derivative of conflict in society. While the conflict is clearly moral, the idea of an intensification of evil appears to imply more. The tropological use of the text takes on ever-more concrete historical features. As the papacy is more clearly labeled Antichrist, Protestant exegeses will more fully identify with the adventual witnesses. Does this imply development or declension in history? While Augustine, clearly a model for Bullinger, expounded both the idea of perennial conflict and of some temporal development of evil in history at the very end of the age, his emphasis was upon the former.[187] Bullinger, and more so the other "Augustinians" after him, differed to the extent that they reckoned with a perceived intensification of evil in history. Hence, the tension: Error and wickedness are perceived as perennial problems yet are believed to increase as time moves toward its goal in salvation history.[188] In Bullinger it appears as though that end were nearing and, thereby lessens, to some extent, the distance between Bullinger and his Anabaptist opponents.

> We have seen that all signs that are said to precede the day of the Lord have been fulfilled. Let us watch therefore. Let us see and hear these things in this wise considered with great and diligent attentiveness, what kind of judge of all things shall come, and what that judgment shall be, by the godly most wished for, to the ungodly horrible and with trembling to be feared.[189]

The fifth section of the series of sermons (Rev.15–22:5) carries us beyond our theme but illustrates some of the tensions just discussed.[190] It is here that Bullinger presents his conception of the millennium, which he places in the past, the period of 1000 years in which the gospel has been preached without significant refutation.[191] If there is any future blessed age, it comes with the restoration of the gospel envisioned in chapter 11 of Revelation.[192] Preaching binds Satan, it completes Christ's victory, and it drives away deception. It makes possible the new freedom in Christ. Bullinger writes, "For in case you yourself are still bound with the chain of the Devil, you have not yet heard the gospel. . . . But concerning the time of this most shining truth of the gospel, it is said that it shall endure in the world a thousand years."[193]

The millennium, or 1000 years during which the gospel was freely preached, probably began at some point during Paul's ministry and ended around the time of Gregory VII when worldly ambition made its full display in the Church.[194] Heresies arose during this time but were successfully refuted. Papal and Turkish power began but were resisted. Ever since the time of Gregory VII, Bullinger argues, Satan has again been unleashed to harass the godly. The adventual witnesses are found throughout this period but especially in the days when the godly are most harassed (i.e., in the last days).[195]

Despite a tension in temporal perspective, it is clear that Bullinger's attention was riveted to the oneness of the promise that gave unity to history. Present moral concerns may have an apocalyptic component but ministers were to be involved with questions of adherence to the covenant, not fantastic prognostications about the future.[196] This concern is formally expressed in the Second Helvetic Confession where Bullinger deals with "Last Things" under chapters on Creation (vii) and Christ (xi).[197] The argument is similar with the Apocalypse. God's promise calls for the continual presence of prophets concomitant with the growth of wickedness in the last days, prophets like Enoch and Elijah or the Evangelist John, who would call people away from idolatry precisely because they are living *coram Deo*.[198]

Two points should be made in summarizing our discussion of Bullinger's use of our text. First, it can be said that his treatment of our theme is largely formal.

After all, the specific text is handled as it is found in the book of Revelation. Bullinger read Revelation through the Gospels, not the Gospels through Revelation. When Bullinger published his sermon "The Last Judgment" (largely a commentary on Matthew's apocalypse) in the opening months when he began his Apocalypse series, our two witnesses are not specifically mentioned.[199]

In 1557, Bullinger produced two further works on the end of the age. Here again Matthew 24 is prominent, although much is taken from Paul and Daniel, and there appears to be an allusion to our theme.[200] Despite such scant treatment, when Bullinger does come to our text in the sermons on Revelation, he has much to say. He uses the text to discuss the ministry in history, a theme that will be expanded upon by later Protestant commentators, several of whom explicitly claim to be following Bullinger. The placement in which the chapter finds itself through his "soft periodization" adds to its significance in the development of Protestant-Catholic polemics. For Bullinger, the adventual witnesses are Christ's messengers and ambassadors, his preachers and pastors.[201] The vision can receive both a general interpretation or can develop more particular implications in light of the given set of historical circumstances. This hermeneutical confluence from the exegetical tendencies of Tyconius together with the anti-papal prophecies of the later Middle Ages has significance now for the development of various sectors of Protestantism. However, in Zürich itself the vision would be continued by Bullinger's successors such as Rudolf Gwalther.[202]

Notes

1. Matthias Senn, "Alltag und Lebensgefühl im Zürich des 16. Jahrhunderts," *Zwingliana*, 14 (1976):251–62; cf. for apocalyptic dating Heinz Schilling, "Job Fincel und die Zeichen der Endzeit," in *Volkserzählung und Reformation* Wolfgang Brückner, ed. (Berlin: Erich Schmidt, 1974), pp. 325–92. Rudolf Pfister, "Reformation, Türken und Islam," *Zwingliana*, 10 (1956):345–75, describes the dilemma which Turkish advance into European precincts posed, the Turk being an outer form of Antichrist parallel to an inner, or papal, Antichrist (pp. 347–53). Also cf. Heinrich Dannenbauer, *Luther als religiöser Volksschriftsteller* (Tübingen: J. C. B. Mohr, 1930); and Robert Scribner, *For the Sake of Simple Folk: Popular Propaganda for the German Reformation* (Cambridge: Cambridge University Press, 1981).

2. Heinrich Heppe, *Dogmatik des deutschen Protestantismus im sechzehnten Jahrhundert*, 3 vols. (Gotha: F. A. Perthes, 1857).

3. References to Bullinger's works are to *Heinrich Bullinger Werke*, Fritz Büsser, ed. (Zürich: Theologischer Verlag, 1972); bibliographical items are cited from sec. 1, vol. 1 (*Heinrich Bullinger Bibliographie*) with the abbreviation, HBBibl I/1, plus the number giving Bullinger's particular work. See also Fritz Büsser, "Probleme und Aufgaben der Bullinger-Forschung," *Bullinger-Tagung 1975*, Ulrich Gäbler and Endre Zsindley, eds. (Zürich, 1977), pp. 7–19. The standard biography remains that of Carl Pestalozzi, *Heinrich Bullinger: Leben und ausgewählte Schriften* (Elberfeld: Friderichs, 1858); more recently J. Wayne Baker, *Heinrich Bullinger and the Covenant: The Other Reformed Tradition* (Athens: Ohio University Press, 1980); and Charles S. McCoy and J. Wayne Baker, *Fountainhead of Federalism. Heinrich Bullinger and the Covenantal Tradition with a Translation of De testamento seu foedere Dei unico et aeterno (1534)* (Louisville, Ky.:

Westminster/John Knox Press, 1991). Both texts find the covenant to be the organizing principle around which Bullinger develops his theology; Edward A. Dowey cautions by illustrating limits, "Heinrich Bullinger as Theologian: Thematic, Comprehensive, Schematic," in *Calvin Studies* 5 (1990):41–60.

4. Bullinger affirms the Christian ministry in the *Decades*: "God indeed might by the secret illumination of the Spirit, without man's ministry (as his power is tied to no creature), regenerate the whole world, and govern the church itself: but he despiseth not his creatures, nor destroyeth the work of his own hands, and doeth all things in order; even so from the first beginning he forthwith spake to the world by patriarchs, then by prophets, afterwards by apostles; neither at this day ceaseth he to give unto the world doctors and pastors: so that it becometh us not to tempt God, that is, not to look for a secret inspiration with the heretics . . . ; but to acknowledge a just order, and that God speaketh unto us by men, of whom he would have us to learn religion" (*The Decades of Henry Bullinger*, Vol. 5, ed. for the Parker Society [Cambridge, 1852], p. 94. See HBBibl I/1 nn. 179–82).

5. This term may at first appear unusual in association with Bullinger as it usually is reserved for "radicality" in the sixteenth century; e.g., Bernard Rothmann's *Restitutionism*, in Robert Stupperich, ed., *Die Schriften Bernard Rothmanns*, Vol. 1 (Münster, 1970). (See the introductory essay on "radicality" in George Williams, *Radical Reformation* [Kirksville, Mo.: Sixteenth Century Journal Publishers, 1992], pp. xix–xxxi; and as a safeguard to transcendence, idem, 13.3.) The term *restituitur* is used in the sermon on Rev. 10:8–11. It appears to be set parallel to *reparandam* and *restorescet* in *Apocalypsim*, cited below (note 7). Bullinger is critical of the doctrine of restorationism (*apokatastasis*), a view he attributes to Anabaptists in Augsburg, Basel, and Moravia (cited in Bullinger, *Antidotus*, 35).

6. Gottfried W. Locher writes of such prophets when the Word of God is preached through rightly called preachers and prophets. Bullinger believed that God's word was itself preached. This, Locher believes, is a brief formula for the underlying sense of knowledge in the Reformation, and, one might add, with pedagogical implications ("Praedicatio verbi dei est verbum dei," *Zwingliana*, 10 [1954]:47–57; cf. Joachim Staedtke, *Theologie des jungen Bullinger* [Zürich: Zwingli Verlag, 1962], pp. 52–79). See further on prophecy in the sixteenth century in Locher, "Prophetie in der Reformation. Elemente, Argumente und Bewegungen," in *Charisma und Institution*, Trutz Rendtorff, ed. (Gütersloh: G. Mohn, 1985), pp. 102–9. On Zwingli's idea that his own day was similar to that of days of prophetic crisis and outpouring in the OT, see Fritz Büsser, "Der Prophet-Gedanken zu Zwinglis Theologie," *Zwingliana* 13 (1969):7–8; cf. Gordon Rupp, "The Swiss Reformers and the Sects," in *The New Cambridge Modern History: The Reformation, 1520–1559*, Vol. 2, G. R. Elton, ed. (Cambridge: Cambridge University Press, 1958), p. 96. The nature of this prophetic activity is described in Bullinger's commentaries on the Hebrew prophets, e.g., *Ieremias fidelissimus et laboriosissimus Dei propheta* . . . (Zürich: Froschouer, 1575) (HBBibl I/1 n. 361). The exemplary prophetic activity of Jeremiah for his own day and for contemporary society is emphasized throughout, e.g., fol. 1r; note Bullinger's conclusions, fol. 8v-9r.

7. Bullinger's debt to patristic and medieval authors for the historical vision and development of ministerial identity evident in these sermons, in particular to the tradition of Tyconius mediated through others and interwoven with Joachite themes, is a story that yet remains to be told fully. It illustrates part of the way in which texts, especially the Old Testament, were reaffirmed in Protestant scholarship, here through the filter of the *figura* of the Apocalypse. Bullinger's sermons on the Apocalypse, *In Apocalypsim conciones centum* (Basel: Oporinus, 1557) might be seen as a summary of his corpus. The series was printed in Basel, not Zürich, by Oporinus, 1557 (HBBibl I/1, no. 327); on the role of

the Zürich Council in monitoring the press, see Hans Ulrich Bächtold, *Heinrich Bullinger vor dem Rat: Zur Gestalfung und Verwaltung des Zürcher Staatswesens in den Jahren 1531 bis 1575* (Bern: Peter Lang, 1982), p. 103. An English translation was rendered early, *A Hundred Sermons upon the Apocalips of Jesu Christe* (London: John Day, 1561) (HBBibl I/1, no. 355). See in Heinrich Bullinger, *Diarium Annales vitae der Jahre 1504–1575*, Emil Egli, ed. (Basel: Basler Buch und Antiquariatshandlung, 1904), p. 50. On its place in the tradition of Apocalypse commentaries, cf. R. H. Charles, *Studies in the Apocalypse*, (Edinburgh: T. & T. Clark, 1913), p. 28; Bousset, *Offenbarung*, pp. 86–89; cf. Richard Bauckham for the influence of Bullinger's series of sermons on the book of Revelation upon English Protestantism, *Tudor Apocalypse* (Oxford: The Sutton "Courtenay" Press, 1978).

8. Several models of unfolding religious-political history in the sixteenth century present themselves: (1) a religious model, attentive to theological argument, that identifies an orthodox reformation and then further devolutions; (2) a model that draws upon the seminal works of Weber, Troeltsch, McNeill, and Williams, attentive to "sociological-theological congeries" of movements (George H. Williams, The Radical Reformation Revisited," *Union Seminary Quarterly Review*, 39/1-2 [1984]:1–24; see p. 3) a model that looks different with its focus upon unfolding social history in general, and in northern as opposed to southern German cities in particular (Heinz Schilling, ed., *Die reformierte Konfessionalisierrung in Deutschland—Das Problem der "Zweiten Reformation"* [Gütersloh: Gerd Mohn, 1986]). For a contemporary summary of these issues, see R. Po-Chia Hsia, "The Myth of the Commune: Recent Historiography on City and Reformation in Germany," *Central European History*, 20 (1987):203–15.

9. Note patterns of alienation and goal definition in Robert King Merton, *Social Theory and Social Structure* (New York: Free Press, 1968), pp. 194–214; and as applied to religious consciousness, Barbara Hargrove, *The Sociology of Religion: Classical and Contemporary Approaches* (Arlington Heights, Ill.: Harlan Davidson, 1989), pp. 270–71. See later chapter in this study.

10. For Zwingli prophetic modeling appears to follow primarily the examples of Isaiah and Jeremiah; this is reflected in the introductions to the Isaiah and Jeremiah commentaries. See Büsser, "Der Prophet," p. 8. In Zwingli's *Der Hirt*, ZW, ed. Emil Egli, Georg Finster, and Walter Köhler (Leipzig: M. Heinsius Nachfolger, 1914), Elijah is one of the preeminent models for ministry (pp. 32–34, 69).

11. Zwingli was taunted and praised as such a prophet, believing his own day to be parallel to that of Isaiah. See Büsser, "Der Prophet." Also cf. Rupp, "The Swiss Reformers and the Sects," in Elton, ed., *The New Cambridge Modern History*, p. 96.

12. Heinrich Bullinger, *De prophetae officio* (Zürich: Froschouer, 1532), sig. Dviii(r)–Eiii(r). BBBibl I/1, no. 33. For commentary and publication of the epilogue see Fritz Büsser, "'De prophetae officio' Eine Gedenkrede Bullingers auf Zwingli," *Festgabe Leonhard von Muralt*, Martin Haas and Rene Hauswirth, eds. (Zürich: Verlag Berichtshaus, 1970), pp. 245–57; G. R. Potter, *Zwingli* (Cambridge: Cambridge University Press, 1976), pp. 211–24.

13. Bullinger, *De prophetae officio* (sig. Eir-v.).

14. Ibid., sig. Aiiv.

15. Ibid., sig. Aiiiv–Bvir. Bullinger deals with the sum of Scripture, the covenant, and Jesus Christ, its guarantor. Rules for interpretation and homiletics are touched upon and highlight emphases in Augustine and Erasmus. Susi Hausamann illustrates the manner in which Bullinger used the rhetorical tradition (*Römerbriefauslegung zwischen Humanismus und Reformation* (Zürich: Zwingli Verlag, 1970), pp. 161–82). She writes that Bullinger follows the humanist's use of rhetoric but grounds it in theology and Scripture. This is

demonstrated by the reference to the three classical tasks of the orator, "docere, delectare, movere," which Bullinger transforms into "docere, hortari, consolari" (p. 179).

16. Ibid., sig. Bvir–Dviiv. The errors of papists and Anabaptists are singled out in addition to the general condemnation of venality and corruption.

17. Bullinger, *De prophetae officio*, sig. Aiiir. See Locher, "Praedicatio verbi dei est verbum dei"; Edward A. Dowey, "Das Wort Gottes als Schrift und Predigt im Zweiten Helvetischen Bekenntnis," in *Glauben und Bekennen: Vierhundert Jahre Confessio Helvetica Posterior*, Joachim Staedtke, ed. (Zürich: Zwingli Verlag, 1966), pp. 235–50, esp. p. 238; Staedtke, *Theologie*, pp. 52–61; and Susi Hausamann, "Anfragen zum Schriftverständnis des jungen Bullinger im Zusammenhang einer Interpretation von 'De scripturae negotio'," in *Heinrich Bullinger 1504–1575: Gesammelte Aufsätze zum 400. Todestag*, Vol. 1 (Zürich: Theologischer Verlag, 1975), pp. 29–48.

18. The identity of the Church is grounded in God's nature, not in a visible community. In the Second Helvetic Confession Bullinger stressed the oneness of the current reform movement with the preaching of the early Church; see Ernst Koch, *Die Theologie der Confessio Helvetica Posterior* (Neukirchen: Neukirchener Verlag, 1968), pp. 216–24, 234, 240. When accused by Cochlaeus of not being in accord with the early Church, Bullinger wrote a defense of his position entitled, *Ad. J. Cochlaei de canonica scriptura et catholice ecclesiae authoritate libellum* (1544). He wrote several works in an effort to demonstrate that the reformed doctrine agreed with that of the early Church, especially in the area of justification by faith alone—an article of faith said to be as old as the world. See *Der alt gloub* (1539), HBBibl I/1, nos. 99–110.

19. Bullinger, *De prophetae officio*, sig. Aivv-Avr.

20. Bullinger's definitive work on the covenant is *De testamento seu foedere Dei unico et eterno* (Zürich: Froschouer, 1534), HBBibl I/1, nos. 54–61. He delineates the conditional nature of the covenant in this work and sets it within the context of God's promise of salvation (*De testamento*, fol. 2–3b). J. Wayne Baker writes: "Bullinger held to a conditional covenant on the one hand and the *sola gratia* encased within a carefully stated doctrine of single predestination on the other" *Heinrich Bullinger and the Covenant*, p. xxiii). Cf. also the discussion, pp. 1–25, 181–215; Baker sees the covenant coming to the center of Bullinger's theological thought as early as 1528, p. 11. The plausibility of such growing weight given the covenant follows from the nature of the Hubmaier-Zwingli debates in Zürich at this time. Both Hubmaier and Zwingli each gravitated toward different metaphors for the Christian life, the symbolism of dying and rebirth in adult baptism for the former, that of the newly covenanted Israel with civic implications for the latter and mentor of Bullinger.

21. Bullinger, *De testamento*, fol. 18r-v. "For the law . . . , as the Lord himself testifies, teaches on the one hand the love of God, on the other the love of neighbor. The same is taught in the chapters of the covenant. Indeed, the Decalogue itself seems to be something like a paraphrase of the conditions of the covenant. For that which is said here in short, I the Lord am all-sufficient, is expounded more copiously in the Decalogue in a similar way: I am the Lord your God who brought you up from the land of Egypt. Again, that very exact word of promise is pronounced: you shall observe my pact (pactum); walk before me and you shall be whole."

22. Bullinger, *De prophetae officio*, sig. Aivv; cf. Baker, *Heinrich Bullinger and the Covenant*, pp. 108–12.

23. Ibid., sig. Dviir.

24. Ibid., sig. Dviiir. The nature of this prophetic activity is described later in Bullinger's commentaries on the Hebraic prophets, e.g., *Ieremias fidelissimus et laboriosissimus Dei propheta . . .* (Zürich: Froschouer, 1575). HBBibl I/1 n. 361. That Jeremiah's

prophetic activity was not only exemplary for his own day but also of current importance is emphasized throughout, e.g, fol. 1r; note Bullinger's conclusions, fols. 8v–9r.

25. Bullinger, *De prophetae officio*, sig. Dviiir. This point is developed, e.g., in Bullinger, *Epitome temporum et rerum ab orbe conditio* . . . (Zürich: Froschouer, 1565), HBBibl I/1, no. 430, fols. 23r–72v.

26. Bullinger, *De prophetae officio*, sig. Aiiir, Bvir–Dviiv.

27. Büsser, "'De prophetae officio' Eine Gedenkrede," p. 252.

28. *Anklag und ernstliches Ermahnen Gottes* (HBBibl I/1, nos. 3,9), dated by references in Bullinger's *Diarium*; Baker, *Heinrich Bullinger and the Covenant*, pp. 102–3.

29. Büsser, "'De prophetae officio' Eine Gedenkrede," p. 253; cf. Baker, *Heinrich Bullinger and the Covenant*, p. xviii (citing Bullinger's *Reformationsgeschichte*, Vol. 3, pp. 293–96).

30. Bullinger, *De prophetae officio*, sig. Dviiv.

31. Ibid., sig. Dviiir.

32. Bullinger, *De fine saeculi & iudicio venturo Domini nostri Iesu Christi* . . . *orationes duae* (Basel: Oporinus, 1557), fol. 57; HBBibl I/1, no. 320. The sermon is on Dan. 7, and the reference alludes to the battle between the saints and the little horn (Dan. 7:20–21).

33. Potter, *Zwingli*, pp. 211–24; cf. Büsser, "'De prophetae officio' Eine Gedenkrede," p. 253.

34. Büsser, pp. 253–54; cf. Siegfried Rother, *Die reliogiösen und geistigen Grundlagen der Politik Huldrych Zwinglis: Ein Beitrag zum Problem des christlichen Staates* (Erlangen: Palm & Enke, 1956), pp. 63–72; on the sread of the Reform movement, see Menna Prestwich, ed., *International Calvinism, 1541–1715.* (Oxford: Clarendon Press, 1985).

35. Bullinger, *De prophetae officio*, sig. Eir–v. See Potter, *Zwingli*, p. 224.

36. Bullinger, *De testamento*, fols. 2r–3v. A sustained treatment is in *Epitome temporum*, fol. 48 *et passim*.

37. Ibid., fol. 5r.

38. Ibid., fol. 6v.

39. Bullinger, *De origine erroris libri duo* (Zürich: Froschouer, 1539). HBBibl I/1, no. 12. Cf. P. Polman, *L'Elément historique dans la controverse religieuse du XVIe siecle* (Gembloux: J. Duculot, 1932), pp. 100–9; Baker, *Heinrich Bullinger and the Covenant*, pp. 81–106.

40. Bullinger, *De origine erroris*, fol. 2r. "In different ways today, many ponder how the church and the realm of Christ might be preserved unharmed from those severe trials by which she is daily attacked. For she is not overthrown and laid waste by means of Turkish weapons only, but rather she is attacked and exceedingly oppressed by the hypocrisy, superstition and overwhelming powers of those who set themselves up as a wall against the house of the Lord, who live by means of the church and desire to be honored as the presiders of the churches."

41. Ibid., fols. 3r–9v.

42. Ibid., fols. 38r–42r.

43. Ibid., fols. 46v–52v.

44. Ibid., fol. 4r. Cf. Polman, *L'Elément*, pp. 165–67; Baker, *Heinrich Bullinger and the Covenant*, pp. 93–94.

45. Bullinger, *De origine erroris*, fols. 54r–59v, 113v–125r.

46. Ibid., fol. 94r.

47. Ibid., fol. 46v.

48. Ibid., fol. 47r.

49. Ibid., fols. 48v, 52v.

50. Ibid., fol. 94r.

51. Ibid., fols. 52v, 54v–63v, 98v–104v.

52. Ibid., fols. 179v–245r.

53. Ibid., fols. 113v–118r.

54. Ibid., fols. 113v–118r.

55. Bullinger, *In Apocalypsim*, sig. Bir; cf. Ulrich Gäbler and Endre Zsindley, eds., *Heinrich Bullinger Briefwechsel, Vol. 1, 1524–1531.* Zürich: Theologischer Verlag, 1973). See letter: [Bullinger] to [Bartholomäus Stocker] and Leo Jud [Kappel], April 17, 1525, pp. 71–74; cf. Staedtke, *Theologie*, p. 72.

56. *Commentarius in II Epist. argumentum posterioris Epistolae ad Thessalonicenses* (Zürich: Froschouer, 1537). HBBibl I/1, no. 84, pp. 528–30.

57. Ibid., p. 530.

58. Bullinger, *De omnibus sanctae scripturae libris expositio*; see Bauckham, *Tudor Apocalypse*, p. 45. Later, in the preface to his sermons on the book of Revelation, Bullinger said that its imagery speaks "in a veiled way" (*sub involucro*) of the facts of history: *In Apocalypsim*, sig. Bir.

59. Bullinger, *In sacrosanctum Jesu Christi Domini nostri Evangelium secundum Matthaeum* (Zürich: Froschouer, 1542), HBBibl I/1, no. 144, fols. 208v–223v.

60. Bullinger, *Das Jüngste Gericht* (Zürich: Froschouer, 1555). HBBibl I/1, no. 281.

61. Idem., *De fine saeculi et iudicio* (HBBibl I/1, no. 320).

62. Idem., *Ieremias fidelissimus et laboriosissimus Dei propheta* . . . (Zürich: Froschouer, 1575) HBBibl I/1 n. 361.

63. Idem., *Daniel sapientissimus Dei propheta* (Zürich: Froschouer, 1565). HBBibl I/1, no. 428. A strong sense of world history in relation to the four world empires is developed in chapters 7 through 12, pp. 73vff. For Bullinger's commentary on Daniel's prophetic weeks, see Baker, *Heinrich Bullinger and the Covenant*, pp. 75–76.

64. Idem., *Epitome temporum*, HBBibl I/1, no. 430.

65. Bullinger, *In Apocalypsim*, sig. B1r-v.

66. Ibid., sig. B1v.

67. Ibid., sig. B1v.

68. Ibid., sig. B1v.

69. With Francis Lambert, Bullinger neglects later medieval interpretations of the Apocalypse in favor of patristic Greek commentaries. This Patristic Greek influence upon Bullinger's work in the sermons on the Apocalypse seems similar to that discussed by Susi Hausamann in her analysis of Bullinger's commentary on Romans. See Hausamann, *Römerbriefauslegung*, pp. 66–88; cf. Polman, *L'Elément*, pp. 95–109.

70. Bullinger, *In Apocalypsim*, sig. B2r-v. Cf. Marjorie Reeves, *The Influence of Prophecy in the Later Middle Ages* (Oxford: Clarendon Press, 1969), pp. 107–8. Reeves underscores the importance of Joachim's "prophecies" of the decline of the papacy for the Protestant attack upon Rome.

71. Pfister, "Türken und Islam," pp. 346–49.

72. Bullinger, *In Apocalypsim*, p. 176.

73. Ibid., p. 176. Luther had identified pope and Turk as the two forms of tyranny (WA DB 7, pp. 412–21) to appear at the end of history—one spiritual (pope), the other corporal (Turk). For many they were adumbrated under the apocalyptic woes (Rev. 9:1–12 and 9:13–11:14) or in league with each other as dragon and beast or beast and beast in chapters 12 and 13 of Revelation.

74. Ibid., p. 6.

75. Ibid., pp. 104–7.

76. Ibid., sig. A6v.

77. Ibid., p. 126. On the qualities of Christ, see pp. 8–19. Bullinger is simply following

the text, but these same qualities are drawn out throughout his series. On Bullinger's Christology, see Edward A. Dowey, "Der theologische Aufbau des zweiten Helvetischen Bekenntnisses," in Joachim Staedtke, ed., *Glauben und Bekennen* (Zürich: Zwingli Verlag, 1966), pp. 219–20.

78. Bullinger, *In Apocalypsim*, sig. A6v.

79. Ibid., sig. A6r–B1r; cf. p. 196.

80. Ibid., pp. 1–27, esp. p. 7.

81. Cf. Numbers 12:5–9.

82. Bullinger, *In Apocalypsim:* "disertam expositionem" (p. 7).

83. Ibid., p. 8.

84. Ibid., p. 5. Because of the consolation found in these visions, Bullinger argues, there is no need for the prophecies of Methodius, Cyril, Merlin, Bridget and others (p. 6).

85. Ibid., p. 14. Bullinger provides his outline for the series on p. 5.

86. Ibid., p. 21.

87. Luther had emphasized the images of consolation in these chapters, the promise of the renewed proclamation of the gospel and of prophets committed to this task, but not to the same extent as is characteristic of Bullinger. WA DB 7, pp. 446–48.

88. Bullinger, *In Apocalypsim*, pp. 155–58.

89. So argues Richard Bauckham of the "theological legitimacy of apocalyptic." It serves to legitimate traditional theodicy and maintain continuity ("The Rise of Apocalyptic," *Themelios*, 32 (1978):10–23, esp. pp. 10, 17, 19); cf. Lerner, "Medieval Prophecy and Religious Dissent," p. 10.

90. Bullinger, *In Apocalypsim*, sig. A4r.

91. Ibid., sig. A4r.

92. Ibid., sig. A2r; cf. pp. 132–36.

93. Ibid., pp. 139–54.

94. Bullinger, *In Apocalypsim*, pp. 102–4. Bullinger delineates the nature of tribulation in several places. For example, in sermon 36 (Rev. 7:13–17) he describes three forms of tribulation: (1) the persecution of tyrants, which produces martyrs; (2) the fear of God, which produces grief over corruption, unrighteousness, and the work of Antichrist; and (3) the mortification of the flesh, which increases a desire for righteousness and the comfort of the world to come.

95. Ibid., pp. 102–4, 123–25.

96. This is clear in the description of the conflict between the witnesses and their adversaries in Rev. 11:7. His sermon on Dan. 7, *De fine seculi* (fol. 57), offers the same perspective.

97. Hastings Robinson, ed., *Original Letters Relative to the English Reformation . . . from the Archives of Zürich* (Cambridge University Press, 1842–1847), vol. 1, pp. 25–26.

98. John Foxe finds a German counterpart for this in Flacius Illyricus. In Foxe such a line of witnesses is more directly connected with Rev. 11:3–13.

99. That the elect suffer in every age is stressed in Bullinger's work, *Der alt gloub*, sig. Bviiiv. Here Abel is the first martyr for the true faith. This is carried through in the Apocalypse while the emphasis is placed upon the first and last ages of the Church: (Bullinger, *In Apocalypsim*, p. 7).

100. Original Letters, Vol. I, p. 169. In light of the censorship applied by Zürich's Small Council to Bullinger's attempts to have Thomas Cramner's *Forty-nine Articles* printed (1553), this Bullinger-English connection is all the more significant. See Hans Ulrich Bächtold, *Heinrich Bullinger vor dem Rat*, pp. 103–14.

101. Ibid., pp. 15, 40.

102. Ibid., p. 61.

103. Ibid., pp. 62–154 (sermons 23–50).

104. Ibid., pp. 63–64; cf. pp. 104–7. Christ's power is one with the essence and nature of God. It is part of and contained in the vision of God as presented in Rev. 4:5–8. On Bullinger's view of governance, see Dowey, "Der Theologische Aufbau," in Staedthe, ed., *Glauben und Bekennen*, pp. 218–19. The seven-sealed book is a summary of God's counsels, works, and judgments (*In Apocalypsim*, pp. 70–71).

105. Bullinger, *In Apocalypsim*, p. 81.

106. Ibid., p. 105.

107. His examples are the Nazarenes and Ebionites (ibid., p. 109).

108. He mentions Valentinianism, Manichaeism, and Montanism (ibid., p. 109).

109. The protagonists are Paul of Samosata and Arius. Bullinger argues that the same tendency reappeared in Michael Servetus (ibid., pp. 109–10).

110. Ibid., p. 10.

111. Rome is the star that falls from the heavens. Her churches were pure until Constantine. After that, decay set in with ambition (ibid., p. 112).

112. The Muslims are described as the Oriental destroyers, "God's whip." Note the association with the prophecies of Daniel (10) and the Sibyl (ibid., p. 121). The real significance of this scourge appears with the year A.D. 1300, a date of millennial importance for Bullinger (ibid., p. 122).

113. Ibid., p. 132.

114. Ibid., p. 133.

115. Theodore Bibliander, *Ad omnium ordinum reipublicae Christianae principes uiros, populumque Christianum, relatio fidelis Theodori Bibliandri* . . . (Basel: Oporinus, 1545). A sense of living in days similar to Noah's runs through this work. On Bullinger's appreciation of Bibliander's commentary, see *In Apocalypsim*, sig. Blr.

116. Ibid., pp. 138–39. The connection between the Council of Constance and our text will figure prominently in the thought of John Foxe.

117. Ibid., p. 58.

118. Bullinger, *In Apocalypsim*, p. 141.

119. Ibid., sig. Blv, B2v, p. 141; Staedtke cites the influence of Luther's *De captivitate Babylonica* (1520), as mentioned in Bullinger's *Diarium* (p. 126), in *Theologie*, pp. 46–47.

120. Francis Lambert, *Exegeseos in sanctum divi Joannis Apocalypsim* (Marburg, 1528). With regard to our two witnesses, Lambert writes that he neither agrees nor disagrees with the possibility that they are Enoch and Elijah or two who will come with their spirit and power. Perhaps they are two clear and distinguished evangelists who appear as John appeared prior to the first Advent of Christ. But he prefers to see them as types of all truthful testimony, which the Church needs to hear at the time of the work of the son of perdition (fol. 188r-v).

121. Sebastian Meyer, *In Apocalypsim Johannis* (Zürich: Froschouer, 1554). The first edition of this commentary appeared in 1539. Meyer writes that the witnesses are those who preach in the spirit of Elijah during the time of the Antichrist (fol. 4lr).

122. Ibid., p. 133; cf. Bullinger, *Epitome temporum*, fols. 5v–6r.

123. Ibid., p. 128; cf. sermons 12, 31, 33, 60, 89.

124. Ibid., pp. 132–33.

125. Ibid., p. 133.

126. Ibid., p. 133; cf. Bullinger, *Epitome temporum*, fols. 52r–53r.

127. Ibid., p. 133.

128. Ibid., p. 134; cf. Bibliander, who associates the witnesses with the Scriptures (*Ad omnium ordinum*, p. 138).

129. Ibid., p. 128; cf. pp. 198–99. The importance of printing in promoting the work of reform is emphasized by Bullinger and other Protestant reformers as part of the restoration of the gospel in the latter days.

130. Ibid., p. 141.

131. Ibid., p. 142.

132. Ibid., p. 142.

133. Ibid., p. 143.

134. Ibid., pp. 263–68.

135. Ibid., pp. 139–40.

136. Ibid., p. 140.

137. Ibid., p. 143.

138. Ibid., pp. 132–36.

139. This is not the old temple of Jerusalem, destroyed for good, but the Church. Bullinger draws our attention to Ezek. 40, the envisioned new temple and those sealed from destruction in Ezek. 9:4 and Rev. 7:3 (ibid., p. 136). Note Hut's use of these texts.

140. Ibid., p. 136.

141. Ibid., pp. 136–37.

142. Ibid., p. 138.

143. Ibid., p. 138.

144. Ibid., p. 138; cf. p. 193. The use of apocalyptic imagery here is similar to the tension between example and historical identity that we encountered earlier in Matthew of Janov. For Protestant speculation on the number 666, see Polman, *L'Elément*, pp. 176–77.

145. Ibid., pp. 139–49 (sermons 47a, 47b, and 48). Luther had led the way in attempting to mark the development of Antichrist in the office of the bishop of Rome. Much of the speculation concerning Antichrist became summarized in the work by Lambert Daneau, *Tractatus de Antichristo . . .* (1576), published in many languages and editions. It is found in his *Opuscula omnia theologica* (Geneva: 1583), pp. 1049–92. See Olivier Fatio, *Methode et theologie: Lambert Daneau et les debuts de la scholastique reformée* (Geneva: Droz, 1976).

146. Bullinger offers a spiritual reason for several of the stated periods. Months rather than years are told to churches that need consolation; days rather than months are mentioned to preachers who need both consolation and strengthening.

147. Bullinger, *In Apocalypsim*, p. 140.

148. Ibid., p. 139.

149. Ibid., p. 139.

150. Ibid., p. 2; cf. p. 133, an elliptical reference to Zwingli?

151. Ibid., p. 115; cf. sig. A2r-v, B3r.

152. Ibid., pp. 140–41.

153. Ibid., p. 141.

154. Ibid., p. 136.

155. Ibid., pp. 147–48.

156. Ibid., p. 148. Bullinger writes: "Thirty years ago, through the grace of God, Mirandola, Reuchlin, Erasmus, Luther, Zwingli, Oecolampadius, Melanchthon, and innumerable others brought light to the world. In them the spirit of life expressing itself after every man's talent, set forth the Scriptures, detected the Romish wickedness, and rebuked the vices of all states, but especially of the clergy."

157. Ibid., p. 149.

158. Ibid., pp. 155–210. Bullinger's fourth division of the series.

159. Ibid., fols. 214r–215v, 208v; cf. *In Apocalypsim*, pp. 112, 120.

160. Bullinger, *In Apocalypsim*, pp. 155–58; cf. p. 167 and *Daniel*, fols. 77r–80v.

161. Ibid., p. 146; cf. sig. B2v.

162. This was held by Luther on the basis of Rev. 10:11, WA (DB) 7, pp. 403ff.

163. Ibid., pp. 164–67.

164. Bullinger, *Daniel*, fol. 124r; Bullinger, *In Apocalypsim*, pp. 172–74. In 2 Thessalonians 2, Paul demonstrated that Christ would not come to Judgment until Antichrist has come first. Jerome and others agreed that Rome, the fourth world empire, the force which restrains evil (2 Thessalonians 2:6), must be taken away first, then Antichrist comes. For further comment on Bullinger's use of Danielic imagery, see Baker, *Heinrich Bullinger and the Covenant*, pp. 75–76, 94–95.

165. Bullinger, *In Apocalypsim*, pp. 172–74. On the origins and development of a "fall" theory of history, particularly in Protestantism, see Erich Seeberg, *Gottfried Arnold. Die Wissenschaft und die Mystik seiner Zeit* (Darmstadt: Wissenschaftliche Buchgesellschaft, 1964; 1st ed., 1923); note the discussion as it applies to Bullinger by Aurelio Garcia Archilla, "Truth in History: The Theology of History and Apologetic Historiography in Heinrich Bullinger" (Ph.D. dissertation, Princeton Theological Seminary, 1989), pp. 245–58.

166. Bullinger, *In Apocalypsim*, pp. 193–94.

167. Ibid., pp. 81–83. "Christ calls the Roman papacy a beast, because in avarice, covetousness, tyranny, cruelty, and even in beastliness, it does not differ at all from the old beast, of whom I have already spoken" (p. 173).

168. Ibid., p. 174.

169. Ibid., pp. 177–78.

170. Ibid., pp. 177–87; on Rev. 13:13–15, the longest in the series.

171. Ibid., pp. 179–87. Bullinger writes, "Who therefore is the first, the two-horned beast, but the Pope? He is also the false prophet. And who is the beast, in whose sight the Pope works wonders, but the Image of the beast, and therefore a beast also, in as much as the empire is raised by the beast, and governed by the spirit of the beast" (p. 179).

172. Ibid., pp. 162–64. John Foxe, among others, will develop Bullinger's argument of parallel periods of persecution and models of adventual witnesses, using such to structure his conception of history.

173. This parallelism is drawn out in sermon 32 (Rev. 6:9–11), pp. 86–87.

174. Bullinger, *In Apocalypsim*, p. 87.

175. Ibid., pp. 88–91. According to Bullinger's sermon on Revelation 14:6–7 the gospel is predicted by law and prophets, fulfilled in Christ and declared by the apostles. In the last days, preachers are to preach the fear and honor of God, that the hour of Judgment is near, that God alone is to be worshipped (pp. 200–201). This vision of consolation parallels other visions of consolation in chapters 7, 10, and 11 of the book of Revelation.

176. Ibid., p. 168.

177. Ibid., p. 196.

178. Ibid., p. 200. Similar signs of consolation are found in chapters 7, 10, 11.

179. Ibid., p. 140; cf. p. 1; and *De testamento*, fols. 2–3v, 16, 17v.

180. Ibid., pp. 140–41.

181. Bullinger, *Reformationsgeschichte*, I, pp. 224, 237, 248.

182. Bullinger, *Der Widertöufferen ursprung fürgang Secten wäsen fürnemen und gemeine jrer leer Artickel* (Zürich: Froschouer, 1561), fols. 42r–44r. HBBibl I/1, no. 395.

183. Bullinger, *De testamento*, fol. 31v. Cf. Edward A. Dowey, "Covenant and History in the Thought of Heinrich Bullinger." (Paper read to the A.S.C.H., December 1962. Unpublished typescript, Princeton Theological Seminary, Princeton, New Jersey, p. 9.)

184. According to Jakob Berchtold-Belart, Bullinger differed from his predecessor,

Zwingli, in having a greater sense of inwardness, other-wordliness, and of the life of the spirit. (*Das Zwinglibild und die Züricherischen Reformationschroniken* [Leipzig: Verlag von M. Heinsius, 1929], pp. 117–67; cf. pp. 118–19). Cf. Joachim Staedtke, "Die Geschicht-sauffassung des Jungen Bullinger," in *Heinrich Bullinger 1504–1575: Gesammelte Aufsätze zum 400. Todestag*, Vol. 1, Ulrich Gäbler and Erland Herkenrath, eds. (Zürich: Theologischer Verlag, 1975), pp. 65–70. Another place in Bullinger's work where this tension between an "outer" and "inner" history occurs in the preface to his commentary on Matthew (*Matthaeus*, sig. Zlr-v).

185. Bullinger, *In Apocalypsim*, pp. 164–95. The longest sermons and most detailed historical work are found in comments on chapter 13 and the nature of the beast.

186. Bullinger's notion of evil "strains" the Augustinian idea of the privative nature of evil by appearing to give to evil a reality of its own. His religious regression, whether defined as the growth of Antichrist in papal dominion or humanist idea of the Dark Ages, gives definition to history by drawing out a moral lesson, which for Bullinger is tied to the concepts and visual constructs in the book of Revelation. Bullinger, *De origine erroris*, fols. 123–139 *et passim*; cf. *In Apocalypsim*, pp. 143–46; cf. Susi Hausamann, *Römerbriefauslegung*, pp. 161–62, 176–85; M. P. Gilmore, *Humanists and Jurists* (Cambridge: Harvard University Press, 1963), pp. 12–14, 18; and Theodor E. Mommsen, "Petrarch's Conception of the 'Dark Ages'," *Speculum*, 17 (1942):226–42.

187. Augustine, *De civitate dei*, pp. 708–15, esp. pp. 712.21–713.54. Evil increases in time for two reasons. (1) Satan becomes more influential in the lives of nonbelievers as he is prevented from controlling the lives of believers; (2) there will occur a final loosing of Satan. Satan, now bound under the present conditions of this age, growing influence of the Church, and Christ's spirit in the world (Rev. 20:1–3), is not able to exercise power fully. After a symbolic 1000 years, and prior to the end of that age, Satan will be loosed and permitted a final fury. Augustine finds four reasons for this: (1) If Satan were never loosed we would never understand the fullness of his power and, contrariwise, the greatness of God's mercy; (2) God does not absolutely protect us from the growth of outward conflict, only from inward temptation; (3) Satan was bound so that faith might grow even in those persons who are weak of spirit; (4) Satan is loosed at the end of the age so that the "city of God" might appreciate more fully the nature of its enemy.

188. Bullinger's affirmation of an historical interpretation of prophecy, perhaps not quite as acute as Luther's, but driven by the same attention to the perceived conflict of the gospel through history, is revealing in its apparent repudiation of medieval mellenarian hopes (represented in his day by certain radical groupings), whereas in its discovery of the history of the Word it laid a foundation for later millenarian thinking in seventeenth-century continental Protestantism, and in Anglo-American biblical exegesis, which found his Apocalypse commentary congenial. To understand Luther on this point, see Robert Barnes, *Prophecy and Gnosis* (Stanford: Stanford University Press, 1988), p. 31.

189. Bullinger, *In Apocalypsim*, p. 257; cf. p. 277.

190. This section comprises sermons 66–95, pp. 210–301.

191. Bullinger, *In Apocalypsim*, p. 263.

192. Ibid., p. 136.

193. Ibid., p. 265.

194. Ibid., p. 78. Saints reign on earth through the virtues of Christ "non quidem corporaliter sicuti imaginantur Chiliastae, & hos sequuti Turcae . . . ." Cf. pp. 265–66.

195. Ibid., p. 201. The millennim is a comparative, not absolute, state. There is a certain tension between a "soft periodization" (cf. Staedtke, "Geschichtsauffassung," in *Heinrich Bullinger 1504–1575*, pp. 70–73) and a levelling of history before Christ who judges all (cf. Dowey, "Covenant and History," pp. 8–9), a tension between history and

the demands of the covenant. See sermon 35 (Rev. 7:2–8) where Bullinger refers to three periods of restoration: (1) an historical period from Cyrus to Pompey, (2) a period from Christ until the coming of Antichrist, (3) a period from the restoration of the gospel until the Last Judgment.

196. Bullinger, *In Apocalypsim*, pp. 43–45. In Bullinger's sermon on the letter to the church at Thyatira, new periods and revelations in history are compared with "Jezebelism"; cf. Baker, *Heinrich Bullinger and the Covenant*, pp. 101–2.

197. Dowey remarks that, rather than concluding with a chapter on eternal life, "this confession is brought to a close among the practical affairs of the church and the Christian life in the world 'sustained and governed by the providence of this wise, eternal, and omnipotent God.'" ("Der theologische Aufbau," in Staedtke, ed., *Glauben und Bekennen*, p. 234) cf. Walter E. Meyer, "Soteriologie, Eschatologie und Christologie in der Confessio Helvetica Posterior," *Zwingliana* 7.6 (1966):391–409.

198. Bullinger holds that this promise was clearly understood in the age of the patriarchs, and that later religions are deviations from it. (*De testamento*, fol. 31v.); cf.

199. One might also say that it provides in microcosm what Bullinger spells out in macrocosm in the following years with respect to the Apocalypse.

200. Bullinger, *De fine saeculi & judicio*, pp. 57–58. The visions of Paul and Daniel are cited as lacking specificity so as to increase faith; cf. Dowey, "Der theologische Aufbau," in Staedtke, ed., *Glauben und Bekennen*, pp. 212, 219–20.

201. Bullinger, *In Apocalypsim*, sig. A4r; cf. Walter Hollweg, *Heinrich Bullingers Hausbuch* (Neukirchen: Kreis Moers, 1956), pp. 18–23.

202. Paula Biel, "Heinrich Bullinger's Death and *Testament*: A Well-Planned Departure," SCJ, 22.1 (1991):3–14; esp. p. 7. In addition to Gwalther, others like Ludwig Lavater and Johannes Stumf will write with similar apocalyptic intent.

6

Rebuilding the Temple

The Company of Prophets

Commenting on our text (Rev. 11:11–13), Heinrich Bullinger noted that he had seen arisen in the previous thirty years a company of prophets (*communis prophetia*) like "Mirandola, Reuchlin, Erasmus, Luther, Zwingli, Oecolampadius and Melanchthon."[1] "Innumerable others" are cited as having taken the mantle. Many stepped forward to prophesy with the new vernacular Bible in hand, thus raising the issue of the definition of prophecy and of prophetic legitimacy.

While the general subject of prophecy is beyond the scope of this study, the question itself, as it was raised in relation to our text, is intriguing and can serve to provide a guide to the contours of prophecy as it was conceived in Reformed circles.[2] In searching for the identity of the two witnesses we have seen how from the start prophetic models were drawn upon from Israel's past. Not only do specific allusions in our text call for such, but the Apocalypse is replete with references to the books of the Old Testament. By raising up an Elijah or Enoch one raised up the company of prophets in the Old Testament. This exegetical effort was consonant with the theological endeavor by Bullinger and others to discover the roots of authentic faith frequently believed to lie in the origins of the covenant. It resonated with the general humanist effort to recover the knowledge mediated through original documents. Each of these lines helped to shape the Protestant emphasis upon the reality of living prophets who call God's people, the New Israel, to life in the New Jerusalem. Such life was to be symbolized in cultic practices that emphasized an aural rather than visual liturgy. One was to listen to the prophesying or preaching of God's prophets, who by the Spirit mediated the present reality of Christ, rather than observe the reenactment of God's sacrifice—Jesus Christ—and all that such had now come to mean in the theologies of the early modern churches. How one conceived of authentic religious mediation lent legitimacy to different forms of Church life and organization.[3]

The nature of prophecy was nuanced differently. Thomas Müntzer, as we have seen, stressed a deepened spiritual insight that drew upon Taulerite mysticism, Joachite–Taborite eschatology, and pointed by way of Hegesippus and Eusebius to a Church grounded in the Spirit rather than the Word. Prophecy was the gift of the living Spirit of God to any person who with an open mind might permit God to write on his or her heart (2 Cor. 3.3.).[4] Hans Hut pointedly added a temporal heightening to this spirit-mysticism.[5] Melchior Hoffman tied prophecy to three entrances of the Spirit into history (Jewish, Gentile, Hussite missions), an awareness of such bearing upon the efficacy of the prophetic message.[6] Luther understood Christ to be the last "prophet" (Deut. 18:18). Prophets since Christ mediate him through the gospel, or the Word. Prophets are discerned by their moral and spiritual qualities, not by the time of their appearances. While convinced by both the moral degeneration he perceived and contemporary social turmoil that he stood on the verge of God's final Judgment, Luther's prophets became preachers of Scripture, not charismatic visionaries.[7] This emphasis on preachers of the Word as discerned in Scripture is pointedly illustrated when, in his 1530 Preface to the Apocalypse, Luther writes that as long as prophecy is given only in images, as often in the Apocalypse, so it is concerned and mute and of no profit. Without a sure word of interpretation, there is no prophecy.

Turning to Zürich, Gussmann argues that it was in this early Reformed setting that Luther was first referred to as Elijah, and by Zwingli. What motivated Zwingli? Was it the same series of events that may have caused Müntzer to begin his apocalyptic timetable, if he had such? The dating is the same, around 1519. In any case, when Zwingli several years later wrote his treatise on the nature of the ministry, *The Shepherd* (*Der Hirt*), there were no references to adventual witnesses. Elijah surfaces as one of the preeminent models for the ministry, but against an Erasmian and moral rather than apocalyptic framework. Zwingli seldom cites the Apocalypse and appears to have had little evident interest in the prophecies of Daniel.[8] The shape of his reform began instead with an emphasis on the sermon rather than the liturgy as he preached on the first call of the gospel (Matthew) and growth of the Christian Church (Acts).

Zwingli's answer to the larger question of prophecy is seen, in part, in the institution of the Prophezei, which in its very structuring heralded the *viva vox evangelii*, the living word of the Gospel rather than the sacramental altar.[9] This institution, symbolic of the Reformed turn from prayer and ritual to prayer and prophecy, functioned without specific apocalyptic concerns.[10] It focused upon the proclamation of the gospel as God's Word was heard through the exposition and application of Scripture.[11] The concerns of the Christian disciple were to be shaped by the leading themes of Scripture, increasingly the rediscovery of the covenant in relation to the current state of society more than by the suppositions of the apocalyptic timetable.[12] Parallels were drawn between contemporary reform of public affairs and the work of the Old Testament prophets who urged national renewal.[13]

In his comments on Revelation 10:11, Bullinger, one with Zwingli in the institution of the Prophezei, finds a legitimate commission for Reformed ministers by recourse to models of prophetic calling in the Old and New Testaments, not through an apostolic order in history. "The evangelical and apostolic doctrine against Antichrist and Mahomet must," he writes, "be restored in the last times before the judgment."[14] The prophetic activity of these ministers is clear. As it touches on the debate over special end-time prophets, Bullinger's definition of prophecy in the sermons on the Apocalypse is helpful in its clarity for the sake of comparison. Bullinger writes that prophecy comes in three different forms—as visions, dreams, or a skillfull exposition of Scripture. The latter is the most usual, and the Apocalypse, he believed, was a good example of such. The minister, or prophet, heralded God's will in light of the covenant and in view of contemporary social deviations from it. This political significance of prophecy, undoubtedly related to the strength of civic humanism in the southwest German cities, helped to ensure that the visions of the Apocalypse would continue to be worked out against a social understanding of the Christian life.[15]

Later in his sermon on Revelation 10:11, Bullinger cites 1 Corinthians 11 and 14 as texts that define prophecy. This evangelical teaching, he argues, translated into all the known languages, overthrows Antichrist.[16] Both Bullinger and Theodor Bibliander, as cited earlier,[17] appear to have found in our text some means for understanding the role of the Church, the commissioning of her prophets, and the nature of their work for the then current religious crisis in society.

The Place of Prophecy

Luther had at first affirmed the priesthood of all believers.[18] Within his conception of calling, Luther appeared increasingly to reserve the office of preacher for those not only endowed by the Spirit and naturally gifted but also trained and duly called. From out of Wittenberg were sent reformers so trained on "church visitations" to ascertain and, as necessary, correct error in the churches of the Lutheran territories.[19] The question of the place of prophecy, of who was appropriately endowed, continued to be a lively issue through the sixteenth century. If looked at together with the various exegeses of our text some of the tensions that arose over the place of prophecy in the Christian community can be discerned.

The use of our text in this connection is found in the work of Francis Lambert of Avignon, who found here support for a wide vision of prophecy as the work of all of God's people. Lambert, formerly a Franciscan, travelled to Zürich in 1522, where he sat under Zwingli's tutelage. Moving then to Wittenberg, Lambert found support from Luther. During Lambert's subsequent sojourn in Strassburg, he heard the Strassburg prophets.[20] From there he came finally to Hesse, in 1526, where he was called by Philip, Landgrave of Hesse, to reorganize the Church.[21]

While his proposals for Church reform were rejected by Philip,[22] Lambert was retained and given a post at the newly established University of Marburg. Here he devoted his efforts to writing several commentaries, particularly on the prophets of the Old Testament. An ardent biblicist and learned philologist, it is tempting to see in Lambert's authorship of such commentaries his intent and his concern for prophetic models discerned in Israel's past, for his intent was pastoral. This temptation is all the stronger in light of Lambert's commentary on the Apocalypse, the earliest "Protestant" commentary on the book of Revelation.[23]

Prophecy was for the strengthening of Christ's Church. How this was to be done is outlined in Revelation 11. The reed given John to measure the temple (Rev. 11:1) is the Word of God. The temple is the Church, the altar Christ, and those worshipping in the temple the people of true faith.[24] Hypocrites are measured out. Here and throughout this commentary we find a strong anti-papal polemic.[25] In turning to the two witnesses, Lambert devotes most of his treatment to a discussion of their spiritual qualities. While the tradition of the Church has often understood these two witnesses as Enoch and Elijah, Lambert cites Jerome's spiritual interpretation approvingly.[26] The two adventual witnesses are faithful prophets and preachers throughout the history of the Church and who speak the truth.

> Two witnesses are sufficient to establish something. Now, since the testimony of two suffices, these two witnesses are types of as many witnesses to the truth as the Church of God will need at the time of the son of perdition. For then, by the providence of God, there will be as many witnesses to teach the truth, confirm the hearts of the faithful, and overcome the son of perdition and all his train as will be enough. This is all we can say with uprightness and certainty, declaring nothing in particular regarding their number or their person. I would yield, if anyone can draw more from the word of the Lord.[27]

At least three things must be noted. First, the focus of the book of Revelation is upon the present life of the Christian. God's witnesses convey his consolation and judgment to the contemporary Church. Scripture is the rod for doing this. It is held by God's prophets, known by the spiritual qualities and prophetic gifts delineated in our text.[28] The witnesses' description offers Lambert the opportunity to draw upon prophetic models from the Old Testament.[29] This contributes to the purpose of the Apocalypse, the strengthening of the Church between the Incarnation and Consummation.[30] The Apocalypse affirms final Judgment, but this does not diminish present concerns. Lambert emphasizes the brevity of life and proximity of the Judgment, which each person faces alone.

Second, the authority of the Apocalypse is the revelation of Jesus Christ. He is its central story. Everything in Revelation has to do with him, even mystically.[31] The Church is Christ's body. The book of Revelation shows us how he rules his Church (the Holy Jerusalem)[32] through Spirit, Word, and ministry. Servants of Christ are servants of his Word, the measuring rod (Rev. 11:1).

Third, there is a strong anti-papal and anti-Turk thrust in this commentary.[33] The two, but chiefly the papacy, constitute the embodiment of the "*antichristus mysticus.*"[34] It is here that time and development enter Lambert's commentary, drawing out the significance of the text. There is a muted sense of development in his discussion of the seals.[35] In line with the recapitulative method, the seven trumpets parallel the seals, constituting an allegorical description of the true proclamation of the mysteries of God as the seals are opened.[36] The first seal is related to the outpouring of the Spirit at Pentecost and the apostolic mission[37]; the second reflects the persecution of the Church by Roman emperors[38]; the third is reflected in the peace of Constantine and the growth of heresy.[39] In each of these the spiritual lesson rather than the historical event is dominant. When Lambert reaches the fourth seal, he discusses the growth of Turkish power.[40] Both pope and Turk are preludes to a deeper spirit of Antichrist growing in the world.[41] The effect of this is that more weight is given to the key imagery of Revelation 11 than seems implied in the general and spiritual interpretation given the text.

Adumbrated under the sixth seal is a picture of the last time, the revival of the gospel and the growth of persecution illustrated in chapters 11 and 13 of Revelation.[42] Following the destruction of Antichrist (the papacy, Islam, and the sects),[43] a brief period of peace on earth follows.[44] This period is correlated with the millennial age of Revelation 20, making Lambert an early Reformed chiliast.[45]

Like Zwingli, Lambert was concerned about the function of prophecy in the Christian Church.[46] The institution of the Prophezei in Hesse was influenced by Lambert's experience in Zürich and Strassburg. However, Lambert appears to have laicized the practice.[47] In a letter to Charles V, Lambert was to argue that prophecy, the interpretation of events to come and events past as well as the interpretation of Scripture for the present, was to be established by every Christian prince in his realm.[48] In his commentary he indicates that his own age is adumbrated by the sixth seal; it is the time for the open revelation of Antichrist in pope and Turk. True preaching at this time faces Antichrist's persecution as is shown in chapters 11 and 13 of the Apocalypse.[49] As the Wittenberg and Zürich divines gathered in Marburg in 1529 to debate the shape of reform, it is intriguing to view their work through the lens of our text.

Lambert's commentary, written before the Augsburg Confession, First Helvetic Confession, and first session of the Council of Trent, appeared in the same year that Luther began his own positive reassessment of the book of Revelation. Both Lambert and Luther found significance in the Apocalypse by drawing upon antipapal polemics, often of medieval origin as well-perceived contemporary experience. Bullinger's series on the Apocalypse, which is dependent upon Lambert, is similar in tenor. It is the definition of Antichrist that helped to establish the applicability of our witnesses in the framework of an otherwise more general reading. This moral reading of history strengthened an intent in the temporal momentum of history of enduring significance for Christendom. While the specific identity of these witnesses is not defined in Lambert, they may be seen as those gathering the Church in Hesse (i.e., Marburg to "prophesy"). These preachers of truth are God's witnesses as they use his rod (Scripture) to reform and rebuild Jerusalem, a theme that grows stronger as temporal hypotheses appear more sure. When the apocalyptic horizon becomes sharper and polemics more bitter, exegetes like Bullinger, Francis Junius, and others who follow this first Protestant "apocalyptic" theologian, will make a closer connection among themselves, the work of the Protestant Reformation, and our text.

Before moving ahead of ourselves, a second early commentary on the Apocalypse by Sebastian Meyer should be mentioned for the light it sheds on the way in which tribulation is to be handled by our witnesses.[50] Meyer, another former Franciscan, became a minister in the city of Bern. Together with Bertold Haller (1492–1528) he took a lead in the Reformation of that city after the disputation of 1528.[51] Casper Megander would further this work of reform by the institution of the Prophezei following the example of Zürich. Meyer's commentary adds a clear historical element to the work of our prophets in what is otherwise a spiritual and allegorical handling of the text. First, however, Meyer underscores the authority of the text of Revelation, which comes both from its author, an apostle, and by virtue of its canonical status.[52] Given the early date and publisher, Froschouer of Zürich, this is remarkable in itself. In developing his own method for approaching the Apocalypse, Meyer notes that one must distinguish different modes of expression and vision in it, an idea Bullinger will expand on in his definition of prophecy. Meyer pointedly lists the first four of Tyconius's rules as a guide.[53] The purpose of the entire Apocalypse is to show us Christ, his priestly work, and method by which he rules and judges.[54]

Meyer's outline of the Apocalypse is thoroughly Christocentric in its structure. The person and work of Christ defines and shapes the imagery of the text, an illustration of the extent to which Meyer applies Tyconius's rules in an effort to make sense of the book's visions. By doing this, Meyer appears to be telling us that the place of prophecy is in that Church that represents Christ. As this is a community in travail, it is one that bears the wounds of Christ, or fills out the sufferings of Christ in its generation.[55] Each portion shows forth some new dimension of Christ and the trials through which his body, the Church, goes in time: his presence in the seven churches (Rev. 2–3), his exaltation and the victory of God's people (Rev. 4–7), the constancy of his gospel and his people (Rev. 8–11), the afflictions of his body (Rev. 12–14), new persecutions (Rev. 15–16), Judgment and damnation (Rev. 17–18), and the marriage of Christ and the Church (Rev. 20–22).[56]

There is some sense of temporal development in the visions of the seals, but Meyer appears to be most interested in the way the first five seals illustrate the events of the life of Christ and find a parallel in the Church's experience through history.[57] The trumpet visions present an occasion for a discussion of the theme of Judgment throughout Scripture. There is little sense of temporal development here until one comes to the fifth trumpet. Muhammad and the papacy ascend out of the bottomless pit (Rev. 9:2) at this point.[58] However, one does not yet find the same desire to correlate vision and event as will be evident in later Protestant writers.

When Meyer comes to the two witnesses, he goes beyond Lambert in his identification of them with the emerging Protestant reform. The witnesses are the few preachers of the gospel throughout history, especially now in the great cities of Germany.

> The two witnesses, he said, signify the paucity of true preachers at the time of persecution by the Antichrist, when faith is already failing and charity is growing cold. In the same way, he might also say to one or the other how, formerly, in the days of Elijah and Micah, the number of false prophets was exceedingly great, but true prophets of the Lord numbered scarcely one or two who dared to stand opposed to the general impiety. So again today, we see in the great cities of Germany, where the pure gospel is taught, that it is done by one or two only and they are totally despised; yet, in these cities a great number of lazy Baalites, haughty in their bearing and voluptuously fed, exercise control.[59]

Meyer draws in a history of martyrdom under the vision of the slaying of the witnesses by the beast (Rev. 11:7). The list points to Hus, Jerome of Prague, Savonarola, the Fraticelli, the poor men of Lyons, and Bohemian Waldensians.

> Of these things you have the example of John Hus and Jerome of Prague, cham-
> pions of the truth of the Gospel, who were burned at the Council of Constance;
> Girolamo Savonarola, of the Order of Preachers, whom pope Alexander VI
> commanded to be burned in Florence of Tuscany and who urged strongly the
> reform of the church preaching to the people from the Apocalypse. . . .[60]

If this is not the first, it is at least one of the earliest, delineations of a "history" of proto-Protestantism under the image of our text. It is a line of development to which Bullinger and the English playwright and apocalypticist John Foxe
will further elaborate. Meyer's history of martyrdom comes in a commentary with
little explicit interest in correlating prophecy and event. The locus of our text is
one of the few such places. This has the effect of drawing a parallel between
Christ's suffering with that of his body, the Church, and our witnesses.[61] Meyer's
tropological, or moral, interests pull in a literal reading of our text where he seeks
to understand reforming efforts of his time. The adventual witnesses are Christ's
body. Under their figure the true Church is imaged much as it had been earlier
for Tyconius, but now it is identified explicitly as those in opposition to the Roman
Antichrist. The image is a vignette of what we will see expanded in Flacius's
Catalogue or John Foxe's *Book of Martyrs*.

The place of prophecy as it was defined in the growing pan-Protestant movement, despite its differences as Lutheran or Reformed after 1529, was with the
Church as the body of Christ and was located in the nascent theological acad-
emies.[62] Again, as with the issue of prophecy itself, while both the growth and
the development of these institutions are beyond the scope of this study, by drawing the topic in at this point in our analysis of Revelation 11 we can discern a key
institutional evolution in relation to the "regularization" of prophecy. In Strassburg
and Geneva, which saw no commentaries on the Apocalypse written by prominent Reformed theologians, particular events promoted this "regularization" at a
time when the Lutheran Church visitations were now underway. Strassburg, already
noted as a center of radical prophetic activity, and of possible significance for the
laicization of the Prophezei, was the place where Melchior Hoffman, having
accepted his role as the Elijah under the rubric of our text, met his end.[63] Reform
in Strassburg, as instituted by Martin Bucer and the city officials, sought to regu-
late any similar or further outbursts of prophetic inspiration.[64] As Spiritualist unrest
increased, the City Council placed interdicts upon unauthorized groups gathering
to read Scripture outside of the control of Synod and Council.[65] In reaction to this
radical prophetism, an official and apocalyptically restrained definition of prophecy was formulated by Bucer and Wolfgang Capito.[66]

Prophecy was carefully defined and its place located in the Academy of Geneva.
Beginning with our text and working out from there it might first be noted that
with John Calvin we find open hostility toward the theme of two adventual witnesses. In his commentary on Hebrews 11:5, Calvin writes:

> It is better to pass over the subtle questions with which curious men harass
> themselves. They ask what became of these two men, Enoch and Elijah. In
> case they may seem to ask empty questions they prophesy that they are kept
> for the final day of the Church so as to be displayed to the world suddenly

then. The Apocalypse of John is cited in support of this. Let us leave this airy philosophy to those with small intellects which cannot find a firm foundation. It should be enough for us that their rapture was a kind of extraordinary death. . . .[67]

Calvin did not have a small intellect and he began his work following the debacle of Münster (1535–1536); both factors need to be kept in mind at this point. The first edition of Calvin's *Institutes* (1536) was written both to explain the evangelical faith and to defend the Reform movement from charges of social sedition and ideas characteristic of religious radicalism.[68] In the Strassburg congregation of French Protestant refugees where Calvin was briefly pastor, some were reportedly Melchiorite sympathizers.[69] Calvin was openly critical of their leaders, whom he identified as Thomas Müntzer, Melchior Hoffman, and Nicholas Storch.[70] It is possible that Calvin had in mind not only "adventual witnesses" like these when he spoke of "curious men [who] harass themselves," but also Michael Servetus (1511–1553), who prophesied of an imminent third Elijah, drawing upon our text, in his *Christianismi Restitutio*.[71] Willem Balke adds that this work may have been a "countermeasure" to Calvin's *Institutes*.[72]

Heinrich Quistorp cites Calvin's "aversion to the Apocalypse,"[73] yet the book remained part of Calvin's canon and he occasionally cited it as authority. However, rather than finding in Enoch and Elijah prophetic figures whose return was to be expected at the end of history, Calvin understands them as models of the meaning and limits of the ministry of the Church. Writing of a second Elijah, Calvin notes, "The task of the second Elijah was, according to Malachi, to enlighten the minds and 'to turn the hearts of the fathers to the children, and the unbelievers to the wisdom of the just.'"[74] After this remark he continues to discuss the work of the minister and the nature of the Church,[75] issues that were vital to him in the fight against the spirit of Antichrist in Rome[76] and the excesses of the Anabaptists.

At one point in his *Institutes*, Calvin writes that "those for whom prophetic doctrine is tasteless ought to be thought of as lacking taste buds."[77] By this he did not imply a search for new revelations or new prophecies. He was willing to see in Luther's work a parallel to Elijah of old but was unwilling to refer to Luther as "the Last Elijah."[78] There was no question of rehabiliting an office of prophecy in any charismatic sense of the word. Word and Spirit were bonded together by Calvin. Both pointed to Christ and by Christ as final prophet (Deut. 18:18; Mark 6:15; John 6:14) both were to be understood.[79] Arguing as had Aquinas in the thirteenth century against the Joachites, Calvin posited no new age of the Spirit. Similarities and differences between the old and new dispensations were clearly articulated, and chiliasm was strongly denied.[80] Rather than looking for new prophets who were to come heralding new eras and prophesying future events, Calvin writes:

> But for my part, as doctrine is the present subject, I would rather explain it [prophecy], as in 1 Cor. 14, to mean outstanding interpreters of prophecies, who, by a unique gift of revelation, applied them to the subjects on hand; but I do not exclude the gift of foretelling, so far as it was connected with teaching.[81]

8 And the voyce which I heard from heauen, spake vnto me againe and said, Go & take ye litle boke which is open in the hand of the Angel, which stadeth vpon the sea & vpon the earth.

9 So I wet vnto the Angel, & said to him, Giue me the litle boke. And he said vnto me, Take it, & eat it vp, and it shal make thy bellie bitter, but it shalbe in thy mouth as swete as honie.

10 Then I toke the litle boke out of the Angels hand, and ate it vp, and it was in my mouth as swete as honie: but when I had eaten it, my bellie was bitter.

11 And he said vnto me, Thou must prophecie againe among the people and nations, and tongues, and to many Kings.

CHAP. XI.

1 The temple is measured. 3 Two witnesses raised vp by the Lord, are murthered by the beast. 11 But after receiued to glorie. 15 Christ is exalted, 16 And God praised by the 24. elders.

1 THen was giuen me a rede, like vnto a rodde, & the Angel stode by, saying, Rise and mette the teple of God, and the altar, and them that worship therein.

2 But the court which is without the temple cast out, and mette it not: for it is giuen vnto the Gentiles, and the holie citie shal they treade vnder fote foure & fortie moneths.

3 But I wil giue power vnto my two witnesses, & they shal prophecie a thousand, two hundreth, & threscore dayes, clothed in a sacke cloth.

4 These are two oliue trees, & two cadelstickes, stading before ye God of ye earth.

5 And if anie ma wil hurte them, fyre procedeth out of their mouthes, and deuoureth their enemies: for if anie man wolde hurt them, thus muste he be killed.

6 These haue power to shut heauen, that it raine not in the dayes of their prophecying, & haue power ouer waters to turne them into blood, and to smite the earth with all maner plagues, as ofte as thei wil.

7 And when they haue finished their testimonie, the beast that cometh out of the bottomles pit, shal make warre against them, and shal ouercome them, and kill them.

8 And their corpses shal lie in the stretes of the great citie, which spiritually is called Sodom and Egypt, where our Lord also was crucified.

9 And they of the people and kinreds, and tongues, and Gentiles shal se their corpses thre dayes and an halfe, and shal not suffer their carkeises to be put in graues.

10 And they that dwell vpon the earth, shal reioyce ouer them and be glad, and shal send giftes one to another: for these two Prophetes vexed them that dwelt on the earth.

11 But after thre dayes and an halfe, the spirit of life comming from God, shal enter into them, & they shal stand vp vpon their fete: and great feare shal come vpon them which sawe them.

12 And they shal heare a great voyce from heauen, saying vnto them, Come vp hither. And they shal ascende vp to heauen in a cloude, and their enemies shal se them.

13 And the same houre shal there be a great earthquake, and the tenth parte of the citie shal fall, and in the earthquake shalbe slaine in nomber seuen thousand: and the remnant shalbe afraid, and giue glo rie to the God of heauen.

14 The seconde wo is past, & beholde the thirde wo wil come anone.

15 And the seuenth Angel blew the trumpet, and there were great voyces in heaue, saying, The kingdomes of this worlde are our Lords, and his Christs, and he shal reigne for euermore.

16 Then the foure & twetie Elders, which sate before God on their seates, fell vpon their faces, and worshipped God,

17 Saying, We giue thee thankes, Lord God almightie, Which art, and Which wast, & Which art to come: for thou hast receiued thy great might, and hast obteined thy kingdome.

18 And the Gentiles were angrie, and thy wrath is come, and the time of the dead, that they shulde be iudged, and that thou shuldest giue rewarde vnto thy seruants the Prophetes, and to the Saintes, and to them that feare thy Name, to smale and great, and shuldest destroye them, which destroye the earth.

19 Then the Temple of God was opened in heauen, and there was sene in his Temple the Arke of his couenat: and there were lightnings, and voyces, and thodrings, and earthquake, and muche haile.

CHAP. XII.

1 There appeareth in heauen a woman clothed with the sunne. 7 Michael fighteth with the dragon, which persecuteth the woman. 11 The victorie is gotten to the comfort of the faithful.

The Two Witnesses and the Rhetoric of Protestantism

A Page from Revelation 11 with text and marginalia as found in *The Geneva Bible. A Facsimile of the 1560 edition*. Introduction by Lloyd E. Berry. Madison, Wis.: The University of Wisconsin Press, 1969. The New Testament, page 118.

Teaching became the form for prophecy at the Academy of Geneva. It is also what was done at weekly meetings of pastors and laity for prayer and the discussion of Scripture.[82] Prophecy as charismatic foretelling was rare and generally limited to the Apostolic Age. The Church during the time of Calvin had Christ; its prophets were tellers of this highest gift. Special prophets and latter-day prophecies were not needed. Peter Martyr, a Florentine reformer at Zürich, Basel, and then Strassburg, cited as evidence the growing numbers of books and numerous teachers of the time.[83]

If apocalyptic visions were distant, "last things" were not. The "day of the Lord" took on a definite but different shape in Calvin's theology from much of what we have encountered thus far in other reformers surveyed. At the level of speculation on the future of the individual soul it found its way into Calvin's work *Psychopannychia* ("soul watchfulness"), 1534, in its way his critique of the radical apocalypticism he encountered in Strassburg, and which was presently causing such social unrest in Münster.[84] For his part, Calvin found in Revelation 14:13 the promise that after death the soul does not sleep but lives in a conscious state in God—and is at rest from labor. The latter clause served to undermine further a theology of purgatory developed elsewhere. Insofar as "last things" took on a corporate or civic dimension in Calvin's thought, they were integrally related to his understanding of how biblical themes were to be understood by those called to be "a kingdom" unto God (Rev. 1:6).

Without denying God's direction in final temporal events, Calvin's references to last things laid primary stress upon God's judgments in time. However, as his reading of the prophetic texts demanded a technical interpretation, Calvin developed a methodology in his exegesis that related biblical promises to patterns of fulfillment. Promises in the Old Testament found their fulfillment in the New Testament and in the establishment of Christ's kingdom. That kingdom began with Christ's first Advent. It continues, though under siege, since that Advent in a tension between promise and fulfillment as that kingdom is increasingly manifest. Richard Müller, using the term "kerygmatic analogy," illustrates the way in which Calvin developed the idea of an extended meaning of the text, permitting its literal reading while, nevertheless, finding, often through the medium of preaching, a contemporary application or meaning of the text. In this way the logic, or dynamism, of the text, though located in history, might carry us into a future meaning.[85]

By applying the logic of this exegetical method with what many have seen as an optimism about the prospects for human betterment or analogy with the growth of Christ's kingdom, Calvin has been seen to contribute to the idea of progress in human history, a kind of historical meliorism wherever the gospel is heard and appropriated.[86] This exegetical integrity gave an inner logic to the idea of the kingdom of God in Martin Bucer's theology, an idea that impressed Calvin during his sojourn in Strassburg.[87] Calvin's meliorism would contribute to an enduring, if less apocalyptic, interest in the nature of Christ's kingdom among the Reformed. A proleptic sharing in Christ's Resurrection and session in glory might be seen to work its way backwards to present times insofar as one believed that the present times stood in the shadow of the end of history.

Circles of Reformed theological thought that took their cue from Calvin excluded special prophets and prophecy, locating such in Christ the last "prophet" whose ministers herald his name. This tended to mean that the tension between whether the gift of the charisma for prophecy was given to the whole congregation of believers (1 Cor. 14:26–32) or alone to those duly trained and approved (1 Tim. 2:2) was one of demonstrable Christ-centered piety rather than Spirit-ecstasy. Christ's heralds were those set against Antichrist. As our text was read in this context a number of implications became clear that would ensure its longevity and contribute to a new form of chiliasm that looked not to a new age following the second Advent of Christ but rather to an age of increasing spiritual, and often derivatively, material improvement prior to Christ's return for his bride, the Church, which has made itself ready for his return (Rev. 19:7).

Among those factors are the following: (1) Antichrist had been identified. The institution of the Reformation in its different communions was predicated upon this symbolic connection; however, one may draw in other theological doctrines or social realities. To deny this identification would require a fundamentally new paradigm for history and explanation for the vicissitudes of the Word in time. (2) Having identified Antichrist as the beast out of the abyss (Rev. 11:7), it appeared that the reformers were, by implication, in some way associated with the witnesses of our text (Rev. 11:3). For over three centuries one reform movement after another had understood themselves in this way. (3) Two possibilities were now open to those who identified with the symbolism of our text. Either the second Advent was imminent, perhaps even three and one-half or seven years away (views explicitly seen in Hut and Hoffman and perhaps of fleeting attraction to Luther), or the Church had at least entered into a new phase of history. (4) Insofar as one sought to retain the imprimatur of orthodoxy in the Latin Western Church, the reformers continued to identify with Augustine's understanding of history. This meant that there was only one final age encompassed by Christ's two advents. Therefore, apart from an imminent Advent the present must be a final lengthening of the day prior to Christ's Advent, as implied in Bede's diurnal symbolism, which caught up in it the symbolic preaching of the witnesses for 1260 days; this was conflated by some with the millennium, which was prior not to Christ's first Resurrection (Rev. 20:5), which for Augustinians meant the spiritual rebirth (or that might be interpreted as the restoration of spiritual truth in the Reformation) but to the second Resurrection and, together with it, the Last Judgment. (5) The nature of this age of the witnesses might be characterized by the mind of spiritual meliorism often associated with Calvin's theology.

There will be many variations on the development of perspective upon our text as noted above. For example, some exegetes will identify two millennial ages, one in the past and another in the present, as related to our text. Eventually, in relation to advances in historical knowledge, the idea will emerge of one future millennial age into which history has entered since the resurrection of the two witnesses. Others will find an age of relative spiritual improvement only after the return of Christ. Some will find in view a continual reformation of the Church as long as pure doctrine is maintained, an historical age without room for significant spiritual change as defined by Augustine, but tinctured with new historicist interests as seen in Bullinger. It is to these perspectives that we now turn. Two are shaped appropriately by French Huguenot commentators in exile, the third by a Reformed theologian of Breslau and then Heidelberg. Each of the three will help to shape new paradigms of historical reflection in relation to our text that will only finally be named in the nineteenth century.

A Visionary Mission

Our great company of prophets will now begin to divide over different visions of the future. The commentaries on the Apocalypse authored by Francis Junius, James Brocard, and David Pareus illustrate the paradigmatic tendencies just noted. Junius's commentary develops most pointedly an anti-papal line common to all Protestant commentaries of his genre, but he does so in a way that points to a millennial growth of the Church after the resurrection of our two witnesses.

Although it has been argued that the notes to the Apocalypse found in the Geneva Bible of 1560[88] may have come from Bullinger's commentary,[89] later editions drew from Francis Junius,[90] spreading Reformed understanding across national boundaries in this area as in so many other points of doctrine. The gloss on our text (1560 edition) identifies the two witnesses as Joshua and Zerubbabel, an interpretation congruent with the muted optimism of Reformed eschatology. It was these two who were charged with the reconstruction of the temple in the days of old Israel's return to Jerusalem following the Babylonian captivity.

> By two witnesses he meaneth all the preachers that shulde buylde vp Gods Church, alluding to Zerubbabel and Iehoshua which were chiefly appointed for this thing, and also to this saying, In the mouthe of two witnesses standeth euerie worde.[91]

That same Bible refers in its notes to Queen Elizabeth as "our Zerubbabel for the erecting of this moste excellent temple."[92] The gloss (Zech. 4:3–14) describes the task. As Joshua and Zerubbabel faced the job of reconstructing the temple after exile, so in the sixteenth century faithful preachers worked to restore the Church. They are opposed by the "beast that cometh out of the bottomless pit." In the gloss the beast is "the Pope which hathe his power out of hel."[93] The names of Elijah and Enoch, seen so frequently in association with Revelation 11, are now replaced by Joshua and Zerubbabel, reflecting the task which lay before the Protestant reformers.

This personally self-confident but acerbic, anti-papal line of interpretation can be traced through the glosses of successive editions of the Geneva Bible.[94] Francis Junius (1545–1602), born in Bourges (France), educated at Lyons, and called as a pastor (1565) to the Walloon congregation of Antwerp, fled the city (1567) in the face of Roman Catholic and Anabaptist opposition. After accompanying Prince William of Orange he was eventually called to Heidelberg (1573) where he assisted Immanuel Tremellius in the translation of a Protestant Latin Bible.[95] The edition of 1599, bearing Junius's notes, was widely read both on the Continent among the Reformed and in English Puritan circles. With respect to our text, Junius notes that there are two histories to the Church. We might describe them as the Church under the cross (Rev. 11:1–13) and the Church victorious (Rev. 11:14–19). The first finds its fuller explanation in Revelation 1–16, the second in Revelation 20, the textual locus for the millennium.

> So this historie hath two parts. One of the state of the Church conflicting with temptations, vnto the 16. Chapter. The other of the state of the same Church obtaining victory, thence vnto the 20. Chapter. The first part hath two members most conveniently distributed into their times, whereof the first containeth an historie of the Christian Church for 1260 yeeres, what time the Gospell of Christ was as it were taken vp from amongst men into heaven: the second containeth an historie of the same Church vnto the victorie perfected. And these two members are briefly, though distinctly, propounded in this Chapter, but are both of them more at large discoursed after in due order.[96]

On the one hand, Junius's commentary follows the historicist tendencies of Nicholas of Lyra. This is clear in Revelation 1–16 (cf. Rev. 11:1–13), the history of the Church under the cross. However, the trials of this Church are told under a polyvalent symbolism as one finds it in chapter 12 of Revelation. The vision of chapter 12 adumbrates the inception, growth, and conflict of the Church in the first century (cf. Rev. 11:2) and later history.[97] That later history is continued in chapter 13 (cf. Rev. 11:7).[98] Junius fills out his view of the Church's past through his description of the seals and trumpets. The fifth (Rev. 9:1) and sixth (Rev. 9:13) trumpets of the Apocalypse both occurred during the period of papal hegemony in society. The fifth trumpet marks the end of the binding of Satan, occurring during the reign of Gregory VII (1075).[99] Following the end of this first millennial period the world was vexed by the dragon for 150 years until the reign of Gregory IX (1227–1241).[100] Conflict continued with the 1260-year ministry of the witnesses ending under Boniface VIII, who literally slew them. The prophetic 1260 days of the witnesses' activity (Rev. 11:3) are added to the approximate length of Christ's life, yielding the year when Boniface was made bishop of Rome (A.D. 1294):

> The beast is the Roman Empire, made long agoe of civill, Ecclesiasticall: the chiefe heade whereof was then Boniface the eight: who . . . called himselfe Lord. . . . He shall persecute most cruelly the holy men, and put them to death, and shall wound and pierce through with cursings both their names and writings. And that this was done to very many godly men by Boniface and others the histories do declare. . . . [101]

Prophecy was revived after Boniface but was opposed again by the dragon and the beasts and would be so until Christ's descent pictured in Revelation 14.[102] This period will be followed by Judgment (Rev. 15–16) and victory (Rev. 17–19). While the slaying of the witnesses was literally fulfilled when certain Christians were hanged in Rome in the thirteenth century, Junius's comments on our text still offer a history of Protestantism and a present agenda for the Church. God's true prophets in the sixteenth century are those who work like Joshua and Zerubbabel to reestablish the true worship of God. The history of this restoration from Boniface VIII until the Consummation is adumbrated by Revelation 11:14–

19, a seeming millennial age.[103] The meanings woven into the text by Junius helped to create a powerful anti-papal thrust and a sense of millennial mission for Protestantism that the movement will bear well through the nineteenth century. The spiritual Temple of God was in process of reconstruction. The Geneva Bible and popular pamphlets heightened the impact of Junius's interpretation:

> Now the Lord is entered into his Kingdome, & hath restored his Church, in which most mightily recouered from the profanation of the Gentiles, he may glorifie himselfe. Namely, that which the Lord ordained when first he ordained his Church, that the faith of the saints doth now behold as accomplished.[104]

With such considerations in mind, the commentary on the book of Revelation by James Brocard presents a different reformed paradigm for the future, and theology is of focal interest.[105] Brocard's work illustrates a blending of Reformed and Joachite elements; as such, the ways in which an earlier radical reading of the Apocalypse helped to shape a growing Reformed understanding of the visions set forth in that book becomes an issue that merits study.[106] Running through the commentary is an apocalyptic or chiliastic hope for restoration in history predicated upon an opening Age of the Holy Spirit consequent to the Protestant Reformation. It outlines a far-reaching vision for Protestant historical and institutional development, which, Jürgen Moltmann argues, influenced the thought of Johannes Cocceius (1603–1669) whose own work helped to alter scholastic Reformed theology by introducing into it the history of salvation and a millenarianism predicated upon the doctrine of successive covenants.[107]

Brocard's work illustrates Reformed theology intermixed to a great degree with Joachite spirituality and historical momentum. Two points stand out in this commentary. First, the Reformed doctrine of predestination is melded with argumentation drawn from Joachite prophetic speculation, thus creating a kind of historical determinism and illustrating a transformationist and progressive historical development toward the kingdom of God. As such, the commentary is a fine example of what Heinrich Quistorp argued was the bias in Calvin's theology toward the triumph of God in time.[108] This is illustrated both in the preface to Brocard's commentary on the Apocalypse and throughout the body of the text. Brocard writes:

> And because we do not only behold God in those things which he hath wrought in the worlde, but also in those thinges which hee hath prepared for us before the worlde was made, and will give us after the world is ended, there ariseth another order from Predestination to glorification: likewise from everlastingness to everlastingness and as before the world was made a kindgome was prepared for us with the Father: so after the worlde is ended, wee shall possesse it everlastingly with the Father.[109]

Additionally, this primacy granted to divine initiative is developed by Brocard so as to see a certain parallelism both in the initial creative activity of God and in the final denouement of history.

> As God in the beginninge woulde have himselfe to bee knowne by his Children, the true, onely, and everlasting God in thinges that he hath made, in the things that he hath done by the holy Ghoste, and was to doe even untill the ende of the world, and in things that he hath spoken touching his Sonne by his

servants in all ages of the world: so in the ende of times, whether also in the course or processe of times he would likewise confirme and repeate the things that hee had set oute in the beginning, that the beleevers might be the rather assured that he is the only God that made the worlde, the Church, and the beleevers.[110]

Having referred briefly to the Reformed provenance of the commentary, it is the more prophetic dimensions that are of interest to us. It is also such speculation that kept Brocard on the move as he faced scholastic Reformed hostility until eventually he found a home in Bremen and protection under Christoph Pezel. Born in 1563 in Venice, Brocard travelled to France but was condemned by the Calvinist National Synod for his prophetic interpretation of Scripture. Expelled from the Netherlands for similar reasons, Brocard found refuge with the Reformed at Bremen. Here he published several works, including a commentary on Genesis, one on the Song of Solomon, and another on the book of Revelation. His life and publication history were clearly bounded by the Age of Philip II of Spain and the Dutch Wars of Independence (1568–1648). This political history adds an additional element of interest to Brocard's work on the book of Revelation. The commentary becomes an early place for analyzing the transition of thought in the late sixteenth and early seventeenth centuries from a transcendent apocalyptic expectation to a more political hope expressive of the new national religious orders reshaping the social and religious map of Europe.[111]

In his exposition on the Apocalypse, Brocard notes three states of history, of which the third, belonging to the Holy Spirit, will be a Sabbath of "opened prophecy."[112] There are seven ages of the world. The sixth age is that of new prophets and the seventh that of the second Advent. There are seven divisions in Brocard's Age of the Son. The seventh began with Luther's preaching of the gospel. There are then seven seasons of the Age of the Holy Spirit, the first from the preaching of Luther to the ascent of the Swiss Reformed movement, the second and third in such places as England and Denmark, the fourth having come with the "French troubles." A fifth season runs from those troubles through the "slaughter of the Gospellers," and a sixth would last until "the conflicte of hostes, when in thicke cloudes of the sky Chryst shalbe present to turne his Judgement agaynst ye Papistes."[113] The source of his vision, Brocard writes in numerous places in his Apocalypse commentary, is the work of "Abbot Joachimus."[114] Reeves argues that "Joachim is the key prophet of the sixth age and the chief medieval influence upon Brocard's thought."[115] In arguing such, Reeves draws out Brocard's use of Ezekiel's wheel, the apocalyptic trumpets, and sacrifice of Elijah on Mt. Carmel, each of these sets of symbols characteristic of the work of Joachim.[116]

Such patterns can be discerned in Brocard's commentary on the book of Genesis. Here he sketches an economy of the Trinity in three ages of history. The first, that of God the Father, is an age of natural law running from Adam through Abraham to Christ; the second age is that of Christ and the gospel. It is a time of preparation and martyrdom, one of conflict with Antichrist. His tyranny is seen in Roman decretals and the papacy. Hope comes through the messengers of the second (spiritual) coming: Joachim of Fiore, the Albigenses, Hus, Savonarola, and, lastly, Luther and the Reformation. The Reformation opens up a third age, that of the Holy Ghost.[117] All of this argumentation is repeated in the commentary on the book of Revelation.[118] In line with such analysis, Moltmann easily and clearly places Brocard in a tradition that includes Joachim, Savonarola, apocalyptic conciliarists on the eve of the Reformation, Martin Cellarius (Borrhaus), Wolfgang Capito, and Anabaptist enthusiasts.[119]

The second point of our analysis has to do with the contemporary religious and attendant social reform movements. These clearly play a role in shaping Brocard's thinking about contemporary history. God's Son comes in the Spirit, preaching renewal.[120] Such thinking is applied to Brocard's own day. Texts from chapters 9–11 of Revelation are used to picture that renewal, comparable to a birthing process, seen in the contemporary persecution of Protestants in France. This renewal is said to begin with the Word, which is given as a measuring rod to all ages now entering the last.[121]

For forty-two months, that is, since the days of Pope Sylvester I (314–335), Gentiles have trodden down the holy city. Throughout this period, paralleled by the 1260 years of the witnesses' preaching in Revelation 11, the gospel was heard. All who have continued in the Gospel are the two apocalyptic prophets[122] but the vision is uniquely applicable to Brocard's own day:

> Now at this tyme when we shall come to the ende of 1260. yeares, ye beginning being taken from Pope Syluester, ye church, and ye gouernment thereof shalbe geuen to those which hold ye testimony of Christ. The new Prophets and ye worthy Petarcha famous for godliness and learning [?] recken ye those 1260. dayes are set for yeres, for ye yere of our Lord 313. unto ye tyme when with power and might Chryst shall bringe his Churche oute of the deserte, then if to those 1260 Yeares thou adde 313. in the which Yeare Syluester tooke the red garment for the blacke, there shall be 1573 Yeares, when both in Fraunce, Holland and Zelande the Gospellers hauing ben troden downe oppressed, put to death, burned and slaine lifted up themselves, and afterward made theyr foes afrayde, as it is sayd hereafter.[123]

Accordingly, Christ will bring the Church out of the desert (the sixth age) by the year 1573, a date based on adding the 1260 day-years to A.D. 313, when the Church became perverted under Sylvester.[124] This occurs together with the emergence of a spiritually empowered ministry. Discussing the two olive trees and candlesticks before God, Brocard writes that these two are the Holy Spirit and Christ. Because true ministers are bearers of these members of the Trinity, they can be referred to by these figures. Thus, Brocard emphasizes a mystical component to our two witnesses. They are "ministers of the Gospel, and of the word of Prophecy."[125] Their power comes from the doctrine and spirit that they bear:

> Men having the Doctrine of the Gospel and the Offyce of Prophecy have euer ben in the Church, although many have not knowne them. Neyther could the Papacy hitherto forbyd them. And whyle the time of 1260 yeares continued, they dyd shut up Heauen that it rayned not. They did shut up Heaven from the Papistes.[126]

For forty years, to the beginning of persecution in France, the gospel has been faithfully preached by these witnesses. This preaching is "the work of Chrysts second coming."[127] Now the prophecies of old begin to be fulfilled. Christ himself reminds us of his words in Matthew 24.[128] The apocalyptic battle begins as the beast arises from the pit "to play the Devill." These events came to pass in France in 1572.[129] Now we stand on the verge of Christ's kingdom:

> The Papistes shall see the Gospellers to possesse Chrystes Kyngdome, and Church, and in them to gouerne all things . . . which may be referred to the third state of Christ.[130]

Not only do contemporary events and Joachite patterns of thinking play a role in Brocard's thought, but it must also be asked about the extent to which he was influenced by the thinking and preaching of the more radical religious figures of his day and of an earlier generation. Perhaps one of the most fruitful lines of analysis would be to explore the relationship between Melchior Hoffman and Brocard—or that of other chiliastic visionaries in the sixteenth century.[131] Another whose thought and preaching might be studied for areas of influence is Bernhard Rothmann, apologist for the Anabaptist kingdom in Münster. Unlike Hoffman, Rothmann believed that the Age of the Gospel, with its emphasis upon patience and suffering, had now been superseded by a third age, which held apostolic aggression to be both valid and virtuous.[132] Others in addition to Hoffman and Rothmann might be cited and valued for comparative analysis. It is difficult to believe that such influence is not there, given the growing impact of popular religious thinking in the period. However, specific citation is difficult to discern because of mutual dependence upon Joachite thought and through the final discrediting of Hoffman.

The tensions evident in the late sixteenth century between theologies of hope dependent upon either an Augustinian/Thomist or Joachite theological perspective are tensions that will now continue to divide Protestantism and Protestant renewal movements into the contemporary period. Both commentaries by Junius and Brocard, as widely different as they are—the first standing within one millennial age and looking to another, and the second more pessimistically located in the present and looking to God's intervention with a millennial age—will now mark the Reformed movement. The commentaries of Junius and Brocard, caught between the worlds of Reformed and radical exegeses, offer promising avenues of analysis for understanding in the way from the dogmatic theologians of the sixteenth century to the apocalyptic theologians of the seventeenth century—and in their own way the onset of modernity.[133]

The chiliastic tendencies among the Reformed, visible already in Francis Lambert, were heightened by Brocard but given fresh respectability particularly with the work of Johann Heinrich Alsted (1588–1638) as well as others.[134] That of Junius would be further developed with enduring significance in the Anglo-American world by Thomas Brightman (1562–1607).

A Perpetual Reformation

We will complete our survey of these various commentaries, each of which sketches a new paradigm of history as worked in relation to our text, by turning next to David Pareus (1548-1622). His commentary retains[135] an anti-chiliastic, anti-

papal line of interpretation.[136] Its purpose is to give a vision of perpetual reformation to the Church with special reference to the Protestant Reformation.[137] In
addition to following Bullinger at many places, Pareus develops a complex recapitulative approach to the imagery of the text.[138]

Pareus writes of the series of seals and trumpets as illustrating similar eras in
the history of the Church. The bowls of wrath are reserved for the end of history.
A large portion of the commentary is devoted to the work of the adventual witnesses. They illustrate Pareus's recapitulative methodology as their work is correlated with the last four great acts of God in history: (1) the calamities of the
Church brought on by tyrants and heretics (especially by Apollyon [the Devil]
and Muhammad) and seen in the six trumpets (Rev. 8,9); (2) the comfort promised the afflicted (Rev. 10); (3) the amplification of the previous calamities, that
is, the conflict of the Church with the Western (!) Antichrist and its cleansing
(Rev. 11:1–15); and (4) the sound of the last trumpet, the call to Judgment and
the great reward.[139] According to Pareus, our text describes:

> the purging of the Evangelical doctrine from Antichristian defilements, with
> the reformation of the Church by the preaching of the two witnesses in the
> latter times of the fifth and sixth trumpets, as also the success of the reforma-
> tion, and what should happen, both to the witnesses, and also to Antichrist.[140]

Its story is divided into two visions, a general command to measure the temple,
that is, to reform the Church (Rev. 11:1–2), and a specific description of the Reformation through the work of the witnesses (Rev. 11:3–14). All is concluded with
the sound of the last trumpet (Rev. 11:15). Four aspects of the work of reformation are detailed in the text as Pareus sees it: (1) a description of the witnesses
(Rev. 11:3–6), (2) their war with the beast (Rev. 11:7–10), (3) the way in which
God's prophets are avenged (Rev. 11:11–13), and (4) the victorious conclusion
with Judgment and divine vindication (Rev. 11:14–15).

Pareus fills in this outline of reform by drawing upon the history of the interpretation of the passage. He rejects Nicholas of Lyra's application of it to the
sixth century as frivolous. John is called to measure the Church (Rev. 11:1-2).[141]
This signifies its reformation through the word of God (the measuring rod) in the
days when it has been destroyed by the Western Antichrist. Arguing against Francis
Ribeira and Catholic theories of the Church's indefectibility, Pareus adds:

> Hence the Papists fiction is refuted, that the visible Church can never degener-
> ate, erre & fal from her integrity. But the thing it self shewes the vanity hereof:
> The old Temple according to Ribera, was a type of the Church: Now we know
> that might be, & was laid wast & destroyed, yea the old Church it self very
> often degenerated: The new Church also shalbe possessed and troden under foot
> by Antichrist, & so need a new measuring, or separation.[142]

Pareus now proceeds to argue that as the old temple needed restoration, so
does the new. Various analogies are drawn between Israel's religious practices
and those of the Church.[143] When he comes to the forty-two months of Gentile
destruction (Rev. 11:2), Pareus applies this period to the time of Antichrist's persecution. Analyzing a variety of opinions,[144] he concludes (agreeing essentially with

Bullinger), that the forty-two months represent a definite figure for an indefinite period:

> From the yeere of Christ thereof 606 [when Boniface III accepted the Church's right of dominion from Phocas], untill this time the holy citie hath been troden under foot by the Romane Gentiles, which is the space of 1073. yeeres, and is yet to be trodden down 223 yeeres more, to wit, untill the yere of Christ 1866. But let this terme bee indefinite, seeing the Lord hath resolved it to himselfe, & undoubtedly will shorten it for the elects sake.[145]

Having sketched the prophecy of a future reformation in general, Pareus turns to the specific program for reform, its instruments, development, success, and history. He notes Theodor Beza's point that this vision is God's promise: When it appears that prophecy is extinct and that Antichrist is victorious, God will restore prophecy so "that the city of God may be rebuilded."[146]Augustine's [*sic*, Tyconius] interpretation that the witnesses are the Old and New Testaments, as well as the opinion of Bede and Brightman, is rejected. The text appears to call for personalities, Pareus writes. Some, he adds, find here two powerful teachers "with the power and spirit of Elias" in the last days. This, however, is uncertain.[147] Pareus concludes:

> I will follow the opinion of Bullinger, and some others of our best interpreters, who understand the two witnesses indefinitely, to be diverse reformers of religion in Antichrist's times.[148]

Parallels are to be found in early movements of restoration. By two, Moses and Aaron, the Israelites were delivered from Egypt. By two, Joshua and Caleb, the promised land was searched out and promise confirmed. By two, Zerubbabel and Joshua, the people were brought back from Babylon—then a physical Babylon; during the time of our commentators, a spiritual one.

> We therefore by these two witnesses doe indefinitely understand, a succession of certaine maintainers of Evangelical truthes against Antichrist. Yet they are said to be two definitely, both because they are but few in respect of the Locusts, of whom the whole Christian world are full: as also because in all matters of judgment two suffice to confirm a testimony, so that we might neither be deceived by the applause of the multitude of Locusts, nor be offended at the fewnes of sincere teachers, wherewith Antichrist upbraides us.[149]

The time of the preaching of the witnesses is said to be 1260 days (Rev. 11:3). This period of time is the same as the forty-two months (Rev. 11:2).[150] Considering a variety of opinions, Pareus follows again an indefinite line; it is enough that God knows the period precisely. If, he adds, one asks why should not some other number be proposed, it is because there is some sense to this figure. It may be applied to the period running from Boniface III forward. At any rate, it refers to a period of oppression mixed with success as the power of Antichrist increases.[151] During all this time Christ's true prophets appear contemptible in their sackcloth garb, but they are dignified by the oil of the Spirit and the light of God's Word, "by which they shall drive away Antichristian darknesse, and kindle againe the lost light of the Gospell in the Church." Arguing from metonymy and metaphor, Pareus explains:

> But first by a certaine metonymia, for, they are two restorers of the Church from under the bondage and yoke of Antichrist, signified by these two olive-trees of old of the Babylonish Captivity. And secondly by a metaphor: for, as they rebuilded Ierusalem beeing formerly wasted by the Babylonians & repaired the temple and typicall worship: so these shall restore the Lords spirituall worship, and repaire the holy citie troden under foot by Antichristian Gentiles.[152]

Pareus next turns to the powers of the two witnesses. Like Bullinger, Pareus uses the prophetic powers associated with Moses and Elijah to describe the spiritual abilities of these two preachers.[153] They are given the promise that before they are slain by the beast their testimony shall be completed. Their conflict will be both religious and civil in nature.[154] The battle will be fought at three levels: preaching, councils, and excommunications, which lead to civil strife. The conflict faced by Wyclif and Hus, the insidiousness of the Inquisition, and the events of the Reformation are all lifted up as instances of the conflict with Antichrist.[155]

The deliverance of the witnesses comes in their resurrection (Rev. 11:11), a sign of hope and encouragement. It signifies not some physical resurrection of Enoch and Elijah, but a promise of perpetual reformation in all of the days of Antichrist.

> But by this vivification is signified a perpetuall restoring of witnesses unto the Church militant, viz: that instead of such whom Antichrist puts to death, the Lord will raise up others to hold forth the testimonie of Christ, and strongly oppose the Beasts kingdome. For when Antichrist shal thinke that all Christ's witnesses are suppressed, then others restored to life shall renew againe the battle against him. . . . So the two witnesses: As for example, John Husse, and Jerome of Prague being killed by the Beast, they lived againe after three days & an half in Luther, Melanchthon, & others, etc.[156]

Bullinger's sermons on the Apocalypse, which began our search on the Reformed use of our text, contributed to the increasingly historicist and anti-papal line of interpretation. The rules for reading a text found in Tyconius, as well as Joachite prophecies of Antichrist, were central to this development. Furthermore, the search for a moral understanding of history, together with a desire to make sense of the vicissitudes of the gospel through time, fostered a growing literalization of the vision inspired by our text.[157] While further tendencies may be discovered in the authors we have discussed, such as those leading to a closer historical and critical analysis of the text,[158] this development will come to fruition only after Protestantism has been significantly marked in its consciousness by the vision of God's two adventual witnesses. Following the works of Junius, Brocard, and Pareus we have seen that vision lay out these different paradigms for historical understanding. Junius's vision caught us up in an increasing second millennial age following the identification of the witnesses. Brocard placed that age beyond the tribulation of the present and Advent of Christ. Pareus's understanding was more recognizably Augustinian, but tinctured by an historicism that would work to keep further speculation alive.

The idea of a perpetual reformation in tension with a muted historicist reading of our text forms a third paradigm for history that develops in relation to the story of our witnesses. Without denying this historicist perspective to Christian history, there is no functional place for an apocalyptic timetable. There appears, instead, a desire to remain rooted in Augustine's understanding of history running from the first to the second Advent as being the last age prior to Judgment with only a recognition granted that we might be nearing the end of that age, as seen in Bullinger's earlier commentary.

Each one of these three paradigms for history was developed in relation to strong civic interests and a desire to shape civil society in different ways. This makes for striking comparison with Luther and visions for the end of history, which appeared within Lutheranism to be less related to immediate interests in social meliorism. The issue of community in relation to the kingdom of God will come to the fore with increasing force following the work on our text by John Foxe. John Foxe added an integral and politically significant national piety to the growing historicization of our text that will bear upon the interests of Anglo, and then Anglo-American, understanding of community and communal values. Each of these historical paradigms, as yet unnamed, will shape issues of Church policy and social governance in the nations of the North Atlantic.

Notes

1. Heinrich Bullinger, *In Apocalypsim conciones centum* (Basel: Oporinus, 1557), p. 148.

2. Philippe Denis shows that the pattern for how to define prophecy in Zürich became a model for the Reformed in the Swiss German and Rhineland centers of Reformation ("La Prophétie dans les églises de la Réforme au XVIe siècle," RHE, 72 [1977]: 289–316). Cf. G. R. Potter, *Zwingli* (Cambridge: Cambridge University Press, 1976), pp. 211–24.

3. Gottfried Locher writes that "the experience of the whole Reformation was that the real presence of the Lord of the church is to be found fundamentally in the *viva vox evangelii* instead of in the sacrament." See "How the Image of Zwingli Has Changed in Recent Research," *Zwingli's Thought: New Perspective* (Leiden: E. J. Brill, 1981), p. 61. Bibliographies on the ecclesiology of the reformers can be found in Emile G. Leonard, *A History of Protestantism. Vol. I: The Reformation*, ed. H. H. Rowley, trans. by J. M. H. Reid (London: Nelson, 1965).

4. Gritsch, "Thomas Müntzer and Luther," pp. 79–83, Abraham Friesen, *Thomas Müntzer, A Destroyer of the Godless* (Berkeley, Calif.: University of California Press, 1990), pp. 108–147.

5. Seebass, "Müntzer's Erbe, Werk, Leben und Theologie des Hans Hut." Theologische habilitationsschrift, Erlangen, Germany, pt. 1, p. 400; cf. Werner Packull, "The Sign of Thau," MQR, 61 (1987):363.

6. Hoffman's sense of covenant closures, while not as developed as Bernhard Rothmann's, appears to imply possibly different duties as well as sensitivity in different historical periods. See Klaus Deppermann, *Melchior Hoffman* (Gottingen: Vandenhoeck und Ruprecht, 1979), pp. 99–100, 217–26.

7. Luther, WA, 10.1 2, p. 194; cf. Hans-Ulrich Hofmann, *Luther und die Johannes-Apokalypse* (Tubingen: Mohr/Siebeck, 1982), pp. 660–61.

8. Christ is the true wisdom and standard in Scripture. See Gottfried Locher, "Zwingli and Erasmus," in *Zwingli's Thought*, p. 245.

9. Begun in June 1525, "prophesyng" took the form of public lectures in the Grossmünster replacing the former canonical hours of Prime, Terce, and Sext. After prayer and the reading of the text for the day in Latin, Hebrew, and Greek, the gathered ministers, canons, and students listened to a sermon in Latin. Then as further citizens from the city gathered, a sermon was delivered in German. See Locher, "In Spirit and in Truth," *Zwingli's Thought*, pp. 27–30; cf. J. Figi, *Die innere Reorganisation des Grossmünstersstiftes in Zürich von 1519 bis 1531* (Affoltern am Albis, 1951), pp. 73–93; and Oskar Farner, *Huldrych Zwingli*, Vol. 3 (Zürich: Zwingli Verlag, 1954), pp. 554–63. Note the role of 1 Cor. 14:34.

10. Rudolf Pfister traces the roots to Bullinger together with the monks at the Kappel cloister in 1523, and to Zwingli since 1525 at the cathedral in Zürich ("Prophezei," in RGG V [Tübingen: J. C. B. Mohr, Paul Siebeck, 1961], col. 638); cf. Emil Egli, art. "Prophesying," in *The New Schaff-Herzog Encyclopedia of Religious Knowledge*, Vol. 9 (New York: Funk and Wagnalls, 1911), p. 278; and F. Schmidt-Clausing, "Das Prophe-zeigebet: Ein Blick über Zwinglis liturgische Werkstatt,"in *Zwingliana*, 12 (1964): 10–34.

11. The Zürich translation of the Bible resulted from the Prophezei, to be revised in every generation. See Die Prophezei," in *Die Züricher Bibel 1531* (Zürich: Theologischer Verlag, 1983), pp. 1383–87.

12. Locher, "Huldrych Zwingli's Concept of History," in *Zwingli's Thought*, pp. 102–3. Zwingli speculates on Antichrist's nature (*De vera et falsa religione commentarius* [1525] in CR, 90, p. 894), but not on the witnesses.

13. Siegfried Rother, *Die religiösen und geistigen Grundlagen der Politik Huldrych Zwingli* (Erlangen: Palm & Enke, 1956), pp. 63–72. Bernd Moeller illustrates the civic nature of Zwingli's reformation through the 1540s after which a growing sense of apocalyptic imminence gained ground perhaps due, in part, to increasing Ottoman's strength in Europe (*Reichsstadt und Reformation*, Eng. trans., *Imperial Cities and the Reformation*, pp. 103–10. Zwingli's influence upon English religious and political thinking is traced by Ruth Wessel-Roth, *Thomas Erastus: Ein Beitrag zur Geschichte der reformierten Kirche und zur von der Staatssouveränität* (Lahr/Baden, 1954).

14. Bullinger, *In Apocalypsim*, p. 132.

15. On the nature of civic humanism and the reworking of apocalyptic and ideological patterns of thought so as to stress a new human responsibility, see Eugenio Garin, *Italian Humanism: Philosophy and Civic Life in the Renaissance* (New York: Harper and Row, 1965); and Hans Baron, *The Crisis of the Italian Renaissance: Civic Humanism and Republican Liberty in an Age of Classicism and Tyranny* (Princeton: Princeton University Press, 1966). On the deep cultural implications of such civic orientation, or lack thereof, in northern German society, see Lionel Rothkrug, "Religious Practices and Collective Perceptions: Hidden Homologies in the Renaissance and Reformation," *Historical Reflections*, 7.1 (Spring 1980).

16. Ibid., p. 135.

17. Theodore Bibliander, *Ad omnium ordinum reip.* (Basel: Oporinus, 1545), pp. 45–60. Bibliander hopes for social renovation through evangelical preaching.

18. Luther's stirring *Address to the Christian Nobility of the German Nation* (1536), based on 1 Peter 2:9, was heard by many as a clarion call to a more democratic understanding of the Church, as is evident from the parish reform movement in Leisnig (1521–1523). Writing to the people of that community (*Gemeine*), Luther affirmed their right to "Judge all Teaching and to Call, Appoint, and Dismiss Teachers," attaching importance

to 1 Corin. 14:30 the scriptural locus for *sitzerrecht* (*lex sedentium*), a text soon to be popular among many radicals (WA, 11, 4011–4016). See George H. Williams, *The Radical Reformation* (Kirksville, Mo.: Sixteenth Century Journal Publishers, 1992), sec. 11.4.

19. Robert Kolb, *Reformers Define the Church, 1530–1580* (St. Louis: Concordia Publishing House, 1991; and cf. Gert Haendler, *Amt und Gemeinde bei Luther in Kontext der Kirchengeschichte* (Stuttgart: Calwer Verlag, 1929).

20. Williams hypothesizes that Lambert may have been influenced in laicizing prophecy by the Strassburg prophets Wolfgang Schultheiss and John Campanus, the latter having written on the topic before 1531. See Williams, *Radical Reformation*, sec. 11.4. See also André Séquenny, ed. *Bibliotheca Dissidentium: Repertoire des Non-Conformistes religieux des seizieme et dix-septième siècles*, Vol. 1 (Baden-Baden: U. Koerner, 1980), p. 14.

21. Gerhard Müller, *Franz Lambert von Avignon und die Reformation in Hessen* (Marburg: N. C. Elwert, 1958), pp. 53–69. The Zürich Prophezei was to influence similar institutions, e.g., in the Palatinate, East Friesland, the Netherlands, and, via John àLasco, England.

22. They were too democratic and "Reformed" for Lutheran tastes (ibid., pp. 35–39).

23. Francis Lambert (d'Avignon), *Exegeseos in sanctum divi Joannis Apocalypsim Libri VII* (Marburg, 1528; Basel, 1539). Of his Franciscan past, Lambert writes that he was "immer noch an den Flüssen des elenden Babels" (p. 53). Bousset argues that Lambert is dependent upon Tyconius, Bede, Haimo, and Strabo. *Offenbarung*, p. 86.

24. Ibid., fol. 180r-v.

25. Ibid., fols. 183r-v–186r.

26. Ibid., fol. 188r.

27. Ibid., p. 188v.

28. Müller cites the first of several "Paradoxa" put forward by Lambert as official points for debate by the Homberg Synod (Oct. 21–23, 1526). The first item: "Titulus primus. Omnia reformanda, que deformata, et per quid" (*Paradoxa*, fol. 2v). Müller writes: "Die heilige Schrift ist seine Autorität. Aus ihr will er ableiten, was deformiert ist, und was reformiert werden muss" (*Franz Lambert*, p. 40). This is the rod for measurement held by the witnesses in Rev. 11:1.

29. Further in the *Paradoxa* (fol. 6r) Lambert writes, "Fürsten und Obrigkeiten sollen mit starker Hand wie Josia ausführen, was jene lehren" (cited by Müller, *Franz Lambert*, pp. 40–41). Contemporary parallels with the rediscovery of the law under Israel's King Josiah, and the reform which followed, will become favorite Protestant themes.

30. Bullinger, *In Apocalypsim*, fols. 189r–191v.

31. Ibid., fol. 1v; cf. his summary at sig. A7v.

32. Ibid., sig. A3r; cf. Müller, *Franz Lambert*, p. 66. Note the trace of Tyconian exegesis in this connection of body and rule.

33. Ibid., sig. A2r, fols. 183v–186r.

34. Wilhelm Bousset, *Die Offenbarung Johannis* (Gottingen: Vandenhoeck und Ruprecht, 1906), p. 86.

35. Lambert, *Exegeseos*, fols. 117v–149v.

36. Ibid., fol. 150r.

37. Ibid., fols. 117v–118r.

38. Ibid., fol. 120v.

39. Ibid., fol. 122r.

40. Ibid., fol. 124v.

41. Ibid., fol. 125r.

42. Ibid., fol. 130.

43. Ibid., fols. 290v–291r. Note how this conflict draws us back to chapters 9–11 of Revelation.

44. Ibid., fols. 283v–284r.

45. Müller, *Franz Lambert*, p. 68.

46. Müller writes that there is not much of Joachim in this work, i.e., the Apocalypse is merely "the history of the church announced beforehand (*Franz Lambert*, pp. 54–55). Marjorie Reeves, on the other hand, finds a Joachite origin for much of Lambert (*The Influence of Prophecy in the Later Middle Ages* (Oxford: Clarendon Press, 1969), pp. 464–65). However, with Lambert's greater allegorical interests, there does appear to be some movement away from Joachim. Müller cites Lambert: "Ipse Dominus Iesus Christus divo Ioanni pro omnium vere fidelium consolatione, sub typis iucundissimis revelare dignatus est, universa quae ab eius passione usque in mundi finem in Ecclesiis Suis erant futura, etiam eo quo facta sunt ordine, et iuxta temporum successum, mazime autem sermonum Dei cursum" (*Exegeseos*, sig. A5r).

47. I am following Philippe Denis, "Prophétie," pp. 295–97. Denis writes that for Lambert all believers are made priests in Christ. After the reading of the lesson anyone was free to offer an interpretation, which had to be carefully prepared and examined beforehand. Furthermore, the center of the church rather than the choir was used for this service.

48. Ibid., p. 297.

49. *Exegeseos*, fol. 130v.

50. Sebastian Meyer, *In apocalypsim Johannis Apostoli* (Zürich: Froschouer, 1539); I refer to the edition of 1554 (Zürich: Froschouer). See Bousset, *Offenbarung*, pp. 86–87.

51. On the bitter anti-papalism and acerbic form of Meyer's efforts at reform, see Steven Ozment, *The Reformation in the Cities* (New Haven: Yale University Press, 1975), pp. 56–61. Ozment cites Oskar Vasella, *Reform und Reformation in der Schweiz. Zur Würdigung der Anfänge der Glaubenskrise* (Münster in Westfalen, 1958), pp. 28–34, 36, 62.

52. Ibid., sig. A2r. The patristic and medieval authorities of Justin Martyr, Irenaeus, Augustine, Jerome, Tyconius, Bede, Haimo, and Rupert of Deutz are cited early (sig. A2r–v, A3v).

53. Ibid., sig. A5v–A6r. See chapter 1 of this text.

54. Ibid., sig. A3v.

55. See 1 Peter 2:21; 3:12–18, ideas which betray Meyer's Franciscan background.

56. Ibid., sig. A5v.

57. Ibid., fols. 21r–23v. The sixth seal is said to be either the calling of the Gentiles or various cataclysms in the Church's history.

58. Ibid., fol. 33r. Meyer does add the unloosing of Satan in A.D. 1000 (fol. 80v).

59. Ibid., fol. 41r.

60. Ibid., fol. 42r.

61. Ibid., sig. A5v–A6r; in particular Tyconius's first rule: "De Dominio et corpore eius." It might be surmised that Meyer is drawing upon a text like Col. 1:24 in which Paul counsels the Christian to accept suffering in order to complete the sufferings of Christ "for the sake of the body, that is the Church."

62. Menna Prestwich, "Introduction," in *International Calvinism, 1541–1715* (Oxford: Clarendon Press, 1985), p. 4.

63. Hofmann's convert Cornelius Polderman was Enoch to Hofmann's Elijah as reported by Obbe Philips, *Bekenntniss*, BRN, 7, p. 126 (Williams's trans. in SAW, pp. 206–25).

64. Denis develops parallels with the Zürich Prophezei ("Prophétie," pp. 292–94). See E. W. Kohls, *Die Schule bei Martin Bucer in ihrem Verhältnis zu Kirche und Obrigikeit*

(Heidelberg: Quelle & Meyer, 1963), pp. 48, 57–58, 65–66; H. Aells, *Martin Bucer* (New Haven: Yale University Press, 1931). On reform in Strassburg, see Miriam Chrisman, *Strasbourg and the Reform* (New Haven: Yale University Press, 1967), pp. 81, 98–114.

65. Chrisman, *Strasbourg and Reform*, pp. 177–201; cf. Manfred Krebs and Hans Georg Rott, eds., *Quellen zur Geschichte der Taüfer, Elsass I und II* (Guttersloh: Gerd Mohn, 1959, 1960), pp. 355, 358–59 for examples. Another example is Wolfgang Schultheyss, who warned the city officials not to neglect prophecy. See his *Ermanung zum geistlichen Urteyl* (1531). I have not yet found any use of our text here in Krebs and Rott, *Elsass I*, pp. 66, 291–97; cf. W. Bellardi, *Wolfgang Schultheyss. Wege und Wandlungen eines Strassburger Spiritualisten und Zeitgenossen Martin Bucers* (Frankfurt: Erwin von Steinbach-Stiftung, 1976), p. 57.

66. Ozment, *Reformation in the Cities*, p. 146–48. On Bucer's theology, see August Lang, *Der Evangelienkommentar Martin Butzers und die Grundzüge seiner Theologie* (Leipzig: 1900), pp. 150ff. On Wolfgang Capito, see James M. Kittleson, *Wolfgang Capito* (Leiden: Brill, 1975), pp. 183ff. I have found no use of our theme in Martin Bucer; nevertheless, his work raises up the civic value of eschatology; see *De Regno Christi libri duo*, 1550, Francois Wendel, ed. (Paris: Presses Universitaires de France; Gütersloh: C. Bertelsmann, 1955).

67. John Calvin, *The Epistle of Paul the Apostle to the Hebrews and the First and Second Epistles of St. Peter*, D. W. Torrance and T. F. Torrance, eds., Calvin's Commentaries XII (Grand Rapids, Mich.: Eerdmans, 1963), pp. 161–62. Compare Calvin's commentary on Genesis 5:22–24.

68. I am following Willem Balke, *Calvin and the Anabaptist Radicals*, trans. by William J. Heynen (Grand Rapids, Mich.: Eerdmans, 1981; Amsterdam, 1973), pp. 39–71; cf. Walter Köhler, "Das Täufertum in Calvins Institutio von 1536," *Mennonitische Geschichtsblätter*, 2 (1936):1–4.

69. Deppermann, *Hoffman*, pp. 331–32.

70. CO, IX, p. 96. Calvin refers to these three self-proclaimed prophets as "Thomas Monetarius," "Melchior Pellionius," and "Nicholas Pelagius," phrases written in defense of the Reformed position against Joachim Westphal's charges that the Reformed were one with the radicals; cf. Balke, *Calvin and the Anabaptist Radicals*, p. 297.

71. Michael Servetus, *Christianismi Restitutio* (Vienna, 1553; repr. Frankfurt: Minerva, 1966). After identifying Rome with Sodom on the basis of Revelation 11 and 17 (p. 447), Servetus writes of the spiritual mystery of the Law, of Christ, and of a third Elijah who will appear before the final resurrection to deal with the need for the restitution of all things (Mal. 4, Matt. 17, Rev. 11).

72. Balke, *Calvin and the Anabaptist Radicals*, p. 200.

73. Heinrich Quistorp, *Die letzten Dinge im Zeugnis Calvins* (Gütersloh: Bertelsmann, 1941), p. 116. In addition to an Erasmian doubt, Calvin's aversion to the Apocalypse was occasioned by what he felt was its misuse by the radicals of the Reformation. See Otto Weber, "Calvins Lehre von der Kirche," in *Die Treue Gottes in der Geschichte der Kirche*. *Vol. 2: Gesammelte Aufsätze* (Neukirchen: Neukirchen Verlag des Erziehungsvereigns, 1968), p. 103.

74. John Calvin, *Institutes of the Christian Religion*, 2 vols., ed., J. T. McNeil, trans. F. L. Battles (Philadelphia: Westminster Press, 1960); see IV.i.6, p. 1020.

75. Calvin, *Institutes*, IV.ii.12.-iii.1 (Battles-McNeill); cf. T. H. L. Parker, *John Calvin: A Biography* (Philadelphia: Westminster Press, 1975), p. 35.

76. Calvin's discussion of the development of the spirit of Antichrist is in *Institutes*, IV.vii.4–25, pp. 1122–45.

77. Calvin, *Institutes*, I.vii.2 (Battles-McNeill), p. 83.

78. Calvin, *Ultima admonitio ad Westphalum, Calvini Opera*, 9:238; I owe this reference to Brian A. Gerrish, *The Old Protestantism and the New* (Chicago: University of Chicago Press, 1982), pp. 45, 289.

79. Calvin, *Institutes*, IV. 1.5–6, sections on education through the Church and meaning and limits of ministry.

80. Ibid., I.ix.1. Most of the 1539 edition was carried into the 1559 edition. See Balke, *Calvin and the Anabaptist Radicals*, pp. 98–115, 299. On Calvin's sense of eschatology and history, see Heinrich Berger, *Calvins Geschichtsauffassung* (Zürich: Zwingli Verlag, 1955), pp. 153–54; and David E. Holwerda, "Eschatology and History: A Look at Calvin's Eschatological Vision," in *Exploring the Heritage of John Calvin: Essays in Honor of John Bratt*, D. E. Holwerda, ed. (Grand Rapids, Mich.: Baker Books, 1976), pp. 111–13, 125–27.

81. John Calvin, *Commentary on Ephesians 4:11* (Torrance, ed., XI) p. 179. Note the continuing role played by 1 Cor. 14 in Zwingli, Luther, Lambert, Bullinger, and now Calvin for regulating prophecy.

82. Denis notes that for the sake of purity and agreement in doctrine, Calvin organized regular "Conferences de l'Ecriture" as part of his *Ecclesiastical Ordinances*. Through such meetings, it was hoped that all of the prophets of the city would speak with one voice in order to expose error and seek agreement around the proper interpretation of Scripture ("Prophétie," p. 299).

83. Peter Martyr noted that there is no need for special prophets since books and teachers are now so numerous (*Loci communes* . . . [Zürich: Froschouer, 1580], I, 19). See Elizabeth L. Eisenstein, *The Printing Press as an Agent of Change: Communication and Cultural Transformations in Early-Modern Europe* (Cambridge: Cambridge University Press, 1979).

84. John Calvin, *Psychopannychia*, in CO V, pp. 170–232; 1st. ed., *Vivere apud Christum non dormire animos sanctos, qui in fide christi decedunt: assertio* (Strassburg, 1542). Possible earlier editions are noted in Walther Zimmerli, ed., *Psychopannychia* (Leipzig, 1932). In Christian speculation, a view drawn from philosophical, ecclesial, and scriptural (Matt. 10:28 and John 8:51) proofs against the idea of the death (thnetopsychism) or sleep of the soul (psychosomnolence) derived from 1 Thess. 4:13. The immortality of the soul (whether natural or contingent), central to medieval penitential and liturgical theology, had been subject to criticism by the medieval apocalypticist Peter John Olivi, and by others, including many Anabaptists, motivated more by the resurrection of the flesh and less by classical doctrines of natural immortality. On doctrines of immortality in the context of sixteenth-century reform, see Williams, *Radical Reformation*, pp. 41–48.

84a. Jaroslav Pelikan notes a paraenetical and polemical use of the Apocalypse in Luther and Calvin. In terms of the former, he sketches the importance of Revelation 14:13. Upon views of the death and afterlife of the individual believer and of Revelation 1:6 upon the social life of the Christian; see "Some Uses of Apocalypse in the Magesterial Reformers," C. A. Patrides and Joseph Wittreich, eds., *The Apocalypse in English Renaissance Thought and Literature* (Ithaca, N.Y.: Cornell University Press, 1984), pp. 74–92.

85. Richard A. Müller, "The Hermeneutic of Promise and Fulfillment in Calvin's Exegesis of the Old Testament Prophecies of the Kingdom," in *The Bible in the Sixteenth Century*, David Steinmetz, ed. (Durham, N.C.: Duke University Press, 1990), pp. 68–82, esp. 71–76.

86. Quistorp, *Die letzten Dinge*, p. 113.

87. Thomas F. Torrance, *Kingdom and Church. A Study in the Theology of the Reformation* (Edinburgh: Oliver and Boyd, 1956). Although Barnes is accurate to my mind on the extent to which apocalyptic ideas were generated and developed by Luther-oriented reformers, it seems clear to me that following the work of Bucer, Bullinger, and Calvin, among others, that a more integral development of eschatological ideas occurred among the Reformed (cf. Robert Barnes, *Prophecy and Gnosis* [Stanford: Stanford University Press, 1988], pp. 3–6 *et passim*) and would be borne out in the different millennial configurations of biblical scholars.

88. *Geneva Bible: A Facsimile of the 1560 Edition*, with an introduction by Lloyd E. Berry (Milwaukee: University of Wisconsin Press, 1969), p. 118, for commentary on Revelation 11:3.

89. Richard Bauckham, *Tudor Apocalypse* (Oxford: The Sutton Courtenay Press, 1978), p. 49.

90. Lewis Lupton, *A History of the Geneva Bible*, Vol. 7 (London: The Olive Tree Press, 1975), pp. 153–77. After 1594, Junius's commentary was increasingly used to supply the notes to the Apocalypse. See Berry, "Introduction to the Facsimile Edition," *Geneva Bible*, p. 15.

91. *Geneva Bible*, p. 118.

92. Ibid., fol. iir.

93. Ibid., fol. 118r.

94. See Lupton, *History of Geneva Bible*, Vol. 7, pp. 153–77.

95. Francis Junius, *Apocalypsis Joannis* (Heidelberg, 1591). The edition I refer to is *Apocalypsis. A Briefe and Learned Commentaire upon the Revelation of Saint John the Apostle and Evangelist, applied unto the historie of the Catholike and Christian Church* (London, 1592), found with the text of the Geneva Bible.

96. *Geneva Bible* (London, 1599), fol. 115r.

97. Ibid., fols. 115v–116r.

98. Ibid., fols. 116r–117r.

99. Ibid., fol. 114r; cf. fol. 120r.

100. Ibid., fol. 114v. On the continuing conflict and the slaying of the witnesses, see fols. 116r–117r.

101. Ibid., fol. 115r.

102. Ibid., fol. 110v.

103. Ibid., fol. 115v.

104. Ibid.

105. The commentary on the Apocalypse to which I have had access is an English edition entitled *The Revelation of S. Ihon reveled* (London, 1582; orig. Latin, 1580); cf. Bousset, p. 95. Brocard belonged first to the French-Reformed and later Dutch Reformed Church. His name is apparently also found as Iacobus Procardus and Iacobus Brocardus, both renderings given by Johannes Wolf, *Lectionum memorabilium et reconditarum centerarii XVI* (Laving, 1600), ii., pp. 752, 937. The name James Brocard is found on the title page of the English translation of his commentary on the Apocalypse, Latin orig., 1580). His works include *De Prophetia Libri Duo* (Lyon, 1581); *The Revelation of S. Ihon reveled . . . Englished by J. Sanford* (London, 1582); *Mystica et Propetica Libri Levitici Interpretatio* (Lyon, 1580); *Mystica et prophetica libri Geneseos interpretatio . . .* (Bremen, 1585).

106. See the article by Jürgen Moltmann, "Jacob Brocard als Vorläufer der Reich-Gottes theologie und der symbolisch-propetischen Schriftausleguing des Johann Cocceius," ZKG, 71 (1960):110–29. In drawing out Brocard's significance, Moltmann illustrates how

Brocard came to know one of the chief reformers of Bremen, Christoph Pezel. Through Pezel, Tholuck argued, Brocard's ideas influenced the development of the "Kingdom of God" theology of Cocceius (pp. 111–12).

107. Ibid., Moltmann draws out the connection, arguing for Brocard's influence upon the anti-papal and recapitulative lines of analysis in Cocceius's exhaustive systematic "septenary" illustrating the totality of his kingdom theology. See Gottlob Schrenk's summary of Cocceius's Apocalypse commentary, *Gottesreich und Bund im älteren Protestantismus, vornehmlich bei Johannes Cocceius* (Gütersloh: C. Bartlesmann, 1923), pp. 335–47.

108. Quistorp, *Die letzten Dinge*, p. 116.

109. Brocard, *Revelation*, fol. 10v.

110. Ibid., fol. 12v. One can only speculate on how such thinking would influence eventual Reformed argumentation and epistemology touching on both the accounts of Creation and the things pertaining to the end of history.

111. Koppel Pinson, *Pietism as a Factor in the Rise of German Nationalism* (New York: Columbia University Press, 1934), pp. 58–59, 78, 180–206.

112. Brocard, *Revelation*, fol. 5r. See Reeves, *Influence of Prophecy*, pp. 488, n. 11; 494–99.

113. Ibid., fol. 5v.

114. Ibid., fol. 17v. Brocard writes that in the sixth Age of the Son, "Chryst sendeth the Abbot Ioachim and many others whom Theleasphorus recordeth, who sayth that the Lordes comming is to bee looked for, and that there must needes be an innovation or renewing, to weete of the Gospell" (fol. 7r).

115. Reeves, *Influence of Prophecy*, p. 495.

116. Ibid., pp. 495–99.

117. Within the threefold economy of the Trinity there are eight ages of history as found in Scripture: (1) that of Abraham, (2) the Law, (3) the prophets, (4) the Evangel, (5) the Apostolic Church, (6) the woman (Church) hidden in the wilderness, (7) that of new prophets, and (8) eternity (Brocard, *Praef. in Gen.*, fols. 20v, 153v; as cited in Moltmann, "Jacob Brocard," p. 120).

118. Brocard, *Revelation*, fol. 5r-v.

119. Moltmann, "Jacob Brocard," pp. 110–29. In addition to his argument, Moltmann supplies helpful information on the commentaries on Genesis and the Song of Solomon.

120. Brocard, *Revelation*, fol. 111r. This Spiritualist exegesis is not only reminiscent of Joachim, but also of Joachim's later disciple, Peter John Olivi, who also held to a second coming in the spirit, in Francis of Assisi.

121. Ibid., fol. 109r. Although peace appeared to come for Protestants in 1570, further measuring was to occur as Christ cleansed his Church (fols. 109v–110r).

122. Ibid. "There are sayd to be two witnesses by reason of the Worde of the Gospell and of Prophecy by reason of the ministerye of the Gospell and of Prophecie, which two have ben in the Church as in very deede it appeareth. But in ye ministry of these two are understoode the People which have continued in the worde of the Gospell, and prophecie with the Woman which fled into the deserte, and haue ben her seede in sustayning the persecutions of the Papistes" (fol. 110v).

123. Brocard, *Revelation*, fol. 110r-v.

124. This merits comparison with the perspective of John Foxe. See as illustrated by Patrick Collinson, *The Birthpangs of Protestant England: Religious and Cultural Change in the Sixteenth and Seventeenth Centuries* (New York: Macmillan, 1988).

125. Brocard, *Revelation*, fol. 110v.

126. Ibid., fol. 111r.

127. Such argumentation is reminiscent of that of Peter John Olivi (c. 1248–1298), a disciple of Joachite thought. Olivi had argued in the thirteenth century that a "second coming of Christ had occurred in the person and preaching of Francis of Assisi."

128. Ibid. "That is as I thinke, after that the Gospel shalbe preached [?] 40. yeres & more. & upon the beginning of the French troubles the worke of Chrysts second comming shalbe declared to haue bene present: when those thinges shall begin to come to passe, whych the Prophetes have reported, and Chryst himselfe hath put us in minde of the 24. cap. Math . . . ."

129. Brocard is referring to the St. Bartholomew's Day massacre, August 23–24, 1572, and following days, during which 2000–100,000 French Huguenots were slain.

130. Brocard, *Revelation*, fol. 113r.

131. Melchior Hoffman, *Ausslegung der heimlichen Offenbarung Joannis* . . . (1530); cf. Packull, "A Reinterpretation of Melchior Hoffman's *Exposition* Against the Background of Spiritualist Franciscan Eschatology with Special Reference to Peter John Olivi," in *The Dutch Dissenters*, Irvin Horst, ed. (Leiden: Brill, 1986), pp. 32–65.

132. Bernard Rothmann, *Die Schriften Bernard Rothmanns, Die Schriften der Münsterischen Täufer und ihrer Gegner*, Robert Stupperich, ed. (Münster, 1970), i, pp. 281, 323–33, 346.

133. Moltmann, "Jacob Brocard," pp. 111–12.

134. Johann Heinrich Alsted, *Diatribe de Mille annis Apocalyptics* (orig., 1627); I have used the edition Francofurti: Conradi Eifridi, 1630. This treatise, a commentary on Rev. 20, is said by the author to connect all of the preceding and subsequent chapters of the Apocalypse. The history of the Church is seen in four periods: (1) John the Baptist to the Jerusalem Council (A.D. 50); (2) A.D 51 to the millennium; (3) the millennial Church; and (4) from the end of the millennium to universal Judgment (pp. 16–25). Our witnesses are found from Boniface III to the years of the Protestant Reformation (pp. 18, 26–65). Alsted's work stands in need of focused attention.

135. David Pareus, *Commentarius in apocalypsim* (Frankfurt, 1618). The edition I used was the *Commentary Upon the Divine Revelation . . . Evangelist John* (Amsterdam, 1644). The substance of this work was delivered as a series of lectures at the Reformed Academy in Heidelberg, 1608, and published ten years later.

136. Bousset, *Offenbarung*, p. 96.

137. Pareus, *Divine Revelation*, p. 242. See Günther Brinkmann, *Die Irenik des David Pareus: Frieden und Einheit ihrer Relevanz zur Warheitfrage* (Hildesheim: Gerstenberg, 1972). We might speculate that this understanding of Reformation served to strengthen Pareus in his endeavor toward toleration and conciliation among Protestants.

138. Bousset, *Offenbarung*, p. 96.

139. Pareus, *Divine Revelation*, pp. 209–10.

140. Ibid., p. 210.

141. Ibid., pp. 212–13. Following Rupert of Deutz, Pareus identifies the little book given John to eat (Rev. 10:2, 8–10) with the measuring rod (Rev. 11:1), the Word of God.

142. Ibid., p. 213.

143. Ibid., pp. 213–16.

144. Ibid., pp. 216–20. Pareus rejects four different interpretations of our text. The manner in which he does this clearly applies to three of the four ways by which the Apocalypse is read as identified in Chapter 1 of our study. He generally agrees with Bullinger that the 42 months (1260 years) ran from A.D. 666 to the Last Judgment historicist. The four rejected positions are: (1) Bellarmine (a specific period of 42 months in the future) (futurist); (2) Junius and the Magdeburg centurators (1260 years from Christ's passion to Boniface VIII) (historicist); (3) Foxe (two periods of persecution in the early

and then last days of the Church) (futurist); and (4) Alcasar (a period of time in the first century) (preterist).

145. Ibid., p. 220.

146. Ibid., p. 221.

147. Ibid., pp. 223–24.

148. Ibid., p. 224.

149. Ibid.

150. Ibid., p. 225.

151. Ibid.

152. Ibid., p. 228.

153. Ibid., pp. 228–31.

154. Ibid., p. 232. He follows the medieval commentator Rupert of Deutz.

155. Ibid., pp. 232–36.

156. Ibid., p. 242; again following Rupert of Deutz.

157. This historicist exegesis stimulated Jesuit preterist (Alcasar) and futurist (Ribeira, Bellarmine) responses, offering a different literalization.

158. R. H. Charles, *Studies in the Apocalypse* (Edinburgh: T. & T. Clark, 1913), p. 33; cf. Bousset, *Offenbarung*, pp. 97–99, 102–6.

7

Self-Conscious Witnesses:
John Foxe and the Martyrs

John Foxe's Martyrs

The spiritual, as distinct from the institutional or political, history of the Christian Church was read by many through the visions and *figurae* of the Apocalypse. By the middle of the sixteenth century, major representatives of Protestantism were contributing to a growing use of our text, finding in it a measure of self-identity and description of Protestant reform. This is particularly visible in England in the account of the martyrs in the writings of John Foxe. His efforts are furthered by Thomas Brightman, Joseph Mede, and Thomas Goodwin.[1] Each of these biblical exegetes developed interpretations of our text that reflected important implications for the shape of Anglo-American piety, polity, and social policy. Here the trope quickly became the letter not only for purposes of self-identity but as a means to plot the way forward to the time when Christ would be visibly King in society.

The pattern for such a moral interpretation of history had been set on the Continent and by British authors reaching back to the days of John Wyclif, or even Bede the Venerable. Such reformers had associated a vision of perseverence in the truth with our text. On the Continent, Heinrich Bullinger had drawn attention to this theme with enduring significance for his English audience in his sermons on the Apocalypse. Preachers will preach and prophets prophesy, he had written. Persecution will come but it will not overwhelm God's ministers until such time as they have finished their testimony. The gospel must be openly preached to all. God appoints a specific work for preachers, keeping them safe for their appointed time. We should thank God, Bullinger wrote in relation to our text, that:

> Many good preachers over a long time, and today D. Luther and
> D. Zwingli and other faithful witnesses of God, could in so wicked a world,
> and under so great a power of Antichrist, execute their ministry for so many
> years in spite of the gates of hell.[2]

Individual prophets may be slain (Rev. 11:7–10), but new ones are raised in order to proclaim the truth.[3] Antichrist does not triumph by Scripture, testimony, or reason, but by force and by using carnal weapons. Preachers will be dealt with cruelly just as Christ and his apostles suffered under old Rome. Indeed, the bodies of the faithful will be left unburied as was happening then. This is a day of martyrs, Bullinger wrote, comparable to the days of Constance when Hus and Jerome of Prague were burnt.[4] Today, Bullinger added, martyrs are falling in England:

> We have heard today after England has gone back under the Roman See and has seen the beginning of a severe persecution of the members of Christ what joy and gladness, what banqueting and triumphs the Papists made in all places. Whenever ministers, or other faithful are burnt, they keep up cheer and banqueting, singing *Te deum Laudamus*. Letters of rejoicing fly to and fro. In some other places when they hear these things they rejoice at the misery of the faithful, but the Lord sees these things and has predicted in this text that they would happen now.[5]

The social reality of persecution of the time, whether from Saracen armies moving into the European heartland[6] or from the restoration of a feared Catholicism by Lutheran or Swiss oriented reformers and political proto-Erastians in England, lent credibility to the imminence of the end of history for many. As Bullinger preached these sermons in Zürich, the city had become a haven for Protestant exiles from England and elsewhere.[7] It was to these English exiles that the series was dedicated in its published Latin version.[8] That the sermons were appreciated can be seen in the exiles' response.[9] At the end of the two years (1554–1556) that Bullinger took to preach out of the Apocalypse, the Englishmen Robert Horn and Richard Chambers wrote to Bullinger, reflecting that "all things seem to be growing worse and worse. So great is the number of martyrs, who in their cheerful profession of the word of God are most cruelly dragged to the flames and to torments."[10] Many editions and translations of Bullinger's sermons on the Apocalypse appeared throughout the balance of the sixteenth century as its influence reached out among those oriented toward the Swiss Reformed movement across Europe.[11] Its significance for English piety lies further in the hypothesis that it may have been used to gloss the book of Revelation in the earliest editions of the Geneva Bible (1560).[12]

Apocalyptic literature was in vogue. It offered a coherent narrative into which experiences of personal turmoil or social unrest could find their place. As Bullinger was delivering his sermons, exegetes and early Protestant historians like John Bale, John Foxe, and Flacius Illyricus were working simultaneously with themes of martyrdom and apocalyptic crisis through history; they did so in the Swiss city of Basel, the very site of the publication of Bullinger's series. Such was the case from Europe's western extremeties all the way to the east and the kingdom of Poland-Lithuania where Cyprian Bazylik, friend of Simon Budny, authored a martyrology which would help to shape historical understanding and social reform in the ever-fissuring Polish reform movement.[13] In the year that a Latin edition of Bullinger's commentary appeared in England, 1561, an English edition was brought out by the Ipswich schoolmaster John Daus.[14] That same year John Parkhurst, Bishop of Norwich, having himself heard the sermons in Zürich, directed the clergy of his diocese to obtain a copy of either the Latin or English edition.[15] A second edition of the English translation appeared, significantly, in 1573, a time of further papal challenge to the legitimacy of Queen Elizabeth's rule.[16]

As in the Lutheran territories and kingdom of France across the English Channel, an apocalyptic horizon became a vivid reality for Protestants in England in the wake of growing religious controversy. This controversy drew upon the narrative of declension and renewal documented from the history of Israel, significant insofar as Christians conceived of their history, that of the New Israel, in line with that older story. As reform was required in the days of Ahab and Hezekiah, or of Joshua and Zerubbabel, so too in the present age. The correlation between the history of the old dispensation and that of the new was no longer seen as merely moral and generally paradigmatic, but as more apocalyptic and literal.[17] The themes associated with Revelation 11 drew into contemporary and apocalyptic reflection that older story of social moral failure and divine responsibility. Judgment, prophetic effort, and temporal speculation appeared in a more focused way through this text. Indeed, there is a striking parallel between Malachi's prophecy of the return of Elijah (Mal. 4:5–6) at the end of the Old Testament and our witnesses in the New Testament in the closing days of the second dispensation. Both call for efforts at restoration or reform under the shadow of imminent Judgment.

The drawing together into a common skein the threads of personal experience, social unrest, biblical narrative, and apocalyptic conscienceness is nowhere seen better than in the work of John Foxe (1516–1587),[18] historian, playwright, and martyrologist. Foxe provided English Protestantism with what many felt to be the accurate spiritual or inside look into history and historical causation. Foxe offered his audience an exciting account of the history of the true Church in his *Book of Martyrs*.[19] His commentary on the book of Revelation illuminates the meaning of that story.[20] Seen in light of this commentary, *The Book of Martyrs* can appear as a lengthy historical excursus upon our theme of two adventural witnesses. Indeed, the periodization is the same, the unevenness to the structure coming only from the diverse biographical information on the particular witnesses that Foxe sought to lift up as exemplars of the truth.

While much could be said about the way in which Foxe helped to further the legitimization and literal-historical interpretation of the book of Revelation,[21] it is the story of his use of our theme that is of primary interest here. The witnesses functioned as part of a comprehensive theodicy for those who sought to lay bare the true story of history.[22] They told of persecution and martyrdom, of reformation and triumph within a divinely ordered progression of history between the two advents of Christ.[23]

In the preface to his *Acts and Monuments*, Foxe writes that his work contains a prophetic history of the Christian Church that has been opened up in recent days through the general study of history.[24] In the introduction to his commentary on Revelation, he adds that the Apocalypse is a prophetic revelation of history. The Church must pay greater heed to prophecies. The book of Revelation "opens up to us the mystery and universal history of the church." It is like a drama ("*spectaculum*") produced on the stage.[25] Foxe objects to those who ignore the content of the prophecies and limit the interpretation of Scripture to the tropological (moral) sense.[26] Foxe's interest in the personalities of the Reformation pushed the question of apocalyptic literalism and particularization as part of his larger interest in the identity of the true Church.[27] It was "an exercise in optimism," showing that reforming martyrs had not died in vain.[28]

The Drama of History

Foxe's scheme of history highlights this concern. The church of the new dispensation was one with the church of old Israel.[29] Current events were to be evaluated in terms of the grid presented in sacred history. As Israel had been refined by affliction in Egypt, so the Christian Church was sifted in the opening years of the Christian era.[30] As Israel had been afflicted by Canaanites in the Promised Land, so the Church was persecuted at the opening of the new dispensation.[31] As rule in Israel had passed from judges to kings, so under Constantine and his successors the Church experienced a similar transition, only to fall prey to priestly rule as had happened to Israel after the Babylonian captivity.[32]

This Church history was united to the political history of our or five empires represented by the metals of gold, silver, bronze, iron, and iron mixed with clay in Nebuchadnezzar's vision of the great image (Dan. 2:31–45).[33] For Foxe, as for others, these metals symbolized the kngdoms of Assyria or Babylonia, Medio-Presia, Greece, and Rome. They were further adumbrated under the first four apocalyptic seals. The fifth seal (Rev. 6:9–11) symbolized Daniel's fifth or godly kingdom, the uncut stone that destroyed the human image (Dan. 2:44–45), or enlarging dominion of the Son of man (by interpretation, Christ) and kingdom of the saints (Dan. 7:13–14, 23–27). It represented the victory of the gospel, spiritually discerned. The fifth seal of the Apocalypse reveals this victory but only under the heavenly altar of God. In other words, the victorious Church of the new dispensation is also the Church of martyrs, the Church under the cross. The Church in time, whose victory is only fully seen through Christ, suffers affliction as did Israel during her Egyptian sojourn.[34]

Two parallel periods of persecution can be chronicled from the outline of Revelation 11–13. The first, pictured under the fifth seal (Rev. 6:9–11) and found in chapter 13, ran from the time of the public ministry of Jesus (A.D. 30) through the time of the emperor Licinius (A.D. 324), a period of 294 years. The second persecution was figured in the forty-two months of Revelation 11:2 during which the holy city is trampled over by the nations. This persecution, like the first, would last 294 years. Foxe adduced this specific number through inspiration on the numerological significance of the periods of time listed in Revelation 11–13: 1260 days (Rev. 11:3; 12:6), a symbolic period of time, times and a half-time (Rev. 12:14), and finally forty-two months (three and a half years [Rev. 11:2; 13:5]).[35]

Between the two persecutions came the millennial age, ending about the year A.D. 1300, the time for the outbreak of the second period of persecution.[36] This period would be dominated by the loosing of Satan (Rev. 20:7) under whom there were to occur ten phases of persecution working their havoc upon the Church together with the subtleties of Antichrist. It was a time of trial for the Church similar to that in the early Church as described by Eusebius of Caesarea. According to Foxe, the ninth phase of the second time of persecution occurred with the Marian exiles. The tenth would be that of Philip II in Spain and Flanders.[37] The second Advent and Last Judgment could be expected following these events.

The fourteenth century showed conditions demonstrating the greater unleashing of satanic activity.[38] Increasing persecution surrounded preachers like Wyclif, Hus, and Jerome of Prague.[39] The century also witnessed the growth of Turkish power, representing for Foxe the second of three apocalyptic woes.[40] This kingdom, Foxe thought, could not be defeated apart from a thorough reformation of the Western Church. Papal idolatry in Christian hearts and churches had weakened Christendom too much throughout Europe.[41]

This matrix of events enabled Foxe to correlate history with the vision of the angel bearing the sixth trumpet (Rev. 9:13–11:15).[42] The first vision under this trumpet was the rise of the Turkish threat. Foxe continues by discussing the appearance of an angel who is said to be standing upon sea and land (Rev. 10:1–7).[43] He lists various interpretations given this figure: the Roman pope (Luther), an angel (Bullinger), the prophet Enoch (Joachim), an angelic messenger (Aretas). He concludes that it is probably Christ and focuses his attention upon the reasons for the angel's appearance: He is to restore prophecy and foreshadow world destruction at the sound of the seventh trumpet and final woe (Rev. 11:15). Foxe admits that the specific time of this end to history is unknown, yet he believes that the future has been given a certain shape that may be discerned in Scripture. Indeed, in an argument that follows Luther, Foxe believed that soon after the restoration of gospel preaching, the Day of Judgment will come.[44] If the end seems delayed, atheists and "Epicureans" being in ascendance, it is because our sense of time cannot be compared to God's. Afflicted by frustration, persecution, even martyrdom, saints are to learn patience, expecting through this their final blessing.[45]

The angel standing upon sea and land (Rev. 10:1–3) swears that now there will be no further delay in God's plan for history. The final series of world events has begun. With almost a sense of apocalyptic resignation, Foxe writes that either the Lord does not live or Christ will come soon in his second Advent.[46] As the prophecies of the first Advent were fulfilled, so, Foxe argues, the prophesied events prior to the second Advent now stand open before our faith.

> In what pertains to the reckoning of time and years, however long it may seem to human expectation that God has delayed for so long the ordained end of these present times, still for us who divide for ourselves the moments of time, that which remains left for the world, whatever it is, should not now seem long; if only we follow and attend to this prophetic caution. . . . Since this is so, let all pious Christians be warned . . . to listen diligently to the word of this angel and to attend to that which he wants, says, and swears.[47]

John is told to take the scroll held by the angel and devour it. He does so, finding it sweet to his mouth but bitter to his stomach, and he is now told to prophesy.[48] In the days of the sixth trumpet this prophecy is to be revived by other "administrators" and "preachers of the Word" pictured in John and his preaching.[49] It is clear, Foxe writes, that the prophecy began to see its fulfillment in the year A.D. 1300. The simplest explanation for current events is to see the power of the Turks shadowed under the release of four destructive angels, the first part of the vision of the sixth trumpet (Rev. 9:14–21), and to recognize in the latter part the restoration of the gospel in Wyclif, Hus, Jerome of Prague, Luther, Zwingli, Oecolampadius, Melanchthon, and Calvin.[50] These all went forth to fight the papal Antichrist.

According to the vision of the Apocalypse, and lifted up pointedly in Augustinian theology, the restoration of the gospel comes during the senectitude of the world, which medieval exegesis had connected with the work of the adventual witnesses and the appearance of the Antichrist.[51] Foxe believed along with his reform-minded contemporaries that that Antichrist had now been identified. Whereas the prevailing medieval opinion had been that Antichrist was still in the future, Foxe not only collected a series of prophecies pointing to the Turk as a possible form of Antichrist but also, and more generally, joined the greater company of Protestant exegetes who identified the papacy as the Great Antichrist.[52]

All of the medieval characteristics assigned to the future Antichrist were now applied to this contemporary manifestation. Thus, one looked for: (1) A final tribulation that would last a symbolic or literal 1260 days or 42 months (e.g., Rev. 11:2–3); (2) an open period of rule of equal length that would be a sign of the impending Judgment; (3) either a person or institution with growing political hegemony in the world would be the focus for such attention. For Foxe, as for many Protestants, the biography of Antichrist, common in the Middle Ages, was transmuted into an account of the history of the papacy.[53] However, Antichrist was not an independent power of evil in the world, nor a part of a transcendent divine force. For Foxe, as for most Protestant exegetes, demonic powers were under the overarching providence of God. The ultimate demonic power was linked to a definite, limited time span. It would appear in history and was related, if not limited, to human misendeavors. Evil and the demonic were not left for an enlarged cosmic role but would be destroyed in time.[54]

Tangible Goodness

This revelation of Antichrist was part of a panoply of signs early and most fully developed by Lutheran theologians following their Elijah, Martin Luther. Luther had set the pattern in his own pointing to the papacy as filling the role of Antichrist and then in seeking justification for this correlation. Melanchthon had provided futher elaboration by discerning and enumerating these types of signs. These consisted of perceived disorders in the natural world, political turmoil in the social order, and troubles in the Church. Throughout the balance of the sixteenth century, theologians like Nikolaus of Amsdorf, Sebastian Franck, Nicolaus Winckler, Philipp Nicolai, and others on the Continent would follow Luther's and Melanchthon's lead.[55] The signs of the end were not all distressing. There was tangible goodness. Foxe found such goodness connected with our text and elsewhere in the book of Revelation. According to Foxe, mysteries "bubble up" everywhere in the Apocalypse, a book that is not easily understood, but filled with promise as well as woe. Such promise is particularly evident in a mysterious way with regard to Revelation 11.

> While this whole book bubbles up everywhere with most divine mysteries, I think there is no part of the book that is more obscure than this very part with which we are now occupied, no part about which interpreters struggle more with their differing opinions.[56]

However, as evil has an historical and tangible reality, so does goodness. Through apocalyptic images of righteousness and purity, the Church is measured and evil ferreted out (Rev. 11:1–2),[57] preaching is revived and righteousness restored according to models provided by ancient Israel. While the days of restoration are introduced by the mighty angel under the sixth trumpet, they are more fully seen in the appearance of the two witnesses (Rev. 11:3–13). Clues to their identity, number[58] and time of appearance[59] are revealed, showing that the witnesses are the positive counterparts of Antichrist. This is the constructive side of apocalyptic polemic and apologetics, in which Protestants attempted to work out a sense of self-definition.

Foxe often follows Bullinger's positions in interpreting the Apocalypse. However, at times he is dissatisfied with the way in which Bullinger holds back from an explicit correspondence between prophecy and event.[60] Having discussed a number of opinions on the identity of the witnesses, Foxe concludes that most papal theologians hold that the two witnesses are Enoch and Elijah, who will appear in the last three and one-half years of the world.[61] Others substitute Moses for one of them because they believe that he also was translated. Still others teach that these are to be pious preachers who will come in the spirit of Enoch and Elijah.

Foxe both accepts and rejects the idea that the witnesses are to be two individuals. He contends that while their number may represent an uncertain multitude, still they are especially evident in two persons.

> In England they may be seen in the person of Wyclif; in Italy, in the person of Marsilius of Padua; in Gaul, in the poor men of Milan; in Bohemia, John Hus and Jerome of Prague; in Saxony, in Luther and Melanchthon; in Switzerland, Zwingli; in Basel, Oecolampadius; and many others.[62]

The witnesses may even include all those who have been oppressed by false accusations: Christian saints, pagan heroes, and Hebrew paragons who suffered after being falsely accused. This list includes individuals such as Socrates and Moses, both described as liberators from oppression. Others are cited down through St. Stephen and the age of the apostles.[63] The two witnesses are those who are persecuted for the truth, libeled as heretics, and condemned by the Church or falsely accused in one way or another.[64]

Foxe wants to say more. As Christ is a person, spoken of as having a body, the Church; as Antichrist is one, yet is said to have many members; so he seems to want to speak of the two witnesses. While neither the time of their persecution is unambiguously defined, nor certain persons designated, nor even their precise testimony or specific number described, still, Foxe insists, there are definite historical figures who fulfill the intent of this prophecy:

> While we may admit that at first glance these enigmas seem more abstruse than that they might easily be interpreted, still . . . as I penetrate more carefully the particular circumstances of this description, and as I compare figures with reality, past events with later events, from the very evidence of events it then appears to me that the correct understanding of this prophecy can only be found in those two unconquered athletes of Christ whom we have described up till now, and [the prophecy] may be properly and definitely applied to the general Council of Constance.[65]

There does appear to be a time that fits what is foreshadowed in Scripture: that of the two Bohemian martyrs, John Hus (c. 1372–1415) and Jerome of Prague (c. 1370–1416). They lived in the portentous days of the fourteenth and fifteenth centuries. While some may scoff at such specificity, Foxe argues that we see in them the beginning of a process which still goes forth and sweeps the Church up in reformation. The primary and most particular example of the prophecy of the adventual witnesses can be seen in those events at the time of the Council of Constance (1414–1419). Called for the purpose of reform in the church (*causa unionis, causa reformationis, causa fidei*) the Council asserted its authority in these matters by sending two it deemed heretics (John Hus and Jerome of Prague) to the stake.

Foxe's handling of the two witnesses is an example of how he seeks to particularize prophecy without negating a more general moral truth.[66] The biographies of Hus and Jerome of Prague receive prominent attention in both *Acts and Monuments* and *Eicasmi*. Foxe follows their histories with lists of people persecuted or martyred for their faith, especially since the coming of Luther and the Protestant Reformation.[67] While the *Acts and Monuments* emphasize the biographies of the martyrs in their particular period of history, the *Eicasmi* illustrates their significance in the hidden purposes of God. Foxe concludes the historical narrative following his interpretation of the identity of the two witnesses by asking how anyone could say that the Antichrist has not come in light of all those who have been persecuted and martyred. In saying this, Foxe points us again to the Council of Constance as the clear evidence for the prophecy's resolution.[68]

In an effort to clarify his conclusions, Foxe draws attention to five circumstances that came together in the persons of Hus and Jerome, proving them to be unique embodiments of our prophetic witnesses. The first piece of evidence relates to the period in which they appeared: the time under the sixth trumpet following the devastation from the East, the era opened by the unsealing of the seventh seal. Foxe rehearses the events prophesied to occur under this trumpet (Rev. 9:13–11:15). He seems overwhelmed by the way in which prophecy and events correlate beginning around 1300—progressive Turkish devastation, papal declension, and, on the other hand, increase in the number of inspired prophets and martyrs. The particular witness of Hus and Jerome and the events surrounding the Council of Constance form part of an apocalyptic picture of history swelling to a climax.[69] Such developments compelled Foxe to alter the traditional Augustinian conception of the millennium: Satan's binding is now seen to have occurred after the first period of persecution in the Church's history. Satan was fully released again in the fourteenth century, which is to be identified with the time of the apocalyptic witnesses.[70]

The second item concerns the fact that in Hus and Jerome we find two powerful prophets working together at the same time in history. For Foxe it is obvious that these are the witnesses. Why, he asks, make an uncertainty out of a certainty? There is nothing repugnant to the idea that the two witnesses are precisely these two. This is open for all to see. The correlation between prophecy and event has reached its climax in these evangelical forerunners or adventual witnesses of a second Advent.[71] Roughly three hundred pages of *Acts and Monuments* deal with Hus and Jerome. Better than one-fifth of *Eicasmi* is concerned with the appearance of the two witnesses. Foxe goes to great lengths in an effort to present the prophecies foretelling all of these events in the fourteenth century and thereafter.[72]

The third circumstance that drives toward a literal application of our prophecy is the fact that these two Bohemians were one in cause as well as in time. They were contemporaries and fulfilled the same mission of giving testimony to the truth at a crucial time in the apocalyptic age. They were forced into the role of prophets by the pope and became cloaked under Old Testament types and allusions referred to in our chapter in Revelation. Like Moses, they began a process of liberation. Like Elijah, they revealed anti-Christian idolatry in the heart of Rome. In line with Jeremiah, they called their people to repentance.[73] Medieval dramas that presented lines of prophets prior to the first or second advents helped to reinforce this sense of living prophecy.[74] Daniel's vision of four empires, the prophecy of Elijah, and the clamor of trumpets out of the Apocalypse gave significance to prophets and martyrs who called out from the brink of the Great Assize (Judgment).[75]

As the witnesses were slain by the beast, yet restored again, so Hus and Jerome were slain and restored. Here Foxe turns to a variety of prophecies of great interest during the Reformation that look toward the restoration of the Church, visions by orthodox and heretical medieval priests and prophets. Included are those of Joachim of Fiore, Arnold of Villanova, Savonarola, and others. Some specifically concern Hus's and Jerome's. The most famous of these is Hus' vision that within a hundred years papal authorities would have to answer for his martyrdom. The rising of the witnesse can be seen allegorically in the restoration of their doctrine in the Protestant Reformation as begun by Luther a century after Hus and Jerome.[76]

The fifth and ultimate item of circumstantial evidence is presented by a mathematical correlation of the prophecy with the events at the Council of Constance. The two sackcloth witnesses prophesy 1260 days. After this they are slain by the beast amidst much rejoicing. Then, after three and one-half days the spirit of God enters them. They stand upon their feet and ascend to heaven. Foxe noted that the period during which the Council of Constance was held lasted precisely the amount of time indicated in the prophecy—three and one-half years. The Council convened in December 1414 and concluded on May 17, 1418, nearly 42 months or 1260 days. Further, from the way in which Hus and Jerome were treated, one may say that they were dressed in sackcloth. Although slain, their resurrection happened in the revival of their message.[77]

Foxe concludes his five points by returning to a more synthetic discussion of the significance of Hus and Jerome as the two witnesses, or at least as exemplary instances of them. Despite persecution and martyrdom, they represent the victory of a providential view of history. Their resurrection in latter-day preaching is the *renovatio* of the last days.[78]

The Trope Becomes the Letter

Foxe's struggle to find a bridge between his spirituality and the events of his day within a providential framework appears clearly in his interpretation of our witnesses. The tropological, or figurative and moral way of conceiving life, was undergoing a literal reconceptualization. Prophecy, under the pressure of current events and an increasing appreciation for particular events in history, was being woven into new apocalyptic patterns reflecting this new appreciation of the empirical event and offered further strength to the literalization of the moral or allegorical truth of Scripture. One could say that the visionary relationship between morality and chronicle plays in the late medieval period was collapsed into historical events in the sixteenth century. From this perspective, it is interesting to note that at least two of those who promoted this kind of literalization, John Bale and John Foxe, wrote plays for the stage as well as commentaries on the book of Revelation.

The Apocalypse lends itself to dramatization. It opens with the words "Blessed is he who reads aloud the words of prophecy, and blessed are those who hear, and who keep what is written therein; for the time is near" (Rev. 1:3). With such advice, the way is already prepared for the move from allegory to history, from pulpit to stage or council chamber and street corner, from prophecy to apocalypticism. For Foxe, as for others, the prophetism of old Israel was filtered through the book of Revelation to create a prophetic tradition in the West parallel to that of Israel.[79] With the appropriation of anti-papal prophecies against an Augustinian temporal perspective that emphasized the deepening of evil prior to Judgment, impulses come to the fore that enhanced the latent tendencies of "prophetic eschatology" to move toward "apocalyptic eschatology."[80] The correlation of Scripture and event was serious business. It concerned ultimate preservation or defection.[81] One of the most frequently cited chronicles of the day argued that it was the duty of Church leaders to occupy themselves with prophecies.[82] Historians like Johannes Sleidanus[83] and Jean Crespin[84] built their accounts around the prophetic texts of the Old and New Testaments. There was an attempt to place the prophecies upon a rational basis, which yet did not lose sight of the moral or tropological implications of the text.[85]

This very effort to locate a moral reading of the text within an apocalyptic framework that could be rationally defended through recourse to historical argument was itself undergoing paradigmatic shift. The tension is nowhere seen more clearly than, first, in Bullinger's commentary on the Apocalypse and now with a clearer literalness in Foxe. The moral vision of the Latin medieval Church had been challenged by a new historiography shaped by humanist appeals to history as empirically measured and rationally conceived. Protestants who themselves would within a hundred years be rent, as now had been Latin Christendom, by the same tension in historical conception in the further devolution of the Reformation, found, for the moment, ready allies in such early chronologists, annalists, and historians as Sleidanus and Crespin.

Augustine's understanding of time and history, summarizing as it did earlier tendencies in Christian thinking, had largely governed Western European patterns of thought. Into this perspective had been factored theories of moral causation with personal and social import which, for purposes of moral rectitude and civic virtue, had been undergoing reconceptualization with republican import in the Florentine and wider Italian Renaissance. Under the impact of this civic humanism,[86] together with a way of reading the literal sense of the Bible, pointedly raised up in the work of the late medievalist Nicholas of Lyra,[87] now with revolutionary religious significance in Luther,[88] one read the judgments envisioned in the Apocalypse through the same literal lens as one perceived moral failure. The truth of Christ now bore a certain immediacy for moral applicability in the personal life of the individual or social life of the community. There was no longer the need to collect religious relics to prove the faith. Such proof was best found in the confessed immediacy of the Spirit, a point ever to dog Luther until the end of his days—and so also for later Protestant "establishmentarians."

How to understand time, and events in time, in the context of the inherited figural patterns associated with the Apocalypse, or visions of Daniel and the other prophets—as interpreted by Christian theology centering around a specific understanding of the person and work of Jesus Christ as that gave coherence to those visions and prophecies—became the issue at hand. For Foxe this meant a life devoted to writing *Acts and Monuments*, a commentary on the book of Revelation, and a dramatic interpretation of the Apocalypse for both the stage and for the popular imagination. His were the days of prodigious events and adventual witnesses. What we see him doing is what other apocalyptic theologians from the sixteenth century into our own era have strived to do, namely work within the figural patterns of Scripture by offering new configurations for fresh coherence as determined by the necessities of theories of moral causation and particular permutations of individual and social events.

New impetus was given to the study of chronologies, as often arranged into annals and histories, which were at first used to prove the figural imagination and then were studied in relation to the evolution of some other ideal or in themselves.[89] Melanchthon's own work with the kingdoms of Daniel, *Chronica Carionis*, and "prophecy of Elias" helped to promote this vision and historical tension within Lutheranism. Conflict in religious vision served to heighten interest in chronology, and vision as illustrated in the conflicting histories of Matthias Flacius and associates in the *Magdeburg Centuries* was met by that of Caesar Baronius (1538–1607) in his work *Annales Ecclesiastici* (1588–1607). Further changes in the service of religious vision by Sebastian Franck, Johannes Sleidanus, David Chytraeus, Georg Nigrinus, and Leonard Krentzheim were published, such work taking on greater urgency with the promulgation of the Gregorian calendar in 1582.

Although it was not until the seventeenth century with the focused interest in human activity in society in Jean Bodin, the comparative chronological interests of Joseph Scaliger, and eventual religiously nonpartisan work of pietist Gottfried Arnold (1666–1714) that the way began to part between historical coherence as offered up in the Augustinian religious vision and an interest in the movement of events, such would not mean their complete or irrevocable sundering for many scholars even at the center of developments in Western European and North Atlantic culture.

Foxe's prophetic framework gave structure to a new understanding of the Reformation in England. It illustrated the way in which believers might know that they stood at the end of history, yet it also provided the calculus by which one might continue to work with the permutations and computations of time and events. This is no where more pointed than in the way in which Foxe drew a parallel between the emperor Constantine and Queen Elizabeth, implying that as Constantine had inaugurated a new era for the Church, so, if this were not history's end, might she.[90] The expectations that this engendered for society were heightened by the ideal itself in the context of competing social and religious movements, and by the increasing politicization of religious life in England under Elizabeth.[91] Once again, as with Luther and the radicals, Bullinger and the company of Reformed preachers—as well as in earlier medieval renewal and reforming efforts—there was established a new correlation between eschatological vision with an apocalyptic figural particularity that bore not only upon the structuring of history but also upon the shaping of organizational life.

Elizabethan Puritanism took shape around acknowledged apocalyptic imagery. Mary's death and Elizabeth's accession to the British throne were viewed as acts of divine deliverance.[92] Our theme continued as a part of that story although tracing it out is not always possible.[93] Yet it did help to define in broad strokes the nature of evolving Protestant self-identity.[94] As it was put so well for English imaginative life two years after the publication of Foxe's commentary on the Apocalypse by the Cambridge Puritan divine Thomas Cartwright, in his influential *Confutation of the Rhemist . . . Testament*—a book written to refute the edition of the Bible translated into English by Roman Catholic scholars in exile at Rheims and produced to mute the influence of the Geneva Bible and other Protestant inspired English translations—our witnesses are identified as the small number who oppose Antichrist "even in [his] . . . hottest persecution."

> Christ shall have his two witnesses always, even in the hottest persecution of Antichrist. Therefore there is no need of Enoch and Elias, neither doth the text speak of them. The coming of Elias was prophesied by Malachi before the coming of Christ, and accomplished in John the Baptist, as our Saviour Christ testifieth. . . . Let the reader therefore judge, whether we be contentious and

incredulous, because we yield not to these various, inconstant, and fabulous opitons of many of the ancient fathers; or rather whether you would not make the world secure of the second coming of Christ, which confirm such fantasies, that it might be thought that Antichrist is not yet come.[95]

For early Puritans, whether of the conforming Anglican party, Presbyterian, or nascent Congregational and Independent parties, all for whom, except perhaps Anglican, Cartwright spoke, his work represented certain assumptions about Christian identity and inspired new understandings of Church polity and implied a more radical representative or democratic ordering of British social life. With respect to the identity assumed, Cartwright argued that misinterpreting the identity of the witnesses could only be linked to what he defined as blind literalism or, called in his day, Judaism. Such an epithet had followed the history of the Jews since one of their own, Paul the convert to Christ, had explained their failure to believe Christ in his day as having been the result of their having been hardened to the truth (Rom. 9:18) and were deceived into believing that the Christ would not come until Elijah had returned in person. Likewise, Cartwright argued, the papists were unable to understand the spiritual significance of the present. They argue that the pope cannot be Antichrist because Enoch and Elijah have not returned in person.[96] Patristic and medieval commentators are cited to underscore the significance of our passage and of the debate over the witnesses' identity in Cartwright's work.[97] The commentary concludes with the point that those who look for literal personages only seek to "make the world secure of the second coming of Christ . . . that it might be thought Antichrist is not yet come."[98] Later Puritan commentators such as William Ames (1576–1633)[99] and Thomas Beard (d. 1632)[100] continue this polemic in the next century by drawing out the same assumptions seen in Cartwright with further significance for British ecclesial and political life.

Foxe's envisioned parallel between Emperor Constantine, referred to out of honor in Orthodox Eusebian theology as "the thirteenth apostle," and Queen Elizabeth was to have enduring significance in the evolution of Anglican theology. Even as that first Christian empire was to define for itself a unique relationship between Christian faith and political rule, such would also be the case in British life. Foxe's martyrology, popularly called his *Book of Martyrs,* helped shape the idea of England as one with Israel of old. Theology, as developed in conformity with the interests of the British Crown, took its lead from theories of state supremacy rather than that of the Church in ecclesiastical affairs. Such leadership granted to the Christian ruler rather than to the Christian teacher or minister, to be referred to as Erastianism following its chief expositor, Thomas Erastus (1524–1583), might be said, anachronistically, to have characterized that first Christian empire under Constantine. As it was hoped that Constantine's rule might open up into a new Christian era on earth, so also with Elizabeth. If the millennium was not at hand, many at least assumed a new day for the Church as Christ's saints would rule in the spirit of King Jesus in ever more far-reaching ways.

Further parallels between those rulers were drawn. As that of Constantine followed three hundred years of persecution and new growth, so that of Elizabeth followed an equal number of years from the first appearance of that "Morning Star of the Reformation," John Wyclif (c. 1330–1384). As tyranny had come upon

Israel from Rome, so fresh religio-political tyranny had come upon God's new Israel from Rome. God's sign to Constantine, *hoc signo vincit* ("by this sign you will conquer"), at the Milvian Bridge near Rome, was repeated for Elizabeth with the defeat of the Spanish Armada. Foxe crafted a winsome vision alike for both English conformist and separatist. Sustained by a martyr's faith, both could perceive God's guiding hand in forging a nation of an elect people whose destiny it now was to extend the benefits of spiritual religion and political expression freed from external constraint.[101] The precise form in which such political expression might work together with the creation of a godly people was now the topic at issue as our two witnesses became embroiled over debates about how Christ might rule in society.

Notes

1. The anti-millennial arguments were dropped in the Thirty-Nine Articles (1563); see Edgar Gibson, *The Thirty-nine Articles of the Church of England* (London: Methuen, 1904), pp. 12–29; Wilhelm Boussett, *Die Offenbarung, Johannis* (Gottingen: Vandenhrech und Ruprecht, 1906), pp. 89–91. The use of the Apocalypse in English Protestantism has been the subject of several recent studies. Bernard Capp offers an overview of such in "The Political Dimension of Apocalyptic Thought," in C. A. Patrides and Joseph Wittreich, eds., *The Apocalypse in English Renaissance Thought and Literature* (Ithaca, N.Y.: Cornell University Press, 1984). He stresses the early connection between an emotional and intellectual appeal of the Apocalypse growing out of the experience of religious upheaval in the sixteenth century. Early developments relating to the medieval tradition that affected England are analyzed in Leslie P. Fairfield (*John Bale: Mythmaker for the English Reformation* [West Lafayette, Ind.: Purdue University Press, 1967] and Richard Bauckham, (*Tudor Apocalypse* [Oxford: The sutton Courtenay Press, 1978]). The continuing effect of such thinking is handled by Bryan Ball (*A Great Expectation: Eschatological Thought in English Protestantism to 1660* [Leiden: Brill, 1975]) and Paul Christianson (*Reformers and Babylon: Apocalyptic Visions from the Reformation to the Eve of the Civil War* [Toronto: University of Toronto Press, 1978], with attention given to English political affairs. Whereas it appears from Ball's study that Reformation apocalyptic thinking flowered in Great Britain, Robert Barnes argues that such was a "weak reflection" of earlier Lutheran theology (*Prophecy and Gnosis* [Stanford: Stanford University Press, 1988], p. 5). Katherine Firth (*The Apocalyptic Tradition in Reformation Britain, 1530–1645* [New York and London: Oxford University Press, 1979]) offers insight through periods of English national reform.

2. Heinrich Bullinger, *In Apocalypsim-conscious centum* (Basel: Oporinus, 1557), p. 144.

3. Bullinger adds that Antichrist's treatment of the prophets is depicted in Rev. 11:7–10, chapters 13, 17, and in Matt. 10, John 16, and Dan. 7 and 11 (ibid., p. 144).

4. Bullinger, *In Apocalypsim*, pp. 144–46.

5. Ibid., p. 146.

6. Rudolf Pfister, "Reformation, Türken und Islam," *Zwingliana*, 19 (1956):364.

7. Christina Garrett raises the question of whether their exile from England to Zürich and other centers on the Continent was one of migration or flight. She argues that the emigration was largely a voluntary movement with a clear purpose, one that would even foreshadow the later migration to North America (*The Marian Exiles. A Study of the Origins of Elizabethan Puritanism* [Cambridge: Cambridge University Press, 1938], pp. 10, 38,

56, 59). The way in which apocalyptic themes became involved in legitimating the vision of both migrations (see below with Thomas Goodwin) should be noted for its rhetorical significance.

8. Bullinger, *In Apocalypsim*, sig. A2r.

9. Hastings Robinson, ed., *Original Letters Relative to the English Reformation . . . from the Archives of Zurich* (Cambridge: Cambridge University Press, 1842–1847), Vol. 1, pp. 158, 169–70; cf. Heinrich Bullinger, *Diarium*, p. 50; and John Strype, *Annals of the Reformation and Establishment of Religion* (Vol. 1) (London: T. Edlin, 1725), pp. 256–57.

10. Robinson, *Original Letters*, Vol. 1, p. 132.

11. Joachim Staedtke, HBBibl I/1, pp. 155–68. See numerical listings, pp. 327–56, and Staedtke's discussion of Bullinger's influence in "Bullingers Bedeutung für die protestantische Welt," *Zwingliana* 11 (1959):372–88; note his conclusion, p. 388.

12. So argues Bauckham, *Tudor Apocalypse*, pp. 49, 53 (n. 51).

13. Cyprian Bazylik, *The History of Harsh Persecution* (Brest-Litovsk, 1563). The book contains the *vita* of John Laski, some-time pastor of the Strangers' Church in London, the features on its title page, "Marian martyrs, including Cranmer and Hooker." See in George H. Williams, *Stanislas Lubieniecki, History of the Polish Reformation, with Nine Related Documents* (Cambridge: Harvard University Press, 1993), Plate 1.

14. Bullinger, HBBibl I/1, no. 355. On Daus, see Bauckham, *Tudor Apocalypse*, p. 53.

15. Hastings Robinson, ed.,,, *The Zürich Letters . . . the Correspondence of Several English Bishops and Others with Some of the Helvetian Reformers* (Cambridge: Cambridge University Press, 1842), pp. 98-9.

16. Staedtke, HBBibl I/1, no. 356 (p. 168). On the differences between the 1561 and 1573 editions, see Bauckham, *Tudor Apocalypse*, p. 298.

17. John Bale gave a moral cast to our text. Still, in the final age the witnesses are not only Moses and Christ (symbolic of law and gospel), but ". . . the true preachers of that gospel and martyrs under Antichrist." *The Image of Both Churches . . . , in Select Works of John Bale*, edited for the Parker Society (Vol. 1) by Henry Christmas (Cambridge: Cambridge University Press, 1849), p. 387. Bale had a strong sense of the impending End (*Image*, pp. 463–64). He follows Lambert's periodization as derivative of the apocalyptic seals to a point, remaining more optimistic about the present age (Fairfield, *John Bale*, pp. 78–80). Katherine Firth argues that Bale, not Tyndale, was the first Englishman to contribute meaningfully to the development of the English apocalyptic tradition (*Apocalyptic Tradition*, p. 38). Cf. Rainer Pineas, "William Tyndale's Use of History as a Weapon of Religious Controversy," HTR, 55 (1962):121–41.

18. The standard biography of John Foxe remains that of J. F. Mozley, *John Foxe and His Book* (London: SPCK, 1940), which corrects the earlier negative assessment by S. R. Maitland. William Haller has written the important study of Foxe's *Acts and Monuments, Foxe's Book of Martyrs and the Elect Nation* (London: Jonathan Cape, 1963). The eschatological and apocalyptic nature of Foxe's thought has been drawn out by V. Norskov Olsen, *John Foxe and the Elizabethan Church* (Berkeley: University of California Press, 1973).

19. John Foxe, *The Acts and Monuments of John Foxe*, 8 vols., Stephen Reed Cattley, ed. (London: R. B. Seeley and W. Burnside, 1841). (Further references to *Acts and Monuments* give volume and page number of this edition unless otherwise stated.) Foxe's influence may be measured in a variety of ways. It should be noted that the *Acts and Monuments* had a marked effect upon the development of drama. Of late sixteenth- and early seventeenth-century English religious plays, twelve draw part or all of their plots

from the *Acts and Monuments*. See Leslie Mahin Oliver "The Acts and Monuments of John Foxe: A Study of the Growth and Influence of a Book" (Ph.D. dissertation, Harvard University, 1945), pp. 4, 221–31.

20. John Foxe, *Eicasmi seu meditationes in sacram Apocalypsim* (London, 1587). The work was published posthumously by the author's son, Samuel. It covers only the first seventeen chapters of the book of Revelation. See Olsen, *John Foxe and the Elizabethan Church*, pp. 43–44; cf. Bousset, *Offenbarung*, p. 89. Bousset cites Foxe's significance for later English apocalyptic speculation, noting his elaborate theory of recapitulation and strong anti-papal thrusts.

21. See Firth, *Apocalyptic Tradition*, pp. 8–16, 28–30; cf. Bauckham, *Tudor Apocalypse*, pp. 42–44, 68–70.

22. Foxe, *Eicasmi*, pp. 176–78. Olsen writes, "The two pictures, the one of a temple and its court, and the other of two witnesses, drawn by the Revelator in chapter 11, illustrate the persecution and restoration of the evangelical church during the latter 300 years" (*John Foxe and the Elizabethan Church*, p. 96).

23. Opposition to Rome becomes almost the sole theological criterion in *Acts and Monuments* for entrance into the line of true witnesses (IV, p. 253); cf. *Eicasmi*, p. 172.

24. Foxe, *Acts and Monuments*, I, pp. 523–32. The structure of *Acts and Monuments* appears roughly similar to the chronology outlined in *Eicasmi* (See Paul Christianson, *Reformers and Babylon* (Toronto: University of Toronto Press, 1978), p. 40; cf. Bauckham, *Tudor Apocalypse*, pp. 83–85). In the earlier editions of *Acts and Monuments* Foxe had followed the traditional Augustinian pattern of beginning the millennial age (Rev. 20: 1–4) with the birth of Christ (*Acts and Monuments* [1563], p. 1). In later editions he modified his position, dating the 1000 years from Constantine to Wyclif (A.D. 324–1324) (*Acts and Monuments* [1570], I, p. 49). The separate books of this work are arranged according to different historical periods of time, each 300 years in length and correlated with Foxe's earlier view of the binding of Satan: Book I treats history to the end of the first period of persecution; Book II, the binding of Satan; Book III, the peace of the church; Book IV, the history of the Church to the days of Wyclif (the time of the loosing of Satan); Book V brings a discourse on the meaning of apocalyptic prophecy, then (through Book VIII) illustrations of martyrdom.

25. Foxe, *Eicasmi*, sig. 3r: "Quo magis admiranda in eo elucet divina ac inefabillis Agni beatissimi omnibus adoranda immensitas, qui ut solus pro sua autoritate ac reverentia potuit librum tot firmatum signaculis aperire, ita apertus hic idem ab illo liber tam admiranda nobis aperuit mysteria, adeoque universam ecclesiae historiam, uno velut spectaculo perlustrandam servis suis proposuit." The drama of the Apocalypse is to be seen on the world stage (p. 4).

26. Ibid., pp. 5, 45–46. Critical of the allegorical approach, which he identifies with Aquinas and finds in Lambert and Bullinger, Foxe writes: " In prophetando, non ita proprie luditur allegoriis, aut si in prophetiis vsu ita veniat quandroque, ut per similium collationem, parabolae adhibeantur: at non ideo tamen sensus historicus per allegorismos & tropologias evertendus est, praesertim ubi res ipsa ad historias nos mittit, non ad allegorias" (p. 46).

27. Paul D. Avis draws helpful distinctions and lines of similarity among several of the protestant reformers in *The Church in the Theology of the Reformers* (Atlanta: John Knox Press; 1981; particularly part I, "The True Church," pp. 13–77. Avis writes: "The very existence of the reform movements and of the evangelical Churches which had broken with Rome hung upon their ability to answer the question 'Which Church is the true Church?' in a satisfactory and convincing way that would both justify their separation from the historic Western Church centered on Rome and safeguard the validity of their sacraments as means of grace and pledges of salvation. Reformation ecclesiology returns

obsessively to the problem of distinguishing between the false Church and the true; the one persecuting, prosperous and triumphalist; the other weak, downtrodden, crucified and even denied the name of Church altogether" (p. 1).

28. The phrase is from William Lamont, *Marginal Prynne, 1600–1669* (London: Routledge & Kegan Paul, 1963), p. 17.

29. Foxe, *Eicasmi*, p. 197. Foxe interprets the image of the woman in Rev. 12:2 as the Church of the old dispensation bearing Christ. Cf. Bale, *The Image*, p. 405.

30. Foxe, *Acts and Monuments*, I, p. 292.

31. Foxe, *Eicasmi*, pp. 383–85.

32. Ibid., p. 385.

33. By interpretation, Nebuchadnezzar's image (golden head, silver chest and arms, bronze belly and thighs, iron legs, feet of mixed iron and clay) was seen to represent four or five empires depending upon whether one divided the feet of mixed iron and clay from the legs of iron. Ambiguity was lent to definitive interpretation not only by this mixed description, but also by the fact that Daniel himself envisions four kingdoms, associated with four beasts, later in his life (Dan. 7:2–28).

34. Foxe, *Eicasmi*, pp. 41–55.

35. Foxe, *Acts and Monuments*, I, p. 290. Foxe writes that he came to his solution through inspiration one Sunday monring. He was to multiply "these months by sabbaths"; with such a methodology at hand, Foxe derived a common figure of 294 from each of the symbolic numerals.

36. Foxe, *Eicasmi*, p. 60.

37. Ibid., pp. 45–50.

38. Ibid., pp. 94–95.

39. Ibid., pp. 150–52. Of interest here is the relatively insignificant attention given Wyclif in the *Eicasmi* compared with the *Acts and Monuments*. In *Eicasmi*, Hus and Jerome of Prague are clearly focal figures. Note the meditations on their personalities and work, pp. 158–76. If there exists Protestant hagiography, surely this is it. Cf. also Luther's somewhat diminished role here in comparison with *Acts and Monuments* where William Clebsch finds him at the heart: "The Elizabethans on Luther," in *Interpreters of Luther*, Jaroslav Pelikan, ed. (Philadelphia: Fortress Press, 1968), p. 97.

40. Ibid., pp. 96–99.

41. Foxe, *Eicasmi*, p. 95; cf. *Acts and Monuments*, III, p. 722; IV, p. 19.

42. Foxe, *Eicasmi*, pp. 68–99. The first trumpet signifies the destruction of Jerusalem by the Romans (pp. 73–74); the second, plagues and other troubles under Aurelius (pp. 74–75); the third, plagues under Decius (pp. 75–79); the fourth, the Roman Empire destroyed by Goths, Vandals, and Lombards (pp. 79–81); the fifth, the woe possibly of the papacy, probably of Muhammadanism (Phocas and Muhammad appearing at the same time) (pp. 82–92); the sixth, the Turks (pp. 95–99). Their power began in Asia in 1051. Their history is traced by Foxe to 1573. Judgment against the persecutors of the true Church is expressed both in the trumpeting angels and imagery of the vial-plagues (cf. pp. 343–88).

43. Foxe, *Eicasmi*, pp. 107–11; *Acts and Monuments, IV*, p. 102.

44. Foxe, *Eicasmi*, pp. 103, 195; cf. *Acts and Monuments*, IV, pp. 95ff. Foxe proposes several dates: 1564, 1570, 1586, and 1594. Marjorie Reeves writes that he at least expected some kind of historical apotheosis under Elizabeth I if not the immediate divine advent (*Joachim of Fiore and the Prophetic Future* [London: SPCK, 1976; New York: Harper and Row, 1977], p. 154).

45. Foxe, *Eicasmi*, intro. and pp. 100–104.

46. Ibid., p. 104.

47. Ibid., pp. 105–6.

48. Ibid., p. 107; cf. *Acts and Monuments*, III, p. 719; IV, p. 252.

49. Ibid., pp. 106–7. "Quo tempore nondum perierat Evangelica veritas, vt nunc sub sexta tuba denuo esset redintegranda. Sed alii administri, & praedicatores verbi pro ratione temporis, ad hoc suscitandi erant, quos sub persona Ioannis, visio hic adumbrat prophetica" (p. 107).

50. Ibid., p. 108.

51. Foxe, *Eicasmi*, pp. 110–16. Foxe discusses pope and Turk as Antichrist, his singular or plural nature, the time and place of his appearance; cf. pp. 223–73 (explanation of the papacy as Antichrist). Christopher Hill demonstrates aspects of the Antichrist tradition in relation to developments in England (*Antichrist in Seventeenth-Century England* [London: Oxford University Press, 1971]); David Brady particularizes this development (*The Contribution of British Writers Between 1560 and 1830 to the Interpretation of Revelation 13:16–18* [*The Number of the Beast*]. *A Study in the History of Exegesis* [Tübingen: Mohr, 1984]).

52. Foxe, *Eicasmi*, pp. 110–11; cf. Buckham, *Tudor Apocalypse*, pp. 91–112.

53. This point is made by Richard Emmerson in *Antichrist in the Middle Ages* (Seattle: University of Washington Press, 1981), pp. 213–14.

54. On the name and identity of Antichrist, see Foxe, *Acts and Monuments*, IV, pp. 96–98. According to Foxe, Antichrist's power was by divine permission and thus expressed a moral, not ontological, dualism (*Eicasmi*, pp. 110–11). Hill claims that in the figure of Antichrist one can find evidence of a Manichaean spirit within Protestantism (*Antichrist in Seventeenth-Century England*, p. 170); cf. Bauckham, *Tudor Apocalypse*, p. 107.

55. Robert Barnes presents detailed accounts of the Lutheran search for signs of the times believed to complement biblical prophecies read so as to find an imminent end to history, in *Prophecies and Gnosis*, pp. 82–93.

56. Foxe, *Eicasmi*, p. 142.

57. Ibid., pp. 117–23. Note the promise of the perpetuity of the Church (p. 117). An historical excursus on the completion of the Church is given, pp. 123–41.

58. Ibid., pp. 142–48. Foxe surveys the history of the exegesis of Rev. 11:3. He generally supports a representative interpretation while looking for more specificity.

59. Foxe offers an extended discussion of the time of their ministry, the 1260 days of Rev. 11:3 (ibid., pp. 149–52).

60. Ibid., p. 144.

61. Ibid., p. 149. Foxe singles out the college established by the Jesuits at Rheims for the education of English Roman Catholics and their planned mission to England. For the controversy, see in A. F. Scott Pearson, *Thomas Cartwright and Elizabethan Puritanism* (Cambridge; Cambridge University Press, 1925; Gloucester, Mass.: Peter Smith, 1966), pp. 198, 200.

62. Ibid., pp. 149, 176–78.

63. Ibid., p. 171.

64. Ibid., pp. 149–50.

65. Ibid., pp. 176–77.

66. Ibid., p. 177.

67. Ibid., pp. 176–78.

68. Ibid., p. 178; cf. Foxe, *Acts and Monuments*, I, pp. 523–32.

69. Ibid., p. 178.

70. Foxe, *Acts and Monuments*, IV, pp. 107ff.; cf. Firth, *Apocalyptic Tradition*, pp. 91–92.

71. Foxe, *Eicasmi*, p. 178f.

72. Foxe, *Acts and Monuments*, III, pp. 98, 105.

73. Foxe, *Eicasmi*, p. 179; cf. pp. 181–84 for prophetic models.

74. Foxe's interest in apocalyptic spirituality is already evident in his play *Christus Triumphans* (1556). (See John Hazel Smith, *Two Latin Comedies by John Foxe the Martyrologist: titus et Gesippus. Christus Triumphans* [Ithaca: Cornell University Press, 1973].) Richard Bauckham has suggested that this play is a preliminary sketch for Foxe's lifelong task of integrating the study of prophecy and history (*Tudor Apocalypse*, pp. 81–88). Foxe particularizes universal principles in historical characters in the play. The conflict between Hierlogus, the Preacher, and Pseudamnus, Antichrist, illustrates Foxe's interest in the personalities of the Reformation.

75. Linus Urban Lucken, *Antichrist and the Prophets of Antichrist in the Chester Cycle* (Washington, D.C.: Catholic University of America Press, 1940), pp. 76–93.

76. Foxe, *Eicasmi*, p. 179; cf. p. 171; *Acts and Monuments*, III, pp. 508–9; IV, pp. 253–59.

77. Foxe, *Eicasmi*, pp. 178f.

78. See Theodore Bibliander, *Ad omnium ordinum reipublicae Christianae . . .* (Basel: Oporinus, 1545), p. 133; or Postel (Geoffrey Atkinson, *Les nouveaux horizons de la Renaissance francaise* [Paris, 1935], p. 57). As we noted, Foxe placed his millennium in the past, yet he was still looking to some kind of apotheosis in the future that included the renewal of evangelical doctrine. Like others as disparate as Bibliander and Postel, Foxe finds adumbrated here and in parallel prophecies such events as the development of printing, new learning, and the restoration of pure doctrine.

79. Paul Hanson's argument on apocalypticism as a development of Hebraic prophetism appears applicable (*The Dawn of Apocalyptic* [Philadelphia: Fortress Press, rev. ed., 1979], pp. 1–31).

80. Hanson isolates three primary factors: (1) self-identification with the classical prophetic tradition; (2) a heightened literalism with respect to the older religious impulses of the tradition; and (3) a new crisis situation. Two terms are introduced to describe the prophetic and apocalyptic moments in such a way as to underscore this connection: "prophetic eschatology" and "apocalyptic eschatology" (ibid., pp. 9–10).

81. Foxe, *Eicasmi*, p. 239; cf. *Acts and Monuments*, I, pp. 523–32.

82. Johann Carion, *Chronica. . . .* (1532). I have used the edition *Chronicon Carionis expositum et auctum . . . a P. Melanchthone et C. Peucero* (Wittenberg: Haeredes Johannis Cratonis, 1580), p. 49. An English edition was issued in 1550 with an appendix by Johannes Funcke. The prophecy of Elijah and Daniel are the principle prophetic sources used, although the reader is told to look further in the Apocalypse for confirmation (fol. xxiv). See Emil Menke-Glückert, *Die Geschichtsschreibung der Reformation* (Leipzig: J. C. Hinrichs, 1912), pp. 21–22.

83. Johannes Sleidanus, *De statu Religionis et Republicae, Carolo Quinto Caesare, Commentarii* (1555); translated into English, 1560); and particularly, *A Briefe Chronicle of the Foure Principall Empyres* (London: Rouland Hall, 1563). On the connection between Foxe and Sleidanus, see Firth, *Apocalyptic Tradition*, p. 71; cf. Menke-Glückert, *Geschichtsschreibung*, p. 23.

84. Jean Crespin, *Histoire des vrays Tesmoins de la verit; de l'évangile, qui de leur sang l'ont signée, depuis Jean Hus usques au temps present* (1570; 1st Latin ed., 1554). S. L. Lee suggests that the title "Acts and Monuments" may have been adopted from a book by Jean Crespin of Geneva entitled, "Actiones et Monimenta Martyrum" (DNB, 20, p. 145). I find little that is directly applicable to our theme here except for the emphasis upon Hus and Jerome of Prague (p. 36), two that are emphasized by Foxe. Firth argues for Foxe's influence on Crespin (*Apocalyptic Tradition*, p. 70).

85. The fresh interest in the Apocalypse as the sixteenth century progresses is noted

by Bauckham (*Tudor Apocalypse*, pp. 68–70) and Firth (*Apocalyptic Tradition*, pp. 8–16). Of interest is the growing attempt by the seventeenth century to develop a science of prophetic speculation parallel to the other developing sciences (See Christopher Hill, *The World Turned Upside Down, Radical Ideas During the English Revolution* [New York: Pengiun, 1975], p. 92).

86. See in the work of Eugenio Garin and Hans Baron (above, Chapter 6) and with ongoing impact upon the Anglo-American world, J. G. A. Pocock, *The Machiavellian Moment: Florentine Political Thought and the Atlantic Republican Tradition* (Princeton: Princeton University Press, 1975).

87. Beryl Smalley, *The Study of the Bible in the Middle Ages* (Oxford: Clarendon Press, 1941).

88. John Headley writes that despite Luther's commitment to the figural understanding of history, his belief in Christ's presence in every moment of history "serves to spring the typological system" (*Luther's View of Church History* [New Haven: Yale University Press, 1963], p. 269). Luther's theology would now stand open not only to new attempts to understand events in the events themselves, and apart from a presumed conceptual framework, but to new perceptions of the immediacy of the Spirit which, when not linked to a high Christology, could move in pantheistic directions.

89. Barnes traces the development of historical reflection in relation to emerging chronologies, prophetic speculation, and temporal reckoning in *Prophecy and Gnosis*, pp. 103–40. A certain end to the attempt to discern an objective history came, in the opinion of Friedrich Meinecke, in the work of Leopold von Ranke (1795–1886). Ranke's statement that each epoch is "immediate to God" reflects Luther's theology, as noted above, and argues that each historical event must be seen in its own particularity.

90. Haller emphasizes Foxe's influence on the idea of England's elect status before God (*Acts and Monuments, Foxe's Book of Martyrs*, p. 224). Others, e.g., Olsen (*John Foxe and the Elizabethan Church* p. 37) and Lamont (*Marginal Prynne*) look to John Napier and Thomas Brightman.

91. Patrick Collinson, *The Elizabethan Puritan Movement* (Berkeley: University of California Press, 1967), pp. 59–97; cf. Paul Christianson, "Reformers and the Church of England," (JEH, 31 (1980):473–74; and John F. Wilson, "Studies in Puritan Millenarianism under the Early Stuarts," Th.D. dissertation, Union Theological Seminary, New York, 1962.

92. This hope is articulated by the Elizabethan apologist John Jewel, *The Works of John Jewel*, 4 vols. (Cambridge: Printed at the University Press, 1847), Vol. 2, p. 1032. We noted that in the edition of the Geneva Bible (1599) the work of Elizabeth is equated with that of the adventual witnesses.

93. Tracing our theme is not always easy. Neither Robert Browne nor Robert Harrison left sufficient writing to illustrate their apocalyptic attitudes. However, in a letter written on the last day of 1588 Browne reveals a chronology that assumes that most of the prophecies of the book of Revelation have been fulfilled and the fall of Antichrist (11:16) is imminent. See Christianson, *Reformers and Babylon*, pp. 47–92; esp. p. 64; cf. B. R. White, *The English Separatist Tradition from the Marian Martyrs to the Pilgrim Fathers* (Oxford: Oxford University Press, 1971), pp. 44–66.

94. Although futurist and preterist readings of the Apocalypse were quickly developed by Catholic exegetes, in part to counter the Protestant historicist use of the text, some Catholics expounded their own historicist line. Ignatius was at times identified with the fifth angel of the Apocalypse (Rev. 9:1–3). Joannes Osorius (1595) and Blasius Viegas (1601) proposed this idea, which was officially adopted at the Council of Tatra (1602). See Marjorie Reeves, "The Abbot Jaochim and the Society and the Society of Jesus," 5 (1961):163–73.

95. Thomas Cartwright, *A Confutation of the Rhemist translation, glosses and annotations on the New Testament* (London, 1589); ed. used, Leavitt, Lord and Co., New York, 1834. The above is Cartwright's gloss on our text (p. 397).

96. Ibid., p. 386.

97. Ibid., pp. 397–98. The approved list includes Bede, Ambrosius Autpertus, Aretas, and others who had taken a spiritual or allegorical view of the passage.

98. Ibid., p. 398.

99. William Ames argues that Robert Bellarmine misinterprets Scripture with his emphasis upon a literal rather than a tropological understanding of the identity of the witnesses, (*Bellarminus Enervatus*, 4 vols. [Oxford, 1629], I, pp. 191–92, 198–200).

100. Thomas Beard, *Antichrist the Pope of Rome: or, The Pope of Rome Is Antichrist* (London, 1625), pp. 44–45, 53–63, 198–212. Christopher Hill finds Beard, schoolmaster of Cromwell, working out of the tradition of Foxe's Martyrology. See *God's Englishman. Oliver Cromwell and the English Revolution* (New York: Harper Torchbooks, 1970), pp. 39–40, 43–44.

101. Patrick Collinson, following Firth (*Apocalyptic Tradition*), illustrates the pervasive apocalyptic thinking of Foxe, which lay behind his ecclesiology. See *The Birthpangs of Protestant England: Religious and Cultural Change in the Sixteenth and Seventeenth Centuries* (London: Macmillan, 1988), p. 14.

8

Forerunners of the Kingdom

From Prophets to Rulers

The question of how to move forward in time was as much a part of John Foxe's legacy as that of the proper identity of the Christian Church in history. As our text was a part of that latter discussion, so it would be in speculation with regard to the shape of the future. The question was not simply academic. It became caught up in issues of politics and governance. If God's saints—by metonymy, our witnesses—had triumphed in the sixteenth century then the nature of their rule was now at issue.

Drawn into debate over how the saints triumph in history were issues of religious legitimacy. Although these factored themselves out in different ways, behind the discussion were assumptions made by the first religious reformers of the sixteenth century, that the Latin medieval Church, far from being indefectible, had in fact lost its privileged role as Christ's body, the Church, in the world. Its papal head, called Antichrist by Luther, had been futher identified with the beast from the abyss of Revelation 11:7, conflated with similar imagery in Revelation 13:16–18. That latter text filled out with detail the insidious nature of the old faith.[1]

Set opposite to this perceived threat, the work of our witnesses defined the work of Protestant ministers. In the history of interpretation surrounding our text, as drawn out with pastoral implications in Heinrich Bullinger, their tasks included drawing the faithful to a perceived morality, the reconstruction of the Church around that moral vision, the conversion of the Jews as a part of a final heralding of the gospel, and the construction of a social order shaped by God's end-time saints.

Into this set of events a number of issues emerged that would divide commentators in Britain. First, there arose debate over who properly represented Foxe's tradition of the true witnesses to the faith. Foxe's commentary on the Apocalypse had been dedicated to John Whitgift (Archbishop of Canterbury, 1583–1604), defender of the establishment who sought, in the main, to conform English ecclesial reform to the interests of the Crown and state. However, many Puritan Nonconformists (Presbytarians, Congregationalists, and Independents) interpreted Foxe's intent differently as supporting their cause.[2] Nevertheless, whichever way we interpret Foxe, the legacy was sufficiently ambiguous so as to catch up the general feeling of legitimacy for a broadly based vision of British Protestant, as against

Roman Catholic, understanding of religious reform.[3] In an age increasingly atuned to local interests with the emergence of the modern nation-state, English sensitivities would reach back to the conflict between Northumbrian Celtic and Kentish Roman Christianity in the seventh century in search of religious legitimacy.

Second, the prophecy of Daniel, interpreted as having foreseen a coming kingdom of the saints (Dan. 7:27), was applied to contemporary social history. English society, undergoing the social and economic transitions characteristic of early modern Europe, was becoming more susceptible to representative and democratic argument. The biblical tradition not only offered examples of covenantal and contractual language, soon to be developed by John Locke, but also a revolutionary vision of democratic rule against an apocalyptic framework of history. The growing tradition of ancient British rights and the civic humanism engendered by the Renaissance contributed to a constitutional crisis that caught up a program of civil reform that opposed king and hierarchies in favor of a divinely inspired republican ethos.[4] The intellectual set of assumptions that drew upon this diverse historical background would be essential to the Anglo-American evangelical vision in the years ahead.

Third, the nature of political rule in Daniel's vision could be interpreted as one of evolutionary growth. As foreseen in the dream of Nebuchadnezzer, a final worldly kingdom would be replaced by God's rule, which would enlarge itself throughout the whole earth (Dan. 2:35). Although already foreseen in argumentation associated with our text in Francis Junius (and others) on the Continent, it is Thomas Brightman who will develop the idea forcefully for Protestantism with an emphasis upon historical progressivism heretofore unseen with such overt cultural implications in relation to our text.[5]

Finally, in this foreseen millennial kingdom, debate would center around how and what way King Jesus would rule. His second Advent implied for some a return to earth to rule for a thousand years (Dan. 7:13–14; Rev. 20:3–6). For others, he would set up a kingdom then return to heaven allowing his saints to rule. Or, for others still, the saints themselves, endowed with Jesus' spirit, would establish and rule that kingdom until his final coming to Judgment (Rev. 20:7–15).[6]

Various commentators carry us and our theme, together with these ambiguities, from Tudor rule (1485–1603) to the Stuart kings (1603 [1649–1660]–1688) of the seventeenth century and "second" English reform with its constitutional crisis and civil wars.[7] John Napier's speculation on our text stands out toward the end of Elizabeth's reign by way of transition.[8] Dissatisfied both with the Elizabethan Settlement of church-state relations and with Foxe's millennial conclusions, Napier laid down a series of premises for interpretation that led him to posit a second and future millennial age beginning in 1541.[9] This was signalled by the victory of the two adventual witnesses who were understood as being the Scriptures or, by metonymy, those reformers who truly held to the Scriptures. Napier was so confident in his approach that he argued that in these last years the witnesses are the instruments for the conversion of thousands. The years since their resurrection mark the inception of the seventh age and the approach of the visible temple and church of God.[10] This apocalyptic confidence seen in Foxe and now Napier would mark British Protestantism well into the nineteenth century.

Three commentators on our text who worked in line with the ideas laid down by Foxe and Napier, and who reflect pointedly on the witnesses in an effort to chart the future, are Thomas Brightman (1562–1607), Joseph Mede (1586–1638), and Thomas Goodwin (1600–1680). Brightman was to restructure Foxe's history by discerning a second millennium following the resurrection of the witnesses, a period characterized by the downfall of the papacy and conversion of the Jews.[11] Mede, working with lines of thought as now pioneered by Foxe and Brightman, projected the millennium into the yet distant future following a yet-to-be fulfilled tribulation marked by the slaying of the witnesses.[12] Goodwin followed Brightman and Mede in places but argued that the apocalyptic temple (Rev. 11:1–2), constructed by the witnesses during the Reformation, needed yet to undergo a second reformation. The witnesses would be slain after this social change, the prelude to the millennium.

The Triumph of the Saints

The triumph of the witness is most clearly visible in a contemporary way in the work of Thomas Brightman.[13] It will be recalled that on the Continent Francis Junius had already worked out a second millennial age. Such is clear with implications for the development of English Puritanism in Brightman. He writes of the witnesses' identity, acknowledging that

> The ancient Fathers that lived farther remote from these two witnesses [wrote that they] were Enoch and Elias, and that they should come and fight with Antichrist in the end of the world. But we that have seene the matter long since accomplished, may determine for a certainty, that the holy ghost had another manner of meaning than this. . . . To dispatch all therefore in a word; we do gather and judge, that these two Prophets are the Holy Scriptures, and the assemblies of the faithful; . . .[14]

Critical of Tridentine Catholicism, Brightman impugns the motives of those who hold that the witnesses are Enoch and Elijah coming at the end of the world. In what represents a debate of increasing acerbity between Roman Catholic and Protestant commentators, particularly since Junius, over the interpretation of our text, Brightman writes at length in his commentary against positions held on our text by Francesco de Ribeira and Robert Bellarmine. In the sixth chapter of this excurses is an argument against Bellarmine's contention (third demonstration) that the pope cannot be Antichrist because Enoch and Elijah have not yet appeared.[15] What is set forth here is for the present "grievous triall" faced by the Church, Brightman argues.[16] He continues, predictably, that those such as Ribeira and the Jesuits who argue that these prophecies belong only to the future are foolishly and wickedly seeking to defend the papacy.[17] Such as these

> catch greedily at this opinion of the Fathers [i.e., that the witnesses are a restored Enoch and Elijah], and make great account of it, thrusting it upon the world, as if it were some Oracle; and no marvaile, seeing it doth withdraw men from the consideration, of those things, which are to be seen with their eyes in this present

day; and this is that onely thing, that they long, and labour greatly to effect, in all their expositions.[18]

The "Popish teachers" are distracted from a proper interpretation of the adventual witnesses. According to Revelation 10:11, prophecy[19] has been restored.[20]

> These things belong not to the last day, but to the sixt trumpet, which [is] . . . now past and gone. As for Iohn he is onely brought in as a Type, not described by any office that he should take upon him, and discharge in his own person in the last Age of the World.[21]

The reality of this restoration is set forth in Revelation 11. This vision pertains to the whole Church and to specific members of it. In the time running from Constantine forward, the Church is small and hidden "tread under foot" for forty-two months (Rev. 11:1–2). The identity of its "principal members" (the two witnesses) depends upon the period of history with which one is concerned. In that history of 1260 years beginning with Constantine, the witnesses represent the true spiritual ministry that often appears mourning (Rev. 11:3–6). Second, they appear in a time of three and a half days, slain and exposed to derision (Rev. 11:7–10). Finally, the witnesses are those who rise again, strike terror in the hearts of their foes, and receive new recognition and honor.[22]

The identity of the witnesses in each of these three periods is related to their faithful handling of Scripture.[23] Brightman's reasoning is polemical and highlights a kind of external identification. But the identification itself can be compared to Luther's handling of Revelation 11. Luther had related the vision to the restoration of the gospel, tying his argumentation to an internal theological justification, something with which Brightman would no doubt agree. Luther, however, refused any close literalization or specific identification with the passage.[24] Brightman argues for the legitimacy of his position in that Scripture refers to itself with a certain personification. This is seen in Chapter 11 of Revelation, Brightman writes, where there is mention of fighting, dying, and rising again.[25]

The witnesses appear in sackcloth. Indeed, the Scriptures have been thus arrayed, Brightman argues. They have been "deformed and put in a mornefull estate" by men. This occurred openly under Emperor Diocletian by means of a terrible persecution. It happened increasingly after Constantine[26] as the Church grew accustomed to a life of ease and happiness. The simple and sincere purity of the Scriptures became defiled,

> the meaning of them began not to bee understood, yea, to be wrested with allegories, and absurd expositions, and any thing almost to bee fathered on them, whatsoever men listed.[27]

Yet, compared with later developments in history,[28] the condition of the Church, related to its use of Scripture, appeared without spot in these early days. The ages that followed saw Scripture increasingly covered "with ashes and dust, and dirt, ..."[29]

The witnesses are two, Brightman adds, "to answer to the two Testaments, old and new; God spake of old by the Prophets, now by his Sonne, Hebrewes 1.1." Yet, even before Christ appeared, the witnesses were always two—"the Law and the Gospell"—which gospel was always in force.[30] These witnesses have two properties: They demonstrate qualities of graciousness and terror, "the one of bounty towards their friends, as I may call it, the other of terrible power over their enemies, both to destroy them." The graciousness or "bounty" of the witnesses is adumbrated under their description as "two olive trees" and "two candlesticks" (Rev. 11:4):

> Seeing then, that in this Type the inward gifts of the Spirit are shadowed forth by the flame of the Candlesticks, the outward by the olive trees, among which the Holy word of God is the principall, these olive trees may not unfitly betoken the Scriptures, as out of whose berries (as it were) oyl is poured to nourish the flame of the Lampes; it being their office to minister Doctrine to the Prophets sufficiently, so as they may be able to nourish the flame of piety in themselves, and in their hearers.[31]

Brightman continues to develop the spiritual significance of the olive tree and candlestick imagery, reflecting upon the varied spiritual state of the Church since Constantine. Even in dark times the witnesses had the might, mirrored in that of Moses and Elijah, to destroy their enemies. These prophetic models illustrate their power. In denouncing impiety and error, the Scriptures "blow fire out of their mouth, . . ." Examples of such are drawn from the accounts of Moses (Num. 16) and Elijah (2 Kings 1) and history. As Moses turned water to blood, so the defiling of the Word of God brings plagues and the scourge. The witnesses are able to open and shut heaven. As long as the Scriptures lay abused and in sackcloth there is a "drought and penury of spirituall dew. . . ."[32] Such was the case for the most part in the 1260 years since Constantine.

> The Prophets are said, to have power, to punish the earth,with what plague they will, because God doth governe and order the world according to his wil revealed in the Scriptures, and that for the good of his Church, and in favour unto it. In the beginning he gave up the earth to Adam while he stood in his entire estate, and he will have al things now againe to serve for the use of his Children, that are restored to their integrity by Christ.[33]

Our text now speaks of the completion of the witnesses' task (Rev. 11:7), after which they are slain. Brightman argues that this occurred in 1546 at the Council of Trent. Here he becomes as intriguingly specific as John Foxe had been with the Council of Constance.[34] Adding the prophetic 1260 years (Rev. 11:3) to the year Constantine ascended the throne (A.D. 304), less 18 years needed to correct the Julian calendar, brought Brightman to the year 1546 and confirmed his apocalyptic hypothesis. How were the witnesses slain at this time? Brightman simply answers that it happened when, at the third session of the Council of Trent, the Greek and Hebrew copies of the Scriptures were cast out in favor of the Latin.

> For herein were the Fountaines of the Hebrue, and Greeke Copies of the Bible refused, and the corrupt Latine translation was established for authentical. Herein were unwritten traditions placed in equall dignity, with the Holy Scriptures. Herein was the power of interpreting the Scriptures, taken away from the Scriptures, and it was alienated and enthralled to the pleasure of men, especially the Pope. The Holy Bookes were never disabled and disgraced so openly & by publike authority from the beginning of the world.[35]

The warfare that broke out in Germany in April 1547 signalled the beginning of the three-and-a-half-year period of Antichrist's victory over the witnesses (Rev. 11:9-10). At this time Protestant forces were put to flight, seen in the failing efforts of John Frederick of Saxony and Ernest Brunswick. While some argue that this period of three and a half years should also be equivalent to the first period which signified 1260 day/years (Rev. 11:3), Brightman contends that they may be viewed differently. This second period of three and a half years "was a time of darknesse,"[36] beginning after the completion of 1260 days of sackcloth prophesying.[37]

> Those pope-holy Fathers triumphed from that time for three whole yeares and a halfe in a confused concourse of all nations, as if they had playd the stout and tall fellowes, and so they addressed themselves to trample the truth that remained under their feet, till at last the wicked conventicle was broken up by the death of Paul 3. Which fell in the yeare, 1546 [*sic.*, 1549]. Novemb. 9. That is, in the third yeare and the halfe after the Scriptures were droden [*sic.*] down.[38]

In the year 1550, after three and a half years of destruction, the Church in Germany was defended by the scholars and others at Magdeburg.

> This was indeed the Spirit of life, which comming from God, put heart againe into the Church, which raised up the Prophets that afore lay dead, and made them stand on their feet, and to be so valiant, that they strooke a terrour into the hearts of their enemies. For besides that franke and bold profession, and protestation, the Author whereof was the Holy Ghost, that was from heaven sent down into their hearts, they stood upon their feet, by resisting Mauricius valiantly, who being sent from Caesar [Charles V], and made the generall in that battel, by publike authority, did at first, fight against them exceeding fiercely . . . . Thus then did the Church now againe stand upright on their feet, which thing made a great feare upon their enemies.[39]

The voice that now calls for the witnesses to ascend together into heaven (Rev. 11:12) implies honor and adornment. Even as Christ had gone through various trials and death, finally to be received and glorified by God, so this was to happen to the Church. The Christian Church, the Scriptures, and knowledge generally could be expected to increase on earth.[40] That there is a voice which bids the prophets to arise indicates that it is another authority which now gives honor to the witnesses. This process began to come to pass, Brightman argues, on August 7, 1555, when King Ferdinand and the rest of the princes in Europe bound themselves by a public decree:

> that the Religion which was contained in the Augustane Confession, should be left free to al men to use it at their pleasure, Sleid. Book 26. This decree, was indeed that voice saying to the Prophets, bidding them come up into heaven.[41]

As John Foxe had advocated the correlation of history and prophecy,[42] so Brightman followed suit. For Brightman the account of the two witnesses accorded accurately with recent European history. The apocalyptic earthquake (Rev. 11:3)[43] signified the general clamor on the part of other European peoples to gain for themselves the privileges of the Peace of Augsburg (1555).[44] The fall of "the tenth part of the city" signifies the diminuation of the "Kingdom of Popery."[45] We see, Brightman concludes, "how this whole Prophecy doth agree most exactly with the Event from top to toe."[46] This is the beginning of the end of the second woe, the conclusion of history under the sixth trumpet.

Now, Brightman continues, humanity faces a time of transition to the last of the three woes and seventh trumpet. Moving into this era does not imply the immediate end of the second woe (Rev. 9:13), that is, enlarged Turkish power throughout the world and continuing religious apostasy visible in Roman idolatry.[47] But the force of that woe has been "empaired, and much weakened . . . at length altogether abolished."[48] The previous trumpets announced times of trial, but why, Brightman asks, should the seventh and last trumpet be referred to as another woe when it signifies the full reformation of the Church? The answer: For the wicked this indeed is woe; it signifies the beginning of their destruction.[49]

The first blast or entrance of the seventh trumpet began, according to Brightman, in the year 1558 in the kingdom of England when Elizabeth became queen. She gave herself and her kingdom to Christ "by way of thankfullnesse," and her efforts begin the outpouring of the vials of God's wrath (Rev. 16:1-17).[50] This was illustrated in the cessation of "Romish" superstitions throughout her realm. The blast of this trumpet was heard more clearly with the addition of various princes of Germany; Gustavus, King of Sweden, and Christianus, King of Denmark. The prophecy of the seventh trumpet reveals the progressive enlargement of Christ's kingdom. Even more,

> that this Kingdom of Christ, that began from this time to be great and manifest, should never be obscured so againe as the former Kingdoms were, which came to an utter ruine in processe of time. For so it is said, and he shall reigne for evermore.[51]

Christ's rule is made manifest when his majesty is visible in Christian kingdoms. It may be seen "after a sort" in Christian kings. "He reigned thus in ancient times, by meanes of Constantine, and the other Godly Emperours."[52] With the advent of recent events Christian dominion will increase in the world. Now is the time spoken of by Daniel (2:44). Not only is the kingdom presently increasing among the Gentiles but soon "the calling of the Iewes" will occur, enlarging it greatly.[53]

Brightman does introduce a note of caution into this crescendo of optimism. His comments throw light on the vehemence that increasingly characterized Puritan polemics under first Tudor and then Stuart policies.[54] He writes that while he believes Elizabeth's reign is "the Type of his [Christ's] eternall Kingdom,"[55] still Christ's truth must not be corrupted nor majesty warped through a reintroduction of anti-Christian superstition. Brightman notes:

> We have made Christ angry against us already, in that we are so farre off from coming to a full and due reformation; but if we shal returne unto our vomit, with what fury will he burne out against us? They therefore that favour the Papist privilege, and that take paines to get them liberty to defile our Holy Kingdom, with bringing in againe their rites and Ceremonies, that are so hateful in the sight of God, do endeavour withall to overthrow our Kingdom . . . .[56]

Christ has begun his kingdom, but he has not tied it to certain countries. Picturing the last three apocalyptic churches (Rev. 2–3) as representative of the Protestant Reformation,[57] Brightman identifies the Church of England with the lukewarm Church of Laodicea (Rev. 3:14).[58] The "apocalyptic spirituality" evident in his reflection adds seriousness to English reform. It does not simply connect English policy with the will of God. That earthly kingdom which no longer represents God's will, will no longer remain a part of his kingdom.

Brightman's allegorical way of conceiving of the two witnesses continued to affect Anglo-American Protestant exegeses and helped to forge that line of thought which, following Daniel Whitby (1638–1726) and Moses Lowman (1680–1752), became identified as postmillennialism.[59] Protestantism, knowledge of the Bible, even all sound learning, became exegetically understood as part of that honor accorded the restored witnesses in Brightman's dawning second millennial age (Rev. 20:5) running on from the end of Foxe's earlier period (A.D. 1300–2300).[60] The significance of this exegetical tradition behind Western views of progress has yet to be told fully.

The Mourning Prophets

Joseph Mede's view of the witnesses' identity was as determinative as Brightman's for later generations.[61] It betrayed a different understanding of the nature of the Church and how it intersected in society. This ecclesiology is seen in Mede's apparent reverence for the patristic Church and is illustrated by his general handling of Revelation 11. Our witnesses are no longer triumphant saints but God's prophets who mournfully decry sin and faithfully preach the gospel.

Mede's two works on the Apocalypse[62] illustrate a more mystical millennialism than that encountered in Brightman as he feared that in Britain, as in Poland-Lithuania and Transylvania, the Reformed understanding of Christianity in Puritanism would give way to Socinianism or Unitarianism.[63] This appears in his greater interest in chronology for determining the millennial timetable. Mede's first book laid out the "synchronisms" or mutual relationships of the various prophecies in the Apocalypse. His second work sought to reconcile this material with historical events and explanations. Revelation 11:2–3, together with the rest of the chapter, was crucial for Mede as he sought to calculate the date for when the millennium would begin. His calculations, calculated for our text, grew out of his effort to discover when the Church had first fallen so that to that date might be added the 1260 prophetic days in the forty-two months to determine the onset of final apocalyptic events and subsequent millennial age.[64]

Numerous people sought Mede's advice on apocalyptic and millennial developments.[65] Increasing sociopolitical tensions and related religious controversy on the onset of the Puritan Revolution (1642) had made the millennium of Napier and Brightman seem less clear. Mede's work helped to give a new reading to history and, relatedly, sustained the optimism toward the future as set forth by Foxe but now with a different view of the Church. More than this, Mede's method for interpreting the book of Revelation was not only of value to those in search of a new ecclesiology, but was also attractive to those who sought to make a science of it.[66] New ways of defining knowledge, reflected not only in Ramist logic but in the Cartesian method and in the empiricism of Francis Bacon, were beginning to affect biblical exegesis. This called for a new systematic reflection upon the structural character of the text, its pattern of imagery, and the philological significance of its terminology—together with a growing appreciation for the complexities of historical interpretation.[67] Our text, believed by Mede to summarize the Apocalypse, caught up all of these new epistemological issues. Mede struggled with them for his generation as he believed that Revelation 11 formed an interface between two lines of prophecy pertaining to universal and ecclesiastical history, prophecies adumbrated under two sets of visions proceeding from the closed (Rev. 5:1) and open (Rev. 10:2) apocalyptic books.[68] While Mede's focus was not upon two particular individuals, rather all true ministers of the gospel, his handling of Revelation 11 implied more.

The prophecy may be said to have a double fulfillment. First, the witnesses are part of the entire history of the Church. The measured court of the temple (Rev. 11:1) depicted the Church in her primitive purity.[69] The description of its outer court, not to be measured and trampled by the Gentiles (Rev. 11:2), illustrated a Church unconformable to divine measure, profaned and polluted since apostolic times. The sackcloth witnesses (Rev. 11:3) are the faithful throughout the Church's wilderness sojourn (Rev. 12:6) and, more particularly, those who face a definite scourge at the end history. They are

> God's true Ministers during all that time [1260 years]: who, when toward the end of their days of mourning they should be about to put off their sack-cloth and leave their lamentation (seeing the Truth they witnessed beginning to take place by publick Reformation) the Beast which ascends out of the Abyss shall slay them, and rejoyce over them as dead three days and an half, that is, so many years.[70]

The witnesses' place in history, and by extension that of the true Church, was understood in the context of Mede's wider system of synchronisms.[71] Garnered from throughout the text following the throne-room vision (Rev. 4.2), these combined the various prophecies in the book of Revelation as occurring within the same temporal period. The seven-sealed scroll (Rev. 5:1,7) revealed the main lines of political history ("Fata Imperii") in its seven seals (Rev. 6:1–8:1) and trumpets (Rev. 8:2–11:15). Mede's rationale was drawn in part from Daniel where the state of Church and general history were shadowed under the great image (Dan. 2:31–45) and four beasts (Dan. 7:1–27).[72]

The six seals are the judgments of Christ upon pagan Rome.[73] Internal slaughters, wars, pestilences and famine are meted out, which slowly destroy Rome.[74] The seventh seal (Rev. 8:1) brings down the Roman Empire. Some may wonder why this should be so in light of the favor now given Christianity. Mede answers, drawing upon the rich biblical tradition:

> For though Josiah were a good King, and made a Reformation, yet must the bloud shed by Manasseh needs be avenged upon the Kingdom of Judah. So

although the Roman Emperors were now become Christians, yet would not God forget their former slaughters of his Servants, but require their bloud at the hands of that Empire.[75]

This destruction is shadowed under the series of seven trumpets (Rev. 8:2–11:15) revealed by the opening of the seventh seal.[76] The first four signify the further destruction of Old Rome[77] through barbarian invasions beginning with the Huns and Vandals.[78] The last three signify the Saracens, Turks, and battle of Armageddon.[79] These are more universal and terrible than the previous four. The seals and trumpets, then, carry us through general history to the reign of Christ (Rev. 11:15–19).

The second line of prophecy is that of the open book (Rev. 10:2, 9–11). This explains the "inner" story of the church ("Fata Ecclesiae") "until both do meet in one in Ecclesia regnante, when all the Kingdoms of the world shall become the Kingdoms of our Lord and of his Christ [Rev. 11:15]."[80] This prophecy draws together the various synchronisms, all of which bear upon what is envisioned in chapter 11 of Revelation.[81] They are seven in number: (1) the woman driven into the wilderness for 1260 days (Rev. 12:6, 13–17), the seven-headed beast given power for forty-two months (Rev. 13:1–10), the outer court of the temple trampled over by the gentiles (Rev. 11:2) and the sackcloth ministry of the witnesses (Rev. 11:3–6)[82]; (2) the two-horned beast (Rev. 13:11) with the beast of ten horns (Rev. 17:7)[83]; (3) the great woman or mystical Babylon (Rev. 17:3), and the same ten-horned beast (Rev. 17:7)[84]; (4) the 144,000 undefiled (Rev. 14:4) with the Babylonian harlot and beast (Rev. 17:2, 18:3)[85]; (5) all of the previously mentioned relationships occur concurrently during the sounding of the first six trumpets[86]; (6) the measuring of the alter and inner courtyard of the temple (Rev. 11:1), the seven-headed dragon (Rev. 12:3) and its war with Michael (Rev. 12:7) over the male child (12:5).[87] This synchronism describes the "inner" history of the primitive Church[88] even as God had begun to judge old Rome, unalterably changed with Constantine's ascension to power (sixth seal). The 1260 days of mournful prophecy (Rev. 11:3; cf. 12:6) begin only after the measuring of the ancient Church.[89] Finally, the seventh synchronism combines the seven bowls of divine wrath (Rev. 16:1) with the fall of the great city of Babylon (Rev. 16:19).[90] These events would occur together with the blowing of the seventh and final trumpet (Rev. 11:15–19).[91]

Mede saw his age adumbrated under the closing years of the sixth trumpet, the end of the 1260 years of sackcloth prophesying by the witnesses.[92] This implied that his own day was summarized in the conflicts illustrated in Revelation 11: The two witnesses are related to those 1260 years. They are models for the proper exposition of God's Word. Mede writes:

> He says two, as I have stated, because the type is of two; as if he had said, I shall give to my Zerubbabel and Joshua, Elias and Elisha, Moses and Aaron. This applies because he calls them witnesses and it is fitting that there be two witnesses for the upholding of very word out of the Law. Just as the number of the tablets of God was two, it is possible to apply them in prophecy to the Old and New Testaments.[93]

Yet, they are more than this. There will yet occur a final slaughter of the witnesses. Our text more fully identifies some prophets rather than others. Such was also true for Brightman. However, by placing these witnesses in the future, or distant past (as in the work of the Jesuit Luis de Alcasar), Mede reconfigured the nature of the contemporary Church and how it was to intersect with society. Mede's view of the Church was drawn to a more mystical and transcendent pole than was Brightman's in the ways in which it implied activity in contemporary society. Brightman's view of the Church was more directly political and Mede's transcendent and mystical. This ecclesiological difference is reflected in particular interpretation of specific texts.[94] For Mede, the final martyrdom of the witnesses has not yet been completed—although "there have been some Preludiums of it in particular Churches."[95] Mede draws our attention to two wars of the beast, both alluded to in our text (Rev. 11:2; 11:7). Both illustrate the particular times and identity of the witnesses. One war occurs

> in medio Testium luctu, during the time of the witnesses mourning-prophecy; another when the Witnesses began to make an end of mourning. The first, while the Court of the Temple was wholly trodden down and prophaned by the Gentiles: the latter, when it began to be purged, and so the cause of the witnesses mourning to be removed.[96]

Mede explains that the first war ("intermedium bellum") is against all of the saints (cf. Rev. 13:7). The second war ("bellum novissimum") is only against the witnesses. The first, seen in its intensity against the Waldensians, is strikingly different from the second. In the earlier conflict the success of the beast is said to be absolute (Rev. 13:7–8). In the later war some will stand as an obstacle to the complete victory of the beast (Rev. 11:9). Again, the first occurred over a period of many years, the second will last only three and a half days. It will be the occasion of the beast's final demise.[97] The second war will be a persecution of Reformed pastors but will not result in the total destruction of the Church.

> These differences I thought good to propound to your consideration, to intimate that the scantling of this last War cannot be well taken from that against the Waldenses and Albigenses, etc. as being of another kind; namely, an extermination of the Reformed Pastors out of their places and Churches, and not a general extermination of the Body of the Reformed People, which are too many to be dealt with according to former violence, and shall remain to terrifie the Beast, and revenge the Clades [calamities] of their Prophets before almost they shall have done rejoycing over them.[98]

In distinction from Brightman, Mede understands there to be a future crisis for the Church, pictured under a second conflict for the adventual witnesses in Revelation 11. This conflict is connected with the conversion of the Jews. Privately, Mede opines, the Jews must be converted before the Second Coming of Christ lest they perish with the enemies of the kingdom. Prior to this advent there will occur some sign or "preludium" of his coming, which will cause the Jewish nation to turn to Christ.[99]

Mede offers some speculation on what this might be in his discussion of the seven vials of divine wrath. Six of these plagues are poured out under the sixth trumpet upon the Antichrist or papal whore.[100] Mede is not definite about what each represents, but he supposes that the first vial was in the preaching of the Waldensians, Albigensians, Wyclif, Hus, and others[101]; the second in Luther's Reformation[102]; the third in Elizabeth's ascension to the English throne.[103] He is less sure about the fourth vial but supposes that it is Rome's loss of influence in Germany.[104] The fifth vial represents the resurrection of the witnesses,[105] an event that occurs in days of darkest conflict.[106] Their death[107] for three and a half years occurs at the end of the 1260 days of mourning prophecy (c. 1625–1715)[108]; their resurrection comes in the new authority and dignity given the Church.[109] The sixth vial now marks the destruction of the Turkish woe.[110] All six of the vials cited are poured out during the period of the sixth trumpet.[111] Again, note the different ecclesiology evident in Mede and Brightman. For Mede the pouring out of these vials charts the course toward the millennial age. For Brightman the succession of vials represents the growing fullness of Christ's rule in the world during a second millennial period (A.D. 1300–2300), following the resurrection of the witnesses.

With this correlation in mind, Mede argues that the time for the conversion of the Jews must be near. Their conversion, like Paul's, would be marked by a miracle. That miracle, Mede suggests, is the defeat of the Turks, possibly the sixth vial following the resurrection of the witnesses.[112] The seventh vial comes with the final woe. In this the second beast, which arose out of the first, is finally destroyed.[113]

The story of the witnesses provides a chronology for the playing out of human affairs on a divine stage.[114] It is a cipher for the history of the Church between the first and second advents of Christ. All that John Foxe had sought is here more particularly determined. The rhetoric for the forces in history is defined in such a way as to fire further historical imagination pressing toward the end of history. Mede placed himself between the chiliasts of the early Church and allegorical or spiritual interpreters of the millennium, an event contained within the blowing of the seventh trumpet. This trumpet signals both the *"Magnus dies Domini,* and *Magnus dies Judicii."*[115] Mede understood his ideas on the millennium to be different from those of Alsted and Piscator, who he felt were guilty of heretical chiliasm. Mede argued that the millennial state of the Church belongs to the era of the second Advent and Day of Judgment. The appearance of the witnesses, revelation of Antichrist, and first resurrection occur before this period and open up the time of the New Jerusalem. This is followed by the war of Gog and Magog, second resurrection, and Last Judgment. The millennial reign of Christ occurs "in or during the Great day of Judgment," not following it.[116]

With the attempt on the part of William Laud and Charles I to impose Episcopacy throughout the realm, apocalyptic perspectives continued to rise, affecting the period of Puritan ascendancy (1638–1660) in England.[117] How our text figured into this development is best left to more focused studies. It is enough to note here that through the interpretation of our text we find a different ecclesiology envisioned of social significance for British society. Napier and Brightman continued to point the way forward for many Presbyterians and Independents.[118] However, Mede's more complex apocalyptic vision, holding that the witnesses had not been fully slain, was also persuasive: Days of crisis still stood before the

Church prior to any great restoration on earth.[119] Its ecclesiological focus remained grounded in a distant ideal, whether in a Constantinian triumph or future hope, but not in contemporary history as was the case for Brightman.

Locating the Restored Temple

Influenced toward Independency by John Cotton, Thomas Goodwin (1600–1680)[120] pastored separatist churches until appointed a member of the Westminster Assembly in 1643. Disillusioned, by 1650 he had become president of Magdalen College, Oxford, but failed to support the Restoration of the British monarchy and episcopally governed Church. In his commentary on the Apocalypse,[121] Goodwin gave definition to current religious strife through his reflection upon the adventual witnesses.[122] Our chapter in Revelation, descriptive, he felt, of a restored temple or church with the true worship of God, was shown to focus upon two events in the closing days of history: the measuring of a newly constructed temple or church at the end of the period of the sixth trumpet[123] and a final slaying of the witnesses, an attack upon those constructing this latter-day temple.[124]

Goodwin believed that the restored temple (Rev. 11:1–2) would find itself established in a generally unreformed place or era. The measuring of this temple implied a "second reformation," a further purification and exclusion of its outer court believed to signify carnal or false Christians. As such, the text offered a powerful vision that called forth historical justification for Independency. It lent legitimacy to those who felt compelled to separate themselves from other Christians who appeared to compromise the moral vision of a true Church. Goodwin writes:

> God being angry, both with the carnal gospellers in the outward court, so profanely mixing themselves with his worshippers, and laying themselves to his building and temple, and also with the carnal gospelling of the two witnesses among them, and with the imperfection of his temple building, not yet answering the pattern, and therefore intending to erect a purer church; he . . . Bids John . . . measure the temple anew . . . to make a new reformation. . . . [125]

This portion of the Church would be separated off and "trodden under" by the Gentiles, i.e., reabsorbed into Rome. Such an interpretation sent a powerful message to the ecclesial-political restorationists of Charles II with political implications for frustrated proto-constitutionalists. It also reminded the nation of how close both Laudian practice and the theology of the Caroline Divines were to Roman Catholicism. The construction of our latter-day temple by God's true witnesses, and its further measurement, illustrates the two reformations seen in recent British history—the first begun under Henry VIII and completed under Elizabeth, and the second begun with the Westminster Assembly but still in process of being fully effected.

> The first reformation he sets out by an inner temple, was imperfect, unfurnished, and, besides, defiled by the adjoining of an outward court into it. The second reformation, more pure, he represents by the inner temple measured again, to be finished and cleansed from that mixture.[126]

Goodwin writes of the importance of finding oneself within that temple, or true Church, explicitly lifting up the example of the newly planted churches in New England. He adds, with implications for ecclesial and colonial identity in the New World, "To get into this temple is the greatest preservative to keep the saints from the over-growing corruptions and defilements of these Gentiles; and it may unto many prove a protection and sanctuary from their power, as to those churches in New England it may be hoped it shall."[127] Mede had argued that the description of the temple was that of the purer patristic Church, the balance of Revelation 11 telling the story of the rest of Church history.[128] Goodwin disagreed. His ecclesiology evinced a more direct social policy than did Mede's, recalling, and with less optimism toward current political structures, the work of Brightman. The description of the apocalyptic temple falls under the sixth trumpet, which age is only terminated with the end of the second woe; the fall of the Turk.[129] Furthermore, there was no pure model of the Christian Church in the first 400 years, particularly after the days of the apostles. The best days of the Church are yet to come.

> For my part, I rest assured that the light which hath broken forth in many of our reformed churches since Calvin's time, and which still increaseth, and shall until Antichrist be consumed, is both in matter of doctrine, interpretation of Scripture, worship, church government, etc., much purer, and might be taken for a truer measure, than what shines in the story and writings of those three latter primitive ages.[130]

Not only does Goodwin single Mede out for criticism, but he also argues against Brightman's understanding of the apocalyptic temple, and the work and slaying of the witnesses. While the measuring of the temple does denote discernment between true and false Christians, this temple is not the Church through history nor is it indicative of a separation from the Roman papacy. Rather, it is a separation within the latter-day temple now being constructed by the witnesses. Goodwin's different conception of the witnesses and their work from that of Brightman gives an apocalyptic dimension to the Presbyterian-Independent quarrel in British Church life. It illustrates a different understanding of divine mediation in contemporary history.[131] The temple's outer court represents a third form of Christianity, a carnal faith, of some interim usefulness, yet calling for further reformation. Goodwin observes:

> This being that exceeding great error and defect laid in the foundation of the churches of the first Reformation, especially in our British churches, namely, the adjoining this outward court of carnal and unregenerate Protestants, and receiving them from the first into the temple, worship, and communion of all ordinances; so that the bounds of the church were extended as far as the commonwealth; which was done out of human prudence, suddenly as to greater the party against the Gentiles [Rome] in the city [Europe]: that as the earth helps the woman, chap. xii., so this, as an outward court, might round about shield the true temple and worshippers in it against the beast.[132]

The controversy over historical visions and related ecclesiology between Brightman and Goodwin in England will divide the churches similarly in New England and be evident in the apocalyptic speculation on our text seen in John

Cotton and Roger Williams. Goodwin writes concerning this further measuring of the temple:

> And then, . . . in this new-begun and second reformation of these churches, the main fundamental principle which is here mentioned, of receiving none into churches but only such worshippers as the need, or light of the word, as far as it gives rules to judge others by, applied by the judgment of men, who yet may err, shall discover to be truly saints. . . . Yet, because that was a true measuring, and this but the finishing of that building . . . like Zerubbabel's finishing the temple; therefore I verily think that the Holy Ghost had an aim of both, as unto two several gradual accomplishments of it.[133]

The witnesses were not slain in 1547 at either the Council of Trent or Schmalkaldic War. The Council (1545–1563) had seen to a reinvigorated Catholicism while the Schmalkaldic War saw the defeat of the Schmalkaldic League, first formed in 1525 by Lutheran princes to protect their religious interests, now in disarray following the battle of Muehlberg and the Wittenberg Capitulation (1547).[134] While our text shows that the witnesses are "the holy people, whose power is at last to be scattered,"[135] they first have the power to oppose the beast, set up a temple in the last days, and even to pour out four vials upon their enemies.[136] This is the first growth of Protestantism. Furthermore, before the witnesses' power is scattered there must occur additional reformation. Goodwin appeals to certain parallels in the history of Israel to make his case. Having left Egypt the Israelites still had to contend with the problem of purity in worship. Goodwin pointedly raises up as examples the rebellion of Nadab (Lev. 10:1–2) and Korah (Num. 16:1–35). Both were guilty of introducing polluted practices into Israel's worship. So, Goodwin argues in figural and apocalyptic language, in England there continues the problem of the full restoration of true worship as raised up in Independent and Separatist ecclesial argumentation:

> All the quarrels between the Popish party, the number of the beast's name, and the witnesses, are reducible to these two heads: (1.) True purity of worship; and, (2.) true holiness, and peculiar election of worshippers.[137]

In the midst of this reform the witnesses will be slain, their power scattered. Their expected restoration foreshadows the last victory of Christ and inauguration of his millennial kingdom. As such, Goodwin opens the way to an ecclesiology that, in spite of a certain measure of contemporary social influence, looks to a perfected age in the future and beyond the yet-to-be expected second Advent. In the millennial language of the nineteenth century it is an early form of Protestant premillennialism such as we saw with James Brocard on the Continent. The resurrection of the witnesses is comparable to that of the spirit of Elijah in John the Baptist.[138] The holy people of God are to rise to new prominence and honor as a tenth of the apocalyptic city falls (Rev. 11:13), that is, first in one of the ten kingdoms of Europe (probably in France[139] or England),[140] then throughout the world.[141] The history of these witnesses constitutes the surest sign of God's work in the world and of the progress of the historical clock as it hastens toward Christ's kingdom.

For when they speak of that day, and the signs of it, you shall generally find it among the ancients that this killing of the two witnesses and their rising, though indeed it hath by them been interpreted of Enoch and Elias, are made the fore-running signs of the approach of that joyful day of Christ's Kingdom, which they called the day of judgment.[142]

Goodwin's sermon, "Zerubbabels Encouragement to Finish the Temple" (prefaced with Rev. 11:4), delivered as a Fast Day sermon in the House of Commons (1642), develops several themes.[143] The witnesses are "candlesticks" before the Lord. They are as "two olive trees," i.e., "eminent Magistrates and Ministers that supply spiritual oil for the New Israel as Zerubbabel and Joshua did for ancient Israel. They are involved in the current sociopolitical turmoil in England. Their reforming efforts

must principally fall upon, not so much the first Reformation, or laying the foundation of the Churches Reformation; as upon a second work of the perfecting and finishing of them: And accordingly, as Zerubbabel there in Zachary is seene with a plummet in his hand, ver. 10. to measure out what remained unfinished for the building of the Temple, so here in the 1 ver. of the 11. of the Revel. John hath a Reed given him (he representing the godly of those ages) and is bidden to measure the Temple of God, and the Alter, and the Worshippers. . . .[144]

Political Spirituality

The popular use of the imagery connected with our text contributed to the growing sense of "prophecy in the air." It illustrates the way in which a biblical text can bring together assumptions about spiritual mediation with a specific construction of history in the service of an ecclesiology, or social organization, with political significance. This evident political spirituality rested upon a long commentary tradition about the identity and work of the two adventual witnesses. Now, in the atmosphere of seventeenth-century England, the work of the witnesses could be construed as symbolically representing the laying of the foundation of the congregational churches,[145] or even some more radical form of social organization.[146] Goodwin had described the work of the witnesses in this regard in the following way:

Thus in the same booke of the Revel. (in which Prophecie of the New Testament, the Holy Ghost borrows all the elegancies and flowers in the story of the Old, thereby to set out the story of the New in succeeding ages) in the 11. chap. ver. 4. the Holy Ghost describes the Two Witnesses, that should oppose the Beast and his party in all (and especially the later) ages, saying, [These are the two olive trees, and the two Candlesticks standing before the God of the earth.] where by the Candlesticks are meant the Churches . . . by the two olive trees the eminent Magistrates and Ministers that supply Oyle, for the maintaining of these Churches light and glory now, as Zerubbabel and Joshua the Priests did then. Yea the Holy Ghost deciphers them not only by the very same Hieroglyphique that is presented here in Zachary, but also he useth the very same words which we find there in the interpretation of the vision, . . . And further, this vision . . . did signifie . . . the first laying of the foundation of the Temple.[147]

Now, Goodwin continues, the time has come to finish that work.

While the theoretical basis of the English reform was held to be scriptural and doctrinal, to believe that one's group was part of a foreseen pattern of events contributed a sense of historical legitimacy.[148] Identifying the witnesses was to determine the time on the prophetic clock. The later that time, the more potentially radical might the work of the witnesses be. How they would rule after their restoration was of increasing debate, the subject of other studies.[149] But our text was attractive to Fifth Monarchy Men and other dissidents. The Welshman Arise Evans believed that the visions of Revelation 8–11 described the Civil War then taking place in England.[150] Upon arriving in London in the 1650s, Laurence Claxton learned that the two witnesses "that I had often read of in Revelation the 11th were now to be seen. . . ."[151]

We needn't dwell on the bizarre and spectacular.[152] Speculation on the identity and time of the witnesses as often as not came together with politics. What began as a mystical vision of theological and reforming impulse became frought with political and ideological import in the social order. The personalities of the witnesses were caught up in questions of political legitimacy and prophetic anarchy.[153] A full reformation called for all of the marks of the Church, which in Puritan Reformed theology had been defined, with some clarity since John Knox (c. 1513–1572) in Scotland and William Perkins (1558–1602) in England, as true preaching, the correct celebration of the sacraments, and scriptural holiness of life.[154] Such was seen symbolically in Christ as true Prophet, Priest, and King.[155] These marks, and their full expression in Christ, were to be discerned in the life of every believer and were to be evident in a state ruled by Christ's witnesses.[156]

By the middle of the seventeenth century this political spirituality was clearly visible in public and popular debate in Britain. Edmund Hall (1620?–1687) saw the "slaying of the witnesses" as the removal of proper magistracy and ministry by the beast, now interpreted as Oliver Cromwell (1651).[157] Even before the Civil War began John de la Marchand and Henry Burton claimed that they were the two witnesses testifying against Antichrist.[158] Others like the weavers Richard Farnham and John Brell followed their lead, claiming to be the adventual prophets.[159] Individuals like Mary Cary,[160] John Tillinghast,[161] Gerrard Winstanley,[162] John Lilburne,[163] and others took our text in both radically political and mystical directions.[164] John Reeve (1608–1658) and Lodowicke Muggleton (1609–1698) claimed to be the two[165] and organized a sect that lasted for three centuries holding to this opinion.[166] Oliver Cromwell's death (1658) hastened the return (1660) of Charles II and episcopacy. For many of the ardent, this was a day of gloom. Christopher Hill writes, "What emerged from twenty years of strife was not the kingdom of God but a world safe for businessmen to make profits in. . . ."[167] Some lost the old hope, some continued to spiritualize it, some took it overseas. For Henry More, however, monarchy and episcopacy, the offices of Moses and Aaron, were now restored. He asks, "Can there be a more fit fulfilling of the prophecy of the resurrection of the witnesses than this?"[168]

Notes

1. David Brady details development for English thought in *The Contribution of British Writers Between 1560 and 1830 to the Interpretation of Revelation 13:16–18* (Tübingen: J. C. B. Mohr [Paul Siebeck], 1983).

2. Christopher Hill draws out the instability of identifying Foxe with the Establishment in "John Reeve and the Origins of Muggletonianism," in *Prophecy and Millenarianism*, Ann Williams, ed. (London: Longman, 1980), p. 308.

3. The thesis of William Haller (*Acts and Monuments, Foxe's Book of Martyrs and the Elect Nation* [London: Jonathan Cape, 1963] with further documentation by Patrick Collinson, *The Birthpangs of Protestant England* (London: Macmillan, 1988).

4. Collinson, *Birthpangs*, p. 1-27; cf. J. G. A. Pocock, ed., *Three British Revolutions, 1641, 1688, 1776* (Princeton: Princeton University Press, 1980); and Pocock, *The Ancient Constitution and the Feudal Law: A Study of English Historical Thought in the Seventeenth Century* (New York: Cambridge University Press, 1987).

5. Most accounts of the history of the idea of progress in the West, while helpful in many respects, fail to deal adequately with the deeper biblical argumentation going on "behind the scenes" of cultural and political debate. See, e.g., Robert Nisbet, *History of the Idea of Progress* (New York: Basic Books, 1980).

6. On the nature of such different models of spiritual meditation and political legitimacy in governance, see William Lamont, *Godly Rule: Politics and Religion, 1603–60* (London: St. Martin's Press, 1969), pp. 12–15, *et passim*.

7. Lamont summarizes these in relation to Foxe in *Godly Rule*; ibid., pp. 12–15; cf. Marjorie Reeves, *Joachim of Fiore and the Prophetic Future* (London: SPCK, 1976; New York: Harper and Row, 1977), pp. 154–55.

8. John Napier, *A Plaine Discovery of the Whole Revelation of Saint John* (Edinburgh: Robert Waldgrave, 1593); cf. Wilhelm Bousset, *Die Offenbarung Johannis* (Gottingen: Vandenhoeck und Ruprecht, 1906), p. 89; and DNB 40, pp. 59–65.

9. Napier lists 36 propositions to guide the reader. In this light he explains by paraphrase and applies historically the rest of the Apocalypse (*A Plaine Discovery*, pp. 1–69, 150).

10. Ibid., pp. 148, 151. The two witnesses are the two testaments and, by metonymy, those who truly profess the Scriptures (ibid., p. 32). They were slain, or their authority denied, for 1260 years by tradition and perversion (p. 146).

11. V. Norskov Olsen cites Brightman as the transitional figure between Foxe and seventeenth-century historiography in *John Foxe and the Elizabethan Church* (Berkeley: University of California Press, 1973), pp. 20, 77–88. Brightman cites Matthias Flacius Illyricus, John Foxe, and John Sleidan as having shown the proper historical understanding of the Church.

12. William Haller, *The Rise of Puritanism* (Philadelphia: University of Pennsylvania Press, 1938), p. 269; cf. Lamont, *Godly Rule*, p. 14; Bryan Ball, *A Great Expectation* (Leiden: Brill, 1975), pp. 172–73; Paul Christianson, *Reformers and Babylon* (Toronto: University of Toronto Press, 1978), p. 245). Olsen writes that Mede "is the link between Brightman and the premillenialism of the seventeenth century" (*John Foxe and the Elizabethan Church*, pp. 20, 84). John Napier and Johann Heinrich Alsted are often included as significant influences.

13. Thomas Brightman, *The Revelation of St. John, Illustrated with Analysis and Scholions* (Amsterdam: Thomas Stafford, 1644; original Latin: *Apocalypsis Apocalypsos* (Frankfurt, 1609). A second Latin ed. was published at Heidelberg in 1613, and English translation at Amsterdam in 1615. Commentaries on Daniel and the Canticles of Solomon

were added to a Latin volume (Basel, 1614) and again (Leiden, 1616). An English version of this later enlarged work appeared in 1635 and again in 1644.

14. Ibid., p. 114. In his introductory summary of chapter 11, Brightman writes: "Prophecying being restored, there was a more full knowledge of the age past, namely, that the Church from Constantines times, 1260. yeares, was hidden in the secret part of the Temple, the Romanes in the meane time boasting of the holy Citie, and out-most Court, vers. 7. And that at the end of those yeares the Bishop of Rome should wage warre against the Church, should cut the throat of the Scriptures with his Councell of Trent, yea, make very carcases of them, triumph over them for three yeares and a halfe, should also, by the helpe of force and armes from Charles the V. tread upon the Saints in Germany, who yet after three yeares and an halfe lived againe in the men of Magdeburgh, and Mauritius stroke the enemies with a great feare, and overthrew the tenth part of the Empire of Rome. ver, 15" (p. 1).

15. Between chapters 17 and 18 Brightman places a lengthy discourse on the nature of Antichrist, arguing pointedly against Robert Bellarmine (1542–1621) who had approached the text similarly to Francesco de Ribeira (1537–1591): "The confuting of that Counterfeit Antichrist, whom Bellarmine describeth, and laboureth to prove by arguments, with all his might. Book 3. touching the Pope of Rome" (ibid., pp. 195–243); esp. 211–14. Bellarmine had defended his position, drawing upon Scripture, the fathers, and reason (*Disputationes de controversiis Christianae fidei adversus huius temporis haereticos* [1596]. The modern edition of Bellarmine is in *Opera Omnia*, ed. by Justinus Fevre, 8 vols. [Frankfurt: Minerva, 1965], Vol. 3, p. 20). Here Brightman offers a full refutation of Bellarmine's use of Scripture, passes quickly by the fathers (whom Brightman says knew less than we know), and argues, finally, that Enoch and Elijah were not translated in order to have to return to earth again but simply to become models of righteousness and of immortality. Cf. Robert W. Richgels, "The Pattern of Controversy in a Counter-Reformation Classic: The Controversies of Robert Bellarmine," SCJ, 11 (1980):3–15.

16. Ibid., sig. A2r-v. On Brightman's preface and purpose, see Katherine Firth, *The Apocalyptic Tradition in Reformation Britain, 1530–1645* (London: Oxford University Press, 1979), p. 165; and Olsen, *John Foxe and the Elizabethan Church*, pp. 87–88.

17. Ibid., sig. A3v.

18. Ibid., p. 114.

19. Ibid., sig. A2r.

20. Ibid., pp. 109–10. Brightman's discussion here is of interest with respect to the witnesses' identity and the new age opening up before the Church: "The preparation [for the restoration of prophecy] . . . was, the taking and eating up of the Booke, . . . the desire after all good learning, wherewith men were inflamed, which gave great hope, that more plentifull light would breake forth every day more and more. But the opinion of those men is fond, who will gather out of these words, that John is to be looked for, together with Enoch, and Elias, to come again at the end of the world" (p. 109).

21. Ibid., p. 110.

22. Ibid.

23. Ibid., p. 114.

24. Luther, WA, 10.I.1, pp. 147.14–148.18.

25. Brightman, *Revelation*, p. 110.

26. The opening of the seventh seal illustrates the nature of the Church and reflects the peace brought to it by Constantine (ibid., pp. 78–82).

27. Ibid., p. 115.

28. The Church's struggle from A.D 300 to the ascendance of Elizabeth I on England's throne is adumbrated under the seven trumpets (ibid., pp. 83–106).

29. The earlier seals, adumbrations of the Church's conflict with old Rome, were opened prior to Constantine (ibid., pp. 67–82). Concerning these successive historical periods, Brightman writes: "Moreover seeing the Seales are as it were pledges of things to come, the Trumpets are evils that rush upon the world with a great noise, the vials such evils, as come sliding in, by litle, and litle . . ." (ibid., p. 68).

30. Ibid., p. 115.

31. Ibid.

32. Ibid., pp. 116–17.

33. Ibid., p. 117. Brightman's position is rather remarkable when it is set parallel to the "spiritual revolutionary" Thomas Müntzer. Both are drawing together the implications of Rev. 11:15 and Dan. 7:27. However, in Müntzer's case it appears that the great crisis or slaying of the witnesses is occurring or soon will occur. For Brightman the greater part of it, if not its entirety, is over and the world is now entering that new age toward which Müntzer may have sought to propel it.

34. John Foxe, *Eicasmi seu meditationes in sacram Apocalypsim* (London, 1587), p. 178.

35. Brightman, *Revelation*, p. 117; cf. p. 120. Brightman continues by describing the destruction of Hebrew books by Antiochus Ephiphanes, similarly by "Diocletian, and other tyrants." As these were types of Antichrist, Brightman appears to be implying the same for Rome.

36. Ibid., p. 118.

37. Ibid., p. 120.

38. Ibid.

39. Ibid., p. 121.

40. This exegetical delineation helps to define an inner theological rationale behind optimistic theories of history, particularly within English Puritanism. See Ernest Tuveson, *Millennium and Utopia* (Berkeley: University of California Press, 1949), and more recently Robert Nisbet, *Idea of Progress*, pp. 124–39. Frank E. Manuel and Fritzie P. Manuel offer a more encyclopedic but less precisely defined perspective particularly in its theological lineaments in *Utopian Thought in the Western World* (Cambridge: Harvard University Press, 1979), pp. 332–36.

41. Brightman, *Revelation*, p. 121. Note here and frequently elsewhere reference made to the historical work of Sleidan.

42. Foxe, *Eicasmi*, p. 239; John Foxe, *The Acts and Monuments of John Foxe*, Stephen Reed Cattley, ed. (London: R. B. Steeley and W. Burnside, 1841), I, pp. 523–32.

43. Brightman, *Revelation*, p. 121. Brightman sets Rev. 11:13 parallel to Rev. 6:12 here.

44. Ibid., Brightman writes: "And indeed there followed a great change, by means of this Decree, throughout all Europe. The men of Austria doe earnestly require of Ferdinandus their King, that the same thing might be granted unto them, that was granted to their fellowes, that were of the Augustane Confession. The Bavarians do importunately request as much of Albertus their Prince" (p. 121).

45. Ibid., pp. 121–22.

46. Ibid., p. 123. Concerning the historical verification of the witnesses' identity, Brightman notes, "The seven last Books of Sleidans Commentaries do helpe us to a more plaine and full exposition upon the fighting, dying and rising againe of these Prophets. The whole Prophecy is of a thousand two hundred fifty and one Iulian yeares, from Dioclesian to the yeare 1555 till which time also, Sleidan proceed both in writing, and in living."

47. Both Boniface II and Muhammad are adumbrated by the star that fell from heaven

(Rev. 9:1), part of the revelation of the fifth trumpet (first woe). The sixth trumpet (second woe) denotes the enlargement of Turkish power and invasion of the West as punishment for Roman idolatry. The direct effect of this conflict bears upon our passage. Brightman argues that a study of the truth is re-kindled in the West, due to this invasion, by which the Scriptures are restored (ibid., pp. 1, 92, 103).

48. Ibid., p. 122.

49. Ibid., p. 122. The precise advent of the third woe is unclear in the text of the Apocalypse (cf. Rev. 11:14; 12:12), a matter that lends itself toward theories of progressive fulfillment.

50. Ibid., pp. 165–76. The first three vials are past: the expulsion of Roman clergy from England (1563); Martin Chemnitz's exposure of papal errors (in his *Examen Concilii Tridentini*) and Parliament's anti-Jesuit acts (1581). The fourth vial is presently being poured out. This is represented by the growing knowledge of the Bible. The last three vials are yet to come: the full destruction of Rome, the conversion of the Jews, and the battle of Armageddon.

51. Ibid., p. 123.

52. Ibid., p. 122.

53. Ibid., pp. 165–76.

54. Brightman himself is difficult to classify in terms of this conflict. He subscribed to the Book of Discipline, appears to have been offended by the Marprelate tracts yet viewed the enforcement of adiaphora as unlawful. He was not a radical separatist but was concerned with purity in the Church. Brightman writes with indignity of those who imprison and revile the reformers, "slaundering them with the odious names of Anabaptists and Puritans" (*Revelation*, p. 51). DNB, 6, p. 339; cf. Peter Lake, *Moderate Puritans and the Elizabethan Church* (Cambridge: Cambridge University Press, 1982), pp. 252–55.

55. Brightman, *Revelation*, p. 123.

56. Ibid., p. 123.

57. Ibid., pp. 13–53. Brightman identifies the seven apocalyptic churches as Ephesus, the Church from the first century to Constantine; Smyrna, from Constantine to Gratian (382); Pergamum, from 380–1300; Thyatira, the struggle between the true and false Church between 1300–1520; Sardis, the German Reformation; Philadelphia, the Reformed movement; Laodicea, the English Reformation. Compare in Olsen (*John Foxe and the Elizabethan Church*, pp. 80–81 and Firth (*Apocalyptic Tradition*, pp. 166–67) on the idealization of the apostolic (Ephesian) Church evident here.

58. Ibid., pp. 40–53. Christianson, in *Reformers and Babylon*, pp. 102–5, draws out the significance of this identification for Brightman as a moderate reformer. By doing things right, the reform of England might hope to surpass the state of the first Church (Firth, *Apocalyptic Tradition*, pp. 167–68).

59. J. A. DeJong, *As the Waters Cover the Sea* (Kempen: J. H. Kok, 1970), pp. 16–29. Tai Liu (*Discord in Zion: The Puritan Divines and the Puritan Revolution 1640–1660* [The Hague, Nijhoff, 1973]) illustrates bewilderment on the millennium in seventeenth-century England (p. 160, n. 21). The millennial views of the period fell into three broad categories, which are analogous to what has come to be referred to as amillennialism, postmillennialism, and premillennialism. See Ball, *Great Expectation*, pp. 160–92; his classification is helpful; cf. R. G. Clouse, "The Rebirth of Millenarianism," in *Puritans, the Millennium and the future of Israel*, Peter Toon, ed. (London: James Clark & Co., 1970), pp. 42–65, and De Jong.

60. Brightman, *Revelation*, pp. 264–68. Others who would promote such optimism were Hugh Broghton, John Wilkinson, and Alexander Leighton (cf. Ball, *Great Expectation*, p. 168).

61. Bousset, *Offenbarung*, p. 90; cf. Ball, *Great Expectation*, pp. 59–61.

62. Joseph Mede, *Clavis Apocalyptica* (1627; repr. 1632 with additions). Parliament authorized its publication in 1642 when it was translated by Richard More and printed in English (1643) as *The Key of the Revelation*. See also *Daniel's Weeks* (1643, 1648, and 1677) and *The Apostasy of the Latter Times* (1641, 1644). Mede's work are found in English translation in *The Works of Joseph Mede*, J. Worthington, ed. (London: Roger Norton, 1677). Subsequent references to Mede are from this edition unless otherwise indicated. It contains works published by Mede before his death (1638) as well as unpublished theological fragments and correspondence. Chapter 12 of Book V gives Mede's summary of the Apocalypse.

63. DNB, 7, p. 178; cf. Clouse, "The Rebirth of Millenarianism," in Toon, ed., *Puritans*, pp. 56–61.

64. DeJong, *As the Waters Cover the Sea*, p. 24.

65. DNB, 37, pp. 178–80; cf. Clouse, "The Rebirth of Millenarianism," in Toon, ed., *Puritans*, pp. 62–65. Ball contends, against Clouse and DeJong, that Mede's millenarianism was not Continentally derived, but wholly original (*Great Expectation*, pp. 159, 174, n. 96). See R. G. Clouse, "The Influence of John Henry Alsted on English Millenarian Thought in the Seventeenth Century," Ph.D. dissertation, State University of Iowa, 1963; cf. DeJong, *As the Waters Cover the Sea*, pp. 21–27; such ideas were "in the air," but between 1627–32 Mede became acquainted with Alsted's Diatribe (cf. Clouse, "The Rebirth of Millenarianism," in Toon, ed., *Puritans*, p. 60. See in this regard Henricus [Johann] Alstedius, *Diatribe de Mille annis Apocalypticis, non illis Chiliastarum & Phantastarum, sed. B. B. Danielis & Johannis* (2d ed.) (Frankfurt: Conradi Eifridi, 1630; 1st ed., 1627). Alsted develops the idea (pp. 104–5) of a twofold coming of Elijah on the basis of Malachi's prophecy (4:1–6) and its cryptic fulfillment in Matthew (17:11).

66. Christopher Hill, *The World Turned Upside Down* (New York: Penguin Books, 1975), p. 92; and Firth, *Apocalyptic Tradition*, pp. 218–19. Marjorie Reeves draws possible Joachite relationships (*The Influence of Prophecy in the Later Middle Ages* (Oxford: Clarendon Press, 1969), pp. 59, 317).

67. Mede, *Clavis*, sig. A3r–E4v. The structural relationships in his seven synchronisms precede his analysis of the text, set out in two parallel lines, the history of Empire and Church. The letters exchanged between Mede and his correspondents (viz., *Works*) offer further insight into his methodology.

68. Ibid., part I: "De Sigillis," pp. 1–119; part 2: "In Bibliaridion," pp. 121–293.

69. Mede, *Works*, V, p. 920.

70. Ibid., V, p. 921.

71. Mede developed a systematic symbolic grammar for understanding the text, but he continued to wrestle with what Michael Murrin has referred to as the polyvalency of apocalyptic terminology. As such, Mede's system could never be finally systematic. Murrin identifies the extrinsic and intrinsic problems for apocalyptic delineation. I am grateful to Murrin for permitting me to see his paper, "Revelation and Two Seventeenth-Century Commentators," (unpublished typescript, University of Chicago, 1982), pp. 1–43.

72. Mede, *Works*, V. pp. 917–18.

73. Mede, *Clavis*, pp. 13–14.

74. The great earthquake, which comes with the sixth seal, signifies the ascendance of Constantine (ibid., pp. 32–33).

75. Mede, *Works*, V. p. 919.

76. Mede, *Clavis*, pp. 65–69.

77. The first trumpet was probably sounded in A.D 395 with the full triumph of Christianity under Theodosius the Great (ibid., p. 71). In his *Works*, Mede writes: "Of

these Seven Trumpets the first Four are lesser ones, and fall chiefly upon the West, and made way for the rising of the Antichristian State of the Beast or Kingdom of the False-Prophet. The last Three are greater and more terrible and more lasting, and therefore distinguished from the former by the name of WOES, verse 13" (V, p. 919).

78. Ibid., pp. 70–88.

79. Ibid., pp. 88–119; cf. *Works*, III, p. 595.

80. Mede, *Works*, V, p. 918.

81. Mede, *Clavis*, sig. A3r.

82. Ibid., sig. B1r–B2v.

83. Ibid., sig. B2v–B3r.

84. Ibid., sig. B3r–B4r.

85. Ibid., pp. 70–88.

86. Ibid., sig. B4r.

87. Ibid., sig. B4r–C1v.

88. Mede writes: "By the Inmost and Measured Court of the Temple, I understand the Church in her Primitive Purity, when as yet the Christian Worship was unprophaned, and answerable to the Divine Rule revealed from above" (*Works*, V, p. 920).

89. Ibid., pp. 920–21.

90. Mede, *Clavis*, sig. C1v–C2v.

91. Further relationships are drawn (ibid., sig. C2r–E4r).

92. Mede argues that the 1260 years probably began between A.D. 365–455, implying an end between 1625–1715 (*Works*, III, p. 600); cf. his use of biblical numbers (pp. 597–98).

93. Mede, *Clavis*, pp. 129–30.

94. Mede's futurist orientation on our theme may be contrasted with that of his older contemporary, the Jesuit Luis de Alcasar (1554–1613). Alcasar (*Vestigatio Arcani Sensus in Apocalypsi* [Antwerp: Heredes Martini Nutii, 1614 and 1619]; edition used, 1619, pp. 516–65) divided the Apocalypse into two series of prophecies: the triumph of Christianity over Judaism (Rev. 1–11), and the conflict of the Church with paganism (Rev. 12–22) with consequent victory under Constantine (Rev. 19:11–21). Our witnesses were Christians who lived during the destruction of Jerusalem (A.D. 70), their death the result of Jewish persecution prior to the elevated authority given the Church (pp. 534–35). Juan Mariana (1619) was to take this preterist understanding of the witnesses one step further and identify them with Peter and Paul (Bousset, *Offenbarung*, p. 95), a view defended by Johannes Munck (*Petrus und Paulus inder Offenbarung Johannis* [Copenhagen: Rosenkilde og Bagger, 1950], pp. 56–81.

95. Ibid., III, p. 596. Note Mede's philogical interests.

96. Ibid., IV, p. 765.

97. Ibid., IV, pp. 765–66.

98. Ibid., IV, p. 766.

99. Ibid., IV, p. 766. Mede finds corroboration for this in Matt. ("the Hebrew Evangelist") 24:30 (pp. 766–68). He suggests that Malachi's prophecy of the returning Elijah (4:5–6) was only partially fulfilled. As John came before the first Advent so another would come before the second. This further "Elijah mission" appears connected with the "preludium" of the Jews' conversion (cf. Brightman, *Revelation*, p. 123).

100. Mede, *Clavis*, pp. 263–64.

101. Ibid., pp. 266–67.

102. Ibid., pp. 267–68.

103. Ibid., pp. 268–69. Note specific acts.

104. Ibid., pp. 269–71.

105. Ibid., p. 271. See his discussion on Rev. 11:13.

106. Mede, *Works*, IV, p. 760. God's exaltation follows periods of greatest darkness.

107. That is, the death of "the publick Fabrick of the Reformation" (ibid., IV, p. 761), "an extermination of the Reformed Pastors out of their places and Churches" (ibid., IV, p. 766).

108. According to Mede, this period has not yet ended. The primary slaying of the witnesses still lies in the future (*Clavis*, p. 136). But the time is specific. Mede writes: "The time of three days and a half is the time during which the Witnesses should lie for dead, without appearance of life or motion; not the time wherein they should be dying or killing; for that may be much longer, and grow also by degrees, . . . The three days and a half are not to be reckoned therefore . . . until all should be dead, and no motion of life anymore appear" (*Works*, IV, pp. 760–1).

109. Mede, *Clavis*, pp. 146–47.

110. Ibid., pp. 271–74.

111. Mede, *Works*, III, p. 596; cf. Brightman, *Revelation*, pp. 165–77, esp. p. 166.

112. Mede, *Works*, IV, pp. 766–68.

113. Ibid., p. 923. The seven vials destroy the second beast, Antichrist, as the first was destroyed under the seal and trumpet judgments; cf. *Clavis*, pp. 263–75.

114. Note the epistolary exchange with William Twisse, moderate Puritan and prolocutor of Westminister Assembly, in Mede, *Works*, IV, pp. 758–61, 764–70.

115. Ibid., III, p. 603; Mede writes: "For I give a third time, in or durante magno Die Judicii, in or during the Great day of Judgment." See pp. 602–4; IV, pp. 770–72, 762; *Clavis*, pp. 275–80; cf. Firth, *Apocalyptic Tradition*, pp. 220–23.

116. The nature of Christ's reign was subject to considerable debate. DeJong delineates among simple chiliasts, complex chiliasts, and extreme literalists. The first two categories correspond to current postmillennialism and premillennialism (*As the Waters Cover the Sea*, pp. 36–42). Ball develops the idea of sequencing as it relates to governance (*Great Expectation*, pp. 159–92). Christianson develops aspects of the growing Puritan and Separatist militance in British society as it related to differing sets of apocalyptic expectations (*Reformers and Babylon*, pp. 179–243).

117. These developments have received close attention in Lamont, *Godly Rule*, pp. 17–135. Note his progression: "Godly Rule," "Godly Prince," "Godly Bishop," "Godly People," "Godly Parliament." Cf. Liu, *Discord in Zion*, and Ball, *Great Expectation*, pp. 157–64.

118. See the *Directory for the Publique Worship of God* (1644) in Bard Thompson *Liturgies of the Western Church* (New York: World Publishing, 1962), pp. 360–61. Compare Brightman, *Revelation*, pp. 125–26. John Owen argued that God was now "shaking" those powers in the world that give their allegiance to Antichrist. See *The Works of John Owen, D. D.* (Edinburgh, 1862), VIII, pp. 256–57. According to Olsen, Brightman's theology serves as the basis for the idea of a redemptive nationalism more so than the apocalyptic ideas of John Foxe. Foxe's work was less tied to the specific politics of a particular people in furthering that vision. See Olsen, *John Foxe and the Elizabethan Church*, pp. 77–87.

119. Note Mede's correspondents in *Works*, IX, pp. 758–72. John Archer and Cromwell's chaplain, Peter Sterry, followed in part Mede's views; see DeJong, *As the Water Covers the Sea*, pp. 36–42; cf. Ball, *Great Expectation*, pp. 127, 129.

120. DNB, 22, pp. 148–50; on Goodwin's influence, see Brady, *Contribution of British Writers*, p. 182–83.

121. Thomas Goodwin, *Exposition upon the Revelation*, in *The Works of Thomas Goodwin, D.D.*, with General Preface by John C. Miller, Vol. 3 (Edinburgh: James Nichol, 1861), pp. 1–205. The commentary was written c. 1639 and published in Goodwin's *Works* (London: Printed by J. D. and S. R. for T. G. [etc.], 1681–1704).

122. Roughly half of the exposition deals with Rev. 11. Goodwin begins the section on our chapter by delineating five general premises that will guide his discussion: (1) The authority of the passages is from Christ who delivers the vision; (2) The fate of the Church as pictured falls at the end of the period of the sixth trumpet; (3) The nature of the Church and what it will face from the beast/whore is described; (4) The events occurring at the end of the history of the fourth monarchy depicted in Dan. 12 are clarified in Rev. 11; (5) The power and nature of the beast is depicted (ibid., pp. 110–16).

123. Ibid., pp. 111–18, 119–41.

124. Ibid., pp. 111–18, 142–80.

125. The Gentiles (Rome) are said to continue to possess this city till the end of their 42 months. However, within this city God's temple (Protestantism) is built (ibid., p. 123). Such appeals for moral separation and the rights of the individual conscience will contribute to future religio-political radicalism.

126. Ibid., p. 128.

127. Ibid., p. 130. This imagery of separation will contribute to the appropriation of typologies of indentification with old Israel and calling and election as raised up, e.g., in the work of Sacvan Bercovitch, *Typologies of Early American Literature* (Amherst: University of Massachusetts Press, 1972) and *The Puritan Origins of the American Self* (New Haven: Yale University Press, 1975); and in Mason I. Lawrence, *The Language of Canaan* (Cambridge: Harvard University Press, 1980).

128. Ibid., pp. 133, 136; cf. Mede, *Works*, V, p. 920; *Clavis*, sig. A3r, B4r–C1v.

129. Ibid., p. 135.

130. Ibid., p. 136.

131. Ibid., pp. 130–31, 138. Some reconciliation with Brightman's views are sought (pp. 153–54), but a different historical vision and related ecclesiology is evident. See R. B. Carter, "The Presbyterian-Independent Controversy . . . with Special Reference to Dr. Thomas Goodwin," Ph.D. dissertation, Edinburgh University, 1961, pp. 294–95; cited in Toon, ed., *Puritans*, pp. 135–36.

132. Ibid., p. 140.

133. Ibid., p. 140.

134. Ibid., p. 138. Goodwin divides the question of the slaying of the witnesses between those like Brightman, who argue that it has occurred, and others like Graserus, Matthias Hoe, Joseph Mede, and Wood, who believe it is yet to occur. Goodwin agrees with the latter (p. 154).

135. Ibid., pp. 142–43. The witnesses are those who in all ages oppose the Antichrist, but our passage describes those in particular who live in the latter times.

136. Ibid., p. 146. The vials are matched with the powers given the witnesses in the text: "For in the days of their prophecy, they 'smite the earth' with plagues, which is the first vial; and turn the 'sea and rivers into blood,' which is the second and third vial; and then 'devour men with fire,' which is the fourth" (p. 154).

137. Ibid., p. 147.

138. Ibid., pp. 180–83. Goodwin sets forth a progressive restoration.

139. France is singled out because of the early preaching of the Waldensians (ibid., pp. 188–89).

140. England is thought to show the best potential for this first sign of renewal. Foxe's *Martyrology* is said to document the trials the English Church has gone through. Here the debate over the true Church has been liveliest: "And they have been put to contend for it more than all the other churches; and this, more or less, ever since the first reaction of the English church at Frankfurt, in Queen Mary's days. And in the contention about it, and through that bitter persecution for it, they even for this cause have prophesied in

sackcloth . . ." (idid., pp. 189–90). Note the reference to Frankfurt and the role it played in the development of the Puritan debate for Richard Cox, John Foxe, and John Knox.

141. Ibid., pp. 158, 192–205.

142. Ibid., p. 192.

143. Thomas Goodwin, *Zerubbabels Encouragement to Finish the Temple: A Sermon Preached Before the Honorable House of Commons, at the Late Solemne Fast, Apr. 27, 1642*. Published by order from that House (London: Printed for R. D. . . . , 1642). The purpose, Church reform, is stated; sig. A2.

144. Ibid., p. 56.

145. Clouse, "The Rebirth of Millenarianism," in Toon, ed., *Puritans*, p. 64 (cf. Christianson, *Reformers and Babylon*, pp. 232–33). This is not simply a return to the apostalic Church, but something greater is implied. See Goodwin, *Exposition upon Revelation*, p. 136; cf. Goodwin, *Works*, II, pp. 145–51.

146. B. S. Capp, "Extreme Millenarianism," in Toon, ed., *Puritans*, pp. 66–90.

147. Goodwin, *Zerubbabel's Encouragement*, pp. 55–56.

148. Illustrations in S. R. Maitland, "Puritan Thaumaturgy," in *Notes on the Contributions of the Rev. George Townsend, M.A., to the new edition of Foxe's Martyrology* (London: J. G. F. & J. Rivington, 1841), pp. 95–117; and Keith Thomas, *Religion and the Decline of Magic: Studies in Popular Beliefs in Sixteenth and Seventeenth Century England* (London: Weidenfeld and Nicolson, 1971), pp. 112, 129ff. Christianson documents factors that came together then, contributing to an increased literalization of the apocalyptic vision: a belief in the reliability of the biblical revelation; a recovery of the knowledge that many in the primitive Church had been chiliasts; a new appreciation of Judaism (long associated with a deprecated chiliasm); and Calvinistic determinism, which looked to the consummation of Christian hope (*Reformers and Babylon*, pp. 175–92.).

149. Ball illustrates the nature of this debate with reference to the exegetical questions involved (*Great Expectation*, pp. 157–92). Note in particular the work of John Archer, influenced by Goodwin, whose ideas appealed to the moderate Fifth Monarchists, in *The Personall Reigne of Christ upon Earth* (London, 1642), pp. 8, 47.

150. Hill, *World Turned Upside Down*, p. 94.

151. Laurence Claxton, *Look about you; or the Right Devil Unfolded* (1659); cited by L. D. Lerner, "Puritanism and the Spiritual Autobiography," *The Hibbert Journal*, 55 (1956):385.

152. Some were unbalanced like Robert Dickons, John Moore, William Geffrey, Ellys Hall, John Richardson, and others who made use of our theme in ways of marginal interest. See Richard Bauckman, *Tudor Apocalypse* (Oxford: The Sutton Courtenay Press, 1978), pp. 185–207.

153. Christianson argues that such militant speculation grows from the idea that saints are to be involved in the political affairs of the last days, showing an active concern for truth (*Reformers and Babylon*, pp. 185–92).

154. Compare Brightman, *Revelation*, p. 123; Mede, *Works*, III, p. 596; and Goodwin, *Exposition upon Revelation*, p. 136.

155. George H. Williams draws attention to the theological, historical, and sociological significance of this triadological image in "Translatio Studii: The Puritans' Conception of Their First University in New England, 1636," Festschrift für Heinrich Bornkamm, ARG, 57:1/2 (1966):152–81.

156. Moderate Protestant postmillennial historicist exegesis of our text continued strong in John Owen and James Durham ("The Latter-day Glory," in Toon, ed., *Puritans*, pp. 39–40). James Durham (*A Commentarie upon the Book of Revelation* [Amsterdam: J. F. Stam, 1660; 1st ed., 1658]), professor of Divinity at Glasgow, emphasized the symbolic identity

of the witnesses as Protestantism (p. 483). In defending the connection, he criticized both futurist and preterist interpretations (specifically Grotius and Jesuit interpreters, pp. 483–84).

157. Edmund Hall, *Manus Testium Mouens, or A presbyteriall glosse upon . . . prophetick texts . . . which point at the great day of the Witnesses rising* (London, 1651). He continues reflection upon our theme in *Discourse of Apostasy and Antichrist;* . . . (1653). Perhaps with our adventual prophets in mind, John Eliot, missionary to the Algonquin tribe, addressed Cromwell as one raised up by the Lord to overthrow Antichrist and bring the Church out of bondage. See John Eliot and Thomas Mayhew, *Tears of Repentance. or, A Further Narrative of the Progress of the Gospel Amongst the Indians in New England* (London: P. Cole, 1653), sig. 42r.

158. They are cited by B. S. Capp in his study of extreme millenarian tendencies withinh Puritanism. See "Extreme Millenarianism," in Toon, ed., *Puritans,* pp. 76–77. Burton wrote *The Sounding of the last two trumpets, the sixth and seventh; or meditations on chapters IX–X. of the Revelations* (London: 1641).

159. See the *Calendar of State Papers, Domestic Series* (1636–37), pp. 459–60, 487–88; (1637–38), p. 66; as cited in Thomas, *Religion and the Decline of Magic,* p. 135.

160. Mary Cary dated the resurrection of the witnesses from the date of the work of the New Model Army (April 4, 1645). See her work, *The Resurrection of the Witnesses* (1648), 'Epistle Dedicatory,' pp. 82–87, 98–99, 153–94. Cited in Christopher Hill, *Antichrist in Seventeenth-Century England* (London: Oxford University Press, 1971), pp. 107–8.

161. John Tillinghast, *Knowledge of the Times; or The Resolution of the Question how long it shall be unto the end of wonders. Dan. XII.* (London: R. J. for L. Chapman, 1654), sig. A4r–A5v, p. 16. His treatise, *Generation Work* (London, 1654), offers an exposition of the seven vials (Rev. 16).

162. Gerrard Winstanley, "The Breaking of the Day" (1648), in *The Works of Gerrard Winstanley,* George H. Sabine, ed. (Ithaca: Cornell University Press, 1941), pp. 85–90.

163. John Lilburne, *The Gospel Treasury Opened,* I, pp. 3, 210–11.

164. Bauckman, *Tudor Apocalypse,* pp. 185–207.

165. Lodowicke Muggleton, *A true interpretation of the eleventh chapter of the Revelation of St. John. . . .* (London? 1662). Reprinted . . . 1751, 1752, 1753 . . . 1833.

166. Founded in c. 1651, this group continued as a small sect until 1868. See Christopher Hill, "John Reeve and the Origins of Muggletonianism," pp. 307–8.

167. Christopher Hill, *Some Intellectual Consequences of the English Revolution* (Madison: University of Wisconsin Press, 1980), p. 34.

168. Henry More, *A Modest Enquiry into the Mystery of Iniquity* (1664), cited in Christopher Hill, *Antichrist,* p. 107.

9

Witnesses in the Wilderness

Faithful Church or Faithful Remnant?

Speculation about our witnesses moved quickly in a variety of directions in seventeenth-century Anglo-American piety. Thomas Goodwin summarized what was hoped by those who carried our theme to the New World, that the temple built by the witnesses in "those churches in New England" might be free of "corruptions and defilements," and constitute a "protection and sanctuary" from the power of the Gentiles (Rev. 11:2), that is, from those churches left unreformed or half-reformed.[1] This was their "errand into the wilderness," of the newly discovered continent.[2] However constituted, it was soon difficult for many to outline the task precisely as it hinged upon the significance one gave to the religious upheaval, or Reformation, in the sixteenth century. Was it an event of temporal moment to be equated with Christ's first Advent or merely another date on the apocalyptic calendar?[3] Put differently, was the Church it birthed the faithful Church—or its members merely a faithful remnant, perhaps only a reforming order in some ways analogous to earlier medieval reform movements?

The adventual witnesses form part of the historical reality mediated to New England Puritanism.[4] The question of their identity and work can be factored out of the conflict between John Cotton and Roger Williams. It is apparent in Cotton Mather's reflections upon religious declension in the American colonies following the failure of the "Half-Way Covenant" (1662) to maintain both piety and communal cohesion in the Massachusetts Bay Colony. Our theme is embedded in Jonathan Edwards's conception of the significance of religious awakening in the colonies of his day.

The debate between John Cotton (1584–1652) and Roger Williams (c. 1604–1683) over the relationship between Church and civil government in the Bay Colony is reflected in their differing attitudes toward the witnesses.[5] Williams argued that the testimony of the witnesses was not complete. They had not been fully slain.[6] Christ's true Church did not yet exist but would only appear with the millennial age following the slaying of the witnesses. Religious uniformity, whether under Stuart or Commonwealth policy in England or magisterial direction in New England, kept the witnesses from performing their duty: namely witnessing.[7] This Williams made clear in *The Bloody Tenent Yet More Bloody* (1652), his reply to John Cotton's criticism, *The Bloudy Tenent, Washed and Made White in the Bloud of the Lamb* (1647).

227

> If the fourtytwo moneths of the Beasts reign, and the two hundred and three-
> score dayes of the prophesie of the Witnesses of Jesus in Sackcloth be expired:
> yet I fear the three days and a halfe of the greatest slaughter of the Witnesses
> is not over: Yet fear not what must be suffered, although the Devill cast (not
> onely some, but) all Christs Witnesses into Prison; yea, although he murther
> and fling out the Karakasses of the Saints to shame and injury, yet the mighty
> Spirit of God will raise them on their feet again and into heavenly glory, out of
> this shame shall they ascent in the flight of their bloody enemies.[8]

Cotton's treatise, *The Bloudy Tenent, Washed*, stressed the responsibility of the
Christian magistrate in fostering and enforcing a proper moral order in civil society. He argued that the destruction of Antichrist is presently occurring through the
work of Christ's restored congregation of believers, Congregationalism in the Massachusetts Bay Colony, as they promoted such a Christian moral order. This implied a fuller restoration of the witnesses' condition.[9] Cotton stressed the fact that

> when the kingdoms of the earth become the Kingdomes of the Lord (Rev. 11:15)
> it is not, by making Christ a temporall king, but by making temporall Kingdomes
> nursing Fathers to his Church.[10]

It was the responsibility of the magistrate to promote and protect the authentic
Church in the era or at least arena of the witnesses' resurrection. By conforming to
divine law, God would establish in Church and state a "visible state of a new
Hierusalem, which shall flourish many yeares upon Earth, before the end of the
world."[11] This outlook offers at least a kernel of that hoped-for millennial kingdom
that might now grow and broaden out in the world.[12] Such historical assumptions
as they were related to our text were too great in their implications for both Church
and state for Williams. Instead, he argued that Protestant communities that established national churches or saw themselves as Christian nations remained "Penin-
sula or necks of land, contiguous and joyned still" to Antichrist's "Christendome."[13]
In other words, from a theological point of view, the Bay Colony, or New England
generally, was no better and no worse than any other geographical region.

In his study reflecting upon the differences between Williams and Cotton,
Rosenmeier has referred to Williams as "the Witness," and Cotton as "the
Teacher."[14] Such a distinction appears appropriate in relation to our text. As a
witness, Williams worked in a disjunctive way in the world, pointing out how the
world and Christian faith differ. The teacher, Cotton, looked for the gradual but
increasing unity between life in the world and redemption. This difference in
historical consciousness is seen particularized in the question of the slaying of
the witnesses.[15] It is one that in different ways will continue to shape the American religious landscape.[16] For Williams, the division between the life of the Spirit
and that of the world[17] will not be healed until the advent of the millennial age
subsequent to a coming slaying of the witnesses.

Heralds of the Seventh Trumpet

Apocalyptic speculation sustained Cotton Mather (1663–1728), giving him new
avenues for hope, at a time when the optimistic vision of what it might be like to

be a part of God's restored Church and community in New England began to break down.[18] However, Mather seems not to have been drawn to the alternative ways of understanding the world that were being developed in those centers of intellectual life in the North Atlantic community in line with Baconian empiricism and Cartesian logic. Instead, he continued to find social coherence through the Bible and book of Revelation in particular.[19] Mather adopted the shape of the future as generally delineated by Joseph Mede and then William Whiston, rather than that of Thomas Brightman or even Thomas Goodwin.[20] This reflected a more pessimistic understanding of what it meant to build a colony in the wilderness of the New World, a loss of the earlier sense of mission or errand that was characteristic of the first two generations of Massachusetts Bay Colony settlers. In *A Midnight Cry*, Mather argued that "we are doubtless very near the Last Hours of the Wicked One, . . ." He feared, in *On Witchcraft*, that a final satanic attack upon the Church might be evident in the outbreak of witchcraft in New England.[21] Such a possible outbreak finds its historical coherence in relation to the view of the world that our text helped to foster.

The witnesses had lately walked the earth and all that remained prior to Judgment in the days of contemporary tribulation was the last blast of the angelic seventh trumpet. Was such related to witchcraft in Salem? The commentary of William Whiston (1667–1752) encouraged a sense of imminence.[22] Joseph Mede had postulated that all but the seventh vial had been poured out upon Rome, symbolized by the beast from the abyss (Rev. 11:7), but he was unsure of specific historical correlations after the third vial. Indeed, the debate was a lively one in Mather's day. Whiston argued that the vials would not be poured out until the sounding of the seventh trumpet. Which might it be? Mede's work implied a period of time for the outpouring of each vial. Hence, history might continue for an unspecified time. Whiston gave grounds for their rapid dispersal, even simultaneous outpouring, therefore a more cataclysmic end.

Applying such thinking to current events drew Mather eventually to think, in line with Whiston, that the persecution of Protestantism in France with the revocation of the Edict of Nantes (1685) was the event that portended a more imminent end. Although Mede placed the pouring of the vials under the sixth trumpet, others, like his student Henry More, placed them under the seventh, thus prolonging present history and further complicating apocalyptic prognostication.[23] Mede's growing sense of imminence followed not only Whiston but also Pierre Jurieu (1637–1713), who lent specificity to our text by arguing that France was the final apocalyptic (tenth) kingdom, that the witnesses were the Vaudois, expelled from their lands or slaughtered in 1686,[24] their restoration (1690) was their resurrection.[25]

Mather heralded Christ's imminent Advent with the publication of books on virtue, writing, "Yea, great will be the army of them that publish them! MDCC.XVI. is a-coming."[26] He believed that such works of what we might call "apocalyptic piety" were essential to Christian character and even appellation in the last days. In anticipation of Christ's Coming, Mather sought to bring all institutions into conformity with his understanding of this latter-day Christian piety. He writes:

I take the works of our day to be:

1. The reviving of primitive Christianity; to study and restore everything. . . . The time for cleansing the Temple comes on. . . . 2. The persuading of the European powers, to shake off the chains of popery. . . . 3. The forming and quickening of that People, that are to be, THE STONE CUT OUT OF THE MOUNTAIN. . . .[27]

This work mirrors the imagery of our text. The agenda for the first point is found in Revelation 11:1–2, the cleansing of the temple and measured separation of true worshippers from false, or Gentiles. The agenda for the second point is found in Revelation 11:3–6, the prophetic work of the witnesses. Mather's third point could easily be derived from a conflation of Revelation 11:11–15 with Daniel 2:44–45, the resurrection of the witnesses with the establishment of God's eternal kingdom following the divine destruction of the kingdoms of this world.

Mather prayed and looked for the promised gift of the Spirit. He felt it was coming and wrote, "There are many Arguments to persuade us that our Glorious LORD will have an Holy City in AMERICA."[28] Yet Middlekauff notes, "A single confusion ate into Mather's confidence—what of the witnesses? Had that event happened in some of the portentous developments on the European continent, or did their slaughter lie in the future as Sewall and others argued?"[29] Having eliminated alternative views as too strained or spiritualizing, Mather followed Mede, identifying Daniel's Day of Judgment (Dan. 7:13–14) with John's millennium (Rev. 20:1–3) thus marking Mather as what would later be called a premillennialist as it is the seemed Advent of Christ that would open the way to the millennium. Such questioning would continue to affect Protestant self-consciousness into and through the years of the Great Awakening, shaping pieties, Church polity, and social organization.

Preachers of Glory in Days of Adversity

The poignancy of the question about the witnesses' identity and all that was connected with it in terms of Protestant identity, the nature of the work of the ministry, and the place of the Church in history, and with respect to the social order, was picked up by others. However, none would be more significant than Jonathan Edwards (1703–1758). Edwards, leader of the Calvinist as opposed to religiously liberal party in colonial American society, developed millennial ideas that would become the key to understanding American social development after 1740. However, this Calvinism, no longer quite that which had been preached in Geneva in the sixteenth century, was characterized by such deepened historical interests by the eighteenth century that a scholar of Edwards, Alan Heimert, was led to write: "The heart and soul of Calvinism was not doctrine, but an implicit faith that God intended to establish this earthly Kingdom—and to do so within the eighteenth century."[30] Edwards's work, developing as it did around the Great Awakening, which seemed to him a portent of increasing millennial splendor, deepened theologically the progressivism inherent in the American religious imagination.

God's kingdom grew through periods of spiritual refreshment and revival. God's witnesses were instruments for effecting this work. They labored by preaching and by spiritual counsel to bring about that kingdom under what has been termed an "afflictive model of progress." Such a model assumed that the gospel glory and imputed righteousness came through times of distress and calamity. Salvation was achieved as the individual soul realized the reality of God's Judgment and found succor in the Saviour. What was true for the individual was in some way true for society. Through trials and affliction God's grace was found and God's kingdom advanced.[31]

As the Great Awakening progressed through the colonies, Edwards began to consider more carefully those last events which were believed to mark the way to God's kingdom in the millennial age.[32] Even when the Great Awakening faltered, Edwards still turned to the Apocalypse for "afflictive" encouragement.[33] Within this spirit he wrote "An Humble Attempt" (1747), an endorsement of a united effort of prayer for the advancement of Christ's kingdom.[34] Edwards defends the proposal by answering a series of objections to it. One of the most serious was that the Advent was not imminent since the witnesses had not been slain. To pray for a hastening of the apocalyptic timetable was not to pray for latter-day glory but for further calamity. Exegetes like Thomas Prince or Samuel Sewall argued that the future kingdom would follow a time of troubles adumbrated under the slaughter of the two witnesses. According to Edwards, such an interpretation of the prophecy undermined and dampened the objectives of the concert of prayer.[35]

The thrust of Edwards's argument is that the witnesses are the faithful, slain in the days leading up to and including the Reformation. The destruction of Antichrist began with the Protestant reformers. With the outpouring of the bowls of wrath the true Church has gained ascendancy.[36] The argument is substantiated by the fact that the book of Revelation describes two great battles, not one: The war of the beast against the witnesses (Rev. 11:7) and a last battle with Antichrist (chapters 16 and 19).[37] The slaughter of the witnesses[38] occurred in a first battle depicted in the witnesses' sackcloth dress (Rev. 11:3). In the second battle Christ rides forth in honor (Rev. 19:11–14; cf. Rev. 16:14–16).[39]

The results of the two conflicts are different. In the first (Rev. 11), the beast overcomes the witnesses.[40] In the last battle the Church will be victorious (Rev. 17:14).[41] The defeat of the witnesses (Rev. 11:8–9) can only be that time when the Church was in its lowest state, when Antichrist (the papacy) "prevailed against the Waldenses, Albigenses and Bohemians."[42] The Reformation best represents the rise and ascent of the witnesses (Rev. 11:11–12). Edwards adds,

> But tis not likely that a time yet remains wherein the Church of Christ will ever be reduced lower by a prevalence of popery, than it was before the Reformation; or so, but that there must remain more appearance, relics and monuments of the true religion, more of a remembrance of it, more of that light in the world, that will endanger popery and will tend to bring a return of Protestant principles.[43]

The fall of Antichrist is adumbrated in the ascent of the witnesses, the Protestant Reformation. Following Moses Lowman, Edwards sees this represented by the fifth vial (Rev. 16:10–11).[44] As the witnesses are said to stand upon their feet again (Rev. 11:11) so Protestantism is able to stand and defend itself. While the Church may be brought low again, it will never be brought as low as in those days immediately preceding the Reformation.[45] Christ's Church is gradually gaining ascendance in the world, but this will come through periods of trouble and even, perhaps, temporary bondage.[46] The fifth, perhaps even the sixth, vial had been poured out; God would not sacrifice these gains, Edwards believed.[47]

Edwards's description of the witnesses helped to define the work of ministry. His reflections parallel those noted by Heinrich Bullinger in the sixteenth century. The witnesses are envisioned as coming with the power of the Word of God, a power that is able to convert or destroy. Their cause is never unavenged. They are able to shut up the heavens. The plagues which they bring (Rev. 11:5–6) are the bowls of wrath (Rev. 16:1–21). These and the witnesses' description carry an allusion to Aaron and Moses. As the land of Egypt and Pharaoh (an image of the Antichrist) were struck down by plagues, so is Antichrist today:

> This is an argument that some of those plagues were executed before the Reformation; for the time of the prophecy of those two witnesses (so small in number) in sackcloth, was chiefly before the Reformation. And [it] was during that time chiefly that they executed that plague here spoken of, viz., of its not raining. For then, above all times after Christ's incarnation, were spiritual showers withheld from the earth.[48]

Early in his career Edwards felt that the first vial had been poured out in the days of Wyclif, Hus, and Jerome of Prague, the second in the Reformation. The "rivers" into which the third was being poured

> are those societies that are fountains of popery, fountains of popish doctrines, fountains of teachers of antichristianism; that continually send forth streams into every part to water the antichristian world. . . . The water is the doctrine; the streams or waterers, are the teachers.[49]

France is referred to as the grand fountain of popery. Later Edwards redates the specific alignment of vials and historical events guided by Moses Lowman's work, but he will lose none of his specificity.[50] Most importantly, all of the martyrs for the true religion are in a way adumbrated under our text. However, given the temporal development of the apocalyptic visions, some may be more precisely seen as such. The question of the identity of the witnesses was clear. They were embodied in fully reformed Protestant ministers who participated with the Spirit in building up God's new social order, his kingdom on earth.[51]

Looking for the Witnesses—Finding the Kingdom

The subject of prophecy, or in its broader lines, eschatology, as we have organized it around the theme of the two adventual witnesses provides a helpful framework for understanding the reform movements of the sixteenth century and their later institutional progeny.[52] Ideas pertaining to the end of personal life, or death, and corporate life, the end of history as we know it (personal and corporate eschatology), as conceived by Christian theorists, were related both to patterns of thought offering social coherence and established lines of moral authenticity. As such eschatological conceptions lent themselves to ways of being reconfigured, marked by the changing warp on which our witnesses were conceived, they permitted new churches and organizations to come into being. The search for the identity of the two witnesses has helped to illustrate this social dynamism. It has taken us down different paths illustrative of the interconnections among piety, polity, and politics. Different nuances in spirituality, often associated with an apocalyptic piety that has redefined the identity of our witnesses, has led to different forms of church structure and different patterns of social activity. By searching for the identity of our witnesses we have come across different conceptions of ways by which the kingdom of God has been conceived.[53]

One way of reading late medieval European history is to find it rent by two competing interpretations of history, both taking their guiding *figurae*, or symbols, from the book of Revelation.[54] The first, or tradition of Tyconius, was incorporated by Augustine, and in line with Jerome's spiritual understanding of the text, into Augustine's larger conception of history in *The City of God*. It elaborated a progressive historical vision that found a certain resolution in a present, or sixth, age of the Church, following upon earlier periods marked by Old Testament history but now unique in its opening by Christ and believed to last for a symbolic 1000 years. The spiritual dimensions of this age were known to the elect for whom the period constituted as well the Apocalypse-inspired seventh or millennial age of spiritual perfection prior to Christ's return for Judgment. While a set of primary apocalyptic images retained a place in history for Augustine, certain secondary images took on a more timeless character, descriptive of the perennial conflict between good and evil in this last age.[55] However, the implications for further historical momentum were always there. Although Christ himself had counselled a general agnosticism respecting the specificities of the end of the age (Matt. 24:36), still he had also left the impression that by keeping watch (Matt. 24:42–44) one might well be prepared for and discern something of the nature of those final events (Mark 13:4–37), which were never rectified by Augustine or his successors like Primasius in a way that was satisfactory to all.

A second interpretive line was embedded in that Church age as foreseen by earlier millennial, or chiliast, interpreters of the text such as Irenaeus, Tertullian, Victorinus, and Lactantius, a progression of symbols by which one might discern events so as to mark the progress of the Church from the present to a millennial age (one thousand years) on earth when Christ would fully rule.[56] These symbols became useful in the High Middle Ages by groups opposed to the Gregorian reforms in Church and society of the eleventh century. Ecclesial reformers like Rupert of Deutz (1070–1129/1135?), Otto of Freising (c. 1110–1158), Anselm of Havelberg (1100–1158), and Gerhoh of Reichersberg (1093–1169) laid out ideas that were later systematically arranged by Joachim of Fiore (c. 1132–1202), providing the Church with a second and historically progressive approach to understanding history through the *figurae* of the book of Revelation.[57]

For both, the primary apocalyptic images of the Second Advent (Acts 1:11; Rev. 16:15), general resurrection of the dead (Dan. 12:2; Rev. 20:13), and Last

Judgment by Christ (Matt. 25:31–33; Rev. 20:12) were interwoven with second-ary images suggestive of religious declension (Matt. 24: 37–39; 2 Thess. 2:3–12), the appearance of a power contrary to Christ, called, on the basis of a collated textual tradition from 1 John with the book of Revelation, the Apocalypse, "Anti-christ" (1 John 2:18; 4:3; 2 John 7; Rev. 11:7; Rev. 13:1–18), the appearance of final, or adventual, prophets (Rev. 10–11:12), and a first resurrection (Rev. 20:6) in distinction from the second and general resurrection. All of these symbols were then set in the context of a wider set of symbols that found historical significance in, first, the two mysterious revelatory scrolls, one larger and opened by Christ (Rev. 5:1, 7–10), one smaller and consumed by a final gospel preacher prior to a final call to repentance and belief (Rev. 10:2, 8–11), and, second, the series of seven seals (Rev. 6–8:5), trumpets (Rev. 8:6–11:19), and bowls of wrath (Rev. 15:7–16:21), which are envisioned serialized or in recapitulated order in the book of Revelation.

In Chapters 3 and 4 of this text we noted the way in which our theme became drawn into the conflict in understanding over the nature of prophecy and the work of prophets in the early years of the Protestant Reformation. This conflict was set within the context of the interplay of the primary and secondary apocalyptic sym-bols alluded to above. These explained the movement of history and, within such, communal identity. Thomas Müntzer and others were to draw understanding and inspiration from lines of thought evident in this late medieval mode of reading the Apocalypse. It can be easily argued that as Müntzer feared the "domestica-tion" of the reform movement under Luther, he turned more fully to Joachite and Taborite patterns of ecclesial radicalism seeking the establishment of a counter-Wittenberg in Bohemia, called for in the "Prague Manifesto." But Müntzer also sought to use consciously a millennialist, or chiliast, argument in his critique of the churches based, in part, upon his reading of the newly humanist discovered pre-Constantinian commentators on the book of Revelation.[58] Müntzer's hope for a new Christian order, fulfilled in the reign of the saints envisioned in his *Sermon Before the Princes*, was never entirely clear on the precise way in which Christ would hold sway in this period, whether through a bodily return and reign or in the deepened spiritual perceptivity of saints now living in a new period of time opened up by final, adventual, preachers (Rev. 11:3–13) and the Last Judgment.

Müntzer's disciple and heir, Hans Hut, one of the most successful Anabaptist preachers of a radically re-visioned Christian order, appears to have perceived Müntzer and his more secularly minded colleague, Heinrich Pfeiffer, as those adventual preachers who, preaching in the style of Enoch and Elijah, would open the way forward, either in themselves or as first examples of a line of similarly endowed prophets, into a new era of Christian history. Although Hut met an early demise, his message was carried on by the ever-more alienated Melchior Hoffman influenced as well by the Strassburg prophets and, perhaps, disciples of Hut with whom he came into contact as they fled growing repression around Augsburg. The vision seems also to have lasted in a Commentary on the Book of Revelation preserved by the Hutterite Brethren allegedly originating with Olivi.[59] When Hoffman met his end the prophetic mantle fell upon the new Enochs, Cornelius Poldermann and Jan Matthijs, who carried the vision further in ever-more idio-syncratic fashion.

Hoffman's forthright preaching and revelatory insights may have been taken from, and were certainly related or at least developed in parallel fashion to, the earlier visionary ideas of Peter John Olivi (c. 1248–1298), ideas that had formed the basis of a socially explosive set of biblical *figurae* combining a Joachite vision of history with Franciscan ecclesial dissent.[60] Hoffman's nuptial theology of baptism, bearing its own relationship with that older medieval pattern of theological union, deepened personally the corporate spiritual implications of the final historical conjunction envisioned in this interpretive tradition as occurring with Christ's second Advent, the return of the bridegroom for his bride, the Church (Eph. 5:21–33; Rev. 19:6–8). Spiritual perceptivity was now said to be deepened for those who lived in the consciousness of the new age. Later Hoffman, like Olivi in his day, would find within a sevenfold scheme of the history of the Church— marked by the successive opening, blaring, and pouring of the sevenfold seals, trumpets, and bowls since the first Advent—a further tripartite periodization of deepening spiritual understanding.[61] Ideas like these rocked the later medieval Church and served to add apocalyptic urgency not only to such dissident groups as the Fraticelli, Beghards, and, perhaps, Waldensians, but also to Taborite and other forms of late medieval radicalism from the thirteenth century through the fifteenth century.

Although much debate continues to turn around actual lines of connection between the medieval Joachite-Olivi tradition and its relation to later forms of dissent in church and society, some things are clear. Of the two lines of eschatological thought that are drawn into the sixteenth century, the Tyconian-Augustinian and Joachite traditions, Hoffman is beholden to both, but more particularly to the latter. His first resurrection is clearly spiritual, and his millennium plays itself out, as it did for Augustine, within a framework bounded by the two resurrections cited in the book of Revelation, for Hoffman, specifically in the apostolic age when Christ's reign was uncontested. However, where he differed from Augustine was in his conception of the Church, which lacked the concrete specificity and sacramental authority appropriated by the Latin Catholic Church of the Middle Ages and in having developed a second millennial period coterminous with his third age of the Spirit, an idea having affinity with the larger Joachite vision of history and historical development.

A renewed apocalyptic tension was briefly attractive to and a part of the eschatological thinking of the early Martin Luther, although he soon withdrew from active and public speculation about such troublesome matters. The Lutherist movement itself was first hailed, at least honorifically, as the fulfillment of that hope envisioned as coming with final adventual preaching.[62] In fact, it can be argued that chiliastic concerns seem not to have divided Luther from Hoffman as much as they did the Lutheran Nikolaus Amsdorf from Hoffman, Amsdorf having taken Hoffman to task on the matter in a series of discussions. Nevertheless, Luther quickly dropped any personal association between himself and such adventual preaching as was hoped to occur in popular imagination, arguing instead that the renewed preaching of the gospel was itself that which would open the way toward the Last Judgment and God's eternal kingdom. This move was quite the opposite of that personal association that was in process of development in Müntzer, Hut, and Hoffman's thinking where a proper spiritual perceptivity led one to look for final prophets as part of a matrix of last things. For Luther, a second model of eschatology loomed larger, one that found its locus of authority more in the gospel message itself rather than in a deepened perception of it borne by special prophets in or on the verge of a new age of history. It was a view that sprang from a sharp sense of the Judgment that awaited every believer, whether at death or the end of time, and, contrariwise, called the Christian to live fully in the orders of this world, unchanged since the days of Noah.[63] Here the prophet functioned as spiritual teacher and "forth-teller." The perennial gospel, which offered hope for all born under the Law, carried its own crisis, or eschatological import, in the person and message of Jesus Christ.

In Chapters 5 and 6 of this text it was noted that that reform which was begun by Luther, with such clear eschatological if not apocalyptic implications, was carried on in the Reformed community, which while it also with Luther consciously sought to re-establish something of the old Israel in the days of God's new community, the Church, and new Israel, the Reformed appeared to do so more in light of the new civic consciousness fostered by the Renaissance, but not apart from a confidence in the final triumph of Christ to restore all things. For both Luther and Calvin the new age was that of the Church. As such it participated in the spiritually suffused millennial perspective laid down by Augustine. But, whereas for Augustine that age was best understood in its other-worldly dimensions and dispensed in its earthly reality by the graces believed to have been given the Church, for the Reformed, at least—and as shadowed in the theological optimism of Calvin, who, despite the ravages of sin, held to the final triumph of Christ in the time and space of the world—that kingdom was felt to be an expression of what one might work toward in the process of personal and corporate sanctification.[64]

Among the Reformed, and with Calvin in particular, the topic of personal eschatology arose, a part of his anti-Anabaptist polemic, becoming an additional aspect of eschatology open to intense debate in the sixteenth century. This personal, rather than corporate, perspective on "last things," the experience of the believer at death (Rev. 14:13), is a topic that could include extreme unction and go on to purgatory, hell, and paradise. It was another dimension of the debate now opened anew between those who believed in the natural immortality of the soul and those who revived a scriptural view that suggested the death or sleep of the soul until the great and corporate resurrection. The importance of such a development can be seen on at least two counts. First is the way in which the death of the soul played a role in radical thinking (i.e., the way in which Christian mortalism combined with millennialist thinking in the latter's stress upon a final Christian age on earth ruled by the saints restored to life). Here the resurrection of the flesh is accented in line with Revelation 20:12–13, there being no place or function for those who have otherwise died, apart from the analogy with Christ's resurrection, no evidence for the implicit nominalism embedded in this perspective for natural immortality. Second, Calvin's thinking about the continued consciousness of the departed soul and the role that such plays in a spiritualized millennial perspective (as saints "under the alter" [Rev. 6:9–11] continue to participate in the life of the Church), had the effect of bringing renewed vigor to an Augustinian seventh age (coterminous with the then present, or sixth, age of the

Church) that opened up at Christ's first Advent. Such was made real, in terms of its spiritual benefits, for the individual at baptism, a sacrament or ordinance reconceived by the Reformed in line with covenant theology.[65] Here, together with that spiritualized but progressive millennial state, our witnesses were conceived in a representative and symbolic way.

Bearing Calvin's idea of personal eschatology in mind, we can return to developments in corporate eschatology which, in Reformed thinking was related to the call to kingdom and priesthood in Revelation 1:6. The terrain of such had been mapped for its past and contemporary significance in the sixteenth century by the heirs of Joachim of Fiore as well as others representative of the wider theological and more recent social Hussite traditions. Future eschatological hope begins to become increasingly subject to further definition and redefinition in the sixteenth century and thereafter. The reason why the scope of eschatological map-making now shifts from the past as it touches upon contemporary events to the present as is defined by and participates in the future probably has as much to do with the fact that Augustine's symbolic millennial period of the Church begins to become ever-more tenuous with the passing of the years, no matter how many epicycles might be added to it, as with any other cause whether social or theological.[66]

The growing momentum to locate God's kingdom was pictured more particularly in the work of Heinrich Bullinger whose series of sermons on the Apocalypse would mark and then help to fill out the lineaments of an ongoing Continental Reformed and later Anglo-American understanding of the nature of Christian eschatology as it pertained to the millennium. Nevertheless, it was the idea of the prophet as "forth-teller" that was dominant in the Lutheran and Reformed communities. Enochs, Elijahs, and Jeremiahs were to fill the new Protestant pulpits instructing the new Israel how to live in the age of Lord Christ, perhaps a first or second millennial age.[67] Such thinking would border on a Christomonism, carrying forward Latin and Western theological tendencies from at least the days of the addition of the *filioque* clause in the eighth century into the modern era. Nevertheless, the idea of a living, even foretelling prophecy (as in Brocard), did not die out in the Reformed community in the interests of such prophecy. Rather, it lived on in tension and remained vibrant in different sectors of thinking and practice to break out anew in twentieth-century charismatic movements.

Such tension could be seen in the unfolding of Reformed thinking around Paul's instruction in 1 Corinthians 14:29–31. Paul, facing the phenomenon of the gift of tongues in the early Church, declared: "Let two or three prophets speak, and let the others weigh what is said. If a revelation [clarification] is made to another sitting (*sedenti*), let the first be silent." Eventually the rule for speaking up in conventicle or synod in the face of opened Scripture would be called the *lex sedentium*, in German: *Sitzerrecht*. In this text Paul was sorting out the rules for prophetic glossolalia and the proper order for congregational (or synodal) interpretation of the meaning of Scripture, sometimes including evidently the participation of the sisters in searching colloquy despite his injunction of silence on women in the same text. Were all of those our witnesses in a kind of Reformed and representative sense?

The first of the "Reformed" to use 1 Corinthians 14:29–31 as the basis of common prophecy (*prophetia communis*) or "prophecying" (the later English Puritan term) was evidently Zwingli. We noted earlier that Zwingli's answer to the larger question of prophecy and prophetic legitimacy is seen, in part, in the institution of the *Prophezei*. Begun in June 1525, "prophesying" first took the form of public lectures in the Grossmünster, replacing the canonical hours of Prime, Terce, and Sext.[68] This institution functioned without specific apocalyptic concerns. It focused upon the proclamation of the gospel and God's law. The parallels were between efforts at reform in a local situation and the work of the prophets in the Old Testament for national renewal. In his commentary on Revelation 10:11, Zwingli's successor, Heinrich Bullinger, would find a commission for Reformed ministers primarily in ancient models in the Old Testament and others added in the New Testament, not, however, through any historical prophetic or apostolic succession. He believed that the "evangelical and apostolic doctrine against Antichrist (the Roman papacy) and Muhammad must be restored in the last times before judgment."[69] Such thinking reinforced a representative interpretation of our text.

Zürich's institution of the Prophezei, a kind of early Bible school and precursor of the University of Zürich, altered the daily office and yearly calendar of the Christian year to raise up a more direct reading and application of the Word. However, it was in Marburg, with the Zwingli-influenced and former Franciscan Francis Lambert of Avignon that a similar though even more charismatically suffused gathering of the Reformed saints would practice a kind of early *lex sedentium*, each speaking the Law of God to oneself and the other as perceived from the direction of the Spirit. Lambert had been in Zürich in 1522–23. In Wittenberg he received support from Luther and married. Successively in Metz and Strassburg, living in apostolic poverty and writing treatises and commentaries on the Old Testament prophets, Lambert was called to Hesse in 1526 by Landgrave Philip in order to reorganize the Church and teach at the newly established University of Marburg. In the synod of Homberg of 1526, a Church order was adopted that drew inspiration from Luther's "congregationalism." Lambert attached importance to lay participation and gave prominence to the *lex sedentium*, a principle of biblically informed inquiry, discourse, and colloquy, which was carried over into the Marburg Colloquy of 1529, in which the prophets of Zürich and the professors of Wittenberg matched scriptural wits over the main issue that divided the Protestant churches, the Eucharist.[70]

Like Zwingli, Lambert was concerned about the function of prophecy in the Church. The institution of the Prophezei in Hesse was influenced not only by Lambert's experience in Zürich, but also by his stay in Strassburg. He had heard in the latter city of the Strassburg prophets and could think of that experience in light of what he had first learned from Zwingli, which situation in Strassburg with its contacts establishes an ongoing debate over the extent to which Joachite ideas permeate Lambert's work. In a letter to Charles V, Lambert was to argue that prophecy—the interpretation of events to come and events past as well as the interpretation of Scripture for the present—should be established by every Christian prince in his realm. In his *Commentary on the Apocalypse*, Lambert indicated that his own age is represented by the opening of the sixth seal of the great wrath (Rev. 6:12–17), the time for the disclosure of Antichrist in Pope and Turk. True preaching therefore faces Antichrist's persecution (as shown in Rev. 11 and 13).

It might be said that at Marburg a democratic sense of the Spirit-induced prophet was merged with the idea of the preacher as teacher. The eschatological significance of such would become more apparent in Reformed communities in the Kingdom of Poland-Lithuania and Transylvania, pointedly raised up in the Pinczovian Confession (1559). The idea of the prophet as teacher would continue well into the future of Protestant consciousness through that confession's emphasis upon the threefold offices of Christ (*triplex munus Christi*), namely Christ as prophet, priest, and king. Each of these offices, as applicable to the believer, found a place for the mystical rule of Christ through new saints as envisioned by the prophet Joel for new prophets (Joel 2:28; Acts 2:17), by Jeremiah of priests (Jer. 31:33; 1 Peter 2:9), and by Daniel for rule (Dan. 7:27; Matt. 25:34). Such offices, given charismatic warrant by Paul (1 Cor. 12:7–11), found expression in the Apocalypse of John (Rev. 1:6; 20:4). Such theology strengthened a representative reading of our text.

Corporate eschatology, always related to an expression of final Judgment, became increasingly bound up with questions of governance made doubly significant then with the internal prompting of the Spirit affirmed (eventually for women as well as for men) in the period of Protestant development from the sixteenth through the nineteenth centuries.[71] This appears to be more true in the areas touched by Reformed theology than in those under Lutheran sway. Luther was critical of the medieval domestication of the eschaton and edited with ironic glosses and a polemical postscript a work by Giovanni Nanni that claimed the papal church as the kingdom of God.[72] However, millenarian thinking played no role in Luther's theology despite his interest in history and apocalyptic symbolism.[73] Rather, corporate eschatology for Luther is found more in a dialectic that parallels his idea of *simul justus et peccator,* or that of two kingdoms. The millennial age and reality of Christ's victory is something that one has, and yet does not have—a kind of realized yet delayed gratification. Each offsets the other.[74] While not differing from Luther on the nature of the millennium, Zwingli and Calvin, and in particular Martin Bucer, drew the Reformed community in a markedly different direction. Their emphasis upon what might be called an eschatology of Resurrection rather than that of Judgment (Luther) tied the idea of election to the realization of the will of God in history and created the theological atmosphere for a progressively actualized kingdom of Christ in time, particularly as later some Reformed theologians developed a diminished understanding of sin.[75]

By contrast with the spiritual and Augustinian conception of the millennium as held, albeit differently, by Luther and then Calvin, and as further developed by the Reformed after Bullinger, the historian Philip Schaff reminds us that throughout most of the history of the Church, chiliasm was identified with millennialism and was usually interpreted as what would be called from the end of the nineteenth century on "premillennialism," i.e, a belief that Christ would come to establish his earthly reign for 1000 years prior to the last Judgment.[76] This view was developed in incipient form by Justin Martyr, Tertullian, Hippolytus, and Irenaeus in the first years of the Church.[77] It was Augustine who (following Origen and Jerome), in opposition to such millenarians, led the way to a spiritual interpretation of the millennium in *The City of God*,[78] a perspective that would as well undermine the political and, if we use the word loosely, "millennial" optimism of the Eusebian-inspired reign of Constantine (sometimes interpreted as an early form of what later would be called "postmillennialism").[79]

The corporate eschatology affirmed by the Reformed, although pointedly critical of the millenarian tendencies of Müntzer and Hut, and of the modified Augustinian position of Melchior Hoffman, would, after the passage of a number of years, come to resemble, at least in architectonics, several of the more radical systems of eschatological thought inherited by European society from the late medieval period and that we have seen in play in the early years of the Reformation. Before offering some speculation on why this was the case, the reasons why the early Reformed distanced themselves from the radicals on this score should be mentioned. Criticism came from two directions. In the first instance there was the predilection for a Church—the nature of which would be defined more by Christological interests similar to Thomas Aquinas rather than to Joachim of Fiore—and the implications that this had for religious knowledge and ecclesial participation. Second, it must be remembered that Bucer, Bullinger, and Calvin all wrote in the aftermath of the Anabaptist debacle of Münster. The first edition of Calvin's *Institutes* (1536), was written both to explain the evangelical faith and to defend the reform movement from charges of social sedition and ideas characteristic of religious radicalism against the larger political framework of a Europe under siege from the Ottoman Empire.[80]

The reasons why the Reformed were drawn to speculation on the corporate dimensions of eschatology are manifold. The first reason certainly grows out of the different eschatological perspective cited above that separated Luther from Bucer and Calvin. Second, in their search for religious peace on the Continent, the Reformed, more internationally dispersed than the Lutherans, were drawn to the visions of ecclesial unity in the Apocalypse. Such seems to be the case with David Pareus.[81] Third, as with all other aspects of knowledge, eschatological matters were drawn into the increasingly prevailing Ramist logic and made subject to it as in the thinking of Johann Heinrich Alsted.[82] Fourth, although the early Reformed were theologically and ideologically committed to an Augustinian understanding of the millennium, finding it as that spiritual condition one entered into in the era between Christ's two comings—distanced as they now were from the first Advent—opened up the position to the kind of deepened spiritual reflection characterized in the Reformed Spiritualist James Brocard.[83] Fifth, the pressures of the age and interests in humanist historiography also pushed the question of literalization, which we find in such tension with an earlier spiritual understanding of our text in the *Sermons on the Apocalypse* of Heinrich Bullinger. The martyrological histories of John Foxe represent such development. Sixth, one aspect of contemporary social pressure lies in the religious polemics of the age, which for Francis Junius (1545–1602) drew out of the Apocalypse a trenchant and acerbic criticism of Roman Catholicism after the Council of Trent.[84] Seventh, as Protestants became involved in the new statecraft of the sixteenth and seventeenth centuries the earlier question of Christian discipline as it applied to the individual and to Christian societies—raised first by Martin Bucer and, pointedly for Edward VI in England (1537–1553), in Bucer's work *On the Kingdom of Christ (De regno Christi)*—emerged as a factor as questions about the "how" of Christ's rule would be raised up in Puritan debates through the seventeenth century and then central to the Protestant missionary effort in the eighteenth and nineteenth centuries.[85]

In Chapters 7 and 8 we noted the development in corporate eschatological or, more particularly, apocalyptic thinking as it related issues of governance to the timing of a literal millennium, point of its beginning and end, the complete or partial binding of Satan, and way in which Christ would rule. Again, Bullinger's *Sermons on the Apocalypse* (1557; English translation, 1561)[86] appeared to have played an important role in shaping discussion from the Kingdom of Poland-Lithuania to England. However, given the influence of the Reformed in English society and their central role in the debate over its political shape, further speculation about the millennium became rich and varied. Individuals like John Foxe, Thomas Brightman, Joseph Mede, and Thomas Goodwin forged ideas drawing as they did upon a wider Continental circle of commentators that would be named in the nineteenth and early twentieth centuries "a-", "post-", and "premillennialism," terms we commonly use today and read back into the earliest phases of corporate eschatological speculation in the early Church and into the radical renewal and reform in the opening days of sixteenth-century Church upheaval.

Working with unresolved issues in the interpretive historical scheme of Bullinger, as developed in relation to the Apocalypse, John Foxe more carefully dated and located in history the millennium as a part of his vast and influential martyrological studies related, as they were, to our text.[87] It is in Foxe's work that we can see the Joachite dimension of Bullinger's interpretive scheme. The rise of evil and "Antichrists" in society begin to overwhelm the Tyconian-Augustinian timeless understanding of the book. So also, a new attempt to understand our witnesses' identity in time is visible. What was held in tension by Bullinger is set in play by Foxe. It is as if Foxe begins a development for Protestantism such as had earlier occurred within Joachite medieval Catholicism. Each "school" (Roman Catholic and Protestant) of Christianity, beginning with a spiritual millennium but under the interests germane to each, made concrete that spiritually millennial age. For medieval Catholicism such was done in the interests of the Church under the vicar of Christ reigning in Rome. For Protestants, members of Christ's extending earthly kingdom, in process of becoming pure in preparation to meet its groom, the Lord Christ, such was done in the interests of national churches and under the vicarage of Christian kings, parliaments, and national legislatures.

Protestant millennialism developed essentially within the same lines of Augustinian interpretation as had medieval Catholicism. Both shared with Augustine the idea of the first resurrection (Rev. 20:4–6) as that which happens at one's baptism and upon confession of faith. It is the spiritual awakening and new birth of one's entering into the fulness of the spiritual life. The second resurrection (Rev. 20:5, 11–15) is that call to Judgment which follows the millennial reign of Christ. However, whereas medieval Latin Christianity had located that millennial reign mystically in heaven under Christ and visibly on earth with his vicar the bishop of Rome, Protestantism now found the place of the millennium in the expanding northern European Protestant kingdoms and nation-states. God's two witnesses, representatively conceived, were bringing in this new age.

What Foxe made more specific in Bullinger, finding his concrete church (and in a way his millennium) wherever the faith was openly preached and then by martyr-witnesses, Thomas Brightman made more real and visual for English Puritanism and thence for Anglo-American piety, in a double millennium, seen earlier in Francis Junius, one that was parallel to that of Foxe's in the past, and a second opened up during the reign of Elizabeth I and in the new technologies of printing and transportation which enabled the Word to go forth.[88] Brightman's views have been described as "a watershed from which two great streams flow in opposite directions."[89] While working in the Augustinian tradition, Brightman divides and periodizes the history of the Church into two millennial ages. Those millennia are fixed and historical. Arguing against the Catholic futurist Francesco de Ribeira, Brightman follows in the historicist school of interpretation so richly carved out by Foxe. Furthermore, there is an implicit optimism woven into Brightman's perspective as he not only finds the Church rewarded in this historical age, but places the traumatic vision of apocalyptic tribulation (Rev. 11:7–10) in the past with the destruction of the papacy and the Turks, which he felt was near completion in his own day.

Brightman's successor in this vision, and innovator in his own right, Daniel Whitby (1638–1726),[90] is the one often credited with formulating the position later to be called "postmillennialism" as it placed the thousand years of Christ's rule in the spiritual reign of his saints, our witnesses, increasing in dominion and spiritual perceptivity prior to the second Advent of Christ (Rev. 19:7). Augustine's spiritual millennium, having been placed once again concretely in history, now became subject to more particular questions touching on the place of worldwide evangelism; the nature of a rapture for believers out of tumultuous, even satanic, historical conditions; and the time of the long-awaited conversion of the Jews (Rom. 11:25–32). While there is some debate over the one to whom the honor of restoring millenarianism properly belongs,[91] it appears most likely that at least for the Anglo-American world it was Whitby's near contemporary, and mystical theologian, Joseph Mede, who would lay down some of the first ideas by a respected theologian, incorporating many of the more debated intricacies of apocalyptic speculation in a system that would later contribute to what would be referred to as "premillennialism" in the nineteenth century.[92] Although for Mede, in contrast to later premillennialists (but with some affinities to later and quite different Jehovah's Witnesses), Chirst returns to establish the millennial kingdom but then returns to heaven while the saints themselves rule upon earth for a thousand years (thereby developing an idea of three advents seen earlier in Peter John Olivi).

In the present chapter we began by briefly tracing the way in which our text was taken up in debates that were central to the development of religious and general cultural consciousness in the colonies of New England. Although of perennial interest, it was the influence of Jonathan Edwards that added focused interest to the agenda outlined by our text.[93] The optimism surrounding the religious revivals of the 1740s, the role they were believed to play in furthering

Christ's kingdom, and reflection upon such evolution as applied to human activity, and specifically a Protestant missions movement that would develop with explosive growth after 1790 (mission, a task entrusted to the witnesses in traditional exegesis), called forth such interest on adventual and millennial issues.

The aftermath of the Great Awakening in the Anglo-American world, at first positive in its support of the older Protestant vision (formed and then re-formed in Puritan debate), carried our theme into the nineteenth century but with increasing dimensions of uncertainty after the American Revolution. It has been argued that as the idea developed, following the Great Awakening, that Christ's millennial kingdom demanded human effort, the religious culture of the late eighteenth century began to delineate what such activity might entail and how it would come into being.[94] This discussion drew attention to our witnesses and their role in bringing in or standing as harbingers of Christ's kingdom, the latter clearly categorized by Samuel Hopkins (1721–1803) in his treatise on the millennium.[95] In its way, Hopkins's work can be seen as adding an inherent human activism to God's agenda in history characteristic of Western moral theology.

The end of the eighteenth century also saw lines of interpretation develop around our text, which conceived of the slaying of the witnesses still to lie in the future as seen in Roger Williams or Cotton Mather, implying both a less direct connection between our text and Protestantism and a future still filled with tribulation rather than dawning millennial bliss. While initially theoretical and somewhat arcane, movements like the Adventists would grow out of similar lines of thought as such distilled in the popular culture in the years of the Second Great Awakening (c. 1787–1825) and the work of William Miller (1782–1849).[96] Additionally, political events on the European continent, particularly the French Revolution and the social disruptions connected with it, served to alter in its way speculation on the nature of corporate eschatology and time of the millennium.[97] These democratic revolutions along with the development of historical and biblical criticism—itself subject to new patterns of understanding that had emerged from a heightened empiricism after Locke and Cartesian logic, as both were undergoing revolutionary change in the speculation of Immanuel Kant—carry us forward into a different speculative landscape that is both more sociologically active and eventually historically pessimistic or uncertain of the nature of Protestantism.[98]

Surprisingly, it was a disaffected Jesuit, Manuel Lacunza (1731–1801), who sets the agenda for further interpretive developments on our text following his expulsion from Chile and settlement in Italy at the time of the dissolution of the Roman Catholic Society of Jesus (Jesuits). There he wrote a commentary under the pseudonym of a Jewish convert to Christianity, Ben Ezra, that was published in 1812 and translated and published in English by the controversial and erstwhile British Presbyterian Edward Irving (1792–1834).[99] Lacunza delineated a still future and final proclamation of the gospel prior to the second Advent of Christ, who would come to earth to reign on earth together with his saints (a view held by some Fifth Monarchists and others in the era of the Puritan Revolution) for a thousand years until the final Judgment.[100] Such views were incorporated into the revival efforts of Edward Irving. More significantly, they are similar to those developed by John Nelson Darby (1800–1882), made popular and further systematized through the Niagara (-on-the-Lake, Ontario) Bible and other prophecy conferences in Great Britain and North America in the latter third of the nineteenth century (1868–).[101] Popular enthusiasm for such came through Christian sectarian and other groups animated, or reanimated, in part by the Second Great Awakening and later urban and prayer revivals in North America and Europe.[102] Together with an enlivened kingdom of God theology and charismatic Pietism in Germany, and the *reveil* in the French-speaking world, popular Protestantism moved almost *en masse* away from the older understanding of millennial issues to a Darbyite premillennialism. In this context the older Protestant vision and self-understanding—organized to the extent it was around our witnesses—was increasingly suffused after the American Civil War not with the transcendence of Jonathan Edwards but with a newly critically informed sense of natural development and divine immanence.[103]

The older Protestant view of the millennium, which conceived of a present spiritually progressive age, continued to have its defenders, weakened as it was by new canons of internal biblical criticism and changes in historical scholarship. Prominent among such defenders was George Stanley Faber (1773–1854) who argued that our two witnesses were the Waldensians and Albigenses. Their death and resurrection were accomplished in their banishment from the Piedmont valleys in 1686 and glorious return three and a half years later.[104] According to Faber, Christ had made two promises to the Church: (1) the Church would exist forever as a visible Church, and (2) it would remain a pure Church.[105] It was important to find this body in history. He did so by pointing to a line of dissenting sectarian bodies in European ecclesiastical life. The theological ancestors of the Albigenses were the Paulicians of Armenia who migrated to Europe where, as Cathars, they were falsely charged with Manichaeism.[106] The two churches, the Albigenses and Waldensians, the latter of great antiquity from the Vaudois, are connected with our text as the two witnessing churches of the Apocalypse.[107]

Faber (and Protestant historicist exegesis) was pointedly challenged on our theme by S. R. Maitland, who argued that the Algibenses and Waldensians were not the apocalyptic witnesses. He signalled thereby both the new awareness of biblical criticism and a less harsh understanding of Roman Catholicism, the communion adopted by his contemporary and former evangelical, then Anglican, John Henry Cardinal Newman (1801–1890). While precursors of Protestantism may have existed prior to Luther and Calvin, Maitland argued that there is not a pure ecclesiastical line running through the Paulicians, Cathars, Albigenses, and Waldensians. Indeed, some of these groups were quite heretical![108] Edward B. Elliott took up the challenge laid down by Maitland and others.[109] His commentary interpreted the entire Apocalypse through the structural elements provided for by our text.[110] Others now followed Grotius and Alcasar earlier, reading other events in the text into the distant past. Some praeterists (those believing that the Apocalypse was written for and speaks best to the first century A.D.), in distinction from Protestant historicists and futurists, offered certain qualifications to this view but suggested little in the way of new speculation. Others continued the futurist line noted earlier in Protestant sectarian interpretation placing the appearance of the witnesses at the end of history, returning traditional Augustinian perspectives to some form of early Church chiliasm, adopting premillennialism.

This latter development in millennial thought followed Joseph Mede's work in the seventeenth century. It constituted the next creative period for apocalyptic speculation, millennialism, and attendant doctrines of the nature of end-time trials and tribulation, raising up and offering as part of an age given to empiricism a greater specificity of meaning within grand historical and dispensational schemes of the linear progression of time. Chiliasm, stigmatized since Origen as too literal and Jewish a vision of the millennium, now gained a new hearing. The way had been prepared by the literalization of the Augustinian vision through decades of largely Anglo-American speculation on it, often understood since Whitby as earthly and spiritually progressive. The historical and the specific nature of that millennium had been accepted, but within an Augustinian framework. It now only took the breakdown of that Protestant vision of history and its spiritual understanding of the Resurrection to occur for the way to be opened widely for a reevaluation of the older and previously rejected chiliasm.

By the beginning of the twentieth century the term "antimillennial" began to appear, probably in reaction to the now popular Protestant (pre-)millennial fervor. Until the middle of the nineteenth century, an Augustinian (but now post-) millennial, or "Whitbian," perspective had held sway, invigorating the Protestant movement and reaching, perhaps, its apex in North America under the Jonathan Edwards-inspired and Presbyterian republican Princeton Theological Seminary, with its chief defender Charles Hodge, and Andover (Academy and Seminary)

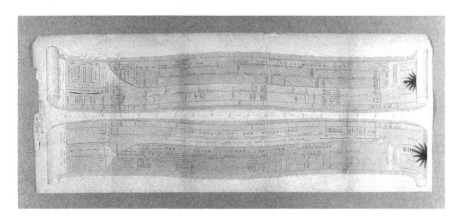

The Two Witnesses and the Structure of Time

Edward Bishop Elliott. *Horae Apocalypticae, or A Commentary on the Apocalypse Critical and Historical.* . . . 3 volumes. London: Seeley, Burnside, and Seeley, 1844. The witnesses' work lends structure to two-thirds of this chart, which depicts history as envisioned by the seven-sealed apocalyptic scroll (Rev. 5:1). The time of their preaching, ca. A.D. 533–1789 or 1800 (1260 years), is additionally and particularly defined by the rise and development of Protestantism.

theologian Moses Stuart (1780-1852) standing contrary to the millenarians or chiliasts.[111] Both Princeton and Andover championed Scottish Commonsense Realism in their epistemological attempt to wed a scientific biblical criticism to a conservative view of the inspiration and authority of the Bible. For many at both institutions, which stood at the center of an American Protestant Orthodoxy as inherited from an earlier Anglo-American Puritanism, that epistemological conception was embedded in a philosophy of history now largely oriented around our witnesses. As that frame of mind that understood the world was being challenged, so also was the historical explanation of momentum in history as it had been fashioned since the sixteenth century.[111a] With two schools of literal millennial interpretation now competing with each other (a developmental vs. cataclysmic millennialism), and the older Protestantism now compromised with theories of natural development, confusion ensued as Darbyite and other popular Protestant groups vied with a Whitbian "post-millennial" perspective that was losing its influence.[112] Such was true particularly among Protestants now attuned to new perspectives on history developing independently, and often in relation to Kantian categories of thought, from that of the older Protestant historiography.

Controversy in the churches and their nascent seminaries broke out in the last third of the nineteenth century not only over issues of the place and value of biblical criticism but also over the implications this, and other sensitivities, bore on the dynamic of the larger Protestant vision worked out in relation to our text. This controversy had effects upon theories of the Church and its missions movement, tied as they conceptually had been to the larger thrusts of our text.[113] Controversy surfaced on the nature of and necessity for the proclamation of the gospel, the task of our witnesses, and in the American Board of Commissioners for Foreign Missions over questions of Congregational identity and the theological subscription of its missionary candidates. It was theologically pointed at Andover Seminary (the "Andover Controversy") when between 1886–1893 debate focused on the doctrine of "future probation," namely that those dying without knowledge of the gospel in this life would gain another chance in the future to accept or reject the gospel prior to Judgment.[114] The controversy was part of the larger debate over the immanence of God, the nature of Christian conversion, and an increasingly secular definition of social transformation rather than millennial transfiguration in history marked by the Andover Liberals.[115] This process was most clearly seen in the development of the social gospel from Washington Gladden (1836–1918), Josiah Strong (1847–1916), Gerald Smith (1868–1929), Lyman Abbott (1835–1922), Richard Ely (1854–1943), and to John Dewey (1859–1952).[116]

By the end of the nineteenth century one begins to observe the prefixes "pre-" and "post-" afixed to the term "millennial." The older (early Church) millennialists were called "premillennial" as they looked for the return of Christ before the millennium; the old Protestant Augustinians were called "postmillennial" as they looked for the return of Christ after the now literalized millennium. Additionally, out of this latter group emerged those who sought to retain Augustinian spiritual categories (i.e., a millennium without the literal and earthly implications). These antimillennialists were called "a-millennialists" by the Dutch Calvinist Gerhardus Vos as against the Darbyites who now were understood by the early twentieth century to be pretribulationist, premillennialist dispensationalists.[117] By the early years of the twentieth century, then, three different millennial options had been defined, pre-millennial, post-millennial, and a-millennial, which, when applied backwards through history, help us to type the perspectives of many of the earlier groups that held consciously to different conceptions of the progression of history.[118]

If we think back upon the first prophesying among the "fore-tellers" and "forth-tellers" in the dawn of that ferment that set the Reformation period in motion in terms of the hopes and, indeed, the expectations that were generated, we can think of those preachers and prophets now in terms of the millennial typology that has been further delineated through reflection and debate upon the direction of the Christian movement and its churches.[119] It was historian and theologian of the New Testament Ernst Käsemann who in this century reaffirmed the centrality of eschatology to Christian thinking and community building by declaring apocalypticism to be the mother of all Christian theology." More recently Jürgen Moltmann has argued similarly about the nurturing and visioning power of Christian apocalypticism.[120]

In terms of the millennial visions that we have now seen sketched, and the way in which debate over the identity of our two witnesses has served as a doorway to those visions, we might summarize as follows: Melchior Hoffman's thought bridges the worlds of Augustine and the millennialists. Thomas Müntzer and Hans Hut would probably be viewed by current standards as premillennialists. However, given the role of the elect in purifying society and, then, depending upon their understanding of the kingdom that was to emerge, they might be classified as proto-postmillennialists. Some things are simply not clear in all of their thinking. Luther and Calvin were clearly by later standards a-millennialists. However, we have noted so much movement in Calvin's own eschatology, and even more in the Reformed movement that was to be, in part, in debt to him—as well as to Martin Bucer and Heinrich Bullinger insofar as eschatology is concerned—that we dare not be too definitive except to say that he clearly divided himself from current (pre-) millennial or chiliast thinking. However, it would probably be equally dangerous to identify Calvin with the progressive rhapsodies of Johann Alsted or Thomas Brightman, which bore such significance for the optimistic development of culture in the North Atlantic world under a post-millennial vision. Certainly the excesses of Münster, the atmosphere in which the first editions of the *Institutes of the Christian Religion* were drafted, were far from the New Jerusalem that Calvin envisioned though both were driven by a kindred Christian hope, if not optimism. Finally, as Reformed apocalypticism was carried to the colonies of North America it had much to do with the shaping of the vision and work of those charged with, or appropriating for themselves, the building up of God's new temple and kingdom in America and in the uttermost parts of the earth (Mark 13:10; Isa. 42:4; 60:9).[121]

Notes

1. Thomas Goodwin, *Exposition upon the Revelation*, in *The works of Thomas Goodwin, D.D.* (Edinburgh: James Nichol, 1861), p. 130.

2. Sacvan Bercovitch, "The Typology of America's Mission," *American Quarterly*, 30 (1978):135–55. The term "Errand in the Wilderness" is found in an election sermon preached by Samuel Danforth on May 11, 1670. See the essay of that title by Perry Miller stressing the moral dimensions of this task in *Errand into the Wilderness*, (Cambridge: Harvard University Press, 1956), pp. 1–15. The wider implications of this errand are draown by Geroge H. Williams, *Wilderness and Paradise in Christian Thought* (New York: Harper and Brothers, 1962), pp. 98–132.

3. Peter Gay draws out the turmoil in historical reflection for Puritan historians in New England who attempted to assess and justify their identity against shifting realities. See *A Loss of Mastery. Puritan Historians in Colonial America* (Berkeley: University of California Press, 1966). His own conclusion is on pp. 25, 117.

4. For examples of the larger apocalyptic framework, see the ministers Thomas Shepard (1605–1649) and John Allin (1596–1671), *A Defence of the Answer made unto the Nine Questions or Positions sent from New England against the reply thereto by Mr. John Ball* (London, 1648) in *The Puritans: A Sourcebook of Their Writings*, Vol. 1, Perry Miller and Thomas H. Johnson, eds. [New York: Harper Torchbooks, 1963], p. 119); Edward Johnson, *A History of New England: From the English Planting in the Yeare 1628 untill the Yeare 1652* . . . (London, 1653); repr. and edited by J. F. Jameson as *Johnson's Wonder-Working Providence* (New York: Charles Scribner's Sons, 1910), p. 52; and Michael Wigglesworth, "The Day of Doom," Miller and Johnson, eds., *The Puritans*, Vol. 2, pp. 587–606; cf. Miller, "The End of the World," pp. 218–19. James Davidson cites examples in his analysis, *The Logic of Millennial Thought. Eighteenth-Century New England* (New Haven: Yale University Press, 1977); cf. Quentin Skinner, "Meaning and Understanding in the History of Ideas," *History and Theory*, 7 (1969). The author develops the idea that the language and concepts that we inherit limit and influence our response to the world as much as reflect it; viz., *The American Puritan Imagination: Essays in Revaluation*, Sacvan Bercovitch, ed. (Cambridge: Cambridge University Press, 1974); and Mason I. Lowance, Jr., *The Language of Canaan* (Cambridge: Harvard University Press, 1981).

5. Questions of exegesis, politics, authoritarianism, and Christology have been seen in this debate: Sacvan Bercovitch, "Typology in Puritan New England: The Williams-Cotton Controversy Reassessed," *American Quarterly*, 19 (1967):166–91; cf. Jesper Rosenmeier, esp. on apocalypticism and typology, "The Teacher and the Witness: John Cotton and Roger Williams," *William and Mary Quarterly*, 25 (1968):408–31, esp. pp. 420–22, 430–31.

6. Roger Williams, *Complete Writings*, 7 vols., Samuel L. Caldwell, ed. (New York: Russell & Russell, 1963). On Williams, see Perry Miller, *Roger Williams: His Contribution to the American Tradition* (Indianapolis: Bobbs-Merrill, 1953). W. Clark Gilpin outlines the vitality of the book of Revelation in Williams's thinking in *The Millenarian Piety of Roger Williams* (Chicago: University of Chicago Press, 1979).

7. This idea was so strong in Williams's mind, Gilpin argues, that Williams published *Christenings Make Not Christians* (1645) in an effort "to dissuade his Puritan colleagues from converting Indians into membership of churches whose imperfect order still linked them by a 'mystical chaine' to Antichrist" (*Millenarian Piety*, p. 97).

8. Williams, *Complete Writings*, Vol. 4, pp. 44–45.

9. As with Goodwin, whom he influenced for Independency, the apocalyptic significance of nascent Congregationalism seems apparent. See John Cotton, *The Churches Resurrection, or the Opening of the Fifth and Sixth Versus of the 20th Chap. of the Revelation* (London, 1642), p. 11. In a sermon on Rev. 13, Cotton argues that "the power and great authority of this Beast [Antichrist]" will probably end in 1655. See *An exposition, upon the Thirteenth Chapter, of the Revelation* (London, 1656), p. 93. See also by Cotton,

The Pouring out of the Seven Vials: or an Exposition of the 16 Chapter of the Revelation, with an Application of it to our Times (London, 1642); cited by Rosenmeier, "The Teacher and the Witness," p. 412.

10. John Cotton, *The Bloudy Tenent, Washed and Made White in the Bloud of the Lamb* (London: Matthew Symmons for Hannah Allen, 1647) pp. 42–43.

11. Ibid., pp. 42–43, 51, 53.

12. Ernest Tuveson presents aspects of the religious exegesis prevailing behind secular laws of society insofar as they were seen operative in the early years of the new American Republic in, *Redeemer Nation* (Chicago: University of Chicago Press, 1968), pp. 26–52; cf. his *Millennium and Utopia* (Berkeley: University of California Press, 1949) tracing religious roots to the idea of progress.

13. Williams, "Christenings Make Not Christians," in Caldwell, ed., *Complete Writings*, Vol. 7, p. 34. The vitality of our theme continues in Williams's treatise *The Hireling Ministry None of Christs* (1652), in *Complete Writings*, Vol. 7, pp. 142–91. He argues critically of required tithes, coining the phrase "no longer pay, no longer pray," and delineating thereby true as opposed to "hireling" ministers. The nature of true ministry is filled out by our text, Foxe's *Martyrology*, and general history: "The Whole Book of Martyrs (or Witnesses) is nothing else but a large Commentary or History, of the Ministry of Witnesses, during all the Reigne of the Beast, to this day" (pp. 160–61; cf. p. 158).

14. Rosenmeier, "The Teacher and the Witness," pp. 408–31.

15. Ibid., p. 410. Rosenmeier, following Ernst Kantorowicz (*The King's Two Bodies: A Study in Medieval Political Theology* [Princeton: Princeton University Press, 1957]), draws the added distinction that Cotton illustrates the medieval conception of the mystical unity of Spirit and Flesh derivative of the Incarnation. His analysis is helpful, realizing that Cotton's emphasis is upon unity in light of the probable past slaying of the witnesses, not merely in the shadow of the first Advent. For Williams there is no such unity. Helpful theological reflection relating to the transformative vision of Cotton and separationist perspective of Williams is given by H. Richard Niebuhr, *Christ and Culture* (New York: Harper and Row, 1951).

16. Our textual interests might be seen to define the different religious outlooks raised up by Jean Miller Schmidt, *Souls or the Social Order: The Two-Party System in American Protestantism* (New York: Carlson Publishing, 1992). Paul Boyer writes of the effect of prophecy on the shaping of American culture in, *When Time Shall Be No More* (Cambridge, MA: Belknap, 1992).

17. Bercovitch, "Typology in Puritan New England," calls attention to the fact that for Cotton both Old and New Testaments provided types and *figurae* for the ordering of life, "a form of typology which links past, present and future in a developmental historiography" (p. 176), whereas for Williams the New Testament was the primary filter through which all such typology was understood, "the events of the Old Testament" signifying "a-temporal states of soul" (p. 175).

18. I am guided by Robert Middlekauff, *The Mathers: Three Generations of Puritan Intellectuals, 1596–1788* (New York: Oxford University Press, 1971), esp. pp. 179–87, 322–27; cf. Phyllis Jones, "Biblical Rhetoric and the Pulpit Literature of Early New England," *Early American Literature* (1976-77):245–58.

19. David D. Hall writes that coherence was found in the mental world of seventeenth-century New England by recourse to "apocalypticism, astrology, natural history, and the meteorology of the Greeks" (p. 76) in *Worlds of Wonder, Days of Judgment: Popular Religious Belief in Early New England* (New York: Knopf, 1989).

20. Middlekauff, *The Mathers*, p. 336.

21. Cotton Mather, *A Midnight Cry* (Boston, 1692), p. 24; cited in K. B. Murdock,

Magnalia Christi Americana (Cambridge: Harvard University Press, 1977), p. 368; see Mather, *On Witchcraft* . . . (Boston, 1692; reprinted by Bell Publishing Co., 1974, New York), pp. 35–36, 59ff; idem, *The Wonders of the Invisible World* (Boston, 1693) p. 15; cited by Murdock, *Magnalia Christi Americana*, p. 368.

22. William Whiston, *An Essay on the Revelation of St. John* (Cambridge, 1706). Middlekauff argues that Mather continued to accept Mede's general vision of the Apocalypse but now drew upon Whiston; cf. Joseph Mede, *Clavis Apocalyptica*, pp. 268–69; Whiston, *Essay*, pp. 42–61; Middlekauff, *The Mathers*, pp. 336–37.

23. Whiston's calculations are based upon Mede's work. See Davidson, *Logic of Millennial Thought*, pp. 55–56, 106.

24. Pierre Jurieu, *The accomplishment of the Scripture prophecies*, . . . (London, 1687; translated from the French edition, 1686), pp. 78–224; see also, *The last efforts of the afflicted innocence* . . . (London, 1682); cf. Davidson, *Logic of Millennial Thought*, p. 56. Note in Middlekauff, Mather's works which reflect this viewpoint, *The Mathers*, p. 339; viz., Mather, *Things to Be Look'd For* and *Midnight Cry*.

25. Middlekauff, *The Mathers*, pp. 344-45. Cf. similar perspectives by James Bicheno (*The Signs of the Times* . . . [London, 1799], esp. parts 1 and 3) and Drue Cressener (*A Demonstration of the first Principles of the Protestant Applications of the Apocalypse* [London: Criswell, 1689]). The slaughter of the witnesses was seen in the revocation of the Edict of Nantes (1685), persecution of Protestant Hungarians, and banishment of the Vaudois from papal Piedmont.

26. Cotton Mather, *Bonifacius. An Essay upon the Good* . . . (Boston, 1710), David Levin, ed. (Cambridge: Harvard University Press, 1966), pp. 15, 18.

27. Ibid., p. 142.

28. Mather, *Theopolis Americana* (Boston, 1710), p. 43; cited in Murdock, *Magnalia Christi Americana*, p. 368.

29. Middlekauff, *The Mathers*, p. 349; note his extensive discussion of fluctuating opinions in chapters 10 and 17. On Samuel Sewall, see *Diary of Samuel Sewall*. Collections of the Massachusetts Historical Society, 5th series, Vols. 5–7 (Boston, 1878–1882); *Phaenomena Quaedam Apocalyptica* (Boston: Bartholomew Green and John Allen, 1697); and *Proposals Touching the Accomplishment of Prophecies Humbly Offered* (Boston: Barthalomew Green, 1713); cf. Davidson, *Logic of Millennial Thought*, pp. 60, 63, 69–70.

30. Modern Edwards scholarship begins with Perry Miller's study, *Jonathan Edwards* (New York: W. Sloane Associates, 1949). Note C. C. Goen, "Jonathan Edwards: A New Departure in Eschatology," CH, 28 (1959):25–40. Goen's early perspective has been added to by others, e.g., Stephen Stein (cited below) and Davidson. Cf. Alan Hiemert (*Religion and the American Mind* [Cambridge: Harvard University Press, 1966]) who contends that two groups vied for cultural hegemony in the eighteenth century, liberals and Calvinists (p. 66).

31. Davidson contrasts gradualistic and afflictive models of historical progress in *The Logic of Millennial Thought* (pp. 28–35, 129, *et passim*). Developing the relation between the individual soul and history, Davidson writes metaphorically, "Just as ontogeny recapitulates phylogeny, so *Seelenheit* recapitulates *Helisgeschichte*" (p. 136)! However, note the caution raised of Davidson's parallel between the soul and society by Christopher R. Smith, who argues that Edwards's understanding of historical progress toward the kingdom was more straightforward than the setbacks of affliction encountered by the soul. See Smith, "Post-millennialism and the Work of Renewal in the Theology of Jonathan Edwards," Ph.D. dissertation, Boston College, 1992.

32. Jonathan Edwards, *Apocalyptic Writings*, Stephen Stein, ed. (New Haven: Yale University Press, 1977), pp. 173–99. After an "Introduction" to Edwards's apocalyptic thought, this volume includes, Edwards's lifelong "Notes on the Apocalypse" and "An

Humble Attempt" (1747). When reference is made to these documents the Stein edition and pagination will be used.

33. Bercovitch argues that "In contrast to European chiliasts, the Puritans and Edwardseans concerned themselves far less with the final event than with the design of gradual fulfillment" ("Typology of America's Mission," p. 139). See Edwards's "Notes," in Stein, ed., *Apocalyptic Writings*, pp. 41, 173–99.

34. Edwards, "An Humble Attempt," in Stein, ed., *Apocalyptic Writings*, pp. 308–436. The text used for the work is Zech. 8:20–22.

35. Edwards, "Humble Attempt," in Stein, ed., *Apocalyptic Writings* pp. 378–94.

36. Edwards, "Notes on the Apocalypse," pp. 201–208; cf. "An Humble Attempt," pp. 378–94.

37. Edwards, "Notes on the Apocalypse," p. 201.

38. Davidson, *Logic of Millennial Thought*, pp. 121, 140–41, 150–51, 153–60, 270.

39. Edwards writes: "In their conflict with Antichrist before, they are represented as leaving their garments stained with their own blood; and therefore, when they get to heaven, they are represented as coming 'out of great tribulation,' having 'washed their robes' and making them 'white in the blood of the Lamb' (Rev. 7:14). But when they come forth to this last battle, they are represented as coming forth on 'white horses, clothed in fine linen, white and clean' (Rev. 19:14)" ("Notes on the Apocalypse," p. 203).

40. Edwards sets this parallel to the war of the little horn against the saints found in Dan. 7:21 and to the war of the beast against the saints in Rev. 13:7. See Edwards, "Notes on the Apocalypse," p. 204.

41. Other passages referred to are Rev. 16:16–17 and 19:16. See Edwards, "Notes on the Apocalypse," pp. 204–205; "An Humble Attempt," pp. 385–88.

42. Edwards, "An Humble Attempt," pp. 390ff.

43. Ibid., pp. 381–83; citation is from "Notes on the Apocalypse," p. 207.

44. For the influence of Lowman and others on Edwards, see Stein, ed., *Apocalyptic Writings*, pp. 54–74.

45. Edwards, "Notes on the Apocalypse," pp. 210–16.

46. Davidson sets the structure of the conversion experience parallel to that of the larger work of redemption: "The same perspective that informed conversion—the smallest awakening—also pervaded thinking about Greater Awakenings and the Work of Redemption as a whole" (*Logic of Millennial Thought*, p. 136).

47. Edwards, "An Humble Attempt," p. 394.

48. Edwards, "Notes on the Apocalypse," p. 105.

49. Ibid., p. 115.

50. Ibid., p. 207.

51. Krister Sairsingh argues that such social considerations in Edwards's theology are developed out of his deeply trinitarian conception of God. See "Jonathan Edwards and the Idea of Divine Glory: His Foundational Trinitarianism and Its Ecclesial Import" (Ph.D. dissertation, Harvard University, 1986).

52. For examples, see, as cited earlier, T. F. Torrance, Hans-Ulrich Hofmann, Robin Bruce Barnes, Heinrich Quistorp, and Klaus Deppermann.

53. At this point is would be of theologicial interest to analyze our theme in relation to the social-theological categories first established by Ernst Troeltsch (mystic-sect-church) and later by H. Richard Niebuhr (*The Social Sources of Denominationalism,* 1929; *Christ and Culture*, 1951), as well as in terms of patterns of alienation and goal definition set forward by Robert King Merton, *Social Theory and Social Structure* (New York: Free Press, 1968), pp. 194–214.

54. See Bernard McGinn, Paula Fredrickson Landes, Marjorie Reeves, and Herbert Grundmann, as cited earlier.

55. For connections see Horst Dieter Rauh, Walter Klaassen, and Karlfried Froehlich, as cited earlier.

56. See early Christian and medieval contributors cited in Chapters 1 and 2.

57. It has been often argued that the order Thomas Aquinas gave to the general or philosophical theological curriculum can be paralleled in the systematic structuring given by Joachim to eschatological and historical thinking.

58. Abraham Friesen and Hans-Jürgen Goetz, eds. *Thomas Müntzer* (Darmstadt: Wissenschaftliche Buchgesellschaft, 1978), pp. 33–52.

59. Werner Packull, "'A Hutterite Book of Medieval Origin' Revisited," MQR, 56 (1982):147–68.

60. Packull works in the tradition of Albrecht Ritschl (*Geschichte des Pietismus in der reformierten Kirche*, Vol. 1 [Bonn: Adolph Marcus, 1880]) and Friedrich Otto zur Linden (*Melchior Hofmann, ein Prophet der Wiedertäufer* [Haarlem: De Erven F. Bohn, 1885]) in tracing a connection between Hoffman and this Franciscan tradition through Ubertino di Casale and Peter John Olivi; see Packull's "Reinterpretation of Melchior Hoffman's Exposition," in *The Dutch Dissenters: A Critical Companion to Their History and Ideas*, Irvin Horst, ed. (Leiden: E. J. Brill, 1986), pp. 32–65; on Olivi, see Franz Ehrle, Carter Partee, David Burr, and Servus Gieben, as cited in Bibliography.

61. Hoffman's pattern of apocalyptic thinking becomes evident with the publication in 1526 of *Das XII Capitel des propheten Danielis ausgelegt und das evangelion des andern sondags . . .* (Stockholm: Königliche Druckerei, 1526). It is deepened and developed in relation to the visions of the Strassburg prophets by 1530 with his publication of *Ausslegung der heimlichen Offenbarung . . .* (Strassbourg: Balthasar Beck, 1530). See works cited earlier. Despite an acknowledged difficulty in proving actual historical contact, Werner O. Packull demonstrates a strong case for, at least, spiritual kinship between Olivi and Hoffman by laying out lines of similarity in their thinking in areas of spiritual identity, patterns of scriptural interpretation (symbolic and numerological), and the threefold comings of Christ (According to Olivi, these three advents came first in the person of Christ, then in Francis, whose appearance was placed between the fifth and sixth apocalyptic periods of Church history [Rev. 7:2], and finally at the end of the seventh to judge: Hoffman discerned three restorations of true faith, first Christ's in Advent, again in Hus [Rev. 7:2], and finally, in apostolic preachers who came at the onset of last judgment). In Packull, "A Reinterpretation of Melchior Hoffman's *Exposition* Against the Background of Spiritualist Franciscan Eschatology with Special Reference to Peter John Olivi," *The Dutch Dissenters*, Irvin Horst, ed., pp. 32–65, Walter Klaassen discusses the two in relation to their second ages, for both an age of Christ and Antichrist, and the third age of the spirit with its implicit call to perfection and to a theology of two spiritual births (p. 26) in "Eschatological Themes in Early Dutch Anabaptism," *The Dutch Dissenters*, Irvin Horst, ed., pp. 18–31.

62. For examples, see in Hans Preuss, *Martin Luther, Der Prophet* (Gütersloh: C. Bertelsmann, 1933), pp. 36–72.

63. Thomas Forsyth Torrance, *Kingdom and Church* (Edinburgh: Oliver and Boyd, 1956), p. 40.

64. Torrance writes, "Calvin, on the other hand [in contrast to Luther], constantly speaks of the resurrection as the chief article of our faith, and even when he speaks of justification the emphasis is laid on our participation in the new humanity in Christ." As found in *Kingdom and Church*, pp. 40–41.

65. This paragraph implies many ways in which eschatological ideas interpenetrate the entire range of Christian sacramental practices and thinking. Material on the corporate significance of eschatology among the Reformed was worked out together with George H. Williams in preparation of his revised edition of *The Radical Reformation* (Kirksville, Mo.: The Sixteenth Century Journal Press, 1992).

66. Augustine did not anticipate the Last Judgment falling beyond A.D. 1000 (*The City of God*, XX.7). Dating the onset of the millennium from the beginning of Paul's ministry, or as late as the fourth century (with Constantine), would push the end of the (a-) millennial period further into the future. Believing that the period was to be followed by a parallel age of tribulation as had been experienced by the Church for the first 300 years of its existence, as was the opinion of John Foxe, might push the expected date for the second Advent as late as the onset of the seventeenth century. Jakob Taubes pushes the question in a more philosophical way in his argument that in the transition from the medieval to Copernican worldview the purpose of life became less that of mirroring a divine pattern on earth and more that of seeking fulfillment in some future earthly ideal, hence an argument for the transmutation of a spiritual conception of the millennium to what will be referred to as postmillenalism, or the progressive realization of a perfected age on earth. See in Taubes, *Abendländische Eschatologie* (Bern: A Francke, 1949), pp. 87–88.

67. Here a parallel might be drawn with the magisterial reformers standing with Aquinas who argued over against the Joachite tradition, represented perhaps by Müntzer, Hut, and Brocard, that the two eras of Old Law and New Law, as understood by Aquinas, appear to leave little room for fresh prophetic insight. Two points stand out in this regard in Aquinas's thinking: First, nothing can be nearer to the final goal than that which immediately drives us to that goal. This is the New Law. Here Aquinas cites Heb. 10:19: We enter the sanctuary by the blood of Jesus. Second, the state and condition of humanity may change; the nature of the New Law may be experienced in different ways depending upon the persons, places, and times. The grace of the Holy Spirit may indwell perfectly or imperfectly. There are degrees of reception of the Spirit, but only one Spirit who leads us to Christ and will only be experienced perfectly in heaven. In Thomas Aquinas, *Summa Theologiae*, 3a, 49, b, 2. (part, question, article, reply).

68. See "Die Prophezei," in J. Figi and O. Farner, eds., *Die Züircher Bibel 1531.*

69. Heinrich Bullinger, *In Apocalypsim conciones centum* (Basel: Oporinus, 1557), p. 132. Later in this sermon Bullinger cites 1 Cor. 11 and 14 as the New Testament texts which further define prophecy. It is the evangelical teaching, translated into all the known languages, that overthrows Antichrist. Bullinger appears to have found in the Apocalypse (chapter 11) some means for understanding the role of the Church and her prophets in the current religious crisis.

70. Gerhard Müller, *Franz Lambert von Avignon* (Marburg: Elwert, 1958). The ideas expressed here were worked out together with G. H. Williams.

71. Bryan W. Ball makes the case for such a refocus upon issues of governance primarily in the domain of English Protestantism in his study, *A Great Expectation: Eschatological Thought in English Protestantism to 1660* (Leiden: E. J. Brill, 1975).

72. WA, 50, pp. 98–105.

73. As in his *Supputatio annorum mundi* (WA, 53, pp. 1–182). A full analysis is found in John Headley, *Luther's View of Church History* (New Haven: Yale University Press, 1963).

74. I am following Torrance here, "Eschatology of the Reformation," pp. 40–52.

75. Ibid., pp. 52–62. Bucer's blueprint for Christian society, *De Regno Christi*, became important both on the Continent as well as in England in further thinking on the corporate Christian task to shape society. However, it would be Calvin's theology, clearly eschatological from the first edition of *Psychopannychia* (1534) through the final edition of the *Institutes of the Christian Religion* where he wrote (citing St. Bernard) that faith is "a kind of transition from eternal predestination to future glory" (III. xiii.4, as found in Torrance).

76. Schaff writes: "The Christian chiliasm is the Jewish chiliasm spiritualized and fixed upon the second, instead of the first, coming of Christ. It distinguishes, moreover, two resurrections, one before and another after the millennium, and makes the millennial

reign of Christ only a prelude to his eternal reign in heaven, from which it is separated by a short interregnum of Satan. The millennium is expected to come not as the legitimate result of a historical process but as a sudden supernatural revelation" (*History of the Christian Church*, Vol. 2 [New York: Charles Scribner's Sons, 1883] pp. 614–15). He continues by citing the Epistle of Barnabas (chap. 15) as the first Apostolic Father to have taught about such a millennium drawing upon Ps. 90:4; 2 Peter 3:8; and Jewish tradition (with no citation from the book of Revelation).

77. For example, Tertullian, *De anima*; Hippolytus, *Demonstratio de Christo et Antichristo* and *In Danielem*.

78. Augustine follows an almost dialogic process as he develops his spiritual understanding of the millennium in contrast to his earlier-held millenarian position in the *The City of God*, XX.7; XX.30; XXII.30. Note his earlier discussion on ages as he considers various twofold, threefold, and sixfold divisions of time, settling for purposes of historical periodization upon the following six ages: (1) Adam to Noah, (2) Noah to Abraham, (3) Abraham to David, (4) David to the Babylonian Captivity, (5) The Captivity to Christ, (6) From Christ to Judgment, (7) A spiritual age coterminous with the sixth age, and, interestingly, an eighth age.

79. As, for example, in Eusebius, *In Praise of Constantine*. See F. Edward Cranz, "Kingdom and Polity in Eusebius of Caesarea," HTR, 45 (1952):47–66.

80. Two points made by Willem Balke. See his *Calvin and the Anabaptist Radicals* (Grand Rapids, Mich.: Eerdmans, 1981), also see Walther Koehler, *Luther und die Kirchengeschichte . . .* (Erlangen: Junge, 1900).

81. Although the work seeks toleration and conciliation among all Protestant groups, from current perspectives Pareus's vision remains marred by its anti-Catholic and anti-chiliastic line of argument. See his *Commentarius in apocalypsim* (Frankfurt, 1618).

82. Alstedius, *Diatribe de Mille annis Apocalypticis . . .* (orig., 1627); I have used the edition Frankfurt: Conradi Eifridi, 1630.

83. See Jürgen Moltmann, *The Church in the Power of the Spirit* (New York: Harper and Row, 1977), and Gottlob Schrenck, *Gottesreich und Bund in älteren Protestantantismus . . .* (Guttersloh: C. Bartelsmann, 1923).

84. *Apocalypsis Joannis* (Heidelberg, 1591). The edition I have used, *Apocalypsis: A Brief and Learned Commentarie . . .* (London, 1592), is found with the text of the Geneva Bible.

85. See in Eastern Orthodox thought, especially John of Damascus with its trinitarian grounding.

86. *In Apocalypsim*.

87. *The Acts and Monuments of John Foxe*, 8 vols. Stephen Reed Cattley ed. (London: R. B. Seeley and W. Burnside, 1841).

88. Thomas Brightman, *Apocalypsis Apocalypseos* (Frankfurt, 1609); English trans. *The Revelation of St. John*). The ascension of Elizabeth I to the English throne was referred to by Brightman as the first blast of the seventh apocalyptic trumpet (Rev. 11:15). Eulogizing the event, Brightman went on to write, "For now is that time begun when Christ shall reign in all the earth, having all his enemies round about subdued unto him, and broken in pieces, of which Daniel speaketh, chap. 2.44. . . , so shall we see out of those things that follow, that the Kingdom among the Gentiles is to be continually added unto this that began now, til it be increased infinitely *by the calling of the Jews*, and be at last translated from thence into heaven" (*Revelation*, pp. 123, 263–73).

89. The phrase is from Ball, *A Great Expectation*, p. 162, n. 27. Ball goes on to note: "Christopher Love, in defending the modified Augustinian view, in 1563, refers to Brightman 'that Orthodox divine', Love, *Heavens Glory*, p. 74, and the millenarians

Nathaniel Homes and John Cotton both refer to Brightman in advocating a coming millennial state, Homes, *Resurrection*, p. 553, Cotton, *Church-Members*, p. 94." See Peter Toon, "The Latter-Day Glory," in Toon, ed., *Puritans, the Millennium and the Future of Israel: Puritan Eschatology 1600–1660* (London: James Clarke, 1970), pp. 23–41.

90. *A Paraphrase and Commentary on the New Testament* (London, 1727). Whitby first laid down his ideas in *A Treatise on the True Millennium*, 1703. The work argued, as the subtitle makes clear, "Shewing that it is not a Reign of Persons Raised from the Dead, but of the Church Flourishing gloriously for a Thousand Years after the Conversion of the Jews, and the Flowing in of all Nations to them Thus Converted to the Christian Faith." Henry Dana Ward, *History and Doctrine of the Millennium* (Boston, 1840), points to Whitby's work as the first explicitly postmillennial formulation of the Apocalypse (cited in Tuveson, *Redeemer Nation*, p. 40). It is, however, Moses Lowman who defines normatively this prophetic system in *A Paraphrase and Notes upon the Revelation of St. John*) (London: J. Noon, 1737). Lowman defines seven "periods of prophecy" after the first Advent: (1) The first age of persecution running from the inception of the Church to A.D. 323; (2) A second age of persecution marked by that of idolatrous European tribes, the division of the Roman Empire and rise of Islam, ending with the victory of Charles Martel over the Saracens near Poitiers, France (A.D. 732); (3) A third age of persecution, the time of the witnesses prophesying in sackcloth for 1260 days (each day being a year), ending in their slaughter by the new Roman Empire or "mystical Babylon," the papacy and medieval church; (4) The millennial age, which begins with the destruction of the "beast" in all of its forms; (5) A brief period of tribulation as satanic fury is once again unleashed; (6) A short and final battle; and (7) The General Resurrection, Judgment and "endless sabbath." A key to dating these events is the conversion of the Jews to Christianity, which event, argued on the basis of Paul's understanding of the promised salvation of the Jews through Christ (Rom. 11), would signal the beginning of the millennium.

91. R. G. Clouse makes the case for the Ramist-trained Calvinist theologian Johann Heinrich Alsted (1588–1638), who taught at Herborn and, later, at Stuhl-Weissenburg in Transylvania. His *Diatribe de mille annis Apocalypticis* (1627; English trans. *Beloved City*, 1643) was important to seventeenth-century English millenarian thinking. See Clouse, "Johann Heinrich Alsted and English Millennialism," HTR 62 (1969):189–207; and "The Rebirth of Millenarianism," in Toon, ed., *Puritans*, pp. 42–65.

92. Mede, *Clavis Apocalyptica*; Parliament authorized the publication of the book in 1642 when it was then translated by Richard More and printed in English (1643) as *The Key of the Revelation*; found in *The Works of Joseph Mede*, J. Worthington, ed. (London: Roger Norton, 1677).

93. David Austin wrote that the prophecy of the two witnesses was fulfilled at the time of the Reformation (*The Millennium* [Elizabethtown: Shepherd Kollock, 1794]. See also John Fry, *The Second Advent*, 2 vols. [London: Ogle, Duncan and Co., 1822]. He writes that Zwingli, Luther, and Calvin are the deliverers of the nations [chap. 54]. Cf. Davidson, *Logic of Millennial Thought*, p. 180). Not all were so optimistic. Aaron Burr, following John Gill, believed that the witnesses had not yet been slain (*A Sermon Preached Before the Synod of New York* [New York, 1756]).

94. Davidson argues that the nineteenth century both inherited a history of millennial logic developed particularly from 1700 to 1763 and predicated new lines of development as issues associated with what the nineteenth century called "premillennial" and "postmillennial" became more clearly delineated. For this to develop Davidson cites the importance of (1) heightened attention given the millennial period, (2) the resurgence of literal exegesis, and (3) the growing Protestant missionary movement. See his *Logic of Millennial Thought*, pp. 260–62.

95. Samuel Hopkins, *A Treatise on the Millennium* (Boston, 1793).

96. Earlier works from the 1790s include Elhanan Winchester, Bishop Thomas Newton, Joseph Priestly, Benjamin Gale, David Austin, and Joshua Spalding. Miller's work is *Evidence form Scripture and History of the Second Coming of Christ, about the Year 1843* (1836).

97. Christopher Dawson shows the effects of the French Revolution upon Protestant and Catholic consciousness, *The Gods of Revolution* (New York: New York University Press, 1972). In terms of our theme, see Bernard Lambert, *Die Weissagungen und Verheissungen, der Kirche Jesu Christi*, Johann Arnold Kanne, ed. (Nuremberg: J. L. Schrag, 1818). The original French edition is *Expositions des predictions et des promesses faites a L'église pour les derniers temps de la Gentilité*, completed 1804, published 1806. See *Weissagungen*, Vol. 1., pp. 40, 159, 163, 171, 175; Vol. II, p. 338. For a Protestant perspective, see Joseph Galloway, *Brief Commentaries on such parts of the Revelation and other prophecies, as immediately refer to the present times* (London: Hatchard, Piccadilly & Rivington, 1802). Galloway was a loyalist in the North American colonies who fled at the time of that revolution and feared Republican France.

98. Wilhelm Bousset, *Die Offenbarung Johannis* (Gottingen: Vandenhoeck und Ruprecht, 1906), pp. 97–99, 104–19.

99. An incomplete copy of Lacunza's work was published in 1812 (first complete edition, 1816), as *The Coming of the Messiah in Glory and Majesty*, by Juan Josafat Ben-Ezra, a converted Jew; translated from the Spanish with a preliminary discourse, by the Rev. Edward Irving (London: L. B. Seeley, 1827).

100. Prior to Christ's reign, Antichrist, a power that dissolves Christ in the Church, would be destroyed by him. The woman of Rev. 12 (contemporary Israel) soon conceives Christ in her womb, i.e., the Jews would soon believe in him. Satan attempts to prevent this conception, perhaps germinated by the preaching of Elijah or another end-time witness. Following the birth of her child (faith) the woman is hidden by Moses and Elijah. The dragon rises against the faithful remnant in the power of the beast. The two witnesses, two religious bodies of the faithful, are slain throughout the world prior to the conversion of the Jews and inauguration of the latter days (ibid., *Coming of the Messiah*, Vol. 2, p. 117).

101. C. Norman Kraus, *Dispensationalism in America* (Richmond, Va.: John Knox Press, 1958); cf. Ernest R. Sandeen, *The Roots of Fundamentalism, British and American Millenarianism* (Chicago: University of Chicago Press, 1970).

102. Garth Rossell and Richard A. G. Dupuis, eds., *The Memoirs of Charles G. Finney* (Grand Rapids, Mich.: Zondervan Publihsers, 1989); see introductory remarks about the rise of voluntaristic agencies in the context of apocalyptic ideas, pp. xix, xxii, *et passim*; cf. Timothy Smith, *Revivalism and Social Reform: American Protestantism on the Eve of the Civil War* (Nashville, Tenn.: Abingdon, 1957).

103. Much of this discussion up to mid-century can be followed in the vast and erudite commentary on the Apocalypse written by Edward Bishop Elliott, *Horae Apocalypticae, or a Commentary on the Apocalypse Critical and Historical . . .* 3 vols. (London: Seeley, Burnside, and Seeley, 1844; repeatedly republished in 1844, 1846, 1847, 1851, 1862). On American developments and the blending of religious, social, and scientific ideas that blurred the boundary between millennial and pragmatic activity, see Robert Weibe, *The Search for Order: 1877–1920* (New York: Hill and Wang, 1967), pp. 137–45; and James H. Moorhead, *American Apocalypse: Yankee Protestants and the Civil War, 1860–1869* (New Haven: Yale University Press, 1978).

104. George Stanley Faber, "Calendar of Prophecy," in *General Works on the Prophecies* (London, 1809–1828).

105. George Stanley Faber, *An Inquiry into the History and Theology of the Ancient Vallenses and Albigenses* (London: R. B. Seeley and W. Burnside, 1838), pp. 1–18.

106. Ibid., pp. 31ff.

107. Ibid., pp. 539. Faber writes: "In truth, if these two churches be not the two apocalyptic Churches, I see not where, between the decuple partition of the Western Empire and the times in which we are now living, the two latter Churches can be found in History: and thence, since the apocalyptic prophecy is evidently a virtual comment upon our Lord's promises, I see not, how these promises can be said to have ever been accomplished."

108. S. R. Maitland, *Facts and Documents Illustrative of the History, Doctrine, and Rites, of the Ancient Albigenses and Waldenses* (London: C.J.G. and F. Rivington, 1832). Note Martin Marty, "Insiders Look at Fundamentalism," *The Christian Century* (November 18, 1981), pp. 1195–97. Marty excoriates modern attempts to delineate a line of witnesses prior to and leading toward Protestantism as represented by the efforts of Moral Majority apologists Ed Dobson and Ed Hindson (*The Fundamentalist Phenomenon: The Resurgence of Conservative Christianity* [New York: Doubleday-Galilee, 1981]).

109. Edward & Elliott, *The Investigator of Monthly Expositor and Register on Prophecy*, J. W. Brooks, ed. (London: Simpkin and Marshall, 1832–1833. See especially Volume 3 for the debate between E. B. Elliott and T. K. Arnold.

110. Elliott, *Horae Apocalypticae*. The work was published repeatedly in 1844, 1846, 1847, 1851, and 1862. See Vol. 1, p. 202; Vol. 2, pp. 179–80. The events portrayed in our passage helped him to set his own position from that of Johann Lorenz Mosheim (1694–1755). See Vol. 2, p. 187.

111. Moses Stuart, *Commentary on the Apocalypse*, 2 vols. (Andover, Mass.: Allen, Morrill and Wardwell, 1845). Note his comment on the witnesses and other apocalyptic topics, Vol. 1, Preface, p. vi; Vol. 2, pp. 213–45. Andover Seminary, established by New England Congregationalists in 1808 to counter religious liberalism arising at Harvard College, attempted to carry into the nineteenth century Edwardsean theology as restated by Samuel Hopkins and in line with Protestant eschatology as inherited from impulses in Brightman and Goodwin through Jonathan Edwards. See also Roland Davis Gunn. "The Andover Case: A Study of Creeds in Nineteenth Century Congregationalism." (Unpublished M.A. Thesis, Andover Newton Theological School, 1993).

111a. On the plane of Scottish Commonsense Realism in the thought of Moses Stuart, see Mark Granquist, "The Role of 'Common Sense' in the Hermeneutics of Moses Stuart," HTR, 83:3 (July, 1990):305–319. The ways in which such a pattern of thinking combined with the millenarian debate to bring about the rise of Fundamentalism in the Anglo-American world, with special reference to the United States, are traced by James Davison Hunter, George M. Marsden, and Ernest Sandeen, among others.

112. Clarence B. Bass, *Backgrounds to Dispensationalism: Its Historical Genesis and Ecclesiastical Implications* (Grand Rapids, Mich.: Baker Book House, 1960); cf. Charles L. Feinberg, *Millennialism: The Two Major Views* (Chicago: Moody Press, 1982 ed.).

113. On millennial missions from 1640 to 1810, see J. A. DeJong, *As the Waters Cover the Sea* (Kampen, the Netherlands: J. H. Kok, 1970); David J. Bosch, *Transforming Mission: Paradigm Shifts in Theology of Mission* (Maryknoll, N.Y.: Orbis Books, 1991), pp. 239–61, 266–345; and William R. Hutchinson, *Errand to the World, American Protestant Thought and Foreign Missions* (Chicago: University of Chicago, 1987), esp. pp. 125–75; and Jean B. Quandt discusses the nature and effects of a modernized version of post-millennialism as such began to alter the traditional definition of mission in "Religion and Social Thought: The Secularization of Postmillennialism," in *American Quarterly*, 25 (1973):390–409.

114. This debate, reflected in a series of articles in the *Andover Review*, led to the

dismissal of E. C. Smyth from the faculty, later voided by the Massachusetts Supreme Court, 1891. See David E. Swift, "The Future Probation Controversy in American Congregationalism, 1886–1893" (Ph.D. dissertation, Yale University, 1947), espeically the general cultural climate (pp. 1–8) and avowed motives (chapter 1).

115. Daniel Day Williams, *The Andover Liberals: A Study in American Theology* (New York: King's Crown, 1941), p. 127.

116. The development and evolution of this liberal theology is clearly presented by H. Richard Niebuhr, *The Kingdom of God in America* (New York: Harper's, 1937). It is defined as focusing on free will, being optimistic, and friendly to science and modern culture. As such evolved, a special place was held open for the place of the city in Christian theological reflection, a precursor to the work of Harvey Cox, *The Secular City: Secularization and Urbanization in Theological Perspective* (New York: Macmillan, 1966 rev. ed.). See Quandt, "Religion and Social Thought," pp. 405–409, esp. n. 71.

117. Surveys of the different dimensions of dispensational theology have been written by Craig A. Blaising, e.g., "Doctrinal Development in Orthodoxy," and "Development of Dispensationalism by Contemporary Dispensationalists," in *Bibliotheca Sacra*, 145 (1988):133–40, 254–80.

118. Developments in postmillennial and premillennial thinking in the late nine-teenth and early twentieth century can be traced in the premillennialist G. N. H. Peters, *The Theocratic Kingdom*, 3 vols. (Grand Rapids, Mich.: Kregel, 1884 repr.); the modern "realized" postmillennialist J. Marcellus Kik, *An Eschatology of Victory* (Phillipsburg, N.J.: Presbyterian and Reformed Publishing Co., 1978); and the amillennialist George L. Murray, *Millennial Studies* (Grand Rapids, Mich.: Baker Book House, 1975).

119. A helpful sketch and discussion of contemporary views on the millennium can be found in *The Meaning of the Millennium: Four Views*, Robert G. Clouse, ed. (Downers Grove, Ill.: InterVarsity Press, 1977); and Millard J. Erickson, *Contemporary Options in Eschatology. A Study of the Millennium* (Grand Rapids, Mich.: Baker Book House, 1977).

120. Käsemann's statement was, "Apocalyptic—since the preaching of Jesus cannot really be described as therapy—was the mother of all Christian theology." Ernst Käsemann, "The Beginnings of Christian Theology," in *Apocalypticism: Journal for Theology and the Church*, Vol. 6, R. W. Funk, ed., J. Leitch, trans., (New York: Herder and Herder, 1961), p. 40; and Jürgen Moltmann, *The Church in the Power of the Spirit* (New York: Harper and Row, 1977), pp. 41–50.

121. The texts are from Isaiah, cited by Jonathan Edwards in connection with his hope for the ever-spreading kingdom of God on earth and expressive of his understanding of the awakening of true religion in North America; in Jonathan Edwards, *Apocalyptic Writings*, Stephen Stein, ed., pp. 28, 142–43.

Epilogue

The Protestant quest for our witnesses helped to bridge current historical experience with the hope found in Christian consummation. This speculation developed out of reflection upon the text as filtered through the history of Church tradition. The earliest commentators tended to identify the witnesses as Enoch and Elijah, finding their appearance at the end of history. It was there that they, like the kingdom which they foreshadowed remained, a part of that future about which one could do little. Together with the work of Tyconius a new way of understanding was opened up. The qualities of these witnesses, drawing as they did upon the history of Israel's prophetic tradition, were stressed and associated with the Church, or the activities of true preachers and prophets. The first, or literal, interpretation had not completely faded; it proved not to be useful in the historical present.

Further interpretative dimensions to our text developed through history and became systematized in the thought of Joachim of Fiore, apparently drawing together the realistic and more general spiritual interpretations in light of focused historical periodization. As a prophetic spirit slipped into apocalypticism, the adventual witnesses were available polemical symbols in the service of Church and social reform. The work of commentators like Nicholas of Lyra tied this ever more firmly to historical, chronological events, given further social or political immediacy in late medieval and Hussite apocalyptic speculation.

Protestants, as joint-heirs to this tradition, and having divided from Rome, faced the problem of communal historical identity, the locus of God's kingdom, and its future consummation. To discover the time and identity of the adventual witnesses became a part of identifying the Church, its social agenda, and future toward which it tended. While doctrine was and remained the perceived point of separation for Protestants from Rome, the development of historical roots related to our text could, and did, aid in institutional development. Most Protestants adopted a representative reading of our text, marked by the early exegesis of Tyconius against a sharpened sense of historical periodization. Protestants were God's adventual witnesses.

However, for Protestants the Christian Church could not be the kingdom of God in quite the same way as had developed within that part of Western Christendom no longer medieval but now Roman Catholic, against which Protestants were now in revolt. Yet the kingdom could not simply be left as an item tabled for the uncertain future. To do so would have been to call into question much of the rhetoric that gave strength to the break from Rome. The search for the witnesses and the way in which they became the door to the future could and did help to define, with differing theological implications, various options for how that future might look. As such, theological reflection was given the opportunity to clarify itself and the nature of the Church's hope with respect to eschatology. As the symbolic numbers in our text could be used to mark time back to a perceived point of defection from the Christian ideal, so could they plot time into the future to the point when Christ's reign would be manifest fully. Finding the time and identity of the witnesses became part of the wider quest for the kingdom of God. It became part of the effort to differentiate the nature of its millennial appearance. This driving impetus continued until new historical perspectives overcame many.[1]

This speculation was not merely a part of the wider search for the kingdom; it tells us, first, something about ourselves and our hopes. A modern deconstruction of the textual tradition reveals this. Our text carried with it a vision for social reform in society together with that wider reform which transcends history itself, a hope integral to the continuing Christian endeavor. The nature of that endeavor has to do with the way in which we read biblical texts, understand the kingdom of God, and live our lives in a given social order. Our reading of the text is always guided by a community of understanding. That community runs through time. By recognizing and following the history of the exegesis of a text in relation to its cultural contexts, we follow something of the trajectory of its meaning.[2]

However, no text is simply a "wax nose" to be manipulated at will. There are limits to its use discerned through the history of its use that are as significant in determining a text's meaning as the meaning of the text itself. There is a multi-valency with some texts, like the one analyzed here, but such should not imply skepticism about the work of interpretation. Quite the contrary; the richness of such texts to call the Church into conversation with itself about its theological self-understanding in a given area across periods of different epistemological paradigms is an opportunity to reflect critically upon accepted social patterns of thought and to the call of faithfulness. In the end, the Church cannot call us to good values if it is not also a source of true knowledge.[3] When we let our text speak to us in our particular circumstances we learn about what it means to be witnesses.[4]

Second, the text we have analyzed tells us about the relationship among piety, polity, and politics. We see through it how people have understood there to be a relationship between religious understandings of authenticity and legitimacy with the ways in which such become built into and embodied in social structures. Behavior in the social order is related to this structuring of patterns of legitimacy. Certain shifts in moral perception and social ordering, such as those attendant to forms of secularity and modernity, have contributed to paradigm shifts in historical understanding. This has lent enhanced social legitimacy to movements different from the established order in history, often movements of "protest" or "reunion." This is simply to say that Christian discipleship, as well as all other forms of discipleship, has always had a social horizon related to the moral ordering of life.[5]

Third, the very fact that we have encountered such malleability in apocalyptic futures should remind us that the economy, or *oikonomia*, of God is more than temporal development, that such is, in fact, mechanistic when compared to the larger organic vision of the kingdom of God. The economy of Christ is greater than its unfolding in history, although through such we learn something of ourselves and the nature of our hope. Augustine is noted for having said in his *Confessions* that "my love is my weight," implying thereby that our loves shape our lives. The heart of the economy of Christ is the way in which it drives us to become participants in the kingdom of God and, thereby, shows our loves for what they are. Inherent in the economy of God is the mystery of what it means to have been made in the image of God, flawed in time, restored through history, saved by grace. Christian hope calls us to a community characterized by the fullness of this economy.[6]

Notes

1. Studies similar to this one could be done tracing the influence of a text from the Apocalypse upon Orthodox history and thought, e.g., coming to a climax in the late seventeenth and early eighteenth centuries with the activity of Peter the Great replacing the Patriarchate with the Holy Synod (1721), or in Roman Catholicism, particularly in Franciscan missionary vision. On this latter, see Marjorie Reeves, *Joachim of Fiore and the Prophetic Future* (London: SPCK, 1976; New York: Harper and Row, 1977).

2. On the possibilities and hazards of this approach, see Karlfried Froehlich's discussion of Church history and the Ebeling thesis ("Church History as the History of the Exposition of Holy Scripture" [1947], published as *Wort Gottes und Tradition: Studien zu einer Hermeneutik der Konfessionen* [Göttingen: Vandenhoek & Ruprecht, 1964]) as a theological *and* historical discipline. "Church History and the Bible," in *Biblical Hermeneutics in Historical Perspective*, Mark Burrows and Paul Rorem, eds. (Grand Rapids, Mich.: Eerdmans, 1991), pp. 1–15; note review cited, Friedrich De Boor, "Kirchengeschichte oder Auslegungsgeschichte?" *Theologische Literaturzeitung* (June 1972): 401–14.

3. Lesslie Newbigin, *Truth to Tell: The Gospel as Public Truth* (Grand Rapids, Mich.: Eerdmans, 1991), p. 2.

4. This textual invitation, analogous to "faith seeking foundation" to use terminology provided by Ronald F. Thiemann (*Revelation and Theology: The Gospel as Narrated Promise* [Notre Dame, Ind.: University of Notre Dame Press, 1985], p. 9, 71–91), calls us to new paths of discourse. Such are opened to the Church as it recovers an understanding of God's prevenient grace and the epistemological implications this has for the life of faith and an understanding of revelation. The internal logic of Christian convictions, by virtue of their inherent religious nature, draw us to deeper moral reflection upon reality than available in other disciplines, although an understanding of the latter is important for an adequate grasp of a field of reflection. Nevertheless, the language of moral discourse cannot be reduced to the level of such disciplines, e.g., as in the use of managerial and psychological language to explain theology and ethics without a resulting constriction of Christian or general religious vision. See Robert N. Bellah et al., *Habits of the Heart* (Berkeley and Los Angeles: University of California Press, 1985). However, merely to adopt a biblical and classical republican language apart from its explication, understanding, and sense of inherent legitimacy leads only to new modes of Restorationism.

5. See the "Draft of a Prologue . . ." for the proposed study on, "Spirit, Order, and Organization," World Council of Churches, Commission on Faith and Order, June 1966. The lines of historical, sociological, and theological analysis laid down in these documents

for understanding movements, referred to as those of "protest" and of "reunion," would be useful to pursue given current and foreseeable social and ecclesial issues. Aspects of the work being edited by Martin Marty et al., *The Fundamentalist Project Series* (Chicago: University of Chicago, 1991–), move in this vein.

6. Community with its implications for the formation of personhood might be explored on parallel with the doctrine of the Trinity; we discover our individual identity in community. See Jean Zizioulas, *Being as Communion: Studies in Personhood and the Church* (Crestwood, N.Y.: St. Vladimir's Seminary Press, 1985); cf. Dietrich Bonhoeffer, *The Communion of Saints* (New York: Harper's, 1963). One might suggest that there can be no end to history apart from the maturation of personhood. See this in light of Francis Fukuyama's reflections in "The End of History?" *The National Interest* (Summer 1989), pp. 3–18.

Abbreviations

AFH	*Archivum Franciscanum Historicum.*
AHR	*American Historical Review.*
ALK	*Archiv für Literatur- und Kirchengeschichte des Mittelalters.*
ANF	*Ante-Nicene Fathers.*
AQ	*American Quarterly.*
ARG	*Archiv für Reformationsgeschichte.*
BJRL	*Bulletin of the John Rylands Library.*
CCL	*Corpus Christianorum. Series Latina.*
CF	*Collectanea Franciscana.*
CH	*Church History.*
CO	Calvin, Jean. *Opera omnia.*
CR	*Corpus reformatorum.*
CSEL	*Corpus scriptorum ecclesiasticorum Latinorum.*
DAB	*Dictionary of American Biography.*
DNB	*Dictionary of National Biography.*
DTC	*Dictionnaire de Théologie catholique.*
EAL	*Early American Literature.*
ERE	*Encyclopedia of Religion and Ethics.*
ERK	*Encyclopedia of Religious Knowledge, The New Schaff-Herzog.*
FS	*Franciscan Studies.*
FzS	*Franziskanische Studien.*
HDB	*Dictionary of the Bible: Dealing with Its Language, Literature, and Contents, Including the Biblical Theology.*
HTR	*The Harvard Theological Review.*
JBL	*Journal of Biblical Literature.*
JEH	*Journal of Ecclesiastical History.*
JETS	*Journal of the Evangelical Theological Society.*
JHI	*Journal of the History of Ideas.*
JMH	*Journal of Medieval History.*
LA	*Lexicon Abbreviaturarum. Latine ed Italiane.*
LthK	*Lexikon für Theologie und Kirche.*
LW	*Luther's Works.* Philadelphia and St. Louis: Fortress and Concordia Press, 1955–67.
ME	*The Mennonite Encyclopedia.*
MH	*Mediaevalia et Humanistica.*
MGH	*Monumenta Germaniae Historica.*
MQR	*Mennonite Quarterly Review.*

MRS	*Medieval and Renaissance Studies.*
NPNF	*Nicene and Post-Nicene Fathers.*
NTA	*New Testament Apocrypha.*
ODC	*The Oxford Dictionary of the Christian Church.*
Parker	*The Parker Society for the Publication of the Works of the Fathers and Early Writers of the Reformed English Church.* 56 vols. Cambridge: The University Press, 1841–1855.
PG	*Patrologiae cursus completus. Series Graeca.*
PL	*Patrologiae cursus completus. Series Latina.*
Quasten	Quasten, Johannes. *Patrology.*
RE3	*Realencyklopädie für protestantische Theologie und Kirche.*
REA	*Revue des études augustiniennes.*
RGG	*Die Religion in Geschichte und Gegenwart.*
RHE	*Revue d'histoire ecclésiastique.*
RTAM	*Recherches de Théologie anciennes et médiévale.*
SAW	George H. Williams and Angel M. Mergal. *Spiritual and Anabaptist Writers.* Philadelphia: Westminster Press, 1958.
SCJ	*Sixteenth Century Journal.*
SJTh	*Scottish Journal of Theology.*
STC1	*A Short Title Catalogue of Books Printed in England, Scotland, and Ireland, and of English Books Printed Abroad, 1475–1640.*
STC2	*Short-Title Catalogue . . . 1641–1700.*
TDNT	*Theological Dictionary of the New Testament.*
WA	*D. Martin Luthers Werke. Kritische Gesamtausgabe.*
WABr	*D. Martin Luthers Werke. Kritische Gesamtausgabe. Briefwechsel.*
WADB	*D. Martin Luthers Werke, Deutsche Bibel.*
ZDG	*Zeitschrift für Deutsche Geistesgeschichte.*
ZHT	*Zeitschrift für historische theologie.*
ZKG	*Zeitschrift für Kirchengeschichte.*
ZkTh	*Zeitschrift für katholoische Theologie.*
ZNW	*Zeitschrift für Neutestamentliche Wissenschaft.*
ZW	Zwingli, Huldreich. *Sämtliche Werke.*

Selected Bibliography

Interpretation of the Book of Revelation: Primary Sources

Alcasar, Ludovici ab. *Vestigatio Arcani Sensus in Apocalypsi*. Antwerp: Heredes Martini Nutii, 1614, 1619.

Alexander of Bremen. *Alexander Minorita Expositio in Apocalypsim*. Edited by Alois Wachtel. Monumenta Germaniae Historica, *Quellen zur Geschichte des Mittelalter*. Weimar: Hermann Böhlau, 1955.

Alstedius, [Johann] Henricus. *Diatribe de Mille annis Apocalyptics* . . . (2d ed.). Frankfurt: Conradi Eifridi, 1630.

Ames, William *Bellarminus Enervatus* (4 vols.). Oxford, 1629.

Anselm of Havelberg. *Diologus, livre 1: Renouveau dans l'Eglise*. Edited by Gaston Salet. Sources Chretiennes, no. 118. Paris: Editiones du Cerf, 1966.

Ante-Nicene Fathers (10 vols.). Edited by Alexander Roberts and James Donaldson. Grand Rapids, Mich.: Eerdmans Publishing Co., 1976.

Anthony of Florence. *Summa Theologica* (4 vols.). Verona: Ex typ. Seminarii apud Augustinum carattonium, 1740. Facsimiie ed. Graz: Akademische Druck und Verlagsanstalt, 1959.

Der Antichrist und die fünfzehn Zeichen (2 vols.). Edited by H. T. Musper. Munich: Prestel-Verlag, 1970.

Der Antichrist und die fünfzehn Zeichen vor dem Jüngsten Gericht (2 vols.). Edited by Karin Boveland, Christoph Peter Burger, and Ruth Steffen. Hamburg: Friedrich Loittig, 1959.

Apocalypse of Elijah. In Texte und Untersuchungen, 17, 3a. *Die Apocalypse des Elias*. Edited by Georg Steindorff. Leipzig: J. C. Hinrichssche Buchhandlung, 1899.

Apocalypsis. Edited by H. T. Musper. *Die Urausgaben der holländischen Apokalypse und biblia pauperum* (3 vols.). Munich: Prestel-Verlag, 1961.

Archer, John. *The Personal Reigne of Christ upon Earth*. London, 1642.

Arnold of Villanova. *Tractatus de tempore adventus Antichristi*. Edited by Heinrich Finke. *Aus den Tagen Bonifaz' VIII: Funde und Forschungen*. Vorreformationsgeschichtliche Forschungen, 2. Münster: Aschendorff, 1902.

Augustine. In D. W. Robertson, translator, *St. Augustine on Christian Doctrine*. Indianapolis: Bobbs-Merril, 1958.

Austin, David. *The Millennium*. Elizabethtown, N.J.: Shepherd Kollock, 1794.

Bale, John. *The Image of Both Churches, Being an Exposition of the Most Wonderful Book of Revelation*. Edited by Henry Christmas. *Select Works of John Bale*. Parker Society, Vol. 1. Cambridge: Cambridge University Press, 1849.

Beard, Thomas. *Antichrist the Pope in Rome: or, The Pope of Rome Is Antichrist*. London, 1625.

Beatus of Liebana. *Beati In Apocalypsin Libri XII.* Edited by Henry A. Sanders. Rome: American Academy in Rome, 1930.

Bede. *Bedae Opera de Temporibus.* Edited by C. W. Jones. Cambridge, Mass.: Mediaeval Academy of America, 1943.

———. *Patres Ecclesiae Anglicanae* (13 vols.). Edited with an English translation by J. A. Giles. London: Whittaker and Co., 1843–1844.

Bellarmine, Robert. *Roberti Bellarmini Politiani Opera Omnia* (8 vols.). Edited by Justinus Fevre. Paris: n.p., 1870–1874. Frankfurt am Main: Minerva, 1965.

Bibliander, Theodore. *Ad omnium ordinum reip. Christianae principes uiros, populumque Christianum,* . . . Basel: Oporinus, 1545.

Bonaventure. *Legenda Major S. Francisci. Ex typographia Collegii S. Bonaventurae. In Analecta Franciscana,* Vol. 10. Quaracchi-Firenze, 1926–1941.

The Book of Enoch. Edited by R. H. Charles. Oxford: Clarendon Press, 1893.

Bossuet, Jacques Benigne. *Oeuvres complètes* . . . (31 vols.). Edited by F. Lachat. Paris: L. Vivès, 1862–1866.

Brightman, Thomas. *Apocalypsis Apocalypseos.* . . . Frankfurt, 1609. Edition used, *The Revelation of St. John, Illustrated with Analysis and Scholions* (1st English ed.). Amsterdam: Thomas Stafford, 1644.

Brocard, James. *The Revelation of S. Ihon reveled.* Translated by James Sanford. London, 1582.

Bucer, Martin. *De Regno Christi.* English translation in *Melanchthon and Bucer* (pp. 174– 394). Translated and edited by W. Pauck. Library of Christian Classics, Vol. 19. Philadelphia: Westminster Press, 1969.

Bullinger, Heinrich. *Ad J. Cochlaei de canonica scriptura et catholice ecclesiae authoritate libellum.* Zürich: Froschouer, 1544.

———. *Der alt gloub.* Zürich: Froschouer, 1939.

———. *In Apocalypsim conciones centum.* Basel: Oporinus, 1557.

———. *Commentarius in II Epist. argumentum posterioris Epistolae ad Thessalonicenses.* Zürich: Froschouer, 1537.

———. *Daniel sapientissimus Dei propheta.* Zürich: Froschouer, 1565.

———. *De fine saeculi et iudicio venturo Domini nostri Jesu Christi . . . orationes duae.* Basel: Oporinus, 1557.

———. *De origine erroris libri duo.* Zürich: Froschouer, 1539.

———. *De propheta libri duo.* Zürich: Froschouer, 1525.

———. *De prophetae officio.* Zürich: Froschouer, 1532.

———. *De testamento seu foedere Dei unico et eterno.* Zürich: Froschouer, 1534.

———. *Diarium annales vitae der Jahre 1504–1575.* Edited by Emil Egli. Basel: Basler Buch und Antiquariatshandlung, 1904.

———. *Epitome temporum et rerum ab orbe conditio . . .* Zürich: Froschouer, 1565.

———. *Heinrich Bullinger Briefwechsel.* Edited by Ulrich Gäbler and Endre Zsindely. Zürich: Theologischer Verlag, 1973.

———. *A Hundred Sermons vpo[n] the Apocalips of Jesu Christe.* . . . Translated by John Daus. London: John Day, 1561.

———. *Ieremias fidelissimus et laboriosissimus Dei propheta.* . . . Zürich: Froschouer, 1575.

———. *Das Jüngste Gericht.* Zürich: Froschouer, 1555.

———. *Oratio secunda . . . ex verbis Apostoli 2 Timoth. 3 docens qua ratione pericula 2 postremi nostri seculi.* . . . Basel: Oporinus, 1557.

———. *In sacrosanctum Jesu Christi Domini nostri Evangelium secundum Matthaeum.* Zürich: Froschouer, 1542.

Burr, Aaron. *A Sermon Preached Before the Synod of New York.* New York: H. Gaine, 1756.

Burton, Henry. *The Sounding of the last two trumpets, the sixth and seventh; or meditations on chapters IX–X of the Revelations.* London, 1641.

Calvin, John. *The Epistles of Paul to the Romans and Thessalonians.* Translated by R. MacKenzie. *Volume 8: Calvin's New Testament Commentaries.* Grand Rapids, Mich.: Eerdmans Publishing Co., 1960.

———. *The Epistle of Paul to the Hebrews and the First and Second Epistles of Peter.* D. W. Torrance and T. F. Torrance, eds., Calvin's Commentaries XII. Grand Rapids, Mich.: Eerdmans Publishing Co., 1963.

———. *Institutes of the Christian Religion,* 2 vols., John T. McNeil, ed., and F. L. Battles, trans. Philadelphia: Westminster Press, 1960.

Carion, Johann. *Chronicon Carionis expositum et auctum . . . a P. Melanthone et C. Peucero.* Wittenberg: Haeredes Johannis Cratonis, 1580. Published first as *Chronica.* Halle, 1532.

Cartwright, Thomas. *A Confutation of the Rhemist translation, glosses and annotations on the New Testament.* London, 1589; edition used, New York: Leavitt, Lord and Co., 1834.

Chytraeus, David. *Explicatio Apocalypsis Johannis apostoli.* Wittenberg: J. Crato, 1564.

Clareno, Angelo. *Historia septem tribulationum.* Edited by F. Ehrle. ALK, 2 (1866).

Cocceius, Johannes. *Cogitationes de apoc. St. Joannis* (1668), In Opera Omni (12 vols.). Amsterdam, 1701–1706.

Corpus Christianorum. Series Latina. Turnholt: Brepols, 1954.

Adso of Montier-en-Der. Adso Dervensis, De ortu et tempore Antichristi. Edited by D. Verhelst. *Continuatio Mediaevalis,* Vol. 45.

Ambrose Autpertus. *Expositio in Apocalypsin.* Edited by Robert Weber. Vol. 27.

Augustine. *De Doctrina Christiana Libri IV.* Vol. 32.

———. *De civitate Dei.* Vols. 47, 48.

Commodianus. *Carmen de duobus populis.* Vol. 128.

Jerome. *In Amos.* Vol. 76.1.

———. *In Esaiam.* Vol. 73.

———. *In Malachiam.* Vol. 76.1.

———. *In Zachariam.* Vol. 76.1.

Corpus Reformatorum, Vols. 5, 8, 11, 21. Edited by Carolus Gottlieb Bretschneider and Henricus Ernestus Bindsel. Halis Saxonum and Brunszigae: C. A. Schwetscheke et filium, 1834–1854.

Corpus Scriptorum Ecclesiasticorum Latinorum, Vol. 1. Editum consilio et impensis Academiae Litterarum Caesareae Vindobonensis, 1866.

Jerome, *Epistolae.* Edited by Isidorus Hilberg. Vol. 54.

Lactantius. *Divinarum Institutionum in Opera Omnia.* Edited by Samuel Brandt. Vol. 19.1.

Tertullian. *De anima.* Edited by Reifferscheid and Wissowa. Vol. 20.

Victorinus of Pettau. *Commentarium in Apocalypsin.* Edited by Johannes Haussleiter. Vol. 49.

Cotton, John. *The Bloudy, Tenent, Washed and Made White in the Bloud of the Lamb.* London: Matthew Symmons for Hannah Allen, 1647.

———. *The Churches Resurrection, or the Opening of the Fifth and Sixth Verses of the 20th Chap. of the Revelation.* London, 1642.

———. *An Exposition, upon the Thirteenth Chapter, of the Revelation* (London, 1656).

————. *The Pouring out of the Seven Vials: or an Exposition, of the 16 Chapter of the Revelation, with an Application of it to our Times.* London, 1645.

Cranach, Lucas. *Passional Christi und Antichristi.* Edited by Wilhelm Scherer. Deutsche Drucke älterer Zeit in Nachbildungen, 3. Berlin: G. Grote'sche Verlagsbuchhandlung, 1885.

Crespin, Jean. *Histoire des vrays Tesmoins de la verit; de l'évangile, qui de leur sang l'ont signée, depuis Jean Hus usques au temps present.* Geneva: P. Auberr, 1570.

Cressener, Drue. *A Demonstration of the first Principles of the Protestant Applications of the Apocalypse.* London: Criswell, 1689.

Daneau, Lambert. *A treatise, touching Antichrist. . . .* London: Thomas Orwin, 1589.

Daubuz, Charles. *A Perpetual Commentary on the Revelation of St. John.* London: B. Tooke, 1720.

Durham, James. *A Commentarie Upon the Book of the Revelation.* Amsterdam: J. F. Stamm, 1660; 1st ed., 1658.

Edwards, Jonathan. *Apocalyptic Writings.* Edited by Stephen Stein. New Haven, Conn.: Yale University Press, 1977.

Eliot, John, and Mayhew, Thomas. *Tears of Repentance, or a Further Narrative of the Progress of the Gospel Amongst the Indians in New England.* London: P. Cole, 1653.

Elliott, Edward Bishop. *Horae Apocalypticae, or a Commentary on the Apocalypse Critical and Historical . . .* (3 vols.). London: Seeley, Burnside, and Seeley, 1844.

————. *The Investigator of Monthly Expositor and Register on Prophecy,* J. W. Brooks, ed. London: Simpkin and Marshall, 1832–1833.

"De Enoch et Haeliae." *Poetarum Latinorum Medii Aevi, 4.1: Rhythmi Aevi Merovingici et Caroli.* Edited by Societas Aperiendas Fontibus Rerum Germanicarum Medii Aevi. Monumenta Germaniae historica. Berlin: Weidmannsche Buchhandlung, 1914.

Faber, George Stanley. *An Inquiry into the History and Theology of the Ancient Vallenses and Albigenses.* London: R. B. Seeley and W. Burnside, 1838.

————. "Calendar of Prophecy," in *General Works on the Prophecies.* London, 1809–1828.

————. *Sacred Calendar of Prophecy* (2 vols.). London: Printed for C. & J. Rivington, 1828.

Field, John, and Wilcox, Thomas. "An Admonition to Parliament." in *The Reformation of the Church: A Collection of Reformed and Puritan Documents on Church Issues* (pp. 83–94). Edited by Iain Murray. London: Banner of Truth Trust, 1965.

Flacius, Matthias (Illyricus). *Catalogus testium veritatis.* Basel: I. Operinum, 1556.

————. *Historia Ecclesiae Christi.* Basel: I. Operinum, 1559–1574.

————. *Novum Testamentum . . . Glossa Commendiaria . . .* Basel: P. Pernam et T. Dietrich, 1570.

Foxe, John. *The Acts and Monuments of John Foxe* (8 vols.). Edited by Stephen Reed Cattley. London: R. B. Seeley and W. Burnside, 1841.

————. *Acts and Monuments. . . .* London: John Day, 1563.

————. *Acts and Monuments . . . newly revised. . . .* London: John Day, 1583.

————. *Christus Triumphans.* Edited by John Hazel Smith. *Two Latin Comedies by John Foxe the Martyrologist.* Ithaca, N.Y.: Cornell University Press, 1973.

————. *Eicasmi seu meditationes in sacram Apocalypsim.* London, 1587.

Fry, John. *The Second Advent* (2 vols.). London: Ogle, Duncan and Co., 1822.

Fulke, William. *Confutation of the Rhemish Testament* [1618]. New York: Leavitt, Lord and Co., 1834.

Funck, Johannes. *Chronologia, hoc est Omnivm temporvm et annorvm ab initio mvndi vsque ad resvrrectionem Domini Nostri Iesv Christi, computatio.* Nuremberg, 1545.

Galloway, Joseph. *Brief commentaries upon such parts of the Revelation, and other prophecies, as immediately refer to the present times.* . . . London: Hatchard, Piccadilly & Rivington, 1802.

Geneva Bible, 1590 Facsimile Edition. Introduced by Lloyd E. Berry. Milwaukee: University of Wisconsin Press, 1969.

Gerhoch von Reichersberg. *De Investigatione Antichristi.* Edited by Ernst Sackur. *Libelli de Lite Imperatorum et Pontificum Saeculis XI et XII*, Vol. 3. Monumenta Germaniae historica. Hanover, 1897.

————. *Opera Inedita.* Edited by O. Van den Eynde. I. Tractatus et libelli. . . . Rome: Spicilegium Pontificii Athenaei Antoniani 8, 1955.

Goodwin, Thomas. *A Sermon of the Fifth Monarchy.* London, 1654.

————. *The Works of Thomas Goodwin, D. D.* With General Preface by John C. Miller. Edinburgh: James Nichol, 1861.

————. *Zerubbabel's Encouragement to Finish the Temple.* . . . London: Printed for R. D., 1642.

Gospel of Nicodemus. Edited by H. C. Kim. Toronto: Pontifical Institute of Mediaeval Studies, 1973.

Gui, Bernard. *Manuel de l'Inquisition.* Edited and translated by G. Mollat. Paris: Société d'édition "les Belles lettres," 1964.

Hall, Edmund. *Manus Testium Mouens, or A presbyteriall glosse upon many of those obscure prophetick texts.* . . . London: n.p., 1651.

Harpsfield, Nicholas (Alan Cope). *Dialogi Sex contra Summi Pontificatus, Monasticae vitae. Sanctorum, Sacrarum Imaginum Opovgnatores, et Pseudomartyres.* Antwerp: Christiphori Plantini, 1566.

Hennecke, Edgar, and Schneemelcher, Wilhelm. *New Testament Apocrypha* (2 vols.). English translation edited by R. McL. Wilson. Philadelphia: Westminster Press, 1965.

Hippolytus. *Commentaire sur Daniel.* Edited by M. Lefevre. Sources Chretiennes, 14. Paris: Editions du Cerf, 1947.

Hoffman, Melchior. *Auslegung der heimlichen Offenbarung* . . . , *1530.* I have relied on references to this work in Fast, *Der linke Flügel* (see II.A.).

————. *Das XII Capitel des propheten Danielis ausgelegt* . . . . Stockholm: Königliche Druckerei, 1526. I have relied on references to this work in Deppermann, *Hoffman* (see II.A.).

————. *Die Ordonanntie Godts.* . . . *1530.* I have relied on the English translation of this work in Williams and Mergal, *Spiritual and Anabaptist Writers* (see II.A.).

————. *Prophetische Gesicht und Offenbarung der götlichen werkung zu diser letsten zeit* . . . *1530.* I have relied on references to this work in Fast, *Der linke Flügel* (see II.A.).

Hopkins, Samuel. *A Treatise on the Millennium.* Boston, 1793.

Hus, Jan. *Historia et Monumenta Joannis Hus atque Hieronymi Pragensis confessorum Christi* (2 vols.). Edited by Matthias Flacius Illyricus. Nuremberg, 1558.

————. *Ioannes Huss De Anatomia Antichristi, Liber unus.* (Argentorati: Joannes Schottus, 1524?–1525?).

The Investigator or Monthly Expositor and Register on Prophecy. Edited by J. W. Brooks. London: Simpkin and Marshall, 1832–1833.

Irenaeus. *Adversus Haereses.* Edited by W. Wigan Harvey. Cambridge, England: Typis Academicis, 1857. Reprint, Ridgewood, N.J.: Gregg, 1965.

Jewel, John. *The Works of John Jewel* (4 vols.). Cambridge: Printed at the University Press, 1845–1850.

Joachim of Fiore. *Expositio magni prophete Abbatis Joachim in Apocalypsim.* Venice: Aedibus Francisci Bindoni, 1527. Reprint, Frankfurt: Minerva, 1964.

———. *Liber Concordiae Novi ac Veteris Testamenti.* Venice, 1519. Reprint, Frankfurt: Minerva, 1964.

———. *Psalterium decem cordarum.* . . . Reprint, Frankfurt: Minerva, 1965.

Johnson, Edward. *Johnson's Wonder-Working Providence, 1628–1651.* Edited by J. Franklin Jameson. New York: Charles Scribner's Sons, 1910.

Junius, Francis. *Apocalypsis Joannis illustrata.* Heidelberg, 1591; English edition: *Apocalypsis: A brief and learned commentarie.* . . . London: by Richard Field for Robert Dexter, 1592.

Jurieu, Pierre. *The accomplishment of the Scripture prophecies.* . . . Translated from the French edition, 1686. London: n.p., 1687.

Krebs, Manfred, and Rott, Hans Georg, eds. *Quellen zur Geschichte der Täufer, Elsass I und II.* Gütersloh, Germany: Gerd Mohn, 1959, 1960.

Lacunza, Manuel. *The Coming of the Messiah in Glory and Majesty.* . . . Translated by Edward Irving. London: L. B. Seeley, 1827.

Lambert, Bernard. *Expositions des predictions et des promesses faites a L'église pour les derniers temps de la Gentilité, 1806.* Published in German as *Die Weissagungen und Verheissungen.* . . . Edited by J. A. Kanne. Nuremberg: J. L. Schrag, 1818.

Lambert (d'Avignon), Francis. *Exegeseos in sanctam divi Joannis Apocalypsim Libri VII.* Marburg, Germany: Academia Marpurgensi praelecti, 1528.

Lapide, Cornelius. *Commentarius in Apocalypsim.* Lyon, 1627.

Lilburne, John. *Lilburne tract: pamphlets and broadsides by or relating to John Lilburne and the Levellers.* London, 1645–1653.

———. *A worke of the beast . . . executed upon John Lilburne . . . the 18 of Aprill 1638.* Printed in the yeare the beast was wounded, 1638.

Lowman, Moses. *A Paraphrase and Notes upon the Revelation of St. John.* London: J. Noon, 1737.

Ludus de Antichristo. Translated by John Wright. *The Play of Antichrist.* Toronto: Pontifical Institute of Medieval Studies, 1967.

Luther, Martin. *Martin Luther's Sämmtliche Werke.* Frankfurt and Erlangen: J. G. Plochman, 1826–1857.

———. *Martin Luthers Werke, Briefwechsel.* Weimar: Hermann Böhlaus Nachfolger, 1930–.

———. *Martin Luthers Werke, Deutsche Bibel.* Weimar: Hermann Böhlaus Nachfolger, 1906–1961.

———. *Martin Luthers Werke, Kritische Gesamtausgabe.* Weimar: Hermann Böhlaus Nachfolger, 1883.

———. *Martin Luthers Werke, Tischreden.* Weimar: Hermann Böhlaus Nachfolger, 1912–1921.

———. *Luthers Briefwechsel* (4 vols.). Edited by E. L. Enders. Frankfurt: I. K. Irmischer, 1884–1932.

———. *Luthers Works.* Philadelphia and St. Louis: Fortress Press and Concordia Press, 1955–1967.

———. *Martin Luthers Werke.* Edited by W. M. L. Dewette. Berlin, 1825–1828.

———. *Supputatio annorum mundi.* Wittenberg: Rhau, 1541.

———. *Three Treatises.* Philadelphia: Fortress Press, 1960.

Maitland, S. R. *Facts and Documents Illustrative of the History, Doctrine, and Rites of the Ancient Albigenses and Waldenses.* London: C. J. G. and F. Rivington, 1832.

Malvenda, Thomas. *De antichristo libri undecim.* Rome: apud Carolum Vulliettum, 1604.

Mather, Cotton. *Bonifacius: An Essay upon the Good.* . . . Edited by David Levin. Cambridge: Harvard University Press, 1966; original edition, Boston, 1710.

———. *Magnalia Christi Americana.* Edited by Kenneth B. Murdock with an introductory essay by George H. Williams. Cambridge: Harvard University Press, 1977.

———. *On Witchcraft.* . . . Boston, 1692; reprinted, New York: Bell Publishing Co. (1974).

Matthew of Janov. *Regulae veteris et novi testamenti* (5 vols.). Edited by Vlastimil Kybal. Oeniponte: Libraria Universitatis Wagnerana, 1911.

Mede, Joseph. *Clavis Apocalyptica ex innatis et insitis visionum characterisbus ervta et demonstrata.* Cantabrigiae [Cambridge], 1627; second edition, Cantabrigiae [Cambridge]: Thomas Buck, 1632.

———. *The Key of the Revelation searched and demonstrated out of the Naturall and Proper Characters of the Visions.* Translated by Richard More, 1643. London: Roger Norton, 1677.

———. *The Works of . . . Joseph Mede, B. D.* Edited by J. Worthington. London: Roger Norton, 1677.

Melanchthon, Philip. *Die Histori Thome Muntzers.* . . . Hagenaw: Durch J. Secerium Getruck, 1525.

Meyer, Sebastian. *In Apocalypsim Johannis.* . . . Zürich: Froschouer, 1554.

Milíč of Kroměříž. *Libellus de Antichristo.* In *Regulae veteris et novi testamenti* (Vol. 3, pp. 368–81). Edited by Vlastimil Kybal. Oeniponte: Libraria Universitatis Wagnerana, 1911.

Miller, William. *Evidence from Scripture and History of the Second Coming of Christ about the year 1843.* Troy, N.Y.: Kemble and Hooper, 1843.

Montanus, F. *Apologia pro Societate Jesu.* Ingolstadt, 1596.

Mosheim, Johann Lorenz. *Ecclesiastical History* . . . (2 vols.). London, 1756. Revised and enlarged in succeeding years.

Muggleton, Ludowicke. *A true interpretation of the eleventh chapter of the Revelation of St. John.* . . . London?, 1662; reprinted, 1751.

Müller, Lydia, ed. *Glaubenszeugnisse oberdeutscher Taufgesinnter.* Leipzig: M. Heinsius Nachfolger, 1938.

Munck, Johannes. *Petrus und Paulus in der Offenbarung Johannis.* Copenhagen: Rosenkilde og Bagger, 1950.

Müntzer, Thomas. *Schriften und Briefe: Kritische Gesamtausgabe.* Edited by Güther Franz. Gütersloh, Germany: Mohn, 1968.

Napier, John. *A Plaine Discovery of the Whole Revelation of Saint John.* Edinburgh: Robert Waldgrave, 1593.

Neander, Augustus. *General History of the Christian Religion and Church.* Translated by J. Torrey (5 vols.). Boston: Crocker and Brewster, 1854.

Newton, Thomas. *Dissertations on the prophecies.* . . . London: J. and R. Tonson and S. Draper, 1754–1758.

Nicene and Post-Nicene Fathers. Edited by Philip Schaff. Reprinted, Grand Rapids, Mich.: Eerdmans Publishing Co., 1974.

Nicholas of Lyra. *Postilla Super Actus Apostolorum Epistolas Canonicales et Apocalypsin.* Mantua: Aloisius de Siliprandis, 1480.

Nikolaus von Dresden. *The Old Color and the New.* Howard Kaminsky et al., editor and translator. Transactions of the American Philosophical Society, new ser. 55, pt. 1. Philadelphia: American Philosophical Society.

Oecomenius. *The Complete Commentary of Oecomenius on the Apocalypse*. Edited by Herman Charles Hoskier. Ann Arbor: University of Michigan Press, 1928.

Osiander, Andreas. *The conjectures of the ende of the worlde*. Translated by George Joye. [Antwerp?]: n.p., 1548; German, 1544.

Otto of Freising. *Chronica. Historia de duabus civitatibus*. Edited by A. Hofmeister. Scriptores Rerum Germanicarum. Hanover, 1912; English Translation, *The Two Cities: A Chronicle of Universal History to the Year 1146 A.D.* Translated by C. C. Mierow. New York: Columbia University Press, 1928.

Pareus, David. In *Divinam Apocalypsin S. Apostoli et Evangelistae Johannis Commentarius*. Heidelberg, 1618. Edition used, *A Commentary Upon the Divine Revelation of the Apostle and Evangelist John*. Translated by Elias Arnold. Amsterdam: printed by C. P., 1644.

Patrologiae cursus completus. . . . Series Graeca (161 vols.). Edited by Jacques Paul Migne. Paris: Seu Petit Montrage, 1857–1866.

    Andreas of Caesarea. *Commentarius in Apocalypsin*. Vol. 106.

    Arethas of Caesarea. *Commentarius in Apocalypsin*. Vol. 106.

    Hippolytus. *Demonstatio de Christo et Antichristo*. Vol. 10.

Patrologiae cursus completus . . . Series Latina (221 vols.). Edited by Jacques Paul Migne. Paris: n.p., 1844–1864.

    Anselm of Havelberg. *Dialogi*. Vol. 188.

    Anselm of Laon. *Enarrationes in Apocalypsin*. Vol. 162.

    Bede. *Explanatio Apocalypsis*. Vol. 93.

    Berengaudus. *Expositio super septem visiones libri Apocalypsis*. Vol. 17.

    ———. *In Expositionem Apocalypsis Admonite*. Vol. 14.

    Bruno of Asti. *Expositio in Apocalypsim*. Vol. 165.

    Caesarius of Arles. *Complexiones in Apocalypsin*. Vol. 70.

    Cassiodorus. *Complexiones in Apocalypsin*. Vol. 70.

    Haimo of Halberstadt. *Expositio in Apocalypsim*. Vol. 117.

    Honorius of Autun. *De Decem Plagis Aegypti*. Vol. 172.

    Martin of Leon. *Expositio libri Apocalypsis*. Vol. 209.

    Primasius of Hadrumetum. *Commentariorum super Apocalypsim*. Vol. 68.

    Quodvultdeus. *De promissionibus et praedictionibus dei*. Vol. 51.

    Richard of St. Victor. *In Apocalypsim Ioannis*. Vol. 196.

    Rupert of Deutz. *Commentariorum in Ioanis Apocalypsin*. Vol. 169.

    Tyconius. *Commentarius in Apocalypsim*. Supplementum 1.

    Walafrid Strabo (Anselm of Laon). *Glossa Ordinaria*. Vol. 114.

Pereyra, Benedict. *Disputationes Super libro Apocalypsis*. Lyon, 1606.

Purvey, John. *Commentarius in Apocalypsin*. . . . Wittenberg: n.p., 1528.

Quodvultdeus. *Quodvultdeus: Livre des promesses et des predictions de Dieu* (Vols. 101–102). Edited by R. Braun. Sources Chretiennes. Paris: Cerf, 1964.

Ribeira, Francisco. *Commentarius in Apocalypsim*. Salamanca, Spain: Excudebat Petrus Lassus, 1585, 1591.

Robinson, Hastings, ed. *Original Letters Relative to the English Reformation . . . from the archives of Zürich*. Published for the Parker Society. Cambridge: Cambridge University Press, 1842–1847.

———. *The Zürich Letters . . . the Correspondence of Several English Bishops and Others with Some of the Helvetian Reformers*. Cambridge: Cambridge University Press, 1842.

Rothmann, Bernhard. *Die Schriften Bernhard Rothmanns. Die Schriften der Münsterischen Täufer und ihrer Gegner*, Vol. 1. Edited by Robert Stupperich: Münster, 1970.

Schornbaum, Karl, ed. *Quellen zur Geschichte der Täufer, Bayern I. Markgraftum Branden-burg* (QgT 2). Gütersloh, Germany: C. Bertelsmann, 1934.

———. *Quellen zur Geschichte der Täufer, Bayern II. Reichsstädte* (QgT 5). Gütersloh, Germany: C. Bertelsmann, 1951.

Servetus, Michael. *Christianismi Restitutio*. Vienna, 1553. Reprinted, Frankfurt: Minerva, 1966.

Sewall, Samuel. *Phaenomena Quaedam Apocalyptica*. Boston: Bartholomew Green and John Allen, 1697.

———. *Proposals Touching the Accomplishment of Prophecies Humbly Offered*. Boston: Bartholomew Green, 1713.

———. *Diary of Samuel Sewall*. Collections of the Massachusetts Historical Society, 5th series, vols. 5–7. Boston, 1878–1887.

Simons, Menno. *Fundamentum. Ein Fundament und klare Ausweisung von der Selig-machenden Lehre unsers Herren Jesu Christi*. 1575; Basel: Horst, 1740. The English text is from *The Complete Writings of Menno Simons*. Edited by J. C. Wenger; translated by L. Verduin. Scottdale, Pa.: Herald Press, 1956.

Sleidanus, Johannes. *A Briefe Chronicle of the Foure Principall Empyres*. Translated by Stephan Wythers. London: Rouland Hall, 1563.

Strand, Kenneth A., ed. *Woodcuts to the Apocalypse in Dürer's Time*. Ann Arbor, Mich.: Ann Arbor Publishers, 1968.

Stuart, Moses. *Commentary on the Apocalypse* (2 vols.). Andover, Mass.: Allen, Morrill and Wardwell, 1845.

Tertullian. *De anima*. Edited by J. H. Waszink. Amsterdam: J. M. Meuleuhoff, 1947.

Thomas Aquinas. *Summa theologiae* (60 vols). Edited by English Dominicans. New York: McGraw-Hill, 1964–1966; also 3 vols. New York: Benziger, 1947–1948.

Tiburtine Oracle. Edited by Paul J. Alexander. *The Oracle of Baalbek: The Tiburtine Sibyl in Greek Dress*. Dumbarton Oaks Studies, vol. 10. Washington, D.C.: Dumbarton Oaks, 1967.

———. Edited by Ernst Sackur. *Sibyllinische Texte und Forschungen, Pseudo and meth-odius, Adso und die Tiburtinische Sibylle*. Halle: Max Niemeyer, 1898; reprinted, Turin: D'Erasmo, 1963.

Tillinghast, John. *Knowledge of the Times, or, The Resolution of the Question. . . .* London: R. J. for L. Chapman, 1654.

———. *Generation Work*. London. M. Simmons for L. Chapman, 1653.

Tyconius. *The Book of Rules of Tyconius*. Edited by F. C. Burkitt. *Texts and Studies*, Vol. 3. Cambridge: Cambridge University Press, 1894.

———. *The Turin Fragments of Tyconius' Commentary on Revelation*. Edited by Francesco Lo Bue. Cambridge: Cambridge University Press, 1963.

Ubertino da Casale. *Arbor vitae crucifixae Jesu*. Venice: Andreas de Bonetis, 1485.

Vitringa, Campegius. *Anakrisis Apocalypseos*. Franeker, The Netherlands: Halmam, 1705.

Whiston, William. *An Essay on the Revelation of St. John*. Cambridge, England: B. Tooke, 1706.

Whitby, Daniel. *A Paraphrase and Commentary on the New Testament*. London, 1727.

Wigglesworth, Michael. *Day of Doom*. Cambridge, England: Printed by S. Green, 1666.

Williams, Roger. *Complete Writings* (7 vols.). Edited by Samuel L. Caldwell. New York: Russell & Russell, 1963.

Winstanley, Gerrard. "The Breaking of the Day." In *The Works of Gerrard Winstanley*. Edited by George H. Sabine. Ithaca, N.Y.: Cornell University Press, 1941.

Wolf, Johann. *De Christiana perseverantia. . . .* Zürich: C. Froschouer, 1578.

———. *Melachim; id est. Regum libri duo posteriores cum commentariis Petri Martyris Vermillii.* . . . Zürich: C. Froschouer, 1571.

Zwingli, Huldreich. *Sämtliche Werke.* Edited by Emil Egli, Georg Finsler, and Walther Köhler. Leipzig: M. Heinsius Nachfolger, 1911.

———. *De vera et falsa religione commentarius.* 1525. CR, 90. English translation, *Commentary on True and False Religion.* Edited by Samuel M. Jackson and Clarence N. Heller. Durham, N.C.: The Labyrinth Press, 1981.

Secondary Sources

Books

Aells, H. *Martin Bucer.* New Haven, Conn.: Yale University Press, 1931.

Aichele, Klaus. *Das Antichristdrama des Mittelalters, der Reformation und Gegenreformation.* The Hague: Martin's Nijhoff, 1974.

Alford, Henry. *The Greek New Testament* (Vol. 4, 3d ed.). Cambridge, England: Rivingtons, 1866.

Allo, P. E.-B. *L'Apocalypse.* Paris: Librairie Victor Lecoffre, 1921.

Althaus, Paul. *The Theology of Martin Luther.* Translated by R. C. Schultz. Philadelphia: Fortress Press, 1966.

Arbusow, Leonid. *Die Einführung der Reformation in Liv-, Est- und Kurland.* Leipzig: M. Heinsius Nachfolger, 1921.

Asendorf, Ulrich. *Eschatologie bei Luther.* Göttingen: Vandenhoeck und Ruprecht, 1967.

Atkinson, Geoffrey. *Les Nouveaux Horizons de la Renaissance Française.* Paris: Libraire E. Droz, 1935.

Atzberger, Leonhard. *Geschichte der christlichen Eschatologie innerhalb der vornicänischen Zeit.* Freiburg im Breisgau, Germany: Herder'sche Verlagshandlung, 1896.

Auerbach, Erich. *Mimesis: The Representation of Reality in Western Literature.* Translated by Willard R. Trask. Princeton, N.J.: Princeton University Press, 1953.

Avis, Paul D. L. *The Church in the Theology of the Reformers.* Atlanta: John Knox Press, 1981.

Bächtold, Hans Ulrich. *Heinrich Bullinger vor dem Rat: Zur Gestaltung und Verwaltung des Zürcher Staatswesens in den Jahren 1531 bis 1575.* Bern: Peter Lang, 1982.

Bainton, Roland. *Hunted Heretic.* Boston: Beacon Press, 1960.

Baker, J. Wayne. *Heinrich Bullinger and the Covenant: The Other Reformed Tradition.* Athens: Ohio University Press, 1980.

Balke, Wilhelm. *Calvin and the Anabaptist Radicals.* Translated by William J. Heynen. Grand Rapids, Mich.: Eerdmans Publishing Co., 1981; Amsterdam, 1973.

Ball, Bryan. *A Great Expectation: Eschatological Thought in English Protestantism to 1660.* Leiden: Brill, 1975.

Barnes, Robin Bruch. *Prophecy and Gnosis: Apocalypticism in the Wake of the Lutheran Reformation.* Stanford, Calif.: Stanford University Press, 1988.

Baron, Hans. *The Crisis of the Italian Renaissance: Civic Humanism and Republican Liberty in an Age of Classicism and Tyranny.* Princeton, N.J.: Princeton University Press, 1966.

Baron, R. *Etudes sur Hugues de Saint-Victor.* Paris: Desclée, De Brouwer, 1963.

Bass, Clarence B. *Backgrounds to Dispensationalism: Its Historical Genesis and Ecclesiastical Implications.* Grand Rapids, Mich.: Baker Book House, 1960.

Bauckhan, Richard. *Tudor Apocalypse.* Oxford: The Sutton Courtenay Press, 1978.

Bauer, Günther. *Anfänge täuferischer Gemeindebildungen in Franken.* Nuremberg: Verein für bayerische Kirchengeschichte, 1966.

Bauman, Clarence. *Gewaltlosigkeit im Täufertum: Eine Untersuchung zur theologischen Ethik des oberdeutschen Täufertums der Reformationszeit.* Leiden: Brill, 1968.

Beasley-Murray, G. R. *Jesus and the Future.* London: Macmillan, 1954.

Becker, Reinhard P., ed. *German Humanism and Reformation.* New York: Continuum Press, 1983.

Beckwith, I. T. *The Apocalypse of John.* New York: Macmillan, 1919.

Beinert, Wolfgang. *Die Kirche-Gottes Heil in der Welt.* Münster: Verlag Aschendorff, 1973.

Beker, J. Christiaan. *Paul the Apostle.* Philadelphia: Fortress Press, 1980.

Bellah, Robert N. et al. *The Good Society.* New York: Knopf, 1991.

———. *Habits of the Heart.* Berkeley and Los Angeles: University of California Press, 1985.

Bellard, Werner. *Wolfgang Schultheyss. Wege und Wondlungen cines Strassburger Spiritualisten und Zeitgenossen Martin Bucers.* Frankfurt: Erwin von Steinbach-Stiflung, 1976.

Bennett, J. A. W., and Smithers, G. V., eds. *Early Middle English Verse and Prose* (2d ed.). Oxford: Clarendon Press, 1968.

Bensing, Manfred. *Thomas Müntzer und der Thüringer Aufstand 1525.* Berlin: VEB Deutscher Verlag der Wissenschaften, 1966.

Benz, Ernst. *Ecclesia Spiritualis: Kirchenidee und Geschichtstheologie der Franziskanischen Reformation.* Stuttgart: W. Kolhammer, 1934.

Berchtold-Belart, Jakob. *Das Zwinglibild und die Züricherischen Reformationschroniken.* Leipzig: Verlag von M. Heinsius, 1929.

Bercovitch, Sacvan, ed. *The American Puritan Imagination: Essays in Revaluation.* Cambridge: Cambridge University Press, 1974.

———. *Typology and Early American Literature.* Amherst: University of Massachusetts Press, 1972.

———. *The Puritan Origins of the American Self.* New Haven: Yale University Press, 1975.

Berger, Heinrich. *Calvins Geschichtsauffassung.* Zürich: Zwingli Verlag, 1955.

Bergsten, Torsten. *Balthasar Hubmaier: Seine Stellung zu Reformation und Täufertum, 1521–1528.* Kassel: J. G. Oncken, 1961. English version translated by I. J. Barnes and edited by W. R. Estep, Jr., *Balthasar Hubmaier: Anabaptist Theologian and Martyr.* Valley Forge, Pa.: Judson Press, 1978.

Berkhof, Louis. *The Kingdom of God.* Grand Rapids, Mich.: Eerdmans Publishing Co., 1951.

Berkhout, Carl T., and Russell, Jeffrey B. *Medieval Heresies: A Bibliography, 1960–1979.* Toronto: Pontifical Institute of Mediaeval Studies, 1981.

Blaising, Craig A., and Bock, Darrell L., eds. *Dispensationalism, Israel and the Church, The Search for Definition.* Grand Rapids, Mich.: Zondervan Publishing House, 1992.

Blickle, Peter. *The Revolution of 1525: The German Peasants' War from a New Perspective.* Translated by Thomas A. Brady, Jr., and H. C. Erik Middelfort. Baltimore: The Johns Hopkins University Press, 1981.

Böhmer, Heinrich. *Studien zu Thomas Müntzer.* Leipzig, 1922.

Bonhoeffer, Dietrich. *The Communion of Saints.* New York: Harper and Row, 1963.

Bonner, Gerald. *Saint Bede in the Tradition of Western Apocalyptic Commentary.* Jarrow Lecture, England, 1966.

Bonner, Leah. *The Stories of Elijah and Elisha as Polemics against Baal Worship.* Leiden: Brill, 1968.

Bornkamm, Heinrich. *Luther in Mid-Career 1521–1530.* Edited and with a foreword by Karin Bornkamm. Translated by E. T. Bachmann. Philadelphia: Fortress Press, 1983.

Bosch, David J. *Transforming Mission: Paradigm Shifts in Theology of Mission.* Maryknoll, N.Y.: Orbis Books, 1991.

Bourdieu, Pierre. *Language and Symbolic Power.* Cambridge: Harvard University Press, 1991.

Bossy, John. *Christianity in the West, 1400–1700.* New York: Oxford University Press, 1985.

Bousset, Wilhelm. *The Antichrist Legend.* Translated by A. H. Keane. London: Hutchinson, 1896.

————. *Die Offenbarung Johannis.* Göttingen: Vandenhoeck und Ruprecht, 1906. Reprint, 1966.

————. *Die Religion des Judentums im späthellenistischen Zeitalter. Handbuch zum NT.* Tübingen, Germany: Mohr, 1926.

Bouwsma, William J. *Concordia Mundi: The Career and Thought of Guillaume Postel, 1510–1581.* Cambridge: Harvard University Press, 1957.

Boyer, Paul. *When Time Shall Be No More.* Cambridge, Ma.: Belknap Press, 1992.

Brady, David. *The Contribution of British Writers Between 1560 and 1830 to the Interpretation of Revelation 13, 16–18 (The Number of the Beast): A Study in the History of Exegesis.* Tübingen, Germany: Mohr, 1983.

Bräuer, Siegfried, and Ullmann, Wolfgang. *Theologische Schriften aus dem Jahr 1523.* Berlin: Evangelische Verlagsanstalt, 1982.

Brinkmann, Günther. *Die Irenik des David Pareus: Frieden und Einheit ihrer Relevanz zur Warheitfrage.* Hildesheim, Germany: Gerstenberg, 1972.

Brodrick, James. *Robert Bellarmine.* London: Burns and Oates, 1961.

Brown, Peter. *Augustine of Hippo: A Biography.* Berkeley: University of California Press, 1969.

————. *The Cult of Saints.* Chicago: University of Chicago Press, 1981.

Brückner, Wolfgang, ed. *Volkserzählung und Reformation.* Berlin: Erich Schmidt, 1974.

Brütsch, Charles. *Die Offenbarung Jesu Christi.* Zürich: Zwingli Verlag, 1970.

Buck, Lawrence P., and Zophy, Jonathan W., eds. *The Social History of the Reformation.* Columbus: Ohio State University Press, 1972.

Burdach, Konrad. *Vom Mittelalter zur Reformation: Forschungen zur Geschichte der Deutschen Bildung.* Berlin: Weidmannsche Buchhandlung, 1913.

Burke, Peter, ed. *A New Kind of History and Other Essays.* New York, 1973.

Büsser, Fritz, ed. *Heinrich Bullinger Werke* (4 vols.). Zürich: Theologischer Verlag, 1972.

————. *Huldrych Zwingli: Reformation als Prophetischer Auftrag.* Göttingen, Germany: Musterschmidt, 1973.

Callaey, Frédégand. *L'idealisme franciscain spirituel au XIVe siècle: Etude sur Ubertin de Casale.* Université de Louvain. Recueil de travaux pub. par les membres des conférences d'histoire et de pihlologie. . . . Louvain: Bureau du Recueil, 1911.

Charles, R. A. *A Critical and Exegetical Commentary on the Revelation of St. John* (2 vols.). The International Critical Commentary. Edinburgh: T. & T. Clark, 1920.

————. *Studies in the Apocalypse.* Edinburgh: T. & T. Clark, 1913.

Chrisman, Miriam Usher. *Strasbourg and the Reform: A Study in the Process of Change.* New Haven, Conn.: Yale University Press, 1967.

Christe, Yves, ed. *L'Apocalypse de Jean.* Geneva: Libraire E. Droz, 1979.

Christianson, Paul. *Reformers and Babylon: English Apocalyptic Visions from the Reformation to the Eve of the Civil War.* Toronto: University of Toronto Press, 1978.

Clasen, Claus-Peter. *Anabaptism: A Social History, 1528–1618.* Ithaca, N.Y.: University of Cornell Press, 1972.

Clavier, Henri. *Etudes sur le Calvinisme.* Paris: Librairie Fischbacher, 1936.

Clemen, Otto, ed. *Beiträge zur Bayrischern Kirchengeschichte*, Vol. 4, 1898.

————. *Flugschriften aus den ersten Jahren der Reformation* (4 vols.). Leipzig: Rudolf Haupt, 1909.

Clouse, Robert G., ed. *The Meaning of the Millennium: Four Views*. Downers Grover, Ill.: InterVarsity Press, 1977.

Cocagnac, A.-M. *Le jugement dernier dans l'art*. Paris: Editions du Cerf, 1955.

Cochrane, Charles. *Christianity and Classical Culture*. New York: Oxford University Press, 1957.

Cohn, Norman. *The Pursuit of the Millennium: Revolutionary Millenarians and Mystical Anarchists of the Middle Ages* (rev. ed.). New York: Oxford University Press, 1970.

Collins John J., ed. *Apocalypse: The Morphology of a Genre, Semeia. Vol. 14*. Missoula, Mont.: Scholar's Press, 1979.

Collinson, Patrick. *The Birthpangs of Protestant England: Religious and Cultural Change in the Sixteenth and Seventeenth Centuries*. London: Macmillan, 1988.

————. *The Elizabethan Puritan Movement*. Berkeley: University of California Press, 1967.

Cornelius, Carl Adolph. *Geschichte des Münsterischen Aufruhrs* (2 vols.). Leipzig: T. D. Wiegel, 1855, 1860.

Court, John M. *Myth and History in the Book of Revelation*. Atlanta: John Knox Press, 1979.

Courvoisier, Jacques. *De la Réforme au Protestantisme: Essai d'ecclesiologie réformée*. Paris: Editions Beauchesne, 1977.

Covey, Cyclone. *The Gentle Radical: A Biography of Roger Williams*. New York: Macmillan, 1966.

Cox, Harvey Gallagher, Jr. *The Secular City: Secularization and Urbanization in Theological Perspectives*. New York: Macmillan Press, 1966, rev. ed.

Cullmann, Oscar. *The Christology of the New Testament* (rev. ed.). Philadelphia: Westminster Press, 1959.

Daley, Brian E. *The Hope of the Early Church. A Handbook of Patristic Eschatology*. Cambridge: Cambridge University Press, 1991.

Daniel, E. Randolph. *The Franciscan Concept of Mission in the High Middle Ages*. Lexington: University of Kentucky Press, 1975.

Dannenbauer, Heinrich. *Luther als religiöser Volksschriftsteller, 1517–1520: Ein Beitrag zu der Frage nach den Ursachen der Reformation*. Tübingen, Germany: Mohr, 1930.

Davidson, James West. *The Logic of Millennial Thought: Eighteenth-Century New England*. New Haven, Conn.: Yale University Press, 1977.

Davies, Horton. *Worship and Theology in England: From Andrewes to Baxter and Fox, 1603–1690*. Princeton, N.J.: Princeton University Press, 1975.

Dawson, Christopher. *The Gods of Revolution*. New York: New York University Press, 1972.

Deane, Herbert A. *The Political and Social Ideas of St. Augustine*. New York: Columbia University Press, 1963.

DeJong, J. A. *As the Waters Cover the Sea*. Kampen, The Netherlands: J. H. Kok, 1970.

Dempf, Alois. *Sacrum Imperium. Geschichts- und Staats- philosophie der politishen Renaissance*. Munich and Berlin: R. Oldenbourg, 1929.

Deppermann, Klaus. *Melchior Hoffman: Soziale Unruhen und apokalyptische Visionen im Zeitalter der Reformation*. Göttingen, Germany: Vandenhoeck und Ruprecht, 1979.

DeVooght, Paul. *L'Hérésie de Jean Hus*. Bibliothèque de la Revue d'histoire ecclésiastique, fasc. 34. Louvain, 1960.

Dobson, Ed. and Hindson, Ed. *The Fundamentalist Phenomenon: The Resurgence of Conservative Christianity*. New York: Doubleday-Galilee, 1981.

Dodd, C. H. *The Bible and Its Background.* London: G. Allen and Unwin, 1931.

Döllinger, J. J. I., ed. *Beiträge zur Sektengeschichte des Mittelalters, II. Dokumente vornehmlich zur Geschichte der Valdesier und Katharer.* Munich: C. H. Beckische Verlagsbuchhandlung, 1890.

Douglas, Mary. *Natural Symbols.* New York: Random House, 1973.

Douie, Decima. *The Nature and Effect of the Heresy of the Fraticelli.* Manchester: University of Manchester Press, 1932.

Dülmen, Richard van, ed. *Das Täuferreich zu Münster 1534–1535: Berichte und Dokumente.* Munich: Deutscher Taschenbuch Verlag, 1974.

Easton, Stewart, C. *Roger Bacon and His Search for a Universal Science.* New York: Columbia University Press, 1952.

Ebeling, Gerhard. *Luther: An Introduction to His Thought.* Translated by R. A. Wilson. Philadelphia: Fortress Press, 1970.

Edwards, Mark. *Luther's Last Battles: Politics and Polemics.* Ithaca, N.Y.: Cornell University Press, 1983.

Ehrismann, Gustav. *Geschichte der deutschen Literatur bis zum Ausgang des Mittelalters* (2 parts in 5 vols.). Munich: Beck, 1918–1935.

Eisenstein, Elizabeth L. *The Printing Press as an Agent of Change: Communication and Cultural Transformations in Early-Modern Europe.* Cambridge: Cambridge University Press, 1979.

Elert, Werner. *The Structure of Lutheranism.* Translated by Walter Hanson. St. Louis: Concordia Press, 1962.

Elliger, Walter. *Thomas Müntzer: Leben und Werk.* Göttingen, Germany: Vandenhoeck und Ruprecht, 1975.

Ellul, Jacques. *Apocalypse: The Book of Revelation.* Translated by George W. Schreiner. New York: Seabury Press, 1977.

Elton, G. R., ed. *The New Cambridge Modern History: The Reformation, 1520–1559.* Cambridge: Cambridge University Press, 1958.

Emmerson, Richard. *Antichrist in the Middle Ages: A Study of Medieval Apocalypticism, Art, and Literature.* Seattle: University of Washington Press, 1981.

Emmerson, Richard K., and Bernard McGinn, eds. *The Apocalypse in the Middle Ages.* Ithaca, N.Y.: Cornell University Press, 1992.

Erickson, Millard J. *Contemporary Options in Eschatology.* Grand Rapids, Mich.: Baker Book House, 1977.

Ernst, U. *Geschichte des Zürcherischen Schulwesens bis gegen Ende des sechzehnten Jahr-hunderts.* Winterhur, Switzerland: Buchdrackerei Bleuler- Mausheer & cie, 1879.

Esser, Cajetan. *Origins of the Franciscan Order.* Translated by A. Daly and I. Lynch. Chicago: Franciscan Herald Press, 1970.

Fackre, Gabriel. *The Christian Story.* Grand Rapids, Mich.: Eerdmans Publishing Co., 1987.

Fairfield, Leslie P. *John Bale: Mythmaker for the English Reformation.* West Lafayette, Ind.: Purdue University Press, 1976.

Falls, Thomas B. *Saint Justin Martyr: Dialogue with Trypho, 49. Vol. 6: The Fathers of the Church.* Washington, D.C.: Catholic University of America, 1948; reprinted 1965.

Farner, Oskar. *Huldrych Zwingli* (4 vols.). Zürich: Zwingli Verlag, 1943–1960.

Fast, Heinold, ed. *Der linke Flügel der Reformation.* Bremen: Schünemann Verlag, 1962.

Fatio, Olivier. *Methode et theologie: Lambert Daneau et les debuts de la scholastique reformée.* Geneva: Libraire E. Droz, 1976.

Feinberg, Charles L. *Millennialism: The Two Major Views.* Chicago: Moody Press, 1982.

Figi, Jacques. *Die innere Reorganisation des Grossmünsterstiftes in Zürich von 1519 bis 1531.* Affoltern am Albis, 1951.

Firth, Katherine R. *The Apocalyptic Tradition in Reformation Britain, 1530–1645.* New York and London: Oxford University Press, 1979.

Fison, J. E. *The Christian Hope.* London: Longman, 1954.

Fleming, John V. *An Introduction to the Franciscan Literature of the Middle Ages.* Chicago: Franciscan Herald Press, 1977.

Fohrer, Georg. *Elia* (rev. ed.). Zürich: Zwingli Verlag, 1968.

Ford, J. Massyngberde. *Revelation.* New York: Doubleday, 1975.

Forell, George W. *Faith Active in Love: An Investigation of the Principles Underlying Luther's Social Ethics.* New York: The American Press, 1954.

Fraenkel, Peter. *Testimonia Patrum: The Function of the Patristic Argument in the Theology of Philip Melanchthon.* Geneva: Libraire E. Droz, 1961.

Franciscains d'Oc, Les Spirituels: ca. 1280–1324. Cahiers de Fanjeaux, Vol. 10. Toulouse: E. Privat, 1975.

Frei, Hans W. *The Eclipse of Biblical Narrative: A Study of Eighteenth and Nineteenth Century Hermeneutics.* New Haven, Conn.: Yale University Press, 1974.

Frend, W. H. C. *The Donatist Church: A Movement of Protest in Roman North Africa.* Oxford: Clarendon Press, 1952.

Friedman, Jerome. *Michael Servetus: A Case Study in Total Heresy.* Geneva: Libraire E. Droz, 1978.

Friedman, Robert. *Die Schriften der Huterischen Täufergemeinschaften.* Wich: Herman Böhlaus Nachfolger, 1965.

Friedrich, Johann. *Astrologie und Reformation.* Munich: Universitäts-Buchhandlung, 1864.

Friesen, Abraham. *Reformation and Utopia.* Wiesbaden: Franz Steiner Verlag, 1974.

———. *Thomas Müntzer, A Destroyer of the Godless. The Making of a Sixteenth-Century Religious Revolutionary.* Berkeley, Calif.: University of California Press, 1990.

———, and Goertz, Hans-Jürgen, eds. *Thomas Müntzer: Wege der Forschung.* Darmstadt: Wissenschaftliche Buchgesellschaft, 1978.

Froehlich, Karlfried. In Mark S. Burrows and Paul Rorem, eds., *Biblical Hermeneutics in Historical Perspective.* Grand Rapids, Mich.: Eerdmans Publishing Co., 1991.

———. *Biblical Interpretation in the Early Church.* Philadelphia: Fortress Press, 1905.

Froom, Leroy. *The Prophetic Faith of Our Fathers* (4 vols.). Washington, D.C.: Review and Herald, 1948.

Funk, Robert W., ed. *Apocalypticism: Journal for Theology and the Church.* Vol. 6. New York: Herder and Herder, 1961.

Funkenstein, Amos. *Heilsplan und natürliche Entwicklung.* Munich: Nymphenburger Verlagsbuchhandlung, 1965.

Gäbler, Ulrich, and Herkenrath, Erland, eds. *Heinrich Bullinger 1504–1575: Gesammelte Aufsätze zum 400. Todestag.* Zürich: Theologischer Verlag, 1975.

Gäbler, Ulrich, and Herkenrath, Erland, eds. *Heinrich Bullinger Briefwechsel: Vol. 1. 1524–1531.* Zürich: Theologischer Verlag, 1973.

Galden, Joseph A. *Typology and Seventeenth-Century Literature.* The Hague: Mouton, 1975.

Gardiner, Harold C. *Mysteries' End: An Investigation of the Last Days of the Medieval Religious State.* New Haven, Conn.: Yale University Press, 1946.

Garin, Eugenio. *Italian Humanism: Philosophy and Civic Life in the Renaissance.* New York: Harper and Row, 1965.

Garrett, Christina Hallowell. *The Marian Exiles: A Study in the Origins of Elizabethan Puritanism.* Cambridge: Cambridge University Press, 1938.

Gay, Peter. *A Loss of Mastery: Puritan Historians in Colonial America.* Berkeley: University of California Press, 1966.

Gerrish, Brian A. *The Old Protestantism and the New.* Chicago: University of Chicago Press, 1982.

Gerrish, Brian A., ed. *Reformers in Profile.* Philadelphia: Fortress Press, 1967.

Ghellinck, Joseph de. *Le mouvement théologique du XIIe siècle.* Bruges: Editions "De Tempel," 1948.

Giamatti, A. Bartlett. *The Earthly Paradise and the Renaissance Epic.* Princeton, N.J.: Princeton University Press, 1966.

Gibson, Edgar C. S. *The Thirty-nine Articles of the Church of England.* London: Methuen, 1904.

Gilmore, M. P. *Humanists and Jurists.* Cambridge: Harvard University Press, 1963.

Gilpin, W. Clark. *The Millenarian Piety of Roger Williams.* Chicago: University of Chicago Press, 1979.

Gilson, Etienne. *The Philosophy of St. Bonaventure.* Translated by Illtyd Trethowan and Frank Sheed. Paterson, N.J.: St. Anthony Guild Press, 1965.

Ginzberg, L. *An Unknown Jewish Sect.* New York: Jewish Theological Seminary, 1976.

Goertz, Hans-Jürgen. *Innere und äussere Ordnung in der Theologie Thomas Müntzers.* Leiden: Brill, 1967.

———, ed. *Radikale Reformation.* Munich: C. H. Beck, 1978.

Göllner, Karl. *Turcica. Die europäischen Türkendrucke des 16. Jahrhunderts.* Bucharest: Editura Academiei R.P.R., 1961.

Goppelt, Leonard. *Typos: The Typological Interpretation of the Old Testament in the New.* Grand Rapids, Mich.: Eerdmans Publishing Co., 1982.

Grant, Michael. *The Ancient Historians.* New York: Schribner, 1970.

Gritsch, Eric W. *Reformer without a Church. The Life and Thought of Thomas Muentzer 1488 [?]–1525.* Philadelphia: Fortress Press, 1967. See his later work: *Thomas Müntzer: A Tragedy of Errors.* Minneapolis, Minn.: Fortress Press, 1989.

Grundmann, Herbert. *Studien über Joachim von Floris.* Leipzig: 1927. Reprint, Darmstadt: Wissenschaftliche Buchgesellschaft, 1966.

Gussmann, Wilhelm D. *Johannes Ecks Vierhundertundvier Artikel zum Reichstag von Augsburg 1580.* Kassel: Edmund Pillardy, 1930.

———. *Quellen und Forschungen zur Geschichte des Augsburgischen Glaubensbekenntaisses*, Vol. 2. Kassel: Edmund Pillardy, 1930.

Haas, Martin, and Hauswirth, Rene, eds. *Festgabe Leonhard von Muralt.* Zürich: Verlag Berichthaus, 1970.

Habig, Marion A., ed. *St. Francis of Assisi: Writings and Early Biographies. English Omnibus of the Sources for the Life of St. Francis.* Chicago: Franciscan Herald Press, 1973.

Haendler, Gert. *Amt und Gemeinde bei Luther in Kontext der Kirchengeschichte.* Stuttgart: Calwer Verlag, 1929.

Hahn, Traugott. *Tyconius-Studien; ein Beitrag zur Kirchen–und Dogmengeschichte des 4. Jahrhunderts.* Aalen, Germany: Scientia Verlag, 1971.

Hailperin, Herman. *Rashi and the Christian Scholars.* Pittsburgh: University of Pittsburgh Press, 1963.

Hall, David D. *Worlds of Wonder, Days of Judgment: Popular Religious Belief in Early New England* (New York: Knopf, 1989).

Haller, William. *Acts and Monuments: Foxe's Book of Martyrs and the Elect Nation.* London: Jonathan Cape, 1963.

———. *The Rise of Puritanism.* Philadelphia: University of Pennsylvania Press, 1938.

Hanson, Paul. *The Dawn of Apocalyptic* (rev. ed.). Philadelphia: Fortress Press, 1979.

———, ed. *Visionaries and Their Apocalypses.* Philadelphia: Fortress Press, 1983.

Hargrave, Barbara. *The Sociology of Religion: Classical and Contemporary Approaches.* Arlington Heights, Ill.: Harlan Davidson, 1989.

Hatch, Nathan. *The Sacred Cause of Liberty.* New Haven, Conn.: Yale University Press, 1977.

Hauerwas, Stanley. *A Community of Character. Toward a Constructive Christian Social Ethic.* Notre Dame, Ind.: University of Notre Dame Press, 1981.

Haugg, Donatus. *Die Zwei Zeugen: Eine exegetische Studie über Apok, 11:1–13.* Münster: Aschendorffsche Verlagsbuchhandlung, 1936.

Hausaman, Susi. *Römerbriefauslegung zwischen Humanismus und Reformation.* Zürich: Zwingli Verlag, 1970.

Headley, John. *Luther's View of Church History.* New Haven, Conn.: Yale University Press, 1963.

Heer, Frederick. *The Intellectual History of Europe.* Translated by Jonathan Steinberg. New York: World Publishing Co., 1953.

Heermann, Horst. *Savonarola: Der Ketzer von San Marco.* Munich: C. Bertelsmann Verlag, 1977.

Heimert, Alan. *Religion and the American Mind.* Cambridge: Harvard University Press, 1966.

Heist, William W. *The Fifteen Signs Before Doomsday.* East Lansing: Michigan State College Press, 1952.

Hendrix, Scott H. *Luther and the Papacy: Stages in a Reformation Conflict.* Philadelphia: Fortress Press, 1981.

Henegan, John J. *The Progress of Dogma According to Anselm of Havelberg.* Rome: Pontifical Gregorian University, 1943.

Heppe, Heinrich. *Dogmatik des deutschen Protestantismus im sechzehnten Jarhundert* (3 vols.). Gotha, Germany: F. A. Perthes, 1857.

Heyer, Fritz. *Der Kirchenbegriff der Schwärmer: Schriften des Vereins für Reformationsgeschichte,* Vol. 56. Leipzig: Heinsius Nachfolger, 1939.

Hill, Christopher. *Antichrist in Seventeenth-Century England.* London: Oxford University Press, 1971.

———. *God's Englishman: Oliver Cromwell and the English Revolution.* New York: Harper Torchbooks, 1970.

———. *Some Intellectual Consequences of the English Revolution.* Madison: University of Wisconsin Press, 1980.

———. *The World Turned Upside Down: Radical Ideas During the English Revolution.* New York: Penguin, 1975.

Hillerbrand, Hans J. *Thomas Müntzer: A Bibliography.* St. Louis: Center for Reformation Research, 1976.

Hinrichs, Carl. *Luther and Müntzer: Ihre Auseinandersetzung über Obrigkeit und Widerstandsrecht, Vol. 29 of Arbeiten zur Kirchengeschichte.* Edited by K. Aland, Eltester, and Rückert. Berlin: Walter de Gruyter, 1952.

Hipler, Franz. *Die Christliche Geschichtsauffasung.* Cologne: J. Bachen, 1884.

Hirth, Georg. *Bilder aus der Lutherzeit; eine Sammlung von Porträts aus der Zeit der Reformation in getreuen Facsimile- Nachbildungen.* Munich: G. Hort, 1883.

Hofmann, Hans-Ulrich. *Luther und die Johannes- Apokalypse: Dargestellt im Rahmen des Auslegungsgeschicte des letzten Buches der Bibel und im Zusamenhang des theologicischen Enturicklung des Reformators.* Tübingen, Germany: Mohr/Paul Siebeck, 1982.

Holl, Karl. "Martin Luther on Luther." Translated by H. C. Erick Midelfort. In Jaroslav Pelikan, ed., *Interpreters of Luther: Essays in Honor of Wilhelm Paruck.* Philadelphia: Fortress Press, 1968.

Hollweg, Walter. *Heinrich Bullingers Hausbuch.* Neukirchen, Germany: Kreis Moers Neukirchener Verlag, 1956.

Horst, Irvin, ed. *The Dutch Dissenters: A Critical Companion to Their History and Ideas with a Bibliographic Survey.* Kirk-historische Bijdragen, Vol. 13. Leiden: Brill, 1986.

Höss, Irmgard. *Georg Spalatin, 1484–1545; ein Leben in der zeit des Humanismus und der Reformation.* Weimar: H. Böhlaus Nachfolger, 1956.

Hunter, James Davison. *Evangelicalism. The Coming Generation* (Chicago: University of Chicago Press, 1987).

Hutchinson, William R. *Errand to the World. American Protestant Thought and Foreign Missions.* Chicago: University of Chicago Press, 1987.

Jones, A. H. M. *Were Ancient Heresies Disguised Social Movements?* Philadelphia: Fortress Press, 1966.

Kaminsky, Howard. *A History of the Hussite Revolution.* Berkeley: University of California Press, 1967.

Kamlah, Wilhelm. *Apokalypse und Geschichtstheologie: Die mittelalterliche Auslegung der Apokalypse vor Joachim von Fiore.* Berlin: Verlag Dr. Emil Ebering, 1935.

———. *Christentum und Geschichtlichkeit.* Stuttgart: W. Kohlhammer, 1951.

Kampers, Franz. *Die Deutsche Kaiseridee in Prophetie und Sage.* Munich: H. Lüneburg, 1896.

Kantorowicz, Ernst H. *The King's Two Bodies: A Study in Mediaeval Political Theology.* Princeton, N.J.: Princeton University Press, 1957.

Kawerau, Peter. *Melchior Hoffman als religiöser Denker.* Haarlem: De Erven F. Bohm, 1954.

Kee, Howard. *Jesus in History: An Approach to the Study of the Gospels* (2d ed.). New York: Harcourt Brace Jovanovich, 1977.

Kennedy, H. A. A. *St. Paul's Conceptions of the Last Things.* London: Hodder and Stoughton, 1904.

Kermode, Frank. *The Sense of an Ending: Studies in the Theory of Fiction.* London: Oxford University Press, 1967.

———. *The Genesis of Secrecy: On the Interpretation of Narrative.* Cambridge: Harvard University Press, 1979.

Kik, J. Marcellus. *An Eschatology of Victory.* Phillipsburg, N.J.: Presbyterian and Reformed Publishing Co., 1978.

Kim, H. C. *The Gospel of Nicodemus.* Toronto: Pontifical Institute of Medieval Studies, 1973.

Kittelson, James M. *Wolfgang Capito: From Humanist to Reformer.* Leiden: Brill, 1975.

Klaassen, Walter. *Living at the End of Ages. Apocalyptic Expectation in the Radical Reformation.* Lanham, Maryland: University Press of America, 1992.

Klein, Peter. *Der ältere Beatus-Kodex Vitr. 14–1 der Biblioteca National zu madrid. Vol. 3: Studien zur Beatus-Illustration und der spanischen Buchmacherei des 10. Jahrhunderts.* Hildesheim: Georg Olms Verlag, 1976.

Kleineidam, Erich. *Universitas Studii Erffordensis. Vol. 2: 1460–1521.* Leipzig: St. Benno, 1969.

Knappen, M. M. *Tudor Puritanism: A Chapter in the History of Idealism.* Chicago: Chicago University Press, 1939; reprinted 1970.

Koch, Ernst. *Die Theologie der Confessio Helvetica Posterior.* Neukirchen, Germany: Neikirchener Verlag, 1968.

Koehler, Walther. *Luther und die Kirchengeschichte nach seinen Schriften, zunächst bis 1521.* Erlangen, Germany: F. Junge, 1900.

Kofler, Leo. *Zur Geschichte der bürgerlichen Gesellschaft* (4th ed.). Neuwied and Berlin: Luchterhand, 1971.

Kohls, Ernst Wilhelm. *Die Schule bei Martin Bucer in ihrem Verhältnis zu Kirche und Obrigkeit.* Heidelberg: Quelle & Meyer, 1963.

Kolb, Robert. *Nikolaus von Amsdorf (1483–1565): Popular Polemics in the Preservation of Luther's Legacy.* Nieuwkoop, The Netherlands: De Graaf, 1978.

———. *Reformers Define the Church, 1530–1580.* St. Louis: Concordia Publishing House, 1991.

Korn, Dietrich. *Das Thema des Jüngsten Tages in der Deutschen Literatur des 17. Jahrhunderts.* Tübingen, Germany: Max Niemeyer, 1957.

Kraus, C. Norman. *Dispensationalism in America.* Richmond, Va.: John Knox Press, 1958.

Kristeller, Paul Oskar. *Renaissance Thought: The Classic, Scholastic, and Humanist Strains.* New York: Harper and Row, 1961.

Krohn, Barthold Nicolaus. *Geschichte der fanatischen und enthusiastischen Wiedertäufer vornehmlich in Niederdeutschland: Melchior Hofmann und die Secte der Hofmannianer.* Leipzig: Bernard Christian Breitkopf, 1758.

Kurze, Dietrich. *Johannes Lichtenberger: Eine Studie zur Geschichte der Prophetie und Astrologie.* Lübeck: Mattheisen, 1960.

Labriolle, Pierre de. *History and Literature of Christianity from Tertullian to Boethius.* Translated by Herbert Wilson. London: Kegan Paul, 1924.

Ladd, George E. *A Commentary on the Revelation.* Grand Rapids, Mich.: Eerdmans Publishing Co., 1972.

Ladner, Gerhart B. *The Idea of Reform: Its Impact on Christian Thought and Action in the Age of the Fathers.* Cambridge: Harvard University Press, 1959; reprinted, New York: Harper Torchbooks, 1967.

Lake, Peter. *Moderate Puritans and the Elizabethan Church.* Cambridge, England: Cambridge University Press, 1982.

Laistner, M. L. W. *The Great Roman Historians.* Berkeley: University of California Press, 1966.

Lambert, Malcolm. *Franciscan Poverty.* London: SPCK, 1961.

———. *Medieval Heresy: Popular Movements from Bogomil to Hus.* New York: Holmes & Meier, 1976.

Lamont, William M. *Godly Rule: Politics and Religion, 1603–60.* London: St. Martin's Press, 1969.

———. *Marginal Pyrnne, 1600–1669.* London: Routledge & Kegan Paul, 1963.

Lamping, A. J. *Ulrichus Velenus and His Treatise Against the Papacy.* Leiden: Brill, 1976.

Lang, August. *Der Evangelienkommentar Martin Butzers und die Grundzüge seiner Theologie.* Leipzig: Dieterich'sche Verlags- Buchhandlung, T. Weicher, 1900.

Leendertz, W. I. *Melchior Hofmann, ein Prophet der Wiedertäufer.* Haarlem: De Erven F. Bohn, 1883.

Leff, Gordon. *Heresy in the Later Middle Ages: The Relation of Heterodoxy to Dissent, c. 1250–c. 1450* (2 vols.). New York: Barnes & Noble, 1967.

Leonard, Emile G. *A History of Protestantism*, 2 vols., trans. by J. M. H. Read. London: Nelson Publishers, 1965.

Lerner, Robert E. *Powers of Prophesy: The Cedar of Lebanon Vision from the Mongol Onslaught to the Dawn of the Enlightenment*. Berkeley: University of California Press, 1983.

Linden, Friedrich Otto zur. *Melchior Hofmann, ein Prophet der Wiedertäufer*. Haarlem: De Erven F. Bohn, 1885.

List, Günther. *Chiliastische Utopie und Radikale Reformation: Die Erneuerung der Idee vom tausend–jährigen Reich im 16. Jahrhundert*. Munich: Wilhelm Fink, 1973.

Littell, Franklin H. *The Origins of Sectarian Protestantism: A Study of Anabaptist Views of the Church* (3d ed.). New York: Macmillan, 1964.

Liu, Tai. *Discord in Zion: The Puritan Divines and the Puritan Revolution, 1640–1660*. The Hague: Nijhoff, 1973.

Locher, Gottfried. *Die Zwinglische Reformation im Rahmen der europäischen Kirchengeschichte*. Göttingen, Germany: Vandenhoeck und Ruprecht, 1979.

Locher, Gottfired W. *Zwingli's Thought: New Perspective*. Leiden: Brill, 1981.

Lohmann, Annemarie. *Zur geistigen Entwicklung Thomas Müntzers*. Leipzig: Teubner, 1931.

Lortz, Joseph. *Die Reformation in Deutschland* (2 vols, 4th ed.). Freiburg: Herder, 1962.

Loserth, Johann. *Wiclif and Hus*. Translated by M. J. Evans. London: Hodder and Stoughton, 1884.

Lowance, Jr., Mason I. *The Language of Canaan*. Cambridge: Harvard University Press, 1980.

Löwith, Karl. *Weltgeschichte und Heilsgeschichte*. Stuttgart: W. Kohlhammer, 1953.

Lubac, Henri de. *Exégèse médiévale: Les quatres sens de l'Ecriture* (2 vols. in 4). Paris: Aubier, 1959–1964.

Lucken, Linus Urban. *Antichrist and the Prophets of Antichrist in the Chester Cycle*. Washington, D.C.: Catholic University of America Press, 1940.

Lukacs, Georg. *Geschichte und Klassenbewusstsein* (2d ed.). Neuwied and Berlin Luchterhand, 1970.

Luneau, Auguste. *L'Histoire du salut chez les Pères de l'Eglise: La doctrine des ages du monde*. Paris: Beauchesne, 1964.

Lupton, Lewis. *A History of the Geneva Bible*. London: The Olive Tree Press, 1975.

McCoy, Charles S. and J. Wayne Baker. *Fountainhead of Federalism. Heinrich Bullinger and the Covenantal Tradition with a Translation of De testamento seu foedere Dei unico et aeterno (1534)*. Louisville, Ky.: Westminster/John Knox Press, 1991.

McFarlane, K. B. *John Wycliffe and the Beginnings of English Nonconformity*. London: The English University Press, 1952.

McGinn, Bernard. *Apocalyptic Spirituality*. New York: Paulist Press, 1979.

———. *Visions of the End: Apocalyptic Traditions in the Middle Ages*. New York: Columbia University Press, 1979.

Male, Emile. *Religious Art in France, the Twelfth Century: A Study of the Origins of Medieval Iconography*. Translated by M. Mathews; edited by H. Bober. Princeton, N.J.: Princeton University Press, 1978.

Manselli, Raoul. *La "Lectura super Apocalypsim" di Pietro Giovanni Olivi*. Rome: Nella Sede Dell' Istituto, 1955.

Manuel, Frank E., and Manuel, Fritzie P. *Utopian Thought in the Western World*. Cambridge: Harvard University Press, 1979.

Manz, Luise. *Der Ordo-Gedanke: Ein Beitrag zur Frage des mittelalterlichen Stöndegedankens.* Vierteljahrschrift für Sozial- und Wirtschaftsgeschichte, Beiheft 33. Stuttgart and Berlin: W. Kohlhammer, 1937.

Markus, R. A. *Saeculum: History and Society in the Theology of St. Augustine of Hippo.* Cambridge: Cambridge University Press, 1970.

Marsden, George M. *Understanding Fundamentalism and Evangelicalism* (Grand Rapids, Mich.: Eerdmans Publishing Co., 1991).

Martin, James P. *The Last Judgment.* Grand Rapids, Mich.: Eerdmans Publishing Co., 1963.

Martin, Peter. *Martin Luther und die Bilder zur Apokalypse.* Hamburg: F. Wittig, 1983.

Masser, Achim. *Bibel und Legendenepik des deutschen Mittelalters.* Berlin: Erich Schmidt Verlag, 1976.

Meinhold, Peter. *Die Genesisvorlesung Luthers und ihre Herausgeber.* Stuttgart: W. Kohlhammer, 1936.

Menke-Glückert, Emil. *Die Geschichtsschreibung der Reformation und Gegen-reformation.* Leipzig: J. C. Hinrichs'sche Buchhandlung, 1912.

Merton, Robert King. *Social Theory and Social Structure.* New York: Free Press, 1968.

Meuthen, Erich. *Kirche und Heilsgeschichte bei Gerhoh von Reichersberg.* Leiden: Brill, 1959.

Meyer, Almut Agnes. *Heilsgewissheit und Endzeiterwartung im deutschen Drama des 16. Jahrhunderts.* Heidelberg: Winter, 1976.

Middlekauff, Robert. *The Mathers: Three Generations of Puritan Intellectuals, 1596–1788.* New York: Oxford University Press, 1971.

Miller, Perry. *Errand into the Wilderness.* Cambridge: Harvard University Press, 1956.

———. *Jonathan Edwards.* New York: W. Sloane Associates, 1949; reprinted, University of Massachusetts Press, 1981.

———. *The New England Mind: From Colony to Province.* Boston: Beacon Press, 1961.

———. *Roger Williams: His Contribution to the American Tradition.* Indianapolis: Bobbs-Merrill, 1953.

———, and Johnson, Thomas H., eds. *The Puritans: A Sourcebook of Their Writings* (2 vols.). New York: Harper Torchbooks, 1963.

Moeller, Bernd, ed. *Bauernkriegs-Studien.* Gütersloh, Germany: Mohn, 1975.

———. *Reichsstadt und Reformation.* Gütersloh, Germany: Mohn, 1962. English translation found in *Imperial Cities and the Reformation: Three Essays.* Edited and translated by H. C. E. Midedlfort and M. U. Edwards. Philadelphia: Fortress Press, 1972.

Moldaenke, Günther. *Schriftverständnis und Schriftdeutung im Zeitalter der Reformation. Vol. 1: Matthias Flacius Illyricus.* Stuttgart: W. Kohlhammer, 1936.

Molnar, Amedeo. *Die Waldensergeschichte und europäisches Ausmass einer Kertzerbewegung.* Göttingen, Germany: Vandenhoeck und Ruprecht, 1980.

———. *A Challenge to Constantinianism: The Waldensian Theology in the Middle Ages.* Geneva: WSCF, 1976.

Moltmann, Jürgen. *The Church in the Power of the Spirit.* New York: Harper and Row, 1977; first edition, German, 1975.

Moneta of Cremona. *Adversus Catharos.* Rome: ex Typographia Palladis, 1743.

Moorman, John. *History of the Franciscan Order.* Oxford: Clarendon Press, 1968.

Moorhead, James H. *American Apocalypse: Yankee Protestants and the Civil War, 1860–1869.* New Haven, Conn.: Yale University Press, 1978.

Morgan, Edmund. *Visible Saints.* Ithaca, N.Y.: Cornell University Press, 1963.

Morgan, Irvonwy. *The Godly Preachers of the Elizabethan Church.* London: Epworth Press, 1965.

Mounce, Robert. *The Book of Revelation.* Grand Rapids, Mich.: Eerdmans Publishing Co., 1977.

Mozley, J. F. *John Foxe and His Book.* London: SPCK, 1940.

Müller, Gerhard. *Franz Lambert von Avignon und die Reformation in Hessen.* Marburg: N. G. Elwert, 1958.

Munck, Johannes. *Petrus und Paulus in der Offenbarung Johannis: Ein Beitrag zur Auslegung der Apokalypse.* Copenhagen: I Kommission hos Rosenkilde og Bagger, 1950.

Murray, George L. *Millennial Studies.* Grand Rapids, Mich.: Baker Book House, 1975.

Murray, Iain. *The Puritan Hope: Revival and Interpretation of Prophecy.* Edinburgh: Banner of Truth Trust, 1971.

Musper, H. T. *Der Antichrist und die fünfzehn Zeichen: Faksimile- Ausgabe des einzigen erhaltenen chiroxylographischen Blockbuchs.* Munich: Prestel Verlag, 1970.

———. *Die Urausgaben der holländischen Apokalypse und Biblia pauperum* (3 vols.). Munich: Prestel Verlag, 1961.

Neuser, Wilhelm. *Hans Hut: Leben und Wirken bis zum Nikolsburger Religionsgespräch.* Berlin: H. Blanke, 1913.

Neuss, W. *Die Apokalypse des hl. Johannes in der altspanischen und altchristlichen Bibel-Illustrationen* (2 vols.). Münster: Aschendorff, 1931.

Newbigin, Lesslie. *Truth to Tell: The Gospel as Public Truth.* Grand Rapids, Mich.: Eerdmans, 1991.

Niebuhr, H. Richard. *Christ and Culture.* New York: Harper and Row, 1951.

———. *The Kingdom of God in America.* New York: Harper's, 1937.

Nigg, Walter. *Das Buch der Ketzer.* Zürich: Artemis Verlag, 1949.

Nipperdey, Thomas. *Reformation, Revolution, Utopie.* Göttingen, Germany: Vandenhoeck und Ruprecht, 1975.

Nisbet, Robert. *History of the Idea of Progress.* New York: Basic Books, 1980.

Nolan, Barbara. *The Gothic Visionary Perspective.* Princeton, N.J.: Princeton University Press, 1977.

Nuttall, Geoffrey. *Visible Saints.* Oxford: Blackwell, 1957.

Oberman, Heiko. *Forerunners of the Reformation.* Philadelphia: Fortress Press, 1966/1981.

———. *The Harvest of Medieval Theology: Gabriel Biel and Late Medieval Nominalism.* Grand Rapids, Mich.: Eerdmans Publishing Co., 1967.

———. *Luther: Mensch zwischen Gott und Teufel.* Berlin: Severin und Siedler, 1982.

O'Connell, John P. *The Eschatology of Saint Jerome.* Mundelein, Ill.: St. Mary's of the Lake Seminary, 1948.

Olsen, V. Norskov. *John Foxe and the Elizabethan Church.* Berkeley: University of California Press, 1973.

Oyer, John S. *Lutheran Reformers Against Anabaptists.* The Hague: Martinus Nijhoff, 1964.

Ozment, Steven E. *The Age of Reform, 1250–1550: An Intellectual and Religious History of Late Medieval and Reformation Europe.* New Haven, Conn.: Yale University Press, 1980.

———. *Mysticism and Dissent: Religious Ideology & Social Protest in the Sixteenth Century.* New Haven, Conn.: Yale University Press, 1973.

———. *The Reformation in the Cities.* New Haven, Conn.: Yale University Press, 1975.

Palacky, Franz. *Geschichte von Böhmen* (Vol. 3). Prague: Kronberger und Weber, 1845.

Parker, T. H. L. *John Calvin: A Biography.* Philadelphia: Westminster Press, 1975.

Pashoud, Francois. *Roma aeterna: Etudes sur le patriotisme romain dans l'Occident latin ā l'époque des grandes invasions.* Rome: Institut suisse de Rome, 1967.

Patrides, C. A. *The Phoenix and the Ladder: The Rise and Decline of the Christian View of History.* Berkeley: University of California Press, 1964.

Patrides, C. A. and Joseph Wittreich, eds. *The Apocalypse in English Renaissance Thought and Literature.* Ithaca, N.Y.: Cornell University Press, 1984.

Pearson, A. F. Scott. *Thomas Cartwright and Elizabethan Puritanism.* Cambridge: Cambridge University Press, 1925; reprinted, Gloucester, Mass.: Peter Smith, 1966.

Pelikan, Jaroslav, ed. *Interpreters of Luther.* Philadelphia: Fortress Press, 1968.

Pestalozzi, Carl. *Heinrich Bullinger: Leben und ausgewählte Schriften.* Elberfeld: R. L. Friderichs, 1858.

Peters, G. N. H. *The Theocratic Kingdom* (3 vols.). Grand Rapids, Mich.: Kregel Publishers, 1884 reprint.

Pettit, Norman. *The Heart Prepared: Grace and Conversion in Puritan Spiritual Life.* New Haven, Conn.: Yale University Press, 1966.

Peuckert, Will-Erich. *Die Grosse Wende: Das apokalyptische Saeculum und Luther.* Hamburg: Claassen und Goverts, 1948.

———. *Die Rosenkreutzer: Zur Geschichte einer Reformation.* Jena: Eugen Diederichs, 1928.

Pfisterer, Karl Dieterich. *The Prism of Scripture: Studies on History and Historicity in the Work of Jonathan Edwards.* Bern: Herbert Lang, 1975.

Phelan, John Leddy. *The Millennial Kingdom of the Franciscans in the New World: A Study of Writings of Geronime de Mendieta (1525–1604).* Berkeley: University of California Press, 1970.

Pinson, Koppel S. *Pietism as a Factor in the Rise of German Nationalism.* New York: Columbia University Press, 1934.

Pocock, J. G. A. *The Ancient Constitution and the Feudal Law: A Study of English Historical Thought in the Seventeenth Century.* New York: Cambridge University Press, 1987.

———. *The Machiavellian Moment: Florentine Political Thought and the Atlantic Republican Tradition.* Princeton, N.J.: Princeton University Press, 1975.

———. *Three British Revolutions, 1641, 1688, 1776.* Princeton, N.J.: Princeton University Press, 1980.

Polman, P. Pontianus. *L'Elément historique dans la controverse religieuse du XVIe siècle.* Gembloux, Belgium: J. Duculot, 1932.

Potter, G. R. *Zwingli.* Cambridge: Cambridge University Press, 1976.

Preger, Wilhelm. *Geschichte der deutschen Mystik im Mittelalter.* (3 vols.). Leipzig: Dörffling und Franke, 1874–1893.

Prestwich, Menna, ed., *International Calvinism, 1541–1715.* Oxford: Clarendon Press, 1985.

Preuss, Hans. *Martin Luther. Der Prophet.* Gütersloh, Germany: C. Bertelsmann, 1933.

———. *Die Vorstellungen vom Antichrist im späteren Mittelalter, bei Luther und in der Konfessionellen Polemik.* Leipzig: J. C. Hinrichs, 1906.

Prigent, Pierre. *Apocalypse 12. Histoire de L'exégèse.* Tübingen, Germany: J. C. B. Mohr, Paul Siebeck, 1959.

Quistrop, Heinrich. *Die letzten Dinge im Zeugnis Calvins.* Gütersloh, Germany: Bertelsmann, 1941; English Translation, *Calvin's Doctrine of Last Things.* Translated by Harold Knight. London: Lutterworth Press, 1955.

Rabb, Theodore K., ed. *The Thirty Years' War* (2d ed.). Washington, D.C.: University Press of America, 1981.

Ratzinger, Joseph. *The Theology of St. Bonaventure.* Translated by Zachary Hayes. Chicago: Franciscan Herald Press, 1971.

Rauh, Horst Dieter. *Das Bild des Antichrist im Mittelalter: Von Tyconius zum deutschen Symbolismus. Vol. 9: Beiträge zur Geschichte der Philosophie und Theologie des Mittelalters,* n.s. Münster: Aschendorff, 1973.

Reeves, Marjorie. *The Influence of Prophecy in the Later Middle Ages: A Study in Joachim-ism.* Oxford: Clarendon Press, 1969.

————. *Joachim of Fiore and the Prophetic Future.* London: SPCK, 1976; New York: Harper and Row, 1977.

Reeves, Marjorie, and Hirsch-Reich, Beatrice. *The Figurae of Joachim of Fiore.* Oxford: Clarendon Press, 1972.

Rendtorff, Trutz, ed. "Prophetie in der Reformation. Elemente, Argumente und Bewegungen." *Charisma und Institution.* Gütersloh: G. Mohn, 1985.

Ricoeur, Paul, in Thompson, John B., Ed. *Hermeneutics and the Human Sciences: Essays in Language. Action, and Interpretation.* Cambridge: Cambridge University Press, and Paris: Editions de la Maison des Sciences de l'Homme, 1981.

Rigaux, Beda. *Saint Paul: Les Épitres aux Thessaloniciens.* Gembloux, Belgium: J. Duculot, 1956.

Ritschl, Albrecht. *Geschichte des Pietismus inder reformierten Kirche,* vol. 1. Bonn: Adolphe Marcus, 1880.

Rosenstiehl, Jean Marc. *L'Apocalypse d'Elie.* Paris: Geuthner, 1972.

Rossell, Garth, and Dupuis, Richard A. G., eds. *The Memoirs of Charles G. Finney.* Grand Rapids, Mich.: Zondervan Publishers, 1989.

Roth, Guenther, and Schluchter, Wolfgang. *Max Weber's Vision of History, Ethics and Methods.* Berkeley: University of California Press, 1979.

Rother, Siegfried. *Die religiösen und geistigen Grundlagen der Politik Huldrych Zwinglis: Ein Beitrag zum Problem des christlichen Staates.* Erlangen, Germany: Palm & Enke, 1956.

Rowley, H. H. *The Relevance of Apocalyptic: A Study of Jewish and Christian Apocalypses from Daniel to the Revelation.* New York: Association Press, 1963.

Rupp, Gordon. *Patterns of Reformation.* Philadelphia: Fortress Press, 1969.

Russell, D. S. *Apocalyptic: Ancient and Modern.* Philadelphia: Fortress Press, 1968.

Salten, F. M. *Mediaeval Drama in Chester.* Toronto: University of Toronto Press, 1955.

Sandeen, Ernest R. *The Roots of Fundamentalism: British and American Millenarianism.* Chicago: University of Chicago Press, 1970.

Schaff, Philip. *The Creeds of Christendom.* (3 vols.). New York: Harper and Brothers, 1877; reprint edition, Grand Rapids, Mich.: Baker Book House, 1977.

————. *History of the Christian Church.* 7 vols. New York: Charles Scribner's Sons, 1882–1910.

Schäufele, Wolfgang. *Das missionarische Bewusstsein und Wirken der Täufer.* Neukirchen, Germany: Neukirchener Verlag, 1966.

Schilling, Heinz, ed. *Die Reformierte Kanfessionalisierrung in Deutschland—Das Problem der "zweiten Reforemations."* Gütersloh: Gerd Mohn, 1986.

Schmid, H. D. *Täufertum und Obrigkeit in Nürnberg.* Nuremberg: Korn & Berg, 1972.

Schmid, Josef, ed. *Der Apokalypse-Kommentar des Andreas von Kaisareia: Studien zur Geschichte des griechischen Apokalypse-Textes* (2 vols.). Munich: Karl Zink Verlag, 1955.

Schmidt, Jean Miller. *Souls or the Social Order: The Two-Party System in American Protestantism.* New York: Carlson Publishing, 1991.

Schmidt, Philipp. *Die Illustration der Lutherbibel, 1522–1700. Ein Stuck abendlandischen Kulter- und Kirchengeschichte mit Verzeichnissen der Bibeln, Bilder und Kunstler.* Basel: F. Reinhardt, 1962.

Schmithals, Walter. *The Apocalyptic Movement: Introduction and Interpretation.* Nashville: Abingdon Press, 1975.

Schrenk, Gottlob. *Gottesreich und Bund im älteren Protestantismus, vornehmlich bei Johannes Cocceius.* Gütersloh, Germany: C. Bartelsmann, 1923.

Schwartz, Edward. *Greichische Geschichtsschreiber.* Leipzig: Koehler & Amelang, 1957.

Schwarz, Reinhard. *Die apokalyptische Theologie Thomas Müntzers und der Taboriten.* Tübingen, Germany: J. C. B. Mohr, 1977.

Scribner, Robert. *For the Sake of Simple Folk: Popular Propaganda for the German Reformation.* Cambridge: Cambridge University Press, 1981.

Seeberg, Erich. *Gottfried Arnold: Die Wissenschaft und die Mystik seiner Zeit. Studien zur Historiographie und zur Mystik.* Darmstadt: Wissenschaftliche Buchgesellschaft, 1964. First edition, 1923.

Seidemann, Johann Karl. *Thomas Müntzer: Eine Biographie.* Dresden: Arnold, 1842.

Séquenny, André, ed. *Bibliotheca Dissidentium: Repertoire des Non-Conformistes religieux des seizième et dix-septième siècles.* Baden-Baden: U. Koerner, 1980.

Sider, Ronald J., ed. *Karlstadt's Battle with Luther: Documents in a Liberal-Radical Debate.* Philadelphia: Fortress Press, 1978.

Smalley, Beryl. *The Study of the Bible in the Middle Ages.* Oxford: Clarendon Press, 1941.

Smirin, Mosei. *Die Volksreformation des Thomas Müntzer und der grosse Bauernkrieg.* Frankfurt am Main: Bundschuh Verlag, 1976.

Smith, John Hazel. *Two Latin Comedies by John Foxe the Martyrologist.* Ithaca, N.Y.: Cornell University Press, 1973.

Smith, Timothy. *Revivalism and Social Reform: American Protestantism on the Eve of the Civil War.* Nashville, Tenn., Abingdon, 1957.

Spinka, Matthew. *John Hus' Concept of the Church.* Princeton, N.J.: Princeton University Press, 1966.

——. *John Hus at the Council of Constance.* New York: Columbia University Press, 1965.

——. *John Hus and the Czech Reform.* Chicago: University of Chicago Press, 1941.

Spitz, Lewis W. "The Impact of the Reformation on Church-State Issues." In *Church and State Under God* (pp. 59–112). Edited by Albert George Huegli. St. Louis: Concordia Publishing House, 1964.

Staedtke, Joachim, ed. *Glauben und Bekennen. 400 Jahre Confessio Helvetica Posterior.* Zürich: Zwingli Verlag, 1966.

——. *Theologie des jungen Bullinger.* Zürich: Zwingli Verlag, 1962.

Staehelin, Ernst, ed. *Die Verkündigung des Reiches Gottes in der Kirche Jesu Christi* (6 vols.). Basel: Freiderich Reinhardt, 1957.

Staehelin, Rudolf. *Zwingli als Prediger.* Basel: Detloft, 1887.

Stayer, James M. *Anabaptists and the Sword.* Lawrence: Coronado Press, 1972.

Steinmetz, David C., ed. *The Bible in the Sixteenth Century.* Durham, N.C.: Duke University Press, 1990.

Strauss, Gerald. *Manifestations of Discontent in Germany on the Eve of the Reformation.* Bloomington: University of Indiana Press, 1971.

Strobel, August. *Untersuchungen zum eschatologischen Verzögerungsproblem: auf Grund der spätjüdisch-urchirstlichen Geschichte von Habakuk 2, 2ff.* Leiden: Brill, 1967.

Strype, John. *Annals of the Reformation and Establishment of Religion* (2d ed.). London: T. Edlin, 1725–1731.

Taubes, Jakob. *Abendländische Eschatologie.* Bern: A. Francke, 1949.

Tellenbach, Gerd. *Church, State and Christian Society at the Time of the Investiture Contest.* Oxford: Blackwell, 1940.

Thiemann, Ronald F. *Constructing a Public Theology: The Church in a Pluralistic Culture.* Louisville, Ky.: Westminster/John Knox Press, 1991.

————. *Revelation and Theology: The Gospel as Narrated Promise.* Notre Dame, Ind.: University of Notre Dame Press, 1985.

Tholuck, August. "Die Verdienste Calvins als Ausleger der heiligen Schrift." In *Vermischte Schriften grössentheils apologetischen Inhalts.* Hamburg: F. Perthes, 1839.

Thomas, Keith. *Religion and the Decline of Magic: Studies in Popular Beliefs in Sixteenth and Seventeenth Century England.* London: Wiedenfeld and Nicolson, 1971.

Thompson, A. Hamilton, ed. *Bede, His Life, Times and Writings.* Oxford: Clarendon Press, 1935.

Thompson, Bard. *Liturgies of the Western Church.* New York: World Publishing, 1962.

Thrupp, Sylvia L. *Millennial Dreams in Action: Studies in Revolutionary Religious Movements.* New York: Schocken Books, 1970.

Tierney, Brian. *Origins of Papal Infallibility: Sovereignty and Tradition in the Middle Ages.* Leiden: Brill, 1972.

Töpfer, Bernhard. *Das Kommende Reich des Friedens.* Berlin: Akademie-Verlag, 1964.

Toon, Peter, ed. *Puritans, the Millennium and the Future of Israel: Puritan Eschatology 1600–1660.* London: James Clark & Co., Ltd., 1970.

Torrance, Thomas F. *Kingdom and Church: A Study in the Theology of the Reformation.* Edinburgh: Oliver and Boyd, 1956.

Trinkaus, Charles, and Oberman, Heiko, eds. *The Pursuit of Holiness in the Late Middle Ages and Renaissance.* Leiden: Brill, 1973.

Trinterud, Leonard. *Elizabethan Puritanism.* New York: Oxford University Press, 1971.

Trites, A. A. *The New Testament Concept of Witness.* SNTS monograph 31. Cambridge: Cambridge University Press, 1977.

Tuveson, Ernest. *Millennium and Utopia.* Berkeley: University of California Press, 1949.

————. *Redeemer Nation.* Chicago: University of Chicago Press, 1968.

Van der Meer, Frederick. *Apocalypse: Visions from the Book of Revelation in Western Art.* London: Thames and Hudson, 1978.

————. *Maiestas Domini: Théophanies de l'Apocalypse dans l'art chrétien. Studi di Antichita Cristiana,* Vol. 13. Rome-Paris: Société d'édition les "Belles Lettres," 1938.

Van Os, Arnold B. *Religious Visions: The Development of the Eschatological Elements in Mediaeval English Religious Literature.* Amsterdam: H. J. Paris, 1932.

Verheus, S. L. *Zeugnis und Gericht: Kirchengeschichtliche Betrachtungen bei Sebastian Franck und Matthias Flacius.* Nieuwkoop: B. DeGraaf, 1971.

Viebig, Johannes, ed. *Matthias Flacius Illyricus, 1575–1975.* Regensburg: Lassleben, 1975.

Volz, Hans. *Die Lutherpredigten des Johannes Mathesius: Kritische Untersuchungen zur Geschichtsschreibung im Zeitalter der Reformation.* Leipzig: M. Heinsius Nachfolger Eger & Sievers, 1930.

Wadstein, Ernst. *Die eschatologische Ideengruppe: Antichrist-'Weltsabbat-'Weltende und Weltgericht, in den Hauptmomenten ihrer christlich-mittelalterlichen Gesamtentwicklung.* Leipzig: O. R. Reisland, 1896.

Wakefield, Walter L., and Evans, Austin P. *Heresies of the High Middle Ages.* New York: Columbia University Press, 1969.

Walvoord, John F. *The Revelation of Jesus Christ* (Chicago: Moody Press, 1966).

Walzer, Michael. *The Revolution of the Saints: A Study in the Origins of Radical Politics.* Cambridge: Harvard University Press, 1966.

Wappler, Paul. *Die Täuferbewegung in Thüringen von 1526–1584.* Jena: Verlag von Gustav Fischer, 1913.

————. *Thomas Müntzer in Zwickau und die "Zwickauer Propheten."* Zwickau, Germany: R. Zückler, 1908. Second edition, Gütersloh, 1966.

Warburg, Aby. *Ausgewalte Schriften und Wurdigungen*. Baden-Baden: Saecula Spiritula, 1979.

Weinstein, Donald. *Savonarola and Florence: Prophecy and Patriotism in the Renaissance*. Princeton, N.J.: Princeton University Press, 1970.

Wessel-Roth, Ruth. *Thomas Erastus: Ein Beitrag zur Geschichte der reformierten Kirche und zur von der Staatssouveränität*. Lahr/Baden, 1954.

West, Delno, ed., *Joachim of Fiore in Christian Thought: Essays on the Influence of the Calabrian Prophet* (2 vols.). New York: Burt Franklin, 1975.

White, B. R. *The English Separatist Tradition from the Marian Martyrs to the Pilgrim Fathers*. Oxford: Oxford University Press, 1971.

White, Helen C. *Tudor Books of Saints and Martyrs*. Madison: University of Wisconsin Press, 1963.

Wiebe, Robert. *The Search for Order: 1877–1920*. New York: Hill and Wang, 1967.

Williams, Ann, ed. *Prophecy and Millenarianism: Essays in Honor of Marjorie Reeves*. London: Longman, 1980.

Williams, Daniel Day. *The Andover Liberals: A Study in American Theology*. New York: King's Crown, 1941.

Williams, George H. *The Radical Reformation*. Philadelphia: Westminster Press, 1962.

———. *The Radical Reformation*. Kirksville, Mo.: Sixteenth Century Journal Publishers, 1992.

———. and Mergal, Angel M. *Spiritual and Anabaptist Writers*. Philadelphia: Westminster Press, 1958.

———. Stanislas Lubieniecki. *History of the Polish Reformation, with Nine Related Documents*. Cambridge: Harvard University Press, 1993.

———. *Wilderness and Paradise in Christian Thought*. New York: Harper and Brothers, 1962.

Wilson, John F. *Pulpit in Parliament: Puritanism during the English Civil Wars 1640–1648*. Princeton, N.J.: Princeton University Press, 1969.

Workman, H. B. *John Wyclif: A Study of the English Medieval Church* (2 vols.). Oxford: Oxford University Press, 1926.

Zeman, Jarold Knox. *The Anabaptists and the Czech Brethren in Moravia, 1526–1678: A Study of Origins and Contacts*. The Hague: Mouton, 1969.

Zizioulas, Jean. *Being as Communion: Studies in Personhood and the Church*. Crestwood, N.Y.: St. Vladimir's Seminary Press, 1985.

Zschäbitz, Gerhard. *Zur mitteldeutschen Wiedertäuferbewegung nach dem Grossen Bauernkrieg*. Berlin: Rütten und Loenig, 1957–1958.

Articles, Dissertations

Albrecht, O., ed. "Luthers Arbeiten an der Uebersetzung und Auslegung des Propheten Daniel in den Jahren 1530 und 1541." ARG, 23 (1926):47ff.

Alexander, Paul J. "Byzantium and the Migration of Literary Works and Motifs: The Legend of the Last Roman Emperor." MH, n.s. 2 (1971):47–68.

———. "The Diffusion of Byzantine Apocalypses in the Medieval West and the Beginnings of Joachimism." In *Prophecy and Millenarianism: Essays in Honor of Marjorie Reeves* (pp. 53–106). Edited by Ann Williams. Harlow, Essex: Longman, 1980.

Alverny, Marie-Thérèse. "Le Cosmos symbolique du XIIe siècle." *Archives d'histoire doctrinale et littéraire du Moyen-Age*, 28 (1953–54):31–81.

Archilla, Aurelio Garcia. "Truth in History: The Theology of History and Apologetic Historiography in Heinrich Bullinger." Unpublished Ph.D. dissertation, Princeton Theological Seminary, Princeton, New Jersey, 1989.

Avis, P. D. L. "The True Church in Reformation Theology." SJTh, 30 (1977):319–45.

Bailey, Richard G. "Melchior Hoffman: Proto-Anabaptist and [first] Printed in Kiel, 1527–1529," CH, 59 n. 2 (1990):175–90.

Barmann, L. F. "Reform Ideology in the Dialogi of Anselm of Havelberg." CH, 30 (1961): 379–95.

Bauckham, Richard. "The Martyrdom of Enoch and Elijah: Jewish or Christian?" JBL, 95 (1976):447–58.

Bauckham, Richard. "The Rise of Apocalyptic." *Themelios*, 3.2 (1978):17ff.

Betts, R. R. "Jerome of Prague." *University of Birmingham Historical Journal* (1947): 1–91.

Benz, Ernst. "Die Geschichtstheologie der Franziskaner-spiritualen des 13. und 14. Jahrhunderts nach neuen Quellen." ZKG, 52 (1933):90–121.

———. "Joachim-Studien III: Thomas von Aquin und Joachim de Fiore." ZKG, 53 (1934):52–116.

———. "Die Kategorien des eschatologischen Zeitbe wusstseins." *Deutsche Vierteljahresschrift für Literaturwissenschaft und Geistesgeschichte*, 11 (1933):200–229.

Bercovitch, Sacvan. "The Typology of America's Mission." AQ, 30 (1978):135–55.

———. "Typology in Puritan New England: The Williams-Cotton Controversy Reassessed." AQ, 19 (1967):166–91.

Betts, R. R. "The Regulae Veteris et Novi Testamenti of Matej z Janova." *The Journal of Theological Studies*, 32 (1931):344–51.

Beumer, J. "Rupert von Deutz und sein Einfluss auf die Kontroverstheologie der Reformationszeit." *Catholica*, 22 (1968):201–16.

Biel, Paula. "Heinrich Bullinger's Death and *Testament*: A Well-Planned Departure." SCJ, 22.1 (1991):3–14.

Bischoff, Guntram. "Early Premonstratensian Eschatology: The Apocalyptic Myth." In *The Spirituality of Western Christendom* (pp. 71–77). Edited by E. Elder. Kalamazoo, Mich.: Cistercian Publications, 1976.

Blaising, Craig A. "Doctorinal Development in Orthodoxy," and "Development of Dispensationalism by Contemporary Dispensatimalists," *Bibliotheca Sacra*, 145 (1988):133–40, 254–80.

Bloomfield, Morton W. "Joachim of Flora: A Critical Survey of his Canon, Teachings, Sources, Bibliography and Influence." *Traditio*, 13 (1957):249–311.

———, and Reeves, Marjorie. "The Penetration of Joachimism into Northern Europe." *Speculum*, 29 (1954):772–93.

Bornkamm, G. "Die Komposition der apokalyptischen Visonen in der Offenbarung Johannis." ZNW, 36 (1937):137–49.

Bossy, John. "Holiness and Society." *Past and Present*, 75 (1977):119–37.

Burr, David. "The Apocalyptic Element in Olivi's Critique of Aristotle." CH, 40 (1971): 15–29.

———. "The Persecution of Peter Olivi." *Transactions of the American Philosophical Society*, 66 (Philadelphia, 1976).

Büsser, Fritz. "Der Prophet-Gedanken zu Zwinglis Theologie." *Zwingliana*, 13 (1969): 7–18.

Capp, B. S. "Extreme Millenarianism." In *Puritans, the Millennium and the Future of Israel: Puritan Eschatology 1600–1660* (pp. 66–90). Edited by Peter Toon. London: James Clarke and Co. Ltd., 1970.

Cargill, Thompson. W.D.J. "Seeing the Reformation in Medieval Perspective." JEH, 25 (1974):297–308.

Cerfaux, Lucien. "Témoins du Christ dans le Livre des Actes." In *Recueil Lucien Cerfaux* (Vol. 2, pp. 175–94). Gembloux, Belgium: J. Duculot, 1954.

Christe, Yves. "Traditions littéraires et iconographiques dans l'interpretation des images apocalyptiques." *L'Apocalypse de Jean. Traditions exégétiques et iconographiques. Actes du Colloque de la Fondation Hardt.* Geneva: Librairie Droz, 1979.

Christianson, Paul. "Reformers and the Church of England under Elizabeth I and the Early Stuarts." JEH, 31 (1980):463–82.

Clasen, Claus-Peter. "Executions of Anabaptists, 1525–1618. A Research Report." MQR, 47 (1973):115–52.

Clemen, Otto. "Das Prager Manifest Thomas Müntzer." ARG, 54 (1933):75–81.

————. "Sechs Briefe aus der Reformationszeit." ZKG, 23 (1902).

Clouse, R. G. "The Influence of John Henry Alsted on English Millenarian Thought in the Seventeenth Century." Ph.D. dissertation, State University of Iowa, 1963. See also his article, "Johann Heinrich Alsted and English Millennialism." HTR, 62 (1969):189–207.

Cranz, F. Edward. "Kingdom and Polity in Eusebius of Caesarea." HTR, 45 (1952): 47–66.

Daniel, E. Randolph. "Apocalyptic Conversion: The Joachite Alternative to the Crusades." *Traditio,* 25 (1969):127–54.

————. "The Double Procession of the Holy Spirit in Joachim of Fiore's Understanding of History." *Speculum,* 55 (1980):469–83.

————. "A Re-examination of the Origins of Franciscan Joachitism." *Speculum,* 43 (1968):671–76.

————. "Spirituality and Poverty: Angelo da Clareno and Ubertino da Casale." MH, 4 (1973):89–98.

Daniélou, Jean. "La typologie millenariste de la semaine dans le Christianisme primitif." *Vigiliae Christianae,* 2 (1948):1–16.

De Boor, Friedrich, "Kirchengeschichte oder Auslegungsgeschichte?" *Theologische Literaturzeitung* (June 1972):401–14.

Denis, Philippe. "La Prophétie dans les églises de la Réforme au XVIe sièle." RHE, 72 (1977):289–316.

Depperman, Klaus. "Melchior Hoffmanns Weg von Luther zu den Täufern." In *Umstrittenes Täufertum 1525–1975.* Göttingen, Germany: Vandenhoeck und Ruprecht, 1977.

Dobschütz, Ernst von. "Vom vierfachen Schriftsinn." In *Harnack-Ehrung* (pp. 1–13). Leipzig: J. C. Hinrichs, 1921.

Dollinger, P. "La Tolérance è Strasburg arc XVIe Siecle." In *Eventail de l'histoire vivante: Hommage a Lucien Febvre* (Vol. 2). Paris: A. Colin, 1953.

Douie, Decima. "Some Treatises against the Fraticelli in the Vatican Library." FS, 38 (1978):10–80.

Dowey, Edward A. "Covenant and History in the Thought of Heinrich Bullinger." Paper read to the A.S.C.H., December 1962. Unpublished typescript, Princeton Theological Seminary, Princeton, New Jersey.

————. "Heinrich Bullinger as Theologian: Thematic, Comprehensive, Schematic," *Calvin Studies,* 5 (1990):41–60.

————. "Der theologische Aufbau des zweiten Helvetischen Bekenntnisses." In *Glauben und Bekennen* (pp. 219–20). Edited by Joachim Staedtke. Zürich: Zwingli Verlag, 1966.

————. "Das Wort Gottes als Schrift und Predigt im Zweiten Helvetischen Bekenntnis." In *Glauben und Bekennen* (pp. 235–50). Edited by Joachim Staedtke. Zürich: Zwingli Verlag, 1966.

Ehrle, Franz. "Petrus Johannis Olivi, Sein Leben und seine Schriften." ALK, 3 (1887):409–552.

————. "Die Spiritualen, ihr Verhältniss zum Franciscanerorden und zu den Fraticellen." ALK (Vol. 1, pp. 509–69). Edited by H. Denifle and F. Ehrle. Freiburg im Breisgau: Herder, 1885–1900.

Eisenstein, Elizabeth L. "The Advent of Printing and the Protestant Revolt: A New Approach to the Disruption of Western Civilization." *Annales. Economies Sociétés, Civilisations*, 26, n. 6 (1971):1355–82.

Emmerson, Richard. "Antichrist as Anti-Saint: The Significance of Abbot Adso's *Libellus de Antichristo.*" *American Benedictine Review*, 30 (1970):175–90.

Faierstein, Morris M. "Why do the Scribes say that Elijah must come first." JBL, 100.1 (1981):75–86.

Feuillet, André. "Interpretation of Chapter 11 of the Apocalypse." In *Johannine Studies.* Translated by T. E. Crane. Staten Island, NY: Alba House, 1964.

Flood, David. "A Study in Joachimism." CF, 41 (1971):131–40.

Florovsky, Georges. "Eschatology in the Patristic Age: An Introduction." *Greek Orthodox Theological Review*, 2 (1956):27–40.

Folliet, G. "La typologie du sabbat chez St. Augustine." REA, 2 (1956):371–91.

Forell, George W. "Justification and Eschatology in Luther's Thought." CH, 38 (1969):164–74.

Fowler, J. T. "The Fifteen Last Days of the World in Medieval Art and Literature." *The Yorkshire Archaeological Journal*, 23 (1914–15):313–37.

Friderich, W. "Kritische Untersuchung der dem Abt Joachim v. Floris zugeschriebenen Kommentare zu Jesajas und Jeremias." *Zeitschrift für Wissenschaftliche Theologie.* Jena, 1859.

Friesen, Abraham. "Social Revolution or Religious Reform? In *Umstrittenes Täufertum 1525–1575* (pp. 223–43). Edited by Hans Jürgen Goertz. Göttingen, Germany: Vandenhoeck und Ruprecht, 1975.

————. "Thomas Müntzer and the Old Testament." MQR, 47 (1973):5–19.

Fukuyama, Francis. "The End of History?" *The National Interest* (Summer 1989), pp. 3–18.

Funkenstein, Amos. "Periodization and Self-Understanding in the Middle Ages and Early Modern Times." MH, n.s. 5 (1974):3–23.

Gelinas, Y. D. "La critique de Thomas d'Aquin sur l'exégèse de Joachim de Flore." In *Tommaso d'Aquino nel suo settimo centenario. Atti del Congresso Inter-nazionale* (Vol. 1, pp. 368–75). Rome-Naples, 1974.

Gieben, Servus. "Bibliographia Oliviana." CF, 38 (1968):167–95.

Goen, C. C. "Jonathan Edwards: A New Departure in Eschatology." CH, 28 (1959):25–40.

Goertz, Hans-Jürgen. "'Lebendiges Wort' und 'totes Ding.' Zum Schriftverständnis Thomas Müntzers im Prager Manifest." ARG, 67 (1976):153–78.

————. "The Mystic with the Hammer: Thomas Müntzer's Theological Basis for Revolution." MQR, 50 (1976):83–113.

Goppelt, Leonhard. "The Existence of the Church in History According to Apostolic and Early Catholic Thought." In *Current Issues in New Testament Interpretation: Essays in Honor of Otto A. Piper* (pp. 193–209). Edited by William Klassen and Graydon F. Snyder. New York: Harper and Brothers, 1962.

Granquist, Mark. "The Role of 'Common Sense' in the Hermenentics of Moses Stuart." HTR, 83:3 (July 1990):305–319.

Gritsch, Eric W. "Thomas Müntzer and the Origins of Protestant Spiritualism." MQR, 37 (1963):172–94.

Groh, John E. "The Kingdom of God in the History of Christianity." CH, 43 (1974): 257–67.

Grundmann, Herbert. "Die Grundzüge der mittelalterlichen Geschichtsanschauung." *Archiv für Kulturgeschichte*, 24 (1934):326–36.

———. "Kirchenfreiheit und Kaisermacht um 1190 in der Sicht Joachims von Fiore." *Deutsches Archiv für die Erforschung des Mittelalters*, 19 (1963):353–96.

Guggisberg, Hans R. "Religious Freedom and the History of the Christian World in Roger Williams' Thought." EAL, 12 (1977):36–48.

Gundry, Stanley N. "Hermeneutics or Zeitgeist as in the History of Eschatologies?" JETS, 20 (1977):45–55.

Gunn, Roland Davis. "The Andover Case: A Study of Creeds in Nineteenth Century Congregationalism." Unpublished M.A. thesis, Andover Newton Theological School, 1983.

Hall, George. "Luther's Eschatology." *The Augustana Quarterly*, 23 (1944):13–21.

Hausamann, Susi. "Anfragen zum Schriftverständnis des jungen Bullinger im Zusammenhang einer Interpretation von 'De scripturae negotio.'" In *Heinrich Bullinger 1504–1575: Gesammelte Aufätze zum 400 Todestag*, Vol. 1. Zürich: Theologische Verlag, 1975.

Hillerbrand, Hans J. "The Antichrist in the Early German Reformation: Reflections on Theology and Propaganda." *Germania Illustrata: Essays on Early Modern Germany Presented to Gerald Strauss* (Vol. 18). Edited by Andrew C. Fix and Susan C. Karant-Nunn. Sixteenth Century Essays and Studies. Kirksville, Mo.: Sixteenth Century Journal Publishers, 1992.

———. "Thomas Muentzer's Last Tract Against Martin Luther: A Translation and Commentary," MQR, 38 (1964):20–36.

Holl, Karl. "Luther und die Schwärmer." In *Gesammelte Aufsätze zur Kirchengeschichte* (Vol. 1, chap. 7, pp. 420–67). Tübingen, Germany: J. C. B. Mohr-Paul Siebeck, 1921.

Holstein, Walter. "Reformation und Mission." ARG, 44 (1953):1–32.

Holwerda, David E. "Eschatology and History: A Look at Calvin's Eschatological Vision." In *Exploring the Heritage of John Calvin: Essays in Honor of John Bratt*. Edited by David E. Holwerda. Grand Rapids, Mich.: Baker Books, 1976.

Horton, Robin. "A Definition of Religion and Its Uses." *Journal of the Royal Anthropological Institute*, 90 (1966):211ff.

Hudson, Anne. "Contributions to a Bibliography of Wycliffite Writings." *Notes and Queries*. n.s. 20 (1973):443–53.

Hurley, Michael. "'Scriptura sola': Wyclif and his Critics." *Traditio*, 16 (1960):301ff.

Johnson, James William. "Chronological Writing: Its Concept and Development." *History and Theory*, II. 2 (1962):124–45.

Jones, Phyllis. "Biblical Rhetoric and the Pulpit Literature of Early New England." EAL, (1976–77):245–58.

Kaminsky, Howard. "Chiliasm and the Hussite Revolution." CH, 26 (1957):43–71.

Keep, David J. "Henry Bullinger, 1504–75: A Sketch of His Life and Work, with Speical Reference to Recent Literature." *London Quarterly and Holborn Review*, 191 (1966):135–46.

Kestenberg-Gladstein, Ruth. "The Third Reich: A Fifteenth-Century Polemic against

Joachimism, and Its Background." *Journal of the Warburg and Courtald Institute*, 18 (1955):245–95.

Klaassen, Walter. "Eschatological Themes in Early Dutch Anabaptism." In Irvin Buckwalter Horst, ed. *The Dutch Dissenters. A Critical Companion to Their History and Ideas.* Leiden: Brill, 1986, pp. 15–31.

Koch, Joseph. "Der Prozess gegen die Postille Olivis zur Apokalypse." RTAM, 5 (1933): 302–15.

Köhler, Walther. "Das Täufertum in Calvins Institutio von 1536." *Mennonitische Geschichtsblätter*, 2 (1936):1–4.

Kölmel, W. "Franziskus in der Geschichtstheologie." FsS, 60 (1978):67–89.

Köstlin, Julius. "Ein Beitrag zur Eschatologie der Reformatoren." *Theologische Studien und Kritiken*, 51 (1978).

Ladner, Gerhart B. "Medieval and Modern Understanding of Symbolism: A Comparison." *Speculum*, 54 (1979):230–31.

Lambert, Malcolm. "The Franciscan Crisis under John XXII." FS, n.s. 32 (1972):123–43.

Landes, Paula Frederickson. "Tyconius and the End of the World." REA, 28 (1982): 59–75.

Leff, Gordon. "The Making of the Myth of a True Church in the Later Middle Ages." *Journal of Medieval and Renaissance Studies*, (1971):1–15.

Lerner, L. D. "Puritanism and the Spiritual Autobiography." *The Hibbert Journal*, 55 (1956):373–86.

Lerner, Robert E. "The Black Death and Western European Eschatological Mentalities." AHR, 86 (1981):533–52.

———. "Refreshment of the Saints: The Time after Antichrist as a Station for Earthly Progress in Medieval Thought." *Traditio*, 32 (1976):97–144.

Lewalter, Ernst. "Eschatologie und Weltgeschichte in der Gedankenwelt Augustins." ZKG, 53 (1934):1–51.

Lindars, Barnabas. "Enoch and Christology." *Expository Times*, 92 (1981):295–99.

Locher, Gottfried W. "Praedicatio verbi dei est verbum dei." *Zwingliana*, 10 (1954): 47–57.

Lotz, David W. "Sola Scriptura: Luther on Biblical Authority." *Interpretation*, 35 (1981): 258–73.

McGinn, Bernard. "Awaiting an End: Research in Medieval Apocalypticism, 1974–1981" (pp. 263–89). MH, n.s. 11. Totowa, NJ: Rowman and Littlefield, 1982.

———. "The Abbot and the Doctors: Scholastic Reactions to the Radical Eschatology of Joachim of Fiore." CH, 40 (1971):30–47.

———. "Angel Pope and Papal Antichrist." CH, 47 (1978):155–73.

———. "Apocalypticism in the Middle Ages: An Historio-graphical Sketch." *Mediaeval Studies*, 37 (1975):252–86.

———. "The Significance of Bonaventure's Theology of History." In *Celebrating the Medieval Heritage: A Colloquy on the Thought of Aquinas and Bonaventure.* Edited by David Tracy. *Journal of Religion, Supplement*, 58 (1978):565–81.

MacKay, T. W. "Early Christian Exegesis of the Apocalypse." In *Studia Biblica 1978* (pp. 257–63). Edited by E. A. Livingstone. Sixth International Congress on Biblical Studies. Sheffield, U.K.: JSOT Press, 1980.

Maitland, S. R. "Puritan Thaumaturgy." In *Notes on the Contributions of the Rev. George Townsend, M.A., to the new edition of Foxe's Martyrology* (pp. 95–117). London: J. G. F. & J. Rivington, 1841.

Manselli, Raoul. "Une grande figure Serignanaise: Pierre Jean Olivi." *Etudes Franciscaines*, 12 (1972):69–83.

Marow, Gottfried. "Thomas Müntzer als Theologe des Gerichts. Das 'Urteil'—ein Schlüsselbegriff seines Denkens." ZKG, 83 (1972):195–225.

Marty, Martin. "Insiders Look at Fundamentalism," *The Christian Century* (November 18, 1981):1195–97.

Martyn, J. L. "We have found Elijah." In *Jews, Greeks and Christians* (pp. 181–219). Edited by R. Hamerston-Kelly and R. Scroggs. Leiden: Brill, 1976.

Matter, E. Ann. "The Pseudo-Alcuinian De Septem sigillis: An Early Latin Apocalypse Exegesis." *Traditio*, 36 (1980):111–38.

May, William. "The Confession of Prous Boneta, Heretic and Heresiarch." In *Essays in Medieval Life and Thought* (pp. 3–30). Edited by John Hine Mundy. New York: Columbia University Press, 1955.

Meier, P. Ludgerus. "Die Rolle der Theologie im Erfurter Quodlibet." RTAM, 17 (1950): 282–302.

Meinhold, Peter. "Die Verarbeitung von Luthers 'Supputatio annorum mundi' in der von Veit Dietrich herausgegebenen Genesisvorlesung." ZKG, 51 (1932):138–60.

———. "Thomas von Aquin und Joachim von Fiore und ihre Deutung der Geschichte." *Speculum*, 27 (1976):66–76.

Meyer, Christian. "Zur Geschichte der Wiedertäufer in Oberschwaben." In *Zeitschrift des Historisches Vereins für Schwaben und Neuberg* (Vol. 1, pp. 207–56). Augsburg: J. A. Schosser'schen Buchhandlung, 1874.

Meyer, Walter E. "Soteriologie, Eschatologie und Christologie in der Confessio Helvetica Posterior." *Zwingliana*, vol. 7.6 (1966):391–409.

Molnar, Amedeo. "Die eschatologische Hoffnung als Grundlage der Böhmischen Reformation." In *Von der Reformation zum Morgen* (pp. 59–187). Edited by Josef L. Hromadka. Leipzig: Koehler und Amelang, 1959.

———. "Le movement préhussite et la fin des temps." *Communio Viatorum*, 1 (1958): 27–32.

Moltmann, Jürgen. "Jacob Brocard als Vorläufer der Reich-Gottestheologie und der symbolisch-prophetischen Schriftauslegung des Johann Cocceius." ZKG, 71 (1960): 110–29.

Mommsen, Theodor E. "Petrarch's Conception of the 'Dark Ages.'" *Speculum*, 17 (1942): 226–42.

Morris, Colin. "Individualism in Twelfth-Century Religion: Some Further Reflections." JEH, 31 (1980):195–206.

Murrin, Michael. "Revelation and Two Seventeenth-Century Commentators." Unpublished typescript, University of Chicago, 1982; as later published in C. A. Patrides and Joseph Wittreich, eds. *The Apocalypse in English Renaissance Thought and Literature*. Ithaca, N.Y.: Cornell University Press, 1984.

Müsing, Hans-Werner. "Karlstadt und die Entstehung der Strassburger Täufergemeinde." In *The Origins and Characteristics of Anabaptism* (pp. 169–95). Edited by Marc Lienhard. The Hague: Martinus Nijhoff, 1972.

Nelson, Janet. "Society, Theodicy and the Origins of Heresy: Toward a Reassessment of the Medieval Evidence." In *Schism, Heresy and Religious Protest* (pp. 65–77). Edited by Derek Baker. Cambridge: Cambridge University Press, 1972.

Neumann, Gerhard J. "Eschatologische und chiliastische Gedanken in der Reformationszeit, besonders bei den Täufern." *Die Welt als Geschichte*, 19 (1959):58–66.

Nimmo, Duncan. "Poverty and Politics: The Motivation of Fourteenth-Century Franciscan Reform in Italy." In *Religious Motivation: Biographical and Sociological Problems for the Church Historian* (pp. 161–78). Edited by Derek Baker. Oxford: Clarendon Press, 1978.

Noll, Mark. "Luther Defends Melchior Hoffman." SCJ, 4 (1973):47–60.

———. "Melchior Hofmann and the Lutherans: 1525–1529." M.A. thesis, Trinity Evangelical Divinity School, Deerfield, Illinois, 1972.

Oberman, Heiko A. "The Preaching of the Word in the Reformation." *Harvard Divinity School Bulletin*, 25 (1960):7–18.

Oliver, Leslie Mahin. "The Acts and Monuments of John Foxe: A Study of the Growth and Influence of a Book." Ph.D. dissertation, Harvard University, 1945.

Packull, Werner O. "Mysticism and the Early South German-Austrian Anabaptist Movement, 1525–1531." Philosophy dissertation, Queens University, Kingston, Canada, 1974.

———. "A Hutterite Book of Medieval Origin Revisted. An Examination of the Hutterite Commentaries on the Book of Revelation and their Anabaptist Origin." MQR, 56 (1982):147–68.

———. "Melchior Hoffman: A Recanted Anabaptist in Schwäbisch Hall?" MQR, 57 (1983).

———. "Melchior Hoffman's Experience in the Livionian Reformation: The Dynamics of Sect Formation." MQR, 59 (1985):130–46.

———. "The Sign of Thau: The Changing Conception of the Seal of God's Elect in Early Anabaptist Thought." MQR, 61 (1987):363–67.

———. "Peter Tasch: From Melchiorite to Bankrupt Wine Merchant." MQR, 62 (1988): 276–95.

Paschoud, François. "La doctrine chrétienne et l'idéologie impériale romaine." In *L'Apocalypse de Jean. Traditions exegetiques et iconographiques. Actes du Colloque de la Fondation Hardt.* Genève: Librairie Droz, 1979.

Paul, Jacques. "Le Joachimisme et les Joachimites au milieu du XIIIe siècle d'après le témoignage de Fra Salimbene." In *Année Charnière-Mutations et Continuites* (pp. 797–813).

Pelikan, Jaroslav. "Luther's Attitude toward John Hus." *Concordia Theological Monthly*, 19 (1948):747–63.

Pfister, Rudolf. "Reformation, Türken und Islam." *Zwingliana*, 10 (1956):343–75.

Pineas, Rainer. "William Tyndale's Use of History as a Weapon of Religious Controversy." HTR, 55 (1962):121–41.

Po-Chia Hsia, R. "The Myth of the Commune: Recent Historiography on City and Reformation in Germany." *Central European History*, 20 (1987):203–15.

Polman, P. Pontianus. "Flacius Illyricus, Historien de l'Eglise." RHE, 27 (1931):27–73.

———. "La methode polemique des premiers adversaries de la Reforme." In *Adversaria Pontiani. Verspreide Geschriften van P. Pontianus Polman* (pp. 1–33). Edited by J. A. H. Bots. Amsterdam: Holland Universiteits Pers, 1976.

Preus, J. Samuel. "Zwingli, Calvin and the Origin of Religion." CH, 46 (1977): 186–202.

Preuss, Hans. "Apokalyptische und prophetische Frömmigkeit seit Ausgang des Mittelalters." *Zeitschrift für den evangelischen Religionsunterricht*, 14 (1907).

Quanbeck, Warren. "Luther and Apocalyptic." In *Luther and Malanchthon*. Edited by Vilmos Vajta. Göttingen, Germany: Vandenhoeck und Ruprecht, 1961.

Quandt, Jean B. "Religion and Social Thought: The Secularization of Post-Millianism," in AQ, 25 (1973):390–409.

Ratzinger, Joseph. "Beobachtungen zum Kirchenbegriff des Tyconius." REA 2 (1958).

Reeves, Marjorie. "The Abbot Joachim and the Society of Jesus." *Mediaeval and Renaissance Studies*, 5 (1961):161–81.

———. "The Abbot Joachim's Sense of History." In *1274-Année Charnière-Mutations et Continuites* (pp. 781–95). Colloques internationaux CNRS, no. 558. Paris, 1977.

——. "History and Eschatology: Medieval and Early Protestant Thought in Some English and Scottish Writings." MH, n.s. 4 (1973):99–123.

——. "History and Prophecy in Medieval Thought." MH, n.s. 5 (1974):51–75.

——. "Joachimist Expectations in the Order of Augustinian Hermits." RTAM, 25 (1958): 111–41.

——. "Joachimist Influences on the Idea of a Last World Emperor." *Traditio*, 17 (1961):323–70.

——. "Some Popular Prophecies from the Fourteenth to the Seventeenth Centuries." In *Popular Belief and Practice* (pp. 107–34). Edited by G. J. Cuming and D. Baker. Cambridge: Cambridge University Press, 1972.

——, and Hirsch-Reich, Beatrice. "The Seven Seals in the Writings of Joachim of Fiore." RTAM, 21 (1954):211–47.

Rettig, H. "Die Zeugnisse des Andreas und Arethas von Caesarea in Kappadocien." *Theologische Studien und Kritiken* (1831):734–76.

Richgels, Robert W. "The Pattern of Controversy in a Counter-Reformation Classic: The Controversies of Robert Bellarmine." SCJ, 11 (1980):3–15.

Ries, Julien. "La bible chez s. Augustin et chez les manichéens." REA, 10 (1964): 309–20.

Ritschl, Albrecht. "Die Entstehung der lutherischen Kirche." ZKG, 1 (1876):51–110.

Rohr, J. "Die Prophetie im letzten Jahrhundert vor der Reformation als Geschichtsquelle und Geschichts-faktor." *Historisches Jahrbuch*, 19 (1898):29–56, 547–66.

Rörich, Timotheus Wilhelm. "Zur Geschichte der Strassburgischen Wiedertäufer in den Jahren 1527 bis 1543." ZHT, 30 (1860):3–121.

Rosenmeier, Jesper. "The Teacher and the Witness: John Cotton and Roger Williams." *William and Mary Quarterly*, 25 (1968):408–31.

Rothkrug, Lionel. *Religious Practices and Collective Perceptions: Hidden Homologies in the Renaissance and Reformation*. In *Historical Reflections*, 7.1 (Spring 1980), 264 pp.

Rupp, Gordon. "Thomas Müntzer: Prophet of Radical Christianity." BJRL, 48 (1965–66):466–87.

——. "The Swiss Reformers and the Sects." In *The New Cambridge Modern History: The Reformation, 1520–1559*. Cambridge: Cambridge University Press.

——. "Word and Spirit in the First Years of the Reformation." ARG, 49 (1958):13–26.

Russell, Jeffrey. "Interpretations of the Origins of Medieval Heresy." *Medieval Studies*, 25 (1963):26–53.

Sairsingh, Krister. "Jonathan Edwards and the Idea of Divine Glory: His Foundational Trinitarianism and Its Ecclesial Import." Ph.D. dissertation, Harvard University, 1986.

Schilling, Heinz. "Job Fincel und die Zeichen der Endzeit." In *Volkserzählung und Reformation*. Edited by Wolfgang Brückner. Berlin: Erich Schmidt, 1974.

Schmid, H. D. "Das Hutsche Täufertum. Ein Beitrag zur Charakterisierung einer Täuferischen Richtung aus der Frühzeit der Täuferbewegung." *Historisches Jahrbuch*, 91 (1971):327–44.

Schmidt, Roderich. "Aetates mundi: Die Weltalter als Gliederungsprinzip der Geschichte." ZKG, 67 (1955):288–317.

Schmidt-Clausing, F. "Das Propheziegebet: Ein Blick über Zwinglis liturgische Werkstatt." *Zwingliana*, 12 (1964):10–34.

Schöffler, H. "Reformation und Geldabwertung." ARG, 38 (1941):55–62.

Schwartz, Hillel. "The End of the Beginning: Millenarian Studies, 1965–1975." *Religious Studies Review*, 2 (1976):1–15.

Schweibert, E. "The Medieval Pattern in Luther's View of the State." CH, 12 (1943).

Scribner, Bob. "The Reformer as Prophet and Saint: 16th-Century Images of Luther." *History Today*, 33 (November 1983):17–21, esp. p. 20.

Seebass, Gottfried. "Apokalyptik/Apokalypsen VII: Reformation und Neuzeit." *Theologische Realenzyklopädie* (Vol. 3, pp. 280–89). New York: Walter de Gruyter, 1978.

———. "Bauernkrieg und Täufertum in Franken." ZKG, 85 (1973):140–56.

———. "Müntzers Erbe, Werk, Leben und Theologie des Hans Hut." *Theologische Habilitationsschrift* (typescript). Erlangen, Germany: 1972. Courtesy of the Mennonite Historical Library, Goshen College, Goshen, Indiana.

———. "Das Zeichen der Erwählten." In *Umstrittenes Taüfertum 1525–1575* (pp. 138–64). Edited by Hans-Jürgen Goertz. Göttingen, Germany: Vandenhoeck und Ruprecht, 1975.

Senn, Matthias. "Alltag und Lebensgefühl im Zürich des 16. Jahrhunderts." *Zwingliana*, 14 (1976):251–62.

Skinner, Quentin. "Meaning and Understanding in the History of Ideas." *History and Theory*, 7 (1969).

Smirin, Mosei. "Thomas Müntzer und die Lehre des Joachim von Fiore." *Sinn and Form*, 4 (1952):69–143.

Smith, Christopher R. "Post-millennialism and the Work of Renewal in the Theology of Jonathan Edwards." Ph.D. dissertation, Boston College, 1992.

Snyder, James. "The Reconstruction of an Early Christian Cycle of Illustrations for the Book of Revelation—The Trier Apocalypse." *Vigilae Christianae*, 18 (1964): 146–62.

Solomon, David M. "The Sentence Commentary of Richard Fishacre and the Apocalypse Commentary of Hugh of St. Cher." *Archivum Fratrum Praedicatorum*, 46 (1966): 367–77.

Sommer, Herbert W. "The Muspilli-Apocalypse." *Germanic Review*, 35 (1960):157–63.

Southern, R. W. "Aspects of the European Tradition of Historical Writings: Vol. 2: Hugh of St. Victor and the Idea of Historical Development." *Transactions of the Royal Historical Society*, 5th series, 21 (1971):159–79.

———. "Aspects of the European Tradition of Historical Writings. Vol. 3: History as Prophecy." *Transactions of the Royal Historical Society*, 5th series, 22 (1972): 159–80.

Staedtke, Joachim. "Bullingers Bedeutung für die protestantische Welt." *Zwingliana*, 11 (1959):372–88.

———. "Der Züricher Prädestinationsstreit von 1560." *Zwingliana*, 9 (1953):536–46.

Stauffer, Ethelbert. "Märtyrertheologie und Täuferbewegung." ZKG, 52 (1933):545–98.

Stayer, James M. "Thomas Müntzer's protestation and Imaginary Faith." MQR, 55 (1981): 99–130.

Stolze, Wilhelm. "Der geistige Hintergrund des Bauern- krieges: Erasmus und Luther." ZKG, 51 (1932):456–79.

Stone, Lawrence. "The Revival of Narrative: Reflection on a New Old History." *Past and Present*, 85 (1974):3–24.

Strauss, Gerald. "The Mental World of a Saxon Preacher." In *Reformation Principle and Practice: Essays in Honor of Arthur Geoffrey Dickens*. Edited by Peter Newman Brooks. London Scolar Press, 1980.

Strobel, Georg Theodor, ed. "Melchior Hofmanns Dialogus von der Disputation zu Flensburg, 1529." *Beiträge zur Literatur, besonders des 16. Jahrhunderts*, Vol. 2 (1787): 499–522.

Stupperich, Martin. "Das Augsburger Interim als apokalyptisches Geschehnis nach den königsberger Schriften Andreas Osianders." AHR, 64 (1973):225–45.

Swift, David E. "The Future Probation Controversy in American Congregationalism, 1886–1893." Unpublished Ph.D. dissertation. New Haven, Conn.: Yale University, 1947.

Thompson, W. D. J. Cargill. "Seeing the Reformation in Medieval Perspective." JEH, 25 (1974):297–308.

Ullmann, Wolfgang. "Das Geschichtsverständnis Thomas Müntzers." In *Thomas Müntzer: Anfragen an Theologie und Kirche*. Edited by Christoph Demke. Berlin: Evangelische Verlagsanstalt, 1977.

Vasilieu, A. "Medieval Ideas of the End of the World: West and East." *Byzantion*, 16 (1942–43):461–502.

Vaucher, Alfred-Félix. "Les 1260 jours prophétiques dans les cercles joachimites." *Andrews University Seminary Studies*, 3 (1965):42–48.

Verhelst, D. "La préhistoire des conceptions d'Adson concernant l'Antichrist." RTAM, 40 (1973):52–103.

Weber, Otto. "Calvins Lehre von der Kirche." In *Die Treue Gottes in der Geschichte der Kirche. Vol. 2: Gesammelte Aufsätze*. Neukirchen, Germany: 1968.

Werner, Ernst. "Popular Ideologies in late Medieval Europe: Taborite Chiliasm and Its Antecedents." *Comparative Studies in Society and History*, 2 (1959–60):344–63.

West, Delno C. "Between Flesh and Spirit: Joachite Pattern and Meaning in the *Chronica* of Fra Salimbene." *Journal of Medieval History*, 3 (1977):339–52.

Whitbread, L. "The Doomsday Theme in Old English Poetry." *Beiträge zur Geschichte der deutschen Sprache und Literatur*, 89 (1967):452–481.

Williams, George H. "Translatio Studii: The Puritans' Conception of Their First University in New England, 1636." ARG, 57 (1966):152–81.

———. The Radical Reformation Revisited." *Union Seminary Quarterly Review*, 39/1–2 (1984):1–24.

Wilson, John F. "Studies in Puritan Millenarianism under the Early Stuarts." Th.D. dissertation, Union Theological Seminary, New York, 1962.

World Council of Churches, Commission on Faith and Order. "Spirit, Order and Organization." Report of Committee IV. Aarhus, Denmark (August 1964). Report, Proposal, and Categories for Case Studies; and "Draft of a Prologue to the Report of the U.S. Study Group—," (typescript) June 1966.

Zeman, J. K. "Restitution and Dissent in the Late Medieval Renewal Movements: The Waldensians, the Hussites and the Bohemian Brethren." *Journal of the American Academy of Religion*, 44 (1976):7–27.

Name and Subject Index

Scripture Index